Question Help offers a number of tutorial tools and learning aids that give students the help they need when they need it. Exercises provide step-by-step instruction, input-specific feedback, and hints, and may link to spreadsheets, sample problems, or the exact spot in the eText that addresses the learning objective of the problem.

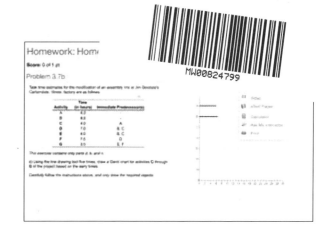

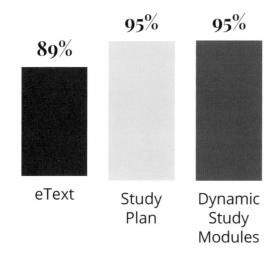

89% eText
95% Study Plan
95% Dynamic Study Modules

% of students who found learning tool helpful

Dynamic Study Modules help students study chapter topics effectively on their own by continuously assessing their **knowledge application** and performance in real time. These are available as graded assignments prior to class, and accessible on smartphones, tablets, and computers.

Pearson eText enhances student learning—both in and outside the classroom. Take notes, highlight, and bookmark important content, or engage with interactive lecture and example videos that bring learning to life (available with select titles). Accessible anytime, anywhere via MyLab or the app.

The **MyLab Gradebook** offers an easy way for students and instructors to view course performance. Item Analysis allows instructors to quickly see trends by analyzing details like the number of students who answered correctly/incorrectly, time on task, and median time spend on a question by question basis. And because it's correlated with the AACSB Standards, instructors can track students' progress toward outcomes that the organization has deemed important in preparing students to be **leaders.**

89% of students would tell their instructor to keep using MyLab Operations Management

For additional details visit: www.pearson.com/mylab/operationsmanagement

SECOND EDITION

MANAGING SUPPLY CHAIN AND OPERATIONS

An Integrative Approach

S. Thomas Foster

Donald L. Staheli Professor and Department Chair
of Marketing and Global Supply Chain
Marriott School of Management
Brigham Young University

Scott Sampson

Hazel S. Thorsell Professor and Area Leader of
Global Supply Chain Management
Marriott School of Management
Brigham Young University

Cindy Wallin

Associate Professor of Global Supply Chain
Management
Marriott School of Management
Brigham Young University

Scott Webb

Assistant Professor of Global Supply Chain
Management
Marriott School of Management
Brigham Young University

New York, NY

Vice President, Business, Economics, and UK Courseware: Donna Battista
Director of Portfolio Management: Stephanie Wall
Editorial Assistant: Linda Siebert Albelli
Vice President, Product Marketing: Roxanne McCarley
Senior Product Marketer: Product Marketer: Kaylee Carlson
Product Marketing Assistant: Marianela Silvestri
Manager of Field Marketing, Business Publishing: Adam Goldstein
Executive Field Marketing Manager: Field Marketing Manager: Nicole Price
Vice President, Production and Digital Studio, Arts and Business: Etain O'Dea
Director of Production, Business: Jeff Holcomb
Managing Producer, Business: Melissa Feimer
Content Producer: Yasmita Hota
Operations Specialist: Carol Melville

Design Lead: Kathryn Foot
Manager, Learning Tools: Brian Surette
Content Developer, Learning Tools: Lindsey Sloan
Managing Producer, Digital Studio and GLP, Media Production and Development: Ashley Santora
Managing Producer, Digital Studio: Diane Lombardo
Digital Studio Producer: Regina DaSilva
Digital Studio Producer: Alana Coles
Digital Content Project Lead: Courtney Kamauf
Project Management: Thistle Hill Publishing Services
Interior and Cover Design: Cenveo® Publisher Services
Cover Art: Steve Vidler/Alamy Stock Photo; Wavebreakmedia/Shutterstock; Daryl Benson/Photodisc/Getty Images; PixieMe/Shutterstock; Foodcollection/Getty Images; Ixefra/Getty Images; Wavebreakmedia/Shutterstock
Printer/Binder: LSC Communications
Cover Printer: LSC Commuications

Library of Congress Cataloging-in-Publication Data
Names: Foster, S. Thomas, author.
Title: Managing supply chain and operations : an integrative approach / S. Thomas Foster, Brigham Young University, Scott Sampson, Brigham Young University, Cindy Wallin, Brigham Young University, Scott Webb, Brigham Young University.
Description: Second Edition. | New York : Pearson, NY. [2017] | Revised edition of the authors' Managing supply chain and operations, [2016] | Includes bibliographical references and index.
Identifiers: LCCN 2017050842| ISBN 9780134739830 (hardcover) | ISBN 0134739833 (hardcover)
Subjects: LCSH: Production management. | Production control. | Business logistics—Management. | Industrial management.
Classification: LCC TS155 .F67 2017 | DDC 658.5—dc23
LC record available at https://lccn.loc.gov/2017050842

ISBN 10: 0-13-473983-3
ISBN 13: 978-0-13-473983-0

For Camille
—T. F.

For Kristen
—S. S.

For David and Joyce Wallin
—C. W.

For my best friend, Mary
—S. W.

About the Authors

S. Thomas Foster is the Donald Staheli Professor and department chair of marketing and global supply chain management at Brigham Young University's Marriott School of Management. He is an internationally recognized expert in quality and global supply chain management and has experience in manufacturing, financial services, and international oil exploration. He has consulted for more than 30 organizations, including Eaton/Cutler Hammer, Hewlett-Packard, Heinz Frozen Foods, Hyundai Corporation, and the U.S. Department of Energy.

Foster has served on the editorial boards of the *Journal of Operation Management* and *Decision Sciences* and is Editor in Chief of the *Quality Management Journal*. He has published more than 80 articles in journals such as *Decision Sciences, Journal of Operations Management, International Journal of Production Research*, and *Quality Management Journal*. His book *Quality Management: Integrating the Supply Chain* is an international best seller. He recently served on the Malcolm Baldrige Board of Overseers and was awarded the prestigious Instructional Innovation Award from the Decision Sciences Institute.

Scott Sampson is the Hazel S. Thorsell Professor of global supply chain management with the Marriott School of Management at Brigham Young University. He teaches MBA, executive MBA, and undergraduate courses in services management and customer relationship management.

Sampson is the author of the books *Understanding Service Businesses* and *Essentials of Service Design and Innovation*. His award-winning research involves service design paradigms, service quality measurement, and service supply chains. He has published research in leading academic journals, including *Management Science, Production and Operations Management, Operations Research, Decision Sciences*, and *Journal of Operations Management*. He received his MBA and PhD degrees from the University of Virginia and taught at Florida State University prior to joining the Brigham Young University faculty.

Cindy Wallin is an associate professor of global supply chain management at Brigham Young University's Marriott School of Management. She earned her PhD in supply chain management from the W. P. Carey School of Business at Arizona State University. Wallin's research focuses on buyer-supplier interfaces in the form of trust-based relationships, information sharing, collaboration, and collaborative inventory management approaches. Her research has been published in various journals, including *Decision Sciences Journal, Journal of Supply Chain Management, Quality Management Journal*, and *Journal of Business Logistics*.

Before pursuing her doctoral studies, Wallin was a commodity team manager for Intel Corporation. During her eight years at Intel, she also held the positions of senior buyer, purchasing manager, stores manager, and commodity manager. Before her graduate studies, Wallin also worked as an auditor for the Defense Contract Audit Agency.

Scott Webb is an associate professor of global supply chain management at Brigham Young University and specializes in logistics management. He received his PhD in logistics and operations management from the Eli Broad College of Business at Michigan State University. In addition to his PhD, he earned an MS degree in logistics management from the Air Force Institute of Technology and a BA in experimental psychology from the College of Idaho.

During his Air Force career, Webb worked on both base- and Pentagon-level assignments. He separated from active duty military service in 2008 at the rank of major and after earning both AF Commendation Medals and the AF Meritorious Service Medal.

Brief Contents

Contents

2 Innovating Supply Chain and Operations   47

Chapter 3   Product and Process Design and Mapping   48

4 Improving Supply Chain and Operations Management Performance 339

Preface

NEW TO THIS EDITION

With this edition of *Managing Supply Chain and Operations: An Integrative Approach*, we wanted to up our game. Every new edition of a textbook must represent a step forward. We feel like we met that goal with this edition. At the same time, you will see that this edition maintains the strengths of the first edition with additional features.

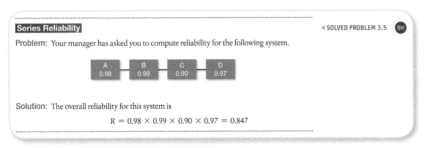

Series Reliability

< SOLVED PROBLEM 3.5 $f(x)$

Problem: Your manager has asked you to compute reliability for the following system.

| A 0.98 | B 0.99 | C 0.90 | D 0.97 |

Solution: The overall reliability for this system is
$$R = 0.98 \times 0.99 \times 0.90 \times 0.97 = 0.847$$

- **Analytics Emphasis** We have added analytics to the core model in the book. We have also honed our focus on analytics. For every quantitative example in the text, we have added analytics icons to show students that they are learning tools they can use in their careers. We have also included discussion of the importance of analytics in the early parts of the book.

- **Cutting Edge** Almost all of the vignettes and examples in the book have been updated. For example, the forecast section includes discussion of the work being done to use social media to forecast trends and preferences. New supply chain and operations vignettes are used to amplify and contextualize the techniques and tools taught in the book. More up-to-date information is provided on our *Managing Supply Chain and Operations* Facebook page, including all source articles for every vignette in the text.

Is Big Data the Key to Better Forecasting?

As you will see in this chapter, a lot of forecasting requires the gathering of historical data, which can be time consuming to gather and to analyze. However, data is everywhere; it comes from social media, search engines, and online retailing. Can this data provide a key to predicting the future? Giselle Guzman thinks it can. She is the founder of Now-Cast Data Corp, a company that uses big data and crowdsourcing to help create financial forecasts and trends.

For example, Now-Cast[1] has found that by scrubbing data on prices from online sources, it can predict inflation much more quickly than the U.S. government can. By monitoring searches on the word *inflation*, it can better gauge consumer expectations and worries relative to price increases.

Giselle has worked closely with eminent researchers in forecasting such as Nobel Laureates Joseph Stiglitz and Lawrence Klein. She believes that there is wisdom in crowds and that their data can be explored and analyzed on a moment-by-moment basis. Analytics can be used to monitor this data, but external variables, such as terrorism or natural disasters, can also be followed to adjust expectations. Next, machine learning can be used to improve forecasting.

While the jury is still out concerning the use of big data in forecasting, it is intriguing to think that this data may be useful in predicting trends like future spending and demand. In this chapter, we introduce you to forecasting methods that use data as a foundation for decision making in firms. We'll return to Now-Cast at the chapter's end.

[1]Pisani, B., "Finding a Better Way to Do Economic Forecasting," CNBC, 24 Mar. 2016.

Supply Chain and Operational Social Responsibility at Apple

As you will learn in this class, supply chain managers concern themselves daily with social responsibility. This involves being sensitive to the rights and dignity of individuals in the global supply chain and putting systems and reporting in place to ensure compliance with company standards in this area. Apple currently has more than 1.6 million people working its supply chain. To manage in a way that is responsive to the needs of all these people is a big job.

To help with managing supply chain and operations social responsibility, Apple has established a supplier code of conduct. The Apple supplier code of conduct addresses safety, working conditions, fair employee treatment, and environmental performance. This requires more than just satisfying local laws. It means meeting world-class requirements for global supply chain practices.

In this chapter, we will introduce supply chain and operations. As a supply chain and operations manager, you will have an opportunity to make the world a better place. We will revisit social responsibility at Apple later in the chapter.

Source: Supplier Responsibility 2016 Progress Report, Apple Corporation, 2016.

- **Streamlined** We have analyzed areas where the first edition could be simplified and have done so for this second edition. This has reduced the number of pages while still providing the same outstanding content coverage. We believe that students will find the text readable.

- **Increased Coverage of Sustainability and Social Responsibility** We have made an effort to increase our discussion of these important topics that resonate with students. This will make your course more relevant for your students.

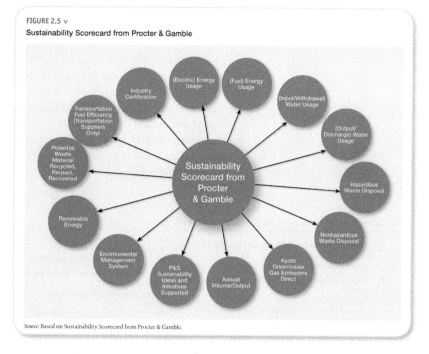

FIGURE 2.5 ∨
Sustainability Scorecard from Procter & Gamble

Source: Based on Sustainability Scorecard from Procter & Gamble.

S OLVING TEACHING AND LEARNING CHALLENGES

The second edition of *Managing Supply Chain and Operations* is targeted toward undergraduate- and graduate-level operations management courses that link to supply chain management in an effective and meaningful way. When we implemented this approach at our own university, we saw a tenfold increase in student enrollment in our major. Students are responding to the global nature of business, which has led to a realization that firms do not act alone to produce products and services. Although it may sound like a cliché, supply chains do compete against other supply chains. This text benefits from the fact that the authors have taught at both research and teaching universities such as Brigham Young, Florida State, Boise State, and Georgia Southern.

This book takes a balanced approach and, although rigorous, is not solely focused on quantitative material. We approach the quantitative material from a managerial perspective, answering the question: "Where does the analytical tool fit into a supply chain and operations (SC&O) management system?" We also recognize that most students in introductory operations courses are not operations or supply chain management majors. Because this course is often a service course, our approach will help students understand how and why this subject area applies to their roles as future managers.

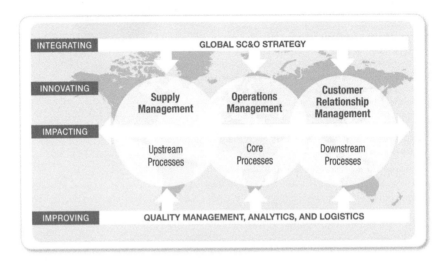

A second motivation for our writing this book emerges from the field. The field of SC&O management has developed from the three academic disciplines of purchasing, logistics, and operations. Faculty members who are coming from these differing fields do not always see the world the same way, which has created some fragmentation within the course. By putting together a world-class team from these three different academic traditions, we have developed the integrative model for SC&O management that brings these areas together. This model presents the glue that integrates these areas to provide a robust and complete textbook for students. Following are other teaching features in the text:

- Each chapter has a defined set of **Learning Objectives**. Because AACSB is requiring faculty to identify learning objectives, we provide them as an aid for faculty and students.

- **Managing Across Majors** boxes directly address how students in different majors and disciplines will use SC&O concepts upon graduation. Making a clear connection between the concepts and how students will use them reinforces the importance and relevance of these concepts.

Managing Across Majors 4.1 Marketing majors, remember that service operations need information from marketing to help identify and understand customer needs.

At the beginning of this chapter, we discussed music-sharing services such as Spotify. After studying service design, you now understand that these companies have created a coproductive environment where customers provide information and preferences. As you use the music-sharing service, you actually help to fine-tune the service the company provides to you.

There are also traditional quality dimensions to this service, such as performance, reliability, cost, and content. The social dimension takes the experience from being primarily technological to relational.

Customers of music-sharing services also prefer paid music. This eliminates commercials and makes the experience less clunky. In addition, socially engaged listeners are much more satisfied than passive listeners. That is, as a listener, you join a community by sharing and borrowing. Also, exclusive content drives users to the service. For example, if one service has Taylor Swift and another doesn't, her fans will flock to the service providing her music.

Data analysis and algorithms allow services to provide music that matches your moods. The social aspect creates an environment not unlike hanging around at a really awesome music shop with your friends. So the next time you chat with your friends about music sharing, explain about providing customer inputs to processes and coproduction.

- **Opening Vignettes** introduce a problem or scenario that an actual company has encountered. At the end of the chapter, we discuss how that company used concepts from the chapter to address its needs. **End-of-Chapter Vignettes** also require assessment and application. These exercises provide students with the skills they will need when they become managers.

SCOR at Ford

A good example of a company that used SCOR to become more effective is Ford Motor Company. The parts, supply, and logistics division of Ford used SCOR to improve its forecasting, inventory planning, electronic supplier communication, and management. Ford's extremely complex supply chain contains thousands of parts, thousands of suppliers, and millions of end consumers. Although Ford's functional areas within purchasing and logistics were individually effective, they were not structured to make integrated supply chain decisions. Ford identified the problems in its as-is state and then used SCOR to map and describe important inventory processes that flowed through the functional silos. Understanding how these processes affected each area of the company helped employees understand the holistic nature of their siloed decisions. Ford managers used SCOR to measure and benchmark these processes against others doing similar processes. Ford was then able to standardize processes and help each business area understand its responsibility for the entire process.

Ford has benefited substantially from using SCOR. Ford's recurring inventory has been greatly reduced due to attention to variation in inventory policies. Focusing on customer requirements has led to a 20 percent reduction in open back orders, improved customer satisfaction, and a 25 percent reduction in forecast inaccuracies. Because employees are focused on the total process rather than their own silo, Ford has reduced total inventory cycle time by 30 percent. Ford's return on investment was calculated to be five times the cost of implementing the SCOR system.

- Each chapter spotlights current events and ties them directly to the chapter's concepts. Students see how managers apply the information they are learning in the field. Every chapter has multiple **SC&O Current Events** boxes that make the material relevant to the students.

Managing Flow for Fast Fashion

We discussed Zara from a strategic perspective in Chapter 2. We now discuss it from a logistics perspective. Zara, the Spanish fast-fashion retailer, uses logistics to ensure that the most recent fashion trends are on store shelves quickly. The secret to Zara's business strategy is the quick turnover of product lines within retail stores. In fact, Zara frequently stocks its shelves with fashion apparel that was displayed on fashion runways only three weeks earlier.

So how does Zara accomplish this fast-fashion supply chain? Zara has created a very cohesive logistics strategy between its factory operations and its retail stores. Zara creates clothing using just-in-time manufacturing and small batch sizes. Zara then ships these batches to retail stores to see what customers prefer. When Zara is informed about what is selling, not selling, or not available at retail stores, the factory produces what customers value most. The factory then uses its excess capacity and agile capabilities to manufacture the most popular styles.

Zara's commitment to a fast and steady tempo paced by order fulfilment to stores allows Zara to keep minimal inventory while still meeting customers' needs. Logisticians for Zara know that it delivers twice weekly from the factories in Bangladesh to the central distribution center in Spain. The shipments are then broken up and delivered to stores, usually in less than 24 hours to European stores and 40 hours to U.S. stores. The logistics costs of rapidly shipping inventory to stores are much more expensive than traditional, slower fashion

- **Global Connections** boxes focus on how SC&O management ties together supply chains across international boundaries. Learning how managers can use global supply chains and how international linkages benefit firms provides students an advantage once they enter the workforce.

- **Using Technology** boxes walk students through the ways managers use technology to solve SC&O problems in the workplace. Step-by-step tutorials break down problems and solutions and provide computer-based fundamentals for SC&O problem solving.

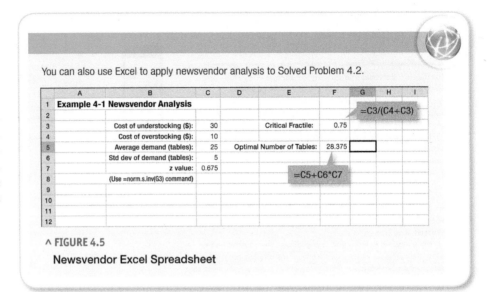

You can also use Excel to apply newsvendor analysis to Solved Problem 4.2.

	A	B	C	D	E	F	G	H	I
1	**Example 4-1 Newsvendor Analysis**								
2							=C3/(C4+C3)		
3		Cost of understocking ($):	30		Critical Fractile:	0.75			
4		Cost of overstocking ($):	10						
5		Average demand (tables):	25		Optimal Number of Tables:	28.375			
6		Std dev of demand (tables):	5						
7		z value:	0.675			=C5+C6*C7			
8		(Use =norm.s.inv(G3) command)							
9									
10									
11									
12									

∧ **FIGURE 4.5**

Newsvendor Excel Spreadsheet

---

f(x) **SOLVED PROBLEM 4.2 >**   **The Newsvendor Problem in Action**

MyLab Operations Management
Video

Problem: In service environments, an inventory issue is capacity. Service operations have a capacity for meeting customer demand according to how they are designed. If there is not enough capacity, customer demand may not turn into sales. Excess capacity comes with a cost as well.

For example, a restaurant chain is opening a new location in a business district. The question is how many tables to design in the restaurant. The key revenue period is the weekday lunch seating, so the restaurant desires to plan capacity for that demand. Lunchtime demand is forecast to be normally distributed with a mean of 25 parties and a standard deviation of 5 parties. (Assume one party per table.) How many tables should the restaurant have?

A naive view would have 25 tables, but that ignores the asymmetric cost structure. The average party spends $40 for lunch, with ingredient costs being 25 percent of that amount.

Solution: Therefore, the cost of insufficient tables (C_U) is $40 - ((40 \times 0.25) = \$30$ per table, which is the average profit contribution per party. Each table takes up 100 square feet of space, and space costs $3 per square foot per month (approximately $0.10 per square foot per day).

Therefore, the cost of an extra table is $100 \times 0.10 = \$10$ per table per day. This cost suggests that an optimal number of tables would have $CF = 30/(10 + 30) = 0.75$, or 75 percent of the cumulative distribution. Looking up 0.75 in the normal cumulative distribution table (see Appendix Table A-2) shows that $z = 0.675$. Therefore, the optimal number of tables is $25 + (0.675 \times 5) = 28.375$, or approximately 28 tables. See FIGURE 4.5 for the formulas and a sample layout for a newsvendor problem.

- The text includes videos in MyLab Operations Management for over 70 **Solved Problems** from the text, allowing students to practice quantitative material prior to coming to class.

End-of-Chapter Resources

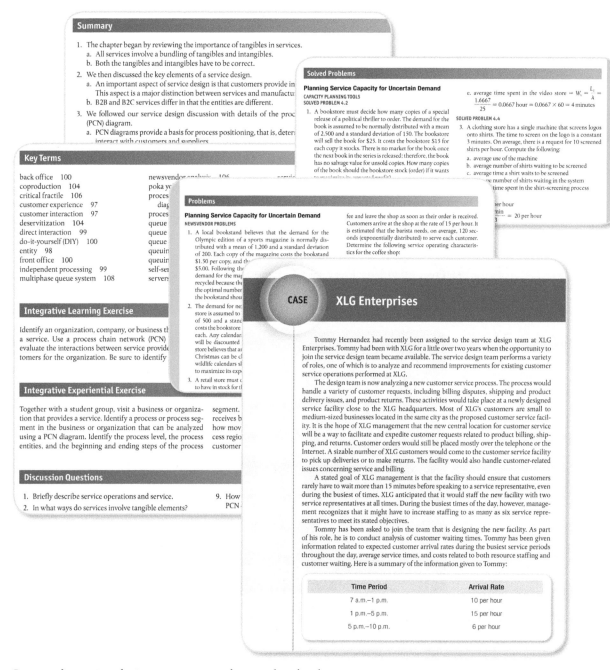

Summary

1. The chapter began by reviewing the importance of tangibles in services.
   a. All services involve a bundling of tangibles and intangibles.
   b. Both the tangibles and intangibles have to be correct.
2. We then discussed the key elements of a service design.
   a. An important aspect of service design is that customers provide in
      This aspect is a major distinction between services and manufactu
   b. B2B and B2C services differ in that the entities are different.
3. We followed our service design discussion with details of the proc
   (PCN) diagram.
   a. PCN diagrams provide a basis for process positioning, that is, deter
      interact with customers and suppliers

Key Terms

back office 100	newsvendor analysis 106
coproduction 104	poka yo
critical fractile 106	proces
customer experience 97	diag
customer interaction 97	proces
deservitization 104	queue
direct interaction 99	queue
do-it-yourself (DIY) 100	queue
entity 98	queuin
front office 100	queuin
independent processing 99	self-se
multiphase queue system 108	servers

Integrative Learning Exercise

Identify an organization, company, or business th
a service. Use a process chain network (PCN)
evaluate the interactions between service provide
tomers for the organization. Be sure to identify

Integrative Experiential Exercise

Together with a student group, visit a business or organization that provides a service. Identify a process or process segment in the business or organization that can be analyzed
using a PCN diagram. Identify the process level, the process
entities, and the beginning and ending steps of the process

Discussion Questions

1. Briefly describe service operations and service.
2. In what ways do services involve tangible elements?

Solved Problems

Planning Service Capacity for Uncertain Demand
CAPACITY PLANNING TOOLS
SOLVED PROBLEM 4.2

1. A bookstore must decide how many copies of a special
release of a political thriller to order. The demand for the
book is assumed to be normally distributed with a mean
of 2,500 and a standard deviation of 150. The bookstore
will sell the book for $25. It costs the bookstore $15 for
each copy it stocks. There is no market for the book once
the next book in the series is released; therefore, the book
has no salvage value for unsold copies. How many copies
of the book should the bookstore stock (order) if it wants

e. average time spent in the video store $= W_s = \frac{L_s}{\lambda} =$
$\frac{1.6667}{25} = 0.0667$ hour $= 0.0667 \times 60 = 4$ minutes

SOLVED PROBLEM 4.4

3. A clothing store has a single machine that screens logos
onto shirts. The time to screen on the logo is a constant
3 minutes. On average, there is a request for 10 screened
shirts per hour. Compute the following:
a. average use of the machine
b. average number of shirts waiting to be screened
c. average time a shirt waits to be screened
   number of shirts waiting in the system
   time spent in the shirt-screening process

r hour
min
= 20 per hour

Problems

Planning Service Capacity for Uncertain Demand
NEWSVENDOR PROBLEMS

1. A local bookstand believes that the demand for the
   Olympic edition of a sports magazine is normally distributed with a mean of 1,200 and a standard deviation
   of 200. Each copy of the magazine costs the bookstand
   $1.50 per copy, and th
   $5.00. Following th
   demand for the maj
   recycled because th
   the optimal number
   the bookstand shou
2. The demand for ne
   store is assumed to
   of 500 and a stand
   costs the bookstore
   each. Any calendar
   will be discounted
   store believes that a
   Christmas can be cl
   wildlife calendars sl
   to maximize its exp
3. A retail store must
   to have in stock for t

fee and leave the shop as soon as their order is received.
Customers arrive at the shop at the rate of 15 per hour. It
is estimated that the barista needs, on average, 120 seconds (exponentially distributed) to serve each customer.
Determine the following service operating characteristics for the coffee shop:

CASE **XLG Enterprises**

Tommy Hernandez had recently been assigned to the service design team at XLG
Enterprises. Tommy had been with XLG for a little over two years when the opportunity to
join the service design team became available. The service design team performs a variety
of roles, one of which is to analyze and recommend improvements for existing customer
service operations performed at XLG.

The design team is now analyzing a new customer service process. The process would
handle a variety of customer requests, including billing disputes, shipping and product
delivery issues, and product returns. These activities would take place at a newly designed
service facility close to the XLG headquarters. Most of XLG's customers are small to
medium-sized businesses located in the same city as the proposed customer service facility. It is the hope of XLG management that the new central location for customer service
will be a way to facilitate and expedite customer requests related to product billing, shipping, and returns. Customer orders would still be placed mostly over the telephone or the
Internet. A sizable number of XLG customers would come to the customer service facility
to pick up deliveries or to make returns. The facility would also handle customer-related
issues concerning service and billing.

A stated goal of XLG management is that the facility should ensure that customers
rarely have to wait more than 15 minutes before speaking to a service representative, even
during the busiest of times. XLG anticipated that it would staff the new facility with two
service representatives at all times. During the busiest times of the day, however, management recognizes that it might have to increase staffing to as many as six service representatives to meet its stated objectives.

Tommy has been asked to join the team that is designing the new facility. As part
of his role, he is to conduct analysis of customer waiting times. Tommy has been given
information related to expected customer arrival rates during the busiest service periods
throughout the day, average service times, and costs related to both resource staffing and
customer waiting. Here is a summary of the information given to Tommy:

Time Period	Arrival Rate
7 a.m.–1 p.m.	10 per hour
1 p.m.–5 p.m.	15 per hour
5 p.m.–10 p.m.	6 per hour

- **Summaries** review the important topics discussed in the chapter.
- **Key Terms** are listed for review purposes. Each list includes page references showing where the concept was first discussed in each chapter.
- **Integrative Learning Exercises** are designed to get students to integrate multiple concepts throughout the chapter.
- **Integrative Experiential Exercises** are designed to get students out into the real world by visiting companies and learning how supply chain and operations concepts are applied.
- **Discussion Questions** test student comprehension of the concepts presented.
- **Solved Problems** detail how to solve model problems using the techniques presented in the chapter.
- **Problems** sharpen students' skills by providing a wide selection of homework material.
- **Cases** challenge students to grapple with a problem. Each case can be used as an in-class exercise, a homework assignment, or a team project.

MYLAB OPERATIONS MANAGEMENT

Reach Every Student by Pairing This Text with Mylab Operations Management

MyLab is the teaching and learning platform that empowers you to reach *every* student. By combining trusted author content with digital tools and a flexible platform, MyLab personalizes the learning experience and improves results for each student. Learn more about MyLab Operations Management at www.pearson.com/mylab/operations-management.

Deliver Trusted Content

You deserve teaching materials that meet your own high standards for your course. That's why we partner with highly respected authors to develop interactive content and course-specific resources that you can trust—and that keep your students engaged.

This text is totally integrated with MyOMLab. Among the features that have proven popular are:

- **Over 80 videos.** Every solved example in the main body of every chapter has a video that shows step-by-step how to solve the problems. Students love this feature of the book. We believe that our videos are best-in-class. We used the talent of BYUTv to develop these videos.

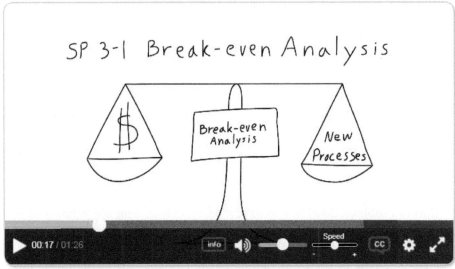

- **Simulations** A series of simulations created by Pearson educational specialists are available for use in your SC&O course at various times. These make great team in-class activities that you can use to drive home key concepts and to make SC&O fun!

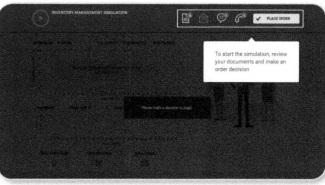

- **Dynamic Study Modules** These are fantastic utilities that help tutor students on key SC&O concepts.

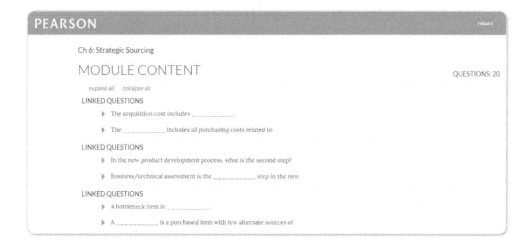

- **E-text** Students can save money by utilizing the e-text and bypassing the need to have a paper text. Red Shelf and other tools are available to make this access very economical for the students. Just contact your Pearson rep to find out about this alternative. We do this at BYU and have saved our students a lot of money.

Empower Each Learner

Each student learns at a different pace. Personalized learning pinpoints the precise areas where each student needs practice, giving all students the support they need—when and where they need it—to be successful.

Teach Your Course Your Way

Your course is unique. Whether you'd like to build your own assignments, teach multiple sections, or set prerequisites, MyLab gives you the flexibility to easily create *your* course to fit *your* needs.

- You can create quizzes using prewritten editable questions from Tom Foster or you can create your own quizzes that students can complete either before, during, or after class.

Improve Student Results

When you teach with MyLab, student performance improves. That's why instructors have chosen MyLab for over 15 years, touching the lives of over 50 million students.

DEVELOPING EMPLOYABILITY SKILLS

This book is designed to provide a basic understanding of supply chain and operations management. For SC&O majors, this is a great platform for other, more advanced classes. For non-majors, in addition to other skills, they will be learning the basic concepts and important tools for managing:

- Logistics
- Purchasing
- Operations Management
- Inventory Management

- Project Management
- Process Management
- Process Improvement
- Six Sigma

This class will provide tools and concepts that you can use on the first day of your job. Pay attention. This is a growing field that is full of excitement and relevance for your future.

Integrative Experiential Exercise

Together with a student group, visit a business or organization that provides a service. Identify a process or process segment in the business or organization that can be analyzed using a PCN diagram. Identify the process level, the process entities, and the beginning and ending steps of the process segment. Be sure to identify the points where the customer receives benefits and the provider incurs costs. Comment on how moving and rearranging steps across and between process regions might affect the value proposition by increasing customer benefits, decreasing provider costs, or both.

Discussion Questions

1. Briefly describe service operations and service.
2. In what ways do services involve tangible elements?
3. Identify the customer input resources and the service provider outputs for the following service operations: accounting, education, computer repair, and healthcare.
4. What is meant by simultaneity in services? What is a major consequence of simultaneity?
5. What are some long-term responses for increasing and decreasing service capacity?
6. What is meant by the term *time-perishable capacity* as it relates to service operations? Provide an example.
7. Customers are generally involved in the service delivery process. What are some negative consequences associated with customer interaction in the service operation?
8. Briefly define and describe how a process chain network (PCN) diagram can be used in designing service delivery systems.

9. How can you shift the focus of your operations using a PCN diagram?
10. What trade-offs are generally made when making capacity decisions?
11. How do capacity choices vary in the near and long terms?
12. How can queuing theory be used to help evaluate capacity decisions for service providers?
13. Queuing psychology identifies ways that service operations managers can improve waits by improving the perception of those customers who do wait. What are some of the fundamental points related to queuing psychology?
14. In waiting lines, sometimes technological advances cannot make it easier to manage queues. How can psychology help with this problem?
15. How does the newsvendor model allow service firms to evaluate capacity decisions?

Expanding Your Career Skills or Building Your Career Skills

As educators and practitioners, we are aware of the changing landscape of the workplace and the needs of managers in various industries. This category of activities encourages students to research data, identify patterns and facts in data, take initiative, work in groups, and clearly communicate their findings to others.

INSTRUCTOR TEACHING RESOURCES

This program comes with the following teaching resources.

Supplements available to instructors at www.pearsonhighered.com	Features of the Supplement
Instructor's Resource Manual, authored by Khurrum Bhutta from Ohio University	• Chapter-by-chapter summaries • A sample syllabus and course outline • Teaching tips • Examples and activities not in the main book • Class discussion questions • Video suggestions
Solutions Manual, authored by Mahesh Srinivasan from The University of Akron	Solutions to all discussion questions, problems, and case questions
Test Bank, authored by Mahesh Srinivasan from The University of Akron	More than 1,000 multiple-choice, true/false, short-answer, and graphing questions with these annotations: • Difficulty level (easy, moderate, difficult) • Type (multiple-choice, true/false, short-answer, essay) • Learning objective • AACSB learning standard (Written and Oral Communication; Ethical Understanding and Reasoning; Analytical Thinking; Information Technology; Interpersonal Relations and Teamwork; Diverse and Multicultural Work; Reflective Thinking; Application of Knowledge)
Computerized TestGen	TestGen allows instructors to: • Customize, save, and generate classroom tests • Edit, add, or delete questions from the test item files • Analyze test results • Organize a database of tests and student results
PowerPoints, authored by Scott Webb from Brigham Young University	Slides include all the figures, tables, and equations in the textbook. PowerPoints meet accessibility standards for students with disabilities. Features include, but are not limited to: • Keyboard and screen reader access • Alternative text for images • High color contrast between background and foreground colors

If assistance is needed, our dedicated technical support team is ready to help with the media supplements that accompany this text. Visit **support.pearson.com/getsupport** for answers to frequently asked questions and toll-free user support phone numbers.

ACKNOWLEDGMENTS

We acknowledge the contributions of many in making this book a success, including graduate assistant support from Erik Chaston, Scott Merrell, Aaron Hefner, Aaron Lund, Heidi Hunsaker, and Brian Andersen. We also wish to thank Phillip Fry for his contributions. Past and current editors have been essential in providing vision, including Chuck Synovec, Donna Battista, and Dan Tylman. Especially, Deepa Chungi has been a wonderful support to this project.

Many outside reviewers have contributed to the quality of this text and include the following:

Nezih Altay, DePaul University
Kwasi Amoako, University of North Carolina
Antonio Arreola-Risa, Texas A&M University
Cliff Asay, University of Wyoming
Dan Ball, Monmouth University
Pamela Barnes, Kansas State University
Hooshang Beheshti, Radford University
Ednilson Bernardes, University of West Virginia
Khurrum Bhutta, Ohio University
Greg Bier, University of Missouri
Terrence Boardman, East Carolina University
Leland Buddress, Portland State University
Dan Bumblauskas, University of Missouri
John Burbridge, Elon University
Paul Choi, California State University
Rich Coleman, Elon University
John Connolly, Latter-Day Saints Business College
Gordon Corzine, University of Massachusetts
Michael Fathi, Georgia Southwestern State University
John Gardner, Brigham Young University
Ray Gehani, The University of Akron
Wooseung Jang, University of Missouri
Amit Kakkad, University of San Diego
Peter Kelle, Louisiana State University
George Kenyon, Lamar University
Gregg Macaluso, University of Colorado

Alan Mackelprang, Georgia Southern University
Bill Maligie, California State University
Hilda Martinez, Clarkson University
Anthony Narsing, Macon State College
Roger Nibler, Portland State University
Glenn Pace, Missouri State University
Gertrude Pannirselvam, Southern Illinois University
Ali Parlakturk, University of North Carolina
Patrick Penfield, Syracuse University
Fred Raafat, San Diego State University
Ana Rosado Feger, Ohio University
Brooke Saladin, Wake Forest University
Michael Santonino, Bethune Cookman University
Mahesh Srinivasan, The University of Akron
Larry Taube, University of North Carolina
Paul Vanderspek, Colorado State University
Jerry Wei, University of Notre Dame
Marek Wermus, Old Dominion University
Angela Wicks, Bryant University
Kaitlin Wowak, University of Notre Dame
John Wu, California State University
Xiaohui Xu, California State Polytechnic University
Helio Yang, San Diego State University
Zach Zacharia, Lehigh University
Wenge Zhu, California State Polytechnic University

Finally, we are thankful for our faith that keeps us continually improving and progressing.

Part 1

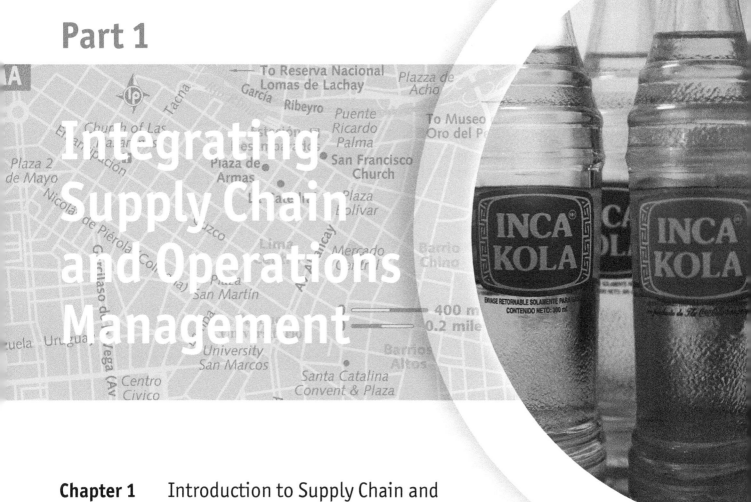

Integrating Supply Chain and Operations Management

1 Introduction to Supply Chain and Operations Management

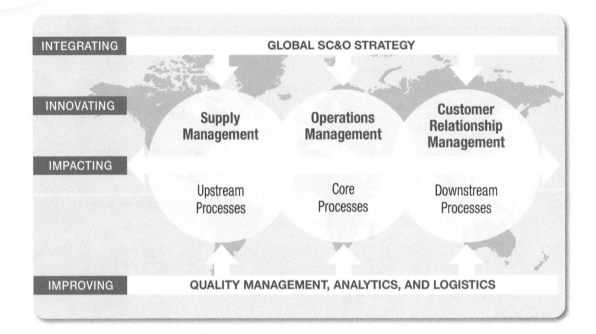

CHAPTER OUTLINE AND LEARNING OBJECTIVES

1 Understand Why You Are Studying Supply Chain and Operations Management

- Explain processes and why they are important to both managers and firms.
- Describe how supply chain globalization is changing the way firms make sourcing decisions.

2 Define, Understand, and Apply the Components of Supply Chain and Operations Management

- Describe supply chain management, supply chain flows, service supply chains, and operations management.
- Combine the basics of supply chain management and operations management, and describe how they work together.

3 Explain the Integrative Model for Supply Chain and Operations Management

- Describe the firm's operating core.
- Explain how upstream and downstream collaboration and strategic integration function within the firm.

4 Explain the Four I's

- Describe the Four I's: (1) impacting, (2) improving, (3) innovating, and (4) integrating.
- Explain how managers use these concepts to increase supply chain and operations effectiveness.

As you will learn in this class, supply chain managers concern themselves daily with social responsibility. This involves being sensitive to the rights and dignity of individuals in the global supply chain and putting systems and reporting in place to ensure compliance with company standards in this area. Apple currently has more than 1.6 million people working its supply chain. To manage in a way that is responsive to the needs of all these people is a big job.

To help with managing supply chain and operations social responsibility, Apple has established a supplier code of conduct. The Apple supplier code of conduct addresses safety, working conditions, fair employee treatment, and environmental performance. This requires more than just satisfying local laws. It means meeting world-class requirements for global supply chain practices.

In this chapter, we will introduce supply chain and operations. As a supply chain and operations manager, you will have an opportunity to make the world a better place. We will revisit social responsibility at Apple later in the chapter.

Source: Supplier Responsibility 2016 Progress Report, Apple Corporation, 2016.

If you listen carefully, that sound you hear is the sound of new jobs being created in supply chain and operations (SC&O) management. These jobs create opportunities for you as students, but SC&O management is not just about jobs. It crosses many international borders and touches the lives of billions of people worldwide. As firms cooperate to create customer value, they also create economic and political alliances that add stability to an unstable world. The supply chain binds not only companies but also cultures, continents, and competencies.

(U) NDERSTAND WHY YOU ARE STUDYING SUPPLY CHAIN AND OPERATIONS MANAGEMENT

Before we begin discussing supply chains and operations, and how they work together, let's define some terms. These terms are commonly used in the SC&O field as well as throughout this text.

Supply chain management is cooperation between different firms to create value for customers. **Operations management** is the administration of transformation processes that create value for customers by meeting their needs or enabling them to meet their own needs. Combining these terms to make **supply chain and operations (SC&O)** emphasizes the linkages between firms that tie operations together with the goal of satisfying customers. The move to SC&O management from just operations management externalizes the view of a productive firm in a way that is healthy for the world, individual firms, and their global competitiveness.

As a student, you might be asking yourself, *Because my major area of study is not SC&O management, why do I need to study this topic?* That is a good question. In leading business schools around the world, students—regardless of their major—study accounting, marketing, finance, human resources, *and* SC&O management. Let's see why.

supply chain management
Firms cooperating to create value for customers.

operations management
Managing transformation processes to convert inputs into products and services.

supply chain and operations (SC&O)
Combining supply chain and operations to serve customers.

TABLE 1.1 >

Functional Areas and Their Roles in Business		
Function	**Responsibilities**	**What the Function Really Means**
Accounting	Auditing and reporting	Accountants are the scorekeepers in business. They provide information for SC&O managers to make informed decisions.
Marketing	Sales and customer management	Marketing proposes new products, performs market studies, and manages sales. Marketing helps SC&O managers make product decisions.
Finance	Investment and resources management	Financial managers decide where to invest the scarce resources of the firm. They obtain financing for SC&O activities.
Human resources (HR)	Selecting, training, and rewarding employees	HR professionals provide employees for SC&O processes to be effective. They consult in training and design reward systems to enhance the effectiveness of SC&O employees.
Supply chain and operations	Managing relationships and creating value	SC&O management is the core of what all firms do. All other areas support SC&O productive activities. SC&O managers are experts in designing, managing, and improving processes that lead to customer satisfaction and delight.

A business manager's responsibility depends on his or her role in the company, and several roles are shown in TABLE 1.1. Accounting and financial managers are responsible for managing and investing the resources of the firm. Marketers help manage customers. Human resources managers are concerned with employees. SC&O leaders help manage both internal and external processes that result in satisfied customers. Even though accountants, marketers, and human resources managers do not deal directly with SC&O procedures, they need to understand how they work so they can make informed decisions for their own departments.

Managing Across Majors 1.1   Watch for boxes that highlight how different business departments use a particular concept, tool, or SC&O idea. These boxes illustrate how departments such as accounting, marketing, and finance incorporate and apply SC&O management in their roles within the firm.

Processes

No matter what your area of study, if you go into a field of business, you must manage *processes*. **Processes** are the means by which all work is performed. You have witnessed processes when you order food at a restaurant or mail a package. In addition, processes are not static; they must continually be changing for the better. Because of global competition, you must continue to improve your processes to stay ahead of your competition. This requirement is not trivial, and you need knowledge and tools to manage and improve processes effectively. When it comes to processes, you must focus on *design*, *management*, *control*, and *improvement*.

Process design consists of configuring inputs and resources in a way that provides value, enhances quality, and is productive. The great thing about process design is that it is proactive. If processes are well designed, other potential problems are avoided. In this book, we have dedicated Chapter 3 to product design and process design and Chapter 4 to service design.

processes
The means by which work is performed.

process design
Configuring inputs and resources in a way that provides value, enhances quality, and is productive.

Process management is the act of executing and controlling the productive functions of a firm. All business involves process management. For example, if you are an accountant, you have established processes for handling accounts receivable. If a payer is late with a payment, you follow established processes to collect the payment.

Process control is the act of monitoring a process for its efficacy, a process that includes dimensions such as cost, timeliness, or quality. Chapters 9, 13, and 14 discuss process management, quality control, inventory control, and planning associated with effectively managing any company function, which will enhance your performance as a manager.

Process improvement is a proactive effort to enhance process performance. Often, managers employ process improvement in response to customer needs or competitive pressures. Many times, process improvement is motivated by a culture based on the human need to do better. For example, even the often-criticized Internal Revenue Service now refers to taxpayers as customers and has worked on processes to provide better advice and service. This policy change has resulted in more than three million people receiving free advice from tax advisors. Chapters 4, 13, and 14 will discuss quality improvement and service enhancement in a way that will provide you with the skills you need to enhance the processes you oversee.

> **Managing Across Majors 1.2** This text provides an overview of supply chains and operations from a process management perspective. No matter what your major is, these tools, philosophies, and techniques will aid in your development as a manager and will provide you with tools and knowledge that you will be able to apply on the very first day of your career.

This text adopts a life-cycle approach and is separated into four themes: (1) integrating SC&O management, (2) innovating SC&O management, (3) impacting SC&O performance, and (4) improving SC&O performance. These four themes build on one another to give you the fundamentals you need to be an effective SC&O manager. As will be discussed in the next section, these processes occur on a global scale.

Supply Chain Globalization

As the opening vignette about Apple demonstrated, SC&O decisions are made in a global environment, and these decisions affect global trade and the world economy. As you can see in FIGURE 1.1, the U.S. trade deficit has gotten larger and larger over time, meaning the United States imports more than it sells to other countries. This imbalance manifests itself in many of the items you use daily. Items such as your toothbrush, your microwave, your computer, and your smartphone were not made in the United States.

Firms use a variety of mechanisms in going global. The first is *licensing*. **Licensing** is the sale of the same product with another trademark in different countries. Through licensing, a U.S. corporation can allow foreign firms to sell in restricted markets while using the original design. This way, firms are able to reach international markets without having to establish international supply chains or marketing arms. For example, when Xerox moved into Europe, it licensed its products to a British company named Rank Xerox. Selling through Rank Xerox allowed Xerox to sell its products in Europe without investing in the infrastructure for European operations.

Firms also seek international markets through joint ventures, or **strategic alliances**, by forming long-term business relationships with suppliers. Firms may decide to partner when two firms have technology, products, or access to markets that each other wants. For example Hewlett Packard (HP) and Canon are partners in printer production. Canon produces the engine of the printer, and HP produces the operating systems, allowing each company to focus on its competencies.

Another approach to capturing international markets is *globalization*. The **globalization** of a firm fundamentally changes the nature of its business by establishing production and marketing facilities in foreign countries. We refer to these firms as multinational corporations. With growing economies in many parts of the world—such as Mexico, India, Brazil,

---

process management
The act of executing and controlling the productive functions of a firm.

process control
The act of monitoring a process for its efficacy.

process improvement
A proactive effort to enhance process performance.

licensing
The sale of a product under another trademark in another region of the world.

strategic alliances
Strategic ventures with partners and suppliers.

globalization
Increasing global presence by establishing operations in other parts of the world.

FIGURE 1.1 >

**U.S. Trade from
1960 to 2010**

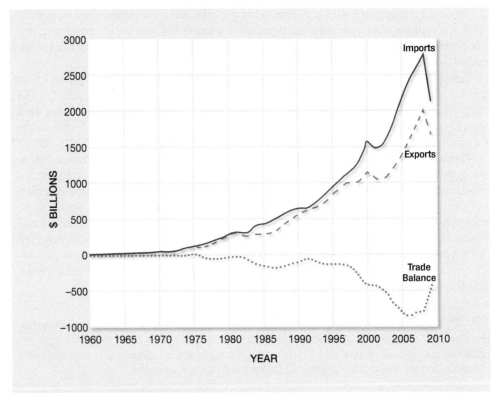

Source: U.S. Department of Commerce, 2012.

Eastern Europe, China, and Russia—a firm may choose to globalize to participate in these markets, depending on its particular needs and goals.

outsourcing
The process of moving production to another firm.

offshoring
Moving production to another country.

nearsourcing
Moving production to a supplier who is geographically closer to where products are sold.

nearshoring
Moving production closer to the same country as consumption.

Outsourcing is the process of moving production of a service, product, or component to another firm. This may be either domestic or overseas. **Offshoring** occurs when a company moves its production to another country. For example, when GM moved production of some cars from Michigan to China, it was offshoring. **Nearsourcing** occurs when production of a product is moved from a supplier that is far away to one that is closer. For example, when one American firm moved its production from a supplier in Malaysia to a supplier in Mexico, it was nearsourcing. Alternatively, **nearshoring** is the act of moving production from far away to a closer location. For example, when Apple announced the production of Mac computers in the United States instead of China, it was nearshoring. SC&O CURRENT EVENTS 1.1 talks about how the Chinese firms are now starting to nearsource.

CHANGES IN ENVIRONMENT Globalization may appear straightforward, but firms often overlook the effects of globalization. Through globalizing, processes are disrupted because there are significant changes to the physical environment, the task environment, and the social environment in which they operate. SC&O managers deal primarily with physical and task environments.

By changing their physical environment, firms locate themselves near to or far away from natural resources. For example, semiconductor firms such as Micron Corporation, which require large amounts of water, probably will not locate in Saudi Arabia or arid parts of Mexico. Instead, they may locate in one of the Asian countries, such as Singapore, to be close to ready supplies of water and expanding markets. Part of the physical environment has to do with **sustainability**, the proactive management of resources in an effort to be environmentally friendly.

sustainability
Proactively managing to save resources and to incorporate "green" production.

The advantage of reducing labor costs is often overemphasized when deciding to change the physical environment. For example, although VW may save money by moving to Mexico, differences in productivity between the United States and Mexico may change the economic equation. A recent study of global drivers of manufacturing competitiveness such as talent-driven innovation, economics, costs, supplier networks, and other factors resulted in the ranking of manufacturing competitiveness shown in FIGURE 1.2.

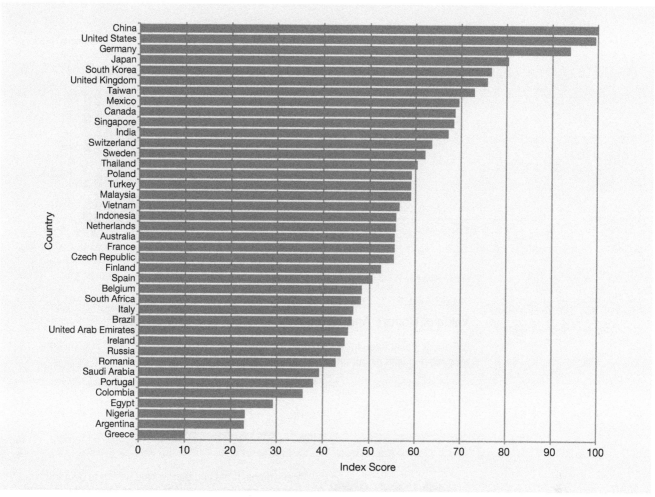

Source: Based on Deloitte Touche Tohmatsu Limited and U.S. Council on Competitiveness, 2013 Global Manufacturing Competitiveness Index.

FIGURE 1.2 ∧

Global Manufacturing Competitiveness Comparisons

Chinese Nearsourcing: An End to Globalization?

< SC&O CURRENT
EVENTS 1.1

Nearsourcing is not limited to American firms moving to American suppliers. Many countries, including Russia, Switzerland, and China, have passed domestic content laws. Domestic content laws require that a certain percentage of a product's components must be produced locally. In addition, sourcing locally can result in lowered costs.

These types of laws have had a significant impact on global commerce. According to the DPB Netherlands Bureau for Economic Policy Analysis, imports of components and raw materials in China have dropped by as much as 15 percent.[1] According to the International Monetary Fund, this trend has been happening for almost ten years.[2]

One example of reduced imports to Chinese manufacturers is Wilton Brands, an American company that manufactures in China. Instead of purchasing nonstick coatings from companies such as Dow Chemical, they now buy these coatings from GMM Coatings, a Chinese company that has gained the ability to make nonstick coatings that are as good as any made anywhere in the world. In addition, over 70 percent of GMM's suppliers are local Chinese companies.

The Chinese government has set a goal that 40 percent of key components to products made in China will come from local sources by 2020 and 70 percent will come from local sources by 2025. In addition, the Chinese government has gone after companies for "dumping" raw materials into the Chinese markets for very low cost. It is expected that this

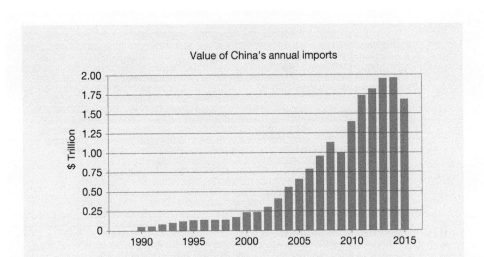

Source: Based on Wind Info. (Imports); CPB Netherlands Bureau for Economic Policy Analysis 2016.

∧ **FIGURE 1.3**

Value of China's Annual Imports

will affect global trade for a long time to come. It will be interesting to see if such actions are reciprocated with global trade barriers being erected.

Source: Based on Trivedi, A., China to World: We Don't Need Your Factories Anymore, *Wall Street Journal*, 18 Oct. 2016, p. 1.

GLOBAL >
CONNECTIONS 1.1

Many times, firms find themselves having to deal with very complex regulatory structures when establishing operations in countries such as Germany, Japan, and Spain. Technological choices vary as firms globalize. What works at home may not serve customers adequately abroad. For example, tobacco producers who globalize find that U.S. mass-production technologies are not flexible enough for the European Economic Community, where regulations concerning tobacco products vary a great deal from country to country. When deciding on where to produce, grow, or assemble their products, supply chain managers must understand the complexities and ramifications of choosing one country over another.

The *task environment* of the firm is the operating structure that the firm encounters when globalizing. The economic structures, skills of the employees, compensation structure, technologies, and government agencies all vary when globalizing. The regulatory structures that firms encounter when globalizing require an understanding of international law. GLOBAL CONNECTIONS BOX 1.1 discusses this requirement in more detail.

D EFINE, UNDERSTAND, AND APPLY THE COMPONENTS OF SUPPLY CHAIN AND OPERATIONS MANAGEMENT

Now that we have defined supply chain management and operations management and have discussed the details of our global marketplace, let's turn our attention to how supply chains and operations management work on their own. We'll also see what happens when managers combine these two concepts.

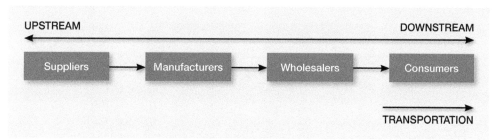

< FIGURE 1.4

A Rudimentary
Supply Chain

Supply Chain Management

It is an important truth that firms no longer compete against one another; today, supply chains compete against other supply chains. What does that mean? Think about a product you are holding now, perhaps some paper. Brazilian farmers harvest fiber and wood chips; shipping companies deliver these raw materials to pulp and paper mills in Vietnam, where workers manufacture the pulp into paper. U.S customer service centers take paper orders, and, based on these orders, trucking companies manage the logistics of shipping the finished paper to wholesalers and retailers. You, the consumer, then go to the store to buy the paper products you need. Procurement activities take place to ensure that the paper producer has everything it needs for maintenance, repair, and operations, the actions that retain a process in a state in which it can perform its required function. The path from Brazil to you, the consumer, is an example of a global supply chain. This supply chain competes with supply chains of other firms that follow their own supply paths. The supply chain that performs the most efficiently wins the customer.

FIGURE 1.4 shows a rudimentary example of a supply chain that has materials flowing from upstream suppliers to downstream customers. In our prior example, the Brazilian farmers are *upstream* suppliers to Vietnamese pulp and paper mills. The U.S. distributors and customers are downstream. In reality, this supply chain is more complex than it initially appears to be. Not only do typical firms have several upstream suppliers, but the suppliers each have many suppliers, which we refer to as tiers of suppliers. Downstream, there are many channels, wholesalers, retailers, and direct customers. Supply chain managers must manage this whole complex network! Add in the complexity of the global movement of materials, information, and monies, and it can get very complicated. SC&O CURRENT EVENTS 1.2 addresses a supply chain disruption at VW.

Supply Chain Disruption at VW

**< SC&O CURRENT
EVENTS 1.2**

Ten years ago, VW was sitting on top of the world. With quality problems at Toyota, they had become the number one producer of automobiles in the world. Then, their world came tumbling down due to a quality/ethical issue that emerged when it was found that they had programmed cars to provide false emission data in their diesel vehicles.

To make matters worse, VW experienced a public dispute with a major supplier that has resulted in a serious supply chain disruption. Supply chain disruptions often occur due to natural events such as tsunamis or earthquakes. They can also result from poor supply chain management.

In VW's case, the emissions scandal hurt its financial performance such that it felt a need to reduce costs by squeezing suppliers. Allegedly, this led VW to cancel its contracts to buy seats and transmission parts from suppliers named Prevent Group and ES Automobilguss. VW lacked alternative suppliers for these parts, so it had to slow or interrupt production of its best-selling Passat and Golf models.

When firms such as VW treat suppliers unfairly or fail to negotiate in good faith, it can result in lost components and supplies, thereby disrupting supply chains and negatively affecting financial results. In this text, we discuss ways of working with suppliers that build trust and reduce supply chain disruptions. Firms with large market power may choose to use that power in a way that puts suppliers at a disadvantage. When suppliers bite back, it can hurt performance.

FIGURE 1.5 >

The Value Chain

value chain
Inbound logistics, transformation processes, and outbound logistics: the core of what a firm does.

Michael Porter, an economist from Harvard, introduced the idea of the *value chain* (FIGURE 1.5) as the basis for the concept of the supply chain. The **value chain** comprises the core activities any firm performs. Firms work with suppliers who provide raw materials and components. These raw materials are brought in through inbound logistics (upstream) processes and are then transformed and shipped to customers through outbound (downstream) logistics. Once the customer has the products, after-sales service is needed to retain the customer.

value-added activities
Process steps that enhance products and services in a way that makes them more valuable for customers.

These "value chain" activities are the core activities where value is created for the customer. **Value-added activities** are process steps that enhance products in a way that makes them more valuable to customers because the products are better suited to meet customer needs. For example, raw iron has a modest value based on its weight alone. Changing that iron into an engine block makes it worth hundreds of dollars. The act of forming the iron into an engine block is an example of a value-adding activity. All other activities—accounting, marketing, finance, human resources, and information systems—are performed in support of these core activities. Adding value to customers is the core of what a firm does and is the primary focus of this course.

Supply Chain Flows

three primary flows of a supply chain
Product flows, monetary flows, and information flows.

Supply chains involve three primary flows. The **three primary flows of a supply chain** (FIGURE 1.6) are (1) *product flows*, (2) *monetary flows*, and (3) *information flows*. We will discuss each of them separately.

product flows
Unidirectional flows of products from upstream to downstream.

Product flows move from upstream to downstream and are generally unidirectional. Firms bring in raw materials, transform them, and ship them to customers. **Reverse logistics** occurs when products move up the supply chain (in special cases such as product returns). One of the current trends in managing product flows is lean production. **Lean** refers to the management of processes in a way that minimizes waste. Chapter 15 addresses lean production in more depth.

reverse logistics
The upstream movement of products through the supply chain.

lean
Managing and improving processes to reduce waste.

monetary flows
The movement of money from downstream to upstream.

Monetary flows are unidirectional but move from downstream to upstream. Customers pay retailers, who pay wholesalers, who pay producers, who pay suppliers, and so forth. The final customer pays for all the economic activity in the supply chain. Understanding this fact will help you understand the importance of adding value. Essentially, if the customer is willing to pay more for a core activity, that activity adds value. It is unlikely that a consumer will be willing to pay more for a purse because the producer has an excellent legal

FIGURE 1.6 >

Three Primary Supply
Chain Flows

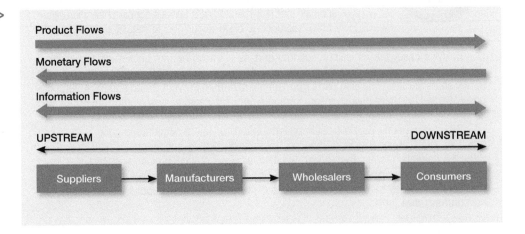

department. **Support processes**, such as legal departments, are activities that support value-added activities.

Information flows are data flows and are bidirectional. **Bidirectional flows** move both upstream and downstream in the normal conduct of supply chain commerce. For example, order information comes from customers or flows upstream. Delivery information flows downstream from suppliers to customers at each stage of the supply chain. Many other types of information flow as well.

....

Managing Across Majors 1.3 Information systems majors need to understand supply chain and operations management because they provide systems that facilitate SC&O effectiveness. **Enterprise resource planning (ERP) systems** are computerized systems and are used to manage supply chain information. We will discuss ERP systems in more detail in Chapter 10.

....

Service Supply Chains

Service supply chain management is often even more complex than manufacturing management because the customers are also the suppliers. Medical patients are both the customer and the supplier. When you go to a doctor's office, you supply the doctor with information *and* you supply the doctor with the raw materials, your own body. As a result, the customer (the patient) provides the doctor (the service provider) with the information and materials necessary for the doctor to provide the customer/patient with the desired service (a healthy body).

That the customer is also the supplier makes service supply chains especially bidirectional, meaning that product resources flow from customers to producers and then back to those same customers. **Service supply chain management** is supply chain management in a service setting. Management of the service supply chain is even further complicated because the service provider is not buffered from the customer the way a nonservice firm is. Although you were probably not present for the production of your phone, clothing, or television, you are often intimately involved in the production of services you purchase. For example, when you order dinner at a restaurant, you provide information about your preferences and are present when the service is provided.

In addition to the direct input customers have on service supply chains, customers as suppliers are more likely to create variation in services than are standard manufacturing customers. *Customer-created variation makes service supply chains and operations very complex to manage.* For example, some fast-food restaurants have self-serve drink stations. Managers have a hard time controlling the customers' experience because the ice-to-drink ratio and number of refills vary from customer to customer. This variation makes it difficult for managers to assess and improve on the customers' experience.

....

Managing Across Majors 1.4 For marketing majors, supply chain management is where marketing meets operations. Service perception often relates to customers' moods and feelings. Customer-created variation is not limited to self-serve kiosks. For example, consider two different couples who go to a highly rated restaurant. If the first couple breaks up over dinner, they may never want to eat at that restaurant again. If the second couple gets engaged there, they may want to come back every year to celebrate. Although managers can make sure that the service and food are impeccable, they cannot control the first couple's distaste for the restaurant any more than they could have planned the second couple's repeat visits.

....

Operations Management

Now that we have discussed supply chain management, let's look at operations management before we combine operations with supply chain. FIGURE 1.7 shows a traditional operations management model. As in the supply chain model, inputs come from suppliers. However, this model emphasizes the conversion or transformation process, which is where raw materials are converted into finished products (or at least finished for that stage of production) using machinery, processes, and labor resources. Operations management involves *integrating* activities and *improving* and *innovating* processes and services, thereby positively *impacting* customers.

---

support processes
Processes, such as legal, that support core processes.

information flows
Data that moves throughout the supply chain.

bidirectional flows
Flows that go both upstream and downstream.

enterprise resource planning (ERP) systems
Computerized systems used to manage supply chain data and information.

service supply chain management
Supply chain management in a service setting.

FIGURE 1.7 >

A Model for Operations Management

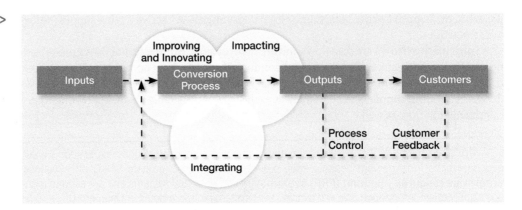

Note in Figure 1.7 that two flows feed back into the productive process. The first of these feedback loops occurs when information is gathered about processes to be able to monitor and improve their efficacy. We call this monitoring activity the control process. Control activities may take the form of process control, cost control, labor control, inventory control, or quality control.

The second feedback loop is where information is gathered from customers, either by the firm or by a third party. All firms gather information from customers. The keys are to be disciplined and to use the gathered information to improve the lives of the customers. World-class firms are able to do so effectively. For example, Ritz-Carlton keeps information about all its customers so that when a customer returns to the Ritz, hotel managers can better anticipate their guests' needs. This text provides the tools and conceptual foundation you will need to better serve customers in your career.

Combining Supply Chain and Operations Management

Now that you are familiar with supply chain and operations management separately, let's unite the two. Combining supply chains with operations externalizes the internal operations of firms. Essentially, supply chain management links the operations of different firms together. Suppliers have transformation processes (operations), and the producing firm has transformation processes. As shown in FIGURE 1.8, the transformative processes of upstream

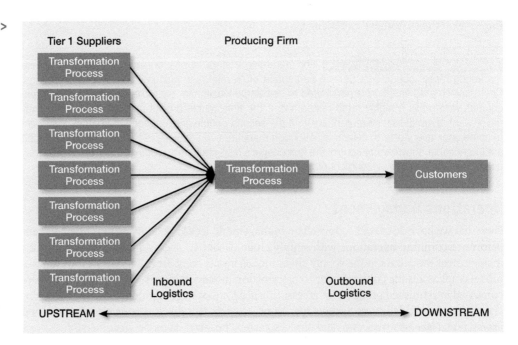

Supply Chain and Operations History		
Date	**SC&O Era**	**Main Contributors**
1700s	*Wealth of Nations*	Adam Smith
1800s	Standardization of parts	Eli Whitney Frederick Taylor
1910s–1930s	Scientific management	Frank and Lillian Gilbreth
	Mass production and standardization	Henry Ford
	Statistical quality control	Walter Shewhart
1940s–1960s	Operations research	George Dantzig and British military intelligence
	Beginning of quality movement in Japan	W. E. Deming, Joseph Juran, and Kaoru Ishikawa
1960s–1980s	Strategic operations management	Wickham Skinner
	Material requirements planning	IBM and Joseph Orlicky
	Just in time	Shigeo Shingo and Taiichi Ohno of Toyota
1990s–2010s	Lean production	Richard Schonberger and others
	In Search of Excellence	Tom Peters
	Supply chain management	Hau Lee and many others
	Services management	James Heskett and many others
	Six Sigma	Thomas Pyzdek, Motorola

< TABLE 1.2

suppliers are tied by supply chain and logistics activities to producers who have transformative processes and eventually to the customers through outbound logistics.

TABLE 1.2 shows the SC&O history that has led us to this point. From the time Adam Smith first introduced his book *Wealth of Nations* until today, the field of SC&O management has been growing and evolving. The growth of supply chain management in recent years has led to radical improvement in performance. For example, average firms spend about 15 percent of costs in supply chain–related activities. World-class firms spend about half that. The opportunity for improvement and cost savings is immense.

Reflecting on Figure 1.8, you can now see that products are created and services are performed through collaborative processes and not through stand-alone operations. This connection between the supply chain and operations is why these two topics are discussed in tandem. Supply chains are the basis for global competition. The ability to share information and compete in a global marketplace allows supply chains to span national borders and encircle the entire world. In other words, global supply chains compete against one another for customers. As a manager, it is your job to juggle these collaborative processes effectively, thus providing outstanding customer service. As a result of this growth in SC&O management, the job market is strong and growing. SC&O CURRENT EVENTS 1.3 gives more detail about career opportunities in this field.

Careers in Supply Chain and Operations

According to Alan Bucio, a business school student, "I think supply chain and operations students have a certain brain-type. I was always the one who organized activities for my friends and [I] like to solve difficult problems."

SC&O management is the hot new major. Schools are ramping up majors and adding concentrations to meet employer demand. SC&O management encompasses fields such as purchasing, logistics, and operations management, and is an exciting business school major for both undergraduate and graduate students. Recent upswings in job openings, comfortable salaries, and prospects for advancement have also caused the academic community to take notice. Salaries have been around $57,400 for graduates of four-year schools and $105,000 for MBA graduates. Firms such as Goldman Sachs, Zara, Ann Taylor, PWC, and many others are scrambling to hire SC&O majors.

The increase in available jobs and the competitive salaries were two reasons that drew Bucio to the field. Bucio spent the summer in an internship with Boeing, where he participated on a factory transformation team. He worked on a project to integrate logistics, supplier management, and production into a single organization, helping to create a strategy for packaging over 3 million items in inventory. He has gone to work for Tesla.

TABLE 1.3 >

Job Titles in Supply Chain and Operations

Supply Management	Operations Management	Customer Management
Supply chain manager	Plant manager	Customer relationship manager
Purchasing manager	Branch operations manager	Product support
Demand planner	Store manager	Customer service
Supplier developer	Project manager	Account manager
Inventory analyst	Production control	Returns manager
Global SC Strategy	**Quality Management**	**Logistics Management**
Chief operating officer (COO)	Business process improvement analyst/ manager	Warehouse manager
Supply network designer	Quality control manager	Export/import manager
Risk manager	Lean/Six Sigma leader	Fleet manager
Sustainability manager	Compliance manager	Reverse logistics manager

Developing Skills for Your Career

As you have begun to see with the Managing Across Majors features, this course in supply chain and operations will help make you more employable, regardless of your major, by providing you core skills that research shows are important for any career. These include critical thinking, knowledge application and analysis, business ethics and social responsibility, and data literacy. We will discuss each of these separately.

CRITICAL THINKING Critical thinking involves purposeful and goal-directed thinking used to define and solve problems and to make decisions or form judgments related to a particular situation or set of circumstances. It involves cognitive, metacognitive, and dispositional components, which may manifest (or be applied) differently in specific contexts. By studying this text, you will be exposed to global business, culture, technologies, and theories that will be new to you. As a result, you will begin to see your world through a different lens.

KNOWLEDGE APPLICATION AND ANALYSIS Knowledge application and analysis is defined as the ability to learn a concept and then apply that knowledge appropriately in another setting to achieve a higher level of understanding. Our discussion of supply chain in this text is global in nature. The study of operations management takes you inside the head of a production and services manager so that you can begin to see the world in new ways.

BUSINESS ETHICS AND SOCIAL RESPONSIBILITY Business ethics are sets of guiding principles that influence the way individuals and organizations behave within the society in which they operate. Corporate social responsibility (CSR) is a form of ethical behavior that requires that organizations understand, identify, and eliminate unethical economic, environmental, and social behaviors. Beginning in Chapters 1 and 2, we discuss the ethical and social aspects of SC&O. You will learn to respond to others intelligently about how business can make the world a better place by alleviating poverty and improving environmental performance.

INFORMATION TECHNOLOGY APPLICATION AND COMPUTING SKILLS Information technology application and computing skills are defined as the ability to select and use appropriate technology to accomplish a given task. The individual is also able to apply computing skills to solve problems and show proficiency with computer software programs. Besides discussing enterprise resource planning systems in depth, as a result of this course, you will improve your skills in Excel. These skills are highly desired by employers.

XPLAIN THE INTEGRATIVE MODEL FOR SUPPLY CHAIN AND OPERATIONS MANAGEMENT

FIGURE 1.9 illustrates the integrative SC&O model, which serves as the basis for the integration of supply chains and operations. This model combines several prior figures provided in this chapter and will begin every chapter in this text. The operating core, upstream collaboration, downstream collaboration, and strategic integration are the key components of this model.

The Operating Core

The horizontal bidirectional arrow in the middle of Figure 1.9 is the supply chain. To the right is the downstream customer, and to the left are the upstream suppliers. The sphere in the center of the model is the operating core. As we discussed earlier, the operating core is where transformation of materials to finished goods takes place. For example, Jansport has internal operations where it produces backpacks (the middle circle). This circle is the operational core. It involves anything from sewing operations to the fabrication of fasteners and buckles. It purchases material, zippers, plastic, patches, and thread from upstream suppliers (the left circle). Jansport must manage the relationships with these upstream suppliers so that these materials arrive on time and to specification. Downstream, Jansport has to manage customer relations with distributors, retailers, and customers (the right circle). Jansport is responsible for making sure that the logistics and quality are correct. All Jansport's decisions throughout the supply chain have to be in alignment with some cohesive strategy.

In addition to operations management, the operating core includes operations strategy, sustainability, product design, process design, process mapping, forecasting, inventory

FIGURE 1.9 >

An Integrative
Model of
Supply Chain
and Operations
Management

management, sales and operations planning, enterprise resource planning, project management, statistical quality control, lean production, Six Sigma processes, and managing change. Look for these operations topics as we move through the text; understanding them is important when making operations decisions within the context of this model.

Upstream Collaboration

Moving upstream in Figure 1.9, the farthest left sphere encompasses working with and collaborating with suppliers. This collaboration is a very important aspect of supply chain management. This text covers this and related topics extensively because managers' relationships with and understanding of their suppliers are an integral aspect of keeping their supply chains operational. Among the topics covered in upstream processes are strategic sourcing or purchasing; supplier selection and development; total cost of ownership; supplier management; supplier scorecards; and supply chain quality management, which deals largely with supplier quality issues.

Downstream Collaboration

Moving downstream from the center in Figure 1.9 is customer relationship management. Although customer relationship management can happen throughout the supply chain, we use this concept to sharpen our focus on downstream processes and customers.

Customer relationship management involves both personal interactions with customers and information systems used in enhancing customer relations. Among the downstream collaboration topics covered in this text are service process design, business-to-business strategies, business-to-consumer strategies, waiting line theory, mass customization, after-sales service, and demand management. There is also a strong focus in this text on customer service and customer satisfaction.

business to business (B2B)
Business transacted between two commercial firms.

business to consumer (B2C)
Business transacted between a business and a consumer.

Managers approach **business to business (B2B)** and **business to consumer (B2C)** collaboration somewhat differently due to the requirements of B2B and B2C markets. B2B is business between two business entities such as a supplier providing components for a personal computer. B2C is business to consumer such as Hershey's selling candy to customers. For example, in B2B collaborations, important topics include information sharing, joint design whereby products are designed collaboratively by suppliers, joint planning, and achieving an understanding relative to needs and requirements. B2C collaboration takes business into mass customization; servitization; and developing an understanding of customer service, including gathering data from customers as a basis for improvement. We will discuss B2B and B2C collaboration in Chapter 4.

Logistics, Analytics, and Quality Management

Notice in Figure 1.9 that performance in the entire supply chain is optimized by *logistics, analytics, and quality management*. Logisticians manage the movement of materials throughout the supply chain. Quality management helps to improve performance and quality. **Analytics** are quantitative tools found throughout the text to aid supply chain and operations professionals in analyzing data and in making better decisions.

analytics
Quantitative tools used to aid SC&O decision making.

Strategic Integration

The foundation and the roof of Figure 1.9 includes the important topics of logistics, quality management, and global supply chain strategy. These topics are represented in this way because they affect the entire supply chain and will be discussed in later chapters.

As you can see, this closed loop in Figure 1.9 encompasses all the core activities that are of importance to SC&O managers. After studying and understanding the intricacies of this diagram, you will be ready to manage employees, suppliers, and customers effectively and to make decisions in today's global business environment.

 XPLAIN THE FOUR I'S

Figure 1.9 includes the **Four I's of SC&O management**, cross-cutting concepts that glue together the supply chain and help to provide a philosophical and theoretical basis for learning SC&O. The Four I's are *impacting, improving, innovating,* and *integrating*.

Four I's of SC&O management
Impacting, improving, innovating, and integrating.

Impacting

As we have already discussed, the core processes and activities affect the customer. **Impacting** means successfully managing core processes that affect the customer. If you manage SC&O processes well, your customers will be satisfied and the company will be successful. Research shows that customer retention (which ties into customer satisfaction) correlates directly to a firm's profitability. Decisions you will make anywhere upstream in SC&O processes affect the customer. If you choose poor suppliers, the customer will definitely be affected. For example, after the media explosion that occurred because their supplier used leaded paint, toy makers Mattel and Fisher Price lost customer trust.

impacting
Effectively managing core processes that affect customers.

Improving

A major focus of this text is on constantly improving SC&O performance. Business managers today are like pole-vaulters running down a lane to perform a jump, but as the pole-vaulter is about to release the pole, competitors and customers quickly raise the bar. In SC&O management, today's requirements become tomorrow's poor performance because the bar is constantly rising.

Improving is a process, not a single event. It is the result of effective process management and design. In this text, we will provide many cutting-edge tools and analytic methods to help you manage improvement.

improving
The act of making processes, products, and people better.

Innovating

An effective process for innovating is necessary for firms to compete effectively. SC&O professionals are known for their innovations in managing global SC&O processes. Companies such as Walmart and Apple are able to become more competitive by innovating their SC&O practices. Apple was an early outsourcer, forming an alliance with Foxconn of Taiwan. Walmart purchases produce directly from farmers in Chile during winter in the Northern Hemisphere.

Improvement tends to be incremental and continuous. **Innovating** is change on a larger scale that has a dramatic effect on business results.

innovating
Large-scale, sudden improvement.

Integrating

integrating
Collaboration and cooperation
between stakeholders in a
supply chain.

Integrating is collaborating and cooperating with all the stakeholders in SC&O processes. These stakeholders include suppliers, operations people, planners, logisticians, customer relationship managers, systems professionals, and customers. Collaboration and coordination between managers and their respective counterparts result in streamlined communication, information sharing, and improved management outcomes. As we have discussed, complexity is a major concern in SC&O management. One of the best ways of managing complexity is through integrating. That is, by communicating and collaborating, teamwork is enhanced and problems are more easily solved.

Supplier Responsibility at Apple

We started the chapter by discussing supplier responsibility at Apple. Now that you have studied this chapter, you can see how firms connect and supply chains compete to satisfy customers. If a supplier is managed improperly or if a supplier to a firm such as Apple employs say, child labor, the blame for that will fall on Apple's shoulders.

As a result, Apple set standards for accountability, labor and human rights, empowering workers, environmental health and safety, and auditing for its suppliers. This means that Apple establishes values regarding issues such as overly long work hours, child labor, safety, bonded labor (slavery), safe water, and many other standards.

As firms such as Apple do this with their supply chain partners, living and work standards around the world should improve. Supply chain professionals can help to make the world a better place.

Summary

1. We began by discussing why you are studying supply chain and operations management.
   a. A key element in studying SC&O management is a focus on process. In our text, we discuss process design, process management, process control, and process improvement.
   b. Process management is made more complex given that SC&O processes are global by nature. Considered here are the physical environment, the task environment, and the social environment in which the SC&O system resides.
2. The supply chain externalizes operations upstream to the suppliers and downstream toward customers.
   a. The three main flows of supply chains are product flows, monetary flows, and information flows.
   b. Service supply chains are bidirectional and complex because of interactions with customers who create process variation.
   c. Operations management involves the management of transformation processes that add value for customers.

3. The integrative model of SC&O management includes considerations of upstream (supplier development) processes, downstream (customer service) processes, optimization of the supply chain through logistics and quality management, and strategic integration.

4. The Four I's provide the glue that allows us to conceptualize SC&O management. The Four I's include impacting customers, improving performance, innovating along the supply chain, and integrating everything strategically. You will find that this text will take you on a journey that is global in nature, important, and exciting!

Key Terms

analytics 17
business to business (B2B) 16
business to consumer (B2C) 16
bidirectional flows 11
enterprise resource planning
    (ERP) systems 11
Four I's of SC&O management 17
globalization 5
information flows 11
innovating 17
impacting 17
improving 17
integrating 18

lean 10
licensing 5
monetary flows 10
nearshoring 6
nearsourcing 6
offshoring 6
operations management 3
outsourcing 6
process control 5
process design 4
processes 4
process improvement 5
process management 5

product flows 10
reverse logistics 10
service supply chain management 11
strategic alliances 5
supply chain and operations
    (SC&O) 3
supply chain management 3
support processes 11
sustainability 6
three primary flows of a supply
    chain 10
value-added activities 10
value chain 10

Integrative Learning Exercise

Describe supply chain management and operations management. Briefly discuss how the functional areas and business disciplines of accounting, finance, marketing, human resources, and information systems are related to supply chain management. Why do students hoping for careers in business need to understand SC&O management?

Integrative Experiential Exercise

As part of a student team, visit a local company. Identify some of the processes performed by the company. How are the processes designed? Identify how a particular process is monitored and controlled. What process improvement activities has the company undertaken in the past year? What challenges and opportunities were encountered during the process improvement? Tie your findings into concepts discussed in this chapter.

Discussion Questions

1. How is operations management different from supply chain management?

2. Why have organizations combined supply chain management and operations management into SC&O management?

3. Identify some of the strategic factors associated with the decision to bring manufacturing back onshore (e.g., nearshoring).

4. What is meant by a process? Why do business students need to understand processes?

5. What are the phases involved with process design? How can process design be expedited?

6. What is process improvement, and how is it related to customer needs?

7. What is meant by globalization? Why is this concept of importance to SC&O managers?

8. Briefly list and define three mechanisms that firms use in globalizing their operations.

9. What is meant by the statement that "companies no longer compete against one another; today, supply chains compete against supply chains"? Why is it important to understand this statement?

10. How do value chain activities differ from support activities? What are a firm's core activities?

11. Identify the three primary flows found in a supply chain. Why is it important for an SC&O manager to understand these flows?

12. In what fundamental way do information flows differ from monetary and product flows in a supply chain?

13. What makes service supply chains more complex to manage than product supply chains?

14. Briefly describe two basic feedback loops found in operations management.

15. Why are many colleges and universities seeing an increase in the number of students who are interested in studying SC&O management?

CASE   Williamston Manufacturing

Trudy Gonzalez was under pressure to put the finishing touches on her presentation to the Williamston Manufacturing executive management committee. Trudy had been with the company, a diversified manufacturing firm, for three years. In that time, she had worked in a variety of areas, most recently in capacity planning. As part of her duties, Trudy was working with a team of employees who were analyzing whether the company should begin to produce products outside the United States. Williamston had several production facilities, but all were located in the Northeast or the Ohio Valley. Many of Williamston's competitors had moved production to Mexico or Asia over the past two decades. Some competitors did all of their manufacturing outside the United States.

Trudy believed that locating production overseas could reduce manufacturing costs, but she was worried about the disruption and fracturing of the company's supply chain with production located so far from key suppliers and end customers. She knew that manufacturing costs were an important consideration in the analysis, but she also understood that managing a supply chain and controlling shipping costs over great distances could eliminate any reductions in labor costs from locating plants outside the United States. Trudy's team needed to make recommendations to the company's executive team by next Wednesday. While she was completing her report, she came across an article titled "The Boomerang Effect" from the April 21, 2012, edition of *The Economist* (available at http://www.economist.com/node/21552898).

Question:

Trudy has hired you as an intern to provide a summary of the article and to relate the issues discussed in the piece to the decisions made by Williamston Manufacturing. Specifically, she wonders how important low wage costs are to manufacturing and whether it is worth chasing after low wages by moving plants outside the United States. What other issues and considerations should be analyzed before making the final recommendation to the executive management committee? Trudy is eagerly awaiting your summary of the article's findings.

2

Supply Chain and Operations Strategy

INTEGRATING	GLOBAL SC&O STRATEGY		
INNOVATING	Supply Management	Operations Management	Customer Relationship Management
IMPACTING	Upstream Processes	Core Processes	Downstream Processes
IMPROVING	QUALITY MANAGEMENT, ANALYTICS, AND LOGISTICS		

CHAPTER OUTLINE AND LEARNING OBJECTIVES

1 Understand and Use Generic SC&O Strategies
- List and explain the three generic strategies.
- Explain how managers use alignment to achieve strategic goals.
- Describe how managers assess customer value.

2 Explain How to Apply SC&O Strategy Process and Content
- Explain Hoshin Kanri strategy and planning.
- Define and differentiate between capabilities and competencies.
- Explain the resource-based view.

3 Explain How Managers Use Supply Chain Strategy to Build Relationships
- Describe how the strategy has changed.
- Describe the types of relationships managers leverage.

4 Execute Strategy
- Describe how managers align strategic levels.
- Explain why and how managers align incentives to achieve optimum levels of output.
- Explain why and how focusing on processes helps managers reach their goals.

5 Understand and Apply Strategic Metrics and Measurements
- Describe correct strategic behavior and how it is implemented.
- Explain how managers use actionable and predictive metrics to achieve their strategic goals.
- List and describe commonly used supply chain metrics.
- Explain why managers need to think about their strategy in a holistic way.

6 Describe the Changing Strategic Environment
- Discuss emerging strategic concerns such as globalization, sustainability, and innovation.

You recently might have heard about Tesla. At the time of this edition, Tesla has announced the production of its Model 3 automobile. Elon Musk, the CEO of Tesla, has been very aggressive in announcing production plans and sales volumes. Of course, these announcements are very strategic and affect every aspect of supply chain and operations.

To launch new products, strategic suppliers and production processes must be put in place. Components must be planned for; new supplier relationships established; and, in the case of Tesla, totally new supplies of elements found. To make this all work requires effective SC&O planning. The launch of the Model 3 has been difficult. At the end of the chapter, we will discuss some of the strategic moves that Tesla has made to try to be successful.

strategy
A long-term plan that defines how the company will win customers, create game-winning capabilities, fit into the competitive environment, and develop relationships.

supply chain strategy
The supply chain portion of the strategic plan.

operations strategy
Allocating resources within the firm to provide value to customers.

SC&O strategy
A strategy that encompasses both supply chain management and operations management.

In this chapter, we will discuss supply chain and operation (SC&O) strategy at the firm level. Strategy involves planning to meet long-term goals and objectives. Leaders establish vision and guide others toward achieving important goals. SC&O strategy addresses many issues that are essential for competitiveness. Much of SC&O strategy has to do with matching resources with business needs. **Strategy** is a long-term plan that defines how the company will win customers, create game-winning capabilities, fit into the competitive environment, and develop relationships. Strategy includes long-term planning that is performed at the highest organizational levels.

Supply chain strategy is the supply chain portion of the strategic plan. It includes developing the ability of the firm to leverage internal relationships, supplier alliances, and customer relationships to create sustained competitive advantage. **Operations strategy** focuses on allocating resources within the firm to provide value to customers. Our use of **SC&O strategy** encompasses both considerations. In this chapter, we will first discuss generic SC&O strategies. We will then discuss process (how to create strategies) and content (what is included in SC&O strategy), followed by the ways in which managers use the competitive landscape to drive strategy, the types of relationships that supply chain managers have with their suppliers, and how managers measure their strategic success. The chapter concludes with a discussion of the changing strategic environment.

U NDERSTAND AND USE GENERIC SC&O STRATEGIES

In this section, we define generic strategies. It is important to understand how firms compete so that managers can align SC&O strategy with overall company goals. In addition to alignment, you will learn about agility and adaptability.

Generic Strategies

Before getting to the nuts and bolts of SC&O strategy, we first must define different strategies and how firms compete. Michael Porter, a Harvard economist, suggests that companies may gain an advantage over their competition in three main ways (FIGURE 2.1). Some companies, such as Walmart, use a **cost strategy** and find ways to reduce costs and provide customers with a lower price than competitors. Others, such as Home Depot,

cost strategy
A generic strategy that focuses on reducing cost.

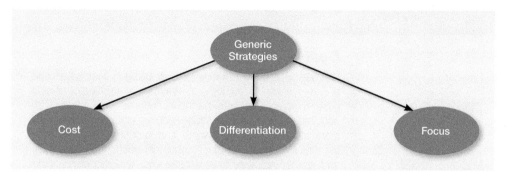

use a **focus strategy** and seek to service only select customers and provide these niche customers with a narrow range of unique products or services. Others, such as Apple, Inc., use a **differentiation strategy** and seek to provide such distinctive products or services that competitors cannot compete with them. In each case, the company focuses on unique ways to gain advantage over competitors and win customers. The company must then develop plans in order to achieve a life-long commitment from customers. SC&O CURRENT EVENTS 2.1 looks at how three very successful firms have adapted these three generic strategies.

focus strategy
A generic strategy that emphasizes select customers or markets.

differentiation strategy
A generic strategy that emphasizes providing special value to customers in a way that is difficult for competitors to replicate.

Alignment

Each generic strategy (cost, focus, and differentiation) must be in alignment with the company's SC&O strategy. **Alignment** means that SC&O decisions will be consistent with the strategic directions for the firm. For example, companies with a low-cost emphasis need processes, systems, labor, and policies that support low cost. The same need for alignment exists for differentiation and focus.

alignment
Consistency among strategic, supply chain, and operational decisions.

FISHER STRATEGY MODEL Alignment in SC&O strategy matches capabilities with the supply chain needs of the customer. The **Fisher strategy model** in TABLE 2.1 shows one example of alignment. In this model, managers match the type of supply chain they use with their customer's needs. As a manager, you might ask yourself if customers want your products to be functional or interactive. Functional products, such as kitchen appliances, tend to be mass produced, and interactive products, such as tailored clothing or custom-made shoes, tend to be customized. Trade-offs between functionality and interactivity have to be made relative to efficiency and responsiveness in the supply chain.

Fisher strategy model
A model developed by Marshall Fisher that matches capabilities with customer needs.

THE IMPORTANCE OF AGILITY Even when firms align their tactics with strategies, strategic planners must be prepared for the dynamics of supply and demand. In other words, SC&O strategic planners must be able to plan for and have the capabilities to adapt to changes in the business environment.

Agility, the ability of a supply chain to respond quickly to short-term changes in demand or supply, is another key SC&O consideration that managers must make when creating strategy. Manufacturers must be prepared to respond to short-term, rapid increases or decreases in demand as well as be able to react to interruptions in supply. Manufacturers that are unprepared for short-term change lose out to manufacturers that are prepared. For example, Spanish fashion retailer Zara understood that fashion changes quickly and created the capabilities to respond in kind. Rather than outsource its production to an Asian manufacturer far away from its target markets, Zara mostly manufactures within its own markets. While other manufacturers take months to design, create, and deliver product, Zara does so in weeks. Manufacturing close to demand allows Zara to adjust to frequently changing customer demand quickly. This agile capability allowed Zara not only to capture market share from less agile competitors but also to reduce marked-down merchandise from an industry average of 50 percent to 15 percent. Its agile capability, in part, has allowed this European company to become the third largest clothing retailer in the world.

agility
The ability of a supply chain to respond quickly to short-term changes in demand or supply.

Examples of Generic Strategies

Cost

Walmart is a good example of how using a cost advantage provides value to customers. Walmart shares point-of-sale cash register data with partners, reduces product lines to only the most profitable stock-keeping units, and reformats store shelves to reduce waste and variability. Walmart also teaches suppliers to produce consumer goods more efficiently and directs suppliers toward more cost-effective outsourcing options. In addition, Walmart is well known for ultra-efficient transportation, fast warehouses, and minimized inventories to provide consumers with the lowest possible supply chain and logistics costs. Walmart's unique, cost-saving capabilities appeal to consumers' desires for low prices. Walmart's low-cost strategy provides it with a competitive advantage over other big-box stores and has allowed it to win and keep customers.

Focus

An example of strategic focus for a retail firm is Home Depot. Home Depot was dreamed up in a coffee shop when Bernie Marcus and Arthur Blank envisioned a hardware store where people could not only buy stuff but they could learn about any home repair or improvement from experienced employees. As the do-it-yourself (DIY) home repair craze has hit America, Home Depot has capitalized, growing from two stores in Atlanta to over 2,200 stores today. Marcus and Blank believe that they have been able to serve a niche—people who like to do home projects.

Differentiation

Apple, Inc. is a good example of a company that wins customers through differentiating its products. Apple does not attempt to make the lowest-priced products or sell products that only select customers will appreciate. Instead, Apple prides itself on making iconic, easy-to-use products.

Contrary to popular perception, the iPhone was not the first smartphone on the market. When Apple introduced the iPhone, however, it also offered consumers the Apple iTunes app store, a system to download Apple-approved applications and content so that customers could easily customize their smartphones. By bundling both the hardware and content into an integrated package, Apple provided customers a product unlike any other on the market. This easy-to-use system soon dominated market share.

Because of the great demand for its highly sought-after products, Apple is able to charge a premium for its products. Apple's capability to create highly differentiated products creates a sustained competitive advantage for the company.

TABLE 2.1 >

Fisher's Supply Chain Alignment Model		
	Functional Products	**Interactive Products**
Efficient Supply Chains	Match	Mismatch
Responsive Supply Chains	Mismatch	Match

Source: Based on data from Fisher, M., "What Is the Right Supply Chain for Your Product?" *Harvard Business Review*, March–April 1997, pp. 105–116.

ADAPTABILITY Although agility may be important to capturing the value in short-term changes, *adaptability* is equally as important when capturing the value of long-term changes. Sometimes, the capability to change your entire supply chain or entire manufacturing strategy keeps a business viable. **Adaptability** is the capability to adjust a supply chain's design (i.e., the supply network, manufacturing capabilities, and distribution network) to meet major structural shifts in the market.[1] For instance, a company should be able to judge when products are moving from an innovative, disruptive product to a more mature product. As products become more mature, companies must be prepared to shift their supply chain to focus more on efficiency and less on responsiveness. To execute an effective change strategy, SC&O strategists must identify the capabilities needed to make this transition.

> **adaptability**
> The capability to adjust a supply chain's design (i.e., the supply network, manufacturing capabilities, and distribution network) to meet major structural shifts in the market.

ORDER WINNERS AND QUALIFIERS Another method for achieving strategic alignment is to identify how the firm generates business. **Order winners** are those attributes that differentiate a company's products.[2] For example, the reason consumers purchase some specific products is low price. To capture those customers, marketing can feature low price. Also, SC&O managers can provide processes, standardization, and high production volumes to support low price. Therefore, identifying how the firm wins orders allows marketing and SC&O to align their efforts in a way that will satisfy the customer.

> **order winners**
> Attributes that differentiate a company's products.

Order qualifiers are those necessary attributes that allow a firm to enter into and compete in a market, and a firm's strategy must account for these necessities. For example, a minimal level of product quality may be required simply to allow a firm to compete. The U.S. automobile industry supports such a marketplace. For example, Kia, made in Korea, had to meet basic quality standards for North America before it was allowed in U.S. markets. Having done so, Kia now competes successfully in the United States. Identifying order qualifiers allows marketing and SC&O to align customer needs with operational choices, such as production technologies and process choices.

> **order qualifiers**
> Necessary attributes that allow a firm to enter into and compete in a market; a firm's strategy must account for these necessities.

Managing Across Majors 2.1 Marketing majors, the order-winning criterion occurs at the point of impact between SC&O and marketing. It can serve as a tool for you to come to agreement on how the firm will compete at a strategic level.

Assessing Customer Value

To achieve alignment in SC&O strategy, SC&O managers need to integrate closely with marketing managers, who are focused on customer needs. The need to win and retain customers motivates all three generic strategies and their alignment with a firm's strategy. Customers provide all the profit and most of the capital for a firm. When a firm is beginning to develop its strategy of how to compete in a market, it must first identify key customers. Managers identify their customers through market studies and conversations between marketing and SC&O managers.

Furthermore, successful companies focus on the concept of the *lifetime value* (LTV) of the key customers rather than on a onetime transaction. LTV examines the potential long-term worth that each customer provides to a company instead of the immediate profit that the customer may contribute. For example, if your new laptop breaks after only a few days of use and the retailer that sold it to you refuses to honor your warranty, not only will you never buy from that store again, but you will also make sure that all your friends know about the store's predatory practices. Even though the electronics retailer received the profit from your one broken laptop, it will miss out on the potential profit that you and your friends may have provided them over your entire lifetime. Strategic decision makers must evaluate and consider the potential LTV of its customers instead of concentrating on the value of a single transaction.

---

[1]Hau L. Lee, "The Triple A Supply Chain" *Harvard Business Review*, Oct. 2004, 1–12.
[2]T. Hill, *Manufacturing Strategy* (Basingstoke: UK, Palgrave, 2009).

Waitrose Attracts the Wrong Customers

Waitrose is a British-based grocery store chain with stores throughout the United Kingdom (UK). The store is known for its high quality. It was the first grocer in the UK to promote and sell organic produce. In addition, it supplies members of the royal family with their groceries. Although it does also carry bargain lines within its stores, Waitrose is generally known as a differentiated brand in the UK.

As a promotion, Waitrose announced that customers that had enrolled in their customer loyalty plan could go to the in-store café and receive free coffee once a day. This initiative was done in order to create a welcoming experience and a differentiated experience from other grocers. It was meant to allow their key customers, middle-aged people with above average incomes, to be part of the Waitrose "family."

Later, Waitrose was forced to change their free coffee policy. To get free coffee, customers now had to buy something. The reason for the change was that the free coffee attracted the wrong type of customers into their stores. While the promotion was meant to attract key customers, it actually attracted a less affluent and less consumption-oriented group of people derogatorily called "chavs." These tech-savvy, loud-dressing, and cash-strapped young people easily signed up for the loyalty card just to get a free cup of coffee every day. Once-loyal key customers complained about not only extensive queues to get their coffee but also the dramatic change in the clientele within the Waitrose stores. Waitrose had attracted the wrong type of customer, and the free coffee meant to differentiate their stores actually hurt their sales. Now, they have also angered their loyal customers because their free cup of coffee is no longer a perk.

Source: Based on "Waitrose Curbs Free Coffee after Customers Complain Deal Is Attracting 'the Wrong Sort of People,'" by Rachel Bishop. Published by *Mirror,* 15 Oct. 2016. http://www.mirror.co.uk/news/uk-news/waitrose-curbs-free-coffee-after-9052033.

SC&O managers understand that customers are not all equally valuable. Some customers simply are not worth the cost or effort to serve. The 80/20 rule, also called *Pareto's law,* suggests that 20 percent of customers account for 80 percent of revenues. The key for strategy makers is to identify the very best customers and provide outstanding service to those top customers. Identifying your top customer is not always simple but, in the end, it is worth the effort (as GLOBAL CONNECTIONS 2.1 demonstrates). Other customers may still provide value, but your best service should be offered to high-value customers.

Strategists must understand key customers' needs for a firm to survive and prosper. Customers are the judge and jury in competitive advantage. No matter how many of your shareholders, your competitors, or the media praise your company, your customer decides your long-term success.

XPLAIN HOW TO APPLY SC&O STRATEGY PROCESS AND CONTENT

strategy process
The method pursued for creating strategy.

strategy content
That which construes a strategy.

We will now turn our attention from generic strategies to developing SC&O strategy. There are two main components to SC&O strategy: *process* and *content*. **Strategy process** is the method pursued for creating strategy. **Strategy content** is what construes the strategy and includes (1) the already-discussed generic strategies, (2) the recognition and consideration of your competitors, (3) the creation and maintenance of supplier relationships, and (4) how you measure and react to your strategies' successes and failures.

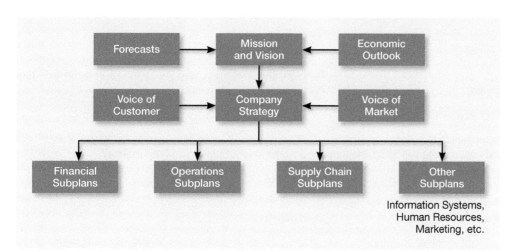

Supply Chain and Operations Strategic Planning Hierarchy

FIGURE 2.2 shows a hierarchy for SC&O strategic planning, and TABLE 2.2 shows definitions of all the steps in the hierarchy. All planning starts with a forecast and requires an understanding of the economic environment. Mission and vision also help inform strategic decision making. Managers use the forecast, mission, and vision, coupled with customer research and market analysis, to set strategic plans. From the strategic plan, *operational subplans* are established in the areas of finance, operations, supply chain management, information systems, human resources, and marketing. These **operational subplans** are portions of the strategic plan pertaining to the differing functional areas of the firm that help ensure attainment of strategic objectives. Strategic alignment occurs when there is consistency in choices made in the subplans to support the overall company strategy.

operational subplans
Portions of the strategic plan pertaining to the differing functional areas of the firm that help ensure attainment of strategic objectives.

Hoshin Kanri Strategic Planning

One planning method that SC&O managers often use is **Hoshin Kanri planning**. *Hoshin* is Japanese for "a compass," which indicates a vision or purpose to all existence. *Kanri* refers to management control; in English, it is generally referred to as policy deployment. Japanese managers have long been using Hoshin Kanri (or Hoshin for short) planning as a means of implementing policy. Implicit in Hoshin is the use of the basic seven tools of quality and quality function deployment. We will discuss the seven tools in more detail in Chapter 13.

Hoshin Kanri planning
Policy deployment through a strategic planning process that utilizes project-based improvement.

In the Hoshin process, after firm leaders develop a three- to five-year plan and senior executives develop the current year's Hoshin objectives, *catchball* occurs. **Catchball** is the strategic back-and-forth dialogue between successive levels of managers and their teams. The development of the Hoshin plan results in the cascading of action plans that are designed to achieve corporate goals.

catchball
Strategic back-and-forth dialogue between successive levels of managers and their teams in Hoshin Kanri.

Many successful companies, such as Solectron and Motorola, use Hoshin planning. By using Hoshin strategic planning processes, Solectron established itself as a market leader in electronic component production.

SC&O Strategy Content

Once a firm completes catchball, it needs to ensure that it possesses *capabilities* to best meet its strategic objectives. A company must first have employees with the skills and training necessary to provide its unique brand of service. Then, a firm ensures that it has the correct assets, policies, and processes needed to provide customers with outstanding service. When a company has capabilities that align with key customers' needs, it can gain competitive advantage.

A firm's SC&O capabilities are key to competitiveness. **Capabilities** are the network of people, knowledge, information systems, tools, and business processes that create value for

capabilities
The network of people, knowledge, information systems, tools, and business processes that create value for customers.

∨ TABLE 2.2

Elements of the Strategic Planning Hierarchy

Planning Step	Definition	What It Really Involves
Forecast	A prediction of future events	Demand patterns, costs, budgets, and so on.
Economic outlook	An examination of how the macroeconomic environment will affect the firm	What do we expect to happen with the overall economy, legal environment, and regulations?
Mission	A statement of the purpose of a firm	Why does the firm exist?
Vision	A statement of possibilities for the company	What are upper management's aspirations for the organization?
Voice of the customer	An understanding of customers' requirements	What are customers' needs, wants, desires, preferences, and expectations?
Voice of the market	An understanding of the competitive environment	What are your competitors up to?
Company strategy	An elicitation of near- and long-term plans for the firm	What are our key objectives for the coming years, and how are we to accomplish them?
Financial subplans	How the company strategy will be financed	What are the needed funding, allocation of scarce resources, risk analysis, and economic decisions? Budgets are set that provide a foundation for what is accomplished from the strategic plan.
Operational subplans	How we support the company strategy operationally	What choices are relative to production technologies, process choice, infrastructure, and capacity?
Supply chain subplans	How we partner to satisfy customers and satisfy company-wide strategic objectives	What strategic partnerships, logistics planning, supplier development, and supply chain performance management options are possible?
Information systems subplans	Planning to provide software, hardware, and support to meet company strategic objectives	What information system projects get priority, and what expenditures will be needed for the coming year?
Human resources subplans	Plans for selecting, training, and developing employees to help achieve company-wide strategic objectives	How many people will be hired and trained during the strategic planning cycle? What plans are needed to meet educational goals for the firm?
Marketing subplans	Based on the company strategy, goals, and plans, sales and promotion for the strategic planning cycle are created.	Based on forecasts, what are the sales goals and resources needed? What plans and budgets should be established for promotional activities, and what marketing channels should be evaluated?

customers. Capabilities vary widely between firms. SC&O CURRENT EVENTS 2.2 discusses capabilities for three retailers.

Another problem many companies face in their strategic content is that they try to master too many capabilities. One such case is General Motors, which has suffered from trying to be "all things to all people" in the auto industry: It has produced vehicles to satisfy every possible consumer desire while not doing anything particularly well. Companies that focus on their **core competencies** hone only those capabilities that tie most closely to their customer values and that provide them with a unique competitive advantage.

A firm's strategic plan might not succeed for many reasons. For instance, a firm might not have the unique resources necessary to compete in its competitive landscape. A firm

core competencies
Abilities that companies compete on that are difficult for competitors to replicate.

An Examination of the Operational and Supply Chain Capabilities of Three Retail Giants

In SC&O Current Events 2.1, we discussed how Walmart's ultra-efficient logistic capabilities complement its low-cost strategy. Home Depot realizes its niche strategy with its unique capability to provide DIY consumers with a place to get all that they need. Apple had a visionary leader in Steve Jobs, who provided customers with innovative and practical products. These qualities are all unique capabilities. Capabilities support strategies because they provide the company with the tools to carry out strategic plans. When a firm develops strategy, it develops an understanding of both its customers and its capabilities. If there is a mismatch between what capabilities provide and what customers expect, the firm will not succeed.

In 1962, three stores were founded: Kmart, Walmart, and Target. Kmart was the early leader in the race for competitive dominance, largely due to its capability to create an exciting shopping experience. Kmart stores frequently had "blue light specials," unexpected sales that were identified by a flashing blue light in the store, to entice buyers to purchase a product immediately. The blue light special was so effective that it quickly became part of the fad culture of the 1960s and 1970s. Kmart was not as concerned about the quality of its sourcing and the cost of its distribution network; it ignored its supply chain and focused on marketing as its core competence.

While Kmart was focusing on an exciting shopping experience, Walmart was creating capabilities to make its supply chain more efficient. Walmart invested in technology, distribution centers, and suppliers that allowed it to provide quality merchandise at a consistently low price. Over time, the customer's excitement for unannounced sales wore off for Kmart, and customers switched to the everyday low prices that Walmart provided them.

Target, at the same time, had developed suppliers that understood its drive to provide fashionable products at reasonable prices. Target's fashion-conscious yet frugal consumers rewarded its unique capabilities.

Kmart had built an effective capability to create a fun shopping experience and built short-term success, but it neglected the capabilities that customers really wanted in the long term. Kmart declared bankruptcy and subsequently merged with the Sears Corporation. Not surprisingly, one of management's key goals after the Kmart and Sears merger was to create more efficiency in the supply chain. Companies must have or be able to gain customer-valued capabilities for this strategy to succeed. When the capabilities they have are no longer valued, such as Kmart's shopping experience, they must be able to change to more successful strategies, such as Sears' efficient supply chain.

This example illustrates two important distinctions. First, effective SC&O firms focus their supply chain strategy on those competencies that create lasting value. Kmart's shopping experience strategy was clearly meant to appeal to consumers emotionally. Consumers can only be entertained for a brief moment before they look for more lasting value. The longer-term strategy of Walmart to focus all its competencies on lowering costs had a much longer-lasting effect on consumers. In addition, Target's competency of focusing on effectively delivering a distinctive product to a targeted consumer segment also provided a longer-term effect.

Second, the effect of a company selecting the wrong supply chain strategy can be deadly. When firms ignore the importance of supply chain, they buy themselves an expensive, wasteful, and ineffective system. Each firm must have a supply chain, and good firms deploy these supply chains strategically.

Coke, Inca Kola and Cultural Fit

Inca Kola is an example of emotion-based switching costs.

Despite being the world's largest beverage provider, Coca-Cola had a very difficult time gaining significant market share in Peru due to a local soda called Inca Kola. Inca Kola was a source of national pride; Peruvians served this sweet soda at birthday parties, soccer matches, and even official government events. Coke initially attempted to take over Peru's market by creating strong relationships with fast-food restaurants and getting commitments from these restaurants to serve only Coke products. Most of the restaurants, however, eventually asked Coke if they could also offer Inca Kola because so many patrons wanted it. Coca-Cola found that consumers were unwilling to switch to a new product because they were culturally invested in Inca Kola. Rather than fight these high customer-switching costs, Coke eventually bought a controlling stake in Lindley Inc., Inca Kola's manufacturer, and Coca-Cola is now a producer of Inca Kola in Peru. When a company does not have the resources or product necessary to compete in an emerging market, competing becomes more difficult. Coca-Cola had to change its supply strategy once it saw that Peruvians would not make the switch from Inca Kola to Coke.

might also not be able to compete because its capabilities are not dynamic enough. Or a firm might find that it simply chose the wrong strategy because it does not fit with the current environment. This is further demonstrated in GLOBAL CONNECTIONS 2.2.

Managing Across Majors 2.2   International business majors, the Inca Kola story illustrates that strategy becomes more difficult in global cultures. You need to understand that country culture plays a role in company strategy.

Ⓢ UPPLY CHAIN STRATEGY

Although companies traditionally focus on understanding customers' values, developing effective competitive capabilities, and fitting within the competitive landscape as the main areas of strategic planning, these elements do not tell the entire story. Companies are quickly realizing that strategic planning must also include planning to create and maintain important business relationships.

Changes in Strategy

For many years, business theories have assumed that managers created strategic advantage within the four walls of the company. The business landscape has changed dramatically, however, as the digital revolution created the opportunity for rapid sharing of information. Almost simultaneously, the markets of Eastern Europe and Asia opened after decades of relative isolation. These new markets and new producers, coupled with information connectivity, created a globally connected world.

The first realization of this global expansion was found in a worldwide web of information. Rapidly shared information meant that coordinated global communication could be quickly established. People quickly connected with friends in far-flung parts of the world. The Internet truly became the World Wide Web.

Lagging behind this information revolution, due to the need for more significant structure and intense business-to-business relationships, was a network of global trade.[3] Every country that desired global trade quickly found that remote manufacturers could cheaply

---

[3]An excellent book about this phenomenon is T. Friedman, *The World Is Flat* (New York: Picador, 2007).

produce and deliver goods to almost any available market. As a result of this realization, most people in North America right now are wearing clothing sewn in Asia.

The ability to manufacture products, materials, or supplies cheaply anywhere in the world and ship them inexpensively to worldwide markets creates a "world wide web of production." Business strategy will never be the same. SC&O management has emerged as a major strategic imperative. Firms must effectively and efficiently tap into the worldwide web of production to be competitive.

Business executives looking for ways to compete in this new reality have discovered that relationship management is the key capability that allows them to maintain sustained competitive advantage. As stated earlier, supply chain strategy is the ability of the firm to leverage internal relationships, supplier partnerships, and customer relationships to create sustained competitive advantage.

There are three main reasons that firms use a supply chain strategy:

1. Leverage relationships to reduce costs
2. Create relationships to appropriate value from a partner with complementary core competencies
3. Establish long-term, intense relationships to create synergistic value

Types of Relationships

Before discussing how businesses leverage relationships, let's first discuss the different types of relationships managers encounter. There are various types of relationships, including *transactional relationships, complementary relationships,* and *synergistic relationships.* Each of these distinctions is important, and managers must understand which strategy best serves their company.

TRANSACTIONAL RELATIONSHIPS A firm that pursues a cost advantage through its supply chain partners generally employs a **transactional relationship**, such as a reverse auction, to find the lowest-cost providers for supplies. For example, for Schneider National trucking company to purchase diesel fuel, it may contact all the known suppliers of diesel and ask them to submit bids to supply the contract. Once the diesel bidding begins, all the suppliers see the lowest bid and can keep bidding until no one bids lower than the lowest bid. Schneider then agrees to purchase the diesel from the lowest bidder. Although transactional relationships have a tendency to keep both the buyer and supplier at arm's length, industries that rely on commodity supplies frequently engage in transactional, cost-reducing relationships.

transactional relationship
An arm's length relationship with supply chain partners that is managed by scripted interactions.

COMPLEMENTARY RELATIONSHIPS A **complementary relationship** occurs when a company that clearly understands its core competencies needs another firm's competencies to maintain world-class service. Generally, such a company understands that it holds a competitive advantage in one area but does not have expertise in another.

Despite Apple's strong research, development, and software development competencies, it does not excel in manufacturing and has therefore turned to the Taiwanese company Foxconn, one of the world's largest manufacturers of consumer technology products, to do its manufacturing. Because Foxconn manufactures for many consumer technology brands inexpensively, establishes intimate relationships with major suppliers, and meets quality expectations, it is an ideal supplier for Apple. Apple's ability to create its products in the United States and to manufacture them in Taiwan gives it the ability to bring high-quality, innovative products to a consumer at a competitive price point.

complementary relationship
A relationship that occurs when companies understand that their core competencies need another firm's competencies in order to maintain world-class service.

SYNERGISTIC RELATIONSHIPS A **synergistic relationship** is a relationship between two companies that are committed to work together in a way that the result is greater than the sum of the individual parts. In a survey of 90 companies, researchers found that ten of these companies committed to an intense, long-lasting relationship in order to create new product ideas, increase their productivity, and create a greater ability to change.[4] Firms that engage in these

synergistic relationship
A relationship between two companies who are committed to working together in a way that the result is greater than the sum of the individual parts.

[4]S. E. Fawcett, A. M. Fawcett, B. J. Watson, and G. M. Magnan, "Peeking Inside the Black Box: Toward an Understanding of Supply Chain Collaboration Dynamics," *Journal of Supply Chain Management* 48, no. 3 (2012): 44–72.

types of relationships generally work very closely with their partners to develop relational capabilities that help create more novel products and find ways to better serve customers.

For instance, Honda has long been considered one of the best automobile manufacturers in the world. As Dave Nelson, the retired senior vice president for Honda, explained, "Ironically, many of Honda's supplier development programs and activities—supplier awards programs or supplier incentives, for example—appear very similar to those found at most automobile manufacturers. But the difference is in how much time, money and effort Honda invests in building and sustaining its supplier relationships. When we select suppliers, we expect to be with them for years."[5]

Honda's return on this commitment to its suppliers is innovation. The Honda Accord's success is partially from process innovations and product innovations that suppliers provide to Honda. Therefore, the synergistic supply chain strategy is about creating relationships that provide value greater than the sum of the parts.

Managers must consider the strategic importance of partnerships when developing strategy. The firm must decide which type of partnership provides the outcome that it is seeking and develop its relationship accordingly. Once the customer, capabilities, competitive environment, and partnerships are understood, a company generally will have most of the pieces needed to create strategic plans.

E XECUTE STRATEGY

The most carefully made plans often underperform. In the business environment, executing your plans often becomes more difficult than creating the plans. We discuss three major points to help you understand how to make your supply chain's strategic plans more effective: (1) aligning strategic levels, (2) aligning incentives, and (3) focusing on process.

Aligning Strategic Levels

First, it is important to understand how the *levels of strategies* within a company all function together. There are three strategic levels in a company: (1) strategies, (2) functional tactics, and (3) operations.

STRATEGIES. Strategies are the means that define how the company will win customers, achieve long-term goals, create game-winning capabilities, fit into the competitive environment, and develop relationships. Strategies form the rationale for tactics and operations because they drive what middle-tier management must accomplish to win and keep customers. For example, once a company determines that it is going to be a low-price competitor, its tactics are also going to focus on cost reduction and efficiency, and its day-to-day operations are going to focus on efficiency. Strategy sets the stage for tactics and operations.

functional strategies or operational subplans
One- to two-year goals that help the firm "win a battle but not necessarily the war." These subplans include events like improving product quality through continuous improvement, reducing costs through improving warehouse flows, or improving supplier relationships through giving awards to key suppliers.

tactics
Short-term steps used to achieve strategic goals.

Functional strategies, or *operational subplans*, are one- to two-year goals that help the firm "win a battle but not necessarily the war." These subplans include events such as improving product quality through continuous improvement, reducing costs through improving warehouse flows, and improving supplier relationships through giving awards to key suppliers. Even though these tactics generally help create sustained, competitive advantage, they are generally part of a bigger, longer-term strategic plan.

FUNCTIONAL TACTICS. There are some well-recognized *tactics* for sourcing, operations, and logistics. To have a good fit between tactics and strategies, managers must understand the right tactics for the given strategy. **Tactics** are short-term steps used in implementing strategies. TABLE 2.3 illustrates how certain, frequently used functional tactics may complement a firm's strategy.

[5]T. M. Laseter, "Balanced Sourcing the Honda Way," *Strategy + Business*, Oct. 1, 1998, www .strategy-business.com/article/13515?gko=ce6a5.

∨ TABLE 2.3

Complementary Tactics for Firm Strategy			
Functional Tactics Related to:	**Purchasing**	**Operations**	**Logistics**
Low-cost strategy	**Purchasing for Nonstrategic Transactions**	**Cost**	**Efficiency**
	The buyer seeks to buy the right supplies or products with an appropriate quality level at the lowest possible prices.	The manufacturer produces products and services in the lowest-cost ways.	The logistician creates logistics systems that maximize efficiency and reduce total logistics costs.
Differentiation Strategy	**Purchasing for Contractual Relationships**	**Quality and Dependability**	**Market Strategy**
	The buyer seeks to build partnerships and appropriate partner's value through the life of the contract relationship.	The manufacturer produces products and services with no defects, and production and service meets or exceeds scheduling deadlines.	The logistician creates logistics systems to reduce the complexity faced by customers.
Niche Strategy (Customer Relationship Strategy)	**Purchasing to Build a Long-Term Alliance**	**Dependability and Flexibility**	**Systems Approach**
	The buyer seeks to build a long-term relationship with a single (or very few) suppliers.	The manufacturer creates the capability for quick changes in products, product mixes, production volume, or service delivery.	The logistician creates a logistics system that can quickly adjust to changing supply chain needs. These systems focus on coordinating flows between supply chain functions and the customer.

When supply chain managers select the correct functional strategies to complement their needs, strategies are supported, and execution becomes easier. Simply having functional tactics is not enough, however. These tactics must be executed correctly.

OPERATIONS Operations are the daily activities that a firm must perform to achieve success. Managers over operations in both service and manufacturing firms generally make sure that schedules are met, enough employees are present to meet customers' needs, and enough shipping is available to deliver the company's goods or services. Companies cannot succeed without effective operations. In addition, for firms to meet strategic goals successfully, tactics must complement strategies, and operations must fit with the firm's functional goals.

Aligning Incentives

After supply chain managers determine strategic levels, they must avoid the dangers of local optimums during execution. A local optimum occurs when a firm rewards each functional area for achieving goals without regard for the company-wide effect of its actions. For instance, sales managers often give their salespeople commissions to sell products and motivate them to sell as many products as possible. Salespeople love having an expansive product line because it allows their product line to appeal to many different consumers. At the same time, manufacturing managers are often given bonuses for meeting cost-reduction goals. One of the easiest ways for manufacturing managers to reduce costs is to reduce the number of products in the product line. Reducing the product variety means that manufacturers can make longer batch runs and require fewer component parts. Therefore, the sales managers incentivize their sales teams to have an extensive product line, whereas production managers incentivize their supply chain team to offer a minimal product line. These goals clearly do not align.

Good strategy aligns the incentives to both the sales team and the SC&O team to create greater profits for the firm. Good execution recognizes that there may be competing incentives and modifies these incentives so that profit, not revenue or cost, is rewarded. Once again, firms must come to agreement about how they win orders.

A number of alignment issues must be addressed in SC&O strategies, including:

- *Information systems:* What kinds of enterprise systems are needed to satisfy the needs of the entire supply chain? How do you link upstream and downstream? What are data relations? What data do you need to manage your supply chain effectively?
- *Logistics:* When will you ship? Does this schedule align with operations expectations? How do you optimize shipping practices to meet customer and manufacturing needs?
- *Suppliers:* Who are your preferred suppliers? What is your process for supplier selection? How do you develop suppliers? How do you link with your suppliers? Do you source globally?
- *Inventory management:* Where do you optimally store inventory? How much? How long? Do you have perishable stocks? Where do you carry safety stocks? Are you maintaining good levels of services?

Focusing on Process

Finally, managers must focus on processes throughout the supply chain rather than individual functions within their supply chain. A manager who focuses on one functional area often incurs trade-offs in other areas. For instance, an inbound logistics manager who decides to reduce transportation costs by fully filling trucks will increase inventory costs for the purchasing manager. An effective way to ensure that a cross-functional viewpoint is taken is to focus on processes.

An often-used model that helps managers consider the holistic effects of their decisions is the supply chain operational reference (SCOR) model. The Supply Chain Council developed the SCOR model to help managers understand and implement strategic supply chain initiatives by focusing managers on five standard supply chain processes found within most supply chains. As shown in FIGURE 2.3, the three main emphases of the SCOR model are

1. Process modeling
2. Performance measurements
3. Best practices

Five well-defined sets of standardized processes that describe the entire supply chain (found in TABLE 2.4) form the SCOR model. When managers have a common understanding of the processes involved in implementing strategy, alignment throughout the supply chain becomes much easier.

FIGURE 2.3 >

The SCOR Model

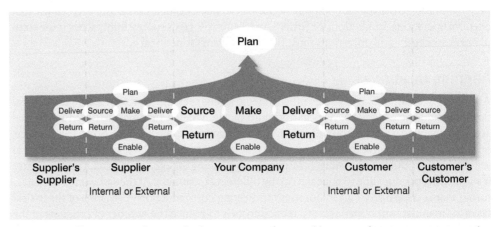

Source: Reprinted by permission from *Supply-Chain Operations Reference Model, Overview of SCOR Version 8.0,* Copyright 2006, Supply-Chain Council.

SCOR Model Processes		< TABLE 2.4
Plan	Balances aggregate demand and supply to develop a course of action that best meets sourcing, production, and delivery requirements.	
Source	Includes activities related to procuring goods and services to meet planned and actual demand.	
Make	Includes activities related to transforming products into a finished state to meet planned or actual demand.	
Deliver	Provides finished goods or services to meet planned or actual demand, typically including order management, transportation management, and distribution management.	
Return	Deals with returning or receiving returned products for any reason and extends into post delivery customer support.	

Source: Reprinted by permission from Lambert, D., *Supply Chain Management: Processes, Partnerships, Performance.* Supply Chain Management Institute, Tempe AZ, 2008.

Furthermore, the SCOR model encourages managers to consider these five processes not only within the company but also outside the company in the interfaces with suppliers and suppliers' suppliers on the upstream side. The SCOR model encourages managers to consider also how these processes influence customers and customers' customers on the downstream side. The SCOR process then suggests that the company should benchmark its processes against firms that are very good at doing similar processes and find where their processes differ. Managers can then compare process measurements and metrics to ensure that their supply chain processes are causing the holistic behaviors needed in a supply chain. In short, the SCOR model gives the manager an effective tool for understanding and controlling how supply chain processes affect the entire supply chain. An application of SCOR is provided in SC&O CURRENT EVENTS 2.3.

SCOR at Ford

< SC&O CURRENT
EVENTS 2.3

A good example of a company that used SCOR to become more effective is Ford Motor Company. The parts, supply, and logistics division of Ford used SCOR to improve its forecasting, inventory planning, electronic supplier communication, and management. Ford's extremely complex supply chain contains thousands of parts, thousands of suppliers, and millions of end consumers. Although Ford's functional areas within purchasing and logistics were individually effective, they were not structured to make integrated supply chain decisions. Ford identified the problems in its as-is state and then used SCOR to map and describe important inventory processes that flowed through the functional silos. Understanding how these processes affected each area of the company helped employees understand the holistic nature of their siloed decisions. Ford managers used SCOR to measure and benchmark these processes against others doing similar processes. Ford was then able to standardize processes and help each business area understand its responsibility for the entire process.

Ford has benefited substantially from using SCOR. Ford's recurring inventory has been greatly reduced due to attention to variation in inventory policies. Focusing on customer requirements has led to a 20 percent reduction in open back orders, improved customer satisfaction, and a 25 percent reduction in forecast inaccuracies. Because employees are focused on the total process rather than their own silo, Ford has reduced total inventory cycle time by 30 percent. Ford's return on investment was calculated to be five times the cost of implementing the SCOR system.

Companies use process thinking because, even though a process flows internally through several functions, the customer only sees the outcome of the process. For example, Harley-Davidson Motor Company almost went bankrupt in the mid-1980s. Its processes were designed to make large batches of motorcycles to keep costs low. Each functional area of the supply chain optimized its own functions to meet company goals. When it became obvious to Harley that this strategy was not working, Harley began to focus on improving its processes. This process focus allowed Harley to view its supply chain holistically. It keyed in on the quality problems it was facing and, using total quality management tools, created a successful supply chain turnaround. Harley's customers appreciated the improved, reliable motorcycles, and the company reaped the benefits.

UNDERSTAND AND APPLY STRATEGIC METRICS AND MEASUREMENTS

The success or failure of a strategy can be assessed only if managers can recognize and measure the results of their strategy. A final obstacle that supply chain managers frequently struggle with is creating effective metrics. Good metrics have two common properties: (1) they drive correct, strategic behavior, and (2) they are actionable and predictive. In addition, an important aspect of measuring the success of the company is creating incentives that reward systems thinking. These strategic measures help managers understand the effectiveness of their strategies.

Correct Strategic Behavior

If a firm decides to be the innovative leader in an industry, it should also create metrics that analyze and predict innovation, but firms often measure the wrong things for the right reasons.[6] A study of a riding lawn-mower manufacturer highlights this point. The lawn-mower manufacturer's marketing department found out that its competitor's innovative tractor designs were attracting more key customers. To appeal to its key demographic, the lawn-mower company created innovation measures to help drive more research and development, and engineers created several different gas caps for five different mowers. The lawn-mower company metrics had driven meaningless innovation because no customer was really buying a new lawn mower because of its cool gas cap.

Great metrics drive not only strategic behavior but also the correct strategic behavior. The lawn-mower company later altered its metrics by measuring innovation only on "customer touch points" (the areas its customers believed influenced their intent to purchase the mower). As a result, the lawn-mower company greatly reduced the complexity of its mowers, which reduced its manufacturing costs. Astonishingly, revenues simultaneously increased as customers were no longer confused about order winners when comparing lawn mowers. The company rededicated itself to a strategy that focused on producing meaningful differentiation and put the metrics in place to drive this correct behavior.

Actionable and Predictive Metrics

A good metric also allows managers to make decisions based on facts. Therefore, an effective metric must provide information that they can act on. As a good rule of thumb, when you develop a measure, ask, What would I do if the metric lowers or rises?

If a clear action plan results from this question, you have probably created a meaningful measure of the strategy. This clear action plan results because you can clearly see the cause-and-effect relationship driving the metric. For instance, project managers commonly use cost and schedule as their metrics. If a project is over the budgeted cost, managers clearly understand that they need to impose greater cost controls. If a project has extended past its initial schedule, project managers must speed up the project. These measures are clearly actionable.

[6]D. Closs, M. Jacobs, M. Swink, and S. Webb, "Competencies for Managing Product Portfolio Complexity: Six Case Studies," *Journal of Operations Management* 25, no. 6 (2008): 590–610.

Commonly Used Supply Chain Metrics

Strategic Metric	Financial Metric	Relationship Metric	Operational Metric
Number of units purchased from supplier	Revenue resulting from supplier	Degree of mutual understanding Trust	Number of joint R&D projects Time to order
Value of products purchased from supplier	Profit generated by supplier	Ratio of investment/marketing/ strategy plans shared Service level	Receipt time (cycle time)
Supplier product innovations (number)	R&D return on investment	Satisfaction level	Parts per million defects
Success rate for new product launches	Marketing return on investment		Agility (response to changes) Invoice accuracy
Process innovations	Total cost of ownership		Productivity ratios
Supply continuity risk	Price stability		
Corporate responsibility	Cost avoidance		
Sustainability	Asset utilization		
Contribution to brand equity	Return on assets Return on investment		

A metric that merely measures completed actions and cannot predict future success is only good for managers interested in the past. Metrics must show trends and thereby trigger appropriate corrective action. Data that direct future actions provide supply chain managers with predictive power and create management by fact. When these leading indicators also help align functional strategies and provide proper incentives to operators, executing strategy becomes scientific rather than a gut reaction.

Commonly Used Supply Chain Metrics

TABLE 2.5 lists a number of commonly used supply chain metrics, including strategic, financial, relationship, and operational metrics. Managers often use these types of metrics to determine the status of a supplier or supply chain partner. Many of these metrics can also be used operationally within the firm.

Systems Thinking

The common theme in strategy alignment, incentive alignment, and measuring important things is the ability to think in a holistic way. Systems thinking makes strategy execution more effective because it allows managers to act in ways that help the entire company. The new SC&O manager is no longer a functional expert; she is a strategic orchestrator. An effective SC&O manager takes a process-oriented approach to management. She realizes that production's end goal is to please the customer. She communicates freely with customers about their expectations and their customer experience. She also seeks to integrate production with distribution to make sure precise distribution processes meet customer targets at the lowest possible prices.

In addition, the SC&O manager works closely with suppliers not only to meet cost targets but also to help suppliers improve their production quality. She focuses on the entire acquisition process to develop strategic advantage rather than just to ensure production has sufficient inventories. The modern SC&O manager worries less about her functional expertise and worries more about leading the entire supply chain.

Managing Across Majors 2.3 Accounting majors, when performing the type of cost accounting called "activity based costing," you must find the drivers of performance to measure the correct things effectively.

Finance majors, you cannot squeeze suppliers to the point that they are insolvent. Good financial management involves finding a price that is good for the customer and the supplier so that they both are successful.

D ESCRIBE THE CHANGING STRATEGIC ENVIRONMENT

Today's SC&O managers also have additional worries beyond creating and executing strategy. Their biggest worry is the rapidly changing environment. Only those firms that are able to accommodate this change will be able to succeed in the future. Four strategic environmental changes that greatly influence SC&O managers have been recently noted. First, because of the advances made in data storage and enterprise systems, data is plentiful and can be useful. Second, all supply chains are becoming increasingly global. Third, sustainability has become increasingly important to SC&O managers. Fourth, innovation is increasingly becoming a necessity. All of these environmental conditions are changing SC&O strategy.

Analytics

In 2000, a gigabyte of data storage cost on average $11. Now, a gigabyte of data storage averages $0.019. In reaction to the reduced costs of holding data, companies have captured and stored so much data that they often do not know what to do with it. However, companies that have been able to use data strategically to make better decisions about SC&O and about customers are creating a competitive advantage for themselves.

A good example of a company that created a strategic advantage using analytics is Ford. The automaker asked a simple question to its data analysts: How common are the parts we use in all of the products throughout the world? After extensive data analysis, the answer came back that there was very little commonality of parts, even in products that were very similar. The data analytics team then pursued a goal to find the right product parts that could be common and worked with supply chain managers to implement common parts. The result of this initiative was over $2 billion in savings.[7]

It is important to realize that it is not the analytics or the data that creates this advantage. The key understanding to unlocking the strategic advantage of data analytics is that all management is decision making. When a manager can effectively manipulate and understand data, she can make better, evidence-based decisions. These smarter decisions lead to better companies.

Globalization

In 2006, U.S. multinational companies had invested $2.5 trillion in foreign direct investment; by 2015, these U.S. multinational companies had doubled foreign direct investment to $5.4 trillion.[8] The real problem for SC&O managers is that, when suppliers, producers, and distributors are located around the world, the supply chain never rests. Real-time information is constantly exchanged, problems occur around the clock, and decisions are required hourly. In addition, to be effective, SC&O managers must be prepared to understand the cultures, economics, and infrastructure of many different countries. Many companies have learned

---

[7]http://sloanreview.mit.edu/projects/the-hard-work-behind-data-analytics-strategy/
[8]Jenniges, Derrick T., and James J. Fetzer (2016) Bureau of Economic Analysis, "Direct Investment Positions for 2015: Country and Industry Detail" July 2016, http://www.bea.gov/scb/pdf/2016/07%20July/0716_direct_investment_positions.pdf.

 **< GLOBAL CONNECTIONS 2.3**

Hanjin Bankruptcy Affects Small and Medium-Sized Retailers

 In August 2016, the Korean shipping company Hanjin declared bankruptcy. This left several Hanjin container ships stranded at sea without being able to unload their freight until a loan could be arranged. There were two major causes for the bankruptcy. First, Hanjin had incurred extensive debt with the expectation of easy loan paybacks due to demand for Asian shipping. That expected demand was diminished due to a worldwide economic slowdown. Second, ship manufacturers had created newer ships with extremely large capacities to carry many more containers than legacy ships. This caused overcapacity in the shipping industry and depressed prices.

After the Hanjin bankruptcy, the largest manufacturers and retailers were able to switch to other shipping companies with little effect on their businesses. However, small and medium-sized manufacturers and retailers were left to compete for the diminished capacity remaining in the shipping industry. This decreased capacity increased shipping rates for smaller companies by as little as 15 percent and by as much as 75 percent. Some smaller companies have even had to switch from shipping via ship to using expensive air shipping to complete their shipments. The effects of Hanjin shipping declaring bankruptcy have increased costs and affected reliability to retailers and manufacturers around the world.

Source: Based on "Even Businesses That Don't Rely on Hanjin Could Be Caught in Cargo Crisis," by Jeremy Quittner. Published by Time Inc. http://fortune.com/2016/09/09/hanjin-cargo-crisis/.

painful lessons as they try to penetrate promising new international markets. The modern strategist must not only be prepared to create strategy but must also be able to accommodate the change and sensitivity that globalization demands. GLOBAL CONNECTIONS 2.3 talks about a supply chain disruption in a global supply chain.

Sustainability

Sustainability is also driving considerable change for the SC&O strategist. In the past, firms could produce and distribute in the most economical way possible without regard for unintended consequences such as pollution. Sustainability is frequently defined as the *ability to operate today in a way that does not threaten the future.* This commitment to sustainable business practices means that strategy must take into account not only the profitability of the firm but also the future effects of the strategies. More and more firms are attempting to adopt sustainable business practices when they realize the economic benefits.

Patagonia is a good example of a company that has shown how sustainable SC&O practices can also be profitable. In 2016, Patagonia announced that the $10 million it earned through black Friday sales would be donated to environmental causes. In addition, Patagonia claims, "We are responsible for all the workers who make our goods and for all that goes into a piece of clothing that bears a Patagonia label." Even though Patagonia is one of the original members of the Fair Labor Association, dedicated to ensuring fair treatment of garment producers, it has its own code of conduct that prevents factories from subcontracting work without permission and requires all suppliers to maintain a quality-improvement plan for workers.[9]

So, what is the reward for a company like Patagonia that gives freely to the environment and works to make sure that people thrive within its supply chain? Patagonia was tied for ranking as the world's most sustainable brand in 2015.[10] This in turn has led to some of the most loyal customers in the marketplace. Customers like to buy Patagonia brands because it makes them feel good about their purchase.

Not all companies are fortunate enough to be in an industry where customers reward sustainability. Because of regulatory pressures, both domestic and international firms

[9]http://www.patagonia.com/blog/2012/04/patagonia-clothing-made-where-how-why/
[10]https://www.theguardian.com/sustainable-business/2015/may/28/sustainability-leaders-report-unilever-patagonia-ikea-nestle

understand that they must integrate environmental concerns into their strategic plans. As Ed Woolard of DuPont Corporation stated:

> As we move closer to zero (emissions), the economic cost which society must ultimately bear may be high (when considering reduction of pollution). Or the energy expenditure necessary to eliminate a given emission may have more ecological impact than trade emissions themselves. Society will have to decide where the balance will be struck and may conclude in some cases that zero emissions is neither in the environment's nor the public's best interest.[11]

Companies have to address many environmental issues. Besides regulatory requirements, firms realize more and more that environmental friendliness is part of being a good corporate citizen. Therefore, tasks such as environmental protection, waste management, product integrity, worker health, government relations, and community relations compose the environmentally related strategic issues that must be addressed. As a result, firms are implementing quality-based environmental management systems, sometimes referred to as **sustainability management**. These systems involve a holistic systems view of the processes causing environmental degradation. Measurements are implemented that identify indicators of environmental performance, with a focus on preventive rather than reactive cleanup.

sustainability management
Improvement-based environmental management systems.

life-cycle costing
Using value analysis to identify total costs from a supply chain–environmental perspective.

Another technique used in environmental management, **life-cycle costing**, uses value analysis to identify the total costs of products from a worldwide perspective.[12] FIGURE 2.4 is an example of life-cycle costing for a typical hamburger. You might ask, How much does a hamburger cost? One answer is that a hamburger can be purchased at Burger King for less than $1. Indeed, that is the immediate price to the consumer. As proposed by some environmentalists, however, if one considers the environmental costs associated with deforestation, degradation to riparian habitats resulting from cattle grazing, and health problems because of the overconsumption of fatty foods, another cost emerges that is much higher than $1. Regardless of one's political stance concerning these issues, the debate will rage for many years, and regulation likely will not decrease over time. Therefore, it is in the best interest of management to address these issues in a proactive manner.

FIGURE 2.5 shows measures from a supplier sustainability scorecard from Procter & Gamble. A **scorecard** is a tool used to monitor the performance of suppliers around the world. More and more, companies are getting serious about ethical and sustainable practices in their supply chains.

scorecard
A strategic tool to communicate strategic metrics. Often used with suppliers.

reverse logistics
Logistics used to move products up the supply chain. Often used in managing recycling.

REVERSE LOGISTICS Another important consideration in sustainability initiatives is **reverse logistics**, the ability of a company to move product upstream while managing waste streams in an effort to reduce the cost of the waste stream or make the waste stream profitable. Reverse logistics will be discussed in more detail in Chapter 11.

CUSTOMER PREFERENCE A final point about sustainability that SC&O managers must consider is customer preference. Customers frequently claim to want environmental products, but they may purchase in ways that are less sustainable than alternatives (FIGURE 2.6). In this case, companies must decide if they are going to try to alter customer lifestyles or if they are going to continue manufacturing for existing customer demand. This decision is one of the most difficult ones that you might make as a strategic planner.

Innovation

Innovation is a requirement that is rapidly encroaching into the SC&O world. For many years, firms could compete on low cost or product quality. SC&O managers have gotten very good at incorporating quality practices, lean supply chain practices, and other tactics that clearly have created great value in terms of lowering costs and increasing quality. It is becoming increasingly clear that to win in tomorrow's supply chain, SC&O managers must also be able to support and help create innovative new products and services. Today's customers expect highly customized

[11]E.S. Woolard speech presented at the Second World Congress on Zero Emissions, Chattanooga, Tennessee, May 31, 1996.
[12]The *Wall Street Journal* provides an interesting article on calculating the carbon footprint of six products at http://online.wsj.com/article/SB122304950601802565.html.

FIGURE 2.4 ∨

The Life-Cycle Cost of a Hamburger

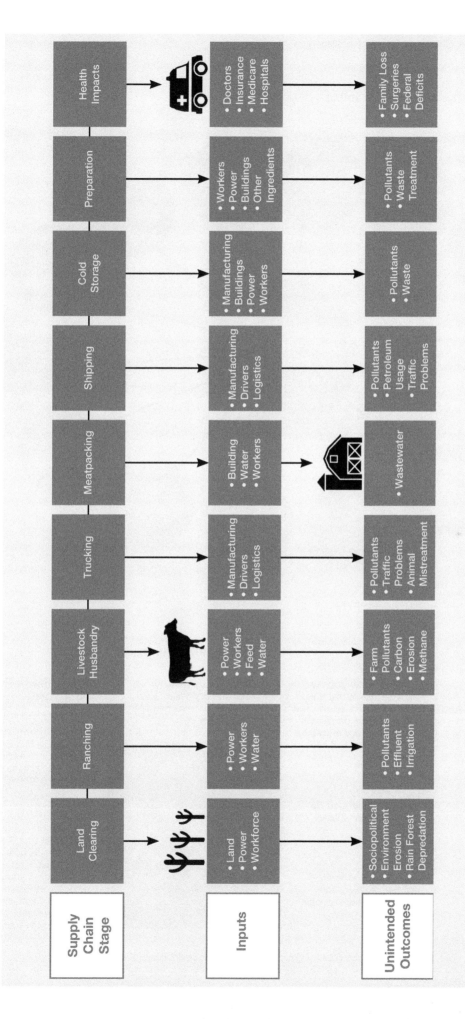

Source: Based on Thomas Gladwin, "Full Cost Pricing of a Cheeseburger," Case Memo, 2013.

FIGURE 2.5 ∨

Sustainability Scorecard from Procter & Gamble

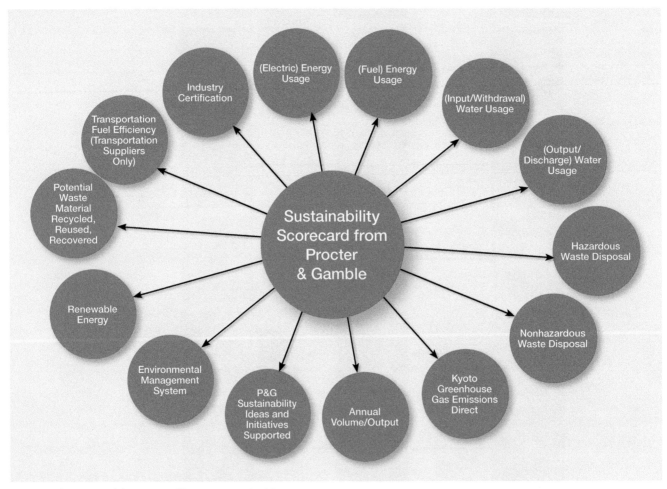

Source: Based on Sustainability Scorecard from Procter & Gamble.

FIGURE 2.6 >

Examples of "Throwaway" Products

Items That Fill Junk Yards

Swiffer WetJet Mops use reusable inserts that bring customers back again and again. The problem is that they replace reusable mops that were just fine.

Lightbulbs. There is now a bulb that lasts 20 years. How can that be profitable?

Razors. Do you realize that before disposable razors and blades, people rarely bought razor equipment?

Umbrellas are cheaply made and don't last. Over 100,000 umbrellas end up in landfills yearly.

Frisbees fly so well they end up in trees.

Solo Cup, a $1.8 billion company, makes products that last as long as one quarter in a football game.

Much furniture, such as that sold at Ikea, is made out of particle board and it doesn't last. By comparison, if you watch the Antiques Roadshow, you will see that some furniture was built to last hundreds of years.

Source: Based on Spencer Bailey, "Keeping Landfills in the Black," *Businessweek*, June 25, 2012, p. 91.

and innovative products. To support these customers, SC&O managers must be able to create flexibility and adaptability into their supply chain strategies to get customized products to market quickly. Tomorrow's SC&O managers must therefore be very good at functional tactics *and* they must be culturally astute, sustainability minded, and innovative.

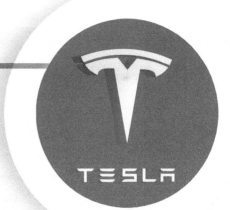

In the beginning of the chapter, we discussed Tesla and its announcement of the Model 3. Upon the announcement of the Model 3 with a base price of $35,000, orders came in at an unexpected pace. It soon became clear that demand would greatly outstrip production capacity. Almost immediately, Tesla started tempering its promise to deliver new models, stating that some orders would take up to two years to deliver.

One strategic design choice by Tesla was to make the car an "iPhone on wheels." This meant a complete change from the traditional approach to car making by taking the focus off the hardware and putting it on the software. That is, the car would only be a foundation for selling ever-better software to the car owner. Physical upgrades might be needed from time to time, but the software platform would allow for selling of upgrades to car owners at regular intervals—just like selling new iPhone apps.

Another strategic choice was to increase productive capacity—immediately and rapidly—at the Fremont, California, plant by investing over $1.25 billion. In addition, new suppliers would be needed, especially in acquiring the chemical element cobalt for the production of lithium batteries. In addition, Tesla has decided to nearsource as many components and materials as it can from U.S. suppliers. Downstream in the supply chain, Tesla has actively installed charging stations to take the place of gas stations.

Only time will tell if Tesla will be successful in its efforts. After studying this chapter, however, you should have more understanding of all the strategic choices facing the managers of Tesla and its supply chain, operations, and services people.

Summary

In this chapter, we have discussed many of the strategic SC&O concerns facing organizations today. These issues are not simple, but strategy lays the groundwork for the smooth functioning and growth of today's firms.

1. We discussed generic strategies such as cost, differentiation, and focus. These forms of competition allow us to provide value to customers.
   a. We discussed how and why a manager's strategy must align with the company's SC&O strategy and specific alignment strategies that managers use.
   b. We also emphasized the importance of assessing customer value and the various methods managers use to do so.

2. Strategy process and content are two major areas of SC&O strategy. The process is how we plan strategy, and the content is what construes the SC&O strategy. The crux is that the topics being discussed are of importance to firms today. Without effective SC&O, firms will fail.

    a. We reviewed Hoshin Kanri strategic planning and provided examples of successful companies that have put this particular strategy to use.

    b. We also discussed SC&O strategy content and emphasized the importance of capabilities and competencies.

3. Managers must also understand how their strategy works within the industry and how changes in the marketplace may affect their strategies.

    a. We described the three types of relationships managers maintain to remain competitive: transactional, complementary, and synergistic.

4. After successful SC&O firms have formed their strategies, they must execute these strategies successfully by:

    a. aligning strategic levels.

    b. aligning incentives.

    c. focusing on processes.

5. Managers also use metrics and measurements to make sure their strategy is working.

    a. Measurements must be able to correct strategic behavior, not simply measure levels of failure.

    b. Measures must explain and predict what is happening to the strategic direction of the firm.

    c. Successful execution also relies on systems thinking. All members of the supply chain must align their functions and operations with the firm's strategic goals.

6. Great SC&O companies that sustain a competitive advantage also understand the changing environment. They create the capabilities to adapt to a constantly changing environment while holding tight to their strategic identity. Wielding adaptability is how successful managers outcompete their competition.

Key Terms

adaptability   25
agility   23
alignment   23
capabilities   27
catchball   27
complementary relationship   31
core competencies   28
cost strategy   22
differentiation strategy   23
Fisher strategy model   23

focus strategy   23
functional strategies   32
Hoshin Kanri planning   27
life-cycle costing   40
operational subplans   27, 32
operations strategy   22
order qualifiers   25
order winners   25
reverse logistics   40
SC&O strategy   22

scorecard   40
strategy   22
strategy content   26
strategy process   26
supply chain strategy   22
sustainability management   40
synergistic relationship   31
tactics   32
transactional relationship   31

Integrative Learning Exercise

Identify a company in your region. Research the company's supply chain and operations planning process. Identify the company's strategic plan and mission. What are the company's core competencies? How does the company integrate the voice of the customer and the voice of the market into its company strategy? Identify at least three functional area subplans (e.g., finance, supply chain operations, information technology, marketing, human resources). How do the subplans support the corporate strategy? How does the company create, foster, and maintain important business relationships?

Integrative Experiential Exercise

Together with a study group, visit a local company. Identify how the company positions itself to gain an advantage over its competitors. Does the company employ a cost strategy, a focus strategy, or a differentiation strategy? Identify the order qualifiers for the market in which the company competes. Identify the order winners the company uses to differentiate its products and services from the competition.

Discussion Questions

1. What is the purpose of strategy?
2. What are the steps of strategic planning?
3. Why is it important for strategic planning to consider the lifetime value of the customer?
4. Why are customers important to the strategic planning process?
5. Why should strategic planners not treat all customers the same?
6. What is the difference between a company's core competency and a skill that the company is really good at doing?
7. How does a firm know which capabilities it should create and foster?
8. What is the five forces model and why is it important to strategic planning?
9. How do relationships create sustained, competitive advantage for firms?
10. How are complementary relationships different from synergistic relationships?
11. How do aligning strategic, functional, and operational plans help strategic execution?
12. How do firms ensure that execution of strategic plans is effective?
13. How does aligning strategic levels help make strategy execution more effective?
14. What role do functional strategies have in strategy execution?
15. How can firms achieve SC&O sustainability?

Zara

Zara is a fast-fashion company from Spain. Although the Spanish economy has struggled, Zara is a rare success story. Fashion is highly perishable, quickly influenced by the latest thing seen on the catwalk or worn by a celebrity. Zara's designers follow such fashion trends closely, but whereas a typical clothing company manufacturing in Asia could take six to nine months to get a new design into the shops, Zara completes the process in around five weeks. It buys some garments and material from Asia, often partly finished or undyed, but approximately half of its clothing is manufactured in-house at its base in La Coruña in northwest Spain or by a cluster of small contractors in the same area. The clothing is delivered by truck to Europe and by air to the stores Zara is now opening in other parts of the world.

Zara avoids mass production. Although some stock is replenished, its clothing, for both men and women, is deliberately made in small batches, which helps create a scarcity value: buy now in case it is gone tomorrow. It also keeps shops looking fresh and reduces markdowns. At Zara, the number of items that end up in a sale is about half the industry average.

Questions:

1. What is Zara's competitive advantage?

2. How has Zara aligned its processes with its marketing requirements?

3. What problems do you see looming for Zara?

4. What opportunities has the company created through excellent SC&O management?

Part 2

Innovating Supply Chain and Operations

3

Product and Process Design and Mapping

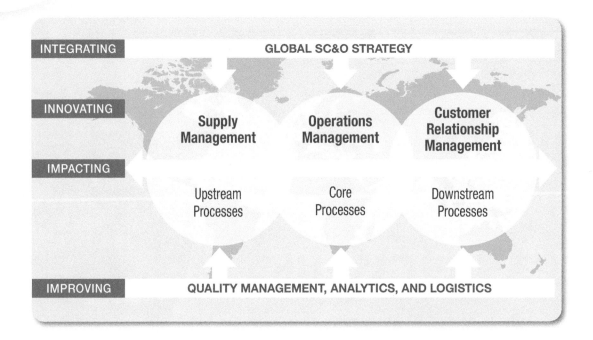

INTEGRATING	GLOBAL SC&O STRATEGY
INNOVATING	**Supply Management** — **Operations Management** — **Customer Relationship Management**
IMPACTING	Upstream Processes — Core Processes — Downstream Processes
IMPROVING	QUALITY MANAGEMENT, ANALYTICS, AND LOGISTICS

CHAPTER OUTLINE AND LEARNING OBJECTIVES

① Understand and Explain the Steps of Process Design

- Explain the differences between process and extended process.
- Describe the different choices that managers face when planning a process.
- List the different components of the process continuum and apply the continuum when choosing a process.
- Apply break-even analysis when choosing processes.

② Understand and Explain the Steps of Process Mapping and Layout Planning

- Define and describe an extended process map for supply chains.
- List and describe hybrid layouts and in what situations managers should apply each type of layout.
- Use line balancing when assigning tasks in the process chain.
- Use matrices to design functional layouts.

③ Illustrate the Different Elements of Product Design

- Describe the product life cycle and the role that complementary products play.
- Explain the role of research and development in a firm.
- Walk through the product design process and explain the function and importance of each step.

④ Understand and Employ Quality Function Deployment

- Understand the importance of concurrent design times, the design for manufacture method, design for maintainability, and design for reliability.

⑤ Apply Green Design Elements to Your Process and Product Design

- Explain why manufacturers design for reuse and why doing so is significant beyond the manufacturing stage.
- Describe why and how manufacturers are incorporating green practices in their process and product designs.

Innovative Designs Sometimes Take Long-Term Commitment[1]

What would you say to producing a jet engine that is more fuel efficient and more powerful than existing models, and you can stand in front of it while conversing on a cell phone? This marvel of engineering wasn't an overnight success. In fact, it took thirty years of applied research by Pratt and Whitney, a maker of jet engines.

Mike McCune is a Pratt and Whitney engineer who has over 60 patents to his credit. He and other engineers developed the PowerPure engine, which uses a turbine fan with gears instead of the shaft that all other jet engines use. This was a simple idea that required a stick-to-itiveness to realize.

Innovative designs such as Pratt and Whitney's PurePower Geared Turbofan require effective product and process design approaches. This product story is unique because it took so long and was so expensive to complete. In this chapter, we will discuss the techniques and approaches used by firms worldwide in producing products such as jet engines. We will return to this example at the end of the chapter.

[1]Coy, P. "The Little Gear That Could Reshape the Jet Engine," *Bloomberg Businessweek,* October 15, 2015, 1–4.

Supply chain and operations (SC&O) manufacturing managers must make two fundamental decisions: (1) what to make, or product design; and (2) how to make it, or process design. **Product design** is the act of creating new products. **Process design** is the selection and implementation of methods for producing products. To ensure the future viability of a company, managers create an ongoing process of renewal. At times, this renewal takes the form of new products and services. At other times, the renewal takes the form of product innovations.

product design
The act of creating new products.

process design
The selection and implementation of methods for producing products and services.

 NDERSTAND AND EXPLAIN THE STEPS OF PROCESS DESIGN

Well-designed products tend to get a lot of attention. Sleek tablets and smartphones, sportswear that tones muscle, and cars that can parallel park on their own are known for their innovative designs, but what about the manufacturing processes for these products? Someone has to design the *process* by which these products are made. The production process is where the rubber meets the road in delivering products and services to the customer. In this chapter, we will separate the manufacturing process and the service process to focus on processes in which there is little interaction with the customer.

Processes and Extended Processes

A **process** is a means of making something that is of value to a customer. Process design used to be straightforward, as pictured in **FIGURE 3.1**. The traditional *operations management input–transformation process–output model* had the transformation process as the core of the company. In the operations management model, everything was done in an environment that was decoupled from customers and suppliers. Management's job was to optimize flows, quality, and productivity within these confined transformation processes.

As we have been discussing, today's world is more complex. Competition is between supply chains; we can no longer confine our vision to the internal workings of a single firm.

process
The means of making something that is of value to a customer.

FIGURE 3.1 >

**Traditional Operations
Management Model**

The realities of SC&O require externalizing our thinking to include our suppliers, our suppliers' suppliers, our internal processes, our distributors, logistical functions, and our customers. **FIGURE 3.2** shows the **extended process**, the chain of activities from raw materials to final customer.

extended process
The chain of activities from raw materials to final customer.

When managers evaluate, innovate, and improve processes, they have to evaluate all these extended processes. For instance, it may harm your firm's supply chain's overall performance if you improve internally to the detriment of your suppliers. When changing processes, managers have to evaluate the effect the changes will have on the entire extended process. For example, one large semiconductor company had a problem in receiving: packages were not clearly addressed. At times, the packages would stack up and negatively affect the company's bottom line. As a result of the company's poor business performance, one employee decided to solve the problem by returning the shipments to their originators. Doing so, however, created problems for both the suppliers and the internal departments that needed the shipments.

Process Choice

When a manager chooses the type of process she wants to use, she must consider several factors. What are the expected production volumes? What technologies will this process need? Is the competitive focus on volume or variety? What are the firm's core competencies? How can she beat her competitors? Most processes can be classified in one of two categories: (1) process layouts or (2) product layouts.

process layout
A physical arrangement of equipment and workstations in which like functions are gathered into work centers.

PROCESS LAYOUTS A **process layout** is a type of layout in which like functions are gathered into work centers. They often use a *jumbled-process flow*. These types of layouts are quite flexible (within a range of similar products) but are less efficient and more costly than product layouts. You will most likely use a process layout when your focus is on variety and product flexibility more than cost or productivity. **FIGURE 3.3** shows an example of a process layout. Notice that everything is laid out by process: drilling is done in one area, milling in another, and painting somewhere else.

A university is a good example of process layout. Universities are usually organized according to field of study, allowing similar researchers to work in similar areas. For example,

FIGURE 3.2 >

The Extended Process

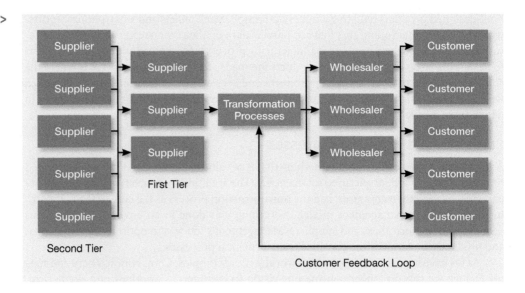

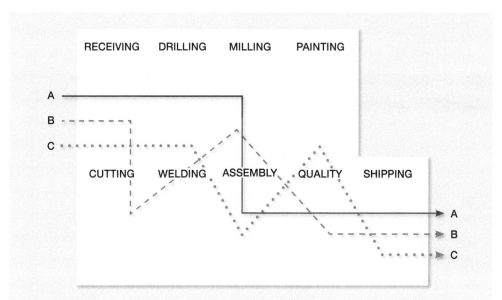

the Fisher College of Business at Ohio State University has five buildings. One building is a hotel that houses guests. Another building is for executive education, another for graduate teaching, another for undergraduate teaching, and yet another for faculty offices. In addition, the business school is kept separate from the law, medicine, and other professional schools.

PRODUCT LAYOUT When a manager needs to keep per unit costs low and produce a high volume of goods, a product layout is best. Product layouts are usually either linear or U-shaped and are laid out according to the requirements of a product. One example of a product layout is a windshield production line (FIGURE 3.4). As another example, an auto production line is laid out according to the requirements of a specific model of car. The car is built in a series of steps, and industrial engineers figure out the best production order for a completed product.

The Process Continuum

FIGURE 3.5 shows a process continuum from project through continuous flow. Process choices fall along a continuum from process layouts to product layouts. The most common types of processes are (1) project, (2) job shop, (3) batch, (4) mass assembly, and (5) continuous flow. We will discuss each type separately.

PROJECT A **project** is a one-shot set of activities resulting in an outcome. Typically, managers use projects when they are creating something new. For example, building a dam on the Yangtze River in China is an example of a very large project (possibly the largest project in history). Whenever managers need a high degree of customization, they undertake a project. Research and development requires projects, so all products and services begin as projects.

JOB SHOP A **job shop** is a low-volume batch processing facility that can produce a variety of products within a fairly narrow range. Like a project, products in a job shop are typically special ordered and are one of a kind, but job shops offer more standardization than a project. A copy shop is an example of a job shop. No two photocopying orders are exactly the same in a copy shop, and a copy shop performs only a fairly narrow set of tasks. You wouldn't go to a copy shop to have welding done, just as you wouldn't go to a machine shop to have your final paper bound.

project
A one-time set of activities resulting in an outcome.

job shop
A processing facility that can produce a variety of products in fairly low quantities.

The building of a dam on the Yangtze River was one of the world's largest construction projects.

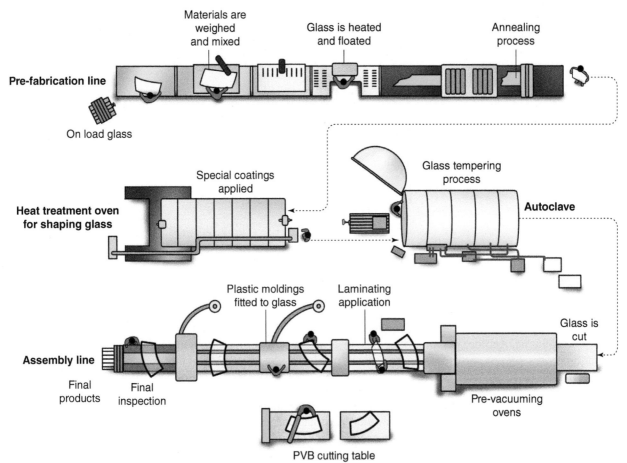

Materials are weighed and mixed

Glass is heated and floated

Annealing process

Pre-fabrication line

On load glass

Special coatings applied

Glass tempering process

Heat treatment oven for shaping glass

Autoclave

Plastic moldings fitted to glass

Laminating application

Glass is cut

Assembly line

Final products   Final inspection

Pre-vacuuming ovens

PVB cutting table

Source: Based on Glass Laminated Windshield Production Line. Published by Xinology Co., Ltd. http://xinology.com:888/Glass-Processing-Equipments-Supplies-Consumables/autoglass/glass-laminated-windshield-production-line/overview/introduction.html

FIGURE 3.4 ∧

An Automobile Windshield Product Layout

batch production
A process type that emphasizes making like products in mid to large quantities.

BATCH PRODUCTION **Batch production** facilities produce products, like processed foods or large appliances, in bunches. In fact, batch is the most commonly used process type for manufacturing products in the world. Because they allow production in higher quantities, batch processes cost less and are more productive than either job shops or projects. A manager who chooses a batch process sets up the production line, produces the product in the quantity required, and then moves to the next product model by reconfiguring the production line.

assembly line
A process type that produces a high volume of products with very little variety.

ASSEMBLY LINE An **assembly line** is used to produce high-volume products when little product variety is required. Examples of assembly lines include automobile and high-volume bread-making lines. These lines are low cost but very inflexible. Assembly lines require higher volumes and more standardization than batch processes.

FIGURE 3.5 >

The Process Continuum

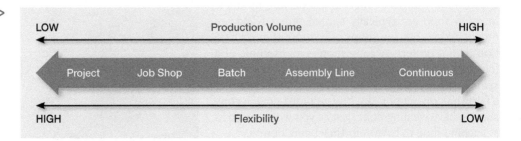

LOW   Production Volume   HIGH

Project   Job Shop   Batch   Assembly Line   Continuous

HIGH   Flexibility   LOW

CONTINUOUS-FLOW PROCESSES A **continuous-flow process** is a specialized facility where products flow from one place to another with little human interaction. Examples include flour mills, petroleum plants, and chemical plants. These capital-intensive processes often require very specialized technologies.

continuous-flow process
A specialized process in which products flow from one place to another with very little human interaction, such as petroleum refining.

PUTTING IT ALL TOGETHER Often, companies don't limit themselves to a single process choice. The same facility may have high-volume mass assembly lines, low-volume special-order job shop areas, and laboratories where projects take place. TABLE 3.1 shows some of the many variables that drive a manager when choosing a process.

Process Decision Variables

Characteristic	Project	Job Shop	Batch	Assembly Line	Continuous
Equipment and Physical Layout Characteristics					
Typical size of facility	Varies	Usually small	Moderate	Often large	Large
Process flow	No pattern	Several dominant patterns	A few dominant patterns	A rigid pattern	Inflexible, dictated by technology
Speed	Varies	Slow	Moderate	Fast	Very fast
Run lengths	Very short	Short	Moderate	Long	Very long
Rate of change	Slow	Slow	Moderate	Moderate to high	Moderate to high
Direct Labor and Work Force Characteristics					
Labor intensiveness	High	Very high	Varies	Low	Very low
Worker skill level	High	High	Mixed	Low	Varies
Worker training requirements	Very high	High	Moderate	Low	Varies
Material and Information Control Characteristics					
Material requirements	Varies	Difficult to predict	More predictable	Predictable	Very predictable
Production information requirements	Very high	High	Varies	Moderate	Low
Scheduling	Uncertain, frequent changes	Uncertain, frequent changes	Varies, frequent expediting	Fixed	Inflexible, dictated by technology
Primary Operating Management Characteristics					
Challenges	Estimating, sequencing tasks, pacing	Estimating, labor utilization, fast response, debottlenecking	Designing procedures, balancing stages, responding to diverse needs	Productivity improvement, adjusting staffing levels, rebalancing when needed	Avoiding downtime, timing expansions, cost minimization

Source: Based on Hayes, R., and Wheelwright, S., *Restoring Our Competitive Edge*, John Wiley & Sons, Inc., 1984.

∧ TABLE 3.1

		LOW	Production Volume		HIGH
Process structure and process life-cycle stage ↓	Product structure and product life-cycle stage →	Low-volume unique (one of a kind) product	Low-volume multiple product	Higher-volume standardized product	High-volume commodity product
Jumbled flow (job shop)	(Project)	Job shop			
Disconnected line flow (batch)			Batch		
Connected line flow (assembly line)				Assembly line	
Continuous flow (continuous)					Continuous

(Vertical axis label: Product Variety — LOW to HIGH)

Source: Based on Hayes, R., and Wheelwright, S., *Restoring our Competitive Edge*, p. 209. John Wiley & Sons, Inc., 1984.

FIGURE 3.6 ∧

A Product/Process Matrix

product/process matrix
A visual model that positions process choice as a trade-off between production volume and product variety.

PRODUCT/PROCESS MATRIX One way to look at process choice is by examining the **product/process matrix**, a visual model that positions process choice as a trade-off between production volume and product variety (**FIGURE 3.6**). Along the diagonal, you can see that projects and job shops tend to have higher customer interaction than mass assembly and that continuous-flow operations tend to produce higher volumes with higher capital intensity. This matrix shows several trade-offs associated with the different processes.

We have discussed differing types of processes and when to select those processes. In the next section, we turn our attention to justifying the investment in those processes you select.

Break-Even Analysis

As stated earlier, a determining factor in moving to a capital-intensive process such as mass assembly is whether expected demand for the products justifies the investment in processes and equipment. It is one thing to select the right process, but you must also justify it economically. One method used to determine the cost effectiveness of a process is *break-even analysis*. **Break-even analysis** is the process of considering fixed costs, variable costs, and expected revenues to determine the viability of an investment in process technologies.

break-even analysis
The process of considering fixed costs, variable costs, and expected revenues to determine the viability of an investment.

A simple case example illustrates break-even analysis. It costs you $10 in materials to set up a lemonade stand. If you were to sell a cup of lemonade for 50 cents, you would need to sell 20 cups to cover your costs. Therefore, 20 cups is your break-even point. If you were to sell more than 20 cups, you would gain profits. If you were to sell fewer than 20 cups, you would operate at a loss. We call the $10 a fixed cost, a cost that does not vary. If you end up buying more lemons and sugar as you sell more lemonade, you will have some variable costs. The 50 cents per cup is revenue, and it can be modeled as

$$\$0.50 \times Q = \$10 \tag{3.1}$$

$$Q = \frac{10}{0.50} = 20 \text{ cups} \tag{3.2}$$

where Q is the break-even quantity.

Now let's suppose that it costs $10 for the lemonade stand and $0.20 per cup for materials (lemons and sugar). The break-even point can now be modeled as

$$\$0.50 \times Q = \$10 + \$0.20 \times Q \tag{3.3}$$

$$Q = \frac{10}{0.30} = 33\tfrac{1}{3} \text{ cups} \tag{3.4}$$

The interpretation is the same as before. With the addition of the variable costs, you now need to sell at least 34 cups to make a profit. The generic form of Equation 3.3 is

$$R \times Q = F_c + (V_c \times Q) \tag{3.5}$$

where

R = revenue per unit sold
Q = quantity
F_c = fixed costs
V_c = variable cost per unit

We will demonstrate Equation 3.5 in SOLVED PROBLEM 3.1.

< SOLVED PROBLEM 3.1 *f(x)*
MyLab Operations Management
Video

Using Break-Even Analysis to Evaluate an Investment in Processes and Equipment

Problem: You are considering investing in a mass assembly production line. The fixed cost for the production line equipment with installation is $3 million. Each unit of product sells for $20 and has a $5 per unit variable cost. Labor, materials, and energy costs are factored into the variable costs. Expected demand is 300,000 units. Should management invest in this production line?

Solution: Using Equation 3.5, we model

$$\$20 \times Q = \$3 \text{ million} + (\$5 \times Q)$$

$$Q = \frac{3 \text{ million}}{15} = 200{,}000 \text{ units}$$

Because 300,000 (expected demand) > 200,000, the investment in the mass production line would be profitable. The expected contribution to profit would be

$$(300{,}000 - 200{,}000) \times \$15 = \$1.5 \text{ million}$$

Management should therefore compare this investment with other opportunities to evaluate whether the return of $1.5 million is acceptable.

Managing Across Majors 3.1 Accounting and Finance majors, break-even analysis is often used with payback period and return on investment to justify investments in projects, plant, and equipment.

< USING
TECHNOLOGY 3.1

Break-Even Analysis in Excel

You can use Excel to solve break-even analysis problems. In **FIGURE 3.7**, fixed, unit, and variable costs are entered in column C using the data from Solved Problem 3.1. The formula to solve the problem is shown in cell F6.

	A	B	C	D	E	F	G	H	I
1									
2									
3						=(C7/(C8-C9))			
4									
5									
6					Break-Even Units:	200000			
7		Fixed Cost ($):	3,000,000						
8		Unit Cost ($):	20	per unit					
9		Variable Cost ($):	5	per unit					
10		Expected Demand:	300,000						
11									

∧ FIGURE 3.7

Break-Even Example

Break-even analysis provides a means of evaluating the economics of a process choice and is an essential part of process selection. Once you have chosen a process and determined its viability, you must design the details of the process. Next, let's turn our attention to laying out processes using process maps and line balancing.

ⓤ NDERSTAND AND EXPLAIN THE STEPS OF PROCESS MAPPING AND LAYOUT PLANNING

process map
A schematic picture of a process using symbols.

A **process map** is a schematic picture of a process using symbols. An important step in designing a process is to develop a map of the process.

The language of process maps can vary from simple to complex. FIGURE 3.8 provides a simple set of symbols.

- A diamond indicates that there is a decision to be made. Often, diamonds identify different paths or sequences in the process map.
- A parallelogram appears whenever materials, forms, or tooling enter or leave the process.
- A rectangle indicates the work that is actually performed.
- A start/stop (or terminator) symbol and the page connector symbol are used for the convenience of the process mapper.

In addition to the symbols, there are a few simple rules for process maps:

1. Use these simple symbols to chart the process from the beginning, with all arcs in the process map leaving and entering a symbol. The arcs represent the progression from one step to the next.
2. Develop a general process map and then fill it out by adding more detail or a subflowchart for each of the elements.
3. Walk through the process by interviewing those who perform it as they do the work.
4. Determine which steps add value and which do not in an effort to simplify the work.

FIGURE 3.9 shows a simple process map used in a city planning department to issue permits allowing applicants to take possession of newly built homes. In FIGURE 3.10, the manager simplified the process by giving the front desk more authority and training to process the forms without assigning them for analyst review. The analyst review did not add value for the organization or the customer, so it could be eliminated.

FIGURE 3.8 >

Process Mapping Symbols

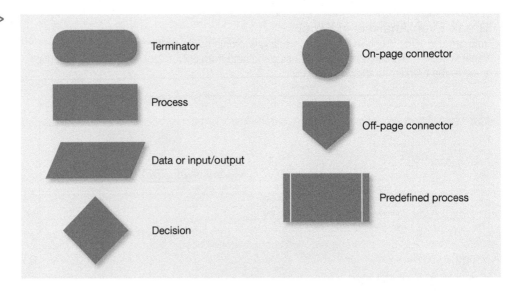

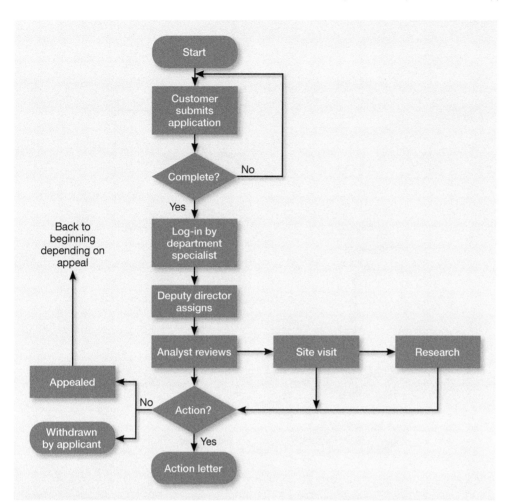

A Process Map of the Home Occupation Process as It Currently Exists Before Any Changes

Extended Process Maps for Supply Chains

The process maps we have discussed so far are for single-company processes. In SC&O, processes cross the bounds between companies. As a result of this link, managers need process maps that cover entire supply chains to use in the improvement of upstream and downstream design of supply chain processes. Both customers and suppliers can collaborate to improve supply chain performance. This type of mapping is extended supply chain mapping. FIGURE 3.11A shows a supply chain map for Mare Technologies. This map shows supplier processes, receiving, internal processes, shipping, and customer service processes. FIGURE 3.11B shows a map of the improved process. Some comparisons of the existing and improved processes are shown in TABLE 3.2.

In the case of Mare Technologies, managers used value-stream maps to study the current supply chain processes and to find ways to improve those processes. This approach can be effective for any supply chain. For example, companies importing parts from China can use these tools to better understand what contributes to long lead times.

Hybrid Layouts

Now that we have discussed process maps, let's discuss advanced types of process designs. Besides basic layouts, such as batch and continuous flow, other layouts are used in specialized situations, including (1) flexible manufacturing systems, (2) cellular layouts, and (3) fixed-position layouts. We will discuss each separately.

FLEXIBLE MANUFACTURING SYSTEMS Earlier, we discussed some of the problems with mass assembly (lack of flexibility) versus job shops (low volumes). As can be seen in

FIGURE 3.10 >

**A Process Map of the
Home Occupation
Process with
Simplification**

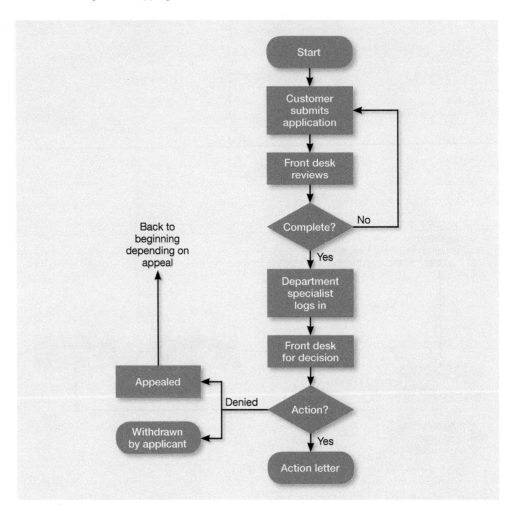

flexible manufacturing system
(FMS)
A process that represents a trade-
off between mass assembly operations and job shops by providing
moderate levels of flexibility with
moderate production volumes.

ladder FMS
An FMS that allows for parts and
assemblies to move in a variety of
different directions to receive the
needed processing.

FIGURE 3.12, one system represents a trade-off between mass assembly operations and job
shops by providing moderate levels of flexibility with moderate production volumes.
As shown, a **flexible manufacturing system (FMS)** is a highly automated production
system that provides moderate volumes with moderate flexibility by making changeovers
almost immediate.

A **ladder FMS**, shown in **FIGURE 3.13**, allows for parts and assemblies to move in different directions to receive the needed processing. In this system, many types of automated
machines may be used at different places in the process.

FMSs are used in many industries, such as aerospace and high-tech manufacturing companies. They are a good fit for manufacturing in moderate volumes. They do, however, require
large outlays in capital. Therefore, the economic question of implementing FMS requires
break-even analysis.

TABLE 3.2 >

Improvements in Mare Technologies' Performance			
Results Metrics	**Prior State**	**Improved State**	**Percentage Improvement**
Lead time (days)	55	42	24
Work in Process (days)	11	1	91
Flexibility	Limited	6.25% increase per week	400 per year
Unit prices	$6440	$5860	9

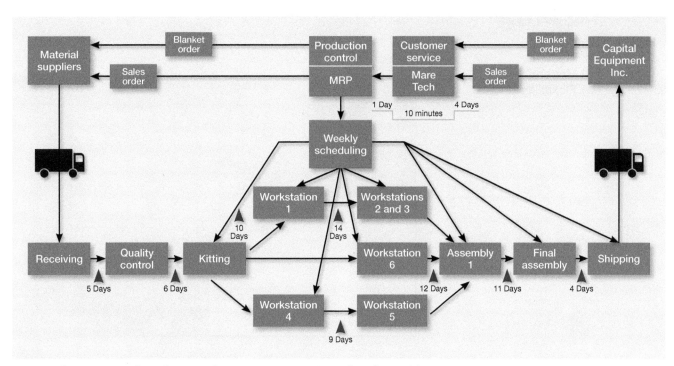

Source: Based on P. Horton and D. DelMonico, "Charting a New Course," *APICS: The Performance Advantage*, Oct. 2004: 43–46.

FIGURE 3.11A ∧

Mare Technologies' Prior-State Extended Value-Stream Map

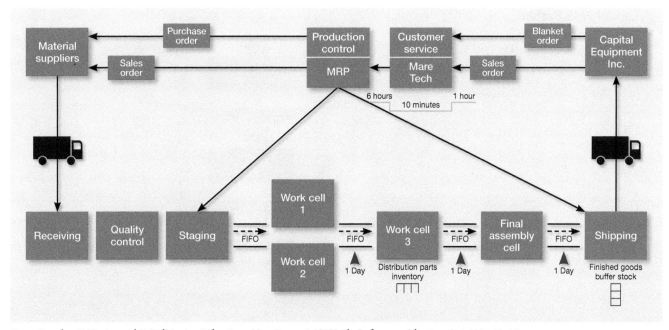

Source: Based on P. Horton and D. DelMonico, "Charting a New Course," *APICS: The Performance Advantage*, Oct. 2004: 43–46.

FIGURE 3.11B ∧

Mare Technologies' Improved-State Extended Value-Stream Map

CELLULAR MANUFACTURING SYSTEMS It is best to think of **cellular manufacturing** units as small job shops. They are usually U-shaped production lines that have combined various types of flexible pieces of equipment so that low-volume production can be performed more efficiently than it can in a job shop. Recall that the job shop we described earlier had an area for drills, mills, and so forth. A work cell could have a drill and a milling machine in the same area so that this work could occur with minimal transportation.

cellular manufacturing
U-shaped production lines that have combined various types of flexible pieces of equipment so that low-volume production can happen more efficiently than it can in a job shop.

Flexible Manufacturing
Systems: Moderate
Volumes with Moderate
Flexibility

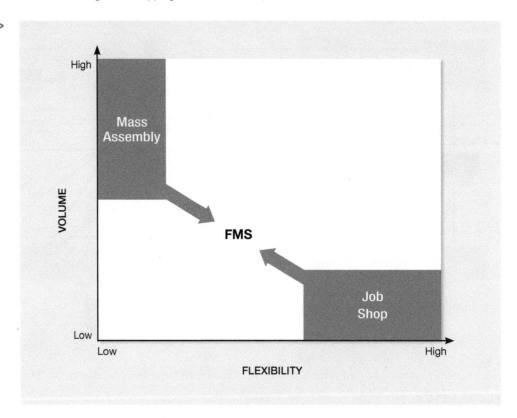

A Ladder FMS System

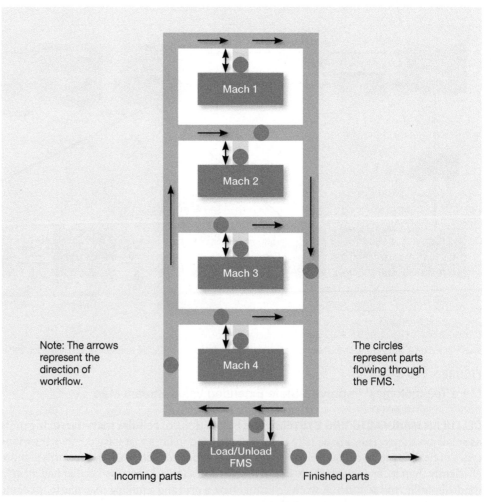

A work cell for producing computer hard drives in a clean room environment.

Harman International in Sandy, Utah, uses work cells in its manufacturing plants. Harman makes Digitech special-effects processors for guitars. In the same work cell, workers can perform different tasks in sequence. Each workstation has a flat-panel monitor to show the operators what operations need to be performed at that stage of production. Having that flat-panel display is useful for Harman because of the variety of products it produces.

FIXED-POSITION LAYOUTS Managers use **fixed-position layouts** in circumstances in which the product stays in a stationary position but equipment, labor, and components are transported from elsewhere into the work area as needed. This layout is sometimes referred to as **stall built**. Some Volvo factories use this approach in making cars. Boeing also uses this approach in constructing hangar-built airplanes.

Line Balancing

For product layouts or assembly line operations in both manufacturing and services, the problem of process design always comes down to assigning tasks to their workstations. Another common question is how many workstations are needed to provide low cost and high efficiency. **Line balancing** is the process of allocating tasks to process workstations in an efficient manner. Line balancing does not optimize layouts in a mathematical sense, but it can lead to finding a good design through the use of **heuristics**, rules used to achieve an objective such as efficiently using machine and labor. Examples of heuristics include *longest operating task time*, *shortest operating task time*, and *most following tasks* (most followers). There are nine steps associated with line balancing:

1. Identify tasks to be performed to produce the product.
2. Determine the task sequence.
3. Determine the task duration.
4. Calculate the takt time.
5. Calculate the theoretical minimum number of workstations.
6. Choose a heuristic such as longest operating time, shortest operating time, or most followers.
7. Apply the heuristic to assign tasks to workstations.
8. Compare your number of workstations with the theoretical minimum number computed in step 5.
9. Look for ways to improve the layout.

fixed-position layouts
Layouts in which the product stays in one place while machines are rolled in and out to perform needed processing steps.

stall built
Another name for a fixed-position layout.

line balancing
A process of allocating tasks to process workstations in an efficient manner.

heuristics
Rules used to achieve an objective, such as efficiently using machines and labor.

takt time
The required cycle time necessary to meet forecasted needs for a product.

Typically, steps 1 through 3 are performed by industrial engineers as a by-product of the design process and work measurement tools. The analyst has to perform step 4 to determine the **takt time**, the required cycle time necessary to meet forecasted needs for a product. Takt time is defined as

$$\text{takt time} = \frac{\text{amount of time available}}{\text{needed production volume}} \tag{3.6}$$

We demonstrate takt time computation in **SOLVED PROBLEM 3.2**.

To complete line balancing, we need to perform some analysis to find the *minimum number of workstations, efficiency,* and *balance delay.* The following formulas are needed to perform this analysis:

$$\text{minimum number of workstations} = \frac{\text{sum of task times}}{\text{takt time}} \tag{3.7}$$

$$\text{efficiency} = \frac{\text{sum of task times}}{(\text{no. of workstations} \times \text{takt time})} \tag{3.8}$$

efficiency
The proportion of time that work is being performed.

balance delay
The proportion of time that the resources in the process are not used.

$$\text{balance delay} = \frac{\text{sum of slack times}}{(\text{no. of workstations} \times \text{takt time})} = (1 - \text{efficiency}) \tag{3.9}$$

The **efficiency** shows the proportion of time that work is being performed. The **balance delay** is the proportion of time that the resources in the process are not used.

$f(x)$ **SOLVED PROBLEM 3.2 >**   **Line Balancing in Action**

MyLab Operations Management
Video

Problem: A manager must use takt times to construct an assembly line with the following tasks:

Task	Task Time (seconds)	Preceding Tasks	Task	Task Times (seconds)	Preceding Tasks
A	110	None	F	80	E
B	40	A	G	80	H
C	50	B	H	40	B
D	90	C	I	40	H
E	30	B	J	50	D, F, G, I

Note: Sum of task times is 610 seconds.

To get started, the takt time must be computed using a needed production volume of 30 per hour. Use the longest operating time (LOT) rule to assign tasks to workstations.

Solution: First, we'll start by computing the takt time using Equation 3.6:

$$\text{takt time} = \frac{60 \text{ seconds} \times 60 \text{ minutes}}{30} = 120 \text{ seconds}$$

As a result, we will use a 120-second cycle time in assigning tasks to a workstation. To assign tasks, we use a heuristic. In this case, the heuristic is LOT. Thus, when we choose between tasks to assign, we choose the task that takes the longest to complete. To apply the heuristic, we first draw a network of the tasks and then assign tasks one by one. Notice that the network shown here is drawn based on the precedence relationships laid out above.

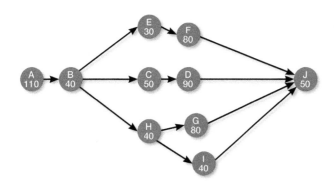

Using the following matrix, we will assign tasks according to the order indicated in the network diagram. As shown, the only possible task that can be assigned first is task A. Because task A has 110 seconds, there are only 10 seconds left in the 120-second takt time. Because there are no tasks with 10 seconds or fewer immediately following task A, this single task becomes the entirety of workstation 1.

Eligible Tasks	Chosen Task (LOT)	Workstation	Task Time	Slack Time
A	A	1	110	120 − 110 = 10

We now have to assign tasks to workstation 2. Because task B is the only task that immediately follows task A, it will be the first task assigned to workstation 2. Because the completion time for task B is 40 seconds, 80 seconds are still left in the takt time. Next, tasks C, E, and H are eligible for selection. Because task C has the longest time, with 50 seconds, it is chosen next. Then, with 30 seconds left in the takt time, only task E is eligible. The sum of the task times for tasks B, C, and E are 40 + 50 + 30 = 120 seconds. Therefore, there is no slack time left.

Eligible Tasks	Chosen Tasks (LOT)	Workstations	Task Times	Slack Times
A	A	1	110	120 − 110 = 10
B	B	2	40	0
C, E, H	C		50	
E	E		30	

For workstation 3, three tasks are eligible: D, F, and H. Of these three tasks, D is the longest, with 90 seconds. Because there are no subsequent tasks with 30 seconds or less, workstation 3 will have only one task with 120 − 90 = 30 seconds slack time.

Eligible Tasks	Chosen Tasks (LOT)	Workstations	Task Times	Slack Times
A	A	1	110	120 − 110 = 10
B	B	2	40	0
C, E, H	C		50	
E	E		30	
D, F, H	D	3	90	30

For workstation 4, tasks F and H are eligible. Because task F has the longest time, with 80 seconds, it is assigned first. Then, with 40 seconds left, task H is an excellent fit. Because 80 + 40 = 120, slack time is 0 for workstation 4.

Eligible Tasks	Chosen Tasks (LOT)	Workstations	Task Times	Slack Times
A	A	1	110	120 − 110 = 10
B	B	2	40	0
C, E, H	C		50	
E	E		30	
D, F, H	D	3	90	30
F, H	F	4	80	0
H	H		40	

Workstation 5 is very similar to workstation 4, only now with tasks G and I. There is no slack.

Eligible Tasks	Chosen Tasks (LOT)	Workstations	Task Times	Slack Times
A	A	1	110	120 − 110 = 10
B	B	2	40	0
C, E, H	C		50	
E	E		30	
D, F, H	D	3	90	30
F, H	F	4	80	0
H	H		40	
G, I	G	5	80	0
I	I		40	

Finally, with only one task left, we will assign task J to workstation 6. The remaining slack time is 120 − 50 = 70 seconds.

Eligible Tasks	Chosen Tasks (LOT)	Workstations	Task Times	Slack Times
A	A	1	110	120 − 110 = 10
B	B	2	40	0
C, E, H	C		50	
E	E		30	
D, F, H	D	3	90	30

F, H	F	4	80	0
H	H		40	
G, I	G	5	80	0
I	I		40	
J	J	6	50	70

As a result of this analysis, we can substitute our numbers into Equations (3.7) through (3.9):

Workstation #: 1   2   3   4   5   6

Tasks:

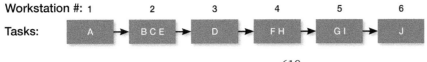

$$\text{theoretical minimum number of workstations} = \frac{610}{120} = 5.083 \cong 6 \text{ workstations}$$

$$\text{efficiency} = \frac{610}{6 \times 120} = 0.85$$

$$\text{balance delay} = \frac{110}{720} = 0.15$$

The minimum number of workstations is 5.083, but we have to round up to six workstations to complete all the tasks needed. Because our line balance resulted in six workstations, we can do no better without fundamentally redesigning how the tasks are performed.

Designing Functional Layouts

We have just discussed a method for laying out assembly lines (product layouts) and now turn to functional (process) layouts. As a reminder, a process layout is one in which like operations are grouped together. Even given this grouping limitation, managers can create functional layouts that are cost effective and somewhat efficient by determining the correct locations for the groupings. In this section, we discuss different methods for arranging job shops and functional layouts.

THE LOAD-DISTANCE MODEL Process layouts are functional in nature and often require flexible layouts for a broad diversity of products. Because these production facilities have jumbled flows, it is helpful to develop a layout that improves efficiency for the majority of products made. For example, if there are frequent trips between painting and milling, those areas should be placed close together. The technique used in laying out functional layouts is called the **load-distance model**. It is an algorithm used to minimize product flow between work centers by minimizing the cost C:

load-distance model
A model used in designing functional layouts where movement is minimized.

$$C = \left(\sum_{i=1}^{n} \sum_{j=1}^{n} L_{ij} D_{ij} \right) K \tag{3.10}$$

where

n = number of work centers
L_{ij} = number of loads transported between work centers i and j
D_{ij} = distance between work centers i and j
K = cost to move one load one unit of distance

For our purposes, we assume that the cost to move from work center A to work center B is the same as the cost to move from work center B to work center A. If the marginal cost of moving varies, a more complex model is needed. We will demonstrate this approach in **SOLVED PROBLEM 3.3**.

SOLVED PROBLEM 3.3 >   **Load-Distance Model in Action**

MyLab Operations Management
Video

Problem: A job shop is arranged as shown with work centers A through L (where each letter represents a different type of process such as drilling, milling, etc.).

A	B	C
D	E	F
G	H	I
J	K	L

Assuming that it costs $1 per unitary distance, the monthly loads (in units) are as follows.

			To		
From	D	G	H	I	J
A	30	60			20
C	60	30	20		40
E	10				50

Using the data in this matrix, find a good layout.

Solution: First, we have to compute the cost (*C*) of the current layout. We do so in the following spreadsheet (note that diagonals count as 1 unit of distance):

Pairing	Loads	Distance	Load × Distance
A–D	30	1	30
A–G	60	2	120
A–J	20	3	60
C–D	60	2	120
C–G	30	2	60
C–H	20	2	40
C–J	40	3	120
E–D	10	1	10
E–J	50	2	100
		C =	660

Next, we sort the layout by the number of loads. The result is the following prioritization:

Pairing	Loads	Distance	Loads × Distance
A–G	60	2	120
C–D	60	2	120

E–J	50	2	100
C–J	40	3	120
A–D	30	1	30
C–G	30	2	60
A–J	20	3	60
C–H	20	2	40
E–D	20	1	10
		$C =$	660

The top priority for rearranging the layout is to place A and G, C and D, and E and J closer together. Doing so requires some creativity; here is one possible layout found using trial and error:

H	D	G
E	C	A
B	J	F
I	K	L

The load-distance calculation for this layout is

Pairing	Loads	Distance	Loads × Distance
A–D	30	1	30
A–G	60	1	60
A–J	20	1	20
C–D	60	1	60
C–G	30	1	30
C–H	20	1	20
C–J	40	1	40
E–D	10	1	10
E–J	50	1	50
		$C =$	320

Because the distances are 1 for all the loads, this one is the low-cost layout. Other low-cost layouts may have other advantages.

FIGURE 3.14 >

Muther's Grid

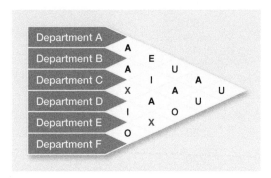

MUTHER'S GRID Although load-distance models are widely used in laying out job shops, their chief limitation is that they focus on cost and distance only. Sometimes, behavioral reasons for locating must be considered. For example, because of odors, you probably would not locate the painting facility immediately adjacent to the lunchroom! To perform this type of analysis, we create a grid, called a **Muther's grid**, which outlines preferences using the following codes:

Muther's grid
A model used in designing functional layouts where behavioral criteria are considered.

Code	Priority of Closeness
A	Absolutely necessary
E	Very important
I	Important
O	Somewhat important
U	Unimportant
X	Undesirable

Obviously, X and A are the highest priorities. Now, we compose a grid like the one in FIGURE 3.14 using the above priorities.

The criteria for determining how to prioritize relationships between departments include the following:

1. Usage of common equipment or facilities
2. Usage of the same labor or information
3. Same work sequence or work flow
4. Need to communicate
5. Makes work unsafe
6. Makes quality of work life poor
7. Similar work

We will demonstrate the use of a Muther's grid in SOLVED PROBLEM 3.4.

 SOLVED PROBLEM 3.4 >   Muther's Grid in Action

MyLab Operations Management Video

Problem: Using the Muther's grid in FIGURE 3.14, identify the most important priorities with an A or X rating and develop a layout.

Solution: Looking at Figure 3.14, we first observe the most important layout considerations: the work areas that must be close together (marked A) and the work areas that must be separate (marked X). They are shown in the following table:

A Priorities	X Priorities
A–B	C–D
B–C	D–F
C–E	
B–E	
A–E	

This method is trial and error. First, place the A's close together:

A Priorities	
C	B
E	A

Next, arrange the **X** priorities, which may require some adjustments to the beginning arrangement. Here is one possibility:

A and X Priorities		
C	B	D
F	E	A

This approach is followed iteratively until you satisfy as many of the priorities as you can. After the A and **X** priorities, proceed to the E and O priorities. The U priorities can generally be disregarded. Experiment with this method to see if you can find a better layout.

ILLUSTRATE THE DIFFERENT ELEMENTS OF PRODUCT DESIGN

Now that we have covered how products are made, we can turn our attention to the products themselves because process design and product design go hand in hand. In product and process design and innovation, we first identify a need that will improve the life of the customer. Then we design a product or service to fit that need. As many inventors know, designing a product or service is harder than it seems. **Design** is a process of applying imagination to invent new products and services. Innovative designs may come in differing ways. **Continuous design** involves designing products that are enhancements to existing products. **Discontinuous design** results in new products that are complete changes from existing products.

We will base our discussions on designing products, process design, and design nuances. Implicit in these design processes are several questions. For example, what are the functions that the customer wants? What are the capabilities of current products? What are the limitations of the materials we have selected for the product? Are better materials available? How much will the product cost to make? How do we price the product to make it successful in the marketplace?

design
A process of applying imagination to invent new products and services.

continuous design
The process of designing products that are enhancements to existing products.

discontinuous design
The process of designing products that are complete changes from existing products.

FIGURE 3.15 >

Phases of the Product
Life Cycle

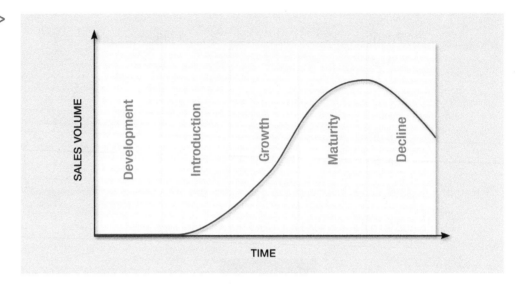

Product Life Cycle

product life cycle
A graphical representation of the life phases that a product experiences.

One of the first things to consider in product design is managing the product life cycle (**FIGURE 3.15**). The **product life cycle** is a graphical representation of the life phases that a product experiences. First, the product is launched. When it is new to the market, demand for the product grows. As the product matures, demand levels out and eventually declines.

Because product life cycles occur naturally, you probably cannot control the rate at which the life cycle occurs. High-tech products such as smartphones have very short product life cycles. The life cycles for more traditional products, such as dining room furniture, may be much longer. When product life cycles dictate, we can plan to introduce new and *complementary products*. **Complementary products** are goods that use similar technologies that can coexist in a family of products. These products extend the life of a product line by offering new features or improvements to prior versions of the product. At times, these improvements are cosmetic; at other times, they are substantive. All-terrain vehicles (ATVs) and snowmobiles are examples of complementary products that have counterseasonal demand. Arctic Cat produces ATVs for consumption in warmer months and snowmobiles for winter use. By doing so, it creates two complementary product life cycles, ensuring that it is producing and selling goods year-round. Managing product life cycles is less about preventing a single product from becoming obsolete and more about making decisions about how to manage a variety of products with different life cycles simultaneously.

complementary products
Goods that use similar technologies that can coexist in a family of products, such as ATVs and snowmobiles.

ATVs and snowmobiles are counter-seasonal, complementary products.

Research and Development

Research and development (R&D) is the process that firms follow to develop new products or improve existing products. Many firms, such as Apple and Hewlett-Packard, may outsource their production and focus primarily on R&D and marketing. Reasons to pursue R&D include the following:

- *Strengthening the bottom line.* R&D provides a lifeblood of new products that produce income.
- *Absorbing productive capacity.* R&D provides new products that allow us to use our productive capacity.
- *Emerging customer needs.* You may need to identify a solution to a problem that makes customers' lives better.
- *Increasing market share.* New product ideas are necessary to maintain or to increase market share.
- *Regulatory mandates.* Changes in the legal environment may make new product development important. An example is when the federal government increased the minimum mileage standards for automobiles.
- *Technological advances.* New technologies may arise. For example, when 5G wireless technology supplanted 4G, the need for more 5G-compatible devices rose.
- *Changes in materials.* New materials, like new technologies, change the way products are designed and manufactured. For example, new carbon fibers are replacing plastics in many products because the fibers are lighter and stronger. R&D helps companies use such changes to their advantage.

APPLIED RESEARCH AND BASIC RESEARCH When we discuss R&D, we need to distinguish between basic research and applied research. **Basic research** is theoretical exploration that is generally not motivated by profit. **Applied research** is practical exploration that often has a profit motive. For example, basic researchers may discover a safer process for nuclear fission. Once they have done so, they will publish research articles in scholarly journals disseminating this knowledge. Applied researchers may then take this knowledge and develop nuclear plants that generate electricity more safely. Generally, the applied researchers may patent their processes so that competing firms cannot exploit their work. R&D then takes the applied research and develops it into commercial applications.

PULL AND PUSH There are two types of R&D. One is referred to as market pull, and the other is technological push. **Market pull** (continuous development) is taking existing products and enhancing them to reinvigorate the product life cycle or to create new complementary products. For example, in 1964, there was one flavor of Doritos chips. Today, more than 100 flavors are being sold worldwide. **Technological push** (discontinuous development) occurs when a new product is sent to market without a clear idea of how it will be used by the customer. When personal computers were first produced, it was impossible to determine how they would be used. Technological push often results in what marketers refer to as *ready-fire-aim*. SC&O CURRENT EVENTS 3.1 discusses how R&D enhances the fortunes of Google.

Product Design Process

Once R&D is complete, the next step is to design processes to produce the products. Although product design does influence process design, there are many different approaches to designing products. Product design approaches vary in some important ways (which we will discuss later), but there are some similarities across the board. For example, design projects are likely to involve a project team rather than a single designer working independently. Preferably, these teams will work closely with customers to ensure that customer needs are met.

FIGURE 3.16 shows a generic approach to designing products. The design process includes nine interrelated phases, beginning with product idea generation and ending with manufacture, delivery, and use. Project managers monitor design projects at each phase for cost and adherence to schedules.

research and development (R&D)
The process that firms follow to develop new products or improve existing products.

basic research
Theoretical exploration that is generally not profit motivated.

applied research
Practical exploration that often has a profit motive.

market pull
Continuous development that takes existing products and enhances them to reinvigorate the product life cycle or to create new complementary products.

technological push
Discontinuous development that occurs when a new product is sent to market without a clear idea of how it will be used by the customer.

Google Contact Lenses

You have probably heard about Google glasses and the fact that they have not been market successes. Some of the failure of the Google Glass has been blamed on poor marketing where early adopters were named Glass Explorers and were required to pay $1,500 for products that are super nerdy looking without a lot of software to do cool things.

Alphabet (the parent of Google) is doubling down with high expenditures on applied R&D on a smart contact lens device. According to Google's packaging patent application, "The eye-mountable device is seated on the pedestal such that the posterior concave side contacts the second end of the pedestal and the eye-mountable device is elevated from the base of the container. The opening of the container can be sealed by a lidstock."

One of the uses for the Google smart contact lens is in disease management. They can perform glucose readings as well as other tests beginning with the eyeball. Sergey Brin (co-founder of Google) stated, "Our dream is to use the latest technology in the miniaturization of electronics to help improve the quality of life for millions of people." It will be interesting to see if these products are received better than Google glasses.

Source: Plummer, Q., "Google Smart Contact Lens to Hit the Market Soon?" *Tech Times,* June 28, 2015.

1. PRODUCT IDEA GENERATION Product idea generation is the first phase. During this phase, internal and external sources provide inputs for new concepts. Internal sources include marketing, management, R&D, and employee suggestions. The primary source for external product ideas is the customer. Original equipment manufacturers and contract manufacturers work closely with customers to develop new products. In other circumstances (e.g., updates to existing products such as household detergents), customer needs are identified to generate product ideas. Other external sources for product ideas can be market-related sources, such as industry experts, consultants, competitors, suppliers, and inventors.

There are fundamental differences between R&D-generated ideas (known as *technology push*) and marketing-generated ideas (known as *marketing pull*). Technology push ideas tend to be ground-breaking, risky, and technologically innovative. An example of R&D-based

FIGURE 3.16 >

The Product Development Process

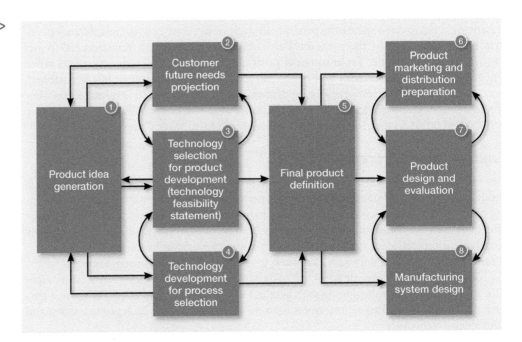

development is the Altair microcomputer. In the mid-1970s, the Micro Instrumentation and Telemetry Systems (MITS) Altair 8800 appeared on the cover of *Popular Electronics* magazine. At the time, there was a very small market for this product. The article, however, inspired two computer whizzes named Paul Allen and Bill Gates to develop a BASIC Interpreter for the Altair. The union of Allen and Gates led to the creation of Microsoft Corporation. Although there was not a large established market for personal computers, they have radically affected business and home life since their introduction.

Marketing pull ideas tend to be more incremental—that is, they build on existing designs—and are better aligned with customer needs than are R&D-generated ideas. For example, at the product idea generation stage, a gap in the market or a customer need should be identified by marketing and design specialists. Preliminary assessment of the marketability of the product is performed by product screeners, and funding is provided for beginning development of a prototype. Recent market-oriented developments in computers have included technological developments such as improved multimedia capabilities and faster speeds, as well as cosmetic changes in casings such as tablet designs and the use of clear plastics. As shown in GLOBAL CONNECTIONS 3.1, new product ideas may need to be tailored to the specific needs of people in differing markets around the world.

2. CUSTOMER FUTURE NEEDS PROJECTION Phase 2 uses data to predict future customer needs. Designers for Intel, the maker of microprocessors for personal computers, are masters at this process. Intel has been able to project and introduce new products that are well timed to fit with changes in the technology that requires them. Intel developed new graphics chips in accordance with the explosion of sophisticated graphics in gaming programs and on the Internet. The company also introduced these microprocessors at a rate that allows for a good balance between software and hardware needs. At the same time, the company has been able to outpace competing microprocessor developers by staying slightly ahead of the technological curve.

The task of the product designer is to offer valuable products that anticipate future changes in customer preferences. There is no single approach to gathering information about future customer needs. Surveys might give insights, but they are usually insufficient to uncover emerging customer needs. Other approaches such as focus groups, listening posts, and observation are useful.

Do Product Development at Tata

< GLOBAL
CONNECTIONS 3.1

One of the most important companies you have never heard of is Tata Motors of India. Imagine the problem faced by an auto producer in India: You have the second most populous country in the world with over 1.2 billion people and a very low per-capita income of just over $600. Obviously, Mercedes and even Ford would not be able to meet the needs of this market. Enter Tata Motors using *disruptive innovation* to create a car called the Nano that sells for just over $3,000. According to Clayton Christensen of Harvard University, disruptive innovations create new markets and disrupt existing markets. The interesting thing is that these disruptive innovations often consist of inferior technologies that undermine existing markets. In the case of Tata Motors, they worked hard to design a car that could service the Indian market at a low cost. Some interesting, cost-saving features of the Nano include:

- The trunk is only accessible from inside the car.
- There is only one windshield wiper.
- There are three lug nuts on the tires instead of four.
- Radios are optional.
- The driver and passenger front seats are the same.
- There is no filler cap. The front hood is opened to put in gasoline.

Essentially, the Tata Nano required rethinking the automobile as we know it. Simplified design with an eye toward cost saving allowed this car to get on the roads in India.

3. TECHNOLOGY SELECTION During technology selection for product development, designers choose the materials and technologies that will provide the best performance for the customer at an acceptable cost. A **technology feasibility statement** is used by designers in the design process to assess issues such as necessary parameters for performance, manufacturing imperatives, limitations in the physical properties of materials, special considerations, changes in manufacturing technologies, and conditions for quality testing the product.

technology feasibility statement
A document used by designers in the design process to assess a variety of issues, such as necessary parameters for performance, manufacturing imperatives, limitations in the physical properties of materials, special considerations, changes in manufacturing technologies, and conditions for quality testing the product.

4. TECHNOLOGY DEVELOPMENT Technology development for process selection chooses those processes used to transform the materials picked in the prior step into final products. Careful technology selection of both automated and manual processes is important from an SC&O perspective because machines, processes, and flows are developed by process engineers that result in a process insensitive to variations in ambient and material-related conditions.

5. FINAL PRODUCTION DEFINITION Final product definition results in final drawings and specifications for the product with product families by identifying base products and derivative products. Process engineers use these drawings to work with suppliers and process designers to produce a final product.

6. MARKETING AND DISTRIBUTION Product marketing and distribution preparation are marketing-related activities such as developing a marketing plan. The marketing department develops a marketing plan that should define customers and distribution streams. The production-related activities are identifying supply chain activities and defining distribution networks. Today, this step often requires the design of after-sales processes such as maintenance, warranties, and repair processes that occur after the customer owns the product.

7. PRODUCT DESIGN AND EVALUATION Product design and evaluation requires definition of the product architecture, design, production, testing of subassemblies, and testing of the system for production. A **product design specification (PDS)** demonstrates the design to be implemented, with its major features, uses, and conditions for use of the product. The PDS contains product characteristics, the expected life of the product, intended customer use, product development special needs, production infrastructure, packaging, and marketing plans.

product design specification (PDS)
A document that demonstrates the design to be implemented and includes major features, uses, and conditions for use of the product.

manufacturing system design
The selection of the process technologies that will result in a low-cost, high-quality product.

8. MANUFACTURING SYSTEM DESIGN **Manufacturing system design** involves the selection of the process technologies that will result in a low-cost, high-quality product. The selection of process technologies is a result of projected demand and the finances of the firm. Processes must be stable and capable of producing products that meet specification. A major development in this area is that firms now desire the ability to change over to new products with a minimum of cost associated with defects. For example, Harman Industries in Utah develops products in-house and produces them there prior to offshoring production eventually to China. This strategy allows Harman to perfect the production process before outsourcing.

9. MANUFACTURE, DELIVERY, AND USE Finally, product manufacture, delivery, and use finish this process. The consumer then enjoys the result of the design process.

With this understanding of the product design process, we now turn to methods for improving designs. One such design tool is quality function deployment.

U NDERSTAND AND EMPLOY QUALITY FUNCTION DEPLOYMENT

quality function deployment (QFD)
A method for translating customer requirements into functional design (also called house of quality).

Once you have determined customer needs, you must then translate those needs into functional product design. **Quality function deployment (QFD)** describes a method for translating customer requirements into functional design. This process of translation is sometimes referred to as the *voice of the customer*.

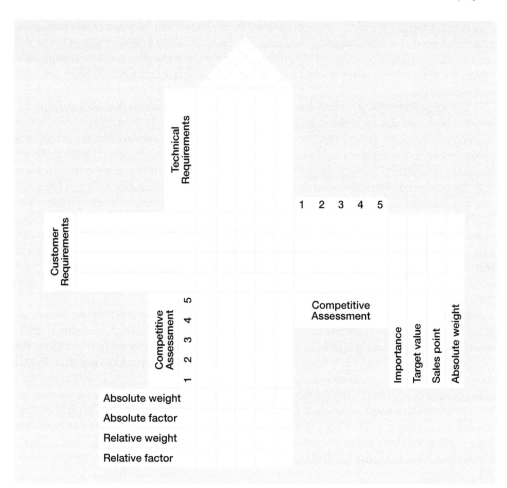

Designers need a means for implementing customer requirements into designs. The house of quality, illustrated in FIGURE 3.17, shows how QFD is used to implement customer requirements into designs. The left side shows customer requirements. The roof on the house of quality lists technical requirements. By using the house of quality, engineering priorities are established that correlate most strongly with customer and market needs.

Concurrent Design Teams

Because performing the design process steps sequentially is very time consuming, the steps are performed simultaneously as often as possible. Performing them at the same time is called **concurrent engineering** and has been very helpful in speeding up the design life cycle. Products such as John Deere tractors and all-new automobiles have been designed using concurrent engineering. Teams, which include program management teams, technical teams, and design-build teams, are a primary component of this approach.

concurrent engineering
Team-based design in which the differing tasks of design are performed simultaneously.

The primary benefits of concurrent engineering are (1) communication among group members and (2) speed. Working on products and processes simultaneously enhances cross-functional communication and reduces the time to get the concept to market. The team concept joins people from various disciplines and improves the cross-fertilization of ideas.

Another benefit of concurrent engineering is increased interaction with the customer. Often, customers are included in concurrent engineering teams to give immediate feedback on product designs.

Design for Manufacture Method

The overriding concept to consider when discussing **design for manufacturing (DFM)** is to *make the product easy to build*. This concept may seem intuitive, but it is sometimes difficult to be intuitive when you are too close to a process (like people who design products). Poor

design for manufacturing (DFM)
A system of design that facilitates the making of products.

ease of manufacturing may be more behavioral or organizational in origin rather than technical. In the old world of designing products, the product design engineer was at the top of the hierarchy of engineers. Lower down the hierarchy were the process design engineers. Often, the different engineers worked in totally different departments, which often impeded communication.

over-the-wall-syndrome
A traditional method for design with poor integration and communication.

This organizational problem has been referred to as the **over-the-wall syndrome**, which is demonstrated by looking at the design process sequentially. First, the product design engineers developed a design. This product design would then be approved by the manager of product design. The design would then go to the manager of process design. Process design engineers would then develop the processes to make the product. If at any point a problem with the product design was found by the process engineers, a request for redesign would be sent to a manager of product design. Product design engineers would solve the problem and send the new product design back to the process designers. The process designers would then continue their work of developing the process. When other problems occurred, they would have to be referred back to the product design engineers. As a result of this back-and-forth method, it often took years to develop a new product and resulted in processes that built poorly functioning products. DFM methods are designed to eliminate the over-the-wall syndrome and radically reduce design cycle times.

product data management (PDM)
A method that helps manage both product data and the product development process by tracking the masses of data needed to design, manufacture, support, and maintain products.

Many firms use enterprise resource planning (ERP) systems to integrate financial, planning, and control systems into a single information architecture. As a result, there is an effort in the business world to include computerized design systems in these ERPs. An important component of such design software is the **product data management (PDM)** tool. PDM is a general extension of techniques commonly known as engineering data management, document management, or other similar names. This tool helps manage both product data and the product development process by tracking the masses of data needed to design, manufacture, support, and maintain products. Companies can then have product-related data in one information system that can be accessed for future product designs. One outcome of PDM is to reduce variation in the components used in different products.

Design for Maintainability

A major concern with new products is ease of maintainability. It is often cheaper to replace a product than to repair it, especially inexpensive products such as electric can openers, portable radios, and other small appliances. The cost of repairing relatively expensive products such as personal computers, automobiles, and large appliances can be very expensive, however.

The decision to repair is essentially an economic decision involving costs, benefits, and trade-offs. This decision becomes particularly difficult when the product life cycle is short. Suppose that you bought a computer for $1,000 a year ago, but you now need more memory, a better sound card, and a larger hard drive. If you go to a discount store, you can purchase those upgrades for about $500. At the same time, for $1,000, you can purchase a new computer that has all the features you need as well as features that are new to the market, such as increased speed and screen clarity. Should you spend $1,000 on a new computer or $500 to upgrade your old computer?

Designers try to make this decision easier for consumers by designing for maintainability. Design for maintainability concepts include components that are easily replaced, components that are easily removed with standard tools, adequate space to perform the maintenance function, nondestructive disassembly, safe maintenance, adequate owner's manuals, and documentation (e.g., wiring diagrams, help facilities, or videos showing how to perform minor repairs).

Many personal computer manufacturers include how-to videos in the computers' memory that demonstrate maintenance functions such as adding memory, connecting interfaces, and other simple maintenance functions. Sears sells Craftsman tractors that include DVDs to demonstrate how to change oil, operate the tractor, and perform other service functions. By providing customers with the necessary information and ease of access to the product that

Besides the creepy clown costume fad that was popular not so long ago, the scariest costume found on Halloween night was from Chris Riley, who created a Samsung Galaxy Note 7 Smartphone costume that emitted smoke. While Samsung makes many fine products, the recall of 4.3 million Samsung smartphones was one of the most spectacular product failures in recent years.

Things got so bad that a Southwest Airlines flight was cancelled due to a smoking Samsung phone. The interesting thing was that the smoking phone was reportedly a replacement phone for a previously recalled Samsung phone. The phones were then banned from all U.S. flights, which means that the phones were more restricted than firearms on flights. Samsung is the largest phone maker in the world, and this failure has erased billions of dollars in value from its stock price.

The phones caught fire due to overheating of a lithium-ion battery with electrodes that were too close together, causing overheating. This failure led to a lot of bad press, many YouTube videos, and social media reports of smoking phones. Eventually the phones were pulled completely from the market. It is apparent that Samsung and other companies can run into reliability issues when they push the limits of existing technologies.

allows for simple or preventive maintenance, customers do not always have to decide between paying for maintenance or buying a new product.

An important issue is ease of delivery for more serious maintenance. Many repairs can be performed only by trained professionals. It is important to recognize that service is also a design issue. At the design phase, after-sale processes must be designed such that maintenance is received simply, rapidly, and cost effectively. Experience has shown that consumers are willing to pay more for products that are supported by outstanding service than for products without such service support.

Designing for Reliability

You can depend on reliable products to work properly when you need them to. Reliability, as it relates to products, results from the interaction of multiple components in a system. SC&O CURRENT EVENTS 3.2 talks about a spectacular product design failure.

Reliability has two dimensions, *failure rate* and *time*, both of which can be applied to components and to systems, respectively. **Component reliability** is the propensity for a part not to fail over a given time. **System reliability** is the probability that a system of components will perform the intended function over a specified period. It is important to recognize the difference in the levels of measurement between component reliability and system reliability. When we talk about component reliability, we refer to a finite aspect of the overall product. System reliability is computed from the aggregation of multiple components.

RELIABILITY MODELS Although there are several reliability models, we will discuss only some of the simpler ones here. The first model is graphic (**FIGURE 3.18**) and is called the **bathtub-shaped hazard function**. The vertical axis on the bathtub function is failure rate, and the horizontal axis is time. This model shows us that a product is more likely to fail either very early in its life or late in its useful life.

Consider this function when you purchase major appliances. It is now common for appliance vendors to offer **service contracts** at an additional cost. Because most major appliances include a first-year warranty that covers all the labor and parts needed to repair the appliance and because most appliances are made to last several years, when you purchase a service contract, you are really insuring the product during the part of its life when it is least likely to fail. In this case, a service contract appears to be a very good deal for the appliance vendor.

component reliability
The propensity for a part not to fail over a given time.

system reliability
The probability that a system of components will perform the intended function over a specified period of time.

bathtub-shaped hazard function
A model that shows that products fail either early or late in their useful life.

service contracts
Contracts that guarantee products if they fail during a given time period.

FIGURE 3.18 >

A Bathtub-Shaped Reliability Curve

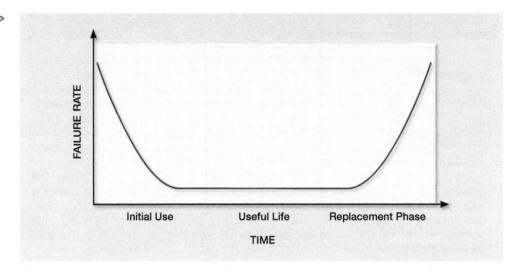

SERIES RELIABILITY Components in a system are in series if the performance of the entire system depends on all the components functioning properly. The components need not be physically wired sequentially for the system to be in series, but all parts must function for the system to function. FIGURE 3.19 shows n components in a series. System reliability for the series is expressed as

$$R_s = P(x_1 x_2 \cdots x_n) \tag{3.11}$$
$$= P(x_1)P(x_2 \mid x_1)P(x_3 \mid x_1 x_2) \cdots P(x_n \mid x_1 x_2 \cdots x_{n-1})$$

where

$$R_s = \text{system reliability}$$
$$P(x) = 1 - \text{probability of failure for component } x_i$$

By the same token, system unreliability can be modeled as

$$Q_s = 1 - R_s \tag{3.12}$$

where Q_s = system unreliability.

These reliability models assume independence between failure events, meaning that the failure of one component does not influence another component to fail. For an example of simple reliability for one component, imagine a component with 99 percent reliability over five years (this component will have a 99 percent chance of lasting five years and only a 1 percent chance of failure). These numbers probably sound good to you, but consider a television set made up of 700 components, with each component having a 99 percent reliability. If it is a series system, where the failure of any one component will cause the entire television to fail, the overall reliability will be $0.99^{700} = 0.00088$ or 0.088 percent reliable. In other words, the television has less than a 1 percent chance of surviving five years, which doesn't sound good at all. Comparing such a television to an automobile with 17,000 parts or a space shuttle with millions of components gives you an understanding of how difficult it is to make a product that will last.

Now let's suppose that we wanted this television with 700 components to have 90 percent overall reliability. If we want $0.90 = R^{700}$, we find that $R = (0.90)^{1/700} = 0.99985$, which is the required component reliability. See Problem 3.5.

FIGURE 3.19 >

A Series of n Components

Series Reliability

< SOLVED PROBLEM 3.5

Problem: Your manager has asked you to compute reliability for the following system.

Solution: The overall reliability for this system is

$$R = 0.98 \times 0.99 \times 0.90 \times 0.97 = 0.847$$

MEASURING RELIABILITY In addition to the series reliability function we have discussed, there are other ways to evaluate reliability. These models take into account historical data and are helpful in evaluating the efficacy of products. Let's discuss some basic reliability functions. Failure rate is measured as

$$\text{failure rate} = \frac{\text{number of failures}}{\text{units tested} \times \text{number of hours tested}} \tag{3.13}$$

Some care should be exercised in using Equation 3.13 because there is no distinction between continuous hours of testing or testing performed at separate times. For example, there is no difference in testing hours if five units are tested for 100 hours each or if one unit is tested for 500 hours. See **SOLVED PROBLEM 3.6.**

Reliability Measurement Failure Rates

< SOLVED PROBLEM 3.6

Problem: Suppose that your manager asked you to test 25 ski exercise machines under strenuous conditions for 100 hours per machine. Of the 25 machines you tested, 3 experienced malfunctions during the test. What is the failure rate for the exercise machines?

Solution:

$$\text{failure rate} = \frac{3}{25 \times 100} = 0.0012 \text{ failure per operating hour}$$

SYSTEM AVAILABILITY Remember that the failure rate is a useful measure for many products. In Solved Problem 3.6, 2,500 hours between failures may not make sense because many products are never used that many hours. A useful measure for maintainability of a product is system availability, which considers both mean time between failures (MTBF) and a new statistic, **mean time to repair (MTTR)**, which is the mean number of hours it takes to repair the product. **System availability (SA)** gives us the "uptime" (or proportion of time the product functions properly) of a product or system. System availability is interesting because it factors the importance of service into reliability calculations. If one supplier can get our system repaired in less time, we want to take that service into account (see **SOLVED PROBLEM 3.7**). The system availability formula is

mean time to repair (MTTR)
The mean number of hours it takes to repair the product.

system availability (SA)
The "uptime" or proportion of time that a product or system functions properly.

$$SA = \frac{MTBF}{MTBF + MTTR} \tag{3.14}$$

where

$$SA = \text{system availability}$$
$$MTBF = \text{mean time between failures}$$
$$MTTR = \text{mean time to repair}$$

 **SOLVED PROBLEM 3.7 >**   **System Availability**

Problem: An analyst has to decide among three suppliers for a server for a network. All other factors being equal, she is going to base her decision on system availability. Given the following data, which supplier should she choose?

Supplier	MTBF (Hours)	MTTR (Hours)
A	67	4
B	45	2
C	36	1

Solution: By Equation 3.14,

$$SA_A = \frac{67}{67 + 4} = 0.944$$

$$SA_B = \frac{45}{45 + 2} = 0.957$$

$$SA_C = \frac{36}{(36 + 1)} = 0.973$$

The analyst should choose supplier C. As you can see, service does matter because C is operable 97.3% of the time.

failure modes and effects analysis (FMEA)
A process used to consider each component of a system, identifying, analyzing, and documenting the possible failure modes within a system and the effects of each failure on the system and the user.

FAILURE MODES AND EFFECTS ANALYSIS Failure modes and effects analysis (FMEA) systematically considers each component of a system, identifying, analyzing, and documenting the possible failure modes within a system and the effects of each failure on the system. It is a method of analysis beginning at the lowest level of detail to which the system is designed and working upward. The FMEA process results in a detailed description of how failures influence system performance and personnel safety. FMEA answers the question, How do the systems or components fail? This analysis was created by the aerospace industry in the 1960s and is used extensively in Six Sigma, a quality improvement method.

FMEA can be applied to five general areas:

1. *Concept.* FMEA is used to analyze a system or its subsystems in the conception of the design.
2. *Process.* FMEA is applied to analyze the assembly and manufacturing processes.
3. *Design.* FMEA is used for analysis of products before mass production of the product starts.
4. *Service.* FMEA is used to test industry processes for failures prior to the release of the product to customers.
5. *Equipment.* FMEA can be used to analyze equipment before the final purchase.

product traceability
A process of tracking products from final use to point of origin.

PRODUCT TRACEABILITY AND RECALL PROCEDURES Although FMEA helps predict where defects will occur and what their effects will be, unforeseen defects sometimes result in dangerous and costly errors that can subject the firm to liability. For example, all aircraft are required to have proper identification techniques and sufficient tracking systems because accidents can result in extreme liability. Product traceability and recall procedures are important aspects of product design. **Product traceability** is a process of tracking products from final use to a point of origin. Because companies are liable for the products they create, it is important to be able to identify the origins of defective products or components through product traceability procedures.

A PPLY GREEN DESIGN TO YOUR PROCESS AND PRODUCT DESIGN

Currently, society demands much more from product designers than just high-quality products. Many manufacturers have turned to a more environmental form of manufacturing that offers positive returns on investment. For example, Siemens, Caterpillar, Xerox, and Hewlett-Packard, among other companies, are using environmentally friendly forms of manufacturing.

The move to green manufacturing began in Germany with requirements for importers to remove packaging materials from German soil. Using a life-cycle approach to product design causes designers to focus not only on incoming materials, manufacturing processes, and customer use but also on the eventual disposal of the product. This life-cycle approach has led to practices known as design for reuse, design for disassembly, and design for remanufacture.

Design for Reuse

Design for reuse is the process of designing products so that they can be used in later generations of products. **Design for disassembly** is related to design for reuse, but with products designed so that they can be taken apart easily. One example is the Kodak FunSaver camera. Initially, the camera was made so that it could be disposed of after use. Although Kodak had experimented with recycling the cameras, the cameras still ended up in landfills. Kodak received a wake-up call when it received the dreaded "wastemaker of the year" award for the disposable cameras, and it responded by converting the design from disposable cameras to recyclable cameras. Initially, the camera had been ultrasonically welded. Through design for disassembly processes, the camera case is now made so that it snaps apart easily. The customer can deliver the camera to the photofinisher, who then returns the camera to Kodak. Kodak has subcontracted with a company named OutSource, a New York State sponsoring organization that employs handicapped people, to take the cameras apart. Camera covers, lenses, and other parts are removed and reused, and miscellaneous plastic parts are ground into pellets that are used in molding new camera parts. Today, 87 percent of the FunSaver camera is either reused or recycled, illustrating the great potential for reuse of products.

In another example, consider that two computers are discarded for every three computers purchased. The method for designing for reuse involves analyzing existing products for materials, identifying other uses for these materials, and developing a disassembly process to sort out these materials. Doing so is good business for the producers of personal computers because, if chemicals used in making personal computers were to find their way into groundwater, the manufacturers could be held liable, and the resulting costs could be in the billions of dollars.

The principles for design for disassembly include using fewer parts and fewer materials, using snap fits instead of screws, making assembly efficient and improving disposal, using design for disassembly experts in concurrent design teams, and eliminating waste through better design.

> **design for disassembly**
> Designing products so that they can be taken apart easily.

Other Green Design Concepts

Central themes to green design are that resources need to be conserved and that waste should be avoided. Waste can be in the form of inputs (wasted materials) and outputs (refuse in landfills). Some green design concepts that aid in reducing waste are the following:

- Use nontoxic materials, such as nonleaded paint, in production.
- Use parts and materials that last longer, reducing the need for replacement parts and wasteful repair.
- Use processes and materials that require less energy. An example of this concept is the use of larger wafers in producing computer chips. These larger wafers require less processing and hence less energy per integrated circuit to produce.
- Conduct life-cycle assessments for the production of products that include carbon footprint assessments.
- Use renewable materials in production whenever possible.

- Make disposable products such as newspapers so that they will decompose when placed in landfills.
- Use processes that conserve water and do not pollute the water. This goal is a major effort in the production of computer chips because water is a major input to production.

As you can see, there is much to consider relative to the environment when designing and producing products. The good news is that society as a whole is becoming more environmentally conscious. As a result of this shift toward green design, innovative firms that employ these approaches are rewarded.

We started this chapter by discussing the PurePower Geared Turbofan at Pratt and Whitney. The project to develop this product involved hundreds of engineers and over $10 billion in investment. At some points, some creative deception was used to keep management from knowing really how much money was being spent.

Several technological issues had to be overcome. Michael McCune had the idea for creating a fan blade that would move slower while still pushing a lot of air. However, the shaft that connected to the motor blades also connected to a low-pressure turbine and a low-pressure compressor. Both the turbine and compressor needed to move at high speed. The way to overcome the slow-moving blades and the other high-pressure parts was to use a gearbox. However, the challenge to overcome was the weight of the gearbox and poor product life. Essentially, adding steel would make it stronger but too heavy.

Because Pratt and Whitney is part of United Technologies (the parent company), it was able to borrow ideas from other parts of the company: gears from Sikorsky, bearings from Pratt and Whitney–Canada, lubricant know-how from the United Technologies Research Center, and components from Timken.

The PurePower Geared Turbofan will now be used on narrow-body planes from Bombadier, Embraer, and Mitsubishi. As a result of successes in design, Pratt and Whitney believes it has a winner on its hands.

Summary

As life cycles for products become shorter, a focus on improving the product design process is necessary to remain competitive. A focus on SC&O, however, requires understanding not only your own processes but also processes that extend to suppliers and customers. In this chapter, we have discussed many aspects of product and process design.

1. We began the chapter by discussing product and process design.
   a. We explained the difference between processes and extended processes that include upstream suppliers and downstream customers.
   b. We defined different process choices on a continuum from projects to continuous flow and the managerial implications of process choice.
   c. Break-even analysis is used when evaluating the choice of the correct processes to use.

2. Next, we presented process mapping.
   a. Process maps use simple symbols to illustrate the flow of a process.
   b. Extended process maps reach throughout the entire process.
   c. Balancing assembly lines is an effective tool for assigning tasks to workstations based on a takt time.
   d. Functional layouts are planned using the load-distance model and Muther's grid.

3. We went on to discuss product design.
   a. We discussed the product life cycle and the importance of complementary products.
   b. R&D is the core of effective product design. It usually takes the form of applied research with an economic motive.

4. We presented quality function deployment, which is used to enhance communication between engineers and marketers, both of whom are key to good product development.

5. Finally, we discussed different elements of green design.
   a. Design for reuse and design for remanufacture are important elements of effective design.
   b. Process design is best when it is waste free.

Companies have implemented these approaches with great results, facilitating huge increases in production capacity along with a reduction in cost. These cost savings can result in higher profits and benefits to customers. For example, the prices of computer chips have dropped consistently. A company that does not become better at design will simply not be competitive in the future.

Key Terms

applied research   71
assembly line   52
balance delay   62
basic research   71
batch production   52
bathtub-shaped hazard function   77
break-even analysis   54
cellular manufacturing   59
complementary products   70
component reliability   77
concurrent engineering   75
continuous design   69
continuous-flow process   53
design   69
design for disassembly   81
design for manufacturing (DFM)   75
discontinuous design   69
efficiency   62
extended process   50

failure modes and effects analysis (FMEA)   80
fixed-position layouts   61
flexible manufacturing system (FMS)   58
heuristics   61
job shop   51
ladder FMS   58
line balancing   61
load-distance model   65
manufacturing system design   74
market pull   71
mean time to repair (MTTR)   79
Muther's grid   68
over-the-wall syndrome   76
process   49
process design   49
process layout   50
process map   56

product data management (PDM)   76
product design   49
product design specification (PDS)   74
product life cycle   70
product/process matrix   54
product traceability   80
project   51
quality function deployment (QFD)   74
research and development (R&D)   71
service contracts   77
stall built   61
system availability (SA)   79
system reliability   77
takt time   62
technological push   71
technology feasibility statement   74

Integrative Learning Exercise

Create a student team and either design a new product or significantly redesign an existing product. Follow the product development process shown in Figure 3.16. Incorporate the voice of the customer in your product design by conducting a quality function deployment exercise.

Integrative Experiential Exercise

Create a student team and visit a company or organization. Examine the type of layout it uses to produce its products or services. Does the layout used by the company exhibit the characteristics of a process, product, or hybrid layout? What objectives were used by the company to design the layout they employ? Describe the layout by performing a process mapping exercise. What improvements would you suggest for the layout to improve efficiency?

Discussion Questions

1. What is meant by *design*? How is it different from *continuous design*?

2. Discuss some well designed products. What positive attributes do they have from a design perspective?

3. What questions must be answered when designing products?

4. Briefly define the product life cycle and identify the life phases that the product experiences.

5. What is meant by a *complementary product*? How can complementary products affect a product line's life?

6. Identify five reasons that firms perform R&D.

7. What is the major difference between basic research and applied research?

8. How is market pull R&D different from technological push R&D?

9. What is meant by *extended process*? How does the extended process differ from the traditional operations management view of a process?

10. Under what circumstances would a process layout be preferred to a product layout?

11. How does batch production differ from a job shop?

12. What is the purpose of process mapping?

13. Briefly discuss the circumstances for which a fixed-position layout might be employed.

14. Under what circumstances might you employ a Muther's grid rather than a load-distance model in designing functional layouts?

15. What is the failure modes and effects analysis (FMEA) process? To what areas can the process be applied?

Solved Problems

Process Design

BREAK-EVEN ANALYSIS
SOLVED PROBLEM 3.1

1. If a company decides to redesign its existing production process, it will incur fixed costs of $10,500,000. The company estimates that the production process redesign will reduce the variable cost of production per unit from $15 to $14. The product's selling price is $20 per unit. What quantity is required for the production process redesign to break-even? If total demand for the product is estimated to be 2,000,000 units, what contribution to profit would the process redesign make?

Solution:

$$\text{break-even quantity} = \frac{\text{fixed costs}}{\text{selling price} - \text{variable cost per unit}}$$

$$\text{break-even quantity} = \frac{10,500,000}{20 - 14} = 1,750,000 \text{ units}$$

If total demand = 2,000,000,
total revenue = $20 × 2,000,000 = $40,000,000, and
total cost = $10,500,000 + $14 × 2,000,000 = $38,500,000, the contribution to profit would therefore be $40,000,000 − $38,500,000 = $1,500,000.

Process Mapping

LINE BALANCING
SOLVED PROBLEM 3.2

2. A company produces a two-slice toaster on an assembly line. The tasks required to assemble the toaster, along with task times (in seconds) and preceding tasks, are shown in the accompanying table. The balanced line needs to achieve an hourly output of 75 toasters per hour.

Task	Task Time (Seconds)	Preceding Tasks
A	40	—
B	15	A
C	10	B
D	20	B
E	35	C
F	30	D
G	15	E, F
H	40	G

a. Calculate the takt time required to achieve a production volume of 75 toasters per hour.

b. Draw the network diagram that graphically illustrates the precedence relationships described above.

c. Use the longest operating time (LOT) heuristic to assign tasks to workstations.

d. Compute the theoretical minimum number of workstations.

e. Compute the efficiency and the balance delay of the line you balanced.

Solution:

a. The takt time is given by Equation 3.6:

$$\text{takt time} = \frac{\text{amount of time available}}{\text{production volume}}$$

The takt time is equal to (60 seconds × 60 minutes)/ 75 = 48 seconds. We will use a 48-second cycle time in assigning tasks to workstations.

b.

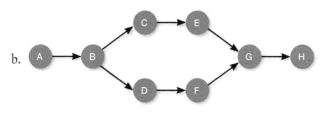

c. Use the network diagram in part b to create the following matrix.

Eligible Tasks	Chosen Task (LOT)	Workstation	Task Time	Slack Time
A	A	1	40	48 − 40 = 8
B	B	2	15	48 − 15 = 33
C, D	D	2	20	33 − 20 = 13
C, F	C	2	10	13 − 10 = 3
E, F	E	3	35	48 − 35 = 13
F	F	4	30	48 − 30 = 18
G	G	4	15	18 − 15 = 3
H	H	5	40	48 − 40 = 8

Note: Each workstation has 48 seconds available to it. We reference the precedence diagram to identify eligible tasks. If there is more than one eligible task, we attempt to assign the task taking the longest operating time to the station if the station has sufficient time. Move to a new workstation when there are tasks yet to be assigned and the current workstation has insufficient time remaining (slack time) to accommodate the task.

d. The formula for the minimum number of workstations is total task time/takt time = 205/48 = 4.27 ≈ 5 workstations (always round up to the next whole value when computing theoretical minimum number of workstations).

e. The efficiency of the line is computed using the equation

$$\frac{\text{total task time}}{\text{no. of workstations} \times \text{takt time}} = \frac{205}{5 \times 48} = 0.8542$$

The balance delay (Equation 3.9) is the complement of the efficiency and is equal to 1 − efficiency = 1 − 0.8542 = 0.1458.

LOAD-DISTANCE MODEL
SOLVED PROBLEM 3.3

3. A job shop with functional departments A through I is currently organized according to the following layout:

A	B	C
D	E	F
G	H	I

Assume that it costs $1/unitary distance and that the weekly loads (in units) are given in the following from/to matrix:

	To				
From	B	D	F	H	I
A	20	15	70	5	5
C	10	90	25	10	10
E	25	30	55	20	10
G	5	20	80	15	5

Use the information given to develop an alternative layout for the job shop that reduces the load-distance cost.

Solution:
We first compute the cost of the current layout:

Pairing	Loads	Distance	Loads × Distance
A–B	20	1	20
A–D	15	1	15
A–F	70	2	140
A–H	5	2	10
A–I	5	2	10
C–B	10	1	10
C–D	90	2	180
C–F	25	1	25
C–H	10	2	20
C–I	10	2	20
E–B	25	1	25
E–D	30	1	30
E–F	55	1	55
E–H	20	1	20
E–I	10	1	10
G–B	5	2	10
G–D	20	1	20
G–F	80	2	160
G–H	15	1	15
G–I	5	2	10
		Total =	805

We next sort by the load-distance cost, recognizing that we pay special attention to the numbers of loads between departments:

Sorted Load-Distance Cost			
Pairing	Loads	Distance	Loads × Distance
C–D	90	2	180
G–F	80	2	160
A–F	70	2	140
E–F	55	1	55
E–D	30	1	30
C–F	25	1	25
E–B	25	1	25
A–B	20	1	20

Pairing	Loads	Distance	Loads × Distance
C–H	10	2	20
C–I	10	2	20
E–H	20	1	20
G–D	20	1	20
A–D	15	1	15
G–H	15	1	15
A–H	5	2	10
A–I	5	2	10
C–B	10	1	10
E–I	10	1	10
G–B	5	2	10
G–I	5	2	10

The top priority for the new layout is to place C–D, G–F, and A–F as close together as possible. The approach is trial and error. The following is one possible layout. The cost of the new layout is 620.

A	B	E
G	F	D
I	H	C

The load-distance cost of the "new" proposed layout is as follows:

Pairing	Loads	Distance	Loads × Distance
A–F	70	1	70
G–F	80	1	80
E–F	55	1	55
C–D	90	1	90
E–D	30	1	30
C–F	25	1	25
E–B	25	1	25
A–B	20	1	20
C–H	10	1	10
C–I	10	2	20
E–H	20	2	40
G–D	20	2	40
A–D	15	2	30

G–H	15	1	15
A–H	5	2	10
A–I	5	2	10
C–B	10	2	20
E–I	10	2	20
G–B	5	1	5
G–I	5	1	5
	Total =		620

RELIABILITY
SOLVED PROBLEM 3.4

4. Compute the overall reliability for the following system.

   Solution:

For the product to function properly, all three components must work properly. Given the failure rates of the three components, the overall reliability is $0.98 \times 0.99 \times 0.99 = 0.96$.

Quality Function Deployment

MEASURING RELIABILITY, FAILURE RATES
SOLVED PROBLEM 3.5

5. Thirty treadmills are each tested for 200 hours in a controlled laboratory environment. If nine treadmills experienced malfunctions during the test, what is the failure rate for the treadmill?

Solution:

$$\text{failure rate} = \frac{\text{number of failures}}{\text{units tested} \times \text{number of hours tested}}$$

$$\text{failure rate} = \frac{9}{30 \times 200} = 0.0015 \text{ failure per operating hour}$$

SYSTEM AVAILABILITY
SOLVED PROBLEM 3.6

6. A decision regarding whether to purchase a generator from supplier A or supplier B will be made on the basis of system availability (SA). Given the following mean time between failures (MTBF) and mean time to repair (MTTR) data, which supplier should be selected?

Supplier	MTBF (hours)	MTTR (hours)
A	60	2
B	70	3

Solution:

$$\text{SA} = \frac{\text{MTBF}}{\text{MTBF} + \text{MTTR}}$$

$$\text{SA(A)} = \frac{60}{60 + 2} = 0.9677$$

$$\text{SA(B)} = \frac{70}{70 + 3} = 0.9589$$

Supplier A should be selected.

Problems

Process Design

BREAK-EVEN ANALYSIS

1. A company is considering an investment in a machine that it believes will speed up production of a product. The machine will cost the company $2,000,000. Products produced using the machine will sell for $25 per unit. The variable cost per unit incurred producing the product is believed to be $10. What quantity of sales is required for the company to break even if it purchases the machine?

2. A decision must be made between two different machines, A and B. The machines will produce the same product, but only one type of machine (either A or B) will be purchased. The company estimates that the selling price per unit for the product will be $30. The variable cost of production per unit if machine A is selected is believed to be $10.

The variable cost of production if machine B is selected is believed to be $14. The fixed cost of machine A is $6,750,000, and the fixed cost of machine B is $5,000,000.
   a. What is the break-even quantity if machine A is selected?
   b. What is the break-even quantity if machine B is selected?
   c. If total demand for the product is believed to be 375,000 units, which machine will make the greater contribution to profit?

3. The fixed costs required to modify an existing production facility's layout is estimated to be $15,000,000. It is believed that the new layout will reduce the variable cost per unit associated with producing the product by $1.25 (from the current $10 per unit to $8.75). If the product

sells for $40 per unit, what must demand be for the modi-
fication to break even?

Process Mapping

LINE BALANCING

4. The following tasks are required to assemble a product.

Task	Task Time (Minutes)	Preceding Task(s)
A	3	None
B	4	A
C	2	A
D	2	B, C
E	3	D

The company believes that the market rate of demand for
the product requires an output of 12 per hour. Calculate
the takt time and then use the longest operating time
(LOT) heuristic to assign tasks to workstations.

5. The following tasks are required to assemble a product.

Task	Task Time (Seconds)	Preceding Task(s)
A	90	None
B	25	A
C	60	B
D	75	B
E	15	C, D
F	35	E

a. What takt time is required to achieve an hourly output
of 30 units per hour?
b. Calculate the minimum number of workstations
required to achieve the desired output.
c. Use the longest operating time (LOT) heuristic to
assign tasks to workstations.
d. What is the efficiency of the line balance you determined in part c?
e. What is the balance delay of the line balance you
determined in part c?

6. The following tasks are required to assemble an alarm
clock radio. The assembly line would like to achieve an
output of 40 finished radios per hour.

Task	Task Time (Seconds)	Preceding Task(s)
A	35	None
B	40	A
C	25	A
D	15	B, C
E	60	D
F	30	E
G	35	C
H	45	F, G
I	15	H

a. What takt time is required to achieve the desired rate
of output?
b. What is the theoretical minimum number of workstations required to achieve the desired rate of output per
hour?
c. Use the longest operating time (LOT) heuristic to
assign tasks to workstations.
d. What is the efficiency of the line balance you determined in part c?
e. What is the balance delay of the line balance you
determined in part c?

LOAD-DISTANCE MODEL

7. The sales offices at MCR Realty are arranged as follows:

A	B	C
D	E	F

Assume that it costs $1/unitary distance and that the
monthly visits (loads) between offices are as shown in the
following from/to matrix.

From	To					
	A	B	C	D	E	F
A	—	15	50	20	5	2
B		—	30	15	25	5
C			—	40	5	15
D				—	20	10
E					—	20
F						—

Using the above data,

a. Compute the cost of the current layout.
b. Sort the layout by load-distance cost.
c. Rearrange the existing layout to achieve a lower-cost layout. What is the cost of the new layout that you established?

8. A job shop has work centers arranged as follows:

A	B	C
D	E	F
G	H	I

Assume that it costs \$1/unitary distance and that the monthly loads are as shown in the following from/to matrix.

				To					
From	A	B	C	D	E	F	G	H	I
A	—	40	70	20	30	10	80	0	2
B		—	40	35	65	45	5	5	0
C			—	90	5	15	0	5	4
D				—	20	50	10	10	0
E					—	20	0	10	4
F						—	0	0	2
G							—	10	0
H								—	0
I									—

The job shop is considering the proposed alternative layout shown below:

A	C	D
G	B	F
E	H	I

a. Calculate the load-distance cost of the current job shop layout.
b. Calculate the load-distance cost of the proposed alternative layout.
c. Based on your analysis, does the proposed layout improve the layout of the job shop based on the load-distance cost?

9. A law firm has its offices arranged according to the following layout:

| A | C | E |
| B | D | F |

The office manager for the law firm estimates that the following number of trips are made daily between offices:

			To			
From	A	B	C	D	E	F
A	—	25	65	40	25	85
B		—	50	10	20	50
C			—	50	20	50
D				—	5	25
E					—	30
F						—

a. Assuming that it costs \$1/unitary distance, compute the load distance cost for the current layout.
b. Suppose that the law office manager proposes the following revised office layout.

| A | D | E |
| F | C | B |

Calculate the load-distance cost for the revised layout.
c. Is the revised layout preferable to the original?

Quality Function Deployment
RELIABILITY

10. A company produces a product consisting of two series components, A and B, arranged as follows:

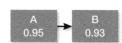

If both components must function for the product to function, what is the product's overall reliability?

11. Calculate the overall reliability of the following product:

FAILURE RATES

12. Fifty electric generators are tested under strenuous conditions by operating each generator for 150 hours. During the test, 12 generators experienced a malfunction that caused the generator not to operate properly. Calculate the failure rate for the generators.

13. Forty professional kitchen mixers were tested in a laboratory by operating each mixer for 50 hours. Six of the

mixers experienced a malfunction during the test. What is the failure rate for the tested mixers?

14. An independent testing agency has randomly sampled 30 computer scanners produced by a major manufacturer. The scanners were subjected to testing that involved operating each of them continuously for 75 hours. During the testing, 5 scanners malfunctioned. Calculate the failure rate for the scanners.

15. Ten large paper shredders were tested under continuous operating conditions for 5 hours each. Four shredders experienced a malfunction during the testing. What is the failure rate for the shredders?

SYSTEM AVAILABILITY

16. A company must purchase a critical piece of industrial equipment from one of two suppliers, A and B. The company's manufacturing engineer is using several criteria, one of which is system availability, to evaluate the suppliers. Given the following mean time between failures (MTBF) and mean time to repair (MTTR) data, calculate the system availability for each supplier.

	Supplier A	Supplier B
MTBF (hours)	150	140
MTTR (hours)	15	12

17. An office manager is deciding on a paper shredder to be purchased for her legal firm. Three suppliers have provided information about their shredders, including MTBF and MTTR for the models under evaluation. Use the information shown in the table to calculate the system availability for each supplier's shredder.

	Supplier A	Supplier B	Supplier C
MTBF (hours)	75	100	80
MTTR (hours)	5	8	4

Which supplier should the office manager select if she chooses the supplier with the best system availability?

18. A company must decide which optical scanner to purchase. Four suppliers are under consideration. The company's purchasing manager has collected the following information from the four suppliers.

	Supplier A	Supplier B	Supplier C	Supplier D
MTBF (hours)	183	196	191	236
MTTR (hours)	3	6	4	8

Given this information, and assuming that the purchasing manager will make her choice based on the supplier who has the highest system availability, which supplier should she select?

CASE   Hamilton Electronics

Josh Martinez realized that something must be done to increase the output of his facility. Josh had started working at Hamilton Electronics as an hourly employee on the production line while he was a college student. As the years passed, Josh remained with Hamilton and assumed a management position on graduating from college. Currently, Josh manages the assembly line for the company's A25 product. The tasks, task times, and precedent relationships to assemble the A25 are as shown in the table below.

Task	Task Time (Seconds)	Preceding Tasks	Task	Task Time (Seconds)	Preceding Tasks
A	15	None	I	10	E
B	20	None	J	15	H, I
C	35	A	K	30	J
D	10	B, C	L	20	K
E	10	B	M	5	K
F	5	D, E	N	10	L, M
G	15	D	O	5	N
H	25	F, G	P	15	O

Currently, tasks have been assigned to four workstations, with each workstation having one employee who performs all tasks assigned to that workstation. The current layout is as follows:

Workstation	Tasks Assigned
1	A, B, C, D
2	E, F, G, H, I
3	J, K
4	L, M, N, O, P

Josh realizes that the current layout will not provide the needed output to meet the increased demand for the product. The company has asked him to revise the existing line to achieve an output rate of 60 units per hour. The company has also told him that an additional workstation and employee can be used if necessary to achieve the desired rate of output.

Questions:

1. What is the maximum hourly output for the line as it is currently balanced?

2. What is the efficiency and balance delay of the current line balance when it is operating at its maximum rate of output?

3. What is the takt time required to achieve an hourly output rate of 60 units per hour?

4. What is the theoretical minimum number of workstations (employees) required to achieve the desired rate of output?

5. Use the longest operating time rule to assign tasks to workstations so that the desired rate of 60 units per hour can be achieved.

6. Calculate the efficiency and the balance delay of the new line balance you developed in question 5.

4 Service Design

Customer Inputs to Music Streaming

The customer plays a key role in services. Consider where you get your music. If you are like most people, you no longer purchase CDs (a tangible product). You probably get your music from a service such as Spotify, Apple Music, or Amazon Prime. These services have all but decimated traditional CD and vinyl record sales.

What makes these services so popular? Although all of these services have very large catalogues of songs—running into the tens of millions— the key to success is how they interact and handle customer inputs and information.

Consumers of these services are happiest when they can engage with the service provider. This can involve sharing music with friends and obtaining playlists from others. According to J.D. Power and Associates, these aspects trump other service dimensions such as selection of songs and sound quality.[1]

When you use social media and a service such as Spotify, the company gathers data about you, such as when you eat lunch and drive home. Using complex algorithms, and knowing the types of music you like to listen to at certain times, they can provide "Daily Lift" tunes after lunch or "Daily Commute" songs when you drive home. They can also predict what new releases you may like and drop them into your music mix. We will return to music streaming services at the end of the chapter.

[1]Power, J.D., "Social Becomes Key Battleground for Streaming Music Providers."

Service design is different from product design in that, in a service system, the product is a process. There are many definitions of service. Some of them are as simple as "anything that isn't manufacturing," but we adopt a more specific definition. **Services operations** are production processes wherein each customer is a supplier of process inputs. **Services** are the result of services operations. Implicit in this definition is the concept that customers are intimately involved in services. Our definition of services refers to what we would more precisely call a service operation, or an operation that processes customer inputs. This definition differs from the often-used (in academia) yet inaccurate assumption that services are intangible products. Services are not only quite tangible, but can involve many tangible elements.

One of the keys you will discover in this chapter is that customers such as you provide information and other inputs to service providers that help them tailor services to your preferences. In this chapter, we look downstream in the supply chain to the customer. In many cases, that customer is you.

services operations
Production processes wherein each customer is a supplier of process inputs.

services
The result of services operations.

Dentistry is an example of a service. Dentists use resources in their work, but they cannot complete their job without a patient's teeth to clean and fix.

U NDERSTAND THE RELATIONSHIPS BETWEEN SERVICES AND TANGIBLES

Services always involve a bundling of tangibles and intangibles. **Tangibles** are products, technology, and other outputs and inputs associated with services. Consider the service example of a dentist

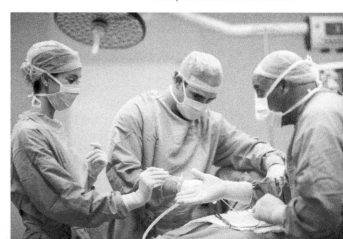

TABLE 4.1 >

Examples of Service Operations		
Service Operation	**Customer Input Resources**	**Service Provider Outputs**
Accounting	Financial records	Financial statements
Air transportation	Passengers and baggage	Transported passengers
Auto repair	Broken car	Repaired car
Consulting	Business problems	Business solutions
Dentistry	Patients' teeth	Mended teeth
Education	Students' minds	Educated minds
Legal services	Legal problems	Legal remedies
Healthcare	Illness and injuries	Healthier patients

tangibles
Products, technology, and other outputs and inputs associated with services.

office. Dentistry includes the production process of cleaning and repairing patients' teeth. Dentists use resources such as equipment, cleaning substances, trained labor, and physical facilities. The most essential resource that dentists use, however, is customers' teeth. Dentists cannot proceed with the teeth-cleaning process until after the customer provides teeth to clean.

Although this dental example may seem humorous, it illustrates the contrasts between service processes and a typical make-to-stock manufacturing operation. For example, a factory that makes dental tools can produce those tools even at times of low demand, and it can keep the tools in inventory until customers purchase them. The factory can wait for dentists to order the tools, but dentists cannot clean teeth in times of low demand; they can only clean teeth simultaneously with demand.

TABLE 4.1 provides examples of customer resources that are processed in service operations. In each case, the provider can prepare for production without customers, but the provider requires customer resources to produce in a substantive, revenue-generating way.

Because production in service operations depends on customer resources, the design of services leads to unique challenges. We begin with the elements of service design.

....

Managing Across Majors 4.1   Marketing majors, remember that service operations need information from marketing to help identify and understand customer needs.

....

IDENTIFY AND APPLY THE KEY ELEMENTS OF SERVICE DESIGN

simultaneity
When the production of services occurs at roughly the same time as customer demand.

An element of service design alluded to in the dentistry example is known as **simultaneity**, which means that the production of services occurs at roughly the same time as customer demand. Instead of producing ahead of demand, service production largely occurs as demand arises. Restaurants can prepare food products and set tables before customers arrive, but the revenue-generating activity of serving customers can occur only when customers arrive and present their demand (and their input resources).

In manufacturing, inventory is a great resource for dealing with fluctuations in demand. Manufacturing firms can often produce relatively constant quantities of goods across times of high demand and low demand. At times of low demand, manufacturers produce goods and store them in inventory, which can be used during times of high demand.

Because of simultaneity, service production usually cannot be inventoried. Instead, managers must rely on extra capacity to meet fluctuations in demand. If the service provider believes that it is important to meet demand even during times of high demand, it needs to set

Capacity Management Options in Services		
Planning Horizon	**Increasing Capacity**	**Decreasing Capacity**
Short term	Work overtime	Underutilize employees
	Hire temporary workers	Assign workers to other areas
	Lease more space	Reduce service offerings
Long term	Hire more employees	Lay off employees
	Add more space	Sell facilities
	Build new facilities	Close unprofitable sites

< TABLE 4.2

the capacity to produce to match the high demand levels. During periods of low demand, it may leave much of the capacity idle.

It is difficult and it can be costly to have variable capacity. Because many elements of capacity cannot change easily on the same short-term basis in which demand fluctuates, managers often make capacity decisions over the long term. For example, demand at many restaurants is higher on weekends than on weekdays, but most restaurants cannot add more seating space only for weekends; they have to add space for long-term use. As shown in TABLE 4.2, the choices relative to service demand depend on the planning horizon.

For example, demand for airline flights fluctuates. Some flights are more popular on weekends than on weekdays, and flights at convenient times are more popular than flights that leave or arrive late at night. Besides passengers and their baggage, one of the primary resources airline companies use is jet airplanes. These jets represent a large fixed cost, a cost that is incurred whether or not passengers are flying on the jet. If an airline has too few jets for times of high demand, it will lose sales. That same airline, however, may also have too many jets for times of low demand and have many empty seats. To adapt to this variable need, some airlines have begun to share planes. Airline companies cannot "save" the high demand seats for planes flying below capacity. The inability to "inventory" unfilled seats to use during times of high demand is an unfortunate condition of service operations. The attribute of service operations known as **time-perishable capacity** means that unused capacity (at times of low demand) is lost forever and cannot be used to meet later demand.

How do airlines deal with time-perishable capacity? One way is to attempt to manage demand by shifting passengers from periods of high demand to periods of low demand. Airlines can do this by offering lower prices for flights with low demand and charging more for popular flights. This pricing practice encourages people who are flexible with their travel plans to adjust their travel and thus fill planes, tempering problems with time-perishable capacity.

time-perishable capacity
Unused capacity (at times of low demand) that is lost forever and cannot be used to meet later demand.

Designing for Service Quality

Providing service quality can be difficult because of the variation that comes from customer interaction. Customers may not always fulfill their responsibilities in the service process, causing the service to fail. For example, if a customer writes the wrong address on a package, the package delivery service is not going to be completed as planned.

Service firms should actively seek to identify failure points: places in the service process that are prone to fail. Then they should identify ways of preventing the failure or at least reducing the likelihood of its occurrence. One way to do so is by designing **poka yoke** (pronounced "poh-kah-yoh-keh"), which is the Japanese term for failsafing.

For example, FedEx realizes that passengers might give incorrect addresses, so it equips its employees with portable terminals that check the accuracy of postal codes listed on package addresses. This practice reduces the likelihood that a package enters the system with an invalid postal code.

Service poka yokes can be used in many businesses. Some fast-food restaurants make the opening of their garbage cans slightly smaller than the size of their food trays, preventing customers from throwing away the trays. ATMs require bank customers to retrieve their bank

poka yoke
The Japanese term for failsafing.

card before giving them cash withdrawals, preventing customers from leaving without their card. Some dry cleaners might require customers to turn the pockets of clothing inside out, thus reducing the likelihood that customers will leave items in the pockets.

Designing for Service Recovery

Despite poka yokes and good intentions, service processes sometimes fail to do what they are designed to do. One response to this problem is **service recovery**, which is an attempt to rectify the problem that the customer experienced with the service. Service recovery is particularly challenging because the failure is not only in the process but in the way it affects the customer's attitude about the service provider.

For example, a guest may stay at a hotel that experiences unforeseen mechanical problems, such as an air-conditioning system that breaks in the middle of the night. Moving the customer to another room would solve only part of the problem and may not make up for the customer's lost sleep. Even providing the guest with a free night's stay might be of little value if the guest is in that town for only one night or if the room is being paid for by an employer.

Although there is no single formula for effective service recovery, the best firms recognize that the need for service recovery is inevitable. An effective recovery system should specify what types of problems are recovered at what levels of the organization, with simple recoveries handled by the frontline employees and more difficult problems handled by managers. Even more important is ensuring that service recovery is coupled with a process to avoid similar service failures in the future.

B2B versus B2C Services

The examples we have considered thus far in this chapter—dentistry, restaurants, and airlines—are service operations that directly meet the needs of consumers who are the beneficiaries of the service. They are business-to-consumer (B2C) operations.

Some service businesses help other businesses meet the needs of their customers. Such arrangements are called business-to-business (B2B) services. An example of a B2B service is management consulting. Management consultants help client businesses meet the needs of their customers more effectively. For example, information technology consultants help businesses with systems analysis needed to develop information systems.

B2B and B2C services are similar in that they process resources that come from customers. Even management consulting requires information about the client's operational needs before the consulting can proceed. Consulting firms can independently acquire expertise and develop other intellectual resources before serving clients, but the actual consulting service begins when a client engages the consultant to solve specific problems. TABLE 4.3 gives examples of B2B and B2C services with varying levels of customer interaction.

Managing Across Majors 4.2   Strategy students, the decisions relating to service design in B2B and B2C operations are very strategic because they need to align with the overall mission of the firm.

TABLE 4.3 >

Examples of B2B and B2C Services		
	B2B	**B2C**
Higher Customer Interaction	Consulting	Doctors
	Training	Attorneys
Lower Customer Interaction	Market research	Mail catalog sales
	Contract field repair	Call centers
	Facilities maintenance	Auto repair

Customer-Interactive Processes

Service operations require customer resources, which implies that, for all services, there is some degree of interaction between the service provider and the customers. This interaction can enable the service provider to understand each customer's specific needs and perhaps develop a productive relationship with customers.

No matter how constructive it can be, **customer interaction** comes with a tremendous cost in terms of *process efficiency*. Customers can vary dramatically in terms of their ability to navigate a service system, the timing of their resources, their ability or willingness to interact with the service operation, and so forth. This customer variation can disrupt the service process and keep it from achieving high levels of productivity and efficiency. As a result of these disruptions, service design usually needs to be robust enough to handle customer variation in a way that is economically and operationally acceptable.

For example, express delivery services need senders to provide accurate addresses. If senders provide incomplete or inaccurate addresses, the delivery service provider may be unable to meet customer expectations for delivery time. That is one reason FedEx, a leading express delivery service provider, provides customers with standard mailing labels.

customer interaction
The degree of customer involvement in the delivery of a service.

service offering
A process in which providers ask customers to participate.

customer experience
The result of a service process in terms of customer emotions.

queue
A waiting line.

Offerings and Experiences

As we discussed in the previous section, a **service offering** is a process in which providers ask customers to participate. Designing service offerings includes (1) developing facilities and resources of the service provider and (2) designing processes that customers will go through to receive the service. These two elements make up the **customer experience**.

Disneyland has a service offering that includes theme-park rides, live entertainment, food services, and souvenir retail. Disney can develop ride equipment, entertainment programs, food items, and other goods as part of the offering, but the service offering is more than that. The service offering also includes designing the processes that customers will go through in receiving the service. People who visit the park are also affected by crowds and lines, and Disney has to focus on making sure that these other elements do not affect customers' experience. One example of service design is figuring out how customers approach a food-service station given that customers will likely have to wait in line. Disney park planners can design waiting lines, or **queues**, in many different ways. One food-service station may have three counters, allowing three customers to place orders and to be served at the same time. Another queue configuration has a separate queue for each counter, which helps lines stay relatively short but may make it difficult for customers to determine which line to enter. A third queue configuration has one queue for all three counters, which can appear longer but which may eliminate the need for customers to choose a line. Disney has done a number of things to improve waiting times, including issuing fast passes at their parks.

Service design is largely about designing the customer experience as it interacts with a firm's operations. Doing so can be challenging because different customer segments may have different needs that require different processes. In GLOBAL CONNECTIONS BOX 4.1, we travel to Spain to see how Zara has successfully fashioned its retail experience.

Disney has made an art out of managing queues.

The Secret Sauce at Zara

The wealthiest person in the world you may never have heard of is Amancio Ortega Gaona, who recently overtook Warren Buffet and Bill Gates to become the second richest person in the world. How did he achieve this success? He was a cofounder and former chairman of Inditex Fashion Group, which owns Zara.

How has Zara been so successful at building a monster company? Look at the customer experience. We have already discussed Zara's formidable design and supply chain capabilities. It is unheard of to be able to get new designs to market in as little as three weeks. Daniel Piette, LVHM fashion director, has called Zara "possibly the most innovative and devastating retailer in the world."

How is the customer experience different at Zara? First, it has to do with frequency of visits. Zara customers visit the store an average of seventeen times per year compared to four for other retailers. Seventeen times may not be enough because Zara replenishes its stock with new items twice per week, on Mondays and Thursdays. When store owners place orders with Zara, they provide information not only on what is highly demanded but also anecdotal information they receive by word of mouth from customers. This information is fed to clothing designers for new designs.

Zara customers are used to fast fashion. For most clothing retail firms, designs are created six months in advance and sent to Asia for production. Zara nearsources (what it calls "proximity" production) to facilities in Spain, Portugal, Turkey, and Morocco. This allows only 10 percent to 15 percent of designs to be created six months in advance of a particular season; another 40 percent are designed prior to the season and the rest of the clothes during the particular season.

This design and supply chain capability has allowed Zara to tailor its services to the "fashionista hunt." Using small batch production, they create the exclusivity that customers desire. If customers do not come to the store, they miss the stock for sale.

The same attention to speed has been applied to the Zara website. Customers can come to Zara.com and see what is new. Included on the website are links to "New In," "TRF" (*trafulac* or "casual"), "Men," "Women," and "Editorials," which include videos and pictures of what is new and cool. When customers order items online, they receive free shipping over $50, and the items are tissue-wrapped in a Zara box. This is the experience that is expected from a high-end retailer.

As you can see with Zara, supply chain management meets the design concepts discussed in this chapter. This approach has provided a secret sauce for success.

UNDERSTAND AND APPLY THE PROCESS CHAIN NETWORK (PCN) TOOL FOR SERVICE DESIGN

process chain network (PCN) diagram
A tool that categorizes flowchart steps according to whether or not they involve interaction between entities such as providers and customers.

The **process chain network (PCN) diagram** is a tool that managers can use when designing service delivery systems. This kind of flowchart evaluates the interactions between service providers and customers.

As we discussed in Chapter 3, flowcharts are graphical diagrams with boxes that represent process steps. The steps are connected by arrows that represent process dependency; an arrow between steps suggests that accomplishing one step depends on accomplishing another step.

entity
A service provider, a customer, or a supplier in a PCN diagram.

A PCN diagram categorizes the flowchart steps according to whether or not they involve interaction between entities such as providers and customers. In PCN diagrams, an **entity** is a service provider, a customer, or a supplier. Entities can also be further up or down the supply chain, such as suppliers' suppliers or customers' customers.

< FIGURE 4.1

Pizza Restaurant PCN Diagram

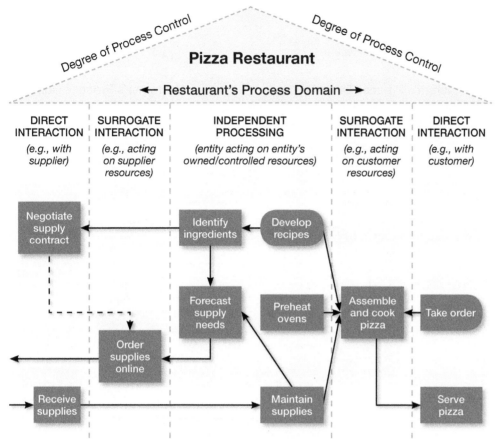

Source: Based on Sampson, S. E., "Visualizing Services Operations," *Journal of Service Research*, 15, 2, pp. 182–198.

FIGURE 4.1 shows an example of a PCN diagram for a pizza restaurant. The pizza restaurant has a **process domain**, which is made of process steps that are the responsibility of the given entity (in this case, a pizza restaurant), as well as interactions with suppliers and customers. A process domain has three regions:

1. The **direct interaction** region includes process steps that involve the pizza restaurant's interacting with another entity, such as a local cheese supplier or a customer.
2. The **surrogate interaction** region includes process steps in which the restaurant acts on the resources coming from another entity without direct interaction. For example, the restaurant may order napkins online.
3. The **independent processing** region includes process steps that the restaurant performs without interacting with other entities, such as developing recipes and turning on the ovens.

The angled "roof" of Figure 4.1 reminds us that organizations have more control over steps they perform independently than they do over steps that require direct interaction with another entity.

process domain
The process steps that are the responsibility of a given entity.

direct interaction
A description of the interaction of two entities in a PCN diagram.

surrogate interaction
The intersection of two entities in a PCN diagram where there is no direct interaction.

independent processing
The steps an entity performs in a PCN diagram where it does not interact with other entities.

Process Chain Networks

In the single-process entity shown in Figure 4.1, the key element of service is the interaction between providers and customers. FIGURE 4.2 shows how the restaurant process incorporates interaction between itself and a customer. The customer is responsible for controlling specific process steps, including traveling to the restaurant and waiting to be seated. The provider is responsible for developing recipes and maintaining supplies. The pizza-ordering process involves coproduction, meaning that the provider and the customer work together

FIGURE 4.2 >

Provider and Customer
PCN Diagram

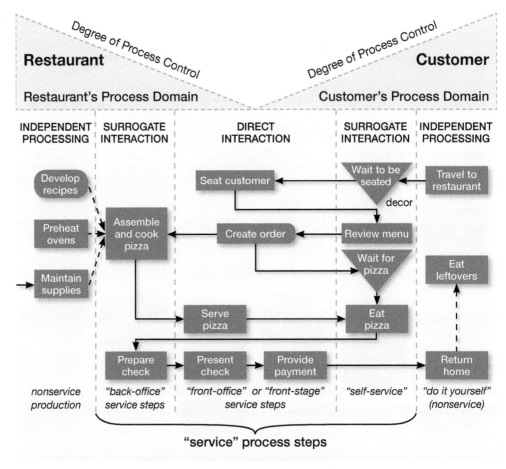

FIGURE 4.2 >

Provider and Customer
PCN Diagram

Source: Based on Sampson, S. E., "Visualizing Services Operations," *Journal of Service Research*, 15, 2, pp. 182–198.

to accomplish the task. Note that both customers and service providers have roles in the process. The customer eats the pizza, the provider prepares the check, and the customer pays. The actor in each step is under the "roof" area that specifies the restaurant's process domain and the customer's process domain.

The N of PCN stands for "network," which means that operating processes typically involve a network of entities. PCN diagrams allow us to visualize service supply chains, which are interactive and interdependent networks of entities.

The lower part of Figure 4.2 shows labels for specific types of process steps. The surrogate and direct interaction steps constitute the service operations. Service steps considered **back office** are performed outside the view of the customer, and those considered **front office** are in view of the customer. **Self-service** is when customers use provider resources to perform steps. When customers perform steps independently, we often call it **do-it-yourself (DIY)**.

....

Managing Across Majors 4.3 Information systems majors, recognize that the interactions between entities are often facilitated by an information system architecture.

....

Process Positioning

The three processing regions of a PCN diagram each have different operating characteristics. Regions of independent processing are more efficient than regions of direct interaction. Because providers have focused competencies and resources, they have greater economies of

back office
A service definition of processes that are buffered from the customer.

front office
Service steps involving the customer with the service provider.

self-service
Steps in a service process where the customer performs steps independently of the service provider.

do-it-yourself
Self-serve.

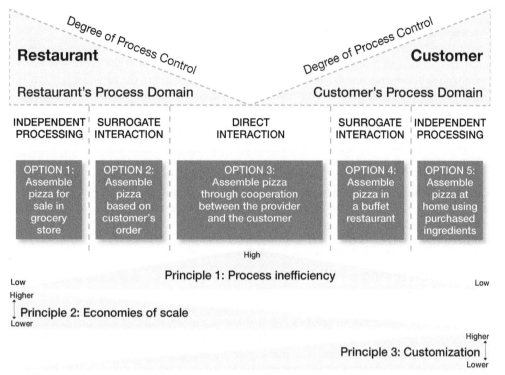

Source: Based on Sampson, S. E., "Visualizing Services Operations," *Journal of Service Research*, 15, 2, pp. 182–198.

scale than their customers. Customers have a greater ability, however, to customize the goods according to their own specific needs. Designers can position process steps in a PCN diagram to achieve improved operating characteristics.

Figure 4.2 showed the step of assembling the pizza in the provider's region of surrogate interaction, but it is just one process option. **FIGURE 4.3** shows other process options. Option 1 means that the pizza company assembles the pizza independently from customers, such as in a remotely located factory. Option 2 is the make-to-order pizza that we have already discussed, where the pizza is produced in the kitchen, away from direct customer interaction. Option 3 is an interactive assembly process, similar to what Subway does with sandwich assembly, with customers choosing from a set number of ingredients. Option 4 is in the customer's process domain, with the customer assembling the pizza using the provider's resources. Option 5 has the customer assembling the pizza using ingredients and utensils that he or she owns.

Three Process Principles

The bottom part of Figure 4.3 highlights three important process principles:

Principle 1: Process inefficiency. The least efficient steps tend to be those that involve direct interaction. For example, pizza assembly time in option 3 takes much longer than in option 1.

Principle 2: Economies of scale. Specialized providers are most likely to have economies of scale, meaning that the fixed costs of obtaining skills and equipment are spread across more units of production. For example, if the pizza restaurant assembles pizzas independently, it can achieve high use of its production equipment.

Principle 3: Customization. The more we allow customers to influence or control the process, the greater their potential for customization. The pizzas in option 5 will be the most varied because the customers are in control of almost everything, from pizza size and shape to cooking time.

How do we know which process positioning is the best? The answer depends on the *competency requirements* of the provider in relation to the *need requirements* of the given customer group (called a customer segment). If customers require a large amount of customization, the process step should be closer to the customer (option 5). If the process requires specialized skills and resources, the process step should be closer to the provider (option 1). If both are required, the process may need to be shared, which may come with a cost of inefficiency.

For example, the making of light-emitting diode (LED) light fixtures requires specialized skills but little customization; therefore, it is positioned in the manufacturer's independent processing region. Solving customers' health problems requires specialized skills of physicians but also tremendous customization, so healthcare tends to involve costly direct interaction. For most people, lawn maintenance requires appropriate competencies but a high amount of customization (each lawn is unique), so customers often buy lawn-mowing equipment and maintain their own lawns (independently from lawn-mower manufacturers).

Steps in Developing a PCN Diagram

The following are basic steps for creating a PCN diagram:

1. Identify a process to analyze. As suggested above, the appropriate unit of analysis is a process or process segment, not a firm. PCN analysis takes place at the process level.
2. Identify the process entities that participate in the given process segment. Usually included are a focal firm and an immediate customer or customer segment. The diagram might also include suppliers, partners, and others involved in the value network.
3. Record the steps that mark the start and end of the chosen process segment. Process segments often start with an identified customer need and end with the fulfillment of that need.
4. Fill in intermediate steps, and show in which process domain and region each step occurs. Included here are steps in the process domains of the focal firm, customers of the focal firm, suppliers of the focal firm, and other entities in the process chain network. As mentioned, the arrows between process steps indicate state dependencies (which may or may not involve product flows).

PCN analysis can also identify the value proposition and elements contributing to that value proposition. The following steps may be included at this stage:

5. Identify the steps where the customer receives benefits (i.e., need-filling value that provides motivation to compensate a focal firm) and where the customer incurs nonmonetary costs (such as inconvenience). We tag customer benefits with ☺ and nonmonetary costs with ☹. These tags identify the process's value proposition to the customer.
6. Identify the steps where the provider firm(s) incurs costs (tagged $-\$$) or receives monetary compensation (tagged $+\$$). Cost steps may include labor costs, component costs, and facility capacity costs. By depicting cost and compensation steps, we get an idea of the profit effect of that given process segment as currently configured.
7. Consider how moving steps across and between process regions would affect the value proposition, either by increasing customer benefits (☺) or by decreasing provider costs ($).

SOLVED PROBLEM 4.1 > **PCN Diagrams in Action**

Problem: You are assigned to develop a PCN diagram that will show interactions between a patient, health clinic, insurance company, and pharmacy.

Solution: A PCN diagram is shown in FIGURE 4.4, where the health clinic is entity 1, the patient is entity 2, the insurance company is entity 3, and the pharmacy is entity 4. Steps are connected across the diagram with circles, which show a connecting letter and the entity number where the connection is found.

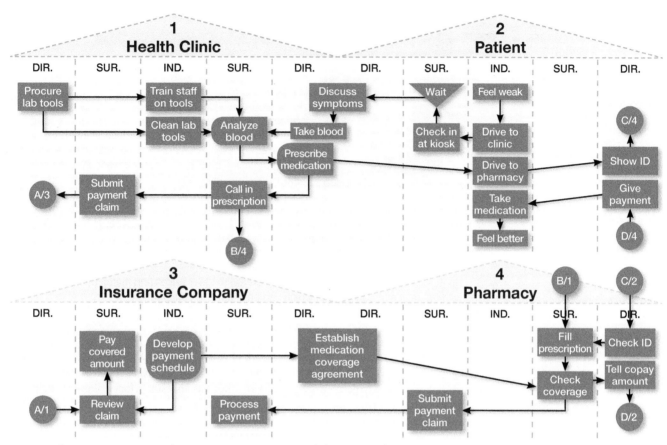

Source: Based on Sampson, S. E., "Visualizing Services Operations," *Journal of Service Research,* 15, 2, pp. 182–198.

∧ **FIGURE 4.4**

An Example of a Healthcare PCN Diagram

ESCRIBE AND USE THE PLANNING SERVICE CAPACITY FOR UNCERTAIN DEMAND

As we saw in the airline example, one challenge in service operations is time-perishable capacity. Overcoming this challenge requires the supply chain and operations (SC&O) manager to plan for uncertain demand and to manage cost trade-offs. A fundamental planning issue is **service capacity planning**, or deciding how much capacity to provide.

service capacity planning
The process of determining the productive capability needed in a service firm.

Capacity Components

Capacity has many components, including physical facilities, equipment, and personnel. The capacity of a fast-food restaurant, for example, is limited by the number of cash registers, number of tables, size of the grill, and number of employees.

Capacity decisions are largely about managing the trade-offs associated with costs to the provider and costs to the customer. Capacity costs are usually a direct cost to the provider and are usually passed on to the customer in terms of higher prices. For example, you might have been to a restaurant that did not have enough servers. If management were to hire more servers, the costs of doing business could increase, leading to an increase in costs to the customers. Managers must consider these indirect costs when planning the service experience.

If capacity is below demand at a given instance, customers will need to wait. Customer waiting is a direct cost to the customer. If customers refuse to wait and instead leave, the restaurant loses that business. As such, waiting costs are an indirect cost to the firm.

Walmart's Loss Is Dollar General's Gain

In trying to match capacity to local markets, Walmart launched a concept called Walmart Express: Put smaller stores in urban areas and provide low prices through Walmart's purchasing power. Think of a Walgreen-sized store selling Walmart products. The idea seemed like a good one; however, Walmart was too rigid in its supply chain purchasing practices to make it work. People don't want to go to a neighborhood store to buy fifty-pound bags of dog food. Enter Dollar General.

In a recent move, Dollar General purchased over forty Walmart Express stores to expand its market. Dollar General is growing at a clip of 1,000 stores a year. That is nearly three stores per day. Dollar General understands its markets and tailors its offerings to lower- to middle-income purchasers. This includes millennials who appreciate the bargains and make up one-fourth of Dollar General's sales.

In this case, you marry smaller format stores with lower prices and match bulk purchasing with the needs of consumers, which can be a winning combination.

Service demand is *variable* and *uncertain*. Think of when you go to a retail store. The need for checkout cashiers can vary greatly throughout the day and week. A mistake such as not properly pricing products can lead to delays in cashier service time that can result in longer lines at the checkout as well as customer frustration. As a result, operational mistakes can use up service capacity because of rework. Therefore, firms must decide how much capacity to provide. Often, employees are somewhat flexible because they can be cross-trained to do different functions. Sometimes, part-time labor can be used, but because demand is uncertain, extra labor might need to be available.

Physical facilities and equipment are somewhat less flexible than other components and represent fixed costs. For example, gas stations must decide how many pumps to install. Because fixed costs dominate the cost structures of most services, using services efficiently becomes key to profitability.

Elements of capacity demand planning are found in the story of Dollar General, which is discussed in SC&O CURRENT EVENTS 4.1.

Some other approaches for managing service capacity include (1) identifying the cost of service capacity and the cost of lost sales, and (2) identifying the appropriate capacity level to meet demand. The tool that we use for this service capacity management issue is called the newsvendor model. Two other approaches for managing service capacity are *coproduction* and *queuing theory*.

coproduction
Customer participation in the service creation process.

Coproduction means that customers participate in the service delivery process and therefore provide their own labor capacity. A common example is self-service retail checkout. The checkout process in retail involves people operating checkout terminals. Retailers need to decide how many checkout terminals and how many cashiers they need at different time intervals. If the retailer provides self-serve checkouts in which customers operate the terminals themselves, the cashier capacity will exactly match demand because the customers are the cashiers!

Deservitization
Reduction of face-to-face interaction in a service setting.

A recent trend in service design and offerings is deservitization. **Deservitization** is the reduction of face-to-face customer contact in service design. In universities, more courses are being added online and in massive open online courses (MOOCs). This reduces interaction between instructors and students in favor of surrogate interactions. Instead of working with human stock brokers, people now use surrogate interaction and make online trades with companies such as TD Ameritrade and E*Trade, where information is provided and users can perform their own analysis. SC&O CURRENT EVENTS 4.2 shows how Nordstrom has pursued this trend toward deservitization.

queuing theory
A method for determining customer service system performance and wait times for customers who must wait in lines.

Another way is to start with a target customer waiting cost and then calculate the amount of capacity needed to meet that target. The tool that managers use for these calculations is *queuing theory*. **Queuing theory** (or waiting line theory) is a method for determining customer service system performance and wait times for customers who must wait in lines. We discuss queuing theory in greater depth later in the chapter.

Deservitization at Nordstrom

Nordstrom has long been revered for providing outstanding service. Legends abound about accepting snow tire refunds in Alaska and mailing personal thank-you cards to customers. Is all of that personalized service mojo resulting in the growth of full service sales? The answer is no. In recent years, almost all of Nordstrom's growth has been in its Nordstrom Rack storefront and not in Nordstrom or Nordstrom.com sales.

In fact, while Rack sales have grown by over 5 percent, mainstream sales have been in decline. The Nordstrom Rack shopping experience is much more similar to Target than Nordstrom. The customer experience is largely self-service and product offerings are off-price.

When the economy sputters or wages remain stagnant, it appears customers are buying Nordstrom fashions at a lower price and foregoing the service. The hope at Nordstrom is that these same customers will gain income over the years and graduate to become Nordstrom customers. Noting this trend, uber-upscale retailer Neiman Marcus has launched www.lastcall.com, where clearance and off-price products can be purchased. It will be interesting to see if these off-price outlets will damage these firms' brand image.

Capacity Planning Tools

There are some basic tools for capacity planning. We will begin with a forecast of demand that can then be used to identify an appropriate capacity level. The costs of excess capacity are traded off against the costs of insufficient capacity through *newsvendor analysis*. Finally, queuing theory will show us the effect of capacity decisions on the amount of customer waiting.

FORECASTING   The basis for service capacity planning is understanding the nature of demand, which is accomplished primarily through demand forecasting. Demand forecasting helps us predict what future demand might be. Forecasting techniques will be covered in Chapter 8. Demand management approaches can also be used to level demand. They are also discussed in Chapter 8.

We must remember that future demand is uncertain, meaning that the forecast represents a probability distribution. The probability distribution of the demand forecast will be used in planning capacity.

Self-checkout stands are an example of customer coproduction.

newsvendor analysis
A method for making capacity decisions in services that measures the trade-offs between the cost of understocking and the cost of overstocking.

NEWSVENDOR ANALYSIS Newsvendor analysis is another way to make capacity decisions under a different set of assumptions. In particular, you may want to trade off the costs of not enough capacity (C_U, or the cost of understocking) against the costs of excess capacity (C_O, or the cost of overstocking). With newsvendor analysis, we make the following assumptions:

1. Excess capacity costs = C_O dollars per time period.
2. If customers have to wait, the cost is C_U per time period. This cost could be lost goodwill or lost sales.
3. Capacity is perishable. In other words, you cannot use today's extra capacity to meet tomorrow's demand.

If these conditions are met, the optimal capacity is the point in the cumulative distribution of demand known as the **critical fractile**, CF:

critical fractile
The optimal capacity level in newsvendor analysis.

$$CF = \frac{C_U}{(C_O + C_U)} \tag{4.1}$$

The newsvendor problem is also called the perishable inventory problem because it is used to calculate the optimal amount of inventory of a perishable item. It is called the newsvendor problem because newspapers are an example of a perishable item. Daily newspapers have a certain value on the day they come out, but little or no value if they are not sold that day.

A newsstand in New York City can purchase newspapers for $0.10 each and sell them for $0.25 each. Daily demand is normally distributed with a mean of 100 and a standard deviation of 20. Newspapers that are not sold at the end of the day are worthless. So the cost having too many (C_O) is $0.10 per paper (the purchase cost), and the cost of having too few (C_U) is $0.15 per paper (the lost profit, which is $0.25 revenue minus $0.10 cost). To find the critical fractile using the newsvendor model use Equation 4.1. Here the critical fractile is $15/(10 + 15) = 0.60$. The 0.60 point on a cumulative normal distribution (see Appendix Table A-2) is $z = 0.255$. Thus, the optimal number of newspapers is $100 + (0.255 \times 20) = 105.1$, or 105 newspapers. A more complete problem is given in SOLVED PROBLEM 4.2.

 SOLVED PROBLEM 4.2 >   The Newsvendor Problem in Action

MyLab Operations Management Video

Problem: In service environments, an inventory issue is capacity. Service operations have a capacity for meeting customer demand according to how they are designed. If there is not enough capacity, customer demand may not turn into sales. Excess capacity comes with a cost as well.

For example, a restaurant chain is opening a new location in a business district. The question is how many tables to design in the restaurant. The key revenue period is the weekday lunch seating, so the restaurant desires to plan capacity for that demand. Lunchtime demand is forecast to be normally distributed with a mean of 25 parties and a standard deviation of 5 parties. (Assume one party per table.) How many tables should the restaurant have?

A naive view would have 25 tables, but that ignores the asymmetric cost structure. The average party spends $40 for lunch, with ingredient costs being 25 percent of that amount.

Solution: Therefore, the cost of insufficient tables (C_U) is $40 - ((40 \times 0.25) = 30 per table, which is the average profit contribution per party. Each table takes up 100 square feet of space, and space costs $3 per square foot per month (approximately $0.10 per square foot per day).

Therefore, the cost of an extra table is $100 \times 0.10 = 10 per table per day. This cost suggests that an optimal number of tables would have $CF = 30/(10 + 30) = 0.75$, or 75 percent of the cumulative distribution. Looking up 0.75 in the normal cumulative distribution table (see Appendix Table A-2) shows that $z = 0.675$. Therefore, the optimal number of tables is $25 + (0.675 \times 5) = 28.375$, or approximately 28 tables. See FIGURE 4.5 for the formulas and a sample layout for a newsvendor problem.

WAITING LINES Queuing theory shows the relationship between capacity levels and expected wait costs. A queue is a waiting line. Queues can take many forms, such as fast-food drive-through lanes, will-call windows at concerts, and process production lines with variation in

You can also use Excel to apply newsvendor analysis to Solved Problem 4.2.

	A	B	C	D	E	F	G	H	I
1	**Example 4-1 Newsvendor Analysis**								
2							=C3/(C4+C3)		
3		Cost of understocking ($):	30		Critical Fractile:	0.75			
4		Cost of overstocking ($):	10						
5		Average demand (tables):	25		Optimal Number of Tables:	28.375			
6		Std dev of demand (tables):	5						
7		z value:	0.675						
8		(Use =norm.s.inv(G3) command)			=C5+C6*C7				
9									
10									
11									
12									

∧ FIGURE 4.5

Newsvendor Excel Spreadsheet

processing times. Queuing theory requires that we have information about the distribution of demand (which we get from forecasting) and about the behavior of the queue system. The remainder of this chapter discusses details of queues and queuing theory.

 # PPLY QUEUING THEORY

Managers and designers use queuing theory when planning service capacity if they are uncertain about demand. This section will show you how managers approach queuing theory with respect to psychology, queue configuration, and wait times.

Queuing Psychology

Queuing psychology recognizes that the customer's cost of waiting is not just about the time customers spend waiting in line but also includes what customers think about the waiting. Uncomfortable waits can seem much longer than they really are. Entertaining waits can seem much shorter. Queuing psychology identifies ways that service operations managers can improve waits by improving the perception of those waits. David Maister provided the following eight points of queuing psychology:[2]

1. Unoccupied waits seem longer than occupied waits.
2. Preprocess waits seem longer than in-process waits.
3. Anxiety makes waits seem longer.
4. Uncertain waits seem longer than waits of a known duration.
5. Unexplained waits seem longer than explained waits.
6. Unfair waits seem longer than equitable waits.
7. The more valuable the service, the longer people are willing to wait.
8. Waiting alone seems longer than waiting with a group.

queuing psychology
The side of queuing theory that emphasizes human behavior.

Queue Systems and Service Stations

There are many options for queue systems. A system may have one queue or multiple queues. Each queue leads to one or more **servers** or **service stations**. For example, at a fast-food restaurant, customers may wait to place their order and then wait again to pay for it. When there are multiple queues and service stations, one after another, we say that it is a

servers or service stations
The person providing service in a queuing system.

[2]Based on D. Maister, "The Psychology of Waiting Lines" (1985), available at http://davidmaister.com/articles/5/52/.

Airport managers often use snake waiting lines with a single queue and multiple servers.

multiphase queue system
A service system involving multiple queues and/or servers.

two-phase system
A configuration of a queuing system with a single waiting line and a different service line.

service system
A service process with waiting line(s) and queue(s).

queue configuration
How a waiting line is organized for a given phase of a system.

queue discipline
A method for determining who goes next in a waiting line.

multiphase queue system. The fast-food restaurant example is a **two-phase system**. The **service system** includes the waiting line(s) and the service station(s).

There may be one station at each phase, or there may be multiple stations in parallel. Some fast-food restaurants have three or more order-processing stations. The **queue configuration** tells how the queue is organized for a given phase of a system. If a service system has one server, there will probably be one queue. If there are multiple servers, there could still be one queue leading to the next available server, or each station could have its own queue.

Sometimes, multiple stations each have their own queue. Customers entering the system need to decide which queue to enter. In some cases, customers may accidentally choose a queue that moves more slowly than other queues. One way to prevent this selection dilemma is to provide a single queue that is shared by all stations, or what is sometimes called a snake. A single queue helps overcome the customers' dilemma of selecting a queue, but snake queues can appear longer.

Some situations use different queues for different classes of customers. For example, at an airline check-in counter, first-class passengers may have a different queue than coach-class customers.

Even with a single queue, there are different ways to determine which customer is next to be served. The **queue discipline** is the method for determining who goes next. One common option is first come, first served. Another option is customers with the most urgent needs going first, as often happens in a hospital emergency room.

Wait Times

How much time customers spend in a queue can be estimated by queuing theory equations, which are provided in TABLE 4.4. These equations are used for three different types of queuing problems that will be introduced sequentially. The equations for simple queues are quite simple, but the equations for more complex queues are beyond the scope of this text.

SINGLE-SERVER QUEUE SYSTEM WITH EXPONENTIAL SERVICE TIMES We have already talked about single-server systems. They are simply queues with a single line and a single server. Exponential service times are those that are distributed with a long tail. Think about your experiences in lines at grocery stores. Most customers are fairly quick, but some take much more time because they may have items with price checks or they are very slow. A simple single-server queue is based on the following assumptions:

- A single server
- A single queue (only one waiting line)
- Random arrival of customers (Poisson arrival process with mean of λ)
- Exponential service times with mean (or average) of $1/\mu$
- First come, first served
- No balking (customers enter the queue regardless of the queue length)

v TABLE 4.4

Queuing Models and Variables

Model I	Single channel/exponential service times	Average line length (length of the queue) $= L_q = \dfrac{\lambda^2}{\mu(\mu - \lambda)}$
		Average time spent in line (waiting in the queue) $= W_q = \dfrac{L_q}{\lambda} = \dfrac{\lambda}{\mu(\mu - \lambda)}$
		Average utilization of the server $= \rho = \dfrac{\lambda}{\mu}$
		Average number of items in system $= L_s = L_q + \dfrac{\lambda}{\mu} = \dfrac{\lambda}{\mu - \lambda}$
		Average time spent in the system $= W_s = \dfrac{L_s}{\lambda} = W_q + \dfrac{1}{\mu} = \dfrac{1}{\mu - \lambda}$
Model II	Single channel/constant service times	Average line length (length of the queue) $= L_q = \dfrac{\lambda^2}{2\mu(\mu - \lambda)}$
		Average time spent in line (waiting in the queue) $= W_q = \dfrac{L_q}{\lambda} = \dfrac{\lambda}{2\mu(\mu - \lambda)}$
		Average utilization of the server $= \rho = \dfrac{\lambda}{\mu}$
		Average number of customers in system $= L_s = L_q + \dfrac{\lambda}{\mu}$
		Average time spent in the system $= W_s = \dfrac{L_s}{\lambda}$
Model III	Multichannel/exponential service times	Average line length (length of the queue) $= L_q = \dfrac{\lambda\mu(\lambda/\mu)^M}{(M - 1)!(M\mu - \lambda)^2} P_0$
		where: $$P_0 = \left[\sum_{n=0}^{M-1} \frac{(\lambda/\mu)^n}{n!} + \frac{(\lambda/\mu)^M}{M!(1 - \lambda/M\mu)} \right]^{-1}$$
		Average time spent in line (waiting in the queue) $= W_q = \dfrac{L_q}{\lambda}$
		Average utilization of the servers $= \dfrac{\lambda}{M\mu}$
		Average number of items in system $= L_s = L_q + \dfrac{\lambda}{\mu}$
		Average time spent in the system $= W_s = \dfrac{L_s}{\lambda}$

λ = arrival rate

μ = service rate

$\rho = \dfrac{\lambda}{\mu}$ = ratio of arrival rate to service rate

P_0 = probability of 0 customers in the system

$\dfrac{1}{\mu}$ = average service time

$\dfrac{1}{\lambda}$ = average time between arrivals

M = number of servers

- No reneging (once you enter the system, you cannot leave)
- An infinite calling population that may enter the queue
- No limits on line length

SOLVED PROBLEM 4.3 shows how to apply these formulas for a single-server/single-queue system.

SOLVED PROBLEM 4.3>

MyLab Operations Management
Video

Model I in Action for a Single-Phase Queue with a Single Server and Exponential Service Times

Problem: The Curtis Fast Food Service is considering installing a drive-through lane (or channel) for its customers, which consists of one lane and one serving window. It is expected that 20 customers will arrive every hour. There is an average 2-minute service time that is exponentially distributed so that an average of 30 customers can be served per hour. Find the following:

a. average line length
b. average time spent in line
c. average utilization of the server
d. average number of customers in the system
e. average time spent in the system

Solution: Using the Model I formulas, we compute the following:

a. average line length (length of the queue) $= L_q = \dfrac{\lambda^2}{\mu(\mu - \lambda)} = \dfrac{20^2}{30(30 - 20)} = 1.33$

   customers

b. average time spent in line (waiting in the queue) $= W_q = \dfrac{L_q}{\lambda} = \dfrac{1.33}{20} = 0.067$

   hour $= 3.99$ minutes

c. average utilization of the server $= \dfrac{\lambda}{\mu} = \dfrac{20}{30} = 0.666$

d. average number of customers in system $= L_s = L_q + \dfrac{\lambda}{\mu} = 1.33 + 0.666 = 2$ customers

e. average time spent in the system $= W_s = \dfrac{L_s}{\lambda} = \dfrac{2}{20} = 0.10$ hour $= 6$ minutes

SINGLE-SERVER QUEUE SYSTEMS WITH CONSTANT SERVICE TIMES The assumptions for the single-server queue system with constant service times are the same as above except that service times are always the same. Consider a drive-through automated car wash where the time for the wash is constant from one car to the next. To compute the necessary statistics, we will use model II in Table 4.4. You will notice that the length of the queue is cut in half. We demonstrate this in SOLVED PROBLEM 4.4.

SOLVED PROBLEM 4.4 >

MyLab Operations Management
Video

Model II in Action for a Single-Phase Queue with a Single Server and Constant Service Times

Problem: The RoboWorld Car Wash services cars in a constant time of 5 minutes. During this time, the cars are washed, waxed, and dried. The service time is constant, with a throughput of 12 per hour. On average, 8 customers arrive per hour. Compute the following:

a. average line length
b. average time spent in line
c. average utilization of the server
d. average number of customers in the system
e. average time spent in the system

Solution:

a. average line length (length of the queue) $= L_q = \dfrac{\lambda^2}{2\mu(\mu - \lambda)} = \dfrac{8^2}{2(12)(12 - 8)} =$ 0.67 customer

b. average time spent in line (waiting in the queue) $= W_q = \dfrac{L_q}{\lambda} = \dfrac{0.67}{8} = 0.0833$ hour $=$ 5 minutes

c. average utilization of the server $= \dfrac{\lambda}{\mu} = \dfrac{8}{12} = 0.67$

d. average number of customers in system $= L_s = L_q + \dfrac{\lambda}{\mu} = 0.67 + 0.67 = 1.33$ customers

e. average time spent in the system $= W_s = \dfrac{L_s}{\lambda} = \dfrac{1.33}{8} = 0.166$ hour $= 10$ minutes

---

MULTISERVER QUEUE SYSTEM WITH EXPONENTIAL SERVICE TIMES What happens when we consider using two servers instead of just one server? To analyze this scenario, we will use model III in Table 4.4. The equations for this model are quite complex, so L_q values are provided in TABLE 4.5. To use Table 4.5, you need to calculate λ / μ, which specifies a particular row of the table (round as necessary). The columns of the table are for different numbers of servers (M). Note that we again assume exponential service times. Use of this model is demonstrated in SOLVED PROBLEM 4.5.

Model III in Action for a Multiserver System with Exponential Service Times

< SOLVED PROBLEM 4.5

MyLab Operations Management
Video

Problem: A bank is trying to figure out how many tellers need to staff the bank windows during lunchtime from 11:30 a.m. to 1:30 p.m. During that time, customers arrive at an average rate of 18 per hour, distributed according to a Poisson distribution. On average, a customer spends 3 minutes with a teller to complete a transaction. Assume that all assumptions of model III are met. The bank manager does not want the average customer wait time to be more than 3 minutes.

a. What is the average customer wait time with one teller?
b. What would the average customer wait time be if the bank had two tellers?
c. How long would customers wait on average with three tellers?

Solution:

$\lambda = 18$ customers per hour (arrival rate)
$\dfrac{1}{\mu} = 3$ minutes per customer (service time)
So,
$\mu = 20$ customers per hour (service rate)
$\dfrac{\lambda}{\mu} = \dfrac{18}{20} = 0.9$

a. For $M = 1$, $L_q = 8.100$ customers (from Table 4.5), so $W_q = L_q/\lambda = 8.1/18 = 0.45$ hour, which is 27 minutes waiting on average ($0.45 * 60 = 27$ minutes).
b. For $M = 2$, $L_q = 0.2285$ customer, so $W_q = L_q/\lambda = 0.2285/18 = 0.0127$ hour, which is 0.76 minute waiting on average. This meets the manager's goal.
c. For $M = 3$, $L_q = 0.03$ customer, so $W_q = L_q/\lambda = 0.03/18 = 0.0017$ hour, or less than 0.1 minute waiting on average, which is almost no wait at all.

In summary, queuing theory is useful because it allows us to estimate system performance as long as we are able to meet assumptions reasonably. As you can see, queuing theory gets somewhat complex when we consider other than just the simplest assumptions. In situations in which the simple assumptions are not reasonable, we need to consider alternate methods of analysis, such as mathematical simulation.

∨ TABLE 4.5

L_q Values for Queuing Model III (Multiserver System)

λ/μ	Number of Servers (M)									
	1	2	3	4	5	6	7	8	9	10
0.10	0.0111									
0.15	0.0264	0.0008								
0.20	0.0500	0.0020								
0.25	0.0833	0.0039								
0.30	0.1285	0.0069								
0.35	0.1884	0.0110								
0.40	0.2666	0.0166								
0.45	0.3681	0.0239	0.0019							
0.50	0.5000	0.0333	0.0030							
0.55	0.6722	0.0449	0.0043							
0.60	0.9000	0.0593	0.0061							
0.65	1.2071	0.0767	0.0084							
0.70	1.6333	0.0976	0.0112							
0.75	2.2500	0.1227	0.0147							
0.80	3.2000	0.1523	0.0189							
0.85	4.8166	0.1873	0.0239	0.0031						
0.90	8.1000	0.2285	0.0300	0.0041						
0.95	18.0500	0.2767	0.0371	0.0053						
1.00		0.3333	0.0454	0.0067						
1.50		1.9286	0.2368	0.0448	0.0086					
2.00			0.0888	0.1730	0.3980	0.0090				
2.50			3.5112	0.5331	0.1304	0.0339	0.0086			
3.00				1.5282	0.3541	0.0991	0.0282	0.0077		
3.50				5.1650	0.8816	0.2485	0.0762	0.0232		
4.00					2.2164	0.5694	0.1801	0.0590	0.0189	
4.50					6.8624	1.2650	0.3910	0.1336	0.0460	0.0155
5.00						2.9375	0.8102	0.2785	0.1006	0.0361
5.50						8.5902	1.6736	0.5527	0.2039	0.0767
6.00							3.6878	1.0707	0.3918	0.1518
6.50							10.3406	2.1019	0.7298	0.2855
7.00								4.4471	1.3471	0.5172
7.50								12.1088	2.5457	0.9198
8.00									5.2264	1.6364
8.50									13.8914	3.0025
9.00										6.0183
9.50										15.6861
10.00										

At the beginning of this chapter, we discussed music-sharing services such as Spotify. After studying service design, you now understand that these companies have created a coproductive environment where customers provide information and preferences. As you use the music-sharing service, you actually help to fine-tune the service the company provides to you.

There are also traditional quality dimensions to this service, such as performance, reliability, cost, and content. The social dimension takes the experience from being primarily technological to relational.

Customers of music-sharing services also prefer paid music. This eliminates commercials and makes the experience less clunky. In addition, socially engaged listeners are much more satisfied than passive listeners. That is, as a listener, you join a community by sharing and borrowing. Also, exclusive content drives users to the service. For example, if one service has Taylor Swift and another doesn't, her fans will flock to the service providing her music.

Data analysis and algorithms allow services to provide music that matches your moods. The social aspect creates an environment not unlike hanging around at a really awesome music shop with your friends. So the next time you chat with your friends about music sharing, explain about providing customer inputs to processes and coproduction.

Summary

1. The chapter began by reviewing the importance of tangibles in services.
   a. All services involve a bundling of tangibles and intangibles.
   b. Both the tangibles and intangibles have to be correct.
2. We then discussed the key elements of a service design.
   a. An important aspect of service design is that customers provide inputs to all services. This aspect is a major distinction between services and manufacturing.
   b. B2B and B2C services differ in that the entities are different.
3. We followed our service design discussion with details of the process chain network (PCN) diagram.
   a. PCN diagrams provide a basis for process positioning, that is, determining best how to interact with customers and suppliers.
   b. PCN diagrams place service processes in the context of supply chains.
4. We then provided tools for managing services with uncertain capacity.
   a. The first tool was the newsvendor model, which is useful for perishable capacity.
   b. Next, we discussed queuing models as a means for optimizing customer service and waiting lines.

Key Terms

Integrative Learning Exercise

Identify an organization, company, or business that provides a service. Use a process chain network (PCN) diagram to evaluate the interactions between service providers and customers for the organization. Be sure to identify the process domain region, the direct interaction region, the surrogate interaction region, and the independent processing region of the service design. If applicable, recommend improvements to the service delivery system that you evaluated.

Integrative Experiential Exercise

Together with a student group, visit a business or organization that provides a service. Identify a process or process segment in the business or organization that can be analyzed using a PCN diagram. Identify the process level, the process entities, and the beginning and ending steps of the process segment. Be sure to identify the points where the customer receives benefits and the provider incurs costs. Comment on how moving and rearranging steps across and between process regions might affect the value proposition by increasing customer benefits, decreasing provider costs, or both.

Discussion Questions

1. Briefly describe service operations and service.

2. In what ways do services involve tangible elements?

3. Identify the customer input resources and the service provider outputs for the following service operations: accounting, education, computer repair, and healthcare.

4. What is meant by simultaneity in services? What is a major consequence of simultaneity?

5. What are some long-term responses for increasing and decreasing service capacity?

6. What is meant by the term *time-perishable capacity* as it relates to service operations? Provide an example.

7. Customers are generally involved in the service delivery process. What are some negative consequences associated with customer interaction in the service operation?

8. Briefly define and describe how a process chain network (PCN) diagram can be used in designing service delivery systems.

9. How can you shift the focus of your operations using a PCN diagram?

10. What trade-offs are generally made when making capacity decisions?

11. How do capacity choices vary in the near and long terms?

12. How can queuing theory be used to help evaluate capacity decisions for service providers?

13. Queuing psychology identifies ways that service operations managers can improve waits by improving the perception of those customers who do wait. What are some of the fundamental points related to queuing psychology?

14. In waiting lines, sometimes technological advances cannot make it easier to manage queues. How can psychology help with this problem?

15. How does the newsvendor model allow service firms to evaluate capacity decisions?

Solved Problems

Planning Service Capacity for Uncertain Demand

CAPACITY PLANNING TOOLS

SOLVED PROBLEM 4.2

1. A bookstore must decide how many copies of a special release of a political thriller to order. The demand for the book is assumed to be normally distributed with a mean of 2,500 and a standard deviation of 150. The bookstore will sell the book for $25. It costs the bookstore $15 for each copy it stocks. There is no market for the book once the next book in the series is released; therefore, the book has no salvage value for unsold copies. How many copies of the book should the bookstore stock (order) if it wants to maximize its expected profit?

    Answer:

    C_U = price − cost = 25 − 15 = $10

    C_O = cost − salvage = 15 − 0 = $15

    $$CF = \frac{C_U}{C_O + C_U} = \frac{10}{10 + 15} = 0.4$$

    $z = -0.25$

    $Q = \mu + z(\sigma) = 2500 + (-0.25)(150) = 2462.5$, or 2463 books

Queuing Theory

WAIT TIMES

SOLVED PROBLEM 4.3

2. A small dollar store has a single checkout aisle staffed by one cashier. Customers arrive at the checkout aisle at the rate of 25 every hour. The cashier is able to process 40 customers per hour. Her service time is estimated to be exponentially distributed. Find the following:

    a. average server utilization
    b. average line length
    c. average time spent in line
    d. average number of customers in the system (in the video store)
    e. average time spent in the video store

    Answer:

    $\lambda = 25$ per hour

    $\mu = 40$ per hour

    a. average server utilization $= \dfrac{\lambda}{\mu} = \dfrac{25}{40} = 0.625$

    b. average line length $= L_q = \dfrac{\lambda^2}{\mu(\mu - \lambda)} = \dfrac{25^2}{40(40 - 25)} =$ 1.042 customers

    c. average time spent in line $= W_q = \dfrac{L_q}{\lambda} = \dfrac{1.042}{25} =$ 0.0417 hour $= 0.0417 \times 60 =$ 2.5 minutes

    d. average number of customers in the system (in the video store) $= L_s = L_q + \dfrac{\lambda}{\mu} = 0.0142 + \dfrac{25}{40} = 1.6667$

    e. average time spent in the video store $= W_s = \dfrac{L_s}{\lambda} = \dfrac{1.6667}{25} = 0.0667$ hour $= 0.0667 \times 60 = 4$ minutes

SOLVED PROBLEM 4.4

3. A clothing store has a single machine that screens logos onto shirts. The time to screen on the logo is a constant 3 minutes. On average, there is a request for 10 screened shirts per hour. Compute the following:

    a. average use of the machine
    b. average number of shirts waiting to be screened
    c. average time a shirt waits to be screened
    d. average number of shirts waiting in the system
    e. average time spent in the shirt-screening process

    Answer:

    $\lambda = 10$ per hour

    $\mu = \dfrac{60 \text{ min}}{3} = 20$ per hour

    a. average utilization of the machine = average utilization of the server $= \dfrac{\lambda}{\mu} = \dfrac{10}{20} = 0.5$

    b. average number of shirts waiting to be screened $= L_q = \dfrac{\lambda^2}{2\mu(\mu - \lambda)} = \dfrac{10^2}{2(20)(20 - 10)} = 0.25$ shirt

    c. average time a shirt waits to be screened $= W_q = \dfrac{L_q}{\lambda} = \dfrac{0.25}{10} = 0.025$ hour $= 0.025 \times 60 =$ 1.5 minutes

    d. average number of shirts waiting in the system $= L_s = L_q + \dfrac{\lambda}{\mu} = .25 + \dfrac{10}{20} = 0.75$ shirt

    e. average time spent in the shirt-screening process $= W_s = \dfrac{L_s}{\lambda} = \dfrac{0.75}{10} = 0.075$ hours $= 0.075 \times 60 =$ 4.5 minutes

SOLVED PROBLEM 4.5

4. Calls arrive at a help desk at the rate of three every 2 minutes. The help desk has four service representatives who are able to handle incoming calls. If a representative can process, on average, one call in 2 minutes, compute the following:

    a. the average utilization of the representatives
    b. average time a caller must wait to have his or her call answered
    c. average amount of time a caller spends in the system.

    Answer:

    $\lambda = 90$ per hour $= \dfrac{60 \text{ min}}{2} \times 3$

    $\mu = 30$ per hour $= \dfrac{60 \text{ min}}{2}$

    $M = 4$

a. average utilization of the representatives $= \dfrac{\lambda}{M\mu} = \dfrac{90}{4 \times 30} = 0.75$.

b. average time a caller must wait to have call answered $=$

$$W_q = \dfrac{L_q}{\lambda}.$$

Using Table 4.5:

$$\dfrac{\lambda}{\mu}\dfrac{90}{30} = 3$$

$$M = 4$$

$L_q = 1.5282$

$$W_q = \dfrac{1.5282}{90} = 0.017 \text{ hour} = 0.017 \times 60 = 1.0188$$

minutes.

c. average amount of time a caller spends in the system $=$

$$W_s = \dfrac{L_s}{\lambda}$$

$$L_s = L_q + \dfrac{\lambda}{\mu} = 1.5283 + \dfrac{90}{30} = 4.5283$$

$$W_s = \dfrac{4.5283}{90} = 0.0503 \text{ hour} = 0.0503 \times 60 = 3.0189 \text{ minutes}$$

Problems

Planning Service Capacity for Uncertain Demand

NEWSVENDOR PROBLEMS

1. A local bookstand believes that the demand for the Olympic edition of a sports magazine is normally distributed with a mean of 1,200 and a standard deviation of 200. Each copy of the magazine costs the bookstand $1.50 per copy, and the bookstand will sell the issue for $5.00. Following the Olympic Games, there will be no demand for the magazine, and all leftover copies will be recycled because they will have no salvage value. What is the optimal number of copies of the Olympic edition that the bookstand should order?

2. The demand for next year's wildlife calendar at a bookstore is assumed to be normally distributed with a mean of 500 and a standard deviation of 75. Each calendar costs the bookstore $5.50 each and will be sold for $12.50 each. Any calendars remaining for sale after Christmas will be discounted and sold for $1.00 each. The bookstore believes that any calendar remaining to be sold after Christmas can be cleared at the $1.00 price. How many wildlife calendars should the bookstore stock if it wants to maximize its expected profit from wildlife calendars?

3. A retail store must decide how many Mother's Day cards to have in stock for this year's Mother's Day. Cards must be ordered months in advance, and there is only an opportunity to order one time. The store believes that the demand for cards will be normally distributed with a mean of 750 and a standard deviation of 50. The cards cost the shop $2.00 each and will be sold for $3.00 each. Any cards remaining after Mother's Day will be destroyed. How many cards should the retail store order for Mother's Day?

Queuing Theory

SINGLE SERVER QUEUING

4. A small coffee shop has a single barista. Because the shop is small, there are no tables or chairs. Consequently, customers wait in a single line to order and receive their coffee and leave the shop as soon as their order is received. Customers arrive at the shop at the rate of 15 per hour. It is estimated that the barista needs, on average, 120 seconds (exponentially distributed) to serve each customer. Determine the following service operating characteristics for the coffee shop:

a. average server utilization

b. average line length in the coffee shop

c. average time spent in line

d. average number of customers in the coffee shop

e. average time spent by customers in the coffee shop (includes waiting time and service time)

5. An ATM located on a college campus is able to process, on average, one customer request every 2 minutes. Assume that the processing times are exponentially distributed and that each person using the ATM makes only one request per visit. If students arrive at the ATM at the rate of 10 per hour throughout the day, find the following:

a. percentage of time the ATM is busy

b. probability the ATM is not in use when a student arrives

c. average number of students waiting to use the ATM

d. average time a student spends waiting in line to use the ATM

e. average time spent waiting and using the ATM

f. average number of students waiting and using the ATM (i.e., the average number of customers in the system)

6. A quick-service restaurant has a single drive-through lane with one worker at the window. It is assumed that the worker can process an order every 4 minutes on average and that the processing (service) times are exponentially distributed. If customers arrive at the drive-through at the rate of 10 per hour, calculate the following service operation performance characteristics:

a. percentage of time the worker at the drive-through is busy

b. average number of cars waiting at the drive-through
c. number of cars, on average, in the drive-through system
d. average time a car spends waiting in the drive-through
e. time, on average, spent in the drive-through system

SINGLE PHASE WITH SINGLE SERVER AND CONSTANT SERVICE TIMES

7. Tourists arrive at a security checkpoint at the rate of 25 per hour. The checkpoint has a single machine that scans all tourists wanting to enter the secure area. Tourists are scanned one at a time according to a first-come, first-served convention. A constant 90 seconds are required to scan a tourist. Compute the following:

   a. percentage of time the scanning machine is busy
   b. average number of tourists waiting in line to be scanned
   c. average time spent in the line waiting to be scanned
   d. average time spent in the system (waiting time and scanning time)
   e. average number of tourists in the system

8. A vanilla milkshake machine requires a constant 3 minutes to make the special shake served at the Burger Shack. The machine can process one vanilla shake at a time. Requests for the special shake occur every 4 minutes, or 15 per hour, on average. Compute the following:

   a. probability that the shake machine is busy
   b. probability that the shake machine is not busy
   c. average amount of time spent waiting to use the shake machine
   d. average amount of time spent in the shake process (waiting and processing time)
   e. average number of shakes ordered but not yet started processing (i.e., waiting for machine)
   f. average number of shakes in process (ordered but not yet delivered to customers)

9. A cleaning tool requires a constant 5 minutes to polish a part. Parts arrive at the tool for processing at the rate of one part every 10 minutes.

   a. On average, what percentage of the time is the cleaning tool busy?

b. On average, how many parts are waiting to be cleaned?
c. On average, how many parts are in the cleaning process?
d. On average, how long does a part spend waiting before beginning processing?
e. On average, how long does a part spend in the cleaning process?

MULTISERVER SYSTEM WITH EXPONENTIAL SERVICE TIMES

10. Customers arrive at teller windows at a bank at the rate of 12 per hour. A teller is able to process 15 customers per hour on average. If the bank has a goal that customer wait time should be no more than 30 seconds to see a teller, how many tellers should the bank have available to process customer requests?

11. A dollar store has four checkout lanes. The clerks in each lane have the same abilities, with each clerk being able to check out a customer in 3 minutes on average. At its busiest times, customers of the dollar store arrive at the checkout counters at the rate of 50 per hour.

    a. What is the average waiting time if all four checkout lanes are being used by the dollar store?
    b. The dollar store is contemplating closing one of the checkout lanes. If it reduces the number of lanes from four to three, how will customer wait time be affected during the busiest store hours?
    c. If the dollar store reduces the number of checkout lanes from four to three, how will the average processing time (service time) change?

12. A company can easily expand its service operation by adding more servers to its process. If each server is able to process 10 customers per hour and customers arrive at the company at the rate of 25 per hour, how many servers should be employed to achieve the standard that no customer should have to wait more than 30 seconds to be served? What is the average utilization of the servers for the number of servers required to meet this service goal?

XLG Enterprises

Tommy Hernandez had recently been assigned to the service design team at XLG Enterprises. Tommy had been with XLG for a little over two years when the opportunity to join the service design team became available. The service design team performs a variety of roles, one of which is to analyze and recommend improvements for existing customer service operations performed at XLG.

The design team is now analyzing a new customer service process. The process would handle a variety of customer requests, including billing disputes, shipping and product delivery issues, and product returns. These activities would take place at a newly designed service facility close to the XLG headquarters. Most of XLG's customers are small to medium-sized businesses located in the same city as the proposed customer service facility. It is the hope of XLG management that the new central location for customer service will be a way to facilitate and expedite customer requests related to product billing, shipping, and returns. Customer orders would still be placed mostly over the telephone or the Internet. A sizable number of XLG customers would come to the customer service facility to pick up deliveries or to make returns. The facility would also handle customer-related issues concerning service and billing.

A stated goal of XLG management is that the facility should ensure that customers rarely have to wait more than 15 minutes before speaking to a service representative, even during the busiest of times. XLG anticipated that it would staff the new facility with two service representatives at all times. During the busiest times of the day, however, management recognizes that it might have to increase staffing to as many as six service representatives to meet its stated objectives.

Tommy has been asked to join the team that is designing the new facility. As part of his role, he is to conduct analysis of customer waiting times. Tommy has been given information related to expected customer arrival rates during the busiest service periods throughout the day, average service times, and costs related to both resource staffing and customer waiting. Here is a summary of the information given to Tommy:

Time Period	Arrival Rate
7 a.m.–1 p.m.	10 per hour
1 p.m.–5 p.m.	15 per hour
5 p.m.–10 p.m.	6 per hour

Average service time per customer representative (all servers are assumed to have the same capabilities)	15 minutes
Cost of waiting (estimated hourly cost for customers in the XLG system, waiting and being served)	$20
Hourly cost of service representative (including benefits)	$25
Average waiting time goal	3 minutes

Tommy remembers studying waiting line analysis in his SC&O management course. A quick review of his old notes helps him recall that the total hourly costs of providing service are comprised of two components: the cost of providing the service and the cost of having customers wait for service. He found the following equation:

$$\text{Total cost} = \text{number of servers} \times \text{cost per server per unit of time} + \text{expected number of customers in the system} \times \text{cost per customer to wait per unit of time}$$

Tommy realizes that management wants an analysis that would help it determine how to staff the facility throughout the day as well as an estimate related to the overall estimated cost of the staffing plan, including customer waiting costs.

Management is eagerly waiting for the results of his analysis, and Tommy has promised it a report early Monday.

Questions:

1. Could the facility operate during the busiest period with only a single service representative?

2. If four service representatives are used during the busiest period, what are the facility's operating characteristics as they relate to waiting lines?

3. If four service representatives are employed, can the company attain its stated goal related to waiting time during the busiest period?

4. How many service representatives should be employed to meet the company's stated service goal for each time segment provided?

5. What are the total costs associated with waiting for the cases in which four, five, or six representatives are employed during the busy period?

5 Customer Relationship Management

INTEGRATING

INNOVATING

IMPACTING

IMPROVING

GLOBAL SC&O STRATEGY

Supply Management

Operations Management

Customer Relationship Management

Upstream Processes

Core Processes

Downstream Processes

QUALITY MANAGEMENT, ANALYTICS, AND LOGISTICS

CHAPTER OUTLINE AND LEARNING OBJECTIVES

1 Understand and Apply Customer Relationships and Systems
- Understand the fundamentals of customer relationship management.
- Explain the importance of customer relationships.

2 Learn the Techniques to Improve Customer Service
- Understand how to meet customer expectations.
- Understand concepts relating to measuring service performance.

- Understand how to identify and recover from service failures.

3 Change Relationships through Servitization
- Understand how firms forward integrate.
- Communicate the perils of servitization.

4 Manage Service Supply Chains
- Understand bi-directional service supply chains.
- Utilize service scripts.

Customer Relationship Management at Amazon

More and more, business-to-consumer (B2C) transactions are facilitated over the Internet. One of the most popular websites for retail is Jeff Bezos's Amazon.com. Amazon does an excellent job of preserving a "single face" to customers through its customer relationship management engine. When you go onto the Amazon website, it is like looking at a mirror into your spending habits, preferences, and aspirations. The "single face" occurs because anyone you deal with at Amazon also has this information about you and can better manage how you interact with the company. This interaction is at the crux of customer relationship management systems. Amazon gathers data, lots of it, about you, the customer. This mass of data that is created by your surfing the Internet is more commonly referred to as big data ("big" because of its sheer volume). Amazon keeps these data in a customer relationship management system. Every time you go onto the Amazon website, the first screen is customized to your needs. We will revisit Amazon at the end of the chapter.

As you can see from the opening vignette, Amazon has data about you that it can use to enhance its relationship with you and potentially generate more sales. However, there is more to customer relationship management than just computer systems. In the coming pages, we will introduce both customer relationships and systems.

U NDERSTAND AND APPLY CUSTOMER RELATIONSHIPS AND SYSTEMS

In addition to creating and maintaining customers, another purpose of business is to remain profitable. These two perspectives are reconciled in the assertion that *the purpose of business is to attain mutually beneficial relationships between providers and customers.* Establishing these mutually beneficial relationships requires careful planning, which is the function of **customer relationship management (CRM)**. You can see CRM's importance to supply chain and operations (SC&O) management in the model at the beginning of the chapter. Operations are at the core, and the customer is downstream in the supply chain. Of special interest are systems that use data to predict future consumer behavior. **Predictive analytics** is the science of using customer data to predict future consumption behavior.

There are two major perspectives of CRM. One perspective stresses the importance of sales force automation, which uses technology to help salespeople identify sales leads, close sales, and identify opportunities to follow up with customers and convince them to buy more. These business functions are accomplished using computer technology called **customer relationship management systems (CRMSs)**. The CRMS perspective of CRM focuses on arming sales employees with data and systems to help them manage their sales contacts more effectively. The other perspective focuses on how managers develop and nurture customer relationships. The main goals of this approach are to (1) understand customer needs, (2) retain customer loyalty, and (3) customize delivery.

In this chapter, you will see that it is no longer sufficient to have a database of customers. You now create relationships with your customers that you nurture, thus allowing you

customer relationship management (CRM)
A methodology for creating mutually beneficial relations between consumers and service providers.

predictive analytics
The science of using customer data to forecast future behavior.

customer relationship management systems (CRMSs)
Information systems used to manage customer-related data.

to create annuity relationships in which customers provide streams of income. In addition, customer management is less transaction-based and is more relationship-based. The SC&O challenge is to provide systems that accomplish effective CRM.

Customer Relationship Management Systems

CRMSs facilitate an overall process of maintaining relationships with individual customers. We usually think of CRM as a broad set of activities to foster positive relationships with customers and CRMSs as the data portions for keeping track of customer requirements. In particular, CRMSs can facilitate the delivery of a unique, customized experience.

Traditional CRMSs are composed of a database that stores information about individual customers and the means for firm employees (and possibly customers) to populate (add data), maintain (update data), and access (report on) the data. In recent years, companies administer CRMSs over the Internet. One popular web-based system is Salesforce.com, which gives client companies access to customer data kept on its servers. SC&O CURRENT EVENTS 5.1 discusses some leading-edge CRMS issues and some of the most popular CRMS software.

Effective use of CRMSs can enhance customer retention. Because it costs six times as much to acquire customers as it does to retain them, it is cost effective to retain current customers (as opposed to continuously finding new ones). Frequent-flier programs and grocery discount cards are examples of information-based methods for retaining customers.

In some cases, customers themselves can access CRMSs. As mentioned at the beginning of the chapter, a common example of a company that gives the customer system access is Amazon. As customers search for and select items, the Amazon system records their preferences and provides customized recommendations. Amazon also gives customers options for customizing the website to their preferences. Predictive analytics provide an opportunity to ship products to customers in anticipation of needs in a B2C environment.

Implementing a CRMS can be very complex, and the investment does not always produce measurable results. To implement a CRMS properly requires an understanding of a business and its customers, competitors, culture, and processes. Many of the project management, team management, and change management techniques we discuss can be extremely helpful for CRMS implementation, which requires strong planning and project management skills.

SC&O CURRENT >
EVENTS 5.1

CRMS in Action

One of the leading-edge efforts in CRM is to mine data from social media to better understand customers and to tailor products and services to satisfy their needs. Such data mining is happening in the business-to-business (B2B) marketplace. Two companies that facilitate firms in accomplishing better mining of big data from social media are Marketo and Salesforce.

Marketo.com is a hip young company that develops marketing automation software that mines social media data to create leads for marketing. Marketo .com also shares cartoons, funny pictures, career-related information, and content to strengthen its brand. These tactics have led Marketo.com to build a network of more than 80,000 Facebook friends to provide data and marketing leads.

Salesforce.com is a company that focuses on social selling. By using Twitter, Salesforce.com can create a network to create personal connections with people. It uses a method it calls social selling, which uses social networks to create sales opportunities. The Salesforce.com application allows customers to gather information from several sources, such as Google Analytics, Facebook, Adobe, and SAP, to deliver the right messages to the right people at the right times.

Application of CRMS falls into three general categories: (1) *acquisition*, (2) *enhancement*, and (3) *retention*:

Acquisition is the acquiring of new customers. CRMSs aid in the acquisition of customers by gathering data that can be used to target customers or identify those who might be likely purchasers of products or services (that may include products). Google employs an acquisition-oriented system. Google collects information from customers in web searches, e-mail messages, and calendar events and provides advertising that should relate. For example, if a user schedules a golf tournament on his or her Google Calendar, Google is likely to provide advertisements for golf equipment.

acquisition
Finding new customers.

Enhancement is improving the experiences of current customers. A classic example of experience enhancement is the data Ritz-Carlton hotels keep about customer preferences. For example, if a guest requests an extra pillow at one Ritz-Carlton hotel, that information is made available to all Ritz-Carlton hotels so that they can anticipate that preference for future stays. Of course, maintaining such detailed records requires identifying each unique customer, which can be accomplished through frequent-guest programs.

enhancement
The improvement of the experience of current customers.

Retention is promoting ongoing and increased business from current customers. Research has shown that loyal customers are more profitable than new customers and casual customers. CRMSs can help retention efforts by tracking customer use and triggering actions to increase use. For example, an auto dealer might offer free auto maintenance service with the purchase of a new car for a certain amount of time after the sale. After the free period, the dealer might provide specials or packages to keep the customer coming back for service.

retention
Promoting ongoing and increased business with current customers.

Managing Across Majors 5.1 Information systems majors, CRMSs require excellent database management systems to flourish.

Customer Relationships

Although CRMSs are key components in customer service, this chapter primarily examines how managers can develop and nurture mutually beneficial relationships. We will consider how the customer-facing aspects of a supply chain can operate in a way that engenders customer loyalty and firm profitability.

A lot of discussion about supply chains focuses on upstream actions such as purchasing and supplier management. CRM focuses our attention downstream, on users and other beneficiaries of the supply chain such as distributors, retailers, and final customers. As we go downstream, we have the opportunity to establish and enhance our relationships with customers, which often falls under the title "customer service." Customer service is important for various reasons, including the following:[1]

- Customers tell twice as many people about bad experiences as good experiences.
- A dissatisfied customer tells eight to ten people about the bad experience.
- Seventy percent of upset customers will remain your customer if you resolve the complaint satisfactorily.
- It's easier to get customers to repeat their business than it is to find new business.
- Service firms rely on repeat customers for 85 percent to 95 percent of their business.
- Eighty percent of new product and service ideas come from customer ideas.
- The cost of keeping an existing customer is a sixth of the cost of attracting a new customer.

Service managers define a **customer** as a beneficiary of a specific supply chain or operation. An **end consumer** is the ultimate beneficiary, or the individual or individuals whose needs are satisfied. The end consumer in a food supply chain is the person who actually buys the food. Throughout the food supply chain, however, are many intermediate customers who benefit from upstream actions and provide benefits to downstream customers. A wheat

customer
The beneficiary of a specific supply chain or operation.

end consumer
The ultimate beneficiary or the individual or individuals whose needs are satisfied by an operation.

[1]Based on A. Kabodian, *The Customer Is Always Right* (Cambridge, MA: Harvard University Press, 1996).

farmer is the customer of a tractor manufacturer, and the wheat farmer benefits from using the tractor. The flour mill is the customer of the wheat farmer, and the bakery is the customer of the flour mill. In each case, the competencies of the provider match the needs of the adjacent customer, motivating the customer to provide resources (usually money) to help meet the needs of the provider.

internal customers
Customers within a firm such as the users of a company print shop.

Customers are either *internal* or *external customers*. **Internal customers** exist within the same firm as the provider. For example, management information systems technicians view the computer users within their company as internal customers. Accounting departments and finance departments often have very little interaction with the bill-paying customer, but they have customers within the firm who use their services daily. Some have used an abstraction of the term *internal customer* to include the person at the next step in an operation. Therefore, the person who works at workstation 3 can be considered the customer of the worker at workstation 2 because that person is the receiver of workstation 2's work or the next step in the supply chain.

external customers
The outside-of-company end beneficiaries of work.

External customers are the outside-of-our-company end beneficiaries of our work. If we satisfy the needs of external customers more effectively than our competition does, our firm is likely to prosper. Surpassing the competition requires an understanding of the needs of customers, their capabilities, and their willingness to partner with us in meeting their needs. Managing and developing customers is a primary focus of an SC&O customer relationship management system.

CRM can be challenging because customers have unique needs, capabilities, and preferences. Firms can gain advantages by understanding and keeping track of individual customer requirements and by dealing with customers on an individual basis. CRMSs play key roles in obtaining, tracking, and applying customer information, hurdling these challenges, and accomplishing CRM's goals.

UNDERSTANDING CUSTOMER REQUIREMENTS   Manufacturing operations usually have an advantage of homogeneity, meaning that production companies can produce similar products in large quantities. Being able to create large quantities of products gives these companies the benefits of economies of scale, meaning that the fixed costs of production are spread across a lot of items. For example, a pencil manufacturer may produce 100,000 mostly identical pencils in a day. This consistency allows the pencil manufacturer to develop high efficiency and consistent quality.

Service operations are, by definition, dependent on customer resources. Those customer resources usually are *heterogeneous*, meaning that each customer provides unique challenges to the service provider. For example, a law firm may handle dozens of unique legal cases in a month. Even specialized law firms, such as those that focus on bankruptcy, experience a broad range of differences in customer requirements and situations. As a result of these differences, service operations enjoy less in the way of economies of scale and have limited opportunities for increased efficiency.

In mass production, managers can keep track of production requirements at an aggregate level, meaning that they decide how many components or finished items they need over specific time periods. Service production managers need to keep track of production requirements at an item level because each item of production is likely to be different from the next. Service managers gather a lot of information about customers and can use that information to better serve them and be more competitive. That is where CRM and CRMSs come in.

INCREASING CUSTOMER LOYALTY   An important goal of CRM is customer retention. Managers can measure customer retention as the percentage of customers who return for more service. You will learn how to increase retention by applying the tools and concepts we discuss in this chapter, such as data gathering and data analysis. In services, where the customers provide inputs to the provider's processes, managers can control variability by maintaining a stable pool of customers who are familiar with their processes.

value
The extent to which a firm meets customer needs.

Customer loyalty comes from meeting customers' needs in a way that goes above and beyond the competition's methods and creates a "superior customer experience." **Value** can be defined as the extent to which a customer's needs are met. "Superior" value might mean with greater convenience, with higher quality, at a more customized level, or even at lower cost.

Enhancing the Customer Experience at Hilton

CRMSs provide an opportunity for companies to manage the customer experience. Some call this *customer experience management.* Usually, purchasing, bill paying, and customer service are disjointed processes. Through proper systems design, all of these experiences can be made to be seamless and highly personalized.

Hilton has made an art of managing the customer experience using a CRMS. The heart of Hilton's CRMS is its smartphone app. According to Dana Shefsby, Hilton's Director of Digital Product Innovation, the phone is the "remote control for your stay." Guests can check in, choose a room, and even use their phone as a room key.

There are things that Hilton has learned after implementing technology. For example, when selecting rooms, guests have shown that the location of facilities outside the hotel, such as museums, stores, or restaurants, influence decision making.

There is an emotional aspect to customer loyalty. Harley-Davidson is one of the best examples of brand loyalty. After all, how many products induce the kind of loyalty that causes people to tattoo the company logo on their bodies? It is difficult to isolate the ethos that results in this type of customer loyalty; Honda, Yamaha, and Kawasaki don't elicit the same passion. Some automobile brands—the Volkswagen Beetle, the Ford Mustang, the Chevrolet Corvette, and, more recently, some hybrid vehicles—create such high levels of customer loyalty that people attend national expositions and jamborees that center on these products. Another example is designer bags or shoes. Women (and men) put their names on waiting lists and drop thousands of dollars just to be able to carry a bag or shoes with a certain logo, such as Fendi or Jimmy Choo. Being able to do so signals those around them that they not only can afford the products but that they are important enough to own them. The relationship between the providers and the customers still needs to be mutually beneficial, however. Customers must be willing to do their part of the relationship, including providing repeat business and perhaps referring other customers. This customer willingness will result from the beneficial relationship with the provider. SC&O CURRENT EVENTS 5.2 shows how a CRMS has helped Hilton hotels.

CUSTOMIZING DELIVERY All service businesses must accommodate each customer's uniqueness, a ubiquitous CRM challenge. Services challenge management because *customers inject variation into processes.* For example, express-lane grocery checkout times vary significantly, especially when people are ringing up their own items. Too many long waits may send them to a competing grocer. Although variation, such as with wait time, creates management problems, it also creates opportunities, such as customization.

....

Managing Across Majors 5.2 Marketing majors, customization creates additional sales opportunities as you gain a better understanding of customer needs.

....

A common theme in applications of CRM is customization, including target marketing and customized user experience. Customization of product design and configuration can be more difficult and more costly than customized user interactions. For example, it is one thing for an auto dealership to customize interactions with a customer and quite another thing to customize an automobile.

Although custom-manufactured individual items could give customers just what they want, producing them is usually cost prohibitive. Service managers consider variation and customization to be the enemies of efficiency and productivity. Learning and cost reduction often come through repetition. Producing distinct items on an individual basis can hinder economies of scale and learning-curve effects.

mass customization
The process in which standardized components and modules are produced and then assembled or configured only when customers need them.

An alternative to custom manufacturing of items is **mass customization**, the process in which standardized components and modules are produced and then assembled or configured only when customers need them. Dell uses mass customization successfully. Although Dell pioneered Internet ordering of custom configurations of personal computers, the configurations were not truly custom; they were made from standard assemblies. A customer could order perhaps four different sizes of hard drives, but no others. It would not make economic sense to require the custom manufacturing of a hard drive for each customer. With four hard drives, three memory configurations, three processors, five monitors, and two mice, however, there are $4 \times 3 \times 3 \times 5 \times 2 = 360$ different "custom" configurations. This Dell example illustrates the blurry line that separates service processes from processes that are not usually considered to be service processes.

The Taco Bell fast-food chain also practices a form of mass customization. It offers several menu items at very low prices. Taco Bell has only a small number of basic components, however, including tortillas, meat, beans, and cheese, which it centrally produces in a very efficient manner. It dices the tomatoes, shreds the lettuce, processes the beans, cooks the meat, and makes the tortillas at central locations. Although Taco Bell customers can customize their meals, they can choose only from a set number of premade ingredients.

Auto dealers usually provide a range of options for various sound systems, video systems, GPS systems, and so forth. These so-called dealer-installed options allow dealers to configure cars at the dealership based on customer preferences, but customers still need to choose from a preestablished set of options.

CRM Processes

A CRMS must fit within a broad set of CRM processes. Customer loyalty comes from providing a complete range of processes that meet customer needs rather than simply providing a single transaction. For example, a university might focus on discrete processes for improvement in an area such as registration, financial aid, or test taking, but these internal processes are not what keep students at a school. To enhance a student's overall experience, universities are implementing new programs for student retention that focus on developing career and job-search skills and giving them the tools they need for life after school. By addressing student needs outside the realm of the classroom, the university begins to look at the whole system relating to the student and not just internal university processes. These types of programs have helped universities retain students.

FIGURE 5.1 shows some important aspects of process design pertaining to CRM that we will address in the coming pages: customization, preventing service failures (through the use

FIGURE 5.1 >

Components of Customer Relationship Management

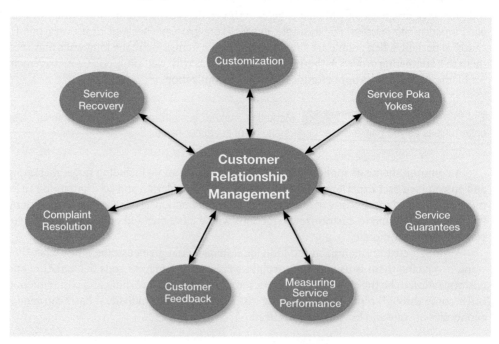

of service poka yokes), guarantees, measuring service performance, customer feedback, complaint resolution, and corrective action or recovery.

 # EARN THE TECHNIQUES TO IMPROVE CUSTOMER SERVICE

The purpose of service process design is to provide excellent customer service. To provide excellent customer service, you must

1. Understand and meet customer expectations.
2. Provide fail-safe services (poka yokes).
3. Provide service guarantees.
4. Measure your performance relative to customer expectations.
5. Manage customer complaints.
6. Recover from service failures.

The following subsections of this chapter cover each of these six topics in more depth.

Understanding and Meeting Customer Expectations

Besides meeting customers' individual needs, SC&O management is concerned with meeting their expectations. The concept of meeting needs is associated with value, and the concept of meeting expectations is associated with quality. For example, a conservative driver might have a strong need for safety and would therefore attribute high value to cars with safety features. That driver might not have a need for quick car acceleration and thus would not value cars with that feature. That driver might still expect a particular sports car to have quick acceleration because high-quality sports cars do have quicker acceleration.

For manufactured items, customers provide their expectations in terms of engineered specifications. In theory, engineers design products based on perceived or assessed customer needs that firms measure through market research. Therefore, quality in manufacturing operations largely means producing items to engineered specification.

Quality in service operations is different from quality in manufacturing operations because of the involvement of customers in the system. Customer involvement has various implications for providing excellent service. First, *each customer may provide his or her own specifications.* For example, what is the appropriate amount of time between when customers finish eating and when a waiter presents the bill at a nice restaurant? Of course, the answer depends on each individual customer. Some customers may expect a quick appearance for the bill, whereas others may consider the quickness a sign that they are being rushed to leave the restaurant.

Second, *customers are often the quality inspectors.* Customers may not articulate their expectations, and they know only if their expectations are not met. Customers are, unfortunately, unreliable inspectors; research has shown that the vast majority of customers who experience a service problem fail to report it. For this reason, firms should have active means of assessing service quality from customers.

Third, *customers are often the cause of service failures.* Firms expect customers to contribute to service production in some way, such as by providing input components or personal effort. (Customer input components were discussed in Chapter 4; examples include dental customers providing their teeth and auto repair customers providing their broken vehicles.) Customers may not understand their role in the service operation, leading to service failure. For example, customers using a self-service checkout station at a grocery store might not understand how to use the technology. Even so, customers tend to blame the service provider for the failure, which may be appropriate if the provider designed the service system inadequately.

Consider, for example, sending packages via FedEx, an overnight delivery service. If packages are misrouted or arrive late, customers will be dissatisfied, even if it is the customer's fault. If a customer provides an invalid address, the delivery is likely to be delayed. It behooves FedEx to provide mechanisms to help avoid inadvertent bad addresses, circumventing customer variance and ensuring that it can meet customer needs as best it can. GLOBAL CONNECTIONS 5.1 discusses difficulties that international air cargo firms experience in trying to satisfy customers.

In recent years, the air cargo industry has experienced a prolonged slump. The industry, with the help of the International Air Transport Association (IATA), sought to improve its performance and relate to its global customers more effectively. According to Tony Tyler, IATA's director general and chief executive officer, "No business or business model survives over the long term without evolving. Air cargo is being buffeted by forces for change. These include changes in the economics of just-in-time manufacturing, longer delivery lead times, innovation by alternative modes of transport and environmental pressures. In the face of these challenges (imposed by customers), air cargo needs to work together as an industry to improve competitiveness and to protect its value proposition."

Tyler also explained that "we need to see air cargo through the eyes of our customers who have high expectations right across the (global) value chain. Air cargo is a premium product. Customers valuing speed or a 100% cool chain need to be certain that their goods will be delivered on time and will be handled appropriately. By working together, I know that we can generate real momentum in the race to drive up quality and (deliver) reliability."

Knowing customers better and using CRM concepts such as those discussed in this chapter can solve these issues.

Source: Based on Tony Tyler, "Partnership to Revitalize Air Cargo." International Air Transport Association, October 17, 2013. http://www.aircargoupdate.com/pdf/2013/nove-dec-2013.pdf.

Providing Fail-Safe Services

The Japanese term *poka yoke* refers to a fail-proof mechanism, or method, for preventing quality failures in manufacturing. In service systems that involve customers, poka yokes can be used to prevent customer failures.

Examples of service poka yokes that deter customer errors include the following:

1. Websites that require users to type their e-mail address twice and thus avoid typographical errors.
2. Automatic teller machines (ATMs) that require users to take their ATM cards before they are given their cash withdrawal to prevent people from forgetting their cards.
3. Parking garages that have a lightweight overhead bar or signal at the entrance to prevent people from entering with tall vehicles that might hit the ceiling in parts of the garage.

The idea behind service poka yokes is to provide a simple mechanism to prevent or reduce the possibility of customer error.

Providing Service Guarantees

Another way to reduce errors is to provide service guarantees. Service guarantees, especially so-called unconditional service guarantees, may be considered a marketing tool, but they can have even bigger effects on ensuring service quality by focusing employee attention on reducing or eliminating the causes of errors. Employees who realize the costs of customers executing the guarantee avoid the cost by improving the service delivery.

Christopher Hart described five essential elements of an unconditional service guarantee:[2]

1. Unconditional, without exceptions
2. Easy to understand and communicate
3. Meaningful (valued by the customer)
4. Easy and painless to invoke
5. Easy to collect

[2]C. W. L. Hart, "The Power of Unconditional Service Guarantees," *Harvard Business Review* 66, no. 4 (1988): 54–63.

Signage that warns truck drivers about clearance heights is an example of a poka yoke. Unfortunately, this particular driver did not heed the warnings, causing this accident.

Of course, unconditional service guarantees are not for all companies. Firms that have perennial quality problems would probably suffer tremendously by introducing a guarantee because they would surely be overwhelmed by customers invoking the guarantee. Companies that are close to providing ideal quality, however, can use a guarantee to motivate continual improvement. One example is Costco. Costco offers a no hassle returns policy on its offerings, which has contributed to the company's success.

Measuring Service Performance

There is a saying that "what gets measured gets managed." It is common for firms to focus their management attention on things that they can measure easily, such as accounting and financial performance, and put less attention on things that are more difficult to measure, such as value realized by customers and customer loyalty. The critical success factors are often these things that are not easily measured. For instance, value provided to customers is not easily measured; we use revenues as an estimate, but revenues are only a rough estimate of the true value we are providing customers.

Managers measure the performance of standard manufacturing processes in terms of the number of items produced, costs of producing the items, and revenues generated by sales. Manufacturers may consider performance measures of throughput (number of items produced per time period), productivity (output per unit of resource, such as per employee), and utilization (percentage of capacity kept occupied in production).

Measuring service performance is much more difficult than measuring manufacturing performance due to the involvement of customers in the production system. Each customer may present different needs, provide different input resources, and have different expectations for the results. Thus, it can be difficult for managers to quantify what is being accomplished in a service production system.

For example, consider how we would measure performance at a law firm. The law firm has various attorneys, and management desires to measure how each attorney performs. One way to measure attorney performance is according to throughput, which we might measure as the number of client cases each attorney handles per week. The problem with this tactic is that each client provides different problems of varying complexity. Although one case may take a week, another case may take three months. Does this variation mean that one attorney is performing better than the other?

In the United States, most law firms evaluate attorney performance according to utilization, measured according to the number of billable hours. A typical law firm might expect attorneys to work 50 hours per week, but the "top" attorneys might bill an average of 60 hours per week, implying 120 percent utilization!

One downside of this utilization approach is that it favors attorneys who are slow and inefficient. In the short run, it can mean more revenue, but in the long run, it may lead to unhappy clients who take their business elsewhere. A similar irony exists in the healthcare industry, where perverse incentives cause hospitals and doctors to perform unnecessary procedures to make more income.

In service systems, it is particularly appropriate to measure performance from customers' perspectives. Law firm clients who are satisfied with the attorney's work are more likely to provide repeat business than clients who are not satisfied. Firms typically measure customer satisfaction by some type of feedback system. Customer feedback systems take many shapes and forms. Some are simple, such as reviewing complaint letters, and others are complex, such as sending out cross-sectional client surveys (surveys that consider the various types of customer segments of the firm). Active-feedback systems involve surveyors personally asking customers for feedback, and passive-feedback systems let customers initiate the feedback, such as by comment cards left in hotel rooms.

satisfaction
The extent to which customer needs are met.

loyalty
The feeling of affiliation a customer has with a firm.

Measures we expect out of a customer feedback system might include *satisfaction* and *loyalty*. **Satisfaction** means meeting customer needs (why the customer engaged the firm) or meeting or exceeding expectations (what the customer previously thought the service would or should provide). **Loyalty** is the feeling of affiliation with the firm or to future behavior that favors the firm, which includes repurchases or referring the service to others.

It is not uncommon for firms to try so hard to gather detailed information that they wind up with feedback that is of little value. For example, firms may want to identify where problems occur in different aspects of the service process by asking customers to rate the performance of numerous areas of the service operation. Firms should not be surprised when the collected data are incomplete because many customers are not willing to complete a long survey.

Research has shown that the vast majority—as much as 96 percent—of unhappy customers complain with their feet (they just leave) rather than with their voice (provide feedback). To retain their customers, firms must identify ways of improving the ability to collect and act on customer feedback.

net promoter score (NPS)
A service feedback rating system.

A simple feedback system that has become popular in recent years is the **net promoter score (NPS)**. This system asks customers a single question: "How likely is it that you would recommend our company to a friend or colleague?" Responses are on an 11-point scale (including zero):

Not at all   Extremely
likely   Neutral   likely
0…..1…..2…..3…..4…..5…..6…..7…..8…..9…..10

The responses are split into three categories:

1. 0 through 6 are the detractors, those who likely will not return
2. 7 and 8 are neutral
3. 9 and 10 are the promoters, those who are likely to promote the firm

$$\text{NPS} = \# \text{ number of promoters} - \# \text{ number of detractors} \tag{5.1}$$

Managers calculate the NPS for a given time period by subtracting the number of detractors from the number of promoters (neutrals are left out of the calculation). For example, if an attorney had 20 clients over a given quarter with 5 promoters, 12 neutrals, and 3 detractors, the net promoter score would be $5 - 3 = 2$. Firms can then compare net promoter scores for an attorney over time to assess changes in performance. **SOLVED PROBLEM 5.1** and USING TECHNOLOGY 5.1 address how hospitals can use this system.

In addition to surveys, social websites and online reviews are important forums for customer feedback. Sometimes the online review systems are set up by the companies that are

Net Promoter Scores in Action

< SOLVED PROBLEM 5.1

Problem: In January, a hospital administered a net promoter score survey to 18 patients as they were leaving the hospital. The following is a table with scores given by the patients:

MyLab Operations Management
Video

3	2	1
2	1	10
5	4	10
7	5	1
10	6	1
10	2	10

Compute the net promoter score for the hospital.

Solution: Observing the above data, there are 5 promoters (scores 9 and 10) and 12 detractors (scores 0 through 6). Using Equation 5.1, we have NPS $= 5 - 12 = -7$. Management must perform a study to see why the score is so low.

selling products and services, and sometimes they are run independently from the companies being reviewed. Either way, online platforms can be an important means for gathering customer feedback, as discussed in SC&O CURRENT EVENTS 5.3.

Managing Customer Complaints

Abraham Lincoln reportedly said, "You can please some of the people some of the time, all of the people some of the time, and some of the people all of the time, but you can never please all of the people all of the time." Because customer happiness can be elusive and hard won, complaint resolution is an important component of a quality management system.

Solving Net Promoter Score Problem Using Excel

< USING
TECHNOLOGY 5.1

FIGURE 5.2 contains the NPS data from Solved Problem 5.1. The survey data are given in the matrix in cells A2 through C7. To compute the NPS, use the *countif* command in Excel. People providing a score of 9 or 10 (> 8) are promoters. People providing a score of 6 or less (< 7) are detractors. Thus, promoter (D9) − detractor (D10) = NPS (E11).

	A	B	C	D	E	F	G
1	**Net Promoter Score Example**						
2	3	2	1				
3	2	1	10				
4	5	4	10				
5	7	5	1				
6	10	6	1		=COUNTIF(A2:C7,">8")		
7	10	2	10				
8							
9			Promoters:	5	=COUNTIF(A2:C7,"<7")		
10			Detractors:	12			
11			Net Promoter Score:	−7	=D9−D10		
12							

^ FIGURE 5.2

Net Promoter Score Calculation in Excel

Online Reviews of Merchandise

Consumers have multiple avenues to express their opinions about products and services they receive: Facebook, Twitter, YouTube, blogs, and so on. Online reviews can provide valuable insight about a product. A survey by E-tailing Group found that 71 percent of online shoppers believed that customer reviews were the most influential factor when buying online.* Online reviews are another opportunity for retailers to gain customer feedback. Instead of scouring the Internet for the information, retailers have created online reviews on their websites.

There are pros and cons to online reviews. Product reviews have been shown to boost loyalty and sales with customers and are overwhelmingly positive. By receiving nearly instantaneous feedback, retailers and designers can respond more quickly to quality issues. Online customers are able to learn about products without seeing and touching them. Some retailers believe that online reviews reduce return rates and increase "conversion," the percentage of browsers who actually buy.

On the downside, there is the potential of a negative review. Leaving reviews up to any user can prove to be unpredictable. As designer Carmen Marc Valvo said, "Style is a very subjective matter."[†] In some industries, such as fashion, producers would prefer leaving the reviews to the experts.

As online sales increase, elite luxury stores such as Neiman Marcus and Nordstrom are changing their tune and are embracing online reviews. Nordstrom was the first in the industry to offer online reviews by adding product reviews to its website. Neiman Marcus has taken a modified approach by only allowing an elite group of customers to post reviews. Luxury stores are known for customer interaction, and they realize that online reviews are a new component of providing quality customer service.

Customers want an objective voice, and reviews give them that. In the end, elite stores may have different motivations for adding online reviews. Some may want the direct customer feedback, and others may do it in an attempt to boost sales.

*http://media2.bazaarvoice.com/documents/Bazaarvoice_Conversation_Index_Volume6.pdf
[†] http://online.wsj.com/news/articles/SB10001424052702304250404575558393667645672

Complaints come in many forms. At least three types of complaints need to be addressed: (1) regulatory complaints from regulatory government agencies, (2) employee complaints, and (3) customer complaints. Although the focus of this chapter is on the customer, it is important to recognize all three types of complaints as potential sources of information for improvement.

Donald Beaver, co-founder of New Pig Corporation, a producer of absorbents in Tipton, Pennsylvania, has a positive attitude about complaints. He states: "You should love complaints more than compliments. A complaint is someone letting you know that you haven't satisfied them yet. They have gold written all over them."[3] Complaints should be viewed as opportunities to improve. Because only a small percentage of customers ultimately complain, they should be taken very seriously. This small percentage of customers may represent a much larger population of dissatisfied customers.

Recovering from Service Failures

Manufacturing operations include elements of quality control to ensure that they produce items according to specifications. Items will often go through component and finished-goods testing to identify problems before items are shipped to customers. Customers

[3]Whiteley, Richard, *A Customer-Driven Company: Moving from Talk to Action* (New York: Perseus Books, 1991), p. 39.

usually have no idea how many times a firm reworks an item before the customers purchase it, and they may not care. What is important to customers is that the finished item performs as expected.

Quality problems that occur in service operations are often harder to handle than those in manufacturing industries because of customer involvement in the production system. A service failure usually means that not only did the service fail to meet expectations but additional damage was incurred vis-à-vis the customer. It is usually not enough to simply bring the service into specification. Attention should be given to the potential damage to the customer, including attitudinal costs. For example, a child in England lost a tooth biting into a take-out pizza that was still in the cooking pan. Replacing the pizza, or even replacing the tooth, does not seem to compensate the child for pain and suffering adequately.

Service recovery efforts demonstrate how firms respond to service failures. **Service failures** are systemic occurrences that result in dissatisfied customers. If managers do not plan service recovery carefully but instead provide recovery on an ad hoc basis, customers will be confused at what may appear to be seemingly random responses to problems. Effective companies plan service recovery as part of their operations, which includes (1) identifying where failures are likely to occur, (2) identifying how failures are detected and reported, and (3) determining how they should be managed. Customers may be frustrated when the only way to get help with a service problem is to demand to talk to a manager. Managers should instruct frontline employees in service recovery procedures and empower them to provide direct and speedy recovery as appropriate. Examples of service recovery are given in **SC&O CURRENT EVENTS 5.4**.

It has been suggested that CRMSs can provide predictive analytics to anticipate problems. One example is at Wells Fargo Bank, where bank employees had fraudulently opened 1.5 million accounts without customer authorization. According to Joe Salesky, "An effective CRMS would have provided the information necessary to show that customers were given products that didn't fit."

service recovery
A process for responding to service failures.

service failures
Systemic occurrences that result in dissatisfied customers.

Service Recovery

< **SC&O CURRENT EVENTS 5.4**

The following are two examples of attempts at service recovery. One has a positive outcome, and one ended a customer's patronage at a particular restaurant.

A mother took her six children to a health clinic for their annual immunization shots. A few days later, the clinic's receptionist called to report that the clinic had given the children an insufficient immunization dosage and that the six children needed to return to receive the remainder of the dosage. The mother responded, "So, who is going to buy the ice cream?" Met with confusion, she explained to the receptionist, "There is no way I am going to get the kids back over there unless someone buys ice cream as consolation." The clinic not only offered to buy ice cream for those six children but also called back the other affected patients and gave them the same offer. Thus, a service failure was turned into a neutral experience and possibly even a positive experience (for the kids).

Some time ago, the same woman went to a nice Italian restaurant for a business dinner. When the food arrived, her meal had a piece of cardboard mixed in with the pasta. When she brought it to the waiter's attention, the waiter apologized and offered to bring a fresh plate of pasta. The time delay a new plate would cause meant that the customer would not eat with the rest of her group. Then, the waiter offered to take the offending pasta off the bill, which was of little personal consolation to the woman because the food was covered by a business expense account. Without a satisfactory resolution, the customer didn't feel the desire to return to the restaurant. Perhaps if the waiter had offered some free ice cream, she may have have felt differently.

CHANGE RELATIONSHIPS THROUGH SERVITIZATION

servitization
The process of integrating service offerings with manufactured products.

forward integration
When a firm moves forward in the supply chain not only to provide products but also to help customers with the use of the products.

Even product manufacturing systems ultimately lead to interactions with customers. Customers may need help using products, or products may fail in some way. Some manufacturers leave the task of supporting customers' use of products to third-party firms. For example, mechanics and dealerships, not auto manufacturers, perform most auto repair. Even if auto manufacturers provide product warranties, they do not do the actual work.

In recent years, a topic catching a lot of attention is **servitization**, which occurs as manufacturing firms begin to provide service in conjunction with their products. Servitization redefines the firms' relationship with its customers. Firms that provide such service move closer to customers by expanding their operations to include more interaction with customers. In one sense, servitization is a form of **forward integration**, meaning that the firm moves forward in the supply chain to not only provide products but also help customers with the use of the products. An example of servitization is provided in GLOBAL CONNECTIONS 5.2.

For example, IBM has long been a manufacturer of computer hardware and software. In a move that illustrates servitization, IBM purchased the consulting arm of Pricewaterhousecoopers to create a new IBM Global Services (IGS) consulting division. IGS consults on the use of IBM hardware and software as well as on the use of equipment produced by other companies.

Xerox has provided servicing and repairs for its copy machines for many years. Xerox not only leases copy machines to customers but also includes technology in the machines so that it can identify problems and even call the Xerox office if a repair technician is needed. This service frees customers from having to worry about the ongoing maintenance of their copy machines. Servitization can also provide benefits to manufacturing companies, which may be under price competition from foreign manufacturers. Servitization allows manufacturers to realize new revenue streams in a related line of business.

An example of a firm that has successfully employed servitization is Apple, Inc. For many years, Apple (or Apple Computer, as it was called) developed and produced computers and related software. Apple moved into online media retail (the Apple Music Store) and physical retail (Apple retail stores). These shifts have given Apple closer ties to customers and tremendous revenue advantages.

Unfortunately, servitization can also be perilous. Sometimes, manufacturing firms that move into related services find it difficult to maintain the profitability they were accustomed to. Dr. Andrew Neeley of Cambridge University in England did a study of 10,028 firms and

**GLOBAL >
CONNECTIONS 5.2**

Servitization at Rolls-Royce

In some cases, manufacturers stop selling the products they manufacture and move to leasing and operating the products for clients. An example is Rolls-Royce, which manufactures jet engines. In the past, Rolls-Royce would sell jet engines to be included in the sale of a jet (such as by Boeing). Lately, though, Rolls-Royce has been instead leasing engines to airlines, charging the airlines for actual use. Under this arrangement, Rolls-Royce is responsible for servicing the engines, including maintenance and repairs.

According to Steve Friedrich, Rolls-Royce's vice president of sales and marketing, civil small and medium engines: "We are proud to celebrate . . . service excellence (at) Rolls-Royce. The customer focus and pioneering approach of 'Power-by-the-Hour' remains at the heart of our CorporateCare program. We continuously seek to enhance our level of service, and this year have significantly expanded our authorized service network and introduced new technologies to improve our Aircraft on Ground responsiveness."

Source: Based on Bartlett, P., "Rolls Royce Negotiating with Key Clients on Power by the Hour." *Seatrade Maritime News*, 8 Sept. 2016.

found that firms that employed servitization were 2.6 times as likely to go bankrupt as those that stayed just in product manufacturing.[4] He also found that, although "servitized firms generate higher revenues[,] they tend to generate lower net profits as a percent[age] of revenues than pure manufacturing firms."

There are various possible explanations for the difficulties firms encounter in servitization. Even though the firms may understand their products, they may not understand the intricacies of managing customer interactions. Also, as we have discussed, the involvement of customers in the service functions can hamper productivity and utilization. Firms that are able to employ servitization successfully, however, can have tremendous competitive advantage.

ANAGE SERVICE SUPPLY CHAINS

Like product supply chains, services often involve a variety of firms working together to meet customer needs. Service operations rely on product supply chains that provide resources used in service delivery. For example, healthcare services depend on complex supply chains to provide pharmaceuticals and equipment used in healthcare delivery.

Service supply chains are different from manufactured product supply chains in some fundamental ways. First, by definition, services involve processing customer resources, making service customers the suppliers. Because customers are also the suppliers, service supply chains are bidirectional, meaning that customers provide resources to service firms and service firms then provide processed resources back to customers. FIGURE 5.3 shows a simple example of a dry-cleaning service supply chain. The customer provides a dirty and damaged garment to the dry-cleaning firm. The dry cleaner does not repair garments, but it outsources that work to a seamstress.

Second, service supply chains tend to be shorter than product supply chains. A given product supply chain can involve many levels of suppliers. Consider the plastic door handle of a car. It began with an oil-drilling operation that produced crude oil, which was refined and processed into plastic resin, delivered in pellets, and shipped to a parts manufacturer, who melted down the pellets and produced a handle with injection molding, which was sent to an auto manufacturer,

service supply chains
Collaboration between service providers and customers to create value.

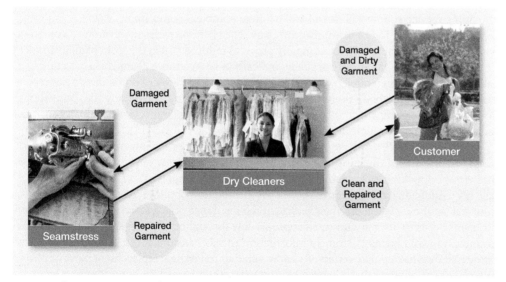

< FIGURE 5.3

A Dry-Cleaning Service Supply Chain

Source: Based on Sampson, S. E., and Spring, M., 2012. "Customer Roles in Service Supply Chains and Opportunities for Innovation." *Journal of Supply Chain Management*, Vol. 48, No. 4.

[4]A. Neely, "Exploring the Financial Consequences of the Servitization of Manufacturing," *Operations Management Research* 1, no. 2 (2008): 103.

FIGURE 5.4 >

**An Auto Insurance
Service Supply Chain**

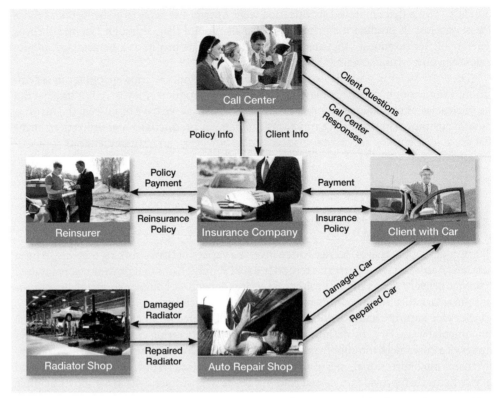

Source: Based on Sampson, S. E., and Spring, M., 2012. "Customer Roles in Service Supply Chains and Opportunities for Innovation." *Journal of Supply Chain Management*, Vol. 48, No. 4.

who put it on a door and shipped the door (with the car) to a dealer, who sold it to a customer. When we compare that process to the service supply chain of a customer bringing his or her car to an auto shop to get a broken door handle replaced, we see that the interactive service supply chain is quite short. That door repair supply chain involves the customer as a supplier of the broken handle, the auto shop as the provider firm, and the customer as the recipient of the repaired handle—only two participants in this simple service supply chain.

Some service supply chains can still be quite complex. For example, **FIGURE 5.4** shows a service supply chain for an insurance company. The client provides the insurance company with payment, and the insurance company provides reduced risk in the form of an insurance policy. A client who has an auto accident and calls in an insurance claim is likely to talk to a call center that has been hired by the insurance company. Insurance companies do not repair cars; rather, local auto body shops handle repairs for insurance claims. Many auto body shops do only superficial repairs and have other repair shops handle mechanical repairs such as radiator repair. This example illustrates the complexity that can exist in a service supply chain.

Service supply chains have more apparent opportunities for integration than product supply chains due to the customer–firm interaction of services. This means that there are numerous opportunities for gathering and using customer information to tailor the service delivery to individual customer needs, which is the function of CRMS. As shown in Figure 5.4, information about customers, their vehicles, their insurance policies, and their accident claim problems needs to be communicated appropriately throughout the service supply chain. For example, to avoid giving customers information that is inaccurate, the call center needs to know exactly what a policy covers. To know whether to use new replacement parts or refurbished parts, the auto body shop needs to know the conditions of the coverage contract.

One method for handling customer complaints and questions is called a service script. **Service scripts** are detailed guides for employees to follow during a service encounter. Encounters such as bank teller interactions are tightly scripted because they are repetitive and standardized. Other interactions such as a visit to a doctor or an auto shop are very loosely scripted; that is, they involve much more customization on the part of the service provider.

service scripts
Detailed service encounter guides for use by service providers.

As discussed at the beginning of the chapter, Amazon is perfecting how to understand its customer needs. Unfortunately, Amazon is a rare case. "With the Internet, companies are still pretty bad about presenting a single face to the customer," says Jeet Singh, chief executive officer of ATG, Inc., based in Cambridge, Massachusetts. "The Internet has blown the multiple touch point issue to the forefront, and in many firms, the left hand doesn't know what the right hand is doing." Many times, customers have to send e-mails or call people who do not have adequate information, making good customer service difficult.

"This situation is driving interest to new customer relationship management approaches with environments that can offer greater central control or management," says Karen Smith, senior analyst with the Boston-based Aberdeen Group. "Organizations are demanding CRM solutions that provide greater visibility into asset management, forecasting and inventory management, product development, procurement, and order and transaction management."

From the corporate side, companies deal with a lot of customers. Knowing everything they need to know is impossible without a CRMS. According to Michael Levin, chief executive officer of e-Steel, "This is not like a cruise line for singles to meet[;] it's a cruise line for couples to have a great time." These complex relationships can happen in the B2B or B2C worlds. Companies who perfect this approach, such as Amazon.com, will win.

Source: Based on "Relationships: Priceless Assets in the Customer Economy," *Businessweek*, www .businessweek.com/adsections/crm/, 2013.

Summary

In this chapter, we discussed customer relationship management, particularly as it relates to SC&O management.

1. We introduced customer relationship management systems and customer relationship management.
   a. CRMSs are information systems for acquiring customers, enhancing relationships with customers, and retaining customers. The broader area of CRM has to do with designing and delivering successful interactions that satisfy customers' needs, including understanding customer requirements to satisfy needs and promote customer loyalty. Sometimes it involves customizing the offering so that customers with different needs can each have needs satisfied.
2. This chapter reviewed ways for improving customer service and meeting customer expectations.
   a. An example is service poka yokes, which are methods for preventing quality failures.
   b. The chapter also reviewed issues surrounding service performance measurement, which is essential to performance improvement. Even well-designed service systems can fail, and service recovery techniques can reduce the negative effects of failure.

3. Manufacturing firms can enhance customer relationships through servitization, wherein manufacturers provide services in conjunction with their products.

4. Finally, this chapter discussed service supply chains, wherein customers are both providers of key process resources and recipients of process results.

Key Terms

acquisition   123
customer   123
customer relationship management
   (CRM)   121
customer relationship management
   systems (CRMSs)   121
end consumer   123
enhancement   123

external customers   124
forward integration   134
internal customers   124
loyalty   130
mass customization   126
net promoter score (NPS)   130
predictive analytics   121
retention   123

satisfaction   130
service failures   133
service recovery   133
service script   136
service supply chains   135
servitization   134
value   124

Integrative Learning Exercise

Think of a time when you experienced a service failure and complained to the service provider. Answer the following questions:
- What was the failure, and how were your expectations not met?
- What was the effect of the failure on your attitude about the service provider?
- Did the service provider offer any recovery?
- What did the provider's action (or inaction) have on your attitude about the provider and on your likelihood of repurchase?

Now assume that you are the team leader for a consulting group that is charged with designing, developing, and implementing an organization's system for customer relations management. Develop an outline of the opportunities you believe that such a system will provide the organization, the challenges inherent in developing the system, and the issues related to implementing and using the system. Be sure to identify the necessary inputs and support staff for the system. What information will be needed? How will it be collected and managed? How will the system improve customer retention?

Integrative Experiential Exercise

As part of a student team, identify a company or an organization in your area that has a customer relationship management system. Visit the company to find out about its system and how it was developed. How has the system helped the organization better understand its customers, both internal and external, and their requirements? Does the system utilize social media? Has it improved the organization's relationship with its customers, and if so, how? Also identify areas where the existing system might be improved.

Discussion Questions

1. Briefly describe the purpose of customer relationship management (CRM).

2. Is CRM primarily focused on upstream or downstream activities in the supply chain?

3. What are the differences between internal and external customers?

4. Why might manufacturing operations have an advantage over service operations in understanding the needs of external customers?

5. How is customer loyalty related to value?

6. How does the uniqueness of each customer present a challenge to customer relationship management?

7. Why might a manufacturing firm select mass customization rather than custom manufacturing as a strategy?

8. Briefly discuss the three general categories of applications of customer relationship management systems (CRMSs).

9. In what ways does customer involvement in service operations affect the quality of service?

10. What is a service poka yoke?

11. Identify some of the essential elements of an unconditional service guarantee.

12. What is meant by the term *service recovery*?

13. Briefly define the term *servitization*.

14. How does servitization redefine a firm's relationship with its customers?

15. In what ways do service supply chains differ from manufacturing supply chains?

Solved Problem

Improving Customer Service

NET PROMOTER SCORE
SOLVED PROBLEM 5.1

1. A rental car agency at an airport administered a net promoter score survey to customers returning rented automobiles. The following scores were tabulated for 15 customers:

5	9	5	3	7	4	2	7	7	2
		7	6	3	3	2			

Compute the net promoter score for the rental car agency.

Solution:
From the above data, we find 1 promoter (scores 9 and 10) and 10 detractors (scores 0 through 6). Therefore, using formula 5.1, NPS = 1 − 10 = −9. Root cause analysis should be employed to see why the score is so low.

Problems

Improving Customer Service

NET PROMOTER SCORE

1. A small coffee shop administered a net promoter score survey to 17 customers. Here are the results of the survey:

6	4	1
10	5	3
8	5	5
10	1	0
3	6	8
10	6	

Compute the NPS for the coffee shop.

2. A regional airline administered a net promoter score survey to 28 passengers traveling between Bozeman, Montana, and Boise, Idaho. Here are the results of the survey:

6	10	5	5
8	7	8	8
10	3	4	4
8	6	3	3
3	4	7	7
7	3	3	3
8	1	2	2

Compute the NPS for the airline.

3. A net promoter score survey was given to users of an Internet site following an online purchase. Here are the results of the survey:

8	7
9	1
4	7
2	5
6	9
3	8
5	1
2	5
3	9

Compute the NPS for the Internet site and make a recommendation to management.

Can CRM Help a New Start-Up Business?

Things were finally starting to fall into place for Cindy Gonzales. Cindy had graduated from the local university with a degree in marketing during a time when many companies were reducing their employee count to save costs during a recent recession. Consequently, she struggled to find a full-time position with a large company in its marketing function. Because Cindy had majored in marketing, she thought that she would have a long career as a marketing or customer service representative for a well-established company. After searching diligently for more than two years and taking short-term internships to gain experience, Cindy thought that perhaps now was the time to start her own business. With some start-up money borrowed from her family, she devoted herself full-time to her own company: selling and delivering assorted baby products to customers.

Although her business started slowly at first, word of her product offerings began to spread, and within a few months Cindy's products and services were being demanded by individuals and day-care center directors who appreciated her product line and dependable delivery service. Although it was a great problem to have, she was becoming overwhelmed by all the activities she had to coordinate to make her business operate. Cindy excelled at the marketing, but she was finding that there was more to operating her business than just selling the products. There were issues with scheduling product deliveries, meeting potential and existing customers, identifying new product offerings, and dealing with issues such as accounting and paying bills. Cindy realized that she could no longer run her business with simply a personal calendar and a notebook. Even the marketing responsibility was growing too fast for her to manage. She was struggling just to respond to customer e-mails, and she was no longer sure how to announce the availability of a new product or service in a way that reached the right target market. She also needed to develop a better delivery schedule for her customers. As her service area began to expand beyond her immediate neighborhood, she realized that she needed to control delivery costs while still maintaining dependable delivery times. She had just opened her e-mail when she realized she could spend the rest of the day and most of tomorrow answering the messages she currently had in her inbox. In addition, she had meetings with suppliers and larger customers (primarily day-care centers) that she could not miss or be late for. She was also beginning to understand that not every customer contributed the same profitability to her business, but she had not yet determined which customers were making her money and which ones might be costing her. Cindy clearly needed help.

Questions:

1. You are Cindy's friend, and you have recently studied customer relationship management, so she has asked you if there is anything that CRM could do to help her small business. Specifically, are there systems that could better manage her e-mail, appointment scheduling, accounting, and even general customer relationships (e.g., corresponding with customers, getting new product announcements out to the correct customers)? She even wondered if something like Facebook or Twitter could help her business.

2. You plan to meet Cindy this coming weekend for pizza and a movie, and she hopes that you will have some recommendations for her. She also knows that there is no perfect customer relationship management system, so she will probably ask you about any downside to the recommendations you make. What advice will you give her?

Part 3

Impacting Supply Chain and Operations Performance

6 Strategic Sourcing

INTEGRATING — GLOBAL SC&O STRATEGY

INNOVATING

Supply Management | **Operations Management** | **Customer Relationship Management**

IMPACTING

Upstream Processes | Core Processes | Downstream Processes

IMPROVING — QUALITY MANAGEMENT, ANALYTICS, AND LOGISTICS

CHAPTER OUTLINE AND LEARNING OBJECTIVES

① Understand the Origins of the Purchasing Profession
- Learn the evolution of purchasing as a field.

② Describe the Impact of Strategic Sourcing on a Firm
- Explain the importance of reducing the cost of purchased products and services.
- Explain the importance of the quality of goods and services.
- Describe the cost of development and design.

③ Apply the Portfolio Approach to Strategic Sourcing
- Apply category segmentation.
- Describe how managers use routine items, leverage items, bottleneck items, and critical items to manage procurement costs.

④ Master the Tools of Strategic Cost Management
- Understand when best to conduct and apply spend analysis, price analysis, cost analysis, and total cost of ownership analysis.
- Apply total cost of ownership analysis when making outsourcing decisions.

Supplier Management at Lenovo

China's Lenovo was once a small player in the PC market with only Chinese customers. Today, Lenovo is a global player with 25 percent of the world market. How has Lenovo done this? Most of its improvement has come through better supplier collaboration and management.

Like many Chinese firms, Lenovo has a strong regional and worldwide supplier base. With many regional suppliers, it deals with many of the same issues that other international firms experience: quality creep, environmental issues, and labor issues. In response, Lenovo has created an 11-point supplier code of conduct:

- Procurement values and ethical dealings
- Human rights
- Supply chain working conditions
- Climate change
- Environmental impact
- Conflict minerals
- Nondiscrimination and nonretaliation
- Supplier diversity
- Public sustainability reports and policies
- Supply chain due diligence
- Grievance notifications

In addition to the emphasis on sustainable policies, Lenovo is working with suppliers to make sure that employees are treated well and that materials used in production are safe. Lenovo also works with suppliers to make sure that firmware used in its products is current and that processes are efficient and result in high quality.

This chapter introduces strategic sourcing and discusses many key issues in finding great suppliers. We will return to Lenovo at the end of the chapter.

The process of procuring the external materials and services that firms need in the operation's transformation process has changed dramatically over the past few decades. As noted in a recent *Wall Street Journal* article, purchasing managers, "once lowly bureaucrats, are shifting onto the front lines."[1] The reason for this shift is clear. Strategic sourcing managers have demonstrated the ability to drive cost savings for their firms, affect product and service quality for their customers, and help improve product and process designs with their suppliers.

Strategic sourcing is defined as the process of planning, evaluating, implementing, and controlling both highly important and routine sourcing decisions. In this chapter, we discuss the evolution from traditional, tactical purchasing to strategic sourcing, the potential effect

strategic sourcing
The process of planning, evaluating, implementing, and controlling both highly important and routine sourcing decisions.

---

[1]Timothy Aeppel, "Global Scramble for Goods Gives Corporate Buyers a Lift," *Wall Street Journal*, Oct. 2, 2007, A1.

of sourcing on a firm's bottom line, and tools that supply managers use when categorizing and analyzing sourcing spend (or purchasing expenditures). We will continue our sourcing discussion in Chapter 7 by exploring the critical steps in the supplier management process.

UNDERSTAND THE ORIGINS OF THE PURCHASING PROFESSION

procurement, purchasing, materials, sourcing, and supply management
Synonyms for the process of buying and working with suppliers.

purchasing agent, purchasing manager, buyer, and supply manager
Synonyms for people who work in purchasing.

The organization within the firm that is responsible for acquiring goods and services from suppliers has been known by many names, including **procurement**, **purchasing**, **materials**, **sourcing**, and **supply management**. The people working in these organizations have likewise been given various titles, including **purchasing agent**, **purchasing manager**, **buyer**, and **supply manager**. Regardless of the label, these organizations and the people working within them are responsible for interacting with suppliers to secure the supply of incoming goods and services needed to produce a final good or service for the customer.

We see the first mention of someone working in a procurement role in the 1800s, when in 1832 Charles Babbage referred to the importance of purchasing and the role of a "materials man."[2] The first book dedicated exclusively to the purchasing function, *The Handling of Railway Supplies—Their Purchase and Disposition,* was subsequently published in 1887. During the early 1900s, industrial purchasing expanded beyond the railroad, and basic purchasing procedures were developed. During both World War I and World War II, an emphasis on obtaining scarce materials led to more interest in the purchasing function; colleges began to offer courses on this subject; and a professional purchasing organization, the National Association of Purchasing Agents, was formed. The importance of purchasing started to grow with the need to manage inventories and quality better, and purchasing managers are now required to "add value." TABLE 6.1 summarizes the evolution of the purchasing profession.

Most firms now look to their procurement functions to provide a competitive advantage by driving cost savings for the firm and providing an uninterrupted supply of the needed products and services of the right quality by selecting and developing the right suppliers. The focus is on a more collaborative approach with key suppliers to develop an integrated supply chain. SC&O CURRENT EVENTS 6.1 shows how one firm is improving communication with its suppliers.

TABLE 6.1 >

Evolution of the Purchasing Profession	
Era	**Focus**
The early years (1850–1910)	Develop basic purchasing procedures.
The war years (1910–1946)	Obtain scarce materials.
Post–World War II (1947–1970)	Reduce prices and meet customer demand.
Global competition (1970–1999)	Add value through better-managed inventories and good-quality materials, along with reducing cost and meeting customer demand.
The new millennium (2000 to the present)	Provide a competitive advantage by driving cost savings for the firm and ensuring an uninterrupted supply of materials. Develop collaborative relationships to achieve an integrated supply chain.

[2]C. Babbage, *On the Economy of Machinery and Manufacturers,* 2nd ed. (London: Charles Knight, 1832), 202, as reported in H. Fearon, "History of Purchasing," *Journal of Purchasing,* Feb. 1968, 44.

< SC&O CURRENT
EVENTS 6.1

Technology Is Changing the Game for ClearOrbit and Its Supply Chain Partners

Procurement is moving from a purely tactical function of cost savings to a more strategic contributor and is becoming more "strategic-minded." Specifically, in addition to cost savings, respondents to a research survey identified three areas in which procurement is making an impact: (1) managing working capital, (2) managing risks to business performance, and (3) expanding into new markets or business lines.

"The opportunity for procurement to contribute to the company's strategic agenda has never been greater," said Tim Minahan, Chief Marketing Officer of Ariba. But to do this, they must forge an even closer alliance with finance and further automate key commerce processes—from sourcing and order through invoice and working-capital management—both within the enterprise and across their supply chain.

ClearOrbit has embraced information technology to improve and automate internal processes for itself, its suppliers, and its customers. Its products emphasize real-time supply chain enabling solutions, such as supplier collaboration applications, automated returns, and warehouse management tools. One of ClearOrbit's partners recently reported a 50 percent increase in warehouse efficiency through the use of ClearOrbit's technology, realizing an immediate benefit and return on investment. And smart sourcing managers know that money saved by one member of the supply chain benefits all members of the supply chain.

Sources: Based on "Technology Changes Game for Procurement," *BusinessWire*, April 17, 2012; http://www.businesswire .com/news/home/20120417005132/en/Technology-Game-Procurement#.U-pznlBdXmw; ClearOrbit Rolls Up More Supply Chain IT Processes 2009, http://pharmaceuticalcommerce.com/information-technology/clearorbit-rolls-up-more-supply-chain-it-processes/.

....

Managing Across Majors 6.1 Strategy students, purchasing has become strategic as companies have realized the benefits of improved sourcing.

....

ESCRIBE THE EFFECT OF STRATEGIC SOURCING ON A FIRM

Purchased goods and services make up 50 to 90 percent of a firm's cost of goods sold.[3] With the responsibility for such a large percentage of cost of goods sold, a procurement organization and its supply managers have a tremendous opportunity to affect the profitability of a firm. That effect can be seen in the cost of purchased products and services, the quality of purchased goods and services, and the cost built into the product or service during development and design.

Reducing the Cost of Purchased Products and Services

The first and most obvious effect that a sourcing manager has on profitability is through the cost of purchased products and services. In fact, a small change in the cost of purchased products and services can have a more significant effect on profits than a large change in sales, as illustrated in **SOLVED PROBLEM 6.1**.

[3]M. L. Emiliani, "Historical Lessons in Purchasing and Supplier Relationship Management," *Journal of Management History*, 16, no. 1 (2010): 116–136.

SOLVED PROBLEM 6.1 >   **Economics of Purchasing**

MyLab Operations Management
Video

Problem: SmileBright Company has decided to hire a new college graduate. Alicia, the purchasing manager, and Samantha, the sales manager, have both submitted requests to hire the new person into their respective departments. Both managers need someone to work on a new electric toothbrush for the company called the Plaque Attack. Plaque Attack is currently projected to have annual sales of $3,000,000, annual materials costs of $2,000,000, and net income of $180,000 (FIGURE 6.1).

FIGURE 6.1 >

Initial Financial Estimates for Plaque Attack

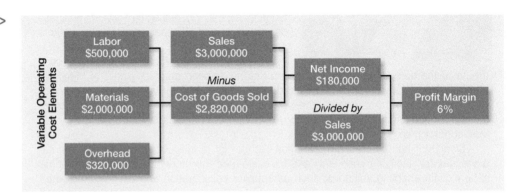

Solution: Alicia estimates that a buyer focused on this product would be able to reduce the cost of materials by 5 percent. Samantha, on the other hand, estimates that a new salesperson could increase the sales of Plaque Attack by 20 percent. Despite the apparent advantage that a new salesperson would have over a new buyer, management has decided to assign the resource based on the estimated effect on profitability.

Let's take the sales perspective first (scenario A). SmileBright currently has a profit margin of 6 percent ($180,000/$3,000,000) on Plaque Attack, which means that for every dollar sold, an additional $0.06 is added to profit. Therefore, if a new salesperson is able to increase sales by 20 percent, an additional $600,000 ($3,000,000 × 20 percent) of Plaque Attack will be sold, and $36,000 ($600,000 × 6 percent) will be added to profits. With profits of $216,000, the profit margin remains at 6 percent (FIGURE 6.2).

Now let's see how a new buyer for the same product might affect the bottom line (scenario B). In this case, we assume no increase in sales but rather a reduction in the cost of materials. If a new buyer is able to reduce the cost of materials by 5 percent, she would save the company $100,000 ($2,000,000 × 5 percent). All $100,000 would go to the bottom line, making the net income $280,000 and increasing the profit margin to 9.3 percent (FIGURE 6.3).

Looking at the two scenarios, we see that sales would need to increase by 56 percent ($100,000 additional profit divided by the profit margin of 6 percent = $1,666,667 in additional sales) to have the same effect on profit as a 5 percent decrease in the cost of

FIGURE 6.2 >

Scenario A for Plaque Attack

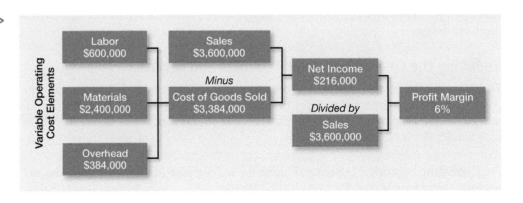

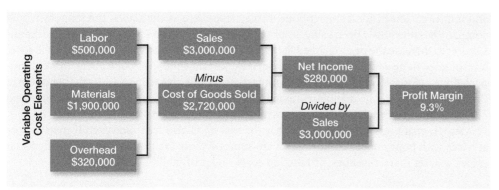

< FIGURE 6.3

Scenario B for Plaque Attack

materials. After understanding how deep an effect that efficient procurement methods can have, companies are giving procurement departments and managers strategic roles.

Managing Across Majors 6.2   Finance and accounting majors, note that savings in the purchasing of materials accrue directly to the bottom line.

The Quality of Purchased Goods and Services

A procurement organization with strategic sourcing in mind is also focused on the quality of goods and services. One need only scan the business news headlines to see the effect product quality, or the lack thereof, can have on a company. For example, the headline "Lead Paint Prompts Mattel to Recall 967,000 Toys" appeared in the *New York Times* around the same time that many other companies had discovered lead paint in products sourced from China.[4] In 2012, Toyota announced a one-time, $1.1 billion pretax charge against earnings to cover the estimated costs associated with its 2010 braking and acceleration problems.[5] In these and many other cases, the quality issues stem from something sourced by the procurement organization. Experienced purchasing managers understand that overall product quality is no better than the weakest supplier.

On the other hand, as illustrated in FIGURE 6.4, sourcing materials and services with higher levels of quality can also affect profitability. Take, for example, a supplier that offers a new

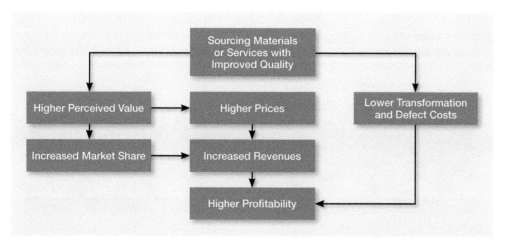

< FIGURE 6.4

Sourcing Improved Quality

[4]*New York Times*, Aug. 2, 2007, http://www.nytimes.com/2007/08/02/business/02toy.html?_r=0.
[5]ABC7.com, "Toyota Recall Settlement Reached over Acceleration Problems: $1.1 Billion," Dec. 26, 2012, http://abclocal.go.com/kabc/story?section=news/consumer/recalls&id=8932615.

and improved screen for a smartphone at the same price as the screen the manufacturing company has previously been using. Improving the quality of the screen may allow the manufacturer to increase the price charged for that phone, thereby increasing revenues at the same level of sales. If the new and improved screen is important enough to consumers, that component alone may drive up sales, and the manufacturer will be able to increase its market share in that phone segment. The manufacturer may also see an effect on profitability from improved quality conformance when defect rates drop and there is less waste due to faulty parts.

Supply managers must be aware that the reverse is also true, however. If materials or services with poor quality conformance are sourced, there are potential negative effects on prices, market share, revenues, production costs, and profitability.

Cost of Development and Design

Approximately 85 percent of an item's or service's cost is determined in the design stage. As noted above, purchased goods and services make up more than 50 percent of a firm's cost of goods sold. Therefore, for a supply manager to maximize the effect he or she can have on the cost and quality of the materials and service procured, the manager must be involved in the design and development process.

....

Managing Across Majors 6.3 Marketing students, you must work with procurement during the product design phase to see how materials cost choices align with customer needs.

....

Before supply managers can add value to the development and design process, however, they must be aware of what the supply base is capable of providing. As supply managers become familiar with the supply base and take time to investigate ongoing innovations, they may find applicable capabilities beyond their expectations. Such was the case for Shell Oil when a simple conversation with one of its strategic suppliers, Hewlett-Packard (HP), led to a joint development effort. Because both companies focus on innovation, the conversation eventually turned to what is new in R&D. The HP manager talked about research into a new wireless printer head the size of a postage stamp that uses sensing technology to pick up vibrations. The information piqued Shell's interest because its deepwater oil explorations use sensing technology to discover rock formations that could hold oil several miles under the ocean. What resulted was HP's early involvement in a system used by Shell to sense, collect, and store geophysical data.[6]

Armed with knowledge of supplier capabilities, supply managers who are involved in new product design can contribute in many ways. They can suggest component parts that are already used in another product within the firm, or they can find a lower-cost or higher-quality component during the design stage. Supply managers can also facilitate early supplier involvement in the design process (**FIGURE 6.5**), which has been found to help reduce cost, reduce concept-to-customer development time, improve quality, and provide innovative

FIGURE 6.5 >

New Product Development Process

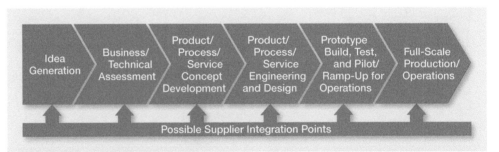

Reprinted by permission from Handfield and Lawson (2007), "Integrating Suppliers into New Product Development," *Research Technology Management* 50(5), 44–51.

[6]Siegfried, "Dig Deep to Uncover Supplier Capabilities," *Inside Supply Management* 23, no. 8 (2012): 18.

Early Supplier Involvement at Japanese Automakers

Toyota, Nissan, and Honda are better than the traditional domestic Big Three at involving suppliers early in the product development process. When suppliers are involved in the new product design and development process, automakers, instead of telling the suppliers what to build, encourage open dialogue and allow parts makers to come to them with ideas that the product planners might not have considered.

"Suppliers are being given significantly more flexibility in meeting quality and piece-price objectives, said John W. Henke, Professor at Oakland University. "Nissan has improved in reducing late engineering changes over all others except Toyota. Nissan, Honda, and Toyota are improving, distancing themselves from Ford, GM, and Chrysler. This certainly will impact supplier engineering as to where suppliers will allocate engineering resources when things get tight—who gets the 'A team'; who gets the newest, best technology; who gets the best support from the supplier; etc.," noted Henke.

technologies that can help capture market share.[7] Although there are many possible supplier integration points in the new product development process, world-class companies are maximizing the benefits of early supplier involvement by forming cross-functional design teams and involving suppliers at the earliest stages of development.[8] SC&O CURRENT EVENTS 6.2 illustrates how Japanese automakers have involved suppliers in the design and development process.

 PPLY THE PORTFOLIO APPROACH TO STRATEGIC SOURCING

Most procurement organizations are responsible for a broad array of purchased goods and services. Because the type and magnitude of spending varies, supply managers must determine how each purchased item should be managed for the best possible outcome for the firm. A **portfolio model** provides a framework for making these strategic management decisions. By applying this model, the supply strategy for a particular purchase can be determined by considering two dimensions: supply risk and profit impact (FIGURE 6.6). **Supply risk** refers to the extent to which the item is difficult to source due to a lack of qualified sources, raw material scarcity, lack of substitutes, logistics cost or complexity, and monopoly or oligopoly conditions. **Profit impact** may result from either the sheer volume of spend for that particular item or the unique additional value from the item. By analyzing purchased materials and services in terms of these two dimensions, we can categorize the items as *routine*, *bottleneck*, *leverage*, or *critical*.

portfolio model
A framework for making purchasing-related strategic management decisions.

supply risk
The extent to which an item is difficult to source due to a lack of qualified sources, raw material scarcity, lack of substitutes, logistics cost or complexity, and monopoly or oligopoly conditions.

profit impact
The result of either the sheer volume of spend for a particular item or the unique added value from an item.

Category Segmentation

The first step in using a portfolio model approach to strategic sourcing is to segment what is being purchased by profit impact and supply risk. The level of profit impact can be determined by a variety of criteria, including the volume purchased (most commonly used), expected growth in demand, percentage of total purchase cost, and effect on product quality. Supply risk can also be measured by a variety of factors, including market conditions, availability or scarcity of the item, number of suppliers, availability of substitutes, ability to store or inventory items, and possible supply interruptions.

[7]Handfield and Lawson, "Integrating Suppliers into New Product Development," *Research Technology Management* 50, no. 5 (2007): 44–51.
[8]Pickerton, "Benchmarking World-Class Purchasing Organizations," *eSide Supply Management* 5, no. 4 (2012).

FIGURE 6.6 >

Portfolio Model

Based on: Kraljic, "Purchasing Must Become Supply Management," *Harvard Business Review*, September/October 1983, 109–117, and Gelderman and van Weele, "Purchasing Portfolio Models: A Critique and Update," *Journal of Supply Chain Management* 41(3), 19–28.

Staatsolie, an oil company, conducted a portfolio analysis of 40 of its purchased items.[9] The sourcing manager first determined the profit impact for each item based on annual purchase value and then created a matrix to evaluate supply risk for each of the items. A sample of that matrix is shown in TABLE 6.2.

∨ TABLE 6.2

Example of Segmentation

Item	Profit Impact	Number of Suppliers*	On-Time Delivery*	Market Conditions*	Available Substitutes: Y = yes, N = no	Supply Risk
Pipe $10\frac{3}{4}''$	$394,000	5	3	3	Y	Low
Packer set $2\frac{3}{8}''$	$398,000	1	5	1	N	Very high
Pipe $3\frac{1}{8}''$	$471,000	5	4	3	Y	Medium
Chemicals treatment plant	$484,000	2	4	3	N	Medium
Drive heads	$621,000	1	3	1	N	Very high
Pipe $6\frac{5}{8}''$	$630,000	5	4	3	Y	Low
Tubing $2\frac{3}{8}''$	$642,000	5	3	2	N	High
Casing $5\frac{1}{2}''$	$1,378,000	5	3	2	N	High

*1 = very bad, 2 = bad, 3 = fair, 4 = good, 5 = very good.

[9]Example based on Gelderman and MacDonald, "Application of Kraljic's Purchasing Portfolio Model in an Undeveloped Logistics Infrastructure," *Journal of Transnational Management* 13, no. 1 (2008): 77–92.

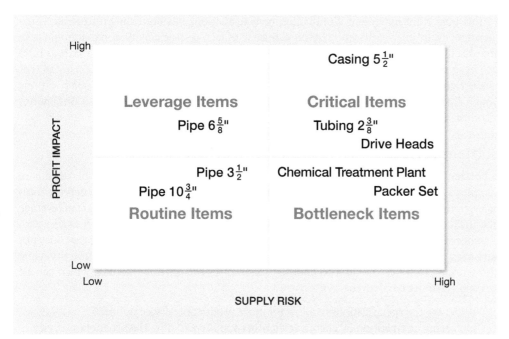

The profit impact and supply risk scores were then used to assign each of the items to a quadrant in the portfolio matrix, as shown in FIGURE 6.7. Once all items are segmented, a sourcing strategy is developed based on the quadrant assignment and whether the items are routine, leverage, bottleneck, or critical.

Routine Items

A **routine item** is typically something of low value, purchased in small volumes and through individual transactions. For this type of expense, there are many alternative products and services and many sources of supply. Because these items do not typically require a high level of purchasing expertise, the appropriate strategy is to simplify the acquisition process. Supply managers can reduce the amount of time and effort expended on procuring these items by automating the purchasing process.

A high-technology manufacturer reported the following strategy for its office supplies, which were categorized as routine items. Rather than having employees fill out a purchase requisition every time they needed toner or paper clips, supply managers simplified the acquisition process by negotiating an ongoing contract with two office supplies providers to achieve volume-based pricing. Administrative employees were then authorized to purchase office supplies for their departments using purchasing credit cards, procuring what was needed at the previously negotiated prices. Once teams established this process, the acquisition of office supplies took place without involving supply managers in the process.

routine item
A basic item or supply.

Leverage Items

A **leverage item** has the potential to affect profit, typically because such items are associated with a high level of expenditures while also having many qualified sources of supply. When supply managers must balance large spending quantities with a broad choice of suppliers, they should work to maximize the commercial advantage for the firm by concentrating business with a limited number of suppliers, thereby achieving volume discounts, and by promoting competitive bidding between qualified suppliers.

Take, for example, buying tomatoes for Heinz ketchup. One approach would be to use a reverse auction (a special type of auction used in purchasing wherein sellers bid for business with customers) to promote competitive bidding for this leverage item. By having suppliers bid on a buyer's need for tomatoes, the supply manager can identify the true market value

leverage item
A purchased item that has the potential to affect profit, typically because it is associated with a high level of expenditures while also having many qualified sources of supply.

for this important ingredient. Conducting reverse auctions has been shown to reduce procurement cycle time significantly because, instead of face-to-face negotiation that might take months, the negotiations take place online in a matter of hours. Significant cost savings have also been reported. This approach should be limited, however, to products and services that can be rigorously specified, where competition exists, and only when supplier qualifications can be evaluated thoroughly. Because a large supply base is needed, reverse auctions are not recommended for bottleneck or critical items.

Bottleneck Items

bottleneck item
A purchased item with few alternate sources of supply, typically due to complex specifications requiring complex manufacturing or service processes, new technologies, or untested processes.

A **bottleneck item** is one in which there are few alternate sources of supply, typically due to complex specifications requiring complex manufacturing or service processes, new technologies, or untested processes. Although these items may not have the profit impact of leverage or critical items, the lack of the item has an effect on operations. Thus, a supply manager who is responsible for a bottleneck item tends to expend a lot of time on something that does not have a large profit impact for the firm. The strategy, then, is to ensure supply continuity while also working to move the item to another quadrant in the portfolio matrix, which can be accomplished in one of three ways:

1. Widening the specifications to allow for more product or service options
2. Increasing competition by encouraging other suppliers to offer the product or service
3. Developing new suppliers

One approach to moving a bottleneck item to another quadrant is to work with design engineers or internal customers to redefine what is needed. A supply manager at a major hospital network reported on her efforts to move casting material from the bottleneck quadrant to the routine quadrant. Her internal customers (the doctors and nurses) had requested casting material in 36 colors to help improve patient satisfaction when a patient received a cast for a broken bone. Some of the colors were in short supply, however, and had to be managed continuously to ensure that inventories were always in place. The supply manager worked with her internal customers to compromise on 12 readily available colors of casting material and thus resolved the bottleneck.

Critical Items

critical item
A purchased good that can have a big effect on profitability but only has a few qualified suppliers.

A **critical item** is an item that can have a big effect on profitability but has only a few qualified suppliers. These items are typified by large expenditures, and the quality and design, which often include complex or rigid specifications, are essential. The best strategy for critical items is to form alliances with the suppliers through trust-based relationships, in-depth information sharing, and joint goal setting. Supply managers should also prepare contingency plans for these items to protect against unforeseen risks (e.g., political unrest, natural disasters, breach of trust, quality failure).

As illustrated in SC&O CURRENT EVENTS 6.3, McDonald's goes to great lengths to develop alliance-based relationships with its critical suppliers. It sees its suppliers as necessary for success and therefore is willing to dedicate the resources necessary to develop these close relationships. Such in-depth relationships take time to develop, however, and the level of trust necessary to share confidential information with suppliers does not mature overnight. Therefore, sourcing managers must take care when assigning products and services to the critical category to ensure that they are truly critical, keeping in mind the level of time and effort that will be necessary to source this type of material effectively.

 **ASTER THE TOOLS OF STRATEGIC COST MANAGEMENT**

Cost management using data analytics has become a critical skill for firms to survive in today's highly competitive environment, but as we've already established, it is not enough for procurement organizations simply to reduce costs. Instead, costs must be managed

Alliances at the Golden Arches

Today, McDonald's golden arches are well known around the world. Someday soon, however, its supply chain management practices and insights may be just as easily recognized. McDonald's business success depends largely on its supplier management strategies. Specifically, McDonald's executives understand the importance of supplier management and, because of its importance, McDonald's has established relationships of trust with its key suppliers.

Strategic Importance of Supplier Alliances

McDonald's practices a three-legged stool approach to fuel sustained growth and profitability. Specifically, McDonald's focuses on its (1) corporate staff, (2) franchisees, and (3) supplier base. McDonald's believes that each of the legs of the stool is as important as the others, which means that its executives take a keen interest in its suppliers' competitiveness and well-being because it understands the value of its suppliers. For example, suppliers get face time with McDonald's USA, LLC, president and chair of the board because McDonald's endeavors to be involved in and improve its processes. One McDonald's executive describes the approach as "from farm to fork." To strengthen its supply base even further, McDonald's expects its suppliers to support one another by sharing insights, technologies, and best practices. It may seem unusual at first glance, but McDonald's has convinced its suppliers that McDonald's is the suppliers' most important customer and that ultimately each supplier's success is linked to how well McDonald's supply chain system delivers customer satisfaction. In addition, McDonald's establishes relationships of trust with its suppliers from day one, which facilitates buyer-to-supplier communication and innovation. McDonald's has decided to focus on a few key points as its secret sauce:

1. All members of the supply chain infuse quality and precision into the process. Suppliers take accountability to meet standards, and restaurants focus on customer service.
2. McDonald's displays deep commitment to its suppliers. Suppliers have business without the worry of competitors cutting their prices; McDonald's is confident it is being delivered the best possible value.
3. McDonald's is very supportive in setting the tone for all the suppliers to work better to make the McDonald's system better. "McDonald's lives and breathes to help its suppliers be successful." Innovations to reduce costs, improve service, or create new products are common for suppliers.

strategically. **Strategic cost management** involves four types of analyses: (1) spend analysis, (2) price analysis, (3) cost analysis, and (4) total cost of ownership analysis.

Spend Analysis

Spend analysis is a review of a firm's entire set of purchases and answers the question, What is the firm spending its money on? This analysis is done at both aggregate and detailed levels. The *spend* (or purchasing expenditure) is most commonly categorized as *direct, indirect,* and *capital*. The **direct spend category** includes any material or service that is part of the final product, whereas the **indirect spend category** includes all the spend that supports the operations of a firm, encompassing everything from cafeteria services to spare parts for factory equipment. **Capital spend**, as the name implies, includes all spend for buildings and large equipment, anything that will be depreciated. Spend analysis can also be used to determine the following:

• Whether or not the firm received the correct amount of products and services given what it paid for them

strategic cost management
Top management focus on price and total ownership costs.

spend analysis
A review of a firm's entire set of purchases. It answers the question, What is the firm spending its money on?

direct spend category
Includes any material or service that is part of the final product.

indirect spend category
Includes all the spending that supports the operations of a firm, encompassing everything from cafeteria services to spare parts for factory equipment.

capital spend
Includes all spending for buildings, large equipment, and anything that will be depreciated.

- Which suppliers received the majority of the business and if they charged an accurate price across divisions
- Whether or not there are opportunities to combine volumes and spending for different business groups, standardize product requirements, reduce the number of suppliers, or take advantage of market conditions to receive better pricing

This analysis is also useful in categorizing purchases into the portfolio model quadrants discussed previously because the quadrant assignment is made based on profit impact, which is most commonly measured as dollars spent for that particular item.

Price Analysis

Price analysis is the process of comparing supplier prices against one another or against external benchmarks. This analysis is most useful when there are many suppliers available in the marketplace, meaning that the purchases are categorized as either routine or commodities in the portfolio model. The primary challenge in conducting price analysis is to be sure you are comparing items with the same specifications, quality levels, lead times, warranties, and so on when analyzing prices. If the items are not identical, the supply manager must account for those features in the price analysis.

A common difference between suppliers of identical items comes in the form of payment terms. Fortunately, these differences can be easily accounted for in a price analysis. SOLVED PROBLEM 6.2 shows how to perform price analysis.

 SOLVED PROBLEM 6.2 >

MyLab Operations Management
Video

Price Analysis in Action

Problem: Let's consider two suppliers that are offering the same part at the same quantity, with the same lead time, but with different payment windows. They have quoted the following pricing and payment terms:

Supplier A: $50.00/unit, payment due in 30 days
Supplier B: $50.35/unit, payment due in 90 days

Perform a price analysis with a 6.5 percent annual cost of capital.

Solution: To compare these two prices equitably, we need to adjust for the different payment windows. We do so by adding an opportunity cost to the supplier that requires earlier payment to account for the interest that we would have been able to make on that money had we been able to keep it in our accounts for the longer payment window. To make the adjustment, we need to determine the following:

1. Number of days earlier supplier A must be paid (longest days to pay − shortest days to pay)

$$90 \text{ days} - 30 \text{ days} = 60 \text{ days}$$

2. Your organization's daily cost of capital
   If we assume an annual cost of capital of 6.5 percent, the daily cost of capital would be

$$\frac{0.065}{365} = 0.000178$$

3. Opportunity cost = number of days earlier × daily cost of capital × purchase price

$$60 \times 0.000178 \times \$50.00 = \$0.534 \tag{6.2}$$

4. The effective price for supplier A:

$$\$50.00 + \$0.534 = \$50.534$$

As a result of the price analysis, we conclude that, although supplier B offers the item at a higher price, the effective price for supplier A was actually higher than supplier B because of the different payment window. The key to price analysis is ensuring that the prices are compared on an equivalent basis. We demonstrate this in Excel in USING TECHNOLOGY 6.1.

Price Analysis in Excel

< USING
TECHNOLOGY 6.1

Here is a spreadsheet that shows the calculations required in Excel to perform price analysis (based on Solved Problem 6.2 data).

	A	B	C	D	E	F	G	H	I	J	K
1	**Price Analysis Example**						=C5/C6				
2											
3	Longest days to pay:		90		Number of days early pay:			60	=C3–C4		
4	Shortest days to pay:		30		Daily cost of capital:		0.000178				
5	Annual cost of capital:		0.065		Opportunity cost:		0.534247				
6	Number of days:		365					=H3*G4*C7			
7	Purchase price:		50		The effective price:		50.53425				
8											
9							=C7+G5				
10											
11											

Cost Analysis

Cost analysis is the process of analyzing each of the individual cost elements that make up the final price. Managers should perform cost analysis when price analysis is impractical or when price analysis alone does not allow a buyer to reach the conclusion that a price is fair and reasonable. These conditions are most likely to occur when there are few alternate sources of supply, as is the case with bottleneck and critical categories in the portfolio model.

A common form of cost analysis is **should cost modeling**, the process of determining what a product should cost based on its component raw material costs, manufacturing costs, production overheads, and reasonable profit margins. From a strategic perspective, knowing approximately what a product should cost enables a supply manager to negotiate a fair price more easily. The extent to which a cost model appropriately reflects the actual cost for the purchased item is a direct function of the quality and availability of information. Because it can be a resource-intensive process, cost analysis is conducted only when price analysis is not sufficient.

Total Cost of Ownership Analysis

The **total cost of ownership (TCO)** is the combination of all costs involved in a product. The goal of **total cost of ownership (TCO) analysis** is to include all costs in an analysis of a purchase, not just the purchase price. This type of analysis applies to all the quadrants in the portfolio model.

Costs in a total cost of ownership model are typically broken into three categories: (1) acquisition costs, (2) ownership costs, and (3) postownership costs. **Acquisition costs** include all costs related to identifying, selecting, ordering, receiving, and paying for a purchased item. Examples include purchase price, planning costs, taxes, financing costs, and transportation costs.

There are still costs associated with a purchased item after acquisition. These **ownership costs** include all costs related to the quality and maintenance of the purchased item. Examples include inventory costs, warehousing costs, and the cost of ongoing supplier management.

cost analysis
Strategic study of cost structures.

should cost modeling
The process of determining what a product should cost based on its component raw material costs, manufacturing costs, production overheads, and reasonable profit margins.

total cost of ownership (TCO)
The sum of acquisition, ownership, and postownership costs.

total cost of ownership (TCO) analysis
Includes all costs in your analysis of a purchase, not just the purchase price, including acquisition costs, ownership costs, and postownership costs.

acquisition costs
Includes all purchasing costs related to identifying, selecting, ordering, receiving, and paying for a purchased item.

ownership costs
Costs relating to the maintenance and operation of products.

postownership costs
All costs related to the customer's use and disposition of a purchased item.

The final category of costs, **postownership costs**, includes all costs related to the customer's use and disposition of the purchased item. Examples of this type of cost are environmental costs, warranty costs, product liability costs, and customer dissatisfaction costs. Any residual value is also included as a postownership cost. We demonstrate total cost of ownership analysis in SOLVED PROBLEM 6.3 and discuss it further in GLOBAL CONNECTIONS 6.1.

 SOLVED PROBLEM 6.3 >

MyLab Operations Management
Video

Total Cost of Ownership

Problem: You have been tasked with procuring a printer and are trying to decide between two different types: ink-jet versus laser printer. A price analysis alone will not answer the question of which would be the better purchase decision because you are comparing printers with very different specifications. Likewise, a cost analysis would not be appropriate because the question you want to answer is not whether the price offered is reasonable in a limited supply market but rather which printer would provide you with the lowest *lifetime cost*. The best approach is to conduct a total cost of ownership analysis to determine the type of printer you should purchase and then conduct a price analysis of competing brands with the same specifications as that printer.

You have collected the following data for the two types of printers you are considering for your small business. You expect to print about 1,000 pages per week and need only black-and-white printing capability.

	Ink-Jet Printer	Laser Printer
Initial cost of printer	$55	$400
Cost of ink or toner	$36/cartridge	$173/cartridge
Pages per cartridge	1,670	10,000
Ink or toner cost per page	$0.022	$0.017
Expected life span	3 years	5 years
Required maintenance	Semiannually	Annually
Cost of maintenance	$35	$35
Electricity used when printing	2.4 kW/hour	2.8 kW/hour
Electricity used in standby mode	0.310 kW/hour	0.323 kW/hour
Cost of kilowatt hour	0.1179	0.1179
Speed of printer	360 pages/hour	1,260 pages/hour
Annual hours printing (52,000/speed of printer)	144.4	41.3
Annual hours in standby (assuming printer is always on; 365 × 24 − hours printing)	8,615.6	8,718.7
Annual cost of electricity (kilowatts used per hour × number of hours × cost per kilowatt hour for printing and standby)	$356	$346

Because both printers are available at local office supply stores, there is no shipping cost for either printer. The laser printer has a longer life span, and it will have a residual value of $100 at the end of three years. The sales tax rate in your city is 7.5 percent, and setup costs are essentially the same.

Solution: Your total cost of ownership model for this sourcing decision is as follows:

	Ink-Jet Printer			Laser Printer		
	Year 1	Year 2	Year 3	Year 1	Year 2	Year 3
Acquisition cost price	$55			$400		
Ownership cost						
• Ink or toner	$1,144	$1,144	$1,144	$884	$884	$884
• Electricity	$356	$356	$356	$346	$346	$346
• Maintenance	$70	$70	$70	$35	$35	$35
Postownership cost						
• Residual value						($100)
Total cost at the end of 3 years			$4,765 plus sales tax			$4,095 plus sales tax

A total cost of ownership analysis is specific to the situation in question and must be recalculated if the situation changes. In the case of comparing two types of printers, if the small business only printed 100 pages per week, the ink-jet printer would have had the lower cost.

Outsourcing to China and Total Cost of Ownership

Over the last decades, trade with China has expanded so that it is one of America's leading trading partners. However, there has been much discussion about the true costs of ownership of products outsourced to China. You have seen what happens when purchasing decisions are based on purchase price alone.

One of the important B2B products purchased by manufacturing firms is a mold. Molds are the inputs used to form plastic and metal products and components.

According to Darcy King, CEO of Unique Tool and Gauge, Inc., the decision to source a mold rests too often on the initial acquisition cost alone, a shortsighted approach. When sourcing molds from China, direct labor costs are very low. However, developing relationships with a number of higher-quality mold builders has required a lot of effort and no small amount of pain along the way. Mold designs from China usually take longer than they do domestically, and they often need rework. Due to high layover and material substitution, Chinese suppliers can be quite unreliable, which means that unforeseen costs are incurred.

According to Harry Moser, former president of GF-AgieCHarmilles, "Companies often ignore the total cost of ownership when deciding where to manufacture." He maintains that firms get caught up with outsourcing and lose sight of real costs.

Total cost of ownership analysis should include consideration of every factor in outsourcing. These factors include the costs of loss of intellectual property and the hidden costs of separating engineering and manufacturing.

Source: Based on King, D., "The True Cost of Outsourcing Molds to China," *Plastic News*, March 31, 2016.

outsource
To procure from a supplier something that a company has been producing internally.

Total Cost of Ownership and Outsourcing Decisions

A total cost of ownership perspective is also important in the strategic decision to **outsource**, or procure from a supplier, something that a company has been producing internally. Once again, the decision needs to be based on more than just the initial price difference. Other considerations include the following:

- The cost of quality
- Inventory costs
- Transportation costs
- The costs of managing new suppliers
- Political implications
- Exchange rate fluctuations

SOLVED PROBLEM 6.4 demonstrates how to use total cost of ownership analysis to determine whether or not you should outsource an item and, if you do, where you should outsource it.

 SOLVED PROBLEM 6.4 >

MyLab Operations Management
Video

Total Cost of Ownership and Outsourcing

Problem: Milwaukee Tool Company, a U.S.-based firm, is considering outsourcing a drill it currently manufactures to either a supplier in Mexico or a supplier in China.[10] The company has analyzed labor, materials, and overhead costs in the three locations (Mexico, China, and the US) to determine the relative production costs and resulting prices. For the suppliers in Mexico and China, supply managers have also calculated the following transportation costs, costs of holding additional inventory, additional overhead within Milwaukee Tool Company needed to manage the outsource suppliers, and costs of receiving lower quality products.

Costs per Unit	United States (Nearsource)	Mexico (Outsource)	China (Outsource)
Price	$91.41	$69.07	$70.22
Shipping cost		$7.22	$7.17
Additional inventory carrying cost		$0.15	$7.58
Additional overhead		$3.45	$7.02
Cost of lower quality		$0.69	$0.70
Estimated total cost	$91.41	$80.58	$92.69

Solution: If Milwaukee Tool Company had based its decision on only the price of the drill, the decision to outsource would seem obvious, and either Mexico or China would be a viable option. Once the other costs are included, however, it becomes clear that only Mexico is a lower cost choice.

[10]Example based on S. Kumar and K. K. Kopitzke, "A Practitioner's Decision Model for the Total Cost of Outsourcing and Application to China, Mexico, and the United States." *Journal of Business Logistics* 29, no. 2 (2008): 107–139.

Researchers have found that, when outsourcing to China, additional costs were found to be 50 percent of the quoted price on average. It is interesting that the buyer's perception was that additional costs were only 25 percent of the quoted price. These findings suggest that, more often than not, buyers are underestimating the costs associated with outsourcing, particularly in global environments.[11] When companies do not measure the costs of global sourcing comprehensively, they significantly underestimate the true costs incurred (see GLOBAL CONNECTIONS 6.1).

[11]K. W. Platts and N. Song, "Overseas Sourcing Decisions—The Total Cost of Sourcing from China," *Supply Chain Management: An International Journal* 15, no. 4 (2010): 320–331.

At the beginning of the chapter, we discussed Lenovo and its modern approaches to suppliers. As a result of these practices, Lenovo now owns 25 percent of the world market in personal computers (PCs). In addition, it has developed 25 key indicators for monitoring supplier performance. During this process, Lenovo has reduced its planning time from 10 hours to 10 minutes.

Lenovo's efforts also face downstream in the supply chain. Lenovo has developed a digital system that utilizes social media for each major customer that communicates order status, information about new products, and other useful information. This kind of collaboration up and down the supply chain has been a winner for Lenovo. Gartner (a well-known supply chain consulting firm) named Lenovo one of the top 25 supply chain companies in the world.

Summary

In this chapter, we introduced key frameworks for strategic sourcing and demonstrated the effect that sourcing managers can have on the profitability of their firms.

1. We began by introducing sourcing and its different historical phases.
   a. There are many job opportunities for students with supply chain training in sourcing jobs.
2. Sourcing managers have the opportunity to have an impact on the bottom-line cost savings. These benefits accrue through:
   a. Improved product and service quality
   b. Supplier involvement in product design
   c. Service design
3. A portfolio approach to supply management can guide a sourcing manager in applying the correct strategy for each category of goods and services:
   a. Routine items
   b. Leverage items
   c. Bottleneck items
   d. Critical items

4. Strategic cost management tools help sourcing managers determine how to pay for the goods and services they are responsible for procuring through conducting spend analysis, price analysis, cost analysis, and total cost of ownership analysis.

5. As you apply these frameworks, you will develop the ability to drive cost savings for your firm, affect product and service quality for your customers, and help improve product and process designs with your suppliers.

Key Terms

acquisition costs   155
bottleneck item   152
buyer   144
capital spend   153
cost analysis   155
critical item   152
direct spend category   153
indirect spend category   153
leverage item   151
materials management   144
outsource   158

ownership costs   155
portfolio model   149
postownership costs   156
price analysis   154
procurement management   144
profit impact   149
purchasing agent   144
purchasing management   144
purchasing manager   144
routine item   151
should cost modeling   155

sourcing management   144
spend analysis   153
strategic cost management   153
strategic sourcing   143
supply management   144
supply manager   144
supply risk   149
total cost of ownership (TCO)   155
total cost of ownership (TCO)
    analysis   155

Integrative Learning Exercise

Visit a business or organization in your community and speak to someone there about the organization's sourcing function. Specifically, investigate whether the organization employs a portfolio approach to strategic sourcing. If it does, describe the approach used. If it does not, describe how such an approach could be implemented and its benefit to the organization.

Integrative Experiential Exercise

Identify a business or organization in your community. Along with a study team, visit the organization and ask about its sourcing decisions. How are sourcing decisions made? How does the organization identify suppliers? How has the sourcing function of the organization evolved since 2000? In what ways does the organization view its sourcing decisions strategically?

Discussion Questions

1. What explains the shift of the procurement function in organizations from a low-level task to a higher-level strategic focus?

2. What is strategic sourcing?

3. How does strategic sourcing that embraces the lean philosophy differ from the traditional approach to sourcing decisions?

4. How must strategic sourcing in a lean supply chain analyze its existing supplier relationships?

5. The role of purchasing organizations has changed over the years. What has been the focus of the purchasing organization since 2000?

6. Researchers who study procurement state that its role in organizations is moving from a purely tactical function focused on cost savings to becoming a strategic contributor. In what ways is procurement becoming more strategic-minded?

7. Briefly describe how it is possible for a small change in the cost of purchased goods and services to have a more significant effect on profits than a large change in sales.

8. Briefly identify the types of purchased goods and services that fall into the direct spend category, the indirect spend category, and the capital spend category.

9. Briefly define routine items and bottleneck items, and contrast the appropriate purchasing strategy for the two.

10. What are leverage items, and how should they be managed?

11. What is the preferred strategy for managing critical items?

12. What is spend analysis, and what questions can it help answer?

13. Identify the purpose of and the primary challenge in conducting total cost of ownership analysis.

14. What is cost analysis, and when should it be used?

15. What is "should cost modeling," and how does it relate to the supply manager's strategic role?

Solved Problems

Effect of Strategic Sourcing on the Firm

ECONOMICS OF PURCHASING
SOLVED PROBLEM 6.1

1. Currently, a product has $5,000,000 in annual sales. The product incurs material costs of $3,500,000, labor costs of $700,000, and overhead of $400,000, resulting in a profit of $400,000. The company wants to decide on one of two alternatives for this product: focus on reducing material cost or focus on increasing product sales. It is estimated that a buyer managing this product could reduce the cost of materials by 4 percent. The company estimates that a new sales manager assigned to this product could increase sales by 12 percent. Calculate the estimated impact on profitability of the two alternatives.

Solution:
Currently, the product has a profit margin of 8 percent.

Labor	$ 700,000
Materials	$3,500,000
Overhead	$400,000
Total cost of goods sold	$4,600,000
Sales	$5,000,000
Net income	$400,000
Profit margin	8.00 percent

Net income/sales = $400,000/$5,000,000 = 0.08 or 8 percent

A focus on reducing material costs by 4 percent produces the following results: Material cost falls to $3,360,000, and cost of goods sold falls to $4,460,000. Net income is therefore $540,000, an increase of $140,000, which brings the profit margin to $540,000/$5,000,000 = 10.8 percent.

A focus on increasing sales by 12 percent produces the following result: New sales = $5,000,000 × 1.12 = $5,600,000. Profit increase ($5,600,000 − $5,000,000) × 0.08 = $48,000.

By reducing material cost 4 percent, there is a $140,000 increase in profits. By increasing sales by 12 percent, there is a $48,000 increase in profit. The company would need to have a 35 percent increase in sales to realize the same increase in profit from a 4 percent reduction in material cost.

Strategic Cost Management

PRICE ANALYSIS
SOLVED PROBLEM 6.2

2. A company must choose between two suppliers to supply a part. The suppliers have the same quality and delivery reliability, so the selection is driven by the price. Supplier A is offering the part for $40.00 per unit. Supplier B has quoted a price of $40.50 per unit. Payment is due in 30 days for supplier A, but supplier B's payment is not due until 120 days. The company's annual cost of capital is approximately 7.5 percent. Based on the different prices and payment windows, which supplier should the company select?

Solution:
Because the suppliers offer different payment periods, the opportunity cost of the supplier requiring the earlier payment must be computed. That computation is as follows:

	Supplier A	Supplier B
Price per unit	$40.00	$40.50
Payment due (in days)	30	120
Annual cost of capital	0.075	
Daily cost of capital	0.0002055	
Days early payment required	90	
Opportunity cost	$0.74	
Effective price	$40.74	

The opportunity cost is the daily cost of capital multiplied by days earlier payment required multiplied by the cost of $40 from supplier A. When the opportunity cost of approximately $0.74 is added to the $40 per unit charge, the total cost of purchasing the product from supplier A becomes $40.74. As a result of the price analysis, we conclude that, even though supplier B offers the product at a higher unit price, the longer payment window provided by supplier B makes the overall price lower. The company should purchase the product from supplier B at a cost of $40.50 per unit.

TOTAL COST OF OWNERSHIP ANALYSIS
SOLVED PROBLEM 6.3

3. A clothing manufacturer uses a cutting machine to cut patterns for men's shirts. Currently, the company is

evaluating which cutting machine to purchase: machine A or machine B. The shirt-making process cuts about 11,000 patterns per day for each of the 250 days it operates annually. After a certain number of cuts, knives on the cutting machine must be replaced. Machine A is produced in and shipped from Japan, whereas machine B is produced in and shipped from Germany. Conduct a total cost of ownership for the cutting machine. The following information is provided:

	Machine A	Machine B
Initial cost	$15,000	$31,000
Shipping cost	$500	$400
Cost of knives	$750	$650
Cuts per knife	11,000	10,000
Useful life	4 years	5 years

Solution to Solved Problem 6.3:

	Machine A			
	Year 1	Year 2	Year 3	Year 4
Acquisition cost (price + shipping)	$15,000 + $500 = $15,500			
Ownership cost of knives	$187,500	$187,500	$187,500	$187,500
Total cost at end of 4 years				$765,500

	Machine B			
	Year 1	Year 2	Year 3	Year 4
Acquisition cost (price + shipping)	$31,000 + $400 = $31,400			
Ownership cost of knives	$178,750	$178,750	$178,750	$178,750
Total cost at end of 4 years				$746,400

The ownership cost is computed by taking the total number of cuts made annually (11,000 per day × 250 days) and dividing by the number of cuts per knife before the knives must be replaced. In this case, even though machine A is cheaper in terms of its initial cost, its four-year total cost of ownership is higher.

TCO AND OUTSOURCING
SOLVED PROBLEM 6.4

4. A company is evaluating whether it should continue to produce a product at its plant in Macon, Georgia, or outsource the plant to either Brazil or India. The company has analyzed the costs of outsourcing the product and believes that the following values capture the costs of outsourcing:

	Brazil	India
Price	$45	$33
Shipping cost	$4.50	$12.00
Additional inventory carrying cost	$1.25	$3.50
Added overhead	$4.00	$3.50
Cost of lower quality	$0.75	$1.2

The price of the item produced at the Macon, Georgia, plant is $62.50. What should the company do?

Solution:

Costs per Unit	Macon (Insource)	Brazil (Outsource)	India (Outsource)
Price	$62.50	$45.00	$33.00
Shipping cost		$4.50	$12.00
Additional inventory carrying cost		$1.25	$3.50
Additional overhead		$4.00	$3.50
Cost of lower quality		$0.75	$1.20
Estimated total cost	$62.50	$55.50	$53.20

Based on this analysis, the lowest cost decision would be to outsource to India.

Problems

Effect of Strategic Sourcing on the Firm

ECONOMICS OF PURCHASING

1. A company wants to evaluate the effects of a reduction in material cost of 3 percent and an increase in sales of 15 percent on a product with the following current characteristics: labor costs of $1,250,000, material costs of $5,000,000, overhead of $710,000, and sales of $8,000,000. What are the effects on net income with a 3 percent reduction in material costs? What is the effect with a 15 percent increase in sales?

2. A company can implement one of two strategies regarding a particular product: hire a marketing firm to increase sales 20 percent or assign a product procurement manager who can reduce material costs for the product by 6 percent. Currently, the product has sales of $10,000,000. The costs of materials are $7,500,000, labor costs are $1,500,000, and overhead costs are $500,000. What are the effects on net income of the two alternative strategies?

3. A purchasing manager is deciding whether to purchase a component part from one of two suppliers. Both suppliers offer the part with the same quality, and there is no difference between the suppliers in terms of delivery schedules and delivery dependability. However, the unit prices and the payment windows quoted by the suppliers are different. The relevant information is as follows:

	Supplier A	Supplier B
Unit price	$100.00	$105.50
Payment window (days)	30	90

The company's annual cost of capital is estimated to be 20 percent. Conduct a price analysis to identify the better supplier in terms of price.

STRATEGIC COST MANAGEMENT

4. Two different suppliers have quoted different unit prices and payment windows for a commodity part used by an industrial company. The purchasing manager for the part will decide on which supplier to use based on a price analysis that adjusts for the difference in the payment windows, thereby reflecting the opportunity cost of making earlier payments. The relevant information is as follows:

	Supplier A	Supplier B
Unit price	$55.00	$55.35
Payment window (days)	30	60

If the annual cost of capital for the company is 6 percent, which supplier is offering the better price given the opportunity cost required by making a payment earlier if supplier A is chosen?

5. The following suppliers all provide an identical part in terms of quality, performance, and delivery, but each supplier quotes a different price and different payment window. If a company's annual cost of capital is 15 percent, which supplier should be selected?

	Supplier A	Supplier B	Supplier C
Unit price	$70	$71	$72
Payment window (days)	30	90	120

TOTAL COST OF OWNERSHIP

6. An office manager is deciding between two competing copiers. The copiers have the same basic features, but the initial prices and cost per copy are different. The following information has been collected for each copier:

	Copier 1	Copier 2
Initial installation and setup cost	$5,000	$6,000
Cost per copy	$0.10	$0.095
Useful life	3 years	3 years

Assume that the company will make approximately 300,000 copies annually, and conduct a total cost of ownership analysis for the two copiers.

7. An electric motor is used to power an assembly line. The motor runs continuously at various speeds and, after a certain number of hours, must be replaced. A food-processing company that uses motors of this type is considering whether to purchase the motors from supplier A or supplier B. Information related to the different costs and useful life of the motors supplied by the two suppliers is as follows:

	Supplier A	Supplier B
Price per motor	$1,000	$800
Useful life (hours)	584	438
Energy cost per hour	$0.25	$0.255

Assume that the food-processing company operates 365 days a year, 24 hours a day, for a total of 8,760 hours of operation annually. Conduct a total cost of ownership analysis for the motors.

8. A company needs to purchase a machine to fabricate a custom part used in its production process. Two machines from two different suppliers are currently under consideration. The company has gathered the following information related to the machines from the two suppliers:

	Machine A	Machine B
Machine price	$7,500	$8,000
Component cost	$200	$185
Component life (units)	5,000	5,500
Machine life (years)	3	4

The component cost refers to the cost to replace a component on the machine after a certain number of units have been produced. For example, with machine A, after 5,000 custom parts have been produced, a component costing $200 must be replaced. The company plans to produce 110,000 custom parts annually. Conduct a total cost of ownership for the two machines.

TOTAL COST OF OWNERSHIP AND OUTSOURCING

9. A company currently produces an electric motor at its main manufacturing facility in Dayton, Ohio. The motor's cost when produced at the Dayton plant is $125 per motor. The company is currently considering outsourcing production to either a plant in Mexico or a plant in Indonesia. The company believes that producing the motor in Mexico will result in additional overhead of 10 percent of the motor's cost to produce it in Dayton. For motors produced in Mexico, the need for additional inventory will probably add $0.50 to each motor's cost, and lower quality will probably cost approximately $1.00. Shipping from Mexico will increase cost by $3.75 per motor. The cost of the motor produced in Mexico will be $106.25. If the motor is produced in Indonesia, it will cost $98.00. The company estimates that the shipping cost from Indonesia will be $7.00 per motor, and the costs of additional inventory and lower quality are estimated at $2.00 and $1.25, respectively. The additional overhead is estimated to be 15 percent of the motor's production cost in Dayton. Conduct a total cost of outsourcing for this item.

CASE   Hazeltonn Industries

Cathy Henderson joined the procurement and logistics staff at Hazeltonn Industries three years ago. Hazeltonn, a company with a solid reputation in the upper Midwest for providing reliable, high-quality, and efficient electric motors and drives, has been considering ways it could use its procurement division to better position itself competitively. Cathy has been assigned to manage the procurement and logistics for a line of electric motors that are used to power assembly lines. These motors are used by a diverse group of industries that appreciate the adjustable speed of the motors as well as their high quality. As more and more industries become interested in sustainability, these motors offer a potential competitive advantage because they are the most efficient motors in the marketplace.

Hazeltonn believes that the motors could create a strong competitive advantage for the company, but it is unsure how to position the company to take advantage of the types of motors that Cathy oversees. Management asked Cathy to conduct a formal analysis of her product line. Specifically, they wanted her to develop a strategic plan for how procurement could improve the strategic position of Hazeltonn. The company is interested in expanding the line of motors that Cathy manages and wonders what role procurement could play in this new product expansion. Management also wants to know how the purchased parts that are used in the motors, especially copper wiring, might affect the firm's success. Finally, management wonders if hiring a new sales manager with the goal of increasing sales by 30 percent would be preferred to reducing material costs for motors by 8 percent.

Cathy understands that she needs to discuss how strategic sourcing can help improve the organization's competitive position. She also understands that she needs to conduct a formal price analysis for the electric motors. An assistant gathered the following economic information related to the costs, labor, and overhead for the electric motors as well as last year's sales:

Labor	$1,500,000
Materials	$6,000,000
Overhead	$960,000
Sales	$9,000,000

Question:

Cathy needs a report by next Tuesday that outlines in general terms how procurement could assist in improving the company's competitive position. Describe what procurement's role might be in new product development, and provide a detailed analysis of the effect of a 30 percent increase in sales versus an 8 percent reduction in material costs.

7

Supplier Management

INTEGRATING	GLOBAL SC&O STRATEGY		
INNOVATING	**Supply Management**	**Operations Management**	**Customer Relationship Management**
IMPACTING	Upstream Processes	Core Processes	Downstream Processes
IMPROVING	QUALITY MANAGEMENT, ANALYTICS, AND LOGISTICS		

CHAPTER OUTLINE AND LEARNING OBJECTIVES

① Understand the Importance of Identifying and Applying the Correct Specification for Materials, Services, and Type of Business Relationship
- Understand the process for scoping and selecting suppliers to support specific needs.

② Make Informed Supplier Selection Decisions
- Create and use a weighted-factor analysis tool.
- Know how to search for potential suppliers.
- Understand how to negotiate agreements with suppliers.

③ Create and Develop Constructive Supplier Relationships
- Identify suppliers with whom you would like to develop a relationship.

- Understand how to assemble a cross-functional team and involve top management to use your company's resources most constructively.
- Be able to identify opportunities for development with potential and existing suppliers, define key metrics, understand cost sharing, and agree on projects and resources.

④ Provide Constructive Supplier Feedback
- Design and implement a supplier scorecard.
- Calculate delivery and cost benefits.
- Leverage supplier rewards and reward criteria.

Supplier Relationships Are Important at Raytheon

Raytheon is a global defense contractor with over $23 billion in sales and 61,000 employees. Raytheon sees itself as a technology and innovation leader in defense, security, and civil markets worldwide. With over 10,000 suppliers, supplier management is a big and important job at Raytheon.

According to Raytheon management, the company has begun an effort to identify key suppliers and to become a preferred customer to those key suppliers. "Just as preferred customers of airlines get upgrades and preferential treatment, customers of choice receive the best terms, manufacturing capacity as needed, and first dibs on new innovations. To reach that level of earned preferential treatment, we have to build stronger bonds and greater trust into supplier relationships," says Mike Shaughnessy, VP of Integrated Supply Chain for Raytheon. Together, he adds, Raytheon and its suppliers can work collaboratively to develop winning technologies while taking costs out of the production and maintenance of products.

This is a big change for Raytheon because their interactions with suppliers have traditionally been more tactical in nature. That is, they have been transactional. In this chapter, we approach supplier relationship management from a strategic perspective. By collaborating with suppliers, it is possible to lower costs, improve schedule performance, and better serve end customers. This chapter discusses tools and ideas to make this happen. We will return to this story at the end of the chapter.

Source: Based on Bob Trebilcock, 2015, Raytheon's Supplier Relationship Management. http://www
.supplychain247.com/article/raytheons_supplier_relationship_management

A firm can perform only as well as the weakest link in its supply chain. The upstream links in the supply chain are known as suppliers or vendors, and it is critical that supply managers take an active role in selecting, developing, and providing feedback to the suppliers in their chain. Strong links based on trust with suppliers in the supply chain can lead to lower costs, a stable supply of materials and services, quality improvement, better risk management, and accelerated innovation.

Supplier management is the processes of forging strong links by first identifying what is needed by the firm and then selecting, developing, and actively managing the supply base. The organization within the firm that is responsible for managing suppliers is typically called procurement, purchasing, or supply management. The people with this responsibility commonly have the title buyer, commodity manager, or supply manager. In this chapter, we discuss each step in the supplier management process along with the tools that a supply manager can use to strengthen supply chains.

supplier management
The processes of forging strong links by identifying what is needed by the firm and then selecting, developing, and actively managing the supply base.

Managing Across Majors 7.1 Information systems students, buyers and suppliers are often connected by electronic data interchange.

Supplier management can be divided into four processes: (1) identifying needs in terms of material, service, and desired relationship; (2) selecting the supplier, which involves searching, evaluating, and negotiating; (3) developing the supplier, which is motivated by either the need to

FIGURE 7.1 >

Supplier Management
Processes

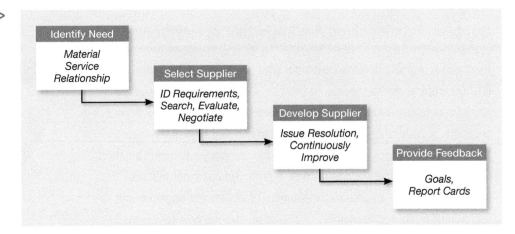

resolve an existing issue or the desire for continuous improvement; and (4) providing feedback to the supplier through goal setting and utilizing report cards. These processes are presented in FIGURE 7.1 as if they are linear in nature, but a supply manager actually uses these processes as needed in each supplier relationship. For example, suppose that a supply manager for an electronics manufacturer manages the relationship with a long-term supplier who has performed well over the years. When there is an unexpected shift in the purchased items needed by the supply manager's firm (i.e., the manufacturer), the supply manager can go back to the selection process and evaluate a new set of suppliers, or she could employ the supplier development process and work with the current supplier to help it cultivate a new capability. We will explore each process and related tools in the order given, but keep in mind the flexible nature of these processes.

(U)NDERSTAND THE IMPORTANCE OF IDENTIFYING AND APPLYING THE CORRECT SPECIFICATION FOR MATERIALS, SERVICES, AND TYPE OF BUSINESS RELATIONSHIP

specification
Documentation that tells buyers (and the assigned supply manager) what to buy and the suppliers what is required of them.

The description of what is needed is called a **specification**. The specification tells the purchasing organization (and the assigned supply manager) what to buy and the suppliers what is required of them. This specification should include a description of the materials and services that a company needs. It is important that the specification also clearly establishes the standards for inspections, tests, and quality checks. The challenge for the supply manager lies in balancing the specification goals of the buying firm and the supplier with the performance and cost of the desired product or service. The supply manager is also responsible for identifying the type of relationship that needs to be in place with the selected supplier.

Identifying the Need for Materials

Specifications for materials can be classified into two broad categories: simple and complex. The categories refer to the specification itself and not the product or service being purchased. For example, let's say that you are responsible for purchasing applesauce for an elementary school cafeteria. You could provide a specification describing the requirements at a general level:

APPLESAUCE, CUP, SHELF STABLE: Individual 4-ounce cups of flavored applesauce with colorful foil lids. Shelf stable in dry storage for a minimum of one year. Each portion to meet one-half cup fruit for USDA child nutrition meal pattern requirement. To be available in various flavors.

This description is an example of a **simple specification**, one given to meet a particular function but not detailing the exact quantities of each ingredient or the precise manner in which the applesauce should be made. On the other hand, it may be important that every one-half cup of fruit served in the cafeteria be exactly the same. If so, instead of the simple specification provided above, you would provide a recipe that details the precise ingredients and the production and packaging process that must be used to produce this product. A recipe is an example of a **complex specification**, one that details the exact quantities of each raw material and the precise manner in which the item should be made. Complex specifications are often very lengthy documents, stretching to more than one hundred pages.

The benefit of a simple specification is that it requires fewer resources and less time to develop than a complex specification. A simple specification may also allow the supplier some flexibility in the materials and production process used, which can result in lower cost. However, a simple specification can introduce more variability in the final product. Therefore, supply managers most often use simple specifications in the following situations:

- When they have a high level of confidence in the supplier's ability to provide what is needed without a lot of detailed explanation
- When precision in the final product is not important
- When the product can be simply specified in terms of a brand name or product number

As might be expected, the benefits of simple specification are the drawbacks of a complex specification, and vice versa. A complex specification is more appropriate in these situations:

- When it is important that all products are precisely the same
- When the supply manager does not have confidence in the supplier
- When the product does not already exist in the marketplace

Identifying the Need for Services

Specifications for services are called a **scope of work**. Although we can still categorize a scope of work as either simple or complex, generally speaking, it is more difficult to communicate what is needed in a service than in a product. Consider a supply manager who needs to hire cleaning services for an office building. A simple scope of work could state: "Daily janitorial services for 120 offices and 10 restrooms at 1234 Juniper St." A complex scope of work details exactly what, where, when, and how each office and restroom are to be cleaned, lists what types of cleaning agents should be used, and includes a checklist for each task. The importance of the service's specifications drives the statement of work's complexity. It may not be important to a supply manager that an office be cleaned in a particular order or with a certain cleaning agent. If a supply manager is creating a statement of work for maintenance of manufacturing equipment, however, the order of the work done and the materials used may be more critical.

Whether you are specifying materials or services, it is important that the specification include some metric for *acceptable performance*. The more precise the supply manager is in specifying what the company needs, the more likely the buying firm is to receive what has been ordered. SC&O CURRENT EVENTS 7.1 illustrates the importance of precise specifications.

Identifying the Need for a Type of Relationship

When a supply manager is in the identify-the-need step, he or she must also specify the desired buyer-supplier relationship. As the procurement function has transformed from clerical to strategic supply management (see Chapter 6), we see a similar evolution in relationships between supply managers and suppliers. Until recently, most buyer-supplier interactions were relatively short term and arm's length in nature. Today, we see collaborative relationships emerging in most industries.

Buyer-supplier relationships, like personal relationships, are varied. FIGURE 7.2 presents a continuum of supply manager–supplier relationships rather than two separate categories. We will describe the two most common points on the continuum, transactional and collaborative, in more detail below.

simple specification
A description given to meet a particular function that does not detail the exact quantities of each ingredient or the precise manner in which a purchased item should be made.

complex specification
A description that details the exact quantities of all purchased raw materials and the precise manner in which an item should be made.

scope of work
A specification for services.

Fighting Fires at Samsung

We will now look at the Samsung Note 7 problem from a supplier management perspective. If you have flown recently, you have probably heard the instruction from the flight crew that you could not be on the flight with a Samsung Note 7 cell phone. That amounts to millions of dollars worth of negative advertising on a regular basis to people who can most afford new cell phones. This fiasco has cost Samsung billions of dollars in profits and has tarnished a company that previously had a stellar reputation as a worldwide leader in cell phones. At a minimum, this is a cautionary tale for other firms about how to interact with suppliers when designing new products.

Samsung has spent months trying to find the root causes of their problems. Initially, Samsung blamed the problems on the battery supplier. However, the whole story is more instructive. Samsung and independent investigators said problems were found in batteries from two different suppliers—the ones that started catching fire right after the phone's launch in August and also those used as replacements. The first battery's outer casing was too small to accommodate the components inside, causing them to short-circuit and overheat, according to the investigations. The second battery's overheating stemmed from other design defects and a missing key component (which is directly related to the importance of understanding the required specifications).

The Note 7 called for a much more powerful battery to satisfy consumers' increasing use of video and games. But Samsung did not want to compromise on the size of the phone. To meet those customer needs, new designs and manufacturing technology were used by the battery suppliers. According to one supplier, "We provided the target for the battery specifications and we are taking responsibility for our failure to ultimately identify and verify the issues arising out of battery design and manufacturing process." Doron Myersdorf, CEO of battery startup StoreDot, suggested it was too simplistic to blame the batteries alone. Instead, it was the specific combination of the battery and smartphone design that caused the fires. "The battery itself might pass all the standalone tests and could be perfectly fine when tested outside the phone," he said. "Once the battery is in this specific design of the phone, with no room to swell, it can create this rare situation." Samsung could have perhaps saved billions of dollars by involving their suppliers in the design process of their phones and then by carefully listening to those same suppliers.

Source: Based on "Samsung Blames Batteries for Galaxy Note 7 Fires" by Sherisse Phan. Published by Cable News Network, 2017. http://money.cnn.com/2017/01/22/technology/samsung-galaxy-note-7-fires-investigation-batteries/.

A supply manager can identify the need for a type of buyer-supplier relationship by examining the characteristics of what the company is purchasing and what it might need from the selected supplier. Those characteristics include the following:

- The likely duration of the relationship
- Whether or not the material or service falls in the critical quadrant of the portfolio matrix (see Chapter 6)
- How difficult it will be to find and procure from another supplier
- How much information will need to be shared
- How important access to technology is
- How much risk exists in the supply chain

FIGURE 7.2 >

Characteristics of Transactional versus Collaborative Relationships

	Continuum of Buyer-Supplier Relationships	
	Transactional	Collaborative
Duration	Short	Long
Critical Item	No	Yes
Switching Costs	Low	High
Information Sharing	No	Yes
Importance of Technology	Low	High
Supply Risk	Low	High

TRANSACTIONAL RELATIONSHIPS Given the characteristics in Figure 7.2, a supply manager should pursue a **transactional relationship** when the buyer has many supplier choices, does not need to share internal company information during the exchange, is purchasing a routine item (refer to the portfolio matrix in Chapter 6), does not require technology innovation from the supplier, and does not expect to experience shortages in supply. Transactional relationships are also referred to as **arm's-length relationships**, implying that the buyer and the supplier remain independent, with little integration of business processes. These relationships typically exist for a relatively short time. An everyday example of a transactional relationship is purchasing groceries or gasoline. In a business-to-business context, the purchase of commodity-type items that are standardized and readily available, like wheat or basic office supplies, are often purchased through transactional relationships.

Let's consider a supply manager who is responsible for procuring furniture for a new office suite. The furniture is expected to last for at least 10 years, and there are no current plans to expand the office building or replace other existing furniture. The supply manager has categorized this purchase as a routine item in the portfolio matrix. She has many suppliers to choose from, so switching costs are low, and the furniture is produced from readily available materials. Access to technology is not important to this purchase, and the only information that needs to be shared is the specification. Given the characteristics of this purchase, the supply manager just needs a transactional relationship with her buyer.

COLLABORATIVE RELATIONSHIPS On the other hand, a manager should seek out a **collaborative relationship** when the buyer has limited supplier options, is procuring a critical item, needs technology innovation, or is concerned about the availability of supply. **Collaboration** implies working together and integrating processes between the buyer and supplier, which requires sharing information, knowledge, and expertise and making specific investments in the buyer-supplier relationship. This type of relationship typically takes time to develop (see GLOBAL CONNECTIONS 7.1).

As a result of the focus on building collaborative buyer-supplier relationships, firms are experiencing improved cooperation, increased capability, better access to technology, a reduction in risk and opportunism, and improved operational performance in the form of better quality, lower inventory levels, faster new product development cycles, higher productivity, lower materials and manufacturing costs, and shorter delivery lead times. For example, suppose that your supply manager is tasked with procuring photolithography equipment for a semiconductor manufacturer. The lead time for this equipment is approximately nine months, and the purchase will include ongoing service to maintain the equipment. Photolithography is a critical step in the manufacture of semiconductor chips, and there are only two international suppliers that can provide the level of technology needed for the supply manager's manufacturing plant. For the supply manager's firm to be on the cutting edge of semiconductor production, it must have access to the supplier's latest technology. Accessing this technology also requires much information sharing between the two firms. With only two available suppliers, both of which are located internationally, the supply risk is high. Given this purchasing situation, the supply manager should pursue a collaborative relationship.

transactional relationship
A relationship in which the buyer has many supplier choices, does not need to share internal company information during the exchange, is purchasing a routine item, does not require technology innovation from the supplier, and does not expect to experience shortages in supply.

arm's-length relationship
A transactional relationship.

collaborative relationship
A buyer-supplier relationship marked by long-term cooperation.

collaboration
Working together and integrating processes between the buyer and supplier, which requires sharing information, knowledge, and expertise and making specific investments in the buyer-supplier relationship.

MAKE INFORMED SUPPLIER SELECTION DECISIONS

With a clear understanding of what is needed in terms of materials, services, and the buyer-supplier relationship, a supply manager can proceed to selecting a supplier. The first step in the selection process is to identify the requirements for the future supplier. Then the search for potential suppliers begins. Once the suppliers have submitted their quotes or proposals, supply managers can evaluate the suppliers. Finally, the supply manager typically chooses a supplier through a negotiation process. The importance of identifying appropriate supplier selection criteria are illustrated in SC&O CURRENT EVENTS 7.2.

Strong Supplier Relationships at Honda and Toyota Lead to Higher Profits

When the consumer price index rose 11 percent over the course of six years, Honda was able to reduce costs by 19 percent with a net competitive gain of 26 percent. During the same time, Toyota saw a 30 percent reduction in component costs via target cost management systems and a codesign approach with suppliers. These numbers are even more impressive when compared with those of Toyota's biggest competitor, which was feeling good about limiting its material costs increases to "only" 7 percent. According to the fifteenth annual North American Automotive—Tier 1 Supplier Working Relations Index® Study, which looks at the automakers' supplier relations and how they affect original equipment manufacturer (OEM) profits, Ford, General Motors, FCA US, and Nissan collectively would have earned $2 billion more in operating profit in just one year had their supplier relations improved as much as Toyota's and Honda's did during that time.

Although some of Honda's and Toyota's competitors set broad, across-the-board cost reduction mandates for their suppliers (which seem to have had the opposite effect), Toyota and Honda have achieved world-class results through global collaboration. These global collaborative initiatives include preproduction design development several years prior to vehicle launch, supplier development programs to help suppliers improve processes continuously, and equity investment in some suppliers to increase alignment for joint success.

One word can explain the difference in supplier relations between Toyota and Honda and the other four automakers, said Henke: commitment. The two top-ranked automakers take supplier relations very seriously and actively work at it throughout their respective organizations, but particularly within their purchasing organizations. This includes the vice president of purchasing down to the buyers who work with the suppliers on a daily basis. They are executing the basics better than the other four automakers. While supplier relationships have many complexities, the issues involved are quite straightforward and the resulting OEM benefits are more than worth the effort to improve.

Speaking to the investment made in its suppliers, Honda reports that its best practices program has increased supplier productivity by about 50 percent, improved quality by 30 percent, and reduced costs by 7 percent. Suppliers who participate in the program agree to share 50 percent of the savings with Honda. Although building a supersupplier relationship requires a great deal of effort—on the parts of both supplier and customer—Toyota and Honda have demonstrated that collaborative relationships based on mutual trust, honesty, integrity, and an objective focus on results can make a competitive difference.

Source: Based on "OEM-Supplier Relations Study Shows Strong Gains for Toyota and Honda, with Ford, Nissan, FCA and GM Falling Well Behind," http://www.prnewswire.com/news-releases/oem-supplier-relations-study-shows-strong-gains-for-toyota-and-honda-with-ford-nissan-fca-and-gm-falling-well-behind-300084605.html.

Identifying Supplier Requirements with Weighted-Factor Analysis

Managers identify many requirements through the specification process. However, beyond clearly identifying what items the company needs, a supply manager must also know how important each of the various aspects of the purchase is in comparison to others. For example, you might identify your requirements for a new car as affordable, safe, and of high quality (meaning that it never breaks down), but what does "affordable" mean to you? Are you willing to trade affordability for safety? In an industrial purchasing situation, a supply manager must have a clear understanding of what the priorities are for a particular material or service that must be procured.

A common approach to identifying requirements and then evaluating suppliers against those requirements is **weighted-factor analysis (WFA)**, which can be performed on a simple spreadsheet. To create a weighted-factor model, it is necessary to (1) identify the key selection factors, (2) determine the relative importance or weight of each factor (the weightings

weighted-factor analysis (WFA)
A multicriteria decision-making method using weights.

Selecting Suppliers at Boeing

Supplier selection is an important aspect of supply chain and operations management. Consider the case of Boeing. In a single year, Boeing purchases 783 million parts and spends $28 billion. Approximately 75 percent of the suppliers who provide those parts are based in the United States; the rest are located around the world.

Potential suppliers for Boeing are evaluated on a range of criteria, including commercial offerings, ability, capacity, integrity, financial health, geographic location, performance, reliability, quality of product, on-time delivery, and overall customer-supplier relations. A key criterion is a proven ability to manage a subtier or distant supply chain. Subtier suppliers are the suppliers who provide raw materials and other items to first-tier or lower-tier Boeing suppliers.

Once the supplier is selected, Boeing personnel are embedded at supplier factories around the world to monitor quality, work with suppliers on process improvements, and ensure adherence to Boeing standards and schedules. Boeing also performs audits of supplier operations.

It appears that the benefits of this new approach are paying off. The parts shortages at their 737 plant are the lowest they've been in five years. Boeing has increased its output of planes to a higher rate than ever before. And Boeing announced a 21 percent increase in annual net profits: to $4 billion.

Sources: Based on "World Class Supplier Quality," http://787updates.newairplane.com/787-Suppliers/World-Class-Supplier-Quality; "Boeing Flying High with Supplier SMARTnerships," Keld Jensen, 2012, http://www.forbes.com/sites/keldjensen/2012/02/09/boeing-flying-high-with-supplier-smartnerships/#573d42dd5779.

should sum to 1 or to 100 percent), and (3) evaluate each supplier on each of the key selection factors. We will review the first two steps here and then discuss the third step, evaluating each supplier, below.

The method often used for WFA is multiple criteria decision making (MCDM). MCDM methods are useful when several criteria (or factors) are considered in making a decision. For example, you may want to consider multiple factors such as pay, quality of work life, and company culture in choosing which job offer to accept. Decisions that involve multiple decision criteria are appropriate for MCDM methods. Another MCDM method is the analytical hierarchy process. Although this process is beyond the scope of this text, it is but one of other, more complex methods for making multicriteria decisions.

For WFA, the first step, identify the key selection factors, is typically performed by a cross-functional team within the firm. The supply manager gathers those who will be affected by the supplier selection decision and asks them for a list of what is most important to them regarding the supplier. This list may include factors related to price, technical ability, quality performance, managerial skills, delivery and flexibility, financial stability, and capacity constraints. For high-level factors, it is also helpful to delineate subfactors. For example, a warehouse manager might evaluate delivery in terms of both lead time and on-time delivery performance. The more specific each subfactor is, the easier it will be to evaluate the suppliers against the chosen criteria.

Once the cross-functional team members have agreed on a list of critical factors, they must then come to agreement on how much weight they will give each of the factors and subfactors. Assigning such weights can be a difficult task because it requires group prioritization in the midst of individual goals. For example, the design engineer might value technical ability over price because the design team is responsible for the overall design of a final product, whereas the finance analyst might prioritize price because he is responsible for meeting the budget for the project. Through understanding one another's goals and keeping the overall goals of the company in mind, the team must agree on how to allocate 100 percentage points across the factors and subfactors. **SOLVED PROBLEM 7.1** illustrates how to complete the first two steps of a WFA.

MyLab Operations Management Video

SOLVED PROBLEM 7.1 >   Creating a Weighted-Factor Analysis

Problem: A commodity team for Carlston, Inc., a plastic extrusion parts producer, was tasked with selecting a new supplier. The team of five had representatives from purchasing (Alicia), engineering (Malcolm), manufacturing (Josh), marketing (Henry), and finance (Samantha). The team is working to define the appropriate evaluation criteria. Members need to agree on the most important criteria and then determine the relative importance of each factor by assigning weights (the weights should add either to 1 or to 100 percent).

Solution: Based on previous experience at Carlston, it was relatively easy to agree on the criteria to be used. Carlston had recently reviewed the characteristics associated with its most successful suppliers and found the most important criteria to be technical ability, managerial capability, quality, delivery performance, and price. Coming to an agreement on the relative importance of each factor, however, was a challenge. At the end of the first commodity team meeting, each of the five managers on the team submitted an initial set of weightings, which are given in TABLE 7.1.

TABLE 7.1 >

WFA Initial Weights for Carlston, Inc.

Factors	Alicia	Malcolm	Josh	Henry	Samantha
Technical	10	30	10	20	15
Management	10	20	20	30	15
Quality	20	15	30	30	20
Delivery	30	20	30	10	20
Price	30	15	10	10	30
Total	100	100	100	100	100

After two rounds of applying a Delphi technique in which managers explained why they had weighted each criterion as they had and then adjusted their own assigned weights with the information provided by the other team members, there were only slight disparities between the weightings, which are shown in TABLE 7.2.

TABLE 7.2 >

WFA after Delphi Weights by Carlston Managers

Factors	Alicia	Malcolm	Josh	Henry	Samantha	Mode
Technical	15	20	15	20	20	20
Management	15	15	15	15	15	15
Quality	25	30	30	25	25	25
Delivery	25	20	25	20	20	20
Price	20	15	15	20	20	20
Total	100	100	100	100	100	100

Because the weights were within five points of one another for each criterion, the team agreed to take the mode weight and use that in the WFA tool. The next step was to break each factor into subfactors (where appropriate) and allocate those weights. With agreement on the overall weight for each factor, the process of allocating the weights to subfactors proceeded relatively quickly, as shown in TABLE 7.3.

WFA Critical Factors and Final Weights for the Carlston Team		
Factors	**Weight**	**Subweight**
Technical	20	
Design		15
Experience		5
Management	15	
Responsiveness		10
Liquidity		5
Quality	25	
Defect rate		20
Practices		5
Delivery	20	
Lead time		10
On-time delivery		10
Price	20	20
Total	100	100

< TABLE 7.3

The WFA tool is now ready for supplier evaluation. Before team members can proceed to that step, however, they have to search for potential suppliers. To ensure objectivity in identifying the most important criteria, it is important to complete the first two steps in the WFA process before the search takes place. Otherwise, a member of the team might be biased in the weighting process, whether consciously or subconsciously, to give a particular supplier an advantage.

Searching for Potential Suppliers

A supply manager has many alternative sources for finding potential suppliers. These sources include the following:

- *Current suppliers.* The best place to start a search is in the buying firm's supplier database. The buying firm has data regarding performance for these suppliers and may have already developed the desired relationship.
- *The Internet.* The Internet provides easy access to many supplier databases and supplier websites.
- *Trade registers.* Trade registers are directories of suppliers for a particular type of product or service compiled by a third party. An example is *Thomas' Register of American Manufacturers.*
- *Trade journals.* Various trade or industry organizations publish journals, and suppliers in those fields often advertise in the journals.

- *Company personnel.* In addition to a firm's supplier database, fellow employees in other functional groups in the company (e.g., engineering, manufacturing, information technology) can be a good source for finding a new supplier.
- *Trade shows.* Trade shows enable interaction with multiple suppliers in one location at one time. They are often a quick and affordable way to be exposed quickly to suppliers.
- *Professional organizations.* Organizations such as the Institute for Supply Management provide opportunities to draw from the knowledge of others working in the same industry to find potential suppliers.

request for quote (RFQ) or request for proposal (RFP)
Contains the specification of what is needed and details the information that must be submitted by a supplier that wishes to be considered for the purchase.

Once the team has compiled a list of potential suppliers, it sends out a **request for quote (RFQ)** or a **request for proposal (RFP)**. The RFQ or RFP contains the specifications of what is needed and details the information that must be submitted by a supplier who wishes to be considered for the purchase. Companies typically use an RFQ when they know exactly what they need, and the supplier can respond with pricing and delivery quotes. An RFP is used when a firm knows what it would like to accomplish but is open to the materials, technology, and so forth used to meet the need. The supplier responds to an RFP with a proposal for how it would meet the specification given as well as the cost and timing to meet the specification. An RFQ or RFP should also ask suppliers to provide financial statements, references, evidence of previous performance, and anything else needed to evaluate the supplier against the factors previously identified.

Supplier Evaluation

Time and resources prohibit an in-depth evaluation of all potential suppliers, so supply managers often perform a first cut or preliminary evaluation of potential suppliers to narrow the list before conducting an in-depth evaluation of the most promising suppliers. Methods to reduce the number of suppliers in the pool include an examination of previous performance and an initial review of the information provided in the supplier quote or proposal.

supplier self-assessment
A survey administered to suppliers to determine fit with purchaser needs.

Once the list of potential suppliers has been narrowed, the selection team can ask the suppliers to complete a more in-depth supplier survey, or **supplier self-assessment**, which includes information about the supplier's principal officers, bank references, credit references, history of sales and profit, number of employees, space currently occupied, current defect rate, on-time delivery performance, and so forth. A member of the finance department might conduct a financial analysis to determine whether or not the supplier is financially stable enough to be reliable. In addition, if time and resources allow, the selection team can conduct a facility visit. Visiting a supplier's plant can be very educational. It allows the team to observe the supplier's process, confirm or reject what was provided in the supplier survey, and determine the likelihood that the supplier will be able to deliver on its commitments.

The team then uses the data collected in the WFA tool to evaluate and compare each of the potential suppliers. Evaluation scores are typically apportioned based on a total of 100 points and then multiplied by their weight. SOLVED PROBLEM 7.2 walks through this evaluation process (the third step of WFA).

 SOLVED PROBLEM 7.2 >

MyLab Operations Management Video

Supplier Evaluation Using Weighted-Factor Analysis

Problem: After identifying the critical factors for the plastic extrusion parts purchase and assigning the weights, Carlston's supplier selection team sent out an RFQ to a list of potential suppliers. The RFQ contained the specifications for the parts in question as well as a request for information related to the critical factors.

After reviewing all the supplier responses, the team identified the top three suppliers—Alpha, Beta, and Gamma—and proceeded with an in-depth evaluation, including creating and administering a supplier self-assessment. The self-assessment asked critical questions to collect data for each of the five areas in the WFA. With agreement about what questions to ask and how the data would be captured and analyzed, evaluating supplier performance was relatively straightforward. Each team member evaluated all three suppliers across all five factors, and then the team met to resolve any differences. TABLE 7.4 shows the evaluation scores for each supplier (scores were based on 100 points).

Supplier Evaluation Scores for the Plastic Extrusion Parts Purchase

< TABLE 7.4

Factors	Alpha's Score	Beta's Score	Gamma's Score
Technical			
Design	95	80	95
Experience	75	85	80
Management			
Responsiveness	90	90	90
Liquidity	65	85	70
Quality			
Defect rate	80	90	95
Practices	75	85	80
Delivery			
Lead time	60	80	85
On-time delivery	65	85	80
Price	70	85	70
Total			

Solution: To calculate the overall score for each supplier, simply multiply the raw scores by the previously determined weights. The resulting WFA model is given in TABLE 7.5.

∨ TABLE 7.5

WFA Evaluation of Suppliers by Carlston

Factors	Weight	Sub-weight	Alpha's Raw Score	Alpha's Weighted Score	Beta's Raw Score	Beta's Weighted Score	Gamma's Raw Score	Gamma's Weighted Score
Technical	0.20							
Design		0.15	95	14.25	80	12.00	95	14.25
Experience		0.05	75	3.75	85	4.25	80	4.00
Management	0.15							
Responsiveness		0.10	90	9.00	90	9.00	90	9.00
Liquidity		0.05	65	3.25	85	4.25	70	3.50
Quality	0.25							
Defect rate		0.20	80	16.00	90	18.00	95	19.00
Practices		0.05	75	3.75	85	4.25	80	4.00
Delivery	0.20							
Lead time		0.10	60	6.00	80	8.00	85	8.50
On-time delivery		0.10	65	6.50	85	8.50	80	8.00
Price	0.20	0.20	70	14.00	85	17.00	70	14.00
Total	1.00	1.00		76.50		85.25		84.25

Based on the comparative evaluation of the three suppliers, the team decided to eliminate Alpha from consideration and proceed with negotiations with Beta and Gamma. The team will make its final supplier selection decision after the negotiations are completed. We demonstrate how to do this in Excel in USING TECHNOLOGY 7.1.

USING >
TECHNOLOGY 7.1

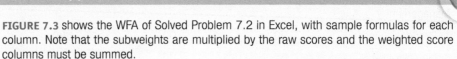

WFA for Supplier Selection

FIGURE 7.3 shows the WFA of Solved Problem 7.2 in Excel, with sample formulas for each column. Note that the subweights are multiplied by the raw scores and the weighted score columns must be summed.

	A	B	C	D	E	F	G	H	I
1	Factors	Weight	Sub-weight	Alpha Raw Score	Alpha Weighted Score	Beta Raw Score	Beta Weighted Score	Gamma Raw Score	Gamma Weighted Score
4	Technical	0.2							
5	Design		0.15	95	14.25	80	12	=C6*F6	14.25
6	Experience		0.05	75	3.75	85	4.25	80	4
7	Management	0.15							
8	Responsiveness		0.1	90	9	90	9	90	9
9	Liquidity		0.05	65	3.25	85	4.25	70	3.5
10	Quality	0.25						=C11*H11	
11	Defect Rate		0.2	80	16	90	18	95	19
12	Practices		0.05	75	3.75	85	4.25	80	4
13	Delivery	0.2							
14	Lead Time		0.1	60	6	80	8	85	8.5
15	On-Time Delivery		0.1	65	6.5	85	8.5	80	8
16	Price	0.2	0.2	70	=C15*D15	85	17	70	14
17	Total	1							

∧ FIGURE 7.3

Weighted Matrix in Excel

Negotiating the Agreement

Negotiation is the final step in the supplier selection process for most purchases, particularly when price is not the only important variable in the selection decision. The negotiation process is also a helpful tool in understanding all issues of the procurement. The formal negotiation process has three steps: (1) preparation, (2) face-to-face negotiation, and (3) debriefing (FIGURE 7.4).

PREPARATION Approximately 90 percent of the time involved in a successful negotiation should be invested in preparation. To negotiate a beneficial agreement successfully, the negotiator must do the following:

- Possess an understanding of the item or service needed
- Analyze the relative bargaining positions of both parties
- Conduct a price or cost analysis
- Know the seller and his or her underlying interest
- Be aware of cultural nuances

FIGURE 7.4 >

Steps in the Negotiation Process

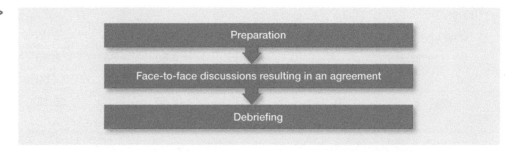

NEGOTIATION PLAN Preparing also involves creating a **negotiation plan**, a preparation tool in which the supply manager outlines all the contract terms that need to be negotiated with the supplier. Most negotiation plans include target and walk-away positions for details such as price, lead time, acceptable defect rates, and the length of the contract. The plan should also help the supply manager prepare any tactics that might be used during the negotiation, including where the negotiation will be held and the order in which issues will be addressed. Depending on the dollar value of the purchase, this negotiation plan may require approval from upper management before the supply manager begins face-to-face negotiations.

negotiation plan
A preparation tool in which the supply manager outlines all the contract terms that need to be negotiated with the supplier.

FACE-TO-FACE NEGOTIATIONS Much has been written about win-win negotiations. **Win-win** does not mean that both parties leave the negotiation equally well off; rather, it means that both the supply manager and the supplier leave the negotiation better off than they would have been without the agreement. To achieve a win-win agreement, both parties try to understand each other's needs and wants, build on common ground, and work together to develop creative solutions that provide additional value. The primary use of *power* in a win-win negotiation is to focus on common rather than personal interests, and the parties in this type of negotiation are likely to engage in open sharing of information.

win-win
A healthy buyer-supplier relationship.

Although win-win exists only when both parties are willing to approach the negotiation from that perspective, the supply manager must also be prepared to negotiate with suppliers who take a win-lose perspective (a position in which one party wants to take all). Properly preparing for win-lose negotiations with suppliers includes being prepared for manipulative tactics and being able to modify tactics when they do not work.

Effective negotiators are well prepared before entering the negotiation. They establish lower and upper ranges for each major issue and are willing to compromise or revise their goals, particularly when new information successfully challenges their position. They view issues independently and explore many options. Effective negotiators focus on the common ground between the parties and have good listening skills. Finally, they think rapidly and clearly under pressure. All these skills take practice to master, so practice negotiation sessions should be included in the preparation phase.

DEBRIEFING SESSIONS After the negotiation, the team should conduct a debriefing session as a means of self-assessment. A **debriefing session** is a meeting that the negotiation team holds soon after the negotiation to provide accurate and timely feedback. The team should identify what was done well and what could be improved, as well as document the lessons learned. Once the debriefing session is completed, the team leader should provide individual and team feedback.

debriefing session
A meeting that the negotiation team holds soon after the negotiation that provides accurate and timely feedback.

CREATE AND DEVELOP CONSTRUCTIVE SUPPLIER RELATIONSHIPS

When a supplier is not able to meet a buying firm's needs, the firm has three choices: (1) produce the material or service within the firm (in-source), (2) find another supplier, or (3) develop the existing supplier. Bringing production in-house and selecting a new supplier are not only resource-intensive options but are sometimes not realistic options either, so a buying firm will often choose instead to develop the existing supplier. FIGURE 7.5 illustrates the steps in the supplier development process. **Supplier development** is the process of helping a supplier improve performance in areas such as cost, delivery, and quality. For example, Toyota has an excellent supplier development program in which it provides consulting from experienced midmanagers to suppliers of parts and components. The result is lowered costs for Toyota and improved performance for the suppliers. We will discuss each of the seven supplier development steps next.

supplier development
The process of helping a supplier improve performance in areas such as cost, delivery, and quality.

Identifying Suppliers to Develop

The first step in the process to develop suppliers is to determine which suppliers a firm should focus on. Developing a supplier takes time and money, so a supply manager must take care to focus development efforts where the buying firm will most benefit. There are many reasons a particular supplier might be the focus of development. Candidates for supplier development include a

FIGURE 7.5 >

Supplier Development Process

1. Identify critical supplier for development
2. Form cross-functional team
3. Meet with supplier's top management team
4. Identify opportunities and probability for development
5. Define key metrics and cost-sharing mechanisms
6. Reach agreement on key projects and joint resource requirements
7. Monitor status of projects and modify strategies as appropriate

Based on Handfield, Krause, Scannell, and Monczka, 1998, "An Empirical Investigation of Supplier Development Reactive and Strategic Process," *Journal of Operations Management* 17(1), 39–58.

supplier who provides a large volume of products or services relative to other suppliers; a supplier who is an existing or potential source of competitive advantage; a supplier who may not be able to meet the firm's competitive needs five years from now; and a supplier who does not meet the firm's current needs in terms of responsiveness, quality, delivery, capacity, or technical capability.

Forming a Cross-Functional Team

The second step is to form a cross-functional team by inviting representatives from the functional areas within the firm that have an interest in the particular supplier's performance to join in the development process. By forming a cross-functional team, the supply manager is able to develop internal consensus on what a company needs from a supplier and what a supplier may need from the firm. Typical members of the supplier development cross-functional team include representatives from supply management, engineering, operations, and quality control.

Involving Top Management

For a buyer-supplier initiative to be successful, management from both companies should be aware of the parameters and display support both verbally and in the form of resource commitment. This third step, resource commitment, although not a formal contract, should be documented and acknowledged (through meeting minutes or written correspondence) so that all are aware of what has been promised. Meeting with the supplier's management also helps establish the trust and collaborative relationship necessary for successful supplier development. Firm managers can also use this initial engagement with top management to ensure strategic alignment on the reasons for the development initiative, establish a positive tone for the interface between the supply manager and supplier representatives, and foster two-way communication.

Identifying Opportunities

The opportunities for development are often linked to the reason the supplier was chosen in the first step. If there is an existing failure on the part of the supplier, such as a high defect rate, addressing that issue would be the primary concern. Or the opportunity might be something to prepare for future projects, perhaps driven by projected requirements and expectations of customers. The important outcome of this fourth step is to agree jointly on areas for development and improvement.

Defining Key Metrics and Cost Sharing

Once it has established the scope of opportunities, the development team (consisting of both buyer and supplier representatives) must define what success looks like, which includes determining if the opportunities are realistic and achievable and establishing agreed-upon measures and improvement goals. An important yet often overlooked aspect of this fifth step is to determine equitable cost- and benefit-sharing arrangements. Problems such as poor communication can occur if these arrangements are not addressed before work on the projects begins. Both the buying firm and supplier will be more motivated to work on the chosen projects if they know beforehand what their benefit or cost will be.

Agreeing on Projects and Resources

Now the real work begins. Unfortunately, many supplier development efforts stall in the fourth or fifth step because that is when resources need to be committed. After defining key metrics and how costs and benefits will be shared, it is time to define and prioritize clearly which projects the team will work on. With the identification of the projects, the team must also identify necessary resources and obtain a commitment from upper management to allocate those resources. The team should also develop specific metrics that demonstrate success for each project. To ensure that projects stay on track, the team should develop visible milestones and time horizons. As SC&O CURRENT EVENTS 7.3 illustrates, many firms are focused on helping their suppliers become more socially and environmentally sustainable through compliance with a supplier code of conduct.

Monitoring Status and Modifying

What gets measured gets done. When a team knows that there will be a review of the committed projects—with measures—it is more likely that progress will be made on those projects. Therefore, routine monitoring by upper management from both firms is important in the supplier development process. Measured monitoring ensures an ongoing two-way exchange of information and provides a means to ask for additional support or to propose modifications to the plan as necessary to maintain momentum or address new findings.

Supplier Code of Conduct at Apple   < SC&O CURRENT
EVENTS 7.3

In Chapter 1, we talked about the Apple Supplier Code of Conduct. We can now discuss how it is managed.

Apple, supported by local third-party experts, audits suppliers to ensure compliance with its Code of Conduct and to identify areas for improvement. Together they interview workers, review hundreds of payroll documents, assess onsite the health and safety conditions of the facilities, and inspect environmental conditions inside and out. Each facility is graded on more than 500 data points corresponding to the Code of Conduct.

Noncompliant suppliers must submit a Corrective Action Plan within two weeks of the audit, outlining how they will fix the problems found. Apple's team of verification specialists then works with suppliers, checking in at thirty-, sixty-, and ninety-day intervals to make sure they're on track. Senior management is notified of any delayed progress.

When suppliers require extra support to comply with the Code of Conduct, Apple sends its team of experts as part of its partnership program. It tailors its approach to help the facility improve through refining business practices and management systems relating to labor, human rights, environment, and health and safety. By working with its suppliers instead of only policing them, Apple reports significant improvements in its Supplier Code of Conduct compliance.

Supplier Scorecard

Supplier Name:
Category:
Annual Volume:
Annual Spend:
Author Name:
Date:

Score	Definition
Excellent	Exceeds the Buyer requirements
Satisfactory	Meets the Buyer requirements
Unsatisfactory	Fails to meet the Buyer requirements

Evaluation Category	Metric	Unit of Measure	Target	Excellent	Satisfactory	Unsatisfactory	Data Source	Data Reporter	1Q05	2Q05	3Q05	4Q05	Average	Trend	Comments	Excellent-Exceeds Requirements	Satisfactory-Meets Requirements	Unsatisfactory-Fails to Meet Requirements
Price	Price	Rating 1-5	3	4-5	2-3	0-1	ERP Reports	Buyer	2.0	2.0	1.0	1.0	1.5	Declining	Prices dropping, but significantly less than competition	Price is lower than competitors	Price is comparable to competitors	Price is higher than competitors
Price	Annual Cost Savings	%	5	>6	4-6	<4	Supplier Report	Supplier	3%	3%	4%	4%	3.5%	Improving	Saving increasing, but raw material and component costs are hindering progress	Annual cost saving target exceeded	Annual cost saving target met	Annual cost saving target not achieved
Price	Price compared to market benchmark	Rating 1-5	3	4-5	2-3	0-1	Supplier Report	Supplier	2.0	2.0	1.0	1.0	1.5	Declining		Price is lower than competitors	Price is comparable to competitors	Price is higher than competitors
Overall Price Ranking		Rating 1-5	3	4-5	2-3	0-1	Buyer completed scorecard	Buyer	2	2	1.0	1.0	1.5	Declining				
Quality	Quality	Rating 1-5	4	4-5	3	0-2	QA Intranet	QA Intranet	3.0	3.0	3.0	2.0	2.8	Declining		Quality rating target exceeded	Quality rating target met	Quality rating target not met
Overall Quality Ranking		Rating 1-5	3	4-5	2-3	0-1	Buyer completed scorecard	Buyer	3	3	2	2	2.5	Declining	Quality is becoming a concern			
Service	Buyer Customer Service Fill Rate	%	100	99-100	<99 with improvement plan	<99 without improvement plan	ERP Reports	Buyer	98.5%	98.5%	100%	100%	99.3%	Improving	Possibly due to increasing production capacity	Buyer customer service fill rate sustained between 99%-100%	Buyer customer service fill rate below 99% and supplier has plans in place to improve supply continuity	Buyer customer service fill rate below 99% and supplier does not have plans in place to improve supply continuity
Service	Supplier % On-time Delivery	%	100	99.5-100	<99.5 with improvement plan	<99.5 without improvement plan	Supplier Report	Supplier	98.5%	98.5%	100%	100%	99.3%	Improving	Possibly due to increasing production capacity	Supplier % on-time delivery sustained between 99.5%-100%	Supplier % on-time delivery below 99.5% and supplier has plans in place to improve supply continuity	Supplier % on-time delivery below 99.5% and supplier does not have plans in place to improve supply continuity
Service	Invoice Accuracy	Rating 1-5	3	4-5	2-3	0-1	Buyer	Buyer	2	2	1	1	1.5	Declining	There has been turnover in accounts payable at the buyer ... could be a potential factor in decline	Invoice accuracy target exceeded	Invoice accuracy target met	Invoice accuracy target not met
Service	Production Capacity Available	Buyer Forecast	150	200	150	<100	Supplier Report	Supplier	150%	170%	180%	200%	175%	Improving	Uncertain why capacity is increasing. Speculation that they may be losing customers	Supplier has 2.0X production capacity to meet annual demand	Supplier has 1.5X production capacity to meet annual demand	Supplier does not have capacity to meet annual demand
Service	Customer Service (i.e. ease of ordering, flexibility, etc...)	Rating 1-5	3	4-5	2-3	0-1	Buyer	Buyer	2	2	1	1	1.5	Declining	There has been turnover in accounts payable at the buyer ... could be a potential factor in decline	All issues are resolved completely and in a timely manner	Reasonable number of interactions to resolve issues	Multiple buyer follow-ups required to resolve issues
Service	Obsolescence	Rating 1-5	3	4-5	2-3	0-1	Supplier Report	Supplier	2	2	1	1	1.5	Declining	Potential factor in problems with price relative to its competitors	No material being held that could become classified as obsolete	Minimal level of material that could be classified as obsolete	Above normal level of material that could be classified as obsolete
Service	Value Added Services	Rating 1-5	3	4-5	2-3	0-1	Buyer	Buyer	3	3	4	4	3.5	Improving	Research & development reports getting increased innovation support from molded caps	Significant services provided that add value to material purchased and improve supplier-buyer relationship	Minimal services provided that materially improve supplier-buyer relationship	No value added services provided beyond contractual requirements
Overall Service Ranking		Rating 1-5	3	4-5	2-3	0-1	Buyer completed scorecard	Buyer	2	2	1	1	1.5	Declining	Invoice accuracy and customer service driving decline in service ranking			
Other	Buyer Policy Compliance	Rating 1-5	3	4-5	2-3	0-1	Buyer	Buyer	3.0	3.0	3.0	3.0	3.0	Steady		Exceeds requirements	Meets requirements	Does not meet requirements
Other	Supplier Diversity (North America Only)	Rating 1-5	3	4-5	2-3	0-1	Buyer	Buyer	3.0	4.0	4.0	4.0	3.8	Improving	Concerns that the pursuit of diverse suppliers is driving costs	Exceeds requirements	Meets requirements	Does not meet requirements
Overall Other Ranking		Rating 1-5	3	4-5	2-3	0-1	Buyer completed scorecard	Buyer	3	3	3	3	3	Steady				
Overall Ranking		Rating 1-5	3	4-5	2-3	0-1	Buyer completed scorecard	Buyer	2	2	1	1	1.5	Declining	Overall there is concern about service and price, and a growing concern about quality.			

▲ FIGURE 7.6

Supplier Scorecard Example

Realizing a competitive advantage from the supply base requires a strategic orientation toward supplier development. Relationship management within the buying firm and between the supply manager and supplier is critical to supplier development success.

ROVIDE CONSTRUCTIVE SUPPLIER FEEDBACK

Supply managers should provide ongoing feedback to their suppliers. This feedback is commonly given in the form of a report card, or a scorecard. A **supplier scorecard** serves two key roles for the supply manager: (1) it identifies the supplier performance metrics that are most critical to the supply manager's organization, and (2) it enables the evaluation of suppliers against key metrics. From the supplier perspective, feedback received via a scorecard does three things: (1) it enables a link between the supplier's own internal performance measures and the strategic objectives of the supply manager, (2) it enables the supplier to identify opportunities for improvement, and (3) it documents the criteria used to define what levels of performance are considered unacceptable. A sample supplier scorecard is shown in FIGURE 7.6.

supplier scorecard
A communication device that serves two key roles for the supply manager: (1) it identifies the supplier performance metrics that are most critical to the supply manager's organization, and (2) it enables the evaluation of suppliers against these key metrics.

Designing and Implementing the Supplier Scorecard

The design and implementation of supplier scorecards involves four fundamental steps (FIGURE 7.7). The first step is to identify ways in which the supplier's performance affects the buying firm's strategic and operational objectives. These key performance measures should be included in the supplier report card. Because the performance measures are tied to the strategic objectives of the buying organization, the scorecard can serve as a mechanism for strategic planning and review.

The second step in the design and implementation of a supplier scorecard is to ensure that the key performance measures identified in the first step are balanced and objective. Balanced scorecards select measures that provide a broad view of performance. The set of metrics must also be objective, focusing on measurable, valued-added results, and should be few in number. A limited number of balanced, objective metrics allows the supplier to use the measures to drive performance. Common categories of performance measures include lead time, on-time delivery, fill rate, accounts payable match rate, order accuracy, quality (defect rate), responsiveness, and cost.

In the third step, the supply manager should engage the supplier in the design and implementation of the scorecard to ensure buy-in. It is best to do so early in the process to allow time for the supplier to provide feedback on the metrics and precisely how they will be measured. The supplier must also buy into the stated goals and objectives and believe that there is mutual benefit in the scorecard process. With buy-in, both parties are more likely to dedicate the resources needed to use the report card as a means for continuous development and a tool to improve collaboration.

< FIGURE 7.7

Design and Implementation of a Supplier Scorecard

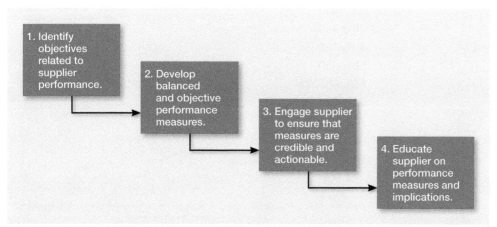

Based on Doolen, Traxler, McBride, 2006, "Using Scorecards for Supplier Performance Improvement: Case Application in a Lean Manufacturing Organization," *Engineering Management Journal*, 18(2), 2–34.

The fourth step in the scorecard design and implementation process is to train suppliers on the final scorecard metrics, the delivery mechanism, and the implications for acceptable or unacceptable performance. Successful scorecard processes also include a mechanism for the suppliers to provide feedback to the supply manager in return and to reconcile any discrepancies in the scorecard data. The supply manager should include an implementation date with instructions to the suppliers. It is also helpful to use the scorecard on a trial basis (with no negative consequences) for a number of weeks or months before implementing any penalties for poor performance.

SOLVED PROBLEM 7.3 shows how to develop a scorecard for a firm in the automotive industry. SC&O CURRENT EVENTS 7.4 discusses scorecard implementation.

 **SOLVED PROBLEM 7.3 >**   **Supplier Scorecard Design**

MyLab Operations Management
Video

Problem: Quality accounts for 40 percent of the overall supplier scorecard for an automotive firm because a primary objective of the firm is to produce a safe, defect-free automobile for its customers.[1] Two of the primary performance metrics in that section are parts per million (PPM) defects and percentage PPM improvement. To ensure that these performance measures are objective, the firm has established the following measurement and scoring criteria.

PPM Defect Rate

$$\text{Performance measurement} = \frac{\text{number of defects}}{\text{total opportunities for defects}} \times 1{,}000{,}000 \qquad (7.1)$$

Allocation of scorecard points:
Points for PPM defect rate will be allocated on the supplier scorecard as follows:

PPM Defect Rate	Scorecard Points
0	20
1–20	19
21–40	18
41–60	17
61–80	16
81–100	15
101–150	14
151–200	13
201–250	12
251–300	11
301–350	10
351–400	9
401–450	8
451–500	7
501–550	6
551–600	5
601–700	4
701–800	3
801–900	2
901–1,000	1
> 1,000	0

[1]Based on an example given in "How to Give a Quality Score to Your Supplier," http://www.metricstream.com/insights/qualityScore.htm.

Percentage PPM Improvement

$$\text{Performance measurement} = \frac{\text{previous PPM defect rate} - \text{current PPM defect rate}}{\text{previous PPM defect rate}} \times 100$$

$$(7.2)$$

Allocation of scorecard points:

Percentage PPM Improvement	Scorecard Points
75–100	5
60–74	4
45–59	3
30–44	2
15–29	1
< 15 (includes negative numbers)	0

The automotive manufacturer met with each of its suppliers 18 months ago to review the proposed scorecard and allow the suppliers to provide feedback on the measures. The scorecard has been functioning well for about a year. Each quarter, the supply managers at the manufacturer collect data from their internal systems, complete the scorecard, and then make it available to the suppliers. The suppliers have 30 days to reconcile their data and the data provided. Changes are made when the supplier can provide evidence that the data provided by the supply manager is incorrect.

Another quarter has come to a close, and the following data are available for one of the suppliers. The supply manager is responsible for calculating the performance measures and updating the scorecard with the points earned.

number of defects: 3
number of parts received: 40,000
PPM defect rate for the prior quarter: 110

Solution:

PPM defect rate: $\dfrac{3}{40,000} \times 1,000,000 = 75$

Allocated scorecard points $= 16$

Percentage PPM improvement: $\dfrac{110 - 75}{110} \times 100 = 32\%$

Allocated scorecard points $= 2$

The supply manager would then fill out the quality section of the scorecard as follows:

First Quarter, Quality Section	Performance Metric	Maximum Possible Points	Performance Achieved	Points Earned
	PPM defect rate	20	75	16
	Percentage PPM improvement	5	32	2

Once all sections of the report card have been populated, the scorecard should be made available to the supplier for its review and reconciliation.

Measurement Leads to Improvement

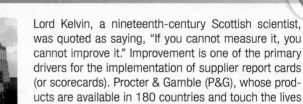

Lord Kelvin, a nineteenth-century Scottish scientist, was quoted as saying, "If you cannot measure it, you cannot improve it." Improvement is one of the primary drivers for the implementation of supplier report cards (or scorecards). Procter & Gamble (P&G), whose products are available in 180 countries and touch the lives of about 4.4 billion people, understands this principle very well. In April 2012, P&G announced that it would even share its environmental sustainability scorecard analysis tools with other companies.

Rick Hughes, P&G's chief purchasing officer, explains that the "scorecard is about collaboration and innovation." The scorecard measures improvements in nine key areas such as water and energy use, waste disposal, and greenhouse gas emissions from year to year. P&G uses these metrics to calculate a supplier rating or score, which can negatively or positively affect a supplier's chances for future opportunities.

The scorecard has been a success for P&G. The company's data shows an aggregate supplier improvement in 55 percent of all the measurable categories. In addition, Hughes elaborates that "about 25 percent of our external business partners offered innovation ideas where they could work with P&G to further improve our environmental footprint." The scorecard has been an integral part of P&G's sustainability efforts, which according to its internal estimates created almost $1 billion of bottom-line savings in 10 years.

P&G's scorecard also facilitates industry-wide collaboration, with P&G serving as a knowledge base and advisor to its suppliers. In addition, the scorecard identifies potential areas for improvement. Using the scorecard, P&G has seen significant improvements and savings with respect to hazardous waste and water usage and disposal, greenhouse gas emissions, and fuel usage. These improvements are not reserved for developing economies, which may have ostensibly more low-hanging fruit. P&G's analysis shows that, although suppliers in Brazil, Russia, India, and China have improved the most, their U.S. counterparts are not far behind.

Supplier report cards or scorecards are an important way for firms to improve supply chain efficiencies and reduce costs. When used most effectively, scorecards can also nurture collaboration and mutual gain. For example, most of P&G's suppliers appreciate the commitment that the company shows toward the environment and sustainable operations. When firms communicate scorecard goals, metrics, and analysis effectively, everyone, including nature, can breathe a little easier.

Source: Based on "P&G Shares Data, Results and Analysis Tool from Supplier Scorecard," Apr. 4, 2012, http://news.pg.com/press-release/pg-corporate-announcements/pg-shares-data-results-and-analysis-tool-supplier-scorecard.

Managing Across Majors 7.2 Finance and accounting majors, scorecards often include financial ratios such as inventory turns and operational measures such as on-time delivery.

Delivery and Cost Assessment

In addition to the quality performance metrics described in Solved Problem 7.3, supply managers often calculate **on-time delivery** percentages (the number of items delivered on time divided by the total number of items delivered) and dollars saved by the supplier through a supplier-initiated cost savings project as part of the scorecard process. If the supplier is responsible for maintaining on-site inventory at the buying firm, the following additional metrics are typically included in the scorecard:

on-time delivery
An important performance metric for suppliers.

- *Percentage of stock outs,* meaning how often the part is not available when needed:

$$\frac{\text{number of times the item is not available when requested}}{\text{total number of times the item is requested}} \qquad (7.3)$$

- *Inventory turnover,* meaning how many times per year the inventory is used and replaced (or "turned over"):

$$\frac{\text{cost of goods sold}}{\text{average inventory value}} \tag{7.4}$$

- *Days of inventory,* meaning that given the annual level of sales as indicated by the cost of goods sold, how many days of inventory are on hand. It is found by first calculating daily cost of goods sold and then dividing by average inventory:

$$\frac{(365 \times \text{average inventory})}{\text{cost of goods sold}} \tag{7.5}$$

It can also be calculated as *weeks of inventory*:

$$\frac{(52 \times \text{average inventory})}{\text{cost of goods sold}} \tag{7.6}$$

Supplier Awards

Supplier scorecards are often used to facilitate **supplier award programs**, which provide the opportunity for buying firms to honor the suppliers who are vital to helping the firm deliver superior quality and value to its end customers for their commitment and outstanding service. SC&O CURRENT EVENTS 7.5 provides an example of a supplier award program.

supplier award programs
Methods for identifying and rewarding outstanding suppliers.

Intel's Award-Winning Supplier: Applied Materials

< SC&O CURRENT EVENTS 7.5

Recently, Intel Corporation recognized 19 suppliers with its Preferred Quality Supplier Award. This award, given annually, is presented to only a handful of Intel's suppliers each year. To determine qualifying suppliers, Intel uses a report card that analyzes its suppliers on several metrics, including performance; cost; quality; availability (e.g., delivery); environmental, social, and governance goals; improvement plans; and business systems. Intel considers only those suppliers who score 80 percent or higher on the report card.

Applied Materials, Inc. was one of the 19 companies selected by Intel. "Intel is very pleased to congratulate Applied Materials for their fifth consecutive Preferred Quality Supplier Award," said Dave Bloss, Director of Intel's Fab Equipment group. "Applied Materials provided Intel with exceptional support for our technology and ramp activities, in addition to a demonstrated commitment to operational excellence. We look forward to Applied Materials' continued success on future Intel technologies."

In response, Dr. Randhir Thakur, executive vice president and general manager of the Silicon Systems Group at Applied Materials, said, "[W]e are extremely pleased to receive our fifth consecutive Intel Preferred Quality Supplier Award. As we celebrate the 50th anniversary of Moore's Law this year, the semiconductor industry is experiencing monumental inflections [also called "tipping points"] enabled by new device designs and materials innovation. We are committed to providing Intel with high-quality products and exceptional levels of support to address these inflections and move the industry forward."

Intel's report card helps it manage all its suppliers and provides data about day-to-day business transactions. Intel also uses the report card to identify potential strategic suppliers for future projects and products. These programs also motivate non-award-winning suppliers to improve quality and strengthen their business relationship with the firm.

Source: Based on "Applied Materials Receives Intel's Preferred Quality Supplier Award," Applied Materials Press Release, March 4, 2015.

In the beginning of this chapter, we saw how Raytheon was proactive in developing its supplier relationships in order to become a customer of choice—the customer that receives the best terms, needed manufacturing capacity, and first dibs on design innovations. By becoming a customer of choice for its suppliers, Raytheon can become the supplier of choice for its customers.

Procurement wanted to transition from tactical relationships, focused on price negotiations and placing purchase orders, to more strategic, collaborative relationships that involved the participation of suppliers up front during the design of a new product, where there are real opportunities to take cost out of a process. This kind of collaboration was a different way of thinking at Raytheon. Not that long ago, the defense contractor was a vertically integrated company that designed and built almost everything it produced. An estimated 80 cents of every dollar of sales was created in house; the other 20 cents came from Raytheon's suppliers in the form of raw materials and parts that Raytheon kitted and fashioned into products.

In this new dynamic marketplace, that ratio has been turned upside down, and supply drives the supply chain: Now, about 70 cents of each dollar of sales emanates from beyond Raytheon's four walls. "Our suppliers are integrated into our processes," says Neil Perry, Director, Supply Chain Learning at Raytheon. "Instead of delivering commodities, like screws, they are delivering completed assemblies that we bring together in our plants." As such, he adds, there is little margin for error. "We have to understand the capabilities of the supply base to ensure that we are in compliance with regulations and quality standards. Reducing risk is an imperative."

Summary

In this chapter, we focused on supplier management. Supplier management can be divided into four processes: (1) identifying the need, (2) selecting the supplier, (3) developing the supplier, and (4) providing feedback to the supplier.

1. When identifying the need, a supply manager must ensure that the specifications include a description of both materials and services that are needed. The supply manager is also responsible for identifying the type of buyer-supplier relationship required.

2. With a clear understanding of what is needed in terms of materials, services, and the buyer-supplier relationship, a supply manager can proceed to selecting a supplier. This process includes identifying the requirements for the future supplier, including:
   a. Searching for potential suppliers
   b. Evaluating potential suppliers
   c. Choosing a supplier

3. When a supplier is not able to meet a buying firm's needs, the supply manager may need to invest in a supplier development process. Following the seven steps of supplier development as presented in this chapter can aid in that effort.

4. We presented a process for providing supplier feedback through the use of a scorecard and suggested some appropriate performance metrics. The scorecard can also be used to manage a supplier award program to recognize the superior performance of the firm's best suppliers and encourage improved performance from other suppliers.

By focusing on all four processes, supply managers can forge strong links with suppliers in their supply chains. These strong links can result in lower costs, a stable supply of materials and services, quality improvement, better risk management, and accelerated innovation.

Key Terms

arm's-length relationship   171
collaboration   171
collaborative relationship   171
complex specification   169
debriefing session   179
negotiation plan   179
on-time delivery   186

request for proposal (RFP)   176
request for quote (RFQ)   176
scope of work   169
simple specification   169
specification   168
supplier award programs   187
supplier development   179

supplier management   167
supplier scorecard   183
supplier self-assessment   176
transactional relationship   171
weighted-factor analysis (WFA)   172
win-win   179

Integrative Learning Exercise

Identify a small company. Visit the company to learn about its supplier management challenges. Assist the company in developing a supplier scorecard that can be used to support the supply manager. Be sure to state clearly the critical performance metrics and how these metrics will be used to evaluate suppliers.

Integrative Experiential Exercise

With a group of students, visit a local company. Ask the company representatives to describe for you how they manage their suppliers. Questions you should ask and discover answers to include the following:

1. In what instances does the company employ a transactional supplier relationship?

2. Does the company now or has it ever employed a collaborative supplier relationship? If so, describe the collaboration. What were the benefits of the collaborative relationship? What challenges had to be overcome to realize the benefits?

3. How does the company identify and select suppliers? Is the company actively involved in developing suppliers?

4. Does the company have a supplier scorecard? How was the scorecard developed? In what ways is it used to evaluate suppliers?

Discussion Questions

1. What advantages result from developing strong links with suppliers in the supply chain?

2. Briefly describe the four processes of supplier management.

3. What is meant by a specification as it relates to supplier management?

4. Under what circumstances should a transactional supplier relationship be pursued?

5. Under what circumstances should a collaborative supplier relationship be pursued?

6. Identify some general steps that can help achieve the full benefits of collaboration.

7. Why is it important for companies to have a strategy in place concerning collaboration? What should the strategy involve?

8. What advantages, in addition to cost savings, can a successful collaborative supplier relationship achieve?

9. What steps are necessary to perform a weighted-factor analysis for evaluating suppliers?

10. What are some alternative sources for identifying potential suppliers?

11. To increase the likelihood of a successful negotiation, where should most of the effort be devoted?

12. What options are available to the buyer when a supplier is unable to meet the buyer's needs and requirements?

13. In what ways does a supplier scorecard help the supply manager?

14. How can the supplier scorecard assist the supplier?

15. Identify the basic steps in the design and implementation of supplier scorecards.

Solved Problems

Supplier Selection

WEIGHTED-FACTOR ANALYSIS
SOLVED PROBLEM 7.1

1. The critical factors for a sourced part have been identified, and weights have been assigned to each factor. The factors and weights are as follows:

Factors	Weights
Design	0.30
Function	0.20
Responsiveness	0.10
Flexibility	0.05
Defect rate	0.15
On-time performance	0.15
Price	0.05

Two suppliers are being considered. The raw scores for the two suppliers are as follows:

Factors	Supplier 1	Supplier 2
Design	75	80
Function	70	60
Responsiveness	85	80
Flexibility	75	75
Defect rate	70	75
On-time performance	75	70
Price	80	85

Compute the weighted-factor analysis score for each supplier.

Solution:
The weighted-factor analysis score is the sum of the weights and the raw scores for each supplier. The results are as follows:

Factors	Supplier 1	Supplier 2
Design	22.5	24.00
Function	14.00	12.00
Responsiveness	8.50	8.00
Flexibility	3.75	3.75
Defect rate	10.50	11.25
On-time performance	11.25	10.50
Price	4.00	4.25
Total	74.50	73.75

The value of 22.5 for supplier 1 on the design factor is equal to supplier 1's raw score of 75 multiplied by the factor weight of 0.30 on design ($75 \times 0.3 = 22.5$). The total scores are the sums of the raw scores multiplied by the weights (a weighted average). In this case, the weighted-factor score for supplier 1 narrowly beats out the weighted-factor score for supplier 2.

Providing Feedback: The Supplier Scorecard

SUPPLIER SCORECARDS
SOLVED PROBLEM 7.3

2. Suppose that a supplier scorecard for a supplier to the electronics industry monitors the number of defects per million parts (PPM) and the percentage improvement in the defects per million parts. The points for PPM are allocated as follows:

PPM Defect	Scorecard Points
0	10
1–50	9
51–100	8
101–150	7
151–200	6
201–250	5
251–300	4
301–350	3

351–400	2
401–450	1
> 450	0

The allocation of scorecard points for percentage PPM improvement is allocated as follows:

90–100	5
80–89	4
70–79	3
60–69	2
50–59	1
< 50	0

The percentage improvement is calculated as

$$\frac{\text{previous PPM defect rate } - \text{ current PPM defect rate}}{\text{previous PPM defect rate}} \times 100$$

The following data have just become available for a particular supplier, and it is necessary to update the supplier scorecard as follows:

number of defects = 12
number of parts received = 150,000
PPM defect rate for the prior period = 175

Solution:

$$\text{PPM defect rate} = \frac{12}{150,000} \times 1,000,000 = 80$$

Allocated scorecard points = 8

$$\text{Percent PPM improvement} = \frac{175 - 80}{175} \times 100 = 54.3$$

Allocated scorecard points = 1

The supplier earns 8 allocated points on the PPM defect rate and 1 allocated point for percentage PPM improvement.

Problems

Supplier Selection

WEIGHTED FACTOR ANALYSIS

1. A company is determining which of two suppliers, supplier A or supplier B, should be used to source a component part. The company has developed the following weights to evaluate the suppliers:

Factors	Weight
Technical	0.15
Management	0.15
Quality	0.20
Delivery	0.25
Price	0.25

The purchasing manager for the company has assigned the following raw scores to the two suppliers:

Factors	Supplier A Raw Score	Supplier B Raw Score
Technical	80	95
Management	90	85
Quality	70	80
Delivery	85	90
Price	95	85

Use a weighted-factor analysis to identify the supplier that the company should use to source the component part.

2. The purchasing department at a large international firm uses weighted-factor analysis as part of its supplier evaluation process. Suppose that the firm has decided to evaluate three potential suppliers. The firm evaluates suppliers based on their technical abilities, management, quality, delivery, and price. The following weights are used in the evaluation:

Factors	Weight	Subweight
Technical	0.20	
Design		0.15
Experience		0.05
Management	0.15	
Experience		0.10
Expertise		0.05
Quality	0.25	
Defect rate		0.15
Best practices		0.10
Delivery	0.20	
Lead time		0.10
On-time performance		0.10
Price	0.20	

Purchasing managers at the firm evaluated each supplier and determined the following raw scores:

Factors	Supplier A Raw Score	Supplier B Raw Score	Supplier C Raw Score
Technical			
Design	90	75	85
Experience	70	80	75
Management			
Experience	85	75	90
Expertise	80	70	85
Quality			
Defect rate	90	70	85
Best practices	65	85	90
Delivery			
Lead time	75	70	60
On-time performance	80	80	70
Price	85	75	80

Use the weights and the raw scores to conduct a weighted-factor analysis of the suppliers.

3. As a part of its supplier evaluation process, a company uses weighted-factor analysis as a way to identify potential suppliers. Analyze the four suppliers in the following table using this method. Based on your analysis, what would you recommend concerning supplier D?

Factors	Weight	Subweight
Technical	0.15	
Design		0.10
Experience		0.05
Management	0.15	
Experience		0.10
Expertise		0.05
Quality	0.30	
Defect rate		0.20
Best practices		0.10
Delivery	0.20	
Lead time		0.10
On-time performance		0.10
Price	0.20	

Table for Problem 3

Factors	Supplier A Raw Score	Supplier B Raw Score	Supplier C Raw Score	Supplier D Raw Score
Technical				
Design	90	85	85	80
Experience	70	80	75	70
Management				
Experience	85	75	90	70
Expertise	80	90	85	80
Quality				
Defect rate	90	70	85	75
Best practices	65	85	90	70
Delivery				
Lead time	75	70	60	65
On-time performance	80	90	70	75
Price	85	90	80	75

Providing Feedback: The Supplier Scorecard

SUPPLIER SCORECARDS

4. A company uses an electronic part. One tool that the company uses to monitor the supplier of the part is a supplier scorecard. The number of defects is carefully monitored each quarter, and the results are used to help assess the supplier's performance. Two primary performance metrics are parts per million (PPM) defects and percentage PPM improvement. The following measurements and scoring criteria are used:

PPM Defect Rate	Scorecard Points
0–50	20
51–100	15
101–150	10
151–200	5
> 200	0

Percentage PPM Improvement	Scorecard Points
75–100	10
50–74	7
25–49	4
< 25	0

Data collected on this electronic part over the last quarter indicated 15 defects and 400,000 parts received, with the PPM defect rate in the prior quarter equal to 50. Calculate the performance measures and update the scorecard using the latest quarter's results.

5. A company distributes a medical device to hospitals and clinics throughout North America. The device is used in a variety of applications. One critical component of the device is its overall quality. The distributor of the device monitors quality using a scorecard that tabulates parts per million (PPM) defects and percentage PPM improvement. The following measurements and scoring criteria are used:

PPM Defect Rate	Scorecard Points
0–100	25
101–200	20
201–300	15
301–400	10
> 400	0

Percentage PPM Improvement	Scorecard Points
90–100	6
70–89	4
50–69	2
< 50	0

In the most recent reporting period, two defects were found out of 10,000 inspected parts. The PPM defect rate in the prior period was 150. Update the supplier scorecard for this device using the most recent data.

6. Quality is a critical component of evaluating supplier performance for an electronics manufacturing firm. Consequently, it monitors supplier part quality using a variety of measurements, two of which are the parts per million (PPM) defect rate and the percentage PPM improvement. These measures are entered into a supplier scorecard every quarter. The following measurement criteria are used:

PPM Defect Rate	Scorecard Points
0–5	10
6–10	9
11–15	8
16–20	7
21–25	6
26–30	5
31–35	4
36–40	3
40–45	2
46–50	1
> 50	0

Percentage PPM Improvement	Scorecard Points
80–100	4
60–79	3
40–59	2
20–39	1
< 20	0

For the most recent reporting period, the number of defects equaled 2, the number of parts received was 200,000, and the PPM defect rate in the prior reporting period was 16. Update the supplier scorecard for the parts per million (PPM) defect rate and the percentage PPM improvement.

Rockhurst Company

Jim Crane was just named the manager of Global Strategic Sourcing for the Rockhurst Company that produces carrying cases and protective covers for electronic devices such as laptops and tablets. Some challenges have arisen related to quality, costs, and delivery reliability of raw materials used in the production process. As a result, the company has received $500,000 in returns in the last three months. Rockhurst is a small company, and this amount represents 10 percent of sales. In the Monday morning planning meeting, the chief executive officer stated, "Jim, it is your responsibility to develop a plan for dealing with these challenges." Jim needs to develop a plan addressing specific issues.

Questions:

You are to assist Jim in developing the following:

1. Describe the steps related to a world-class supplier management process.

2. Define the desired buyer-supplier relationship. Should a transactional relationship or a collaborative relationship with suppliers be used?

3. Identify a process for reviewing existing suppliers and evaluating potential new ones.

4. Identify alternative sources for identifying new suppliers.

5. Develop a model for supplier development.

6. Discuss how a supplier scorecard should be developed to provide supplier feedback.

7. Define measurements that can be used to improve supplier performance.

8

Demand Management and Forecasting

INTEGRATING	GLOBAL SC&O STRATEGY		
INNOVATING	Supply Management	Operations Management	Customer Relationship Management
IMPACTING	Upstream Processes	Core Processes	Downstream Processes
IMPROVING	QUALITY MANAGEMENT, ANALYTICS, AND LOGISTICS		

CHAPTER OUTLINE AND LEARNING OBJECTIVES

1 **Apply the Fundamentals of Demand Management**
- Understand different tools for managing demand.

2 **Understand and Apply Time Series Forecasting**
- List and understand the components of a time series.
- Define and describe the bullwhip effect on forecasts.
- Distinguish among different types of forecasting models, including judgmental and experiential forecasting.

3 **Understand and Apply Naive Forecasting Methods**
- Perform short-term forecasts using simple moving average, weighted moving average, single exponential smoothing, and double exponential smoothing.
- Describe how forecasters measure and manage error.

4 **Understand and Apply Time Series Forecasting Using Regression**
- Perform longer-term forecasts using simple linear regression.
- Describe and apply linear regression with seasonality.
- Explain how forecasters use econometrics and regression models.

Is Big Data the Key to Better Forecasting?

As you will see in this chapter, a lot of forecasting requires the gathering of historical data, which can be time consuming to gather and to analyze. However, data is everywhere; it comes from social media, search engines, and online retailing. Can this data provide a key to predicting the future? Giselle Guzman thinks it can. She is the founder of Now-Cast Data Corp, a company that uses big data and crowdsourcing to help create financial forecasts and trends.

For example, Now-Cast[1] has found that by scrubbing data on prices from online sources, it can predict inflation much more quickly than the U.S. government can. By monitoring searches on the word *inflation*, it can better gauge consumer expectations and worries relative to price increases.

Giselle has worked closely with eminent researchers in forecasting such as Nobel Laureates Joseph Stiglitz and Lawrence Klein. She believes that there is wisdom in crowds and that their data can be explored and analyzed on a moment-by-moment basis. Analytics can be used to monitor this data, but external variables, such as terrorism or natural disasters, can also be followed to adjust expectations. Next, machine learning can be used to improve forecasting.

While the jury is still out concerning the use of big data in forecasting, it is intriguing to think that this data may be useful in predicting trends like future spending and demand. In this chapter, we introduce you to forecasting methods that use data as a foundation for decision making in firms. We'll return to Now-Cast at the chapter's end.

[1]Pisani, B., "Finding a Better Way to Do Economic Forecasting," CNBC, 24 Mar. 2016.

"Tonight's weather forecast is
confusing, followed tomorrow
morning by downright bewildering."

Accuracy in forecasting is often elusive.

All business planning starts with a forecast. You need a *forecast* to determine how much financing you need, how much plant and equipment you need, how many employees you need, what type of systems to put in place, and everything else. Managers must make decisions based on data. The problem is that *all forecasts are wrong.*

Possibly the most common complaint in business is the inaccuracy of forecasts. This chapter is written based on the premise that all forecasts are wrong. Does that mean that we eliminate them? Does it mean that we distrust them? Of course not.

What it means is that, as a manager, you need to understand business forecasting for supply chain and operational purposes. If you understand the forecasting process, you can understand the assumptions behind a forecast—its strengths and weaknesses—to use the data for better-informed decision making. A **forecast** is an assertion about the future whose outcome you have not yet seen. **Forecasting** is the process of creating that assertion about the future.

A product or service has **independent demand** when the demand does not rely on the demand for some other item. We contrast this with **dependent demand**, where the demand is calculated from the demand of some other parent or sibling item. Parent-dependent demand is illustrated in this example: We know that if we were to produce 1,000 motorcycles, we would need $1,000 \times 2 = 2,000$ tires.

Because it is not linked to some other product or service, independent demand is forecasted demand. In the above example, the finished motorcycles have independent demand, the focus of this chapter. Chapter 10 will discuss dependent (or calculated demand) in the context of material requirements planning systems, which are an important component of any enterprise resource planning system.

A PPLY THE FUNDAMENTALS OF DEMAND MANAGEMENT

Before talking about analytic forecasting methods, we first need to discuss *demand management*. **Demand management** is a proactive balancing of scarce business resources with demand. Consider the case of the Dodson Property and Casualty Insurance Company. Dodson writes commercial policies for businesses. Property and casualty insurance companies help insure businesses against risks that occur in the normal course of business. In the past, the company had gained business by attending two national insurance meetings, which occured in March and October. The policies were underwritten soon after. In addition to gaining new business during the two meetings, the company renewed existing policies on the policy anniversary dates that coincided with the national meetings. The forecast for sales in the coming year is shown in FIGURE 8.1. As shown in the figure, the company has to make staffing choices. The number of employees needed is directly related to the number of policies that are sold and renewed in any year.

The question for management is, How many employees should it staff? Should the company staff at low levels and then work overtime during peak periods like accounting groups do during year-end closing and tax time? Should it staff at the average level and have too much labor during lulls and work overtime during peaks? Or should it staff at the peaks so that it provides excellent customer service? Should it consider hiring temporary labor?

Instead of varying labor levels, Dodson looked at the peaks in demand. It could seek other insurance products or other sales channels that would result in a steadying of demand. In Dodson's case, it decided to stagger renewal dates so that renewals occurred evenly throughout the year. Staggering renewal dates is one approach to demand management.

forecast
An assertion about the future whose outcome has not yet been seen.

forecasting
The process of creating an assertion about the future.

independent demand
Forecasted demand.

dependent demand
Demand that is calculated from a parent item.

demand management
A proactive balancing of scarce business resources with demand.

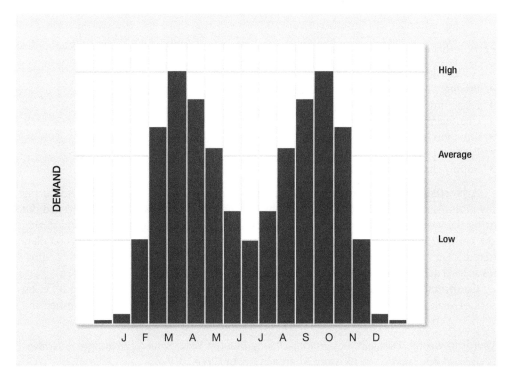

< FIGURE 8.1

Demand for Insurance Policies at Dodson

Theater managers use mid-week promotions to draw moviegoers during the mid-week lulls.

churn
The loss and replacement of customers.

A variety of factors must be considered in demand management, including expected demand, forecasted sales growth, and *churn*. **Churn** is the expected loss of customers that must be replaced with new customers. Churn can be beneficial, such as when you lose unprofitable customers and replace them with profitable customers. Alternatively, churn can result from poor service, resulting in low levels of customer retention.

According to the Aberdeen Group:

> Demand forecasting is essentially a linear process of translating input assumptions into a forecast of expected sales; demand management, by contrast, is a highly iterative process that involves driving to a revenue and profit target through prioritization of customers, channels, products, geographies, and the demand stimulation programs available to the enterprise.[2]

Key tools that companies have for demand management include the following:

- Advertising and promotion
- Pricing
- Designing counterseasonal products
- Channel management
- Outsourcing
- Product phasing
- Supply chain management

advertising and promotion
Different methods for managing demand.

Advertising and promotion can help to level demand by increasing demand during slow periods. In movie theaters, certain nights are discounted so that demand is evened out during the week. A related mechanism of **pricing** allows firms to increase demand during slow periods. Hotels and resorts offer off-season discounts for slow periods. Auto retailers often discount heavily at the end of the quarter. These promotions offer a chance for companies to level demand and consume resources during slow periods.

pricing
A method for increasing demand during slow periods.

Counterseasonal products offer a means to level capacity demands during differing times of year. A company like Arctic Cat produces snowmobiles during the summer and

counterseasonal products
A means to level capacity demands during differing times of year.

[2]Aberdeen Group, *Demand Management: Driving Business Value Beyond Forecasting: A Demand Management Benchmark Study* (Boston: Aberdeen Group, 2004, p. 9).

Through product phasing, Digitech moved the manufacturing of products such as these special-effects boxes overseas once domestic employees became familiar with this product's production.

all-terrain vehicles (ATVs) during the winter. These products can then be shipped and sold during their appropriate seasons.

Channel management allows marketers to use differing marketing channels that may complement each other to level demand. For example, a men's deodorant company may use retail outlets to sell during peak times and direct sales to level demand during the year. Wing Enterprises sells Little Giant Ladders. They are sold in many retail outlets and are a seasonal product. The company then uses late-night television infomercials during other times. Some producers of consumer products resort to auction outlets such as eBay to sell products during slow periods.

Outsourcing provides a supply chain alternative for periods of peak demand. If productive capacity is needed on a temporary basis, outsourcing is a way to produce additional products during these busy periods.

Product phasing allows firms to manage demand and their capacity. Harman Industries in Sandy, Utah, produces high-end sound-reinforcement products. One line of products is the Digitech family of guitar special-effects boxes. When the company introduces a new product to the market, it produces the product in its Sandy production facility. When employees become familiar with producing a particular product and as newer products are introduced, the production of mature products is moved to partners in China.

Supply chain management coordination offers the possibility of improving uncertainty in forecasts. Consider the example of a supply chain in FIGURE 8.2. The demand at the end user is 1,000 units. Every stage upstream, however, increases its production by 8 percent to allow for uncertainty due to poor coordination. The excess stock made at each stage is then $360 + 260 + 166 + 80 = 866$ units, which is nearly as much as the original demand of 1,000 units! This extra stock adds cost and delays into the supply chain. To make schedules more stable for upstream suppliers, communication and collaboration are needed.

A variety of methods for demand management are available to producers of goods and services at every stage of the supply chain. Sometimes, leveling demand may involve investing in finished goods or work-in-process inventory, and in some cases, this investment has

channel management
Using differing marketing channels to complement each other to level demand.

outsourcing
The act of moving production to a supplier.

product phasing
Introducing new products in a sequence that allows for an effective use of capacity.

< **FIGURE 8.2**

Uncertainty in the Supply Chain

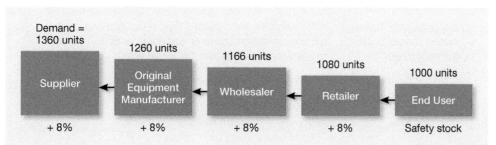

a positive payback, especially where demand is very uncertain or uneven. The art aspect of demand management comes from combining the differing methods mentioned in this chapter in a way that makes sense for your particular situation.

UNDERSTAND AND APPLY TIME SERIES FORECASTING

Now that we have discussed demand management, we can turn to forecasting. When you forecast, you use a time series. Time series forecasting is forecasting over time, but managers can also forecast based on other variables, such as expenditures on advertising or income. TABLE 8.1 shows the steps in time series forecasting.

When we plot time series data, many different trends appear (FIGURE 8.3). The positive and negative linear trends in Figure 8.3 mean that a least squares regression line can be fitted to the data with a slope that is significantly different from zero. Shown next are positive and negative curvilinear trends. Although a statistically significant straight line could be fitted to these time series, the curving lines are a much better fit. In the bottom two graphs, we see a seasonal pattern and no trend. The one on the left is actually a time series of temperatures from the National Weather Service over two years, and the one on the right is a time series of data that seems to have neither a repetitive pattern nor a positive or negative slope.

Components of a Time Series

Time series have four components: (1) *trend*, (2) *cyclical*, (3) *seasonal*, and (4) *irregular*. **Trend** is the average rate of change in a time series. In a linear time series, trend is often referred to as the slope of a time series. **Cyclical effects** are long-term, repetitive patterns in a time series that are often macroeconomic in nature, such as the business cycle or the boom-bust cycle of the world economy. They sometimes last 20 years or longer and are difficult to identify in data. **Seasonal patterns** (or **seasonality**) are repetitive patterns that occur during some fixed time period such as a day, week, month, or year. Seasonal patterns occur in retail over a year's time, with the highest level of sales during the holidays. Daily patterns of traffic flow on an urban highway or weekly demand patterns for bank tellers or movies are also examples of seasonal patterns. As we will see later, these patterns are relatively easy to identify from the data. The **irregular component** or **noise component** is random variation that occurs in any time series. Because this variation is random, it cannot be forecasted, only measured.

trend
The average rate of change in a time series. In linear regression, it is often referred to as the slope.

cyclical effects
Long-term, repetitive patterns in a time series that are often macroeconomic in nature, such as the business cycle or the boom-bust cycle of the world economy. These effects sometimes last 20 years or longer and are difficult to identify in data.

seasonal patterns or seasonality
Variation that is repetitive and occur during some fixed time period, such as a day, week, month, or year.

irregular component or noise component
Random variation that occurs in any time series.

TABLE 8.1 >

Forecasting Steps	
Step	**Application**
1. Identify the purpose for your forecast.	Are you forecasting demand, staffing levels, units, costs, or budgets?
2. Determine the time horizon for the forecast.	Is it near term, midterm, or long term?
3. Select a forecasting technique.	Which model will you use: judgmental, short term, or longer term?
4. Get good data, fit the models, and choose the right model.	After modeling the data on a time series plot and checking for and removing outliers or bad data, try different models to see which has the best "fit" (least error).
5. Build out the forecast.	Take the model with the best fit and extrapolate into the future.
6. Check your forecast periodically.	A model that works well with historical data does not guarantee that it will work well into the future.

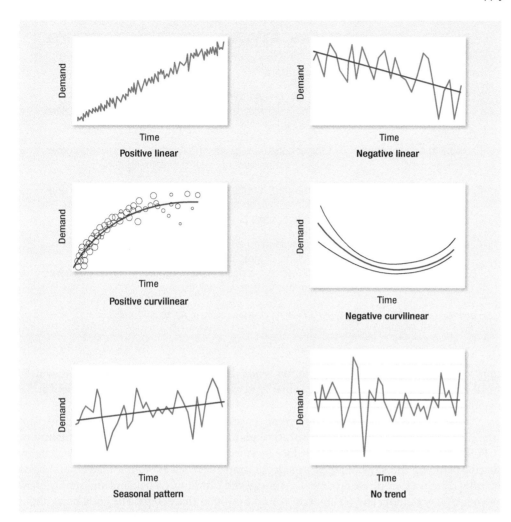

Forecasting and Bullwhips

The **bullwhip effect** (called the Forrester effect in the 1960s) occurs as a result of forecasts in a supply chain or distribution channel. Even modest demand fluctuation can become greatly amplified as you move up the supply chain, which is also true with forecasting data. Because different firms have different forecasts, the *noise* is amplified as it moves up the supply chain (FIGURE 8.4), resulting in an amplification of demand variation as you move upstream in the

bullwhip effect
Increasing upstream supply chain variation resulting from forecasts in a supply chain or distribution channel.

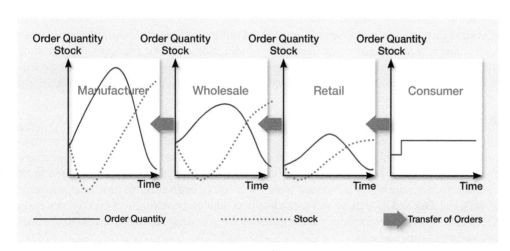

< FIGURE 8.4

Bullwhip Effect

TABLE 8.2 >

Collaborative Planning, Forecasting, and Replenishment Activities	
Step	**Application**
1. Strategy and planning	Establish ground rules for collaborative relationships. Determine product mix and placement, and develop plans for the period.
2. Demand and supply management	Project consumer (point-of-sale) demand as well as order shipment requirements over the planning horizon.
3. Execution	Place orders, prepare and deliver shipments, receive and stock products on retail shelves, record sales transactions, and make payments.
4. Analysis	Monitor planning and execution activities for exception conditions. Aggregate results and calculate key performance metrics. Share insights and adjust plans for continuously improved results.

Source: Based on CPFR Advisory Team, *CPFR: An Overview*, Tempe, AZ: VICS, 2004.

supply chain. Just as a small hand motion sends the tip of a bullwhip to modulate widely, small variations in demand at the consumer level can create large variation in demand at the manufacturer level.

As we introduced in Chapter 2, one route toward ameliorating the effect of this upstream amplification of error is called **collaborative planning, forecasting, and replenishment (CPFR)**. The objective of CPFR is to reduce inventory levels throughout the supply chain by sharing planning and scheduling information. Companies such as Walmart have had success in using data in a four-phase process: (1) strategy and planning, (2) demand and supply management, (3) execution, and (4) analysis. TABLE 8.2 outlines these steps. The good news about bullwhips is that many firms have been able to reduce their effects with better collaboration.

collaborative planning, forecasting, and replenishment (CPFR) A method for moderating the impacts of the bullwhip effect by sharing planning and scheduling information.

Types of Forecasting Models

Now that we have discussed the process of forecasting, we can introduce various forecasting models. We start with judgmental or experience-based forecasting and then move to naive and causal models. Although some of these models are very simple, they can be powerful forecasting tools. When possible, it is best to use the simplest forecasting methods available. Generally, they are more understandable and often just as accurate as more sophisticated methods.

The purpose in introducing these models to you is not to make you an expert forecaster in one introductory chapter. Rather, the goal is to help you apply some simple models but also sensitize you to the tools and assumptions behind these models so that you, as a manager, can understand where forecasts come from, their weaknesses, and their strengths. After reading this chapter, you should be equipped to question forecasts you receive from forecasting statisticians and be prepared to do what-if analysis so that you can make better informed decisions.

Judgmental or Experiential Forecasting

Sometimes managers need to forecast with no data or when statistical methods may be inappropriate for a particular situation. At times, exogenous or external political considerations could affect demand. For example, forecasting sales of Samsung cell phones became more complicated after the highly publicized Note 7 failures. To be an effective forecaster, you must understand data and models as well as the business and legal environment you operate in. In the following pages, we introduce some qualitative forecasting approaches that can be used in a variety of situations.

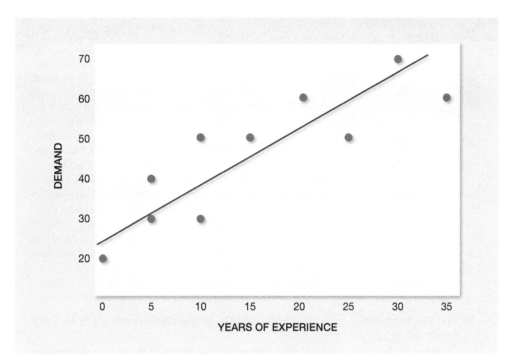

STRING METHOD Probably the simplest form of judgmental forecasting is the **string method** of forecasting. This method does not require any statistical knowledge; it takes a time series of data in the form of a scatter plot and fits a line to it using a string. The string method is one of the simplest methods of judgmental forecasting. FIGURE 8.5 shows a scatter plot with a string drawn across the data to create a forecast.

string method
A simple approach to forecasting using a string to identify trend.

GREENFIELD FORECASTING METHODS There are several **greenfield forecasting methods**. Forecasters use this term to describe a class of techniques used to launch new products or services where no prior demand data are available. Such is the case when the product is not simply an upgrade to a prior product, as in the launch of the second edition of this book, but when there is no way to forecast demand, as in the launch of the first iPad in 2010, which created a new market segment. Big data may prove helpful for greenfield forecasting (see SC&O CURRENT EVENTS 8.1).

greenfield forecasting methods
Forecasting approaches used in new product launches.

DELPHI METHOD The best-known qualitative technique is the **Delphi method**. With this technique, a group of experts achieves consensus through an iterative process. Here is an example of how this process might work for forecasting:

Delphi method
An iterative forecasting method using professional judgment.

1. A facilitator gathers a group of experts to forecast quarterly sales over the next two years.
2. The facilitator asks each expert to fill in a sheet with eight quarterly forecasts for the next two years based on her or his understanding of the market and then dismisses the group.
3. The facilitator takes the input from each expert and creates a summary spreadsheet with mean forecasts, high and low values, and standard deviations of all the forecasts.
4. A subsequent meeting of the experts is called after some time has passed. The facilitator asks the experts to review the summary spreadsheets and revise their forecasts based on this new information. The facilitator gathers the new forecasts from the experts.
5. Steps 3 and 4 are repeated until "consensus" is reached. Consensus does not mean that everyone agrees. Consensus may mean that there is only a 20 percent difference between the high estimates and the low estimates.
6. When consensus is reached, you have your forecast by averaging the final results.

The two key roles in the Delphi method are the (1) experts and (2) facilitator. The experts should be chosen carefully by decision makers to provide diversity of experience for the decisions to be made. The facilitator must have the experience to choose a team and analyze data properly.

Is Forecasting an Art or a Science?

Every day on the news, you hear about predictions or forecasts about the future—inflation is predicted to increase, deflation is on the rise, or Brexit will never pass (although it did). Some of these forecasts are right and others are wrong. Philip Tetlock, a University of Pennsylvania professor in psychology and political science, has studied nearly 28,000 predictions by so-called experts and has found that the predictions are not much better than flipping a coin.

As we will discuss, forecasts are inherently unreliable for a variety of reasons. Sometimes data are messy. At times, it is difficult to get the right data. Some data are biased—either too conservatively or too aggressively. As a result of inaccuracy forecasts, sometimes CEOs and other managers do not trust the forecasts they are given. In other cases, top managers may exert undue influence on their forecasts in an effort to attract investors. According to Ken Lamneck,[3] CEO of Insight Enterprises Inc., he has pretty much decided to ignore quantitative forecasts in favor of querying other CEOs and using expert judgment to make decisions.

To improve accuracy, Phil Tetlock, an expert on forecasting, recommends the following steps:[4]

- Find the right forecasters. Through his research, he identified superforecasters. Some people are better than others!
- Collaborate. He found that when forecasters combine efforts, they improve accuracy by 10 to 20 percent.
- Debias. Reducing bias in forecasts improves performance.
- Emphasize superforecasters and reduce conservatism in forecasting. Some forecasters are too careful in making predictions.

[3]R. Silverman, J. Lublin, and R. Feintzeig, "In Uncertain Times, CEOs Lose Faith in Forecasts," *The Wall Street Journal*, 12 July 2016.
[4]Based on *Superforecasting: The Art and Science of Prediction* by P. Tetlock and D. Gardner. Published by Broadway Books, 2016.

---

nominal group techniques (NGTs)
Brainstorming and team techniques that remove the influence of power and position.

structured brainstorming
Brainstorming methods following a strict script or format.

NOMINAL GROUP TECHNIQUES Nominal group techniques (NGTs) are a group of team brainstorming approaches that are similar to Delphi except that they involve active vocal participation by team members as opposed to written participation. An example of an NGT is 10/4 voting. In a 10/4 voting activity, moderators use **structured brainstorming**, in which participants go around in a round-robin format to brainstorm ideas. After the facilitator posts the ideas on flip-chart paper, for example, the team members vote on various ideas. The "10" in 10/4 voting is for the total of 10 points each participant must use up. The "4" comes from the rule that participants cannot allocate more than 4 points to any single idea. The advantage of NGTs is that they elicit everyone's input so that everyone has an equal voice.

grassroots forecasting
Going to the market to get information for new product launches.

GRASSROOTS FORECASTING Grassroots forecasting is a greenfield forecasting technique that involves getting as close to the market as possible. Companies use grassroots forecasting when they elicit input from regional marketers. Firms then aggregate these forecasts to create a final forecast.

BEHAVIORAL/JUDGMENTAL FORECASTING While it has been shown that some people can beat computer-based forecasting methods, there are limitations.[5] For example, research has shown that people tend to be overly optimistic when performing short-term forecasts.[6] Alternatively, they tend to be too pessimistic when performing long-term forecasts. People also tend to forecast the best using intuition when historic patterns are linear.

[5]E. Mahmoud, "Accuracy in Forecasting: A Survey," *Journal of Forecasting*, 3, no. 4 (1984): 139–159.
[6]H. Linstone and T. Marray, *The Delphi Method, Techniques and Applications* (Boston, MA: Addison-Wesley, 1975).

UNDERSTAND AND APPLY NAIVE FORECASTING METHODS

We next discuss naive forecasting methods. **Naive forecasting methods** are considered naive because they make no attempt at explaining *why* demand is increasing or decreasing. That is, there is no attempt at explaining why variation occurs in a time series. All these methods do is take historical mathematical relationships and extrapolate them into the future. Most of these methods involve some kind of weighted average of historical data. The methods are (1) simple moving average, (2) weighted moving average, (3) single exponential smoothing, and (4) double exponential smoothing.

naive forecasting methods
Forecasting methods that make no attempt at explaining why demand is increasing or decreasing.

Simple Moving Average

Forecasters compute a **simple moving average (SMA)** by calculating the mean of recent periodic demand. First, they determine the number of periods (n) they want to use in computing their average. For example, they may decide to use a three-period simple moving average. To do so, they simply take the prior three periods of demand and average them. The simple moving average equation is

simple moving average (SMA)
A naive forecasting technique where prior demand is averaged.

$$F_{t+1} = \frac{a_t + a_{t-1} + \ldots + a_{t-n}}{n} \tag{8.1}$$

where

F_{t+1} = forecast for the coming period $t + 1$
a_t = actual demand for period t
n = number of periods used to compute the moving average

Using the Moving Average

Problem: For the following data, compute a three-period simple moving average and find a forecast for period 13. Here, a_t is the actual demand for period t, and F_t is the forecast for period t.

< SOLVED PROBLEM 8.1 f(x)

MyLab Operations Management
Video

Period	a_t
1	24
2	26
3	27
4	22
5	30
6	28
7	37
8	41
9	28
10	43
11	50
12	52

Solution: We found the following solution. Notice that forecasts for the first three periods were not possible because they required three months' worth of data to get started.

Period	a_t	Calculation	F_t (SMA)
1	24		
2	26		
3	27		
4	22	(24 + 26 + 27)/3 =	25.67
5	30	(26 + 27 + 22)/3 =	25.00
6	28	(27 + 22 + 30)/3 =	26.33
7	37	(22 + 30 + 28)/3 =	26.67
8	41	(30 + 28 + 37)/3 =	31.67
9	28	(28 + 37 + 41)/3 =	35.33
10	43	(37 + 41 + 28)/3 =	35.33
11	50	(41 + 28 + 43)/3 =	37.33
12	52	(28 + 43 + 50)/3 =	40.33
		(43 + 50 + 52)/3 =	48.33

The forecast for period 13 is $(43 + 50 + 52)/3 = 48.33$.

Weighted Moving Average

weighted moving average (WMA) A naive forecasting model in which previous period data have different weights. Usually, the heavier weight is on the most recent data.

The **weighted moving average (WMA)** is similar to the SMA except that more recent periods are weighted more heavily based on the notion that more recent periods are likely better predictors of current demand. The formula for weighted moving average is

$$F_{t+1} = w_t a_t + w_{t-1} a_{t-1} + \ldots + w_{t-n} a_{t-n} \qquad (8.2)$$

where

w_t = weight for period t (note that the weights sum to 1)
a_t = actual demand for period t
n = the number of periods used in computing the WMA

A note of caution: With WMA, the weights must equal 1 or else the model will be biased. As already stated, the heavier weights are usually applied to the most recent periods.

 SOLVED PROBLEM 8.2 >   **Weighted Moving Average**

MyLab Operations Management Video

Problem: Using the data from Solved Problem 8.1, develop a weighted moving average forecast with the weights 0.5, 0.3, and 0.2, where the heaviest weights are placed on the most recent data.

Solution: The following table shows the result. Note that again we do not have forecasts for the first three periods. Here, a_t is the actual demand for period t, and F_t is the forecast for period t.

Period	a_t	Calculation	F_t (WMA)
1	24		
2	26		
3	27		
4	22	$(27 \times 0.5 + 26 \times 0.3 + 24 \times 0.2) =$	26.10
5	30	$(22 \times 0.5 + 27 \times 0.3 + 26 \times 0.2) =$	24.30
6	28	$(30 \times 0.5 + 22 \times 0.3 + 27 \times 0.2) =$	27.00
7	37	$(28 \times 0.5 + 30 \times 0.3 + 22 \times 0.2) =$	27.40
8	41	$(37 \times 0.5 + 28 \times 0.3 + 30 \times 0.2) =$	32.90
9	28	$(41 \times 0.5 + 37 \times 0.3 + 28 \times 0.2) =$	37.20
10	43	$(28 \times 0.5 + 41 \times 0.3 + 37 \times 0.2) =$	33.70
11	50	$(43 \times 0.5 + 28 \times 0.3 + 41 \times 0.2) =$	38.10
12	52	$(50 \times 0.5 + 43 \times 0.3 + 28 \times 0.2) =$	43.50
		$(52 \times 0.5 + 50 \times 0.3 + 43 \times 0.2) =$	49.60

As you can see, the forecast for period 13 is 49.60.

Single Exponential Smoothing

With simple moving average and weighted moving average, we have created a smoothing of the time series. The forecasts are sometimes better predictors of actual demand than the previous period's actual sales. How can that be? The reason for this phenomenon is the **smoothing effect**, the result of smoothing out random variation in a time series. FIGURE 8.6 shows the plot of the actual demand and forecasts from Solved Problems 8.1 and 8.2. For periods 9 and 10,

smoothing effect
The result of reducing random variation in a time series.

< FIGURE 8.6

Plots from Solved Problems 8.1 and 8.2 to Show Smoothing Effect

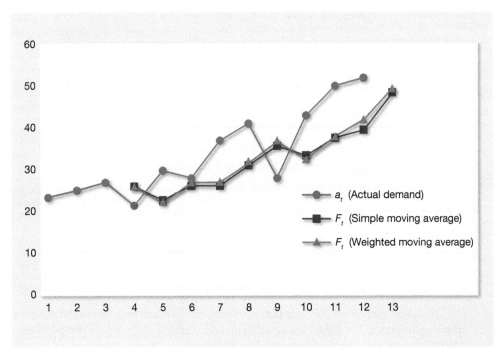

note how the prior forecast is a better predictor of actual demand than the prior actual demand. When we discussed time series, we stated that they contain noise. With our smoothing forecasts, we smooth out the irregular (noise) component of the time series. The prior forecasts may still be of interest to us, especially when our data are "noisy" (full of random error).

single exponential smoothing (SES)
A naive forecasting model that averages prior demand with a prior forecast.

Single exponential smoothing (SES) takes advantage of prior forecasts by taking a weighted average of prior forecasts and actual sales and creating new forecasts. The single exponential smoothing model is expressed as

$$F_{t+1} = \alpha a_t + (1 - \alpha)F_t \tag{8.3}$$

where

$$
\begin{aligned}
F_{t+1} &= \text{forecast for the next period } t + 1 \\
\alpha &= \text{smoothing constant } (0 \le \alpha \le 1) \\
a_t &= \text{actual demand for period } t \\
F_t &= \text{forecast for period } t
\end{aligned}
$$

smoothing constant
A constant (represented by α) that ranges between 0 and 1 in an exponential smoothing model.

The **smoothing constant** ranges between 0 and 1. A larger smoothing constant places a heavier weight on prior actual demand, whereas a smaller one places a heavier weight on the prior forecast. Another equivalent form of the single exponential smoothing model is

$$F_{t+1} = F_t + \alpha(a_t - F_t) \tag{8.4}$$

SOLVED PROBLEM 8.3 shows how the single exponential smoothing model is implemented.

 SOLVED PROBLEM 8.3 >

MyLab Operations Management Video

Single Exponential Smoothing

Problem: Using the data from Solved Problem 8.2 and Equation 8.3, use a single exponential smoothing model with a smoothing constant $(\alpha) = 0.3$ to develop a short-term forecast for period 13. Use 24 as the initial forecast for period 1.

Solution:

Period	a_t	Calculation	F_t (SES)
1	24		
2	26	$(0.3 \times 24) + (0.7 \times 24) =$	24.00
3	27	$(0.3 \times 26) + (0.7 \times 24) =$	24.60
4	22	$(0.3 \times 27) + (0.7 \times 24.60) =$	25.32
5	30	$(0.3 \times 22) + (0.7 \times 25.32) =$	24.32
6	28	$(0.3 \times 30) + (0.7 \times 24.32) =$	26.03
7	37	$(0.3 \times 28) + (0.7 \times 26.03) =$	26.62
8	41	$(0.3 \times 37) + (0.7 \times 26.62) =$	29.73
9	28	$(0.3 \times 41) + (0.7 \times 29.73) =$	33.11
10	43	$(0.3 \times 28) + (0.7 \times 33.11) =$	31.58
11	50	$(0.3 \times 43) + (0.7 \times 31.58) =$	35.01
12	52	$(0.3 \times 50) + (0.7 \times 35.01) =$	39.50
		$(0.3 \times 52) + (0.7 \times 39.50) =$	43.25

Note that we needed only one period to start our forecast. Because we did not have a forecast for period 1, we used the actual demand for period 1 as our first period forecast. As you can see, the forecast for period 13 is 43.25.

Double Exponential Smoothing

Double exponential smoothing (DES) gets closer to trend by smoothing out the irregular component in a time series with stable demand. DES is useful when there is a pronounced trend in the data. It may provide greater smoothing when there is a pronounced trend (single exponential smoothing does not work as well when there is a strong trend in the data). The formula for double exponential smoothing is

$$FD_t = \alpha F_t + (1 - \alpha)FD_{t-1} \qquad (8.5)$$

where

> FD_t = the double exponential smoothing forecast for period t
> α = smoothing constant
> F_t = the single exponential smoothed forecast for period t

Using Equation 8.5, we see the double exponential smoothed forecast for the next period is a weighted average of the single exponential smoothing forecast and the previous period's double exponential smoothed forecast, providing a second level of smoothing. The single exponential smoothing model adjusts the trend for the previous period. The double exponential smoothing model eliminates this lag and brings the forecast to the correct base for a current period forecast. We demonstrate this elimination from double exponential smoothing in SOLVED PROBLEM 8.4.

double exponential smoothing (DES)
A naive model that gets closer to a trend by smoothing out the irregular component in a time series with stable demand.

....

Double Exponential Smoothing

Problem: Using the data from Solved Problem 8.3, perform double exponential smoothing and develop a forecast for period 13. Once again, use $\alpha = 0.3$. Again, use 24.00 as the first period DES forecast seed value.

< SOLVED PROBLEM 8.4

MyLab Operations Management
Video

Solution:

Period	a_t	F_t(SES)	Calculations	F_t(DES)
1	24			
2	26	24.00	(0.3 × 24) + (0.7 × 24) =	24.00
3	27	24.60	(0.3 × 24.60) + (0.7 × 24) =	24.18
4	22	25.32	(0.3 × 25.32) + (0.7 × 24.18) =	24.52
5	30	24.32	(0.3 × 24.32) + (0.7 × 24.52) =	24.46
6	28	26.03	(0.3 × 26.03) + (0.7 × 24.46) =	24.93
7	37	26.62	(0.3 × 26.62) + (0.7 × 24.93) =	25.44
8	41	29.73	(0.3 × 29.73) + (0.7 × 25.44) =	26.73
9	28	33.11	(0.3 × 33.11) + (0.7 × 26.73) =	28.64
10	43	31.58	(0.3 × 31.58) + (0.7 × 28.64) =	29.52
11	50	35.01	(0.3 × 35.01) + (0.7 × 29.52) =	31.17
12	52	39.50	(0.3 × 39.50) + (0.7 × 31.17) =	33.67
		43.25	(0.3 × 43.25) + (0.7 × 33.67) =	36.54

As demonstrated in Figure 8.6, we used the beginning actual sales of 24 to initiate the single and double exponential smoothing forecasts in period 1. The double exponential smoothed forecast for period 13 is 36.54. FIGURE 8.7 shows the graphs and the smoothing effects for the single and double exponential smoothing models.

FIGURE 8.7 >

Graph of Single and Double Exponential Smoothing Effects

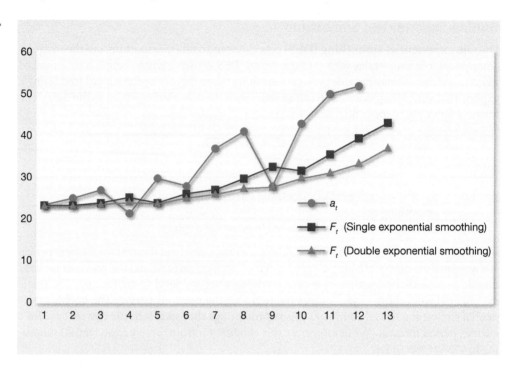

mean absolute deviation (MAD)
A measure of forecasting error that tells the average error in a forecast.

mean squared error (MSE)
A measure of forecasting error used in computing variance.

bias
The tendency to forecast either too high or too low.

mean average percentage error (MAPE)
A measure of forecasting error that tracks the average percentage of error.

Measures of Forecasting Error

We have now introduced four naive forecasting models: (1) simple moving average, (2) weighted moving average, (3) single exponential smoothing, and (4) double exponential smoothing. How, though, can you tell which forecasting model is best?

To identify the best model, we introduce the concept of *fit*. Forecasters determine fit by the amount of error they measure when comparing their forecast models with actual sales. In this chapter, we discuss four measures of forecasting error: (1) **mean absolute deviation (MAD)**, (2) **mean squared error (MSE)**, (3) **bias**, and (4) **mean average percentage error (MAPE)**. TABLE 8.3

∨ TABLE 8.3

Measures of Forecasting Error			
Measure of Forecasting Error	**Definition**	**Equation Formula and Equation Number**	**Application**
Mean absolute deviation (MAD)	The average amount that the forecast is off target	$\text{MAD} = \dfrac{\sum_{i=1}^{n} |a_t - F_t|_i}{n}$ (8.6)	A forecast for a style of shoes sold was off by 12 units (on average). That does not tell us whether we were too high or too low. It is just an absolute value.
Mean squared error (MSE)	The square of the amount that the forecast is off target	$\text{MSE} = \dfrac{\sum_{i=1}^{n} (a_t - F_t)_i^2}{n}$ (8.7)	The square of the forecast errors for a different style of shoes was 110. This information is hard to interpret, but it is often used by statisticians to compute variances.
Bias	Tendency to forecast too high or too low	$\text{Bias} = \dfrac{\sum_{i=1}^{n} (F_t - a_t)}{n}$ (8.8)	When we compared the forecast for another style of shoes, we computed a bias of −3, which means that, on average, our forecast was low by 3 units.
Mean average percentage error (MAPE)	The average percentage error	$\text{MAPE} = \dfrac{\sum_{i=1}^{n} \dfrac{|a_t - F_t|_i}{a_t}}{n}$ (8.9)	On average, our forecast for even a different style of shoes is off by 15 percent. Again, this doesn't tell us if we are too high or too low.

defines these four measures (note that the definitions of the variables in the formulas are the same as we have used in the chapter so far). These measures of forecasting error are presented in SOLVED PROBLEM 8.5.

....

Measures of Forecasting Error

< SOLVED PROBLEM 8.5   ⓕ⁽ˣ⁾

MyLab Operations Management
Video

Problem: In this chapter, we introduced four naive forecasting models. Compute the MAD, MSE, bias, and MAPE for each of the four previous solved problems (Solved Problems 8.1–8.4). So that you compare apples with apples, compute the error measures for periods 4 through 12 (some models did not forecast for periods 1–3).

Solution: We present the results in the following sequence: simple moving average (SMA), weighted moving average (WMA), single exponential smoothing (SES), and double exponential smoothing (DES):

Period	a_t	F_t (SMA)	Absolute Deviation	Squared Error	$F_t - a_t$ (for Computing Bias)	Average Percentage Error
4	22	25.67	3.67	13.44	3.67	0.17
5	30	25.00	5.00	25.00	−5.00	0.17
6	28	26.33	1.67	2.78	−1.67	0.06
7	37	26.67	10.33	106.78	−10.33	0.28
8	41	31.67	9.33	87.11	−9.33	0.23
9	28	35.33	7.33	53.78	7.33	0.26
10	43	35.33	7.67	58.78	−7.67	0.18
11	50	37.33	12.67	160.44	−12.67	0.25
12	52	40.33	11.67	136.11	−11.67	0.22
		Means =	7.70	71.58	− 5.26	0.20

Period	a_t	F_t (WMA)	Absolute Deviation	Squared Error	$F_t - a_t$ (for Computing Bias)	Average Percentage Error
4	22	26.1	4.10	16.81	4.10	0.19
5	30	24.3	5.70	32.49	−5.70	0.19
6	28	27	1.00	1.00	−1.00	0.04
7	37	27.4	9.60	92.16	−9.60	0.26
8	41	32.9	8.10	65.61	−8.10	0.20
9	28	37.2	9.20	84.64	9.20	0.33
10	43	33.7	9.30	86.49	−9.30	0.22
11	50	38.1	11.90	141.61	−11.90	0.24
12	52	43.5	8.50	72.25	−8.50	0.16
		Means =	7.49	65.90	− 4.53	0.20

Period	a_t	F_t (SES)	Absolute Deviation	Squared Error	$F_t - a_t$ (for Computing Bias)	Average Percentage Error
4	22	25.32	3.32	11.02	3.32	0.15
5	30	24.32	5.68	32.22	−5.68	0.19
6	28	26.03	1.97	3.89	−1.97	0.07
7	37	26.62	10.38	107.77	−10.38	0.28
8	41	29.73	11.27	126.94	−11.27	0.27
9	28	33.11	5.11	26.14	5.11	0.18
10	43	31.58	11.42	130.43	−11.42	0.27
11	50	35.01	14.99	224.84	−14.99	0.30
12	52	39.50	12.50	156.15	−12.50	0.24
		Means =	8.52	91.05	−6.64	0.22

Period	a_t	F_t (DES)	Absolute Deviation	Squared Error	$F_t - a_t$ (for Computing Bias)	Average Percentage Error
4	22	24.52	2.52	6.36	2.52	0.11
5	30	24.46	5.54	30.66	−5.54	0.18
6	28	24.93	3.07	9.41	−3.07	0.11
7	37	25.44	11.56	133.68	−11.56	0.31
8	41	26.73	14.27	203.73	−14.27	0.35
9	28	28.64	0.64	0.41	0.64	0.02
10	43	29.52	13.48	181.62	−13.48	0.31
11	50	31.17	18.83	354.64	−18.83	0.38
12	52	33.67	18.33	336.03	−18.33	0.35
		Means =	9.81	139.62	−9.10	0.24

After comparing our measures of forecasting error, we can see that our weighted moving average model had the best fit with MAD = 7.49, MSE = 65.90, bias = −4.53 (underforecasting), and MAPE = 0.20. It is interesting that all the models had negative bias due to the pronounced trend.

U NDERSTAND AND APPLY TIME SERIES FORECASTING USING REGRESSION

causal models
Forecasting methods using regression.

We now turn to *causal models*. **Causal models** are regression models in which forecasters attempt to explain variation in demand. Although we object mildly to the use of the term *causal*, we will use it here because these models show the strength of association between variables, but this association does not necessarily establish cause and effect. One type of causal model is simple linear regression. In simple linear regression, the first step is to identify the

independent variable (x) and the **dependent variable (y)** (not to be confused with independent and dependent demand discussed earlier in the chapter). The dependent variable is the focus of the regression model or what is being predicted. Conversely, the independent variable is the variable that is used to explain variation in the dependent variable.

For example, take two variables such as rainfall and crop yield. There are two possible ways to draw a causal relationship:

rain → crops (to be read as rainfall influences crop yield)

or

crops → rain (crop yield influences rainfall)

Which assertion seems more reasonable? You could make a tenuous case that more crop yield could cause more humidity, thereby resulting in more rainfall, but that might seem like a stretch. It is much more reasonable to assert that rainfall influences crop yield. At first, more rain results in more crops (a positive relationship). However, after a certain point (say, where flooding begins), more rain could result in fewer crops yielded (a negative relationship). Therefore, the relationship between rain (x) and crop yield (y) might follow a concave curve where first there is a positive relationship and later (at higher water levels) ruined crops.

Time Series Forecasts Using Simple Linear Regression

For time series forecasts, the independent variable (x) is time, and the dependent variable (y) is what the model is predicting (e.g., demand; FIGURE 8.8). For these types of forecasts, firms prefer **simple linear regression**, a regression model with only one independent variable. Alternatively, **multiple linear regression** is a regression model with more than one independent variable.

In a simple linear regression forecasting model, the period's demand is expressed as

$$F_t = a + bx_i \qquad (8.10)$$

where

F_t = forecast for period t
a = y intercept
b = slope
x_i = independent value for period i

independent variable (x)
The explanatory variable in a regression model.

dependent variable (y)
The predicted variable in a regression model.

simple linear regression
A regression model with only one independent variable.

multiple linear regression
A regression model with more than one independent variable.

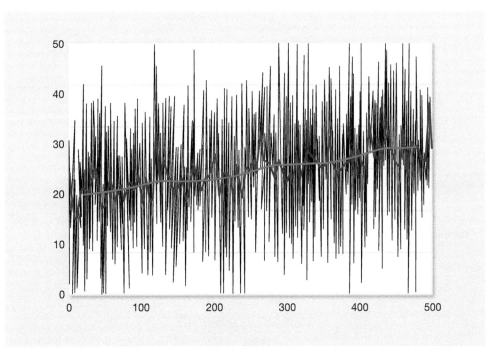

< FIGURE 8.8

Time Series Fitted with a Regression Line

Coefficients a and b are computed in the following order:

$$b = \frac{n\left(\sum xy\right) - \left(\sum x\right)\left(\sum y\right)}{n\left(\sum x^2\right) - \left(\sum x\right)^2} \tag{8.11}$$

$$a = \bar{y} - b\bar{x} \tag{8.12}$$

where

   n = number of paired observations

We demonstrate simple linear regression in **SOLVED PROBLEM 8.6**.

   **SOLVED PROBLEM 8.6 >**   **Using Simple Linear Regression**

MyLab Operations Management
Video

Problem: We acquired the last four years of sales data for a retail outlet in the Mall at Peachtree Center in Atlanta, Georgia. For these data (all values in thousands of dollars), compute a regression equation and make a forecast for the first quarter in year 5 (quarterly period 17). First, plot the data to see what the time series looks like.

Year	Quarter	Period (x)	Demand (y)
1	1	1	23
	2	2	27
	3	3	44
	4	4	55
2	1	5	37
	2	6	45
	3	7	69
	4	8	80
3	1	9	54
	2	10	63
	3	11	93
	4	12	97
4	1	13	67
	2	14	77
	3	15	105
	4	16	111

Solution: The plot for the data, shown on the next page, has a positive linear trend with some seasonality. It appears that we can fit a least squares regression line to these data.

The slope and intercepts are computed as follows:

$$b = \frac{n\left(\sum xy\right) - \left(\sum x\right)\left(\sum y\right)}{n\left(\sum x^2\right) - \left(\sum x\right)^2}$$

$$b = \frac{16(10,610) - (136)(1047)}{16(1496) - 136^2}$$

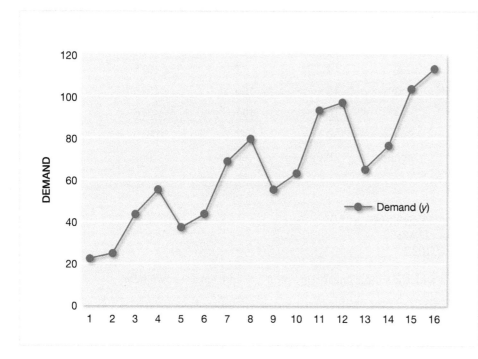

$$b = 5.03$$
$$a = \bar{y} - b\bar{x}$$
$$a = 65.44 - 5.03 \times 8.5 = 22.68$$

Using Equation 8.9, we calculate the trend as

$$F_t = a + bx_i = 22.68 + 5.03x_i$$

For period 17, we substitute 17 for x_i and obtain

$$F_t = a + bx_i = 22.68 + 5.03(17) = 108.2$$

Therefore, the forecast for quarter 17 is 108.2. The analysis is given in the following table.

n = 16					
Year	Quarter	Period (x)	Demand (y)	$x \times y$	x^2
1	1	1	23	23	1
	2	2	27	54	4
	3	3	44	132	9
	4	4	55	220	16
2	1	5	37	185	25
	2	6	45	270	36
	3	7	69	483	49
	4	8	80	640	64
3	1	9	54	486	81
	2	10	63	630	100
	3	11	93	1023	121
	4	12	97	1164	144

(continued)

n = 16 (continued)					
4	1	13	67	871	169
	2	14	77	1078	196
	3	15	105	1575	225
	4	16	111	1,776	256
	Sums:	136	1,047	10,610	1,496
	Means:	8.50	65.44		

$$b = 27{,}368/5440 = 5.03$$
$$a = 22.675$$
$$F_t = 108.2$$

The plot with the simple linear regression line appears as shown here.

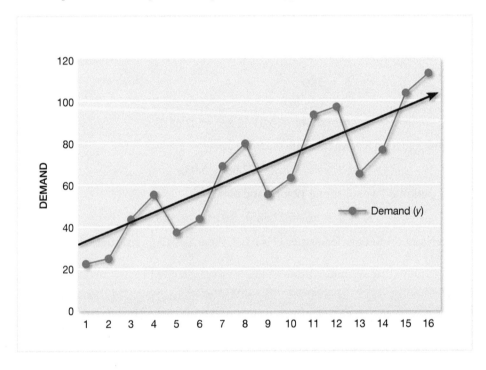

SC&O CURRENT EVENTS 8.2 talks about an application of predictive analytics called saber-metrics. It is more commonly known as *moneyball*.

Linear Regression with Seasonality

In Solved Problem 8.6, we noticed that the data appeared to exhibit seasonality, that is, a repetitive pattern occurring in regular time intervals. Earlier in the chapter, we mentioned that it was fairly simple to account for seasonality in a forecast. Although the math is simple, the method for **deseasonalizing a forecast** or **decomposing a time series** involves a series of procedural steps:

deseasonalizing a forecast or decomposing a time series
The act of removing seasonal variation from a time series to estimate trend more closely.

1. Compute seasonal indexes for the data.
2. Deseasonalize the data.
3. Perform a forecast using the deseasonalized data to find the trend.
4. Reseasonalize the deseasonalized forecast.

Managers use regression for predictive purposes. In a time series, time is the independent variable. However, other variables can be used to predict future outcomes. A novel use of forecasting and regression methodologies was immortalized in a book by Michael Lewis, and later a movie starring Brad Pitt, called *Moneyball*. Moneyball became famous when the Oakland Athletics (A's) were able to make the Major League Baseball playoffs in 2002 and 2003 with the third lowest salary in baseball. Billy Beane, the general manager of the A's, employed a predictive approach to regression nicknamed *sabermetrics*.

Using regression to predict success in baseball, the A's focused on hiring underpriced players who had high on-base and slugging percentages. This approach countered the traditional thinking of baseball insiders who favored statistics such as stolen bases, runs batted in, and batting averages. Beane found that these variables were statistically and significantly related to offensive success. **FIGURE 8.9** shows the A's salary compared with the rest of Major League Baseball.

[7]L. Scagliarini, "Moneyball and How Data Analysis Can Level the Playing Field," *icrunchdata*, 28 Oct. 2016.

We demonstrate these steps in **SOLVED PROBLEM 8.7**. Note that the simple linear regression formulas are the same as those used before (Equations 8.10–8.12). In addition, you need to compute seasonal indexes using the **ratio-to-moving-average method** for each season. We use the following formula to compute a reseasonalized forecast:

$$RSF_t = (a + bx_i)(SI_i) \tag{8.13}$$

ratio-to-moving-average method
A method for computing seasonal indexes.

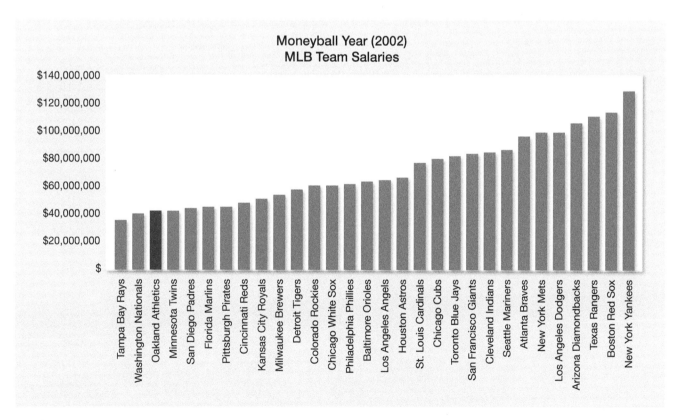

∧ **FIGURE 8.9**

Causal Forecasting Methods Were Used Successfully by the Oakland Athletics, a Major League Baseball Team

where

$$RSF_t = \text{reseasonalized forecast}$$
$$a = y \text{ intercept}$$
$$b = \text{slope}$$
$$x_i = \text{predicted independent value for period } i$$
$$SI_i = \text{seasonal index for period } i$$

 SOLVED PROBLEM 8.7 >

MyLab Operations Management
Video

Deseasonalizing a Time Series

Problem: Using the same time series from Solved Problem 8.6 for the retail outlet in the Mall at Peachtree Center in Atlanta, Georgia, develop a forecast for periods 17 through 20 using classical decomposition of a time series.

Solution: We will follow each of the steps outlined above.

1. Compute seasonal indexes for the data.

   Using the following table,* we take the data for each quarter and compute a yearly average. The periodic index is computed by dividing each quarter's demand (y) by its yearly average demand. Therefore, the periodic seasonal index for period 1 is $23/37.25 = 0.62$. By the same token, the periodic seasonal index for period 14 is $77/90 = 0.86$. Then, each seasonal index (SI) is computed using Equation 8.13 by averaging the periodic SIs for the appropriate seasons. Therefore, the SI for the first quarter is $(0.62 + 0.64 + 0.70 + 0.74)/4 = 0.68$. By the same token, the SI for the third quarter is $(1.18 + 1.19 + 1.21 + 1.17)/4 = 1.19$. The SIs are given below.

Year	Quarter	Period (x)	Demand (y)	Yearly Average	Periodic SI
1	1	1	23		0.62
	2	2	27		0.72
	3	3	44		1.18
	4	4	55	37.25	1.48
2	1	5	37		0.64
	2	6	45		0.78
	3	7	69		1.19
	4	8	80	57.75	1.39
3	1	9	54		0.70
	2	10	63		0.82
	3	11	93		1.21
	4	12	97	76.75	1.26
4	1	13	67		0.74
	2	14	77		0.86
	3	15	105		1.17
	4	16	111	90.00	1.23

*Solutions found in these tables were computed using unrounded numbers. The numbers are concatenated in these tables for simplicity.

Quarter	Seasonal Indexes (*SIs*)
1	0.6765
2	0.7951
3	1.1886
4	1.3397

2. Deseasonalize the demand data.

To deseasonalize the data, divide the periodic demand by its seasonal index, which has the effect of inflating the below-average season forecasts and deflating the above-average season forecasts. For example, the seasonally adjusted demand (SAD) for period 1 is $23/0.6765 = 34.00$, as shown in the table below. The other periodic SADs are computed in the same manner.

Period (*x*)	Demand (*y*)	*SI*	Seasonally Adjusted Demand (SAD)
1	23	0.6765	34.00
2	27	0.7951	33.96
3	44	1.1886	37.02
4	55	1.3397	41.05
5	37	0.6765	54.69
6	45	0.7951	56.60
7	69	1.1886	58.05
8	80	1.3397	59.71
9	54	0.6765	79.82
10	63	0.7951	79.23
11	93	1.1886	78.24
12	97	1.3397	72.40
13	67	0.6765	99.03
14	77	0.7951	96.84
15	105	1.1886	88.34
16	111	1.3397	82.85

The deseasonalized data are shown in the figure on the next page. Note that the variation in the deseasonalized data are much less pronounced than in the original data with seasonality. Perform a forecast using the deseasonalized data to find the trend.

This step follows the simple linear regression process we demonstrated in Solved Problem 8.6, except that we use the seasonally adjusted demand data in developing the forecast. The slope and intercepts are computed as follows:

$$b = \frac{n\left(\sum xy\right) - \left(\sum x\right)\left(\sum y\right)}{n\left(\sum x^2\right) - \left(\sum x\right)^2}$$

The calculations are shown in the table below.

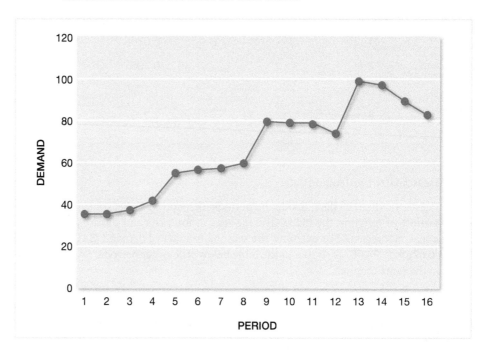

Period (x)	Seasonally Adjusted Demand (y_a)	$x \times y_a$	x^2	Deseasonalized Forecast
1	34.00	34.00	1	33.36
2	33.96	67.91	4	37.68
3	37.02	111.05	9	42.00
4	41.05	164.21	16	46.31
5	54.69	273.45	25	50.63
6	56.60	339.57	36	54.95
7	58.05	406.36	49	59.26
8	59.71	477.70	64	63.58
9	79.82	718.36	81	67.90
10	79.23	792.34	100	72.22
11	78.24	860.68	121	76.53
12	72.40	868.82	144	80.85
13	99.03	1,287.43	169	85.17
14	96.84	1,355.78	196	89.48
15	88.34	1,325.09	225	93.80
16	82.85	1,325.63	256	98.12
Sums:	136	1051.84	10,408.38	1496.00
Means:	8.5	65.74		

$$b = \frac{16(10,408.38) - (136)(1051.84)}{16(1496) - 136^2}$$

$$b = 4.32$$

$$a = \bar{y} - b\bar{x}$$

$$a = 65.74 - 4.32 \times 8.5 = 29.05$$

Using Equation 8.10, the trend is computed as

$$F_t = a + bx_i = 29.05 + 4.32x_i$$

3. Reseasonalizing the deseasonalized forecast.

We use Equation 8.13 to reseasonalize the forecast $RSF_t = (a + bx_i)(SI_i)$ as shown in the table below. The deseasonalized forecast was found in the usual way ($Ft = a + bx_i$). The reseasonalized forecast was found by multiplying the deseasonalized forecast number by the related seasonal index. The forecasts for periods 17 through 20 are given in periods 17 through 20 in the seasonally adjusted demands and reseasonalized forecast columns in the table below.

n = 16				
Period (x)	Seasonally Adjusted Demand (Y_a)(SI)	Deseasonalized Forecast (DF_t)	SI	Reseasonalized Forecast ($DF_t \times SI_t$)
1	34.00	33.36	0.6765	22.57
2	33.96	37.68	0.7951	29.96
3	37.02	42.00	1.1886	49.92
4	41.05	46.31	1.3397	62.05
5	54.69	50.63	0.6765	34.25
6	56.60	54.95	0.7951	43.69
7	58.05	59.26	1.1886	70.44
8	59.71	63.58	1.3397	85.18
9	79.82	67.90	0.6765	45.94
10	79.23	72.22	0.7951	57.42
11	78.24	76.53	1.1886	90.97
12	72.40	80.85	1.3397	108.32
13	99.03	85.17	0.6765	57.62
14	96.84	89.48	0.7951	71.15
15	88.34	93.80	1.1886	111.49
16	82.85	98.12	1.3397	131.45
17	102.43*		0.6765	69.30*
18	106.75*		0.7951	84.88*
19	111.07*		1.1886	132.02*
20	115.39*		1.3397	154.59*

* Forecasted values.

The reseasonalized forecast is shown on the next page. The typical measures of forecasting error, such as MAD, MSE, bias, and MAPE, can be used to assess the fit of this model for periods 1 through 16, as we did before.

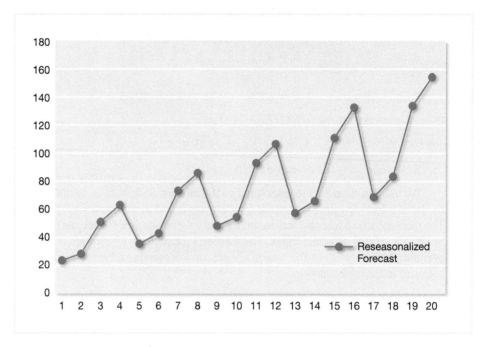

Econometric and Multiple Regression Models

In this section of the chapter, we have discussed simple linear regression and decomposition of a time series. Thousands of firms and organizations around the world use these forecasting tools. Although there are models that are more complex, such as multiple linear regression models and econometric models, the models discussed here give you a good idea of some of the forecasting tools used by statisticians. As shown in SC&O CURRENT EVENTS 8.3, however, it takes more than quantitative models to create accurate forecasts. Managers must understand what is going on in the world around them to avoid bias. We demonstrate simple linear regression in USING TECHNOLOGY 8.1.

SC&O CURRENT >
EVENTS 8.3

When Is Optimism Bad?

In this chapter, we have discussed positive and negative bias. In the case of positive bias, people tend to overforecast. In overforecasting, one of two things can be happening: Either the forecaster is too optimistic or, for some reason, the thing being forecasted is performing worse than expected.

The International Monetary Fund (IMF) is an organization of 189 countries working to foster international financial stability and to reduce poverty. One of the things that the IMF does is lend money to governments to help them promote economic growth. Such lending is a bit like business loans to nations. As with any loan, if you lend money to someone who is not capable of paying back the loan, the net effect is bad for the lender and for the loan holder if he, she, or the nation is forced into default. This has been the case when countries such as Greece have been forced to accept austerity at the hands of the IMF.

Among the chief inputs for determining the creditworthiness of a country are economic forecasts. However, it appears that the IMF may suffer from optimism biases in its forecasts. In the graph in FIGURE 8.10, the IMF forecasted better economic growth than was experienced. The right-facing bars show where the forecasts have been too high, and the left bar for China shows that the IMF has tended to underforecast relative to China. Again, Chinese growth has long been high (see Figure 8.10).

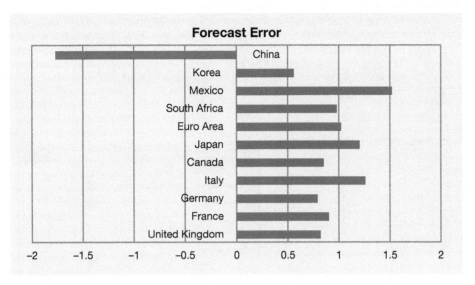

∧ **FIGURE 8.10**

Dealing with Uncertainty

Evidently, the IMF has been struggling with forecast bias. There is room for improvement, however, in reducing or eliminating optimism bias.

Using Excel to Perform Simple Linear Regression

In Microsoft Office, simple linear regression is easy to perform using Data Analysis Tools under the *Data* tab. Be sure to go to File → Options to choose the *Data Analysis Add-in* if you haven't done so already. **FIGURE 8.11** shows the data we have been using in the previous regression examples in this chapter. First, open the *Data* tab and click on *Data Analysis*. The dialog box in Figure 8.11 will appear. Choose *Regression* and click OK.

∧ **FIGURE 8.11**

Excel Window 1

After clicking OK, a *Regression* dialog box will open. As shown in **FIGURE 8.12**, enter the ranges for the *x* (independent) and *y* (dependent) variables. In our problem, the *x* variable is *Period*, so use the values of the range for numbers 1 through 16. For the *y* variable, input the range of demand values (from 23 to 111). You are given other choices, but you need only click on OK.

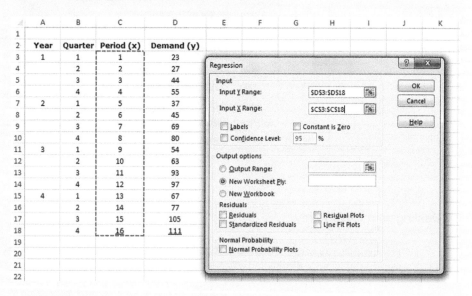

∧ **FIGURE 8.12**

Excel Window 2

When you click OK, the table shown in **FIGURE 8.13** appears. The numbers of interest are the "Significance of F," the "Intercept" coefficient, and the "X Variable 1" coefficient. Interpreting this output, the significance value of 5.00596E-06 is less than 0.05. Therefore, the model is statistically significant. The intercept is 22.675 (or 22.68 rounded), and the slope is 5.03 (labeled as X Variable 1), confirming the analysis we performed earlier in the chapter. Therefore, the simple linear regression model is $y = 22.68 + 5.03x_i$.

	A	B	C	D	E	F	G	H	I	J
1	SUMMARY OUTPUT									
2										
3	*Regression Statistics*									
4	Multiple R	0.885770345								
5	R Square	0.784589105								
6	Adjusted R Square	0.769202612								
7	Standard Error	12.99069237								
8	Observations	16								
9										
10	ANOVA									
11		*df*	*SS*	*MS*	*F*	*Significance F*				
12	Regression	1	8605.324265	8605.324265	50.9920701	5.00596E-06				
13	Residual	14	2362.613235	168.7580882						
14	Total	15	10967.9375							
15										
16		*Coefficients*	*Standard Error*	*t Stat*	*P-value*	*Lower 95%*	*Upper 95%*	*Lower 95.0%*	*Upper 95.0%*	
17	Intercept	22.675	6.81237655	3.328500683	0.004972173	8.063905462	37.28609454	8.063905462	37.28609454	
18	X Variable 1	5.030882353	0.704519211	7.140873203	5.00596E-06	3.519838928	6.541925778	3.519838928	6.541925778	
19										

∧ **FIGURE 8.13**

Excel Window 3

FIGURE 8.14 contains the analysis needed for decomposing the time series. The columns in this spreadsheet are arranged in a way that makes the analysis described earlier in the chapter convenient to perform.

									n= 16						
Year	Quarter	Period (x)	Demand (y)	Yearly Average	Periodic SI	SI	Seasonally Adjusted Demand (SAD)		Period (x)	Seasonally Adjusted Demand	(X x Y$_s$)	X^2	De-seasonalized Forecast	SI	Re-seasonalized Forecast
1	1	1	23		0.62	0.68	34.00		1	34.00	34.00	1	33.36	0.68	22.57
	2	2	27		0.72	0.80	33.96		2	33.96	67.91	4	37.68	0.80	29.96
	3	3	44		1.18	1.19	37.02		3	37.02	111.05	9	42.00	1.19	49.92
	4	4	55	37.25	1.48	1.34	41.05		4	41.05	164.21	16	46.31	1.34	62.05
2	1	5	37		0.64	0.68	54.69		5	54.69	273.45	25	50.63	0.68	34.25
	2	6	45		0.78	0.80	56.60		6	56.60	339.57	36	54.95	0.80	43.69
	3	7	69		1.19	1.19	58.05		7	58.05	406.36	49	59.26	1.19	70.44
	4	8	80	57.75	1.39	1.34	59.71		8	59.71	477.70	64	63.58	1.34	85.18
3	1	9	54		0.70	0.68	79.82		9	79.82	718.36	81	67.90	0.68	45.94
	2	10	63		0.82	0.80	79.23		10	79.23	792.34	100	72.22	0.80	57.42
	3	11	93		1.21	1.19	78.24		11	78.24	860.68	121	76.53	1.19	90.97
	4	12	97	76.75	1.26	1.34	72.40		12	72.40	868.82	144	80.85	1.34	108.32
4	1	13	67		0.74	0.68	99.03		13	99.03	1287.43	169	85.17	0.68	57.62
	2	14	77		0.86	0.80	96.84		14	96.84	1355.78	196	89.48	0.80	71.15
	3	15	105		1.17	1.19	88.34		15	88.34	1325.09	225	93.80	1.19	111.49
	4	16	111	90.00	1.23	1.34	82.85		16	82.85	1325.63	256	98.12	1.34	131.45
Qtr	SI							Sums:	136	1051.84	10408.38	1496.00			
1	0.6765							Means:	8.5	65.74					
2	0.7951														
3	1.1886							b =		23484.36		= 4.32			
4	1.3397									5440					
								a=		29.04547794					

∧ **FIGURE 8.14**

Excel Window 4

In the beginning of the chapter, we discussed a new approach to forecasting that includes "scraping" social media data, news sources, and crowdsourcing. In the past, the markets have waited breathlessly for government data to confirm or disconfirm market expectations. These announcements from the government can cause the stock market to vary wildly. One of the problems with the government forecasts is that they are often based on data that are months old.

An expectation that inflation will increase might be preceded by an increase in Google searches on the word *inflation*. Also, pricing data for many (or most) products are available on the Internet. Thus, it is reasonable not to have to wait for government "mystery shoppers" to obtain pricing information. According to economist Michael Strain,[8] "You could have every transaction on Amazon, every search on Google, every resume that was downloaded, that's really useful stuff. When a big outside event disrupts the economy, those are hard things to forecast. By definition, you can't build them into your forecasting model because they haven't happened yet."

This is an exciting time for forecasting. We may be moving from an era where data are limited and causal factors affecting business are rare. With social media and other sources of data, researchers and forecasters have new opportunities to predict the future more accurately. As a manager, it is important that you understand forecasting and can question assumptions to support better decision making for your organization.

[8] J. Zumbrun, "Economic Forecasting Is Getting More Up-to-the-Minute," *The Wall Street Journal*, 24 Aug. 2015.

Summary

In this chapter, we introduced the art of demand management and forecasting.

1. The demand management tools included advertising, pricing, designing counterseasonal products, channel management, outsourcing, product phasing, and supply chain management. We saw how information moving up the supply chain can help reduce variation and the bullwhip effect. One approach to improve communcation is collaborative planning, forecasting, and replenishment (CPFR).

2. We then introduced several forecasting approaches and models.
   a. Judgmental forecasting approaches include the string method, greenfield forecasting techniques, Delphi method, nominal group techniques, and grassroots forecasting.
   b. The naive models are so named because they do not attempt to explain why variation occurs in terms of causality. They simply take mathematical patterns that existed in the past and if there is good "fit," we conclude that the same model will work well in the future.
   c. We introduced MAD, MSE, bias, and MAPE as measures of forecasting error and used them to assess the fit of the model.

3. We discussed simple linear regression. An extension of regression is the decomposition of a time series to account for seasonality.

   TABLE 8.4 summarizes all the models outlined in this chapter. They are just one step in the direction of making you familiar with the models and tools you need to be a better manager.

TABLE 8.4 >

Summary of Forecasting Models

Model	Purpose
$F_{t+1} = \dfrac{a_1 + a_{t-1} + \cdots + a_{t-n}}{n}$	Simple moving average
$F_{t+1} = w_t a_t + w_{t-1} + \cdots + a_{t-n}$	Weighted moving average
$F_{t+1} = \alpha a_t + (1 - \alpha)F_t$	Single exponential smoothing
$F_{t+1} = F_t + \alpha(a_t - F_t)$	Alternative single exponential smoothing formulation
$FD_t = \alpha F_t + (1 - \alpha)FD_{t-1}$	Double exponential smoothing model
$\text{MAD} = \dfrac{\sum_{i=1}^{n}\lvert a_t - F_t\rvert_i}{n}$	Mean absolute deviation
$\text{MSE} = \dfrac{\sum_{i=1}^{n}(a_t - F_t)_i^2}{n}$	Mean squared error
$\text{Bias} = \dfrac{\sum_{i=1}^{n}(F_t - a_t)}{n}$	Bias (forecasting too high or too low)
$\text{MAPE} = \dfrac{\sum_{i=1}^{n}\dfrac{\lvert a_t - F_t\rvert_i}{a_t}}{n}$	Mean absolute percentage error
$F_t = a + bx_i$	Simple linear regression equation
$b = \dfrac{n(\sum xy) - (\sum x)(\sum y)}{n(\sum x^2) - (\sum x)^2}$	Slope
$a = \bar{y} - b\bar{x}$	y intercept
$RSF_t = (a + bx_i)(SI_i)$	Reseasonalized forecast

Key Terms

advertising and promotion   198
bias   210
bullwhip effect   201
causal models   212
channel management   199
churn   198
collaborative planning, forecasting, and
      replenishment (CPFR)   202
counterseasonal products   198
cyclical effects   200
decomposing a time series   216
Delphi method   203
demand management   197
dependent demand   197
dependent variable (y)   213
deseasonalizing a forecast   216
double exponential smoothing
      (DES)   209

forecast   197
forecasting   197
grassroots forecasting   204
greenfield forecasting
      methods   203
independent demand   197
independent variable (x)   213
irregular component   200
mean absolute deviation
      (MAD)   210
mean average percentage error
      (MAPE)   210
mean squared error (MSE)   210
multiple linear regression   213
naive forecasting methods   205
noise component   200
nominal group techniques
      (NGTs)   204

outsourcing   199
pricing   198
product phasing   199
ratio-to-moving-average method   217
seasonality   200
seasonal patterns   200
simple linear regression   213
simple moving average
      (SMA)   205
single exponential smoothing
      (SES)   208
smoothing constant   208
smoothing effect   207
string method   203
structured brainstorming   204
trend   200
weighted moving average
      (WMA)   206

Integrative Learning Exercise

Identify two products or services, one that is established and the other that is new to the market and for which there is no past historical sales data. Discuss how you would forecast demand for the different products or services you identified. What forecasting techniques might be appropriate for the established product or service? What forecasting techniques might you use to determine the demand for the new product or service? Why are your choices of forecasting techniques different for the two products or services?

Integrative Experiential Exercise

Together with your student team, visit a company or organization near your campus. Ask company representatives how they use forecasting to predict the demand for their products or services. Identify the types of forecasting techniques they use and how they measure the accuracy of their forecasting models. For what purposes do they use their forecasting tools?

Discussion Questions

1. What is a forecast? How are forecasts related to business planning?

2. Briefly contrast independent demand with dependent demand. Why is the difference between the two important in terms of forecasting?

3. Briefly describe demand management and three tools that companies can use for demand management.

4. Briefly describe how counterseasonal products can offer a way to level capacity demands during the year.

5. In what ways can coordinating the supply chain improve forecasting?

6. How is a trend different from a seasonal pattern in a time series?

7. How is forecasting in the supply chain related to the bullwhip effect?

8. What is the objective of collaborative planning, forecasting, and replenishment?

9. In what situations might judgmental or experiential forecasting be appropriate?

10. What is the Delphi method? How is it used in forecasting?

11. What is meant by the naive forecasting method?

12. How does a weighted moving average forecast differ from a simple moving average forecast?

13. How does increasing and decreasing the smoothing constant α in a single exponential smoothing model affect the forecast?

14. Under what circumstances would double exponential smoothing be preferred to single exponential smoothing in forecasting?

15. Briefly describe the concept of bias as it relates to forecasting.

Solved Problems

Naive Forecasting Methods

SIMPLE MOVING AVERAGE
SOLVED PROBLEM 8.1

1. Using the following data, compute a four-period simple moving average and a forecast for period 11.

Period	a_t
1	106
2	93
3	95
4	94
5	106
6	103
7	103
8	96
9	106
10	96

Solution:

Period	a_t	Calculation	F_t (SMA)
1	106		
2	93		
3	95		
4	94		
5	106	(106 + 93 + 95 + 94)/4 =	97.00
6	103	(93 + 95 + 94 + 106)/4 =	97.00
7	103	(95 + 94 + 106 + 103)/4 =	99.50
8	96	(94 + 106 + 103 + 103)/4 =	101.50
9	106	(106 + 103 + 103 + 96)/4 =	102.00
10	96	(103 + 103 + 96 + 106)/4 =	102.00
		(103 + 96 + 106 + 96)/4 =	100.25

Forecasts for the first four periods are not possible because four months of data are needed to get started. The forecast for period 11 is (103 + 96 + 106 + 96)/4 = 100.25.

Weighted moving average

SOLVED PROBLEM 8.2

2. Use the following data to develop a weighted moving average forecast with the weights 0.6, 0.3, and 0.1, using the heaviest weights for the most recent data.

Period	a_t
1	106
2	93
3	95
4	94
5	106
6	103
7	103
8	96
9	106
10	96

Solution:

Period	a_t	Calculation	F_t (WMA)
1	106		
2	93		

3	95		
4	94	$(95 \times 0.6 + 93 \times 0.3 + 106 \times 0.1) =$	95.50
5	106	$(94 \times 0.6 + 95 \times 0.3 + 93 \times 0.1) =$	94.20
6	103	$(106 \times 0.6 + 94 \times 0.3 + 95 \times 0.1) =$	101.30
7	103	$(103 \times 0.6 + 106 \times 0.3 + 94 \times 0.1) =$	103.00
8	96	$(103 \times 0.6 + 103 \times 0.3 + 106 \times 0.1) =$	103.30
9	106	$(96 \times 0.6 + 103 \times 0.3 + 103 \times 0.1) =$	98.80
10	96	$(106 \times 0.6 + 96 \times 0.3 + 103 \times 0.1) =$	102.70
		$(96 \times 0.6 + 106 \times 0.3 + 96 \times 0.1) =$	99.00

Again, the first three periods are not forecasted. The forecast for period 11 is 99.00.

Single exponential smoothing

SOLVED PROBLEM 8.3

3. Use the following data to develop a single exponential smoothing forecast. Use a smoothing constant $(\alpha) = 0.25$. Use 106 as the initial forecast.

Period	a_t
1	106
2	93
3	95
4	94
5	106
6	103
7	103
8	96
9	106
10	96

Solution:

Period	a_t	Calculation	F_t (SES)
1	106		
2	93	$(0.25 \times 106) + (0.75 \times 106) =$	106
3	95	$(0.25 \times 93) + (0.75 \times 106) =$	102.75
4	94	$(0.25 \times 95) + (0.75 \times 102.75) =$	100.81
5	106	$(0.25 \times 94) + (0.75 \times 100.81) =$	99.11
6	103	$(0.25 \times 106) + (0.75 \times 99.11) =$	100.83
7	103	$(0.25 \times 103) + (0.75 \times 100.83) =$	101.37
8	96	$(0.25 \times 103) + (0.75 \times 101.37) =$	101.78
9	106	$(0.25 \times 96) + (0.75 \times 101.78) =$	100.34
10	96	$(0.25 \times 106) + (0.75 \times 100.34) =$	101.75
		$(0.25 \times 96) + (0.75 \times 101.75) =$	100.31

The forecast for period 11 is 100.31.

Double exponential smoothing

SOLVED PROBLEM 8.4

4. Use the following data to develop a double exponential smoothing forecast. Use $\alpha = 0.30$. Use 104 as the seed forecast (period 1) for both SES and DES.

Period	a_t
1	104
2	107
3	106
4	130
5	128
6	137
7	109
8	150
9	147
10	170

Solution:

Period	a_t	F_t (SES)	Calculations	F_t (DES)
1	104			
2	107	104.00	(0.3 × 104) + (0.7 × 104) =	104.00
3	106	104.90	(0.3 × 104.90) + (0.7 × 104) =	104.27
4	130	105.23	(0.3 × 105.23) + (0.7 × 104.27) =	104.56
5	128	112.66	(0.3 × 112.66) + (0.7 × 104.56) =	106.99
6	137	117.26	(0.3 × 117.26) + (0.7 × 106.99) =	110.07
7	109	123.18	(0.3 × 123.18) + (0.7 × 110.07) =	114.00
8	150	118.93	(0.3 × 118.93) + (0.7 × 114) =	115.48
9	147	128.25	(0.3 × 128.25) + (0.7 × 115.48) =	119.31
10	170	133.88	(0.3 × 133.88) + (0.7 × 119.31) =	123.68
		144.71	(0.3 × 144.71) + (0.7 × 123.68) =	129.99

Measures of forecasting error

SOLVED PROBLEM 8.5

5. A forecasting procedure has produced the following forecasts for periods 4 through 12. The actual observations (a_t) and the forecasted values (F_t) are shown for each period. Use the information to compute the mean absolute deviation (MAD), the mean squared error (MSE), the bias, and the mean average percentage error (MAPE).

Period	a_t	F_t
4	96	87
5	79	73
6	96	91
7	85	76
8	89	80
9	92	70
10	86	87
11	94	92
12	78	80

Solution:

Period	a_t	F_t	Absolute Deviation	Squared Error	$F_t - a_t$	Average Percentage Error
4	96	87	9	81	−9	0.09
5	79	73	6	36	−6	0.08
6	96	91	5	25	−5	0.05
7	85	76	9	81	−9	0.11
8	89	80	9	81	−9	0.10
9	92	70	22	484	−22	0.24
10	86	87	1	1	1	0.01
11	94	92	2	4	−2	0.02
12	78	80	2	4	2	0.03
		Means	7.22	88.56	−6.56	0.08
			MAD	MSE	Bias	MAPE

Notice the large error for period 9 is magnified in the MSE, which squares errors in the calculation.

Time Series Forecasting Using Regression

SIMPLE LINEAR REGRESSION
SOLVED PROBLEM 8.6

6. The demand for a product for the past 10 months (periods) is shown below. Use the demand data to develop a simple linear regression and produce a forecast for period 11.

Period (x)	Demand (y)
1	105
2	150
3	164
4	149
5	222
6	220
7	198
8	239
9	246
10	327

Solution:

The plot of the data shows a positive linear trend:

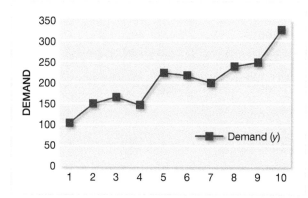

The slope and intercept are computed from the following calculations:

Period (x)	Demand (y)	$x \times y$	x^2
1	105	105	1
2	150	300	4
3	164	492	9
4	149	596	16
5	222	1,110	25
6	220	1,320	36
7	198	1,386	49
8	239	1,912	64
9	246	2,214	81
10	327	3,270	100
Sums	**55**	2,020	12,705	385
Means	**5.5**	202		

$$b = \frac{(10)(12{,}705) - (55)(2020)}{(10)(385) - (55)(55)}$$

$b = 19.33$
$a = 202 - 19.33(5.5) = 95.67$

The trend is calculated as $F_t = 95.67 + 19.33(x_t)$.

For period 11, we substitute 11 for x_t and obtain $F_t = 95.67 + 19.33(11) = 308.30$. The plot of the demand with the simple linear regression line is shown below:

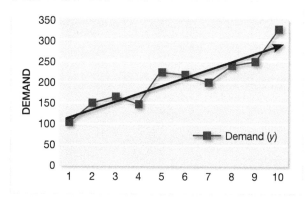

Linear regression with seasonality

SOLVED PROBLEM 8.7

7. The following demand data were collected quarterly for the past four years.

Year	Quarter	Period (x)	Demand (y)
1	1	1	200
	2	2	100
	3	3	190
	4	4	105
2	1	5	240
	2	6	95
	3	7	250
	4	8	110

continued

Year	Quarter	Period (x)	Demand (y)
3	1	9	260
	2	10	120
	3	11	265
	4	12	115
4	1	13	300
	2	14	140
	3	15	280
	4	16	150

Plot the data and determine if a linear regression model with seasonality is appropriate. If it is, determine the seasonal indexes, deseasonalize the data, perform a forecast using the deseasonalized data to find the trend, and reseasonalize the deseasonalized forecast. Finally, produce a forecast for periods 17 through 20.

Solution:
The plot of the demand data reveals an upward trend with seasonality:

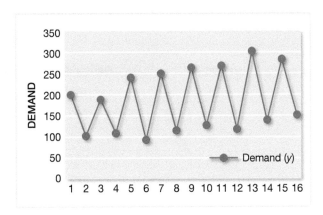

First, the yearly averages and the periodic seasonal indexes (SIs) are computed as follows:

Year	Quarter	Period (x)	Demand (y)	Yearly Average	Periodic SI
1	1	1	200		1.34
	2	2	100		0.67
	3	3	190		1.28
	4	4	105	148.75	0.71
2	1	5	240		1.38
	2	6	95		0.55
	3	7	250		1.44
	4	8	110	173.75	0.63
3	1	9	260		1.37
	2	10	120		0.63
	3	11	265		1.39
	4	12	115	190	0.61
4	1	13	300		1.38
	2	14	140		0.64
	3	15	280		1.29
	4	16	150	217.5	0.69

The *SIs* for the four quarters are computed by averaging the periodic *SIs* for the respective quarters. The results are as follows:

Quarter	SI
1	1.3684
2	0.6236
3	1.3496
4	0.6585

To deseasonalize the data, divide the demand by its seasonal index:

Period (x)	Demand (y)	SI	Seasonally Adjusted Demand (Y_a)
1	200	1.3684	146.16
2	100	0.6236	160.37
3	190	1.3496	140.79
4	105	0.6585	159.46
5	240	1.3684	175.39
6	95	0.6236	152.35
7	250	1.3496	185.25
8	110	0.6585	167.05
9	260	1.3684	190.00
10	120	0.6236	192.44
11	265	1.3496	196.36
12	115	0.6585	174.65
13	300	1.3684	219.24
14	140	0.6236	224.51
15	280	1.3496	207.47
16	150	0.6585	227.80

The deseasonalized data are shown below:

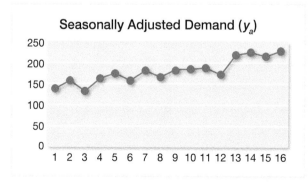

Seasonally Adjusted Demand (y_a)

The simple linear regression process is performed again using the seasonally adjusted demand data to develop the forecast. The slope and intercept are:

$$b = \frac{(16)(26{,}591.56) - (136)(2919.28)}{(16)(1496) - (136)(139)} = 5.2286$$

$$a = 182.45 - 5.2286(8.5) = 138.01$$

Use the formula $F_t = 138.01 + 5.2286(x_i)$ to get the following deseasonalized forecast by substituting the period for x_i:

Period (x)	Deseasonalized Forecast
1	143.24
2	148.47
3	153.70
4	158.93
5	164.15
6	169.38
7	174.61
8	179.84
9	185.07
10	190.30
11	195.53
12	200.75
13	205.98
14	211.21
15	216.44
16	221.67

The reseasonalized forecast is found by multiplying the deseasonalized forecast by the seasonal index.

Period (x)	Deseasonalized Forecast	SI	Reseasonalized Forecast
1	143.24	1.3684	196.01
2	148.47	0.6236	92.58
3	153.70	1.3496	207.42
4	158.93	0.6585	104.65

continued

Period (x)	Deseasonalized Forecast	SI	Reseasonalized Forecast
5	164.15	1.3684	224.63
6	169.38	0.6236	105.62
7	174.61	1.3496	235.65
8	179.84	0.6585	118.42
9	185.07	1.3684	253.25
10	190.30	0.6236	118.66
11	195.53	1.3496	263.87
12	200.75	0.6585	132.19
13	205.98	1.3684	281.87
14	211.21	0.6236	131.71
15	216.44	1.3496	292.10
16	221.67	0.6585	145.96

The forecasts for periods 17 through 20 follow:

Period	Deseasonalized Forecast	SI	Reseasonalized Forecast
17	226.89	1.3684	310.5
18	232.12	0.6236	144.7
19	237.35	1.3496	320.3
20	242.58	0.6585	159.7

The reseasonalized forecast is shown below:

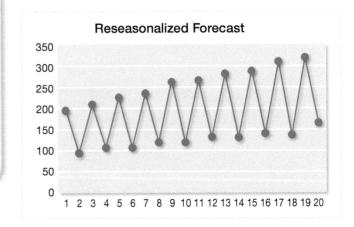

Reseasonalized Forecast

Problems

Naive Forecasting Models

SIMPLE MOVING AVERAGE

1. Use the following information to compute a three-period simple moving average and find a forecast for period 10. Note: a_t is the actual demand for the period.

Period	a_t
1	149
2	134
3	131
4	147
5	163
6	109
7	189
8	191
9	162

2. A company has the following demand (a_t) for the previous nine weeks. Use the information to develop a four-period simple moving average and a forecast for period 10.

Period	a_t
1	403
2	422
3	325
4	428
5	332
6	317
7	376
8	478
9	382

3. The demand for a consumer product is fairly constant from week to week. The previous nine weeks of demand are shown below. *Note: a_t is the actual period's demand.* Use the information to produce a three-period moving average and a forecast for period 10.

Period	a_t
1	455
2	410
3	340
4	338
5	433
6	356
7	371
8	363
9	440

4. A company has experienced the following demand for a product over the most recent nine months. Use the information to produce a two-period simple moving average and a forecast for period 10. *Note: a_t is the actual demand for the period.*

Period	a_t
1	928
2	861
3	872
4	852
5	855
6	658
7	640
8	716
9	527

WEIGHTED MOVING AVERAGE

5. Use the following information to compute a three-period weighted moving average forecast with the weights 0.5, 0.3, and 0.2, where the largest weight is placed on the most recent data. Also, find a forecast for period 10. *Note: a_t is the actual demand for the period.*

Period	a_t
1	149
2	134
3	131
4	147
5	163
6	109
7	189
8	191
9	162

6. A company has the following demand (a_t) for the previous nine weeks. Use the information to develop a four-period weighted moving average using the weights 0.4, 0.3, 0.2, and 0.1, with the largest weights applied to the most current data. Be sure to compute a forecast for period 10.

Period	a_t
1	403
2	422
3	325
4	428
5	332
6	317
7	376
8	478
9	382

7. The demand for a consumer product is fairly constant from week to week. The previous nine weeks of demand are shown below (a_t is the actual period's demand). Use the information to produce a weighted moving average with the following weights: 0.45, 0.35, and 0.20. More recent periods receive a larger weight. Produce a forecast for period 10.

Period	a_t
1	455
2	410
3	340
4	338
5	433
6	356
7	371
8	363
9	440

8. A company has experienced the following demand for a product over the most recent nine months. Develop a weighted moving average using the weights 0.6 and 0.4 applied to the most recent periods, respectively. What is your forecast for period 10? *Note:* a_t is the actual demand for the period.

Period	a_t
1	928
2	861
3	872
4	852
5	855
6	658
7	640
8	716
9	527

SINGLE EXPONENTIAL SMOOTHING

9. Use the following information to compute a single exponential smoothing model forecast with a smoothing constant ($\alpha = 0.10$) to produce a forecast for period 10. *Note:* a_t is the actual demand for the period. Use 149 as the initial forecast.

Period	a_t
1	149
2	134
3	131

4	147
5	163
6	109
7	189
8	191
9	162

10. A company has the following demand (a_t) for the previous nine weeks. Use the information to develop a single exponential forecast for period 10 using a smoothing constant, α, equal to 0.25. Use 403 as the initial forecast.

Period	a_t
1	403
2	422
3	325
4	428
5	332
6	317
7	376
8	478
9	382

11. The demand for a consumer product is fairly constant from week to week. The previous nine weeks of demand are shown below. Use the information to produce a single exponential smoothing forecast for period 10 using a smoothing constant, α, equal to 0.30. *Note:* a_t is the actual period's demand. Use 455 as the initial forecast.

Period	a_t
1	455
2	410
3	340
4	338
5	433
6	356
7	371
8	363
9	440

12. A company has experienced the following demand for a product over the most recent nine months. Use the information to produce a single exponential smoothing model for period 10. Use a smoothing constant, α, equal to 0.40. *Note:* a_t is the actual demand for the period. Use 928 as the initial forecast.

Period	a_t
1	928
2	861
3	872
4	852
5	855
6	658
7	640
8	716
9	527

DOUBLE EXPONENTIAL SMOOTHING

13. The following data represent the actual demand for a company's product for the previous 12 months. Use the data to develop a double exponential smoothing forecast for period 13. Use a smoothing constant, α, equal to 0.20. Use 72 as the forecast value to begin.

Period	a_t
1	72
2	71
3	82
4	75
5	74
6	73
7	75
8	67
9	76
10	79
11	65
12	76

14. Use the following demand data (a_t) to produce a double exponential smoothing forecast for period 13. Use a smoothing constant, α, equal to 0.30. Use 262 as the initial SES and DES forecasts.

Period	a_t
1	262
2	237
3	228
4	265
5	261
6	239
7	264
8	271
9	268
10	278
11	318
12	282

15. Use the following 12 periods of demand to produce a double exponential smoothing forecast for period 13. Use a smoothing constant, α, equal to 0.35. Use 536 as the initial forecast value.

Period	a_t
1	536
2	573
3	568
4	640
5	746
6	619
7	772
8	704
9	899
10	863
11	822
12	864

16. The following 12 periods of actual demand are to be used to produce a double exponential smoothing forecast for period 13. Use a smoothing constant, α, equal to 0.25. Use 57 as the initial forecast value.

Period	a_t
1	57
2	54
3	51
4	50
5	50
6	47
7	46
8	38
9	37
10	33
11	39
12	35

FORECASTING ERROR

17. Compute the mean absolute deviation (MAD), the mean squared error (MSE), the bias, and the mean average percentage error (MAPE) for the following forecast. *Note:* The actual demand values are designated by a_t and the forecast values by F_t.

Period	a_t	F_t
1	616	599
2	598	572
3	597	646
4	582	699
5	607	623
6	611	596
7	615	566

18. A company has the following actual (a_t) and forecast (F_t) values for one of its products. Compute the mean absolute deviation (MAD), the mean squared error (MSE), the bias, and the mean average percentage error (MAPE).

Period	a_t	F_t
1	468	493
2	434	510
3	450	532
4	480	469
5	447	506
6	483	484
7	485	465
8	473	469

19. The Washington Company has the following actual (a_t) and forecast (F_t) values for its primary product. Compute the mean absolute deviation (MAD), the mean squared error (MSE), the bias, and the mean average percentage error (MAPE).

Period	a_t	F_t
1	1,829	2,050
2	1,901	1,900
3	1,814	1,995
4	1,887	2,208
5	1,896	1,787
6	1,814	2,103
7	1,877	1,787
8	1,898	1,914
9	1,904	2,042
10	1,912	2,024

20. Compute the mean absolute deviation (MAD), the mean squared error (MSE), the bias, and the mean average percentage error (MAPE) for the following forecast. *Note:* The actual demand values are designated by a_t and the forecast values by F_t.

Period	a_t	F_t
1	2,835	2,900
2	2,970	3,090
3	2,995	3,100
4	2,935	2,860
5	2,715	3,160

6	2,940	2,870
7	2,855	3,280
8	2,925	2,760
9	2,880	3,050
10	2,955	2,940
11	2,965	2,790
12	2,805	3,030

9	149
10	137
11	128
12	115

Time Series Forecasting Using Regression

SIMPLE LINEAR REGRESSION

21. For the following 12 periods of historical data, compute a simple linear regression equation and develop a forecast for the next four periods.

Period	a_t
1	108
2	112
3	107
4	118
5	131
6	126
7	138
8	145
9	159
10	138
11	153
12	159

22. A company wants to develop a simple linear regression model for one of its products. Use the following 12 periods of historical data to develop the regression equation and use it to forecast the next three periods.

Period	a_t
1	207
2	193
3	188
4	175
5	164
6	154
7	161
8	168

23. Develop a simple linear regression model based on the following 12 periods of historical data. Then compute the forecast for the next five periods.

Period	a_t
1	557
2	546
3	566
4	562
5	582
6	566
7	565
8	579
9	589
10	608
11	580
12	603

24. The Wellington Company wants to develop a simple linear regression model for one of its products. Use the following 12 periods of historical data to develop the regression equation and to forecast the next three periods.

Period	a_t
1	946
2	905
3	837
4	779
5	794
6	643
7	670
8	608
9	488
10	649
11	446
12	437

REGRESSION WITH SEASONALITY

25. Quarterly data for the most recent three years of a product's demand are shown below. Use the data to develop a forecast for periods 13 through 16 using classical decomposition of a time series.

Period	a_t
1	575
2	590
3	610
4	485
5	605
6	638
7	691
8	538
9	666
10	680
11	695
12	555

26. A company has collected the following quarterly demand data for one of its products. Use the information provided to develop a forecast for periods 13 through 16 using classical decomposition of a time series.

Period	a_t
1	1,178
2	1,239
3	1,311
4	1,067
5	1,361
6	1,467
7	1,623
8	1,291
9	1,631
10	1,700
11	1,772
12	1,443

27. The Wintergreen Company produces a product whose demand is highly seasonal. The most recent 16 quarters of demand data are shown below. Use the product's actual demand for the most recent 16 quarters to produce a

forecast for periods 17 through 20 using classical decomposition of a time series forecasting.

Period	a_t
1	421
2	183
3	466
4	113
5	629
6	277
7	693
8	170
9	736
10	323
11	813
12	197
13	789
14	350
15	876
16	214

28. The following quarterly data show the demand for the most recent four years for a product. Develop a forecast for quarters 17 through 20 using the classical decomposition of a time series.

Period	a_t
1	1,566
2	670
3	1,810
4	434
5	1,448
6	668
7	1,741
8	391
9	1,127
10	533
11	1,332
12	340
13	830
14	389
15	945
16	220

Demand Planning at BIOCNG

Teresa Miller is responsible for demand planning at BIOCNG Enterprises. As part of her planning activities, she must develop a demand forecast for the next four quarters. She will then use her demand forecast to plan and manage the company's production schedules. Teresa has the historical demand (sales) figures shown in the table below. She will have to present her demand analysis and forecast to the company's planning team. Consequently, she will want to have both graphical and table summaries of her findings, together with some measure of forecast accuracy.

Question:

1. Your role is to provide assistance to Teresa and help her prepare a forecast for the next four quarters (quarters 3 and 4 of 2020 and quarters 1 and 2 of 2021). As part of the analysis, your report should identify an appropriate forecasting technique, develop a forecasting model, use the forecasting model to generate forecasts for the historical quarters as well as for the planning quarters, and provide an assessment of the forecasting model's accuracy.

Period	Sales
1Q-2016	571,216
2Q-2016	446,781
3Q-2016	462,418
4Q-2016	532,339
1Q-2017	750,308
2Q-2017	569,922
3Q-2017	562,211
4Q-2017	546,235
1Q-2018	753,131
2Q-2018	567,191
3Q-2018	573,539
4Q-2018	558,543
1Q-2019	805,850
2Q-2019	643,072
3Q-2019	660,513
4Q-2019	640,426
1Q-2020	917,147
2Q-2020	717,715

9

Inventory Management Fundamentals and Independent Demand

Consider the case of the Target retail customer who goes to the store to buy an item and finds that it is not in stock. Target managers must balance the costs of carrying excess inventory with the cost of stockouts. Stockouts can result in lost and dissatisfied customers. Target is the second largest U.S. importer of containerized freight. This freight must be distributed to regional warehouses, which then provide stock to individual stores. Imagine the problem of trying to stock the right amount of winter clothing when an unexpected snowstorm hits the East Coast and the weather is mild in the Rocky Mountains. This is the task before inventory professionals at Target.

Many people think that inventory is just another cost. As we will show in this chapter, inventory is an asset that needs to be managed properly. It is important to carry the right quantities in the right locations. We will return to this Target story at the end of the chapter.

D EFINE THE ROLES AND TYPES OF INVENTORY

In this chapter, we will discuss inventory management fundamentals. You have probably not spent much time thinking about *inventory*, but inventory and its management have a huge effect on your life. When you started the semester, you purchased school supplies and books from inventories. When you went online or to your bookstore, you expected them to have what you needed in stock. If it wasn't there, you may have been forced to spend more time and money to find what you needed. Inventory affects us and how businesses run in many ways, and with increasing numbers of supply chain distribution channels, inventory decisions are making more and more of a difference to a company's bottom line. Carry too much inventory and you will incur high costs. Carry too little inventory and you will lose sales, incur supply chain disruptions, and risk going out of business. Such is the balancing act that many companies face as they decide how much inventory to carry.

Inventory is a store of goods and stocks for some future (either near-term or long-term) use. Effective **inventory management** uses tools and strategies to achieve a balance between costs and customer service.

inventory
A store of goods and stocks for some future (either near-term or long-term) use.

inventory management
Using tools and strategies to achieve a balance between inventory costs and customer service.

The Role of Inventory

Inventory is an asset. If you look at the balance sheet of any company, you will see inventory listed among its assets. The assets of many companies are largely made up of inventory. Since 1950, inventory has made up 20 to 25 percent of U.S. gross national product.[1] Think of retail giants such as the Gap or Toys 'R' Us. More than 20 percent of their assets are tied up in inventory. These large percentages mean that if these companies—with all their core activities such as purchasing, advertising, and merchandising—manage inventories poorly, they will not be competitive. Inventory is big money. Intermountain Hospital, a large hospital system, hired a new vice president of supply chain to help improve its inventory management. He convinced management to hire him for zero salary in the first year if the firm would pay

---

[1]*Economic Report of the President* (2010). http://www.whitehouse.gov/administration/eop/cea/economic-report-of-the-President/2010.

him 10 percent of the savings that he generated in improvements. During his first months, he focused on inventory. He found a large amount of excess inventory in the form of just-in-case items for various doctors and surgeons. Reductions in inventory resulted in $100,000,000 in savings in the first year for the hospital system. This arrangement obviously was very lucrative for this executive!

In the following paragraphs, we will discuss the reasons for carrying inventory, including (1) improving service levels, (2) tempering uncertainty, (3) managing production lead times, (4) creating economies of scale, and (5) buffering processes.

IMPROVING SERVICE LEVELS Probably the most important reason for carrying inventory is to provide a high level of service to your customers. From an inventory supply chain perspective, **service level** for any item is the probability that an item will be available in stock for order fulfillment when it is needed during lead time. Inventory could be needed for sale; for use in a stage of production; or as a supply, such as soap in a dispenser in a restroom. If the item is out of stock 5 percent of the time there is a reorder, there is a 95 percent service level.

service level
The probability that an item will be available in stock for order fulfillment when it is needed during lead time.

Managing Across Majors 9.1 Marketing majors, if you want to provide good service to your customers, you should pay attention to inventories. You will lose customers if your inventory levels are too low for key items.

TEMPERING UNCERTAINTY Firms face many kinds of uncertainty. Hush Puppy shoes, for example, experienced unexpectedly high demand in the mid-1990s. Sales of the shoes were down to 30,000 pairs a year, and the brand owner, Wolverine, considered phasing out the brand. Suddenly, after the shoes became popular in downtown New York City clubs, sales increased to 430,000 pairs,[2] and Wolverine had to scramble to meet demand. Alternatively, sales of products can unexpectedly drop. Tiger Woods's PGA Tour video game, for example, saw a 68 percent drop in sales over the prior year after revelations of his infidelity and his poor performance on the links.[3]

Uncertainty can be product-specific or due to macroeconomic factors, such as economic downturns or booms. Other types of uncertainty in a global supply chain include exchange rate fluctuation, political instability, and risk of interrupted supply due to unforeseen events such as terrorist threats, natural disasters, and difficulties in shipping. When global instability is present, firms may hedge. **Hedging** is building up inventory in anticipation of unforeseen global supply chain interruptions. For example, if you expect the exchange rate in currency to become markedly less favorable, you may decide to buy inventory in anticipation of the weakening of your purchasing currency.

hedging
Building up inventory in anticipation of unforeseen global supply chain interruptions.

Managing Across Majors 9.2 Global finance majors, there are reasons to hedge other than exchange rate fluctuation. To avoid cost increases, you should be aware of reasons such as shipping problems and disruptions.

MANAGING PRODUCTION LEAD TIMES When there is variation in demand and your firm makes many products that require setups, the amount of time it takes to produce products can become unacceptably long. **Lead time** is the period between placing and receiving an order. When operating under the assumption that your lead times will lengthen, you can use inventory as a tool to keep these times short by having inventory available for sale. One mechanism for managing lead times is **production smoothing**, or producing extra inventory during periods of low demand, which is then consumed during periods of high demand.

lead time
The period between placing and receiving an order.

production smoothing
Producing extra inventory during periods of low demand, which is then consumed during periods of high demand.

----

[2]M. Gladwell, *The Tipping Point: How Little Things Can Make a Big Difference* (Boston: Little, Brown, 2000): 3.
[3]E. Kay, "Tiger Woods Still the World's Richest Athlete, Despite Plummeting Endorsements and Video Game Sales," *San Francisco Examiner*, July 21, 2010.

The trick to production smoothing is to build stocks in anticipation of higher demand and to stock at levels that will meet—but not exceed—anticipated demand. Another approach to managing lead times is to use fixed time period models for inventory management. **Fixed time period models** call for inventory orders at regular time intervals, such as weekly or monthly, to stabilize purchasing and shipping schedules.

fixed time period models
Inventory models for ordering in regular time intervals, such as weekly or monthly, to stabilize purchasing and shipping schedules.

CREATING ECONOMIES OF SCALE Inventory is often a mechanism for reducing the average per-unit cost for production; if you produce more, fixed overhead costs are amortized across more units. Large lot sizes allow for lower per-unit price and savings over time. At times, these savings may exceed the costs of storing the additional inventory.

BUFFERING PROCESSES A breakdown at one stage of production can cause downstream and upstream production problems at all stages in a lean supply chain. For example, there were downstream stoppages after the September 11, 2001, terror attacks. When shipping routes were interrupted, plants were temporarily closed and production was halted. Inventories that are kept at the intersection of differing stages of production to maintain continuity of processing are called **buffers**. Buffers allow production to continue downstream despite upstream supply interruptions. As an inventory manager, you should use buffer stocks only when analysis shows that the cost of maintaining the buffer inventory is less than losses associated with not keeping stock on hand. SC&O CURRENT EVENTS 9.1 shows why buffer stocks may be needed to avoid supply chain disruptions.

buffers
Inventories that are kept at the intersection of differing stages of production to maintain continuity of processing.

Types of Inventory

To understand inventory management, we first need to understand the various types of inventory. Using some aspects of the upstream/downstream model from this text, we will identify and define the different types of inventory. For our purposes, we separate inventory into four

Buffer Stocks and Supply Chain Disruption: Hanjin

< SC&O CURRENT
EVENTS 9.1

One of the most important considerations in planning buffer or safety stocks is global supply chain risk. Buffer stocks are kept in anticipation of risk. One example of supply chain risk is the bankruptcy of the world's seventh largest shipping company, Hanjin Sooho. Just in time for Christmas shipments, the Korean company claimed bankruptcy, stranding as many as 80 vessels with over 500,000 containers at an estimated value of $14 billion. Some of the ships were seized in ports such as Shanghai and other ships were at sea.

While many of the shipments were scheduled out of China, some companies such as Samsung were left exposed. Samsung used Hanjin for as many as 40 percent of its shipments, and LG shipped 20 percent of its products via Hanjin. Potential purchasers can hedge by using either of two buffer stock strategies—safety stock or safety lead time. However, as we will see later in this chapter, both options come at a cost.

One of the reasons for the bankruptcy was a slowing in the growth of international trade. Since 2000, the world shipping fleet has quadrupled in size while international trade has not kept pace. The shipping behemoth Maersk is also flowing with red ink, and other companies are struggling.

What does this mean for companies who depend on these companies to ship their products? It means that they will experience increased levels of risk of global supply chain disruptions. Winter promotions for retailers and component parts for U.S. manufacturers often come from China and are ordered months in advance. If shipping becomes nonviable because of economics, companies must plan inventories appropriately. This also affects purchasing and logistics professionals because expedited orders and alternative shipment have to be arranged. Retailers JCPenney, Target, Best Buy, and Walmart were especially hard hit in anticipation of Christmas sales.

FIGURE 9.1 >

Types of Inventory

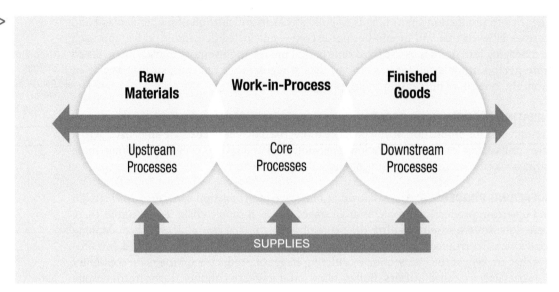

main categories: (1) raw materials, (2) work-in-process, (3) finished goods, and (4) supplies. We will also introduce consignment inventory and vendor-managed inventory, which we discuss later in the chapter.

RAW MATERIALS INVENTORY As shown in FIGURE 9.1, upstream inventory managers receive raw materials from their suppliers. **Raw materials** are inputs to production that take the form of either fundamental supplies, such as iron or wood, or subassemblies and components received from suppliers. For example, incoming raw materials may include precut glass for windows or wood moldings for windowpanes. Managers must determine if they will hold the stock or if the supplier will handle the raw material inventory for them.

raw materials
Inputs to production that take the form of either fundamental supplies, such as iron or wood, or subassemblies and components received from suppliers.

WORK-IN-PROCESS INVENTORY Within the production process, **work-in-process (WIP) inventory** usually comes in three forms: (1) inventory that is waiting to be processed, (2) inventory that is being processed, and (3) inventory that is waiting to be moved for future processing. Note that only stage 2 is a value-added activity. The other stages (1 and 3) are places in the process where productivity improvement efforts are often centralized to reduce delays and waiting times. For example, incoming raw steel is received into inventory (1). The steel is then processed (2) into mailboxes, and the finished mailboxes are placed into a waiting area for painting (3). If processing is highly efficient, reductions in waiting time in stages 1 and 3 provide the greatest opportunity for improvement in process lead times.

work-in-process (WIP) inventory
Inventory that has been received and is in the production phase.

FINISHED GOODS INVENTORY Downstream, inventory managers have **finished goods inventory**, products that are waiting to be sold to the customer. Managing finished goods inventory can be done in different ways, such as make to stock and make to order. **Make-to-stock inventory** is made to be placed into inventory for sale at a later date, such as M&M candy that is placed into inventory to be shipped later to a Kroger warehouse. **Make-to-order inventory** is sent directly to the customer and is not placed in inventory; an example is personalized M&Ms that can be ordered from www.mymms.com and sent directly to the consumer. Each approach has its own strengths and weaknesses and is usually tied to strategic SC&O decisions, such as how you win orders in the marketplace. If you win orders on the basis of flexibility and variety, make-to-order inventory is more likely to be your approach to keeping finished goods in stock.

finished goods inventory
Products that are waiting to be sold to the customer.

make-to-stock inventory
Inventory that is completed and placed into inventory for sale at a later date.

make-to-order inventory
Products sent directly to the customer and not placed in finished goods inventory.

SUPPLIES The fourth class of inventory is **supplies**, materials that are stored to support the functioning of the business. Supplies can be anything from floor wax to pens to party favors. Many firms keep large amounts of supplies in inventory. Think about your university or college; professors keep stores of supplies in their offices, department offices keep supplies for

supplies
Materials stored to support the functioning of the business.

the department, and the campus bookstore keeps inventory for the entire university. The value of supplies is not trivial. Think of how much money must be tied up in supplies within the federal government.

NDERSTAND IMPORTANT INVENTORY CONCEPTS

We will now discuss important inventory management concepts for SC&O managers. They include inventory velocity, consignment inventory, and vendor-managed inventory. These topics provide context for understanding some of the more current approaches to managing inventory.

Inventory Velocity

More and more, firms are stressing the importance of **inventory velocity**, the rate at which firms dispose of their inventory. The inventory manager's main goal is to use inventory in a way that it enters and exits the operating system very rapidly, which may not always mean simply carrying less all the time. One measure of inventory velocity is the inventory turnover model. Inventory turnovers are measured as

inventory velocity
The rate at which firms use up their inventory.

$$\text{inventory turnover} = \frac{\text{cost of goods sold}}{\text{average inventory}} \qquad (9.1)$$

The average length of an inventory cycle can be computed by dividing the inventory turnover into the number of days in the work year. We demonstrate this model in SOLVED PROBLEM 9.1.

·····

Computing Inventory Turnover

Problem: The Buffalo Iron Works has the following accounting data relative to inventory (in dollars) and cost of goods sold. Compute the inventory turnover.

< SOLVED PROBLEM 9.1

**MyLab Operations Management
Video**

Month	Average Inventory (in Thousands of Dollars)	Cost of Goods Sold (in Thousands of Dollars)
January	8,000	7,500
February	8,050	7,200
March	9,200	8,000
April	9,800	9,200
May	9,600	9,100
June	7,800	7,100
July	7,500	7,000
August	7,500	6,800
September	7,800	7,000
October	8,100	7,400
November	8,200	7,450
December	8,040	7,200

Solution: The average inventory for the year is found by averaging the totals in the second column, which is $8,299,167 in inventory. Summing the third column, we get a total of $90,950,000. Using Equation 9.1, we obtain an inventory turnover rate of

$$\text{Inventory turnovers} = \frac{90,950,000}{8,299,167} = 11 \text{ turns,}$$

which means that the inventory is consumed about 11 times per year. If there are 365 days in a work year, the company consumes its entire inventory every 365/11, or approximately every 33 days (see Equation 7.5).

Inventory velocity can be enhanced by reducing the amount of inventory on hand relative to sales and costs of goods sold. Another way to increase inventory velocity is to reduce the amount of time a firm "owns" the inventory, which can be accomplished by using consignment and vendor-managed inventory. We will discuss each of these separately.

Consignment Inventory

consignment inventory
Stock that is owned by the supplier but is in the physical possession of the buyer.

Consignment inventory is stock that is owned by the supplier but is in the physical possession of the buyer. Consignment can work well with unproven new products, existing products in new marketing channels, or risky products where it is unclear that there is a strong sales opportunity. Consignment inventory gives the supplier an available sales channel, and the buyer does not have to invest in the inventory, providing benefits to both parties. Such is the case of Nikon, a company that sells photolithography equipment to Intel for use in semiconductor fabrication (**FIGURE 9.2**). Intel manages and orders the inventory that is held in case it is needed for spare parts to repair equipment. Nikon, however, owns the parts as they are stored in Intel's warehouse. This arrangement can be advantageous for both Nikon and Intel because Intel is relieved of managing the inventory and Nikon improves its relationship with a major customer. On the other hand, in a business-to-consumer environment, consignment suppliers may not get the best treatment from retail buyers, who may view the consignment items as less profitable or risky. For example, a music store may sell Fender guitars based on a contract with Fender and accept a smaller brand such as Reverend guitars on consignment. Because the main part of the business is Fender guitars, the consignment guitars will probably receive less attention from store owners.

FIGURE 9.2 >

Three-Dimensional Consignment and Vendor-Managed Inventory Model

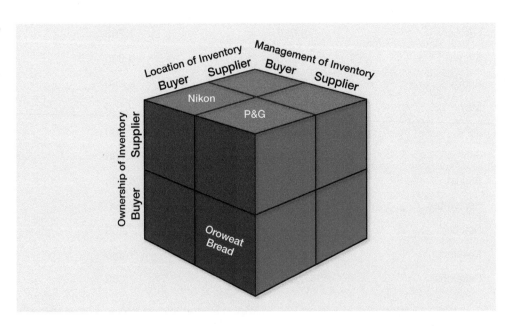

Vendor-Managed Inventory

Vendor-managed inventory (VMI) was made popular by companies such as Walmart and Procter & Gamble (P&G).[4] In VMI, the supplier manages the inventory items, and the buyer houses the inventory. When using VMI, the supplier monitors the buyer's inventory and manages the stock levels. In some retail situations, the retailer tells a supplier, such as Oroweat Bread, that it has allowed a certain placement in terms of shelf feet and location. It is then up to the Oroweat Bread vendor to keep the shelves full of its products and to demonstrate profitability for the retailer. The buyer does relinquish some control but achieves economies that allow it to focus its efforts in other areas such as customer service.

VMI often exists within a consignment arrangement wherein ownership is postponed until after the sale of the product. In the case of P&G and Walmart, P&G manages and owns its product until it is sold at Walmart. Obviously, the products are stocked in a Walmart store, so the "buyer" stores the product. Walmart, however, does not pay for the products until they are sold to the final customer.

> **vendor-managed inventory (VMI)** An arrangement by which the supplier manages the inventory items and the buyer houses the inventory.

....

Managing Across Majors 9.3 Finance majors, notice that postponing ownership by using VMI can result in reduced need to finance inventories for a retailer, thereby lowering costs. Suppliers may be willing to do so if the buyer has enough purchasing power.

....

Inventory and Bullwhips

In Chapter 8, we discussed the results of the bullwhip effect on demand management, shown in **FIGURE 9.3**. Recall that the bullwhip effect results in exaggerated variation in demand as you move up the supply chain. As you move upstream, the amplitude changes also affect inventory levels. As was discussed with demand management, communication, information sharing, and collaboration are necessary for costs to be contained along the supply chain. A result of inventory reduction management can be that suppliers are sometimes required to carry higher levels of inventory so that they can meet the short lead time demands of their customers. A solution is better sharing of production data coupled with enhanced communication.

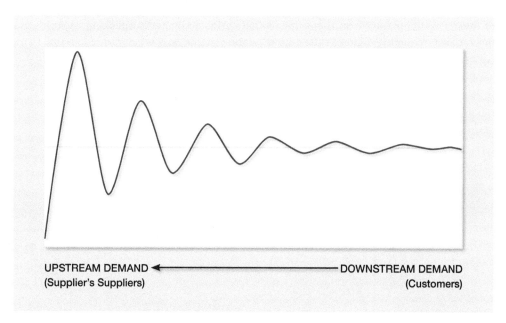

< **FIGURE 9.3**

The Bullwhip Effect

UPSTREAM DEMAND ◄————————————► DOWNSTREAM DEMAND
(Supplier's Suppliers)   (Customers)

[4] M. Waller, E. Johnson, and T. Davis, "Vendor-Managed Inventory in the Retail Supply Chain," *Journal of Business Logistics*, 20: 183–203.

NDERSTAND, PERFORM, AND APPLY DEMAND ANALYSIS

Now that we have discussed inventory from a managerial perspective, let's define a few terms. First, we will discuss dependent demand, independent demand, and ABC analysis, and then we will explain the two types of review systems, continuous and periodic.

Dependent versus Independent Demand

dependent demand
Calculated from the demand for a parent item.

In inventory, there are two types of demand: dependent and independent. **Dependent demand** is calculated from the demand for a parent item. For example, 100 bicycles require 200 tires. Thus, the demand for tires is calculated from the number of bicycles and is dependent demand. The number of tires depends on the number of bicycles, the *parent* items. Managers calculate this type of demand with enterprise resource planning (ERP) systems, which we will discuss in Chapter 10. In this chapter, we focus on inventory systems for independent demand. **Independent demand** is the inventory requirement for final products, such as the finished bicycles mentioned above. Spare parts are also independent demand items. Independent demand is typically *forecasted*, not calculated from a parent item.

independent demand
Inventory requirement for final products and spare parts.

Independent demand systems are used to answer two questions, sometimes referred to as the **operating doctrine of inventory management**:

operating doctrine of inventory management
A doctrine that asks two questions of SC&O managers: How much do we order (Q), and when do we place the order (R)?

1. How much do we order (Q)?
2. When do we place the order (R)?

These queries can be expressed with the single phrase "quantity and timing."

ABC Analysis

ABC analysis
A method for categorizing inventory based on a criterion such as usage or value.

One tool often associated with dependent demand is **ABC analysis**, a method for categorizing inventory based on a criterion such as usage or value. FIGURE 9.4 shows that the A items are the most consumed; the B items are the second most consumed; and the C items, although making up a majority of the stock, account for the least consumption. This classification is based on Pareto's law, which suggests that 20 percent of customers account for 80 percent of revenue. The application of Pareto's law here is that a small percentage of items in stock account for a large proportion of the company's inventory value. The application of this concept is useful because managers often classify stock similarly. One reason is for purposes of **cycle counting**, the practice of performing regularly scheduled counts of inventory items based on their ABC classifications. Generally speaking, A items are inventoried frequently, B items intermittently, and C items only when needed. In one firm, A items are counted weekly, B items are counted quarterly, and C items only annually for tax purposes.

cycle counting
A repetitive procedure for counting inventory on a regular basis—often quarterly or annually. Often coupled with ABC analysis.

FIGURE 9.4 >

ABC Inventory Classification

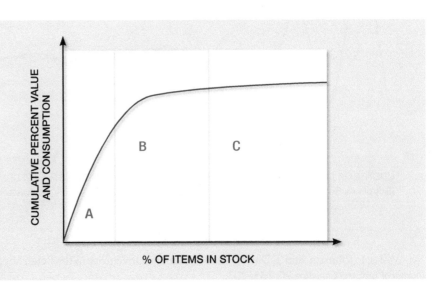

Performing a cycle count.

The process for performing ABC analysis is as follows:

1. Determine a criterion for classifying stock (we will use the example of dollar value of stock).
2. Find the value of items in stock multiplied by their annual volume of usage.
3. Calculate the percentage of total usage per dollar by item.
4. Rank the items based on your calculations in steps 2 and 3.
5. Classify the items as A, B, or C.

Note that sometimes you may want to carry more safety stock for A items. We demonstrate how to perform ABC analysis in **SOLVED PROBLEM 9.2**.

....

Performing ABC Inventory Analysis

Problem: For the following items, perform an ABC analysis based on revenues generated by each item:

< SOLVED PROBLEM 9.2

MyLab Operations Management
Video

Camille's Inventory	In Stock
Apples	150
Toothbrushes	100
Paper towels	200
Flowers	50
Squash	30
Magazines	200
Mushrooms	100
Balloons	400

Camille's Inventory	
Item	**Item Price**
Mushrooms	$15.00
Toothbrushes	$4.00
Balloons	$1.00
Magazines	$1.00
Paper towels	$1.50
Flowers	$0.50
Apples	$0.10
Squash	$0.25

Solution: First, calculate total revenue by finding the revenue for each item.

Camille's Inventory			
Item	**Item Price**	**Amount**	**Item Revenue**
Mushrooms	$15.00	100	$1,500.00
Toothbrushes	$4.00	100	$400.00
Balloons	$1.00	400	$400.00
Paper towels	$1.50	200	$300.00
Magazines	$1.00	200	$200.00
Flowers	$0.50	50	$25.00
Apples	$0.10	150	$15.00
Squash	$0.25	30	$7.50

Next, calculate the percentage for each item. In this case, divide the total revenue generated by the items by the total revenue created from all inventory items.

Camille's Inventory				
Item	**Item Price**	**Amount**	**Item Revenue**	**Revenue (%)**
Mushrooms	$15.00	100	$1,500.00	53
Toothbrushes	$4.00	100	$400.00	14
Balloons	$1.00	400	$400.00	14
Paper towels	$1.50	200	$300.00	11
Magazines	$1.00	200	$200.00	7
Flowers	$0.50	50	$25.00	1
Apples	$0.10	150	$15.00	1
Squash	$0.25	30	$7.50	0
Total revenue:			$2,847.50	

At this point, you can use a bit of discretion in deciding where to categorize items. In this example, we will use the following breakdown:

Category	Percentage of Revenue
A	50–100
B	10–50
C	0–10

Every case may be unique, so the percentages you use should be specific to your case. Most ABC analyses are done using something similar to the following breakdown:

Category	Percentage of Revenue
A	70–100
B	20–70
C	0–20

	Camille's Inventory				
	Item	**Item Price**	**Amount**	**Item Revenue**	**Revenue (%)**
A	Mushrooms	$15.00	100	$1,500.00	53
	Toothbrushes	$4.00	100	$400.00	14
B	Balloons	$1.00	400	$400.00	14
	Paper towels	$1.50	200	$300.00	11
	Magazines	$1.00	200	$200.00	7
	Flowers	$0.50	50	$25.00	1
C	Apples	$0.10	150	$15.00	1
	Squash	$0.25	30	$7.50	0
	Total revenue:			$2,847.50	

As you can see, mushrooms fall into classification A; toothbrushes, balloons, and paper towels fall into classification B; and magazines, flowers, apples, and squash fall into classification C.

Supporting the Pareto principle, we can see that, although you may have a small amount of a certain item, it may create the largest amount of revenue. Camille may think that because she has the largest number of balloons, she should spend all her time tracking and selling balloons, but in reality, the mushrooms earn the largest amount of revenue.

Review Systems

Inventory can be managed using *single-period*, *periodic review*, or *continuous review* inventory systems. Each system has its own strengths and weaknesses. Recall that single-period (newsvendor) models were introduced in Chapter 4. We will introduce periodic and continuous review models in the following sections.

Periodic inventory systems are used to calculate order quantities (Q) when orders are placed at fixed intervals, such as weekly or monthly, allowing purchasers to combine several orders into one and thus save time and sometimes shipping expense. Using periodic review systems is similar to going shopping on a weekly basis.

The continuous inventory system, on the other hand, is like going to the store to buy a new 50-pound bag of sugar when the old bag runs out. **Continuous review systems** (also known as perpetual systems) involve monitoring inventory levels for items held in stock until the items reach a predetermined level known as a *reorder point (R)*. Once the reorder point is reached, an order is placed for a predetermined amount known as an *order quantity (Q)*. Together, the reorder point and the order quantity answer the two questions in the operating doctrine of inventory. These calculations can be useful because they allow for purchasing an economically optimal quantity of an item at any point.

FIGURE 9.5 shows a graph of an inventory cycle in a continuous inventory system. It is sometimes referred to as a *sawtooth chart* because it resembles the tines on a saw. Note that continuous inventory systems are also referred to as **Q/R systems** because they give us the answers to the quantity (Q) and timing (R) operating doctrine questions. The theoretical inventory cycle in Figure 9.5 is for a continuous inventory system where there is no variation in daily demand (constant demand). In other words, this company sells 10 units of product every day of the year with no variation. Although one could argue that this situation is generally not very realistic, this visual model is instructive.

At time t_0, an order for Q = 200 of the mythical item is received. Immediately, the firm starts using 10 units every day or 1 unit every (24 hours × 60 minutes)/10 units, or 144 minutes. When the inventory is depleted down to 40 units at time t_1, the inventory manager places an order for another 200 units. Notice that it takes four days from time t_1 to t_2. These four days are called the *lead time (L)*, the time from placing an order until you receive the order. The time

FIGURE 9.5 >

The Inventory Cycle Sawtooth Chart with Constant Demand

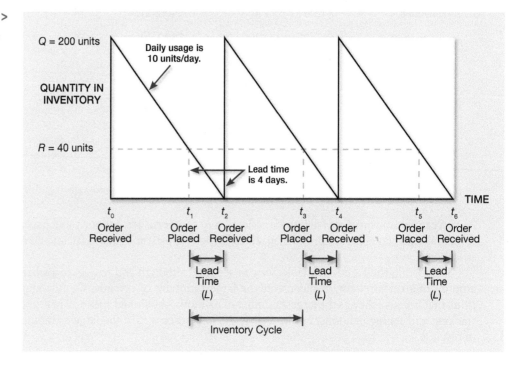

Inventory management involves having the right quantities available at the right time.

between orders (t_1 to t_3) is called an *inventory cycle*. We can now introduce models for computing order quantities (Q) and reorder points (R). Note that orders are placed at 40 units because that is the amount to be used during lead time.

The choice of either continuous or periodic systems is one of balancing purchasing resources against the savings incurred by ordering optimal quantities. As shown in SC&O CURRENT EVENTS 9.2, it may also be a function of other considerations, such as product variety.

Handling Product Variety at Apple

< SC&O CURRENT
EVENTS 9.2

When Apple decided to expand its offerings to include a new white-colored phone, just this small addition to the product line played havoc with Apple's inventory keeping.

Any Apple product launch means another near-immediate strain on inventory. The suddenly missing-in-action white iPhone model may have been the reason that Apple ceased taking preorders for its iPhone only a few hours after first offering it via its website and why it stopped offering the option to pre-order and pick it up on the official launch day. What initially appeared to be a mere website overload problem had the makings of an outright supply shortage. As apple.com stated, "Those pre-ordering an iPhone today won't be able to get their hands on it until a month after the launch date."

What does this inventory shortage have to do with the introduction of the white iPhone? Some customers who really wanted that white model would wait for it, whereas others who did not have as strong a preference would go with the black model rather than wait. It meant that Apple experienced significantly higher than expected sales of the black iPhone for as long as the white iPhone was missing in action. In other words, the lack of the white model was placing an unexpected strain on availability of the black model as well. If Apple had decided from the start that there was going to be only a black iPhone, it would have manufactured twice as many of the black model instead of splitting its manufacturing orders between black models and white models.

XPLAIN AND APPLY INVENTORY MODELS

Now let's implement some of these inventory concepts through modeling. Among the models introduced are the basic economic order quantity (which can be used for quality discounts and computing reorder points), the periodic review inventory model, and the finite replenishment rate model. Each of these introductions is accompanied by an example and solved problems at the end of the chapter.

The Basic Economic Order Quantity Model

Managers use the *basic economic order quantity (EOQ) model* to compute an optimal order quantity (Q). To introduce this model, we first discuss **relevant costs** of inventory, the costs that adjust if you change the amount ordered. For example, ordering 12 cases of paper towels at a time instead of 6 cases means that you will place half as many orders for paper towels during a year. On the other hand, your costs of carrying inventory will increase because you are carrying twice as much in stock. Other operating costs, such as your rent, your electricity, or your labor costs, do not change. Therefore, the relevant costs to be considered in annualized inventory costs are

relevant costs
Inventory-related costs that adjust if you change the amount ordered.

$$TC = S\frac{D}{Q} + iC\frac{Q}{2} \tag{9.2}$$

where

TC = total annualized costs of inventory, which includes annualized ordering and inventory holding costs
S = ordering or setup cost, which includes the cost of administering order placement or configuring a production line
D = annual demand for the product or component in question
Q = order quantity for the item in question each time an order is placed
i = carrying charge as a proportion (such as the interest rate paid to borrow money to finance inventory)
C = item cost to purchase one unit

Note that we do not consider cost of the items multiplied by demand at this point because we are not considering quantity discounts. Demand is assumed to follow a normal distribution. We demonstrate the use of this model in **SOLVED PROBLEM 9.3** and then explain the different components of the model.

 SOLVED PROBLEM 9.3 >   **Total Annualized Inventory Costs**

MyLab Operations Management
Video

Problem: Compute the total annualized inventory costs when the order costs (S) are $20 per order placed, the annual demand (D) is 10,000, the carrying charge (i) is 15 percent, the order quantity (Q) is 231, and the cost of the item is $50.

Solution: Using Equation 9.2, we find the following total annualized inventory cost:

$$TC = 20\frac{10,000}{231} + 0.15(50)\frac{231}{2} = \$1,732.05$$

Breaking the total cost model into its components, $S(D/Q)$ is the cost of placing one order (S) multiplied by the total number of orders per year (D/Q), and $iC(Q/2)$ is the cost of carrying one item for one year in inventory (iC) multiplied by average inventory ($Q/2$). Using, these variables, the formula for finding the optimal order quantity (Q^*) is:[5]

$$Q^* = \sqrt{\frac{2SD}{iC}} \tag{9.3}$$

We will demonstrate below how we derived this Q^* model (note that * denotes optimality).

[5]The method we use for deriving the EOQ is very intuitive. The same model can be found using calculus by taking the first derivative of the model of total annualized inventory costs (TC).

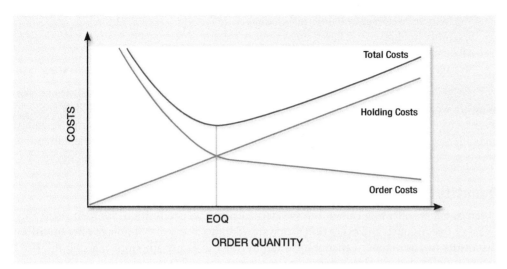

In FIGURE 9.6, the holding costs [$iC(Q/2)$] increase as the order quantity increases. In other words, if you order larger amounts at a time, you will end up holding more inventory. On the other hand, ordering costs [$S(D/Q)$] decrease as order quantities get bigger because as order quantities get bigger, fewer orders are placed annually. As you can see in Figure 9.6, the total cost curve when combining these costs (Equation 9.2) is minimized when holding and ordering costs are equal. Thus,

$$iC\frac{Q}{2} = s\frac{D}{Q}.$$ (9.4)

Solving for Q,

$$Q^2 = \frac{2SD}{iC}.$$ (9.5)

Therefore, the optimal order quantity is

$$Q^* = \sqrt{\frac{2SD}{iC}}.$$ (9.6)

By definition, the **economic order quantity (EOQ)** is the order quantity (Q) at which total annualized inventory-related costs (Equation 9.2) are minimized. We demonstrate the EOQ in SOLVED PROBLEM 9.4.

economic order quantity (EOQ)
The order quantity (Q) at which total annualized inventory-related costs are minimized.

....

The Economic Order Quantity in Action

Problem: Compute the EOQ where the order costs (S) are $20 per order placed, the annual demand (D) is 10,000, the carrying charge (i) is 15 percent, and the cost of the item is $50.

Solution: Using Equation 9.3:

$$Q^* = \sqrt{\frac{2(20)(10,000)}{0.15(50)}} = 230.9 \approx 231$$

Therefore, the optimal order quantity is 231.

....

< **SOLVED PROBLEM 9.4** $f(x)$

MyLab Operations Management
Video

EOQ ASSUMPTIONS Having now introduced the EOQ model, let's review some assumptions behind the model.

- Demand is known and constant.
- There is no variation in lead times. They are fixed and constant.
- Ordering costs are identifiable, and they do not change.

- The item price is fixed and does not change.
- Inventory holding cost is based on average inventory.
- All demand for products will be satisfied (there will be no back orders).
- Managers must order only full order quantities and cannot accept partial deliveries.

Reviewing these assumptions, you may conclude that none of them are very realistic and ask, Why are we studying these EOQ models if they do not reflect reality? These models not only teach us a great deal about inventory; they are also very flexible. We will discuss this flexibility and different variations in the EOQ model. In particular, we will look at cases when discounts are given for large purchases and when managers consider replenishing their inventory needs.

Quantity Discounts

quantity discounts
Lowered prices given when higher amounts of an item are purchased.

Often, suppliers offer inducements to sweeten the purchase proposition. Sometimes they are offers of free product, and other times they are quantity discounts. Suppliers offer **quantity discounts** to customers to encourage them to order in larger amounts, relaxing the EOQ assumption that price is fixed. Managers can easily use the EOQ model to evaluate whether or not they should accept quantity discounts. Consider, for example, a specialized apron. In this case, if the purchaser orders 6 or more aprons, the price is $12 each. If more than 48 aprons are ordered, the price per apron drops to $9.

To use the EOQ model when evaluating whether or not you should accept a quantity discount, apply the following two-step approach:

1. Calculate the EOQ using Equation 9.6 at lowest price. If the lowest-cost EOQ results in an order quantity that feasibly gives you the lowest price, stop! You have found the best deal. If the order quantity is not feasible, compute the EOQ at the next lowest prices until you find a feasible quantity and cost.
2. Compute the total annualized ordering costs for the EOQ and the price break quantities using the formula

$$TC = DC \; + \; S\frac{D}{Q} \; + \; iC\frac{Q}{2} \tag{9.7}$$

Equation 9.7 is Equation 9.2 with the addition of annual demand (D) multiplied by the cost of a single item (C) for each price break quantity above the EOQ. Compare the computed total costs and choose the lowest. Order this amount.

Companies like Home Depot offer quantity discounts online. These discounts could include certain percentages off for large purchases or simply free shipping if consumers spend a certain amount.

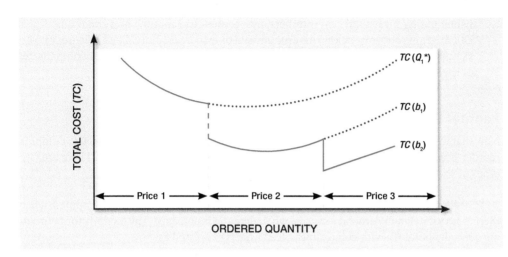

As you can see in FIGURE 9.7, quantity discounts are useful because the savings in purchasing items may overcome diseconomies caused by incurring higher carrying costs. IKEA uses quantity discounts in purchasing and carries high levels of inventory in regional warehouses as a result of quantity discounts. IKEA management believes that this gives the company a cost advantage over competitors. We demonstrate how to use this powerful approach in SOLVED PROBLEM 9.5.

Using EOQ with Quantity Discounts

< SOLVED PROBLEM 9.5 🄵

MyLab Operations Management Video

Problem: Compute the EOQ where the order costs (S) are $20 per order placed, the annual demand (D) is 10,000, the carrying charge (i) is 15 percent, and the cost of the item is $50. In addition, suppose that the following quantity discounts are offered:

Order Quantities	Discount
100–199	$3
200–299	$5
300–499	$8
500 or more	$12

Solution: Using Equation 9.3, we compute the following economic order quantity (EOQ) at the lowest cost ($50 – $12 = $38 is the lowest cost):

$$Q = \sqrt{\frac{2(20)(10,000)}{0.15(38)}} = 264.9 \approx 265,$$

which fits into the 200 or more range. The result is a price of $45, which does not qualify for the lowest price and is therefore not feasible. At $45, the EOQ is 243 units. So we will ignore the 100 or more price in favor of saving $5 or more. The total cost for 243 is computed using Equation 9.7:

$$TC(265) = 10,000(\$45) + (20)\frac{10,000}{265} + 0.15(\$45)\frac{265}{2} = \$451,649.10$$

Now, we need to compute total costs for the price breaks at quantities of 300 and 500:

$$TC(300) = 10,000(\$42) + (20)\frac{10,000}{300} + 0.15(\$42)\frac{300}{2} = \$421,611.67$$

$$TC(500) = 10,000(\$38) + (20)\frac{10,000}{500} + 0.15(\$38)\frac{500}{2} = \$381,825.00$$

By comparing these total cost numbers, it becomes clear that the best order quantity is 500. Anything above or below this amount will only increase annualized inventory costs. As this example shows, there are times when the price savings more than compensates for the increased carrying costs.

Reorder Points

reorder point
A signal to replenish an item in inventory.

deterministic reorder points
Reorder points computed when there is no variation in demand.

Now that we have learned how to compute order quantities, we need to learn how to compute reorder points. A **reorder point** is a signal to replenish an item in inventory. There are two types of reorder points, deterministic and stochastic (or *probabilistic*).

DETERMINISTIC REORDER POINTS **Deterministic reorder points** are computed when there is no variation in demand—that is, when demand is constant. The formula for computing a reorder point (R) with deterministic lead time is expressed as

$$R = d \times L \tag{9.8}$$

where

R = reorder point
D = periodic demand (e.g., daily, weekly, or monthly)
L = lead time (expressed in the same time units as d)

We illustrate how to compute deterministic reorder points in SOLVED PROBLEM 9.6.

 SOLVED PROBLEM 9.6 >

MyLab Operations Management Video

Computing a Reorder Point with Deterministic Lead Time

Problem: Compute the reorder point (R), where daily demand (d) is 20 and lead time (L) is six days.

Solution: The solution is found rather simply by using Equation 9.8:

$$R = 20 \times 6 = 120$$

Therefore, the reorder point is 120. Thus, when our inventory level gets down to 120 units, we should place an order for the quantity (Q*). Because the lead time never changes and demand never changes (i.e., it is deterministic), we will receive the needed new stock just as we are running out of the units in inventory.

stochastic reorder points
Reorder points used in the more realistic case where demand, while awaiting an order, is variable.

safety stock
Extra stock held in anticipation of variable demand.

stockout
The situation that occurs when a customer places an order and there is no stock available to fulfill the order.

STOCHASTIC REORDER POINTS **Stochastic reorder points** are used in the more realistic case where demand is variable while we are awaiting our order. FIGURE 9.8 shows a new saw-tooth diagram. Compare this diagram with Figure 9.5; notice how the teeth in the saw "blades" are no longer straight. That is because demand is now variable, meaning that the orders from customers for the item are received at differing rates of time and in differing quantities. In Figure 9.8, we handle this variation by adding **safety stock**, extra stock held in anticipation of variable demand. In essence, we add some extra (safety) stock to lower the probability of failing to satisfy customer demand. We express this probability as a service level, the probability that a customer will not experience a **stockout**, which occurs when a customer places an order and there is no stock available to fill the order.

Safety stock can be expensive if you carry too much extra stock. Therefore, safety stock calculations must always weigh the cost of carrying the extra stock versus the costs of not satisfying customers. If a customer attempts to buy something that is not in stock, you may lose the profit from that single transaction as well as future sales.

The concept of the service level is important because it links our inventory decisions with the concept of customer service. The reason for carrying safety stock is that customers and their satisfaction are important to us as a firm. For this reason, we may be willing to invest some money in carrying more inventory than would seem optimal without this concern for the customer.

The stochastic reorder point with safety stock is computed using the following formula:

$$R_s = R + SS \tag{9.9}$$

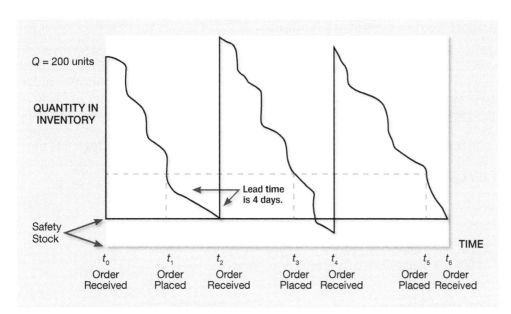

where

R_s = stochastic reorder point

R = deterministic reorder point (Equation 9.8)

SS = safety stock $z\sigma_{dL}$, where z is the number of standard deviations from average demand. Use Table A-2 in the appendix and σ_{dL} = standard deviation of demand during lead time, a measure of dispersion.

In this context, stockouts occur only during lead time. That is, managers experience stockouts only during the time between when they place an order and when they receive that order from a supplier. Hence, inventory managers place special emphasis on this perilous time between order and receipt, when a stockout may occur. A 95 percent service level means that stockouts may occur only five times during the phase of 100 inventory cycles. See **SOLVED PROBLEM 9.7**.

....

Reorder Point with Stochastic Demand during Lead Time

Problem: Compute the reorder point (R) where the daily demand (d) is 20, the service level is 98 percent, lead time (L) is 6 days, and the standard deviation of demand during lead time (σ_{dL}) is 3. Compute the annualized cost of this safety stock.

Solution: The solution is found by using Equations 9.8 and 9.9:

$$R_s = (20 \times 6) + (2.06 \times 3) = 126.18 = 127$$

Therefore, the reorder point is 127. We rounded up to ensure that we achieve at least a 98 percent service level. The $z = 2.06$ value is found by using Table A-2 and finding the z value associated with a 98 percent probability in a one-tailed distribution. When our inventory level gets down to 127 units, we place an order for the quantity (Q^*). Notice that, compared to Solved Problem 9.6, we are carrying seven additional units of inventory as safety stock. The cost of this extra safety stock can easily be computed as

$$\text{annualized cost of safety stock} = BiC \tag{9.10}$$

where

B = the amount of safety (or buffer) stock

i = the opportunity cost of capital (as in the EOQ computations)

C = the per unit cost of the item

We already calculated $B = 7$ above. If the opportunity cost of capital is 10 percent and the cost of the item is \$100, the annualized cost of carrying inventory is $7 \times .10 \times \$100 = \$70$ per year. You now have to compare the \$70 cost of carrying inventory with the cost of not carrying inventory. If the cost of not carrying inventory is, in your estimation, more than \$70, the safety stock may be a good investment.

....

< **SOLVED PROBLEM 9.7**

MyLab Operations Management
Video

Periodic Review Inventory Models

Now that we have discussed the Q/R inventory model, let's turn to periodic review inventory models. Some firms may be limited by technology, staffing, or circumstances, forcing them to place orders on a regularly periodic basis, such as once a week or once a month. We see this kind of periodic activity in our own lives. Most families perform their grocery shopping at regular time intervals. People order routine health checks such as mammograms or prostate tests on a periodic basis and buy their holiday decorations only once a year.

To compute an order quantity, we account for the time between orders (TBO), lead time (L), and the amount of inventory on hand at the time an order is placed. We begin by computing the **uncertainty period**, the time when a stockout may occur, as

$$UP = TBO + L \tag{9.11}$$

uncertainty period
Used with periodic inventory models, the time between orders (*TBO*) + order lead time.

where

UP = the uncertainty period
TBO = the time between orders (such as 7 days or 28 days)
L = lead time

Understanding the uncertainty period, we can now compute the order quantity using

$$Q = \bar{d}(UP) + z\sigma_{ddup}\sqrt{UP} - I \tag{9.12}$$

where

Q = the order quantity
$\bar{d}$ = average daily demand (the bar over the d denotes "average")
UP = the uncertainty period = $TBO + L$, or the amount of time we're unsure about running out of stock
z = the standard deviation of daily demand given a desired service level
σ_{ddup} = the standard deviation of the uncertainty period demand
I = the on-hand inventory at the time the order is placed

We demonstrate the use of this model in **SOLVED PROBLEM 9.8**.

---

f(x) **SOLVED PROBLEM 9.8**

MyLab Operations Management
Video

Using the Periodic Review Inventory Model

Problem: Compute the reorder point (R) where the daily demand is 20, the service level is 98 percent, orders are placed every 28 days, the lead time (L) is 6 days, the standard deviation of daily demand during the uncertainty period (σ_{ddup}) is 15, and 100 units are on hand.

Solution: Using Equation 9.11, we find that the uncertainty period is 28 days + 6 days = 34 days. As in Solved Problem 9.7, the z value comes from Table A-2 in the appendix where the probability in the right tail of the distribution is .48 (z = 2.06). With this number, we can compute our order quantity using Equation 9.12:

$$Q = 20(34) + 2.06(15)\sqrt{34} - 100 = 760$$

As a result, an order should be placed for 760 units for the coming 28 days. The order will be received in six days.

A Finite Replenishment Rate Inventory Model

finite replenishment rate inventory model
An inventory model used when product cannot be received at the full order quantity.

The **finite replenishment rate inventory model** is a complicated name for a fairly simple idea. With every component, firms are faced with a make-versus-buy decision. That is, managers must choose whether they want to make any component or buy it. Part of the decision depends on how much capacity a firm has available. If it has the available capacity and decides to produce a component, inventory managers may need to use this model.

The finite replenishment rate inventory model is used when product cannot be received at the full order quantity. For example, if you need 500 units of a component on Monday and only 250 are available due to limited capacity, what should you do? Could you receive 250 on Monday and another 250 on Wednesday and still satisfy your needs? The finite replenishment rate model helps answer this question.

The EOQ computation for a fixed production rate is similar to the basic EOQ, with two more pieces of needed information: (1) the periodic production rate (p, often a daily rate) and (2) the periodic demand (d, also often a daily rate of demand). These variables are used to create a finite correction factor $[1 - d/p]$ that is included in the EOQ model as follows:

$$Q^{frr} = \sqrt{\frac{2SD}{iC[1 - (d/p)]}} \qquad (9.13)$$

We demonstrate the finite replenishment rate problem in **SOLVED PROBLEM 9.9**.

....

Using the Finite Replenishment Rate Model

Problem: Compute the EOQ with finite replenishment where the order costs (S) are $20 per order placed, annual demand (D) is 10,000, the carrying charge (i) is 15 percent, and the cost of the item is $50. The firm operates 250 days per year, and the daily production rate is 50.

Solution: Using Equation 9.13, we compute the following EOQ:

$$Q^{frr} = \sqrt{\frac{2(20)(10,000)}{0.15(50)\left[1 - \frac{40}{50}\right]}} = 516.40$$

Note that the daily demand rate is 10,000/250 days $= 40$ units/day. Because the most cost effective lot size is 516 and the daily production rate is 50, the required length of a production run is 516/50, or 10.32 days.

....

< SOLVED PROBLEM 9.9

MyLab Operations Management Video

As you have seen, the EOQ model can be adapted to many different situations, and we have relaxed several of the EOQ assumptions. There are many other EOQ models and many variations for particular situations. The models presented in this chapter are representative of a vast array of inventory models that can be used to help you make better inventory decisions. Remember that inventory in and of itself is not the problem. Poorly informed decision making and out-of-control inventory systems are the problems. That is where skilled management enters the picture.

In this chapter, we have discussed inventory management. We now reflect on the Target example introduced at the start of the chapter. In the chapter-opening vignette, we introduced the SC&O strategic challenges at Target. After reading this chapter, you should have a better understanding of how companies such as Target can approach their SC&O planning. Target[6] imports over 500,000 containers of merchandise a year from China, making them the second largest U.S. importer of containerized freight. After receiving merchandise

[6] Wahba, P. "This is How Target Is Solving Its Out-Of-Stock Problems," *Fortune*, March 2, 2016.

through customs, the freight is shipped to regional warehouses and then distributed to stores. In recent years, Target has emphasized finding strategic ways to improve its process flow between warehouses and regional distribution centers. It has also worked closely with strategically important vendors to see that products reach the warehouse on the exact day they are needed—not too early or too late.

The inventory problem at Target stores is not trivial. Through customer surveys, Target found that 75 percent of customers experienced stockouts during a recent year. Besides using inventory models like those in this chapter, Target has reduced its product selection in inventory, flavors, and brands of products. According to Target CEO Brian Cornell, "We will never be famous for selling bottled water or laundry soap. [However,] we have to always be in stock because we know these items are key."

Using this approach, Target has reduced its assortments by 15 percent and has reduced stockouts by 40 percent.

Summary

In this chapter, we have discussed the importance of inventory and managing inventory properly. You might be surprised by the depth of your new understanding of the importance of inventory. Here are some key points:

1. Managing the differing types of inventory properly can make your company more responsive to customer needs and business requirements.

2. Inventory has several uses, including improving service levels, tempering uncertainty, managing production lead times, creating economies of scale, and buffering supply chain processes.

3. We discussed inventory velocity and inventory turnovers. Vendor-managed inventory is a trend in many industries, and poor inventory management exacerbates the bullwhip effect.

4. We discussed basic tools in inventory management, including understanding independent demand, ABC analysis, and continuous periodic review systems. The choice of tool depends on the realities of your inventory needs.

5. We introduced and explained several inventory management models such as economic order quantity, quantity discounts, and reorder points. We also discussed more advanced models such as periodic review models and finite replenishment rate models.

6. World-class firms manage their inventories well. That does not always mean having no inventory. It means right-sizing your inventory to drive better business performance.

Formulas	Equation Number	Definition
$\text{inventory turnover} = \dfrac{\text{cost of goods sold}}{\text{average inventory}}$	9.1	Inventory turns
$TC = S\dfrac{D}{Q} + iC\dfrac{Q}{2}$	9.2	Total annualized inventory costs
$Q^* = \sqrt{\dfrac{2SD}{iC}}$	9.3	Simple EOQ model

	9.7	Total costs of inventory calculation for quantity discounts
$TC = DC + S\dfrac{D}{Q} + iC\dfrac{Q}{2}$		
$R = d \times L$	9.8	Deterministic reorder point
$R_s = R + SS$	9.9	Stochastic reorder point
$UP = TBO + L$	9.11	Uncertainty period
$Q = \bar{d}(UP) + z\sigma_{ddup}\sqrt{UP} - I$	9.12	Fixed time period inventory model
$Q^{frr} = \sqrt{\dfrac{2SD}{iC\left[1 - \dfrac{d}{p}\right]}}$	9.13	Finite replenishment rate model

Key Terms

ABC analysis 250
buffers 245
consignment inventory 248
continuous review systems 254
cycle counting 250
dependent demand 250
deterministic reorder points 260
economic order quantity (EOQ) 257
finished goods inventory 246
finite replenishment rate inventory
    model 262
fixed time period models 245

hedging 244
independent demand 250
inventory 243
inventory management 243
inventory velocity 247
lead time 244
make-to-order inventory 246
make-to-stock inventory 246
operating doctrine 250
periodic inventory systems 254
production smoothing 244
Q/R systems 254

quantity discounts 258
raw materials 246
relevant costs 256
reorder point 260
safety stock 260
service level 244
stochastic reorder points 260
stockout 260
supplies 246
uncertainty period 262
vendor-managed inventory (VMI) 249
work-in-process (WIP) inventory 246

Integrative Learning Exercise

Inventory is expensive. Consequently, companies look for ways to reduce inventory yet maintain high levels of customer service. With a team, evaluate strategies and approaches by which companies could possibly reduce inventory levels while maintaining competitive customer service levels. The following questions might help focus your discussion.

1. How could improvements in forecasting demand affect inventory decisions?

2. Could reductions in lead time provide an opportunity to reduce inventory without compromising customer service levels?

3. Could the use of technology help control and manage inventory better?

4. How might strategies such as vendor-managed inventory be used to control inventory costs better?

Integrative Experiential Exercise

All companies have inventory. Visit a company near your campus or in your neighborhood and interview an inventory manager or the individual who is responsible for ordering items used by the company. Ask this person the following questions:

1. What tools or techniques do you use to determine the best order quantity?

2. How do you know when to place an order to replenish inventory?

3. Do you employ safety stocks? If so, how do you decide how much safety stock to hold?

4. What are the biggest challenges your company faces in managing its inventory?

Discussion Questions

1. Briefly describe the balancing act that companies face as they decide how much inventory to carry.

2. What is meant by a service level from an inventory perspective?

3. What are some examples of global supply chain uncertainty? How might a firm protect itself against this uncertainty?

4. What is hedging? How can hedging be used to reduce supply chain uncertainty?

5. What is the purpose of buffer inventory? How can a lack of buffer inventory hurt a company's performance?

6. In what forms might you find work-in-process inventory?

7. If a company's order-winning criteria involve increased flexibility and greater product variety, is the company more likely to employ a make-to-stock or a make-to-order finished goods inventory approach? Why?

8. What actions can a company take to improve its inventory velocity?

9. What is meant by consignment inventory? Under what circumstances does consignment inventory work well?

10. Briefly contrast dependent and independent demand.

11. What are the two primary questions related to independent demand inventory systems?

12. How is the reorder decision made in a continuous review inventory system?

13. In a continuous review inventory system, what is meant by lead time? How is it different from an inventory cycle?

14. What is the difference between a service level and a stockout?

15. What is ABC analysis? Briefly describe how it is used in inventory management.

Solved Problems

Inventory Management

INVENTORY VELOCITY
SOLVED PROBLEM 9.1

1. A company reported the following inventory and cost of goods sold data for last year. Calculate the inventory turnover ratio for this company.

Month	Average Inventory ($)	Cost of Goods Sold ($)
January	10,022,550	6,213,000
February	9,761,500	8,457,200
March	9,985,000	15,976,600
April	10,491,650	15,102,400
May	9,739,950	6,663,200
June	9,993,750	10,513,700
July	9,747,650	10,105,500
August	10,454,400	16,135,700
September	9,844,150	8,822,800
October	10,393,500	15,099,100
November	9,581,250	9,246,600
December	9,916,550	13,816,900

Solution:
We calculate the average annual inventory by the average monthly inventory values. This annual average is $9,994,325. The cost of goods sold for the year is the sum of the monthly cost of goods sold values, or $136,152,700. The inventory turnover is cost of goods sold/average inventory = $136,152,700/9,994,325 = 13.623 turns per year. Using 365 days in a year, the company consumes its inventory every 365/13.623, or 26.8, days.

Demand Analysis

TOTAL ANNUALIZED INVENTORY COSTS
SOLVED PROBLEM 9.2

2. Calculate the total annualized inventory costs when the cost per order (S) is $50, the annual demand for the item is 6,000, the carrying charge is 20 percent of the item's $12 per unit cost, and the order quantity is 500.

Solution:
Using Equation 9.2, we find that the total annualized inventory costs are $50 × (6,000/500) + 0.2 × 12 × (500/2) = $1,200.

Inventory Models

THE BASIC ECONOMIC ORDER QUANTITY MODEL
SOLVED PROBLEM 9.3

3. Calculate the EOQ when the cost per order (S) is $75, the annual demand ($D$) is 15,000, and the carrying charge is 25 percent of the item's $25 cost.

Solution:
Using Equation 9.3, the EOQ is calculated as

$$Q^* = \sqrt{\frac{2(75)(15,000)}{(0.25) \times 25)}} = 600$$

The optimal quantity is 600 units.

COMPUTING A REORDER POINT WITH DETERMINISTIC LEAD TIME
SOLVED PROBLEM 9.4

4. Calculate the reorder point, R, for the case where daily demand is 75 units and the item's lead time is five days.

Solution:
Using Equation 9.4, we find that the reorder point, R, is equal to $75 \times 5 = 375$.

REORDER POINT WITH STOCHASTIC DEMAND
SOLVED PROBLEM 9.5

5. Compute the reorder point, R, when daily demand is 50, the lead time is four days, the standard deviation of demand during lead time is 6, and the desired service level is 95 percent.

Solution:
Using Equation 9.8, we calculate the reorder point as $R = (50 \times 4) + (1.65 \times 6) = 209.9$, or 210 (where $z = 1.65$ from Appendix Table A-2).

FIXED TIME PERIOD INVENTORY MODELS
SOLVED PROBLEM 9.6

6. Calculate the order quantity, Q, for the periodic review inventory model when the average daily demand is 40, the desired service level is 90 percent, orders are placed every five days, and the lead time is four days. Assume that the standard deviation of demand during the uncertainty period is 10 and that the on-hand inventory at the next order period is 25.

Solution:
The order quantity is found to be $Q = [40 \times (5 + 4)] + [1.29 \times 10 \times \sqrt{9}] - 25 = 360 + 38.7 - 25 = 373.7$, or 374.

EOQ WITH QUANTITY DISCOUNTS
SOLVED PROBLEM 9.7

7. A company sources a part from a supplier that has offered the following quantity discount:

Order Quantity	Price per Unit
0–999	$20
1,000–2,499	$19
2,500 or more	$18

The company incurs a $300 cost for each order placed. The annual demand for the part is 24,000 units. The company believes that its carrying charge is 20 percent of the item's cost. What order quantity minimizes the company's total inventory-related cost?

Solution:
Begin by calculating the EOQ for the lowest-offered price of $18. If the calculated EOQ falls in the order quantity

range for this price, you have found the optimal order quantity. For the price of $18 (using Equation 9.3),

$$Q^* = \sqrt{\frac{2 \times 300 \times 24{,}000}{0.2 \times 18}} = 2{,}000$$

This quantity will not qualify the company to receive the unit price of $18 and is therefore not a feasible quantity at $18. We now must calculate the EOQ for the next higher price of $19. At a price of $19,

$$Q^* = \sqrt{\frac{2 \times 300 \times 24{,}000}{0.2 \times 19}} = 1{,}947$$

This quantity falls in the range for that unit price. It is feasible, but it may not be optimal. We must now calculate the total cost of the feasible EOQ = 1,947 and compare that total cost to the total cost at the minimum order size required to obtain all lower unit prices (using Equation 9.7):

$$\text{total cost}_{(Q=1{,}947)} = \left(\frac{1{,}947}{2}\right) \times (0.2 \times 19)$$
$$+ \left(\frac{24{,}000}{1{,}947}\right) \times 300 + 24{,}000 \times (19)$$
$$= \$463{,}397.30$$

$$\text{total cost}_{(Q=2{,}500)} = \left(\frac{2{,}500}{2}\right) \times (0.2 \times 18)$$
$$+ \left(\frac{24{,}000}{2{,}500}\right) \times 300 + 24{,}000 \times (18)$$
$$= \$439{,}380$$

Because the lower total price occurs at an order quantity of 2,500 with a unit price of $18, the company's decision should be to order 2,500.

FINITE REPLENISHMENT RATE INVENTORY MODELS
SOLVED PROBLEM 9.8

8. Calculate the finite replenishment rate quantity for the case where the daily demand is 150, the daily production rate is 200, and carrying charges are 25 percent of the item's $20 cost. Assume that there are 360 days of demand annually and that the cost of ordering is $150 per order.

Solution:
Note that annual demand is 150 per day $\times$ 360 days = 54,000. Using Equation 9.13, we calculate the finite replenishment rate quantity as

$$\sqrt{\frac{2(150)(54{,}000)}{(0.25 \times 20) \times \left[1 - \left(\frac{150}{200}\right)\right]}} = 3{,}600.$$

So the length of the production run is 3,600/200 = 18 days.

ABC ANALYSIS
SOLVED PROBLEM 9.9

9. The following inventory record was taken from a company's inventory database. Use the information to conduct an ABC analysis.

Item	Item Cost ($)	No. in Stock
M-12	20.00	250
Q-34	125.00	400
Z-11	50.00	25
K-64	35.00	60
T-55	40.00	30
P-29	250.00	50
U-13	8.00	15,000
R-97	75.00	15

Item	Item Cost ($)	No. in Stock	Value ($)	Percentage of Total
M-12	20.00	250	20 × 250 = 5,000	2.59
Q-34	125.00	400	125 × 400 = 50,000	25.88
Z-11	50.00	25	50 × 25 = 1,250	0.65
K-64	35.00	60	35 × 60 = 2,100	1.09
T-55	40.00	30	40 × 30 = 1,200	0.62
P-29	250.00	50	250 × 50 = 12,500	6.47
U-13	8.00	15,000	8 × 15,000 = 120,000	62.12
R-97	75.00	15	75.00 × 15 = 1,125	0.58
			Total **$193,175**	

Solution:

First, compute the dollar value of the in-stock inventory for each item by multiplying the item's cost by the number of items in stock.

Use the Total column to identify A, B, and C items. The items with the largest percentages are assigned to category A.

Item	Item Cost ($)	No. in Stock	Value ($)
M-12	20.00	250	20 × 250 = 5,000
Q-34	125.00	400	125 × 400 = 50,000
Z-11	50.00	25	50 × 25 = 1,250
K-64	35.00	60	35 × 60 = 2,100
T-55	40.00	30	40 × 30 = 1,200
P-29	250.00	50	250 × 50 = 12,500
U-13	8.00	15,000	8 × 15,000 = 120,000
R-97	75.00	15	75 × 15 = 1,125
		Total	**$193,175**

Category	Item	Percentage of Total
A	U-13	62.12
B	Q-34	32.35
	P-29	
C	M-12	5.53
	K-64	
	Z-11	
	T-55	
	R-97	

Next, calculate the percentage that each item's dollar value is of the total dollar value.

In this analysis, one of the eight items makes up 62.12 percent of the total dollar value invested in inventory. Item U-13 is an A item. The B items comprise 32.35 percent of the inventory investment. The C items represent over half (five) of the eight items and account for only 5.53 percent of the inventory investment.

Problems

Inventory Management

INVENTORY VELOCITY

1. A company reports that its average inventory last year was $17,500,000 and its cost of goods sold was $148,750,000. What was the company's inventory turnover last year?

2. According to its financial reports, a company shows average inventory last year of $23,500,000 with cost of goods sold equal to $109,100,000. How fast did the company turn its inventory last year?

3. Last year, an online retailer of tennis equipment carried an average inventory of $8,000,000. The retailer reported sales revenue of $30,000,000 last year with a cost of goods sold of $18,000,000. Use this information to calculate the inventory turnover for the retailer last year.

4. Topeka Tool Works reports the monthly values for its inventory and cost of goods sold for the most recent twelve months as follows:

Month	Inventory ($ 000)	Cost of Goods Sold ($ 000)	Month	Inventory ($ 000)	Cost of Goods Sold ($ 000)
January	1,550	1,225	July	1,250	1,100
February	1,850	2,150	August	1,400	1,150
March	1,300	1,550	September	1,700	1,700
April	1,400	975	October	1,800	1,350
May	2,000	1,350	November	1,200	1,400
June	1,650	1,550	December	900	1,000

Calculate the company's inventory turnover.

Demand Analysis

ABC ANALYSIS

5. A company uses ABC analysis to help manage its inventory. Its current stock of inventory reflects the following items, item cost, and quantity.

Item Part No.	Item Cost	Quantity in Stock
142-AZ	$546.00	318
4392-GF	$45.00	1,250
86935-ES	$15.35	3,546
173-DC	$653.00	1,876
999-BA	$199.00	526
7846-NM	$23.00	973
2765-OP	$385.00	790
103-VX	$12.50	4,875
2648-YT	$16.75	5,185

Which items would you classify as A items? As B items? As C items?

6. A company is preparing for a cycle count of its inventory. The company's ERP inventory report showed the following values for the products under review.

Item No.	Item Cost	No. in Stock
CD-143	17.00	587
FR-46	1,500.00	25
GP-123	63.00	635
MPZ-65	300.00	12
NWM-8	657.75	2,050
KL-35	2,525.00	39
PF-18	789.99	353
RD-82	850.00	79
ZW-6	37.99	629
CP-40	5,000.00	7
BX-2	7.50	7,506
LG-94	75.00	1,200
WU-09	22.50	2,364
TY-187	325.00	46
QX-22	195.99	851

Which items would you classify as being A items? As B items? As C items? Quantitatively justify your answer.

Inventory Models

TOTAL COST OF INVENTORY

7. Compute the total annualized inventory costs when the cost per order (S) is $75, the annual demand (D) is 120,000, the annual carrying charge (i) is 25 percent, the order quantity (Q) is 1,200, and the item's cost is $50.

8. What is the total annualized inventory cost for the case where the order quantity (Q) is 1,200, the item's cost is $100, the carrying charge (i) is 10 percent, the cost to place an order is $50, and the annual demand for the item (D) is 9,000 units?

9. A company incurs an ordering cost of $90 each time it places an order, regardless of the order size. The item's cost is $25, and the annual carrying charge for the item is 20 percent. If annual demand for this item is 2,500 and the company's order quantity (Q) is 300, calculate its total annualized cost of inventory.

BASIC EOQ

10. Compute the EOQ when the cost per order (S) is $180, the annual demand (D) is 5,000, the carrying charge (i) is 20 percent, and the cost of the item is $25.

11. What is the economic order quantity for the case where the annual demand (D) is 15,000, the carrying charge (i) is 25 percent, the item's cost is $150, and the cost of placing an order (S) is $200?

12. A company orders a product from an outside supplier. The annual demand for the product is 75,000 units, and each time an order is placed the company incurs an ordering cost of $100. The company's annual carrying charge is 20 percent of the item's cost of $150 per unit. What order quantity minimizes the company's total annualized inventory-related costs?

13. A coffee shop uses approximately 250 pounds of a particular type of coffee every week. The shop is open 52 weeks a year. The annual carrying charge for the coffee is 20 percent. If 1 pound of coffee costs the shop $12.00 and the cost associated with each order is $39, how many pounds of this coffee should be ordered each time an order is placed if the shop wants to minimize its total annualized inventory-related costs?

QUANTITY DISCOUNTS

14. The following quantity discount is offered to a company that purchases 120,000 units of the product annually.

Order Quantity	Price per Unit
0–1,999	$50
2,000–3,999	$49
4,000 or more	$46

Each time an order is placed, the company incurs a cost of $75. If the company's carrying charge is 25 percent of the price of the item, what order quantity should it use to minimize its total inventory-related costs?

15. Suppose that the annual demand for a component is approximately 60,000 units. The company orders the component from a supplier who has offered the following quantity discount schedule.

Order Quantity	Price per Unit
0–999	$30
1,000–1,999	$29
2,000–3,999	$28
4,000 or more	$27

If the company's carrying charge is 15 percent of the item's price and the cost per order is $150, determine the order quantity that would minimize the total related inventory costs for this component.

16. As part of its procurement strategy, a company is evaluating whether it should switch to a new supplier. Part of the evaluation will focus on the price schedules that the two suppliers are offering. Supplier A offers the company the following quantity discount schedule.

Order Quantity	Price per Unit
0–4,999	$25
5,000–9,999	$24
10,000 or more	$22

Supplier B is offering the following quantity discount schedule.

Order Quantity	Price per Unit
0–3,999	$26
4,000–7,999	$25
8,000–12,499	$23
12,500 or more	$21

The annual demand for the product is 240,000 units. The cost of placing an order, independent of the supplier or the order quantity, is $250, and the carrying charge is estimated to be 20 percent of the item's price. Which supplier and what order quantity should the company use if its objective is to minimize its total inventory-related costs?

DETERMINISTIC REORDER POINTS

17. Compute the reorder point (R) when daily demand (d) is 125 and lead time (L) is four days.

18. What is the reorder point (R) for a product whose weekly usage is 500 and whose lead time (L) is three weeks?

19. A company uses a product at the rate of approximately 250 units per day. If the company's lead time is three days, what is the reorder point for this item?

STOCHASTIC REORDER POINT

20. Compute the reorder point when daily demand is 60, the service level is 90 percent, the lead time is four days, and the standard deviation of demand during lead time is 9.

21. Calculate the reorder point and the annualized cost of safety stock when daily demand is 125, the lead time is three days, the standard deviation of demand during lead time is 30, the desired service level is 95 percent, the opportunity cost of capital is 25 percent, and the item's unit cost is $50.

22. A part is demanded at the rate of 400 per week. The part is purchased from a supplier in Asia, and the lead time is five weeks. The standard deviation of demand during the lead time is 50 units. If the company wants to have a service level of 97.5 percent, how much safety stock should the company hold for this part? If the opportunity cost of capital for the company is estimated to be 20 percent and the part costs $75, what is the annualized cost of the safety stock required to achieve the desired service level?

23. Dayton Electronics demands a part at a daily rate of 40 units. The lead time for replenishment is four days for this item. The standard deviation of demand during the lead time is 8. Dayton Electronics prides itself on having a high level of customer service and strives to achieve a service level of 99 percent. How much safety stock should Dayton Electronics hold for this item? What will be the annualized cost of this safety stock if the opportunity cost of capital for Dayton Electronics is 15 percent and the item costs $125?

PERIODIC REVIEW INVENTORY MODELS

24. A company uses the periodic review inventory model to calculate its order quantity for a product that has a daily demand of 40 with a lead time of nine days. The company places orders every 16 days for this product. The standard deviation of daily demand during the uncertainty period is estimated to be 100. If the company wants to achieve a service level of 95 percent for this product, what should its order quantity be if there are 75 units on hand at the next order?

25. A company manages its inventory for a specific item using the periodic review inventory model with seven days between orders. It is currently time to place an order, and the company notes that there are 200 items on hand. The item to be replenished has a lead time of two days with a daily demand of 400 units. The standard deviation of daily demand during the uncertainty period has been calculated to be 60. If the company wants to have at least a 90 percent service level for this item, what should its order quantity be?

26. A hair salon orders shampoo every week from its supplier. The salon uses the periodic review model to determine the quantity to order weekly. The supplier ships the product from its warehouse in the Midwest, and the lead time to receive an order of shampoo is three weeks. Having enough shampoo is critical to the hair salon, so it wants an order quantity that will ensure that a stockout occurs no more than 1 percent of the time. If the salon uses 70 bottles of shampoo on average every week, with a daily standard deviation of demand of 10 bottles over a four-week period, how many bottles of shampoo should be ordered this week if five bottles are on hand?

27. A company uses the periodic review inventory model to calculate its reorder quantity. The company currently places orders weekly. The item is produced and shipped from Asia with a lead time of eight weeks. The company currently has 1,000 items on hand. If the company uses the product at the rate of 250 per week, with a standard deviation of daily usage of 50 over the uncertainty period, what order quantity is needed to achieve a service level of 98 percent?

28. Suppose that the company in Problem 27 has spoken to its supplier, and a new shipping arrangement has been implemented that reduces the lead time from eight weeks to four weeks. How does the reduced lead time affect the company's order quantity? Assume that all other information remains unchanged.

FINITE REPLENISHMENT RATE MODEL

29. A company produces a part that is used in its production process. The company produces the part at a rate of 300 units per day. The daily demand for the product is 180 units. The annual demand for the part is 54,000 units and occurs consistently over the 300 days that the company operates yearly. The company incurs a setup cost of $300 each time the item is produced. The cost of carrying the item in inventory is estimated to be 25 percent of the item's $100 cost. How many units should the company produce each production run to minimize its inventory-associated costs?

30. A company uses the finite replenishment model to determine the optimal quantity to produce. There are 250 days a year over which demand and production occur. The daily demand is 480, and the production rate is 800 per day. The setup cost for production is $600 per setup. Assuming that the carrying cost is 20 percent of the item's $50 cost, what is the length, in days, of a production run if the company produces the replenishment quantity that minimizes its inventory-related costs?

31. Each day, a company uses 120 bags of industrial cleaner. The bags can be shipped to the company each day at a rate of 200. The cost of placing an order is $90, and the carrying charge is 15 percent of the item's $30 cost. The company operates 360 days per year. Calculate the order quantity that minimizes the company's inventory-associated costs. How many days are there between orders for the order quantity you calculated?

Managing Inventory at Nordstrom

Many companies have implemented online shopping, but Nordstrom has combined online shopping with inventory management to serve customers better. While Walmart allows customers to buy online and to pick up items at nearby stores, and Target tells customers if products are available in a particular store, Nordstrom went with a slightly different approach. Managers at Nordstrom combined online shopping capabilities with modern inventory management systems to accommodate customer needs better.

Here's how Nordstrom's system works. Let's say you want a certain pair of Prada shoes. You go online to check if they are at your local store. While the shoes may be available in some stores, they may not be available at your city's Nordstrom. You are in luck, however. Those Prada mules can be overnighted to you from any Nordstrom store. Even if your closest store is out of the shoes you want, you can still wear them the day after you order them.

This approach has had a powerful effect on Nordstrom financially. Shipping items to other stores and customers means that fewer products are discounted at the end of season because online customers can search inventories from anywhere. Also, customers can access bargains at Nordstrom Rack (their discount arm of Nordstrom) online.

One drawback to this system is that if a store clerk enters inventory data incorrectly, the entire system will be in error and customers will be left dissatisfied.

Besides adding to Nordstrom's bottom line, the web-based sales system has increased inventory turnovers from 4.8 to 5.4. Faster inventory turnover is very good for the retail world. According to a Nordstrom manager, "[W]e can sell more without having to buy more inventory. That plays through to margins and ultimately, earnings."

Questions:

1. How was Nordstrom's approach different from that of other retailers?

2. Briefly describe the different costs associated with inventory in retailing.

3. How did Nordstrom's approach enable its stores to increase same-store sales?

4. How was Nordstrom able to increase customer service without increasing inventory?

5. Did inventory turnovers improve for Nordstrom as a result of its new strategy? Why is increasing inventory turnover important for a retailer?

10

Sales and Operations Planning and Enterprise Resource Planning

INTEGRATING

INNOVATING

IMPACTING

IMPROVING

GLOBAL SC&O STRATEGY

Supply Management

Operations Management

Customer Relationship Management

Upstream Processes

Core Processes

Downstream Processes

QUALITY MANAGEMENT, ANALYTICS, AND LOGISTICS

CHAPTER OUTLINE AND LEARNING OBJECTIVES

1 Apply Sales and Operations Planning
- Define aggregation and disaggregation.
- Name the steps in and describe the hierarchy of a disaggregation process.
- Describe the components of and be able to perform sales and operations planning.

2 Define and Explain How Capacity Functions in Operations Management
- Explain how bottlenecks form and how managers resolve their effects.
- Identify and apply the best operating level.

3 Understand and Apply Capacity Planning
- Describe and apply the capacity planning process.
- Identify when and how to apply modeling and rough-cut capacity planning.

4 Understand the Main Functionality of an Enterprise Resource Planning System
- Identify difficulties associated with implementing an ERP system.

5 Understand and Apply Material Requirements Planning
- Identify and define MRP inputs.
- Understand how managers use an MRP record.
- Apply MRP logic.
- Understand and leverage MRP outputs.

Enterprise Resource Planning at Rolls-Royce

Besides being the premier makers of luxury automobiles, Rolls-Royce is a builder of airplane engines. The civil aerospace division, which builds engines, developed an enterprise resource planning (ERP) system to manage its complex web of processes such as sales, customer relationship management, inventory, purchasing, vendor integration, accounting, payroll, and material requirements to run the whole business.

To be successful in implementing its ERP, Rolls-Royce identified a need for a cohesive communications structure. To accomplish this new structure, Rolls-Royce made radical changes to its business. These radical changes included implementing an ERP system.

Implementing an ERP system is a daunting task for a firm the size of Rolls-Royce. As a result, Rolls-Royce partnered with Electronic Data Systems, a consultancy firm. Electronic Data Systems produced a sound architectural framework for the project, thus allowing Rolls-Royce to concentrate its efforts on manufacturing turbine engines for aerospace. In this chapter, we will discuss ERP systems such as the system implemented by Rolls-Royce. We will return to Rolls-Royce at the end of the chapter.

Source: Based on Goodwin, B., *Rolls Royce Cloud HR Project Will Pay for Itself in Two Years,* Computerweekly .com, March 16, 2016.

sales and operations planning (SOP)
System helping managers make decisions related to the creation of schedules that balance demand and supply.

enterprise resource planning (ERP) system
A powerful database system used to manage the whole enterprise, including finances, material requirements planning, human resources, production, customer relationship management, accounting, and most everything else.

material requirements planning (MRP) system
The production engine of an ERP system.

aggregation
Creating a high-level overview of planning, which involves groups or families of products and is usually done at a divisional level.

disaggregation
Breaking product families into individual products and components of products.

Life in business is often about setting timetables and taking action, things that this chapter focuses on. Two of the chief ways to schedule production are sales and operations planning and enterprise resource planning. These methods have different but related purposes. **Sales and operations planning (SOP)** is a process that helps managers make decisions relating to the creation of schedules that balance demand and supply. An **enterprise resource planning (ERP) system** is a powerful database system used to manage the whole enterprise, including finances, material requirements planning, human resources, production, customer relationship management, accounting, and most everything else. The **material requirements planning (MRP) system** is the production engine of an ERP system and is emphasized in this chapter. We discuss MRP systems at length at the end of this chapter. First, however, let's illustrate how firms plan production and explore the related topic of capacity planning. The worldwide use of data is discussed in GLOBAL CONNECTIONS 10.1.

A PPLY SALES AND OPERATIONS PLANNING

SOP is synonymous with aggregate planning. Much like ERP, SOP is a process that resides in an interconnected world where customers, companies, and suppliers share information. To understand SOP, we should clarify the concepts of aggregation and disaggregation. **Aggregation** conceptualizes the high-level overview of planning, which involves groups or families of products and is usually done at a divisional level. These high-level plans are then disaggregated. **Disaggregation** breaks down product families into individual products and

One of the by-products of all these ERP systems, coupled with worldwide outsourcing, is a need to communicate more effectively with suppliers and customers. This communication has been enhanced by T1 communications lines crossing the oceans and linking the continents.

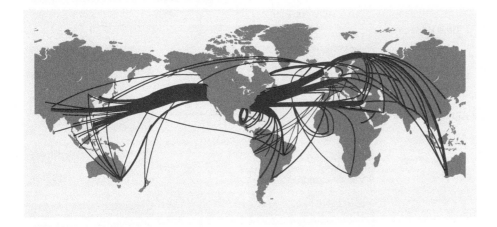

World Telecom Map
Based on TeleGeography, http://www
.telegeography.com

One way firms share planning systems is through **electronic data interchange (EDI)**, the computer-to-computer interchange of formatted messages such as documents, planning information, and monetary instruments. EDI often connects suppliers and customers throughout the supply chain.

EDI requires adherence to strict communications protocols that can be costly. Another approach to sharing data can be through **business-to-business integration (B2Bi)**, which uses third-party facilitators who format planning information in a way that even a small company with limited resources can access and use via the Internet. More and more, ERP systems are cloud-based. Cloud computing provides the opportunity for companies to obtain the benefits of ERP without the investment in hardware and software. This also provides the advantage that data is accessible from any location or any device.

Regardless of the format that managers use in communicating with suppliers and customers, the reality of the connected world is that SC&O managers need to share real-time information to reduce lead times and improve customer service. When we discuss ERP, you should imagine these systems in a connected world where companies have access to data from customers, and suppliers have access to planning data.

electronic data interchange (EDI)
The computer-to-computer interchange of formatted messages such as documents, planning information, and monetary instruments.

business-to-business integration (B2Bi)
Using third-party facilitators who format planning information in a way that even a small company with limited resources can access and use via the Internet.

components of products. From a planning horizon standpoint, SOP may go several months to a year into the future, whereas disaggregated plans may be made and completed on a daily or an hourly basis.

Production Planning

FIGURE 10.1 shows a hierarchical planning process that results in disaggregation. Notice that, at the top levels, products are aggregated together. As you move down the hierarchy, products are broken into individual components and subassemblies, and time horizons go from months down to days. We will define business plans, sales and operations plans, master production schedules, material requirements plans, and production activity control in the following paragraphs.

At the aggregate level, the hierarchical production planning process starts with strategies, policies, competitive intelligence, and forecasts. These inputs outline the present and future needs and requirements for the firm as a whole. These are then stratified into operational subplans.

FIGURE 10.1 >

Hierarchical Production Planning

business plan
A document that provides guidance for each of the operational subplans in areas such as finance, human resources, marketing, and SC&O management.

aggregate capacity plan
A quick analysis to make sure that capacity exists at the aggregate level to produce the units projected in the sales and operations plan.

master production schedule (MPS)
Portion of the ERP that disaggregates the sales and operations plan from product families to individual products to determine when they will be produced.

rough-cut capacity planning (RCCP)
A planning system that focuses on bottlenecks to ensure that the MPS does not overload production processes or facilities and can be produced given current capacity limitations.

detailed capacity plan
A plan performed on a computer to ensure that daily production plans are reasonable.

production activity control
A method used to coordinate the way that jobs are done on a daily basis, such as loading work centers, sequencing and prioritizing jobs, identifying job start times, job assignments to workstations, and other detailed scheduling.

capacity loading analysis
A method for planning capacity on a daily basis.

BUSINESS PLAN The **business plan** provides guidance for each of the operational subplans in areas such as finance, human resources, marketing, and SC&O planning. This plan usually projects up to one or more years into the future. At this level, planning is focused on outputs of product groups, divisions, or families. The inputs to the business plan include mission, policies, procedures, strategic objectives, competitive intelligence, and an understanding of the legal and regulatory environment.

SALES AND OPERATION PLAN The sales and operations plan is the production portion of the business plan and focuses on output of product families. The feasibility check on the sales and operations plan is the **aggregate capacity plan**, a quick back-of-the-envelope analysis to make sure that capacity exists at the aggregate level to produce the units projected in the sales and operations plan.

MASTER PRODUCTION SCHEDULE The **master production schedule (MPS)** disaggregates the SOP from product families to individual products to determine when they will be produced. The feasibility check of the MPS is **rough-cut capacity planning (RCCP)**, which focuses on bottlenecks to ensure that the MPS does not overload production processes or facilities and can be produced given current capacity limitations. The MPS provides a link between marketing and supply chain professionals by allowing order promising to customers.

MATERIAL REQUIREMENTS PLANNING The *material requirements plan (MRP)* is where product requirements are exploded into individual components and subassemblies. The feasibility check for the MRP is the **detailed capacity plan**, which is performed on a computer to ensure that daily production plans are reasonable.

PRODUCTION ACTIVITY CONTROL Managers use **production activity control** to coordinate the way that jobs are done on a daily basis, such as loading work centers, sequencing and prioritizing jobs, identifying job start times, job assignments to workstations, and other detailed scheduling. **Capacity loading analysis** is a method for planning daily capacity needs.

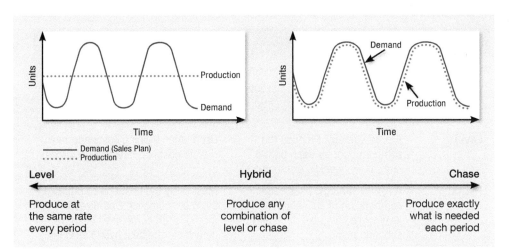

....

Managing Across Majors 10.1 Information systems majors, this chapter should help you understand the operations side of ERP.

....

Performing Sales and Operations Planning

With this brief introduction to hierarchical planning, we can now move to differing sales and operations strategies. There are two *pure production planning strategies* in SOP: *chase* and *level*. Hybrid plans involve a combination of level and chase, as FIGURE 10.2 illustrates.

A **chase SOP** production plan is a plan in which the exact amount demanded is produced each month. In the simplest case, managers can achieve this balance by varying workforce numbers or hiring temporary workers to accommodate demand levels. A chase plan can work only if the tasks performed require little training or specialized expertise, such as a simple assembly that requires little expertise. Other variants on this strategy are to work overtime or to subcontract during peak times.

The advantages of the chase strategy are that managers are able to hold little inventory and exactly meet customer demand. However, the costs of overtime, training, hiring, and laying off employees can be very high. Also, possibly the best workers will not necessarily gravitate toward firms that employ this strategy. As a result of constant hiring and then being let go, worker morale may be very low.

One company that uses this approach is Hallmark. During the winter season, Hallmark warehouse managers hire extra workers when demand is high. These temporary workers typically work through the holiday season and then are released once the holidays are over.

A **level SOP** production plan is accomplished by varying inventory levels, including periods in which negative inventory levels, or stockouts, are incurred. Typically, when a stockout occurs, back orders are allowed. **Back orders** are orders that are held in abeyance until more stock arrives. When the new stock arrives, the past-due orders are fulfilled. The advantages of the level strategy are that production is smoothed and labor instability is kept to a minimum. On the other hand, inventory carrying and stockout costs may be very high.

A **hybrid SOP** production plan involves any combination of the above pure strategies (level and chase). It may involve some varying of workforces, overtime, and subcontracting coupled with varying inventory levels. Due to simplicity and our own purposes, we will demonstrate only the pure plans here. Keep in mind, however, that applying a hybrid plan can negate the disadvantages of the pure plans and is usually the route managers take.

TABLE 10.1 provides a synopsis of SOP. SOLVED PROBLEMS 10.1 and 10.2 illustrate how to use chase and level plans, respectively, and TABLE 10.2 lists the steps involved in such planning.

chase SOP
A planning strategy in which the exact amount demanded is produced each month.

level SOP
A planning strategy that is accomplished by varying inventory levels.

back orders
Orders that are held in abeyance until more stock arrives.

hybrid SOP
A planning strategy that involves any combination of the *pure strategies* (level and chase).

TABLE 10.1 >

Sales and Operations Plans

Plan	Synopsis	What It Really Means
Chase	A pure strategy. Produce exactly what is needed for each period.	Used in any company that uses seasonal laborers, such as agriculture, food processing, or holiday workers.
Level	A pure strategy. Produce the same amount for each period (e.g., daily, weekly, or monthly).	Used when training costs and the morale costs of varying workforces are high.
Hybrid	A hybrid strategy. Uses some combination of chase and level while using overtime and subcontracting.	Most likely the best choice but also the most complex. Optimization methods are sometimes used to determine the best hybrid strategy.
Yield management	An approach that does not require allocation of resources. Instead, inducements are offered to spike demand during periods of low demand.	Involves interaction between marketing and SC&O planning to make it work; has a danger of cannibalizing business from yourself.

TABLE 10.2 >

SOP Strategy Steps

Step	Action
1	Determine type of plan: level, chase, or hybrid.
2	Based on the type of plan, post the needed periodic production quantities.
3	Compute ending inventory levels and stockouts.
4	Compute workforce-level changes.
5	Compute ending totals for each of the above items.
6	Find the total of inventory, shortage, hiring, and layoff costs.

SOLVED PROBLEM 10.1 >

MyLab Operations Management
Video

A Chase Plan in Action

Problem: You must perform a chase sales and operations plan for your firm. You have also been asked to compute the costs associated with this plan. To keep your analysis simple, do not consider overtime or subcontracting as options. A single worker can produce 100 units of the product per month. The hiring cost for an employee is $500, and the layoff cost for an employee is $2,000 due to severance and unemployment benefits costs. In addition, it costs $5 to carry a unit of inventory from one period to the next. Stockouts cost $20 per unit because of the potential for losing customers. Compute total costs for the chase plan. The predicted demand is as follows:

Plan: Chase

Month	1	2	3	4	5	6	Total
Demand	3,000	4,000	4,000	5,000	6,000	2,000	24,000

Solution: After research, you find that a chase plan means that you will have to produce exactly what is demanded each month. Therefore, you construct the following schedule:

Plan: Chase							
Month	1	2	3	4	5	6	Total
Demand	3,000	4,000	4,000	5,000	6,000	2,000	24,000
Production	3,000	4,000	4,000	5,000	6,000	2,000	24,000

You now need to compute the effect that this schedule will have on labor and inventory levels. Because you are producing exactly what is needed, ending inventory is always zero, as shown below:

Plan: Chase							
Month	1	2	3	4	5	6	Total
Demand	3,000	4,000	4,000	5,000	6,000	2,000	24,000
Production	3,000	4,000	4,000	5,000	6,000	2,000	24,000
Ending inventory	0	0	0	0	0	0	0
Stockouts	0	0	0	0	0	0	0
Labor (30 beginning, recall that each laborer can produce 100 units per month)							
Workers	30	40	40	50	60	20	240
Hires	0	10	0	10	10	0	30
Layoffs	0	0	0	0	0	40	40

We can now compute the costs for the chase plan:

Inventory carrying costs = $0
Stockout costs = $0
Hiring costs = 30 × $500 = $15,000
Layoff costs = 40 × $2,000 = $80,000
Total chase costs = $95,000

As you can see, the costs of the chase strategy are $95,000.

....
....

A Level Plan in Action

< SOLVED PROBLEM 10.2

Problem: Your plant manager now wants you to perform a level sales and operations plan for a product family. As before, the demand is given as follows:

MyLab Operations Management
Video

Plan: Level							
Month	1	2	3	4	5	6	Total
Demand	3,000	4,000	4,000	5,000	6,000	2,000	24,000

Solution: Because 24,000/6 = 4,000 units, that will be your level production quantity. The amount is shown as follows. Note that demand and production levels are no longer equal.

Plan: Level							
Month	**1**	**2**	**3**	**4**	**5**	**6**	**Total**
Demand	3,000	4,000	4,000	5,000	6,000	2,000	24,000
Production	4,000	4,000	4,000	4,000	4,000	4,000	24,000

You know that you will have to hire 10 more workers because 40 total workers are needed. After that, however, no more changes in workforce levels will be needed. You will see increased inventory carrying and stockouts as follows:

Plan: Level							
Month	**1**	**2**	**3**	**4**	**5**	**6**	**Total**
Demand	3,000	4,000	4,000	5,000	6,000	2,000	24,000
Production	4,000	4,000	4,000	4,000	4,000	4,000	24,000
Ending inventory	1,000	1,000	1,000	0	0	0	3,000
Stockouts	0	0	0	0	2,000	0	2,000
Labor (30 beginning)							
Workers	40	40	40	40	40	40	240
Hires	10	0	0	0	0	0	10
Layoffs	0	0	0	0	0	0	0

As before, the hiring cost for an employee is $500, and the layoff cost for an employee is $2,000 due to severance and unemployment benefits costs. In addition, it costs $5 to carry a unit of inventory from one period to the next. Stockouts cost $20 each because of the potential for losing customers. We now compute total costs for the level plan:

Inventory carrying costs = 3,000 × $5 = $15,000
Stockout costs = 2,000 × $20 = $40,000
Hiring costs = 10 × $500 = $5,000
Layoff costs = $0
Total level costs = $60,000

The difference in cost is $95,000 (see chase cost, Solved Problem 10.1) − $60,000 (level cost) = $35,000. Therefore, the level plan is less costly.

As we discussed in Chapter 8, another way to manage production when demand varies is by yield management. Managers use **yield management** to manage demand by offering discounts during periods of low demand and charging higher prices during times of high demand, which levels demand through pricing. This approach is often used in airlines that change ticket prices according to demand.

yield management
Using mechanisms such as pricing to level demand.

Airlines practice yield management when they offer discounted ticket prices during slower seasons.

DEFINE AND EXPLAIN HOW CAPACITY FUNCTIONS IN OPERATIONS MANAGEMENT

Capacity is the productive capability of a firm. It is not an exaggeration to say that there is no more important strategic decision than planning capacity. If your capacity is too constrained, you become a slave to your bottlenecks. If you underutilize capacity, you end up with costs that are too high. Decisions that you make relative to capacity affect customer service, your cost structures, future and current resource allocations, and how effectively you will compete, and they affect what you will emphasize in your global supply chain. As shown in TABLE 10.3, there are differing types of capacity.

Capacity can be measured either in terms of *inputs* or *outputs*. Examples of inputs are seats in an airplane, beds in a hospital, and number of servers in a restaurant. Examples of outputs are the ability to produce 600 units per hour, 35 pages per minute on a printer, and a

capacity
The productive capability of a firm.

< TABLE 10.3

Types of Capacity		
Type	**Definition**	**What It Really Means**
Design capacity	The capacity that a machine or system should realize given optimal operating conditions.	Often the capacity specified by the manufacturer of a machine. An example is a printer that is rated at up to 35 pages per minute (ppm).
Available capacity	Design capacity less scrap and rework.	The above printer prints up to 35 pages per minute with a 5 percent jamming rate; therefore, available capacity = 0.95 × 35 = 33.25 ppm.
Actual capacity	Design capacity minus scrap and rework; also factors in inefficiencies inherent in the system.	The printer is inactive 20 percent of the time due to time associated with the operator loading paper and getting jobs prepared for printing; therefore, actual capacity = 35 × 0.95 (jamming) × 0.80 (operator time) = 26.6 ppm.

FIGURE 10.3 >

Capacity Bottlenecks

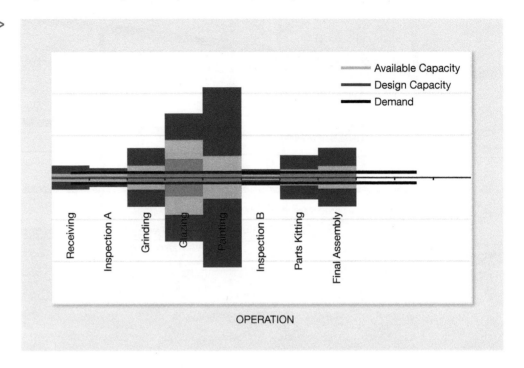

farm that produces 3.4 tons of alfalfa hay per acre, per year. Remember that capacity is rated and measured in differing ways depending on whether managers are focusing on inputs or outputs.

Bottlenecks

bottleneck
A department, step, or machine in a process that constrains throughput.

A **bottleneck** is the department, step, or machine in a process that constrains throughput. FIGURE 10.3 shows a graph of a process with 8 steps. A quick review of this process reveals that the inspections constrain throughput. Increasing capacity is not as much about building whole new production facilities and plants. Often, capacity can be added at the bottleneck by adding more labor, machinery, or some other resource. Therefore, capacity expansion is often a matter of studying bottlenecks and finding ways to increase throughput in those bottlenecks. This approach to managing bottlenecks is sometimes called the **theory of constraints**.

theory of constraints
A method for managing capacity.

Best Operating Level

best operating level
The rate of capacity utilization that minimizes average product cost.

economy of scale
Producing more so that the average cost of production for the item decreases.

diseconomies of scale
When the production of more units results in higher average cost per item.

The **best operating level** is the rate of capacity utilization that minimizes average product cost. Note in FIGURE 10.4 that, for low levels of production volume, average per-unit cost is high. As more is produced, the costs lessen, which economists refer to as an **economy of scale**. That is, as production volumes increase, average unit costs decrease. The minimum average cost point in Figure 10.4 is called the best operating level. As production exceeds the best operating level, quality problems may occur, machines may break down, and general confusion may occur. The result is **diseconomies of scale**, or an increase in per-unit average cost. This interesting concept implies that 100 percent of design capacity utilization is rarely preferable.

Therapists sharing an office is a good example of best operating level. With four available offices, the office easily accommodates four therapists. Bringing in a total of four therapists to fill the offices reduces the cost per therapist by allowing them to split the rent four ways. Because some of the therapists work only work part time, a fifth therapist is brought in to lower costs further. Although there are some rare conflicts, splitting the rent five ways results in additional scale economies. When a sixth therapist joins the office group, however, several conflicts emerge in scheduling offices: Some therapists must either lose appointments or rent an adjoining room. Going with the sixth therapist results in a diseconomy of scale for the

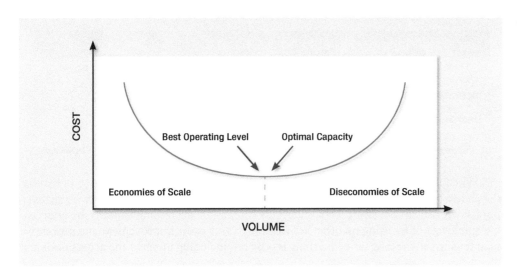

< FIGURE 10.4

Best Operating Level

small group, so the therapists scale back to five. In manufacturing, too much capacity utilization results in broken-down machinery, piles of work-in-process inventory, missed delivery dates, and other problems that can increase average per-unit cost. Therefore, sometimes trial and error is required to identify the best operating level.

A rule of thumb is that the best operating level is around 85 percent for manufacturing and around 60 percent for services. This lower best operating level for services is a result of the high level of customer contact in services and the need to tailor services to the needs of the customer. Because manufacturing is buffered from the customer, higher levels of capacity utilization are possible and desirable. Service managers, on the other hand, manage capacity through labor schedules. Poorly managed service capacity often affects customers negatively. As a manager, you can use these rules of thumb to plan capacity utilization to find the best operating level.

Poor service can result from poor capacity management.

UNDERSTAND AND APPLY CAPACITY PLANNING

One of the primary jobs of management is to take forecasted planning information and turn it into concrete capacity plans. Think of the launch of the new Xbox console. Based on prior launches, Microsoft might have an idea of what demand will be. Now, as the production manager for this product, you have to find the capacity to produce what your customers demand. Do you produce the product yourself, or do you outsource to other partners?

In Figure 10.1, we presented differing types of capacity plans as feasibility checks in the hierarchical planning process. We now discuss capacity at the firm level and demonstrate how to model capacity.

As you can see in TABLE 10.4, there are two primary facets to consider in capacity planning: time horizon and direction of change. The problems related to capacity do not always have to do with expanding capacity in a growing company. The more difficult scenario comes when you have to manage capacity in a shrinking market.

TABLE 10.4 >

Capacity Planning Facets and Scenarios		
	Short Term	**Long Term**
Increasing Capacity	Stretching	Expansion
Decreasing Capacity	Shrinking	Contraction

When increasing capacity in the short term, your options are limited, such as making the choice between asking your current set of employees to work overtime or hiring temporary workers. In the short term, managers can handle decreasing capacity by underusing employees or focusing on other activities such as process improvement and preventive maintenance. In the long term, anything is possible, including mergers and acquisitions and divestitures.

Another consideration in planning capacity is how aggressive a firm will be in adding capacity in a growing company. The choices vary from "wait and see" to the "field of dreams" approach. ("Field of dreams" refers to a 1989 movie starring Kevin Costner where the character, Ray Kinsella, builds a baseball field on his farm in the hope of luring the ghosts of the 1919 Chicago White Sox team, including Shoeless Joe Jackson, to his field. The catchphrase of the movie is, "Build it and they will come.") FIGURE 10.5 shows four approaches commonly used in managing capacity. **Leading capacity** is aggressive because capacity is added incrementally in anticipation of increasing demand. **Lagging capacity** is much more cautious than leading capacity because capacity is increased only when increasing demand justifies the increase in capacity. **Matching capacity** is more fluid, and capacity is increased at relatively the same rate that demand increases. **Mass capacity expansion** is the high-risk, high-reward "field of dreams" approach.

You might ask, Which approach is best? Of course, the correct answer is the standard business student response, "It depends." The correct approach depends on the market, competitive pressures, and customer demand for your products. The answer will probably be different for a conservative insurance company compared to a leading-edge high-tech firm. Of course, there are implicit trade-offs that must be considered in this risk/reward calculation.

leading capacity
Capacity is added incrementally in anticipation of increasing demand.

lagging capacity
Capacity is increased only when increasing demand justifies the increase in capacity.

matching capacity
Capacity is increased at relatively the same rate that demand increases.

mass capacity expansion
Large-scale capacity expansion with the expectation of high customer demand.

Capacity Planning Process

Generally speaking, firms follow a path to planning capacity that involves a combination of the following steps:

1. Project future capacity needs.
2. Determine if current capacity is sufficient.
3. Explore different alternatives for changing capacity levels based on short-term and long-term needs (refer again to Table 10.4).
4. Perform financial, supply chain, and market analyses of each alternative.

FIGURE 10.5 >

Capacity Planning Strategies

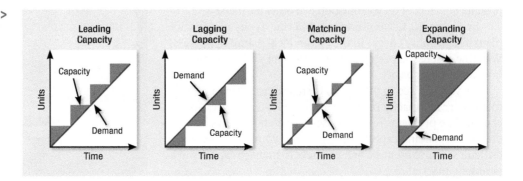

Capacity Management at American Airlines

As you read about capacity planning, keep in mind that managers' capacity decisions seriously affect the profitability of companies. For example, faulty capacity planning is costing American Airlines $1 billion annually, according to a report by a veteran airline analyst. According to Bob McAdoo of Avondale Partners, capacity is a big deal at American Airlines (AA). States McAdoo, "More important than its costs are AA's capacity decisions, its market selection and its unwillingness to halt or reduce flying in markets that are losers." In a recent year, AA's 10 worst markets caused the airline to lose nearly half a billion dollars. Those routes included New York to Los Angeles, New York to London, and several others. To see how capacity is measured in the airline industry, United flies three round trips daily from Chicago to London with 549 seats as opposed to AA's four round trips with 980 seats. This additional capacity costs AA an excess $75 million per year. These decisions are difficult for AA because it believes that the international routes add to its prestige, but these routes come at a high price. Comparatively, United's revenue per available seat mile is 10.9 cents, whereas AA's is 8.7 cents.

American Airlines has been driven to bankruptcy as a result of inefficient management capacity. For example, AA loses $70 million per year on its 10 daily flights from New York to Los Angeles. The New York to San Francisco flight loses $54 million per year. Such capacity issues have severely affected AA's profitability.

Source: Based on T. Reed, "American Loses on Bad Capacity Planning: Analyst," *The Street*, May 16, 2011.

5. Perform a qualitative "screening study" for each of the alternatives.
6. Choose and implement the alternative that best satisfies short-term and long-term objectives.
7. Perform a post-implementation review.

Capacity planning follows the hierarchical disaggregation discussed earlier in the chapter (refer again to Figure 10.1). At higher levels, managers perform product family- and division-level analysis. Eventually, they manage capacity on a daily basis using workcenter capacity loading analysis. SC&O CURRENT EVENTS 10.1 shows how detrimental poorly managed capacity can be to a firm.

Modeling Capacity

We have already discussed the differences between the three types of capacity (design, available, and actual). We now use these measures to determine our effectiveness in using a firm's capacity. All three are examples of widely used, single-factor capacity measures that can be applied to any type of capacity situation. **Capacity utilization** is a measure of what proportion of design capacity is actually being used during a time period. The **efficiency percentage** takes into account some of the problems with the design capacity measure; because less than full capacity utilization is often preferable, the adjusted number gives us a better measure of capacity usage. The **output gap measure** provides a variance measure against design capacity. In equation form:

$$capacity\ utilization\ \% = \frac{actual\ output}{design\ capacity} \times 100 \qquad (10.1)$$

$$efficiency\ \% = \frac{actual\ output}{actual\ capacity} \times 100 \qquad (10.2)$$

capacity utilization
A measure of what proportion of design capacity is actually being used during a time period.

efficiency percentage
A metric that accounts for some of the problems with the design capacity measure; because less than full capacity utilization is often preferable, the adjusted number gives us a better measure of capacity usage.

output gap measure
A metric that provides a variance measure against design capacity.

$$\text{output gap measure \%} = \frac{\text{actual output} - \text{design capacity}}{\text{design capacity}} \times 100 \qquad (10.3)$$

SOLVED PROBLEM 10.3 shows these three measures in action.

 SOLVED PROBLEM 10.3 >   **Modeling Capacity Measures**

MyLab Operations Management
Video

Problem: A process is designed to produce 1,000 units per hour with a 1 percent scrap rate and 12 percent inherent inefficiencies, including worker fatigue. Assuming that actual output is 790 units, compute the design capacity, available capacity, actual capacity (refer to Table 10.3), capacity utilization percent, efficiency percent, and output gap measure.

Solution:

design capacity $= 1{,}000$ units
available capacity $= 1{,}000 \times (1 - 0.01) = 990$ units
actual capacity $= 1{,}000 \times (1 - 0.01) \times (1 - 0.12) = 871.2$ units

$$\text{capacity utilization \%} = \frac{790}{1000} \times 100 = 79\%$$

$$\text{efficiency \%} = \frac{790}{871.2} \times 100 = 90.68\%$$

$$\text{output gap measure \%} = \frac{790 - 1000}{1000} \times 100 = -21\%$$

Managing Across Majors 10.2   Human resources management majors, capacity inefficiency affects the amount of labor you will need to hire to meet required demand.

Rough-Cut Capacity Planning

When discussing SOP strategies, we introduced rough-cut capacity planning (RCCP). Once an SOP strategy is in place, RCCP is a quick analysis at the product family level to ensure that there is enough capacity to meet customer demand. Managers accomplish RCCP by comparing available labor to labor requirements for a particular product family. We show how managers apply RCCP in SOLVED PROBLEM 10.4.

 SOLVED PROBLEM 10.4 >   **Rough-Cut Capacity Planning in Action**

MyLab Operations Management
Video

Problem: The following table provides demand for three products from a sales and operations plan. Also provided are standard hours for the three products. These standard hours do not include different possible product variations. Assuming that the company has 32,000 labor hours available in the coming 90 days, determine the feasibility of this plan using RCCP.

Labor Requirements for the 90-Day Sales and Operations Plan		
Product	**Units Demanded**	**Standard Hours (in hours/unit)**
A	15,000	0.95
B	20,000	0.45
C	12,000	0.33
D	5,000	1.22

Solution: Using the above data, multiply the units demanded by the related standard hours, which yields the following solution for the labor required:

Labor Requirements for the 90-Day Sales and Operations Plan			
Product	Units Demanded	Standard Units (in hours/unit)	Labor Required (in hours)
A	15,000	0.95	14,250
B	20,000	0.45	9,000
C	12,000	0.33	3,960
D	5,000	1.22	6,100
		Total:	33,310

We see that there is a need for 33,310 hours of labor. Because 32,000 hours are available, management needs to find a means to expand capacity by 1,310 hours.

Ⓤ NDERSTAND THE MAIN FUNCTIONALITY OF AN ENTERPRISE RESOURCE PLANNING SYSTEM

ERP systems are a fact of life in business today. The benefits of data integration, connectivity, and the ability to analyze *big data* make ERP systems very intriguing. It is fair to say that all large and most average- to small-sized companies use ERP systems of some sort to manage resources. In this section, we introduce ERP systems. In the next section, we focus on the SC&O portion of ERP, the material requirements planning (MRP) system.

We should mention that not all ERP implementations have gone well. Trus Joist Macmillan originally budgeted $10 million to implement an SAP system (a brand of ERP system). After it had spent more than $100 million without any tangible benefits, it had lost so much value that it became a buyout target and was taken over. SC&O CURRENT EVENTS 10.2 discusses ERP security impacts from moving to the cloud.

In its origin, ERP was an extension of MRP. Today, ERP systems refer to large database systems that tie together nearly all the disparate information systems firmwide. TABLE 10.5 shows some of the functions often included in ERP systems.

The Cloudy Future of ERP

< SC&O CURRENT EVENTS 10.2

One of the newest trends in ERP is the movement of ERP to cloud systems. The benefits of using cloud systems include less investment in hardware, less software maintenance and the outsourcing of information systems infrastructure. However, you need to look closely at the security capabilities of your cloud provider. With much talk of hacking—whether Russian, American, or Chinese—managers need to worry about information security.

According to the United States Computer Emergency Readiness Team (US-CERT), several organizations using ERP systems are vulnerable to cyberattack. First, ERP specialists are often database administrators with very little experience in cybersecurity. Second, ERP systems are very complex, with as many as tens of thousands of settings that make cybersecurity difficult. In addition, companies often lack the resources to monitor their ERP systems properly.

Without naming particular systems, password protection, token generation at sign-on, and authentication protocols can all be problematic. From a behavioral point of view, firms should never let associates access ERP systems from personally owned computers, tablets, or smartphones, and employees should not be given the use of company computers when they leave a company. One firm found their systems hacked when a former employee pawned his work computer.

According to Gartner, an IT consulting giant, "[D]elaying security measures in an effort to avoid disrupting business can be a false economy." This means that a failure to properly secure your data may ultimately put your business's entire future at risk.

UNDERSTAND AND APPLY MATERIAL REQUIREMENTS MANAGEMENT

Now that we have introduced ERP systems, we are ready to drill down to their operational cores. The operational core of an ERP system is the MRP system. It is called an ERP *engine* because it is where *explosion* takes place. **MRP explosion** is the process of calculating requirements for components and subassemblies from the demand for finished products.

MRP explosion
The process of calculating requirements for components and subassemblies from the demand for finished products.

dependent demand
Demand that is calculated from the requirements for some parent item.

MRP systems are used in circumstances where the demand for one item is predicated on the demand for another item, or **dependent demand**. Take the case of the iPhone (FIGURE 10.6). If your firm wants to ship 500 iPhones on the 20th week of the year, parts must be purchased and fabricated in the weeks leading up to the shipping date. The task of scheduling everything to make shipments is the job of the MRP system.

MRP Inputs

The three primary inputs to an MRP system are (1) the master production schedule, (2) the inventory status file, and (3) the bill of materials (FIGURE 10.7). These files provide the information that the MRP system needs to operate properly. We will define each input separately.

TABLE 10.5 >

ERP Modules	
ERP Function	**Detailed Processes**
Financial and accounting systems	Accounts payable/receivables, general ledger, cash management, budgeting, activity-based costing, financial analytics
Manufacturing systems	Bills of materials, material requirements planning, scheduling, capacity planning, SOP, operations analytics
Human resources systems	Payroll, recruiting, diversity planning, benefits, 401k plans, talent management, workforce deployment
Supply chain management systems	Inventory management, purchasing, supply chain performance optimization, warehouse management systems, logistics (inbound and outbound), transportation management
Customer relationship management systems	Marketing, sales, call center support, services management, customer records

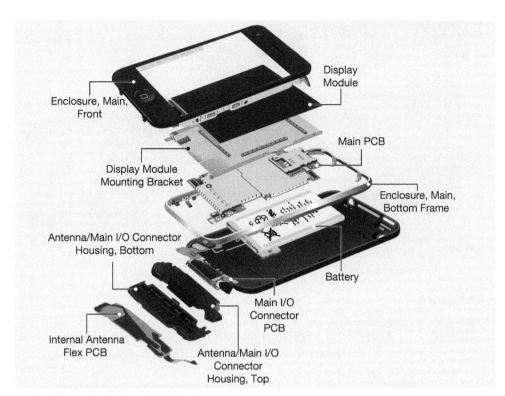

Reprinted by permission from IHS Technology

< FIGURE 10.6

Exploded View of an iPhone

The master production schedule (MPS), discussed earlier in the chapter, gives demand for finished products. As you may recall, the MPS is based on product families. The MRP system requires information regarding what variations of products will be produced exactly and when they are needed.

The **inventory status file** knows when items will be in stock as well as the current inventory levels. Because the inventory status file must be accurate, an active **cycle counting** process is usually required. In this process, products are categorized as A, B, or C and are counted on a regular basis, with the A items being counted most often.

The **bill of materials (BOM)** shows how a product is manufactured. It shows what components are used in the manufacture of the finished product, the quantities needed, lead times for each stage of production, and the order of assembly. In FIGURE 10.8, the final assembly A is the parent item at level 0. Final assembly requires three weeks and is completed by combining one item B with three item Cs. The lead times for items B and C are two weeks and four weeks, respectively. Items B and C are ordered lot for lot (exactly the amount required in each period) and in lots of 200, respectively. Item B is a parent of items D and E, and item C is a parent of item F. Items D, E, and F each have their respective lead times (*L*), quantities (*Q*), and lot sizes.

inventory status file
A database that knows when items will be in stock as well as the current inventory levels.

cycle counting
An inventory management approach based on regularly scheduled counts of different classes of inventory (e.g., ABC).

bill of materials (BOM)
A data file that shows how a product is manufactured, including what components are used in the manufacture of the finished product, the quantities needed, lead times for each stage of production, and the order of assembly.

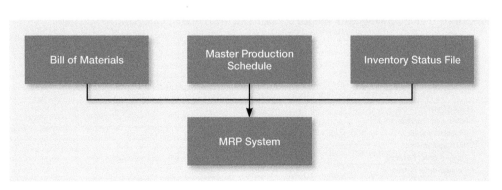

< FIGURE 10.7

Three Primary MRP Inputs

FIGURE 10.8 >

A Simple Product
Structure Tree Bill of
Materials

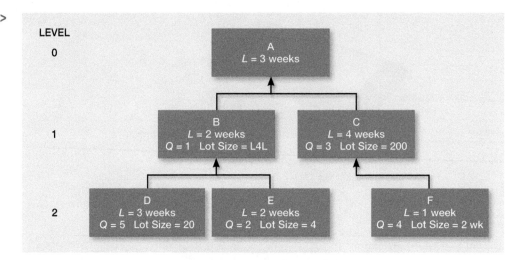

MRP Record

FIGURE 10.9 shows a rudimentary MRP record. Each row of the MRP record has special importance in performing the explosion process mentioned earlier. The upper part of the MRP record (week number, item, lead time, and order quantity) is general information that managers use when computing requirements. The lower half of the record is for computing gross requirements, scheduled receipts, projected on hand, net requirements, planned order receipts, and planned order releases. TABLE 10.6 defines each of these elements of the MRP record. The MRP record computations are demonstrated in SOLVED PROBLEM 10.5.

FIGURE 10.9 >

An MRP Record

Week #	1	2	3	4	5	6	7	8
Item LT =								
Quantity								
Item LT =								
Gross Requirements								
Scheduled Receipts								
Projected on Hand								
Net Requirements								
Planned-order Receipts								
Planned-order Releases								

 SOLVED PROBLEM 10.5 >

MyLab Operations Management
Video

MRP Record Computations

Problem: Item A has a gross requirement for 600 in week 6. There are 200 on hand and a scheduled receipt of 100 in week 4. The lead time is two weeks. The order quantity is lot for lot, which means that you should order only what is needed, when it is needed. Fill out the MRP record for item A.

Solution: The following MRP record contains all the required calculations and data:

Week #		1	2	3	4	5	6	7	8
Item A LT = 2									
Quantity: lot for lot									
Gross Requirements							600		
Scheduled Receipts					100				
Projected on Hand	200	200	200	200	300	300	0		
Net Requirements							300		
Planned-order Receipts							300		
Planned-order Releases					300				

Notice that the inventory is carried through from the beginning. The scheduled receipt is reflective of an order that had already been placed. The *time phasing* takes place between the planned order receipt and its planned order release two weeks earlier (remember that lead time was two weeks). So we will plan to place an order in week four for 300 units of item A.

MRP Logic

Now let's walk through the details of MRP explosion. The basis of explosion is MRP logic. **MRP logic** is the process of time phasing and calculating requirements for lower-level items from parent items. **Time phasing** is moving backward through time from the delivery date for the completed product to enable releasing orders only when they are needed. **Parent items** are items that occur in higher levels in a BOM. We will demonstrate with a rolling cart example. FIGURE 10.10 shows a drawing of a rolling cart. The bottom part of the drawing shows the parts used in assembling a rolling cart.

FIGURE 10.11 shows a product structure tree BOM for the rolling cart. Note that the final product is at level 0 of the BOM. The subassemblies are at level 1, and the components are at level 2. SOLVED PROBLEM 10.6 shows how to use MRP logic to calculate requirements for this product.

MRP logic
The process of time phasing and calculating requirements for lower-level items from parent items.

time phasing
Moving backward through time from the delivery date for the completed product to enable releasing orders only when they are needed.

parent items
Items that occur at higher levels in a bill of materials.

MRP Record Elements Defined		
Element	**Definition**	
Gross requirements	The quantity required at the end of each period to meet customer requirements. Demand for the end items comes from the MPS. Gross requirements for lower-level items are calculated from the planned order releases for parent items.	
Scheduled receipts	The quantity that has already been ordered and will be received at the beginning of the period. It is an *open order* that is yet to be received.	
Projected on hand	The amount of inventory that will be on hand at the end of the period. This amount is available for the succeeding period and is calculated as scheduled receipts plus planned order receipts plus the prior period's on-hand inventory minus current period gross requirements.	
Net requirements	The amount that is needed to satisfy gross requirements when everything else is taken into account. It is calculated as gross requirements minus scheduled receipts minus the projected on-hand inventory from the prior period.	
Planned order receipts	The amount that is *planned* to be ordered and to be received at the beginning of the period. The order is yet to be placed.	
Planned order releases	The amount that is *planned* to be ordered so that it may be released at the right time. Between planned order receipts and planned order releases is where *time phasing* takes place. When this order is officially placed, it becomes a scheduled receipt and is deleted from planned order receipts and planned order releases.	

< TABLE 10.6

FIGURE 10.10 >

**Detailed Drawing of a
Rolling Cart**

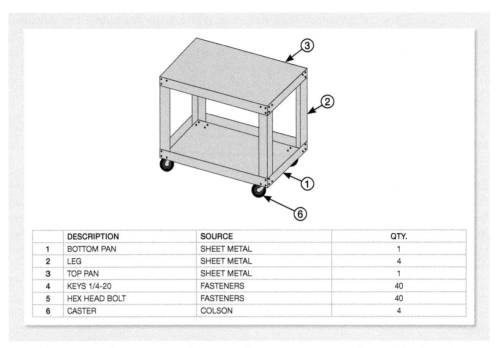

	DESCRIPTION	SOURCE	QTY.
1	BOTTOM PAN	SHEET METAL	1
2	LEG	SHEET METAL	4
3	TOP PAN	SHEET METAL	1
4	KEYS 1/4-20	FASTENERS	40
5	HEX HEAD BOLT	FASTENERS	40
6	CASTER	COLSON	4

Reprinted by permission from "3-D CAD: Modeling a Nest of Parts," Precision Matters, The FABRICATOR, March 2011.

 **SOLVED PROBLEM 10.6 >**

**MyLab Operations Management
Video**

Rolling Cart MRP Logic

Problem: Using the product structure tree BOM of Figure 10.11 (p. 294), calculate the requirements for all subassemblies and components using MRP logic. There is a gross requirement for 500 completed rolling carts in week 8. Other lead times and quantities are given in the following table:

Item	BOM Level	Required Quantity	Lead Time	Beginning On-Hand Inventory	Schedule Receipts	Order Quantities
Rolling cart (completed)	0	N/A	1 week	100	None	Lot for lot
Base assembly	1	1	2 weeks	50	None	Lot for lot
Top	1	1	1 week	0	200 in week 3	150
Legs and bolts sub-assembly	1	4	1 week	0	None	Lot for lot
Base	2	1	1 week	0	None	Lot for lot
Casters	2	4	3 weeks	0	None	Lot for lot
Legs	2	4	1 week	0	None	Lot for lot
Hex bolts	2	5	1 week	3,000	None	1,500

Solution: The solution is given in the following MRP records:

This calculation of requirements for components and subassemblies is referred to as MRP explosion. Note that this example is simple. The real power of MRP comes when planning production for many products simultaneously.

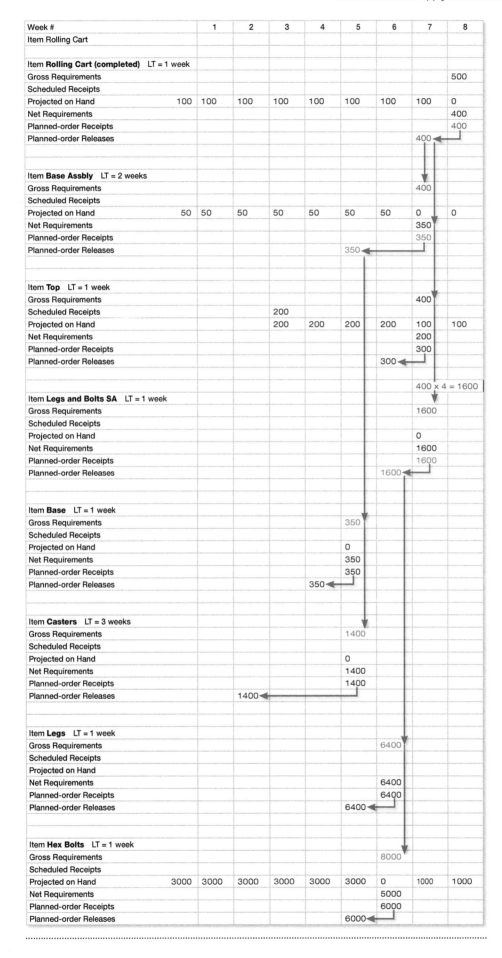

MRP Table for Solved Problem 10.6

Week #		1	2	3	4	5	6	7	8
Item Rolling Cart									
Item Rolling Cart (completed) LT = 1 week									
Gross Requirements								500	
Scheduled Receipts									
Projected on Hand	100	100	100	100	100	100	100	100	0
Net Requirements								400	
Planned-order Receipts								400	
Planned-order Releases								400	
Item Base Assbly LT = 2 weeks									
Gross Requirements								400	
Scheduled Receipts									
Projected on Hand	50	50	50	50	50	50	50	0	0
Net Requirements								350	
Planned-order Receipts								350	
Planned-order Releases						350			
Item Top LT = 1 week									
Gross Requirements								400	
Scheduled Receipts				200					
Projected on Hand			200	200	200	200	200	100	100
Net Requirements								200	
Planned-order Receipts								300	
Planned-order Releases							300		
							400 x 4 = 1600		
Item Legs and Bolts SA LT = 1 week									
Gross Requirements								1600	
Scheduled Receipts									
Projected on Hand								0	
Net Requirements								1600	
Planned-order Receipts								1600	
Planned-order Releases							1600		
Item Base LT = 1 week									
Gross Requirements						350			
Scheduled Receipts									
Projected on Hand						0			
Net Requirements						350			
Planned-order Receipts						350			
Planned-order Releases					350				
Item Casters LT = 3 weeks									
Gross Requirements						1400			
Scheduled Receipts									
Projected on Hand						0			
Net Requirements						1400			
Planned-order Receipts						1400			
Planned-order Releases			1400						
Item Legs LT = 1 week									
Gross Requirements							6400		
Scheduled Receipts									
Projected on Hand									
Net Requirements							6400		
Planned-order Receipts							6400		
Planned-order Releases						6400			
Item Hex Bolts LT = 1 week									
Gross Requirements							8000		
Scheduled Receipts									
Projected on Hand	3000	3000	3000	3000	3000	3000	0	1000	1000
Net Requirements							5000		
Planned-order Receipts							6000		
Planned-order Releases						6000			

FIGURE 10.11 >

Product Structure Tree BOM for the Rolling Cart for Solved Problem 10.6

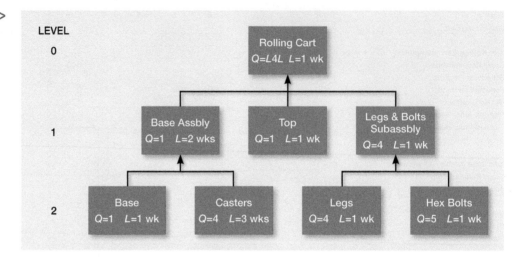

MRP Outputs

Now you have the information you need to understand how MRP works and its importance in scheduling operations. We previously talked about the inputs to an MRP system. As a result of MRP explosion, we are able to generate production planning documents, including the following:

- Planned order receipt schedules
- Planned order release schedules
- Documents outlining changes to prior schedules such as priority planning
- Performance reports, including stockouts and expedited orders
- Exceptions, including late orders and back orders

MRP systems have long been in use and are seen as necessary staples for any planning system. Within an ERP system, the MRP system provides information that can be input into financial, accounting, and human resources systems to help plan for future needs.

In the beginning of the chapter, we discussed the development of an ERP system at Rolls-Royce. The steps required to accomplish the ERP implementation included the following:

- Bridging the legacy systems and data cleanup to provide more trust in the management of information
- Training senior management, particularly the executive group, to be responsible for the overall direction of the company, even though they lacked technical knowledge of the ERP system
- Managing effective relationships and leading teams in both technical and noncomputer based environments
- Manufacturing simulation exercises

- Completing transactional training
- Streamlining shop floor communication with line workers with an exercise that occurred during the implementation of software updates (the exercise required line workers to attend workshops to learn new computer skills to process work)

As with any large implementation, Rolls-Royce overcame many obstacles to achieve success in implementation. As a result of implementing the ERP, Rolls-Royce has reported the following benefits:

- Faster global product changes
- Greater plant and resource utilization
- Improved product quality and profitability
- Better customer responsiveness
- Reduced scrap and rework
- Labor savings
- Reductions in overhead costs

Summary

In this chapter, we have introduced important planning-related topics. In the aggregate, these decisions are highly strategic and can run into the billions of dollars.

1. We introduced sales and operations planning (SOP).
   a. Chase SOP strategies are used when producing exactly what is demanded during every period.
   b. Level SOP strategies vary inventory levels to keep production at a level rate.
2. Capacity is the productive capability of a firm.
   a. Bottlenecks are the capacity constraint in processes.
   b. The best operating level in capacity planning is around 85 percent for manufacturing and around 60 percent for services.
3. Enterprise resource planning (ERP) systems are used to manage information in a firm.
   a. ERP systems combine databases such as material requirements planning, inventory, human resources, accounting, and finance.
4. Materials requirements planning (MRP) systems are where the process of explosion takes place.
   a. The main inputs into an MRP system are the inventory status file, the bill of materials, and the master production schedule.
   b. We presented MRP logic to show how MRP systems work.
   c. ERP systems are not only for manufacturing companies. All these topics apply to services firms as well. Anywhere that capacity and information are important, you will find these systems.

Key Terms

aggregate capacity plan   276
aggregation   274
back orders   277
best operating level   282
bill of materials (BOM)   289
bottleneck   282
business plan   276
business-to-business integration
   (B2Bi)   275
capacity   281
capacity loading analysis   276
capacity utilization   285
chase SOP   277
cycle counting   289
dependent demand   288

detailed capacity plan   276
disaggregation   274
diseconomies of scale   282
economy of scale   282
efficiency percentage   285
electronic data interchange
   (EDI)   275
enterprise resource planning (ERP)
   system   274
hybrid SOP   277
inventory status file   289
lagging capacity   284
leading capacity   284
level SOP   277
mass capacity expansion   284

master production schedule (MPS)   276
matching capacity   284
material requirements planning (MRP)
   system   274
MRP explosion   288
MRP logic   291
output gap measure   285
parent items   291
production activity control   276
rough-cut capacity plan (RCCP)   276
sales and operations planning
   (SOP)   274
theory of constraints   282
time phasing   291
yield management   280

Integrative Learning Exercise

Successful businesses continually look for ways to gain a competitive advantage. Working with a team of students, identify ways that improvements to sales and operations planning can help establish a competitive advantage for a company. In what ways is SOP related to the other functional areas of the business, especially marketing? How does enterprise resource planning fit into the sales and operations process? What challenges accompany the implementation of an ERP system?

Integrative Experiential Exercise

All companies do some form of sales and operations planning. Visit a company near your campus and interview a manager or the individual who is responsible for SOP. Answer the following questions:

1. What tools or techniques do you use to balance demand and supply?

2. Does the company integrate its planning efforts with other functional areas such as marketing?

3. What are the biggest challenges to developing a feasible plan?

4. Does the company use an ERP system?

5. What difficulties did or will the company have to overcome to implement and use an ERP system?

Discussion Questions

1. Briefly describe sales and operations planning and enterprise resource planning.

2. Briefly compare electronic data interchange with business-to-business integration.

3. In sales and operations planning, what is meant by the terms *aggregation* and *disaggregation*?

4. In what ways does the business plan differ from the sales and operations plan?

5. What is the master production schedule? How is its feasibility verified?

6. What activities comprise production activity control?

7. What are chase SOP and level SOP plans? What are the advantages and disadvantages of each approach to SOP?

8. What is yield management? How might yield management be used to manage demand in the airline industry?

9. What is capacity? In what ways do capacity decisions affect a company's performance?

10. What is a bottleneck? Why is it important to know the bottleneck when evaluating capacity?

11. Briefly discuss the concept of best operating level. What might happen if a firm's production exceeds the best operating level?

12. In what ways can capacity be increased in the short term?

13. Briefly describe the four common approaches to managing capacity.

14. Do capacity utilization and efficiency describe the same thing? If not, how are they different?

15. What is rough-cut capacity planning? What role does it play in sales and operation planning?

Solved Problems

Sales and Operating Planning

CHASE SOP
SOLVED PROBLEM 10.1

1. A firm has the following predicted demand for the next six months:

Month	1	2	3	4	5	6
Demand	10,000	9,000	8,000	7,000	11,000	9,000

A worker is able to produce 50 units per month. The cost to hire each additional worker is $1,000 per worker, and layoff costs are $2,000 per worker. The cost to carry an item in inventory is $10 per unit per month. A stockout is estimated to cost the firm $50 per unit out of stock. At the start of the planning process, 100 workers are employed. Assuming that overtime and subcontracting are not available options for the firm, develop a chase sales and operations plan.

Solution:

Plan: Chase

Month	Demand	Beginning Inventory	Production	Ending Inventory	Stock-outs
1	10,000	0	10,000	0	0
2	9,000	0	9,000	0	0
3	8,000	0	8,000	0	0
4	7,000	0	7,000	0	0
5	11,000	0	11,000	0	0
6	9,000	0	9,000	0	0

Labor = 100 beginning

Month	Workers Required	Hires	Layoffs
1	200	100	0
2	180	0	20
3	160	0	20
4	140	0	20
5	220	80	0
6	180	0	40

The cost for the chase plan is computed as follows:

Total inventory carrying costs = total ending inventory × $10 = 0 × $10 = $0

Total stockout costs = total stockouts × $50 = 0 × $50 = $0

Hiring costs = workers hired × $1,000 = (100 + 80) × $1,000 = $180,000

Layoff costs = workers laid off × $2,000 = (20 + 20 + 20 + 40) × $2,000 = $200,000

Total chase plan costs = $380,000

LEVEL SOP
SOLVED PROBLEM 10.2

2. A firm has the following predicted demand for the next six months:

Month	1	2	3	4	5	6
Demand	10,000	6,000	8,000	7,000	11,000	9,000

A worker is able to produce 50 units per month. The cost to hire each additional worker is $1,000 per worker, and layoff costs are $2,000 per worker. The cost to carry an item in inventory is $10 per unit per month. A stockout is estimated to cost the firm $50 per unit out of stock. At the start of the planning process, 100 workers are employed. Assuming that overtime and subcontracting are not available options for the firm, develop a level sales and operations plan.

Solution:
The monthly production quantity is the monthly average of the total demand = 51,000/6 = 8,500 per month. (Note: A negative beginning inventory denotes a stockout that is carried forward.)

Month	Demand	Beginning Inventory	Production	Ending Inventory	Stock-outs
1	10,000	0	8,500	0	1,500
2	6,000	−1,500	8,500	1,000	0
3	8,000	1,000	8,500	1,500	0
4	7,000	1,500	8,500	3,000	0
5	11,000	3,000	8,500	500	0
6	9,000	500	8,500	0	0

Labor = 100 beginning

Month	Workers Required	Hires	Layoffs
1	170	70	0
2	170	0	0
3	170	0	0
4	170	0	0
5	170	0	0
6	170	0	0

The cost for the level plan is computed as follows:

Total inventory carrying cost = total ending inventory $\times$ \$10 = 6,000 $\times$ \$10 = \$60,000

Total stockout costs = total stockouts $\times$ \$50 = 1,500 $\times$ \$50 = \$75,000

Total hiring costs = workers hired $\times$ \$1,000 = 70 $\times$ \$1,000 = \$70,000

Total layoff costs = workers laid off $\times$ \$2,000 = 0 $\times$ \$2,000 = \$0

Total plan costs = \$205,000

Capacity Planning

MODELING CAPACITY
SOLVED PROBLEM 10.3

3. A process has been designed to produce 1,500 units per hour with a scrap rate of 1.5 percent and 9 percent inherent inefficiencies, including worker fatigue. Assuming that actual output is 1,275 unit per hour, compute design capacity, available capacity, actual capacity, capacity utilization percentage, efficiency percentage, and the output gap measure.

Solution:
Design capacity = 1,500 units per hour

Available capacity = 1,500 $\times$ (1 − 0.015) = 1,477.5 units per hour

Actual capacity = 1,500 $\times$ (1 − 0.015) $\times$ (1 − 0.09) = 1,344.5 units per hour

Capacity utilization % = $\frac{1,275}{1,500} \times 100 = 85\%$

Capacity efficiency % = $\frac{1,275}{1,344.5} \times 100 = 94.8\%$

Output gap measure % = $\frac{1,275 - 1,500}{1,500} \times 100 = -15\%$

ROUGH-CUT CAPACITY PLANNING
SOLVED PROBLEM 10.4

4. The following table provides demand for the next quarter and standard hours for four products selected from a sales and operations plan. If the company has 55,000 labor hours available for the next quarter, determine the feasibility of this sales and operation plan using rough-cut capacity planning.

Product	Units Demanded	Standard Hours (in hours/unit)
A	20,000	0.75
B	12,000	1.3
C	8,000	0.25
D	25,000	0.9

Solution:
The units demanded for each product are multiplied by the corresponding standard hours. The resulting labor hours required for each product and the total labor hours required are as follows:

Product	Units Demanded	Standard Hours (in hours/unit)	Labor Hours Required
A	20,000	0.75	15,000
B	12,000	1.3	15,600
C	8,000	0.25	2,000
D	25,000	0.9	22,500
		Total =	55,100

The total labor hours required by these four products for the next quarter is 55,100 hours. Because the firm has only 55,000 hours next quarter, it must expand hours available by (55,100 − 55,000) = 100 hours to make the sales and operation plan feasible.

Materials Requirement Management

MRP RECORD
SOLVED PROBLEM 10.5

5. Item A has a gross requirement for 800 in week 4. There are currently 100 of item A on hand and a scheduled receipt for 100 in week 3. The order quantity for item A is lot for lot, and item A has a lead time of two weeks. Complete the MRP record for item A.

Solution:
The following contains the required calculations:

Week	1	2	3	4
Item A: lead time = 2				
Quantity: lot for lot				
Gross requirements				800
Scheduled receipts			100	
Projected on-hand inventory 100	100	100	200	0
Net requirements				600
Planned order receipts				600
Planned order releases		600		

6. Use the following product structure tree diagram for product 1 and the information provided to explode the requirements for all subassemblies and components using MRP logic.

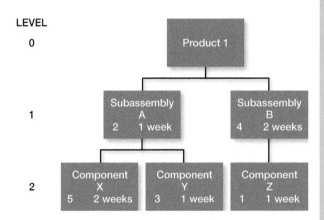

7. There is a gross requirement for 500 completed units of product 1 in week 6. The lead times, scheduled receipts, and order quantities for the subassemblies and component parts are as follows:

Item	BOM Level	Required Quantity	Lead Time	Beginning On-Hand Quantity	Scheduled Receipts	Order Quantity
Product 1	0		1 week	100	None	Lot for lot
Subassembly A	1	2	1 week	200	None	200
Subassembly B	1	4	2 weeks	0	100 in week 2	100
Component X	2	5	2 weeks	0	None	Lot for lot
Component Y	2	3	1 week	500	500 in week 1	500
Component Z	2	1	1 week	0	100 in week 1	100

Solution:
The solution is provided in the following MRP records:

Week	1	2	3	4	5	6
Product 1: lead time = 1						
Quantity: lot for lot						
Gross requirements						500

(*continued*)

Week	1	2	3	4	5	6
Scheduled receipts						
Projected on-hand inventory	100	100	100	100	100	100
Net requirements						400
Planned order receipts						400
Planned order releases					400	

Week	1	2	3	4	5	6
Subassembly A: lead time = 1						
Quantity: 200						
Gross requirements					800	
Scheduled receipts						
Projected on-hand inventory	200	200	200	200		
Net requirements					600	
Planned order receipts					600	
Planned order releases				600		

Week	1	2	3	4	5	6
Subassembly B: lead time = 2						
Quantity: 100						
Gross requirements					1,600	
Scheduled receipts		100				
Projected on-hand inventory	0	100	100	100		
Net requirements					1,500	
Planned order receipts					1,500	
Planned order releases			1,500			

Week	1	2	3	4	5	6
Component X: lead time = 2						
Quantity: lot for lot						
Gross requirements				3,000		
Scheduled receipts						
Projected on-hand inventory	0					
Net requirements				3,000		
Planned order receipts				3,000		
Planned order releases		3,000				

Week	1	2	3	4	5	6
Component Y: lead time = 1						
Quantity: 500						
Gross requirements				1,800		
Scheduled receipts	500					
Projected on-hand inventory 500	1,000	1,000	1,000	200	200	200
Net requirements				800		
Planned order receipts				1,000		
Planned order releases			1,000			

Week	1	2	3	4	5	6
Component Z: lead time = 1						
Quantity: 100						
Gross requirements			1,500			
Scheduled receipts	100					
Projected on-hand inventory 0	100	100				
Net requirements			1,400			
Planned order receipts			1,400			
Planned order releases		1,400				

Problems

Sales and Operations Planning

CHASE SOP

1. A company has predicted the following demands for the next six months:

Month	1	2	3	4	5	6	Total
Demand	15,000	18,000	15,000	20,000	22,000	24,000	114,000

A single worker working for one month can produce 125 units. The beginning workforce is 50 workers. It costs the company $1,500 to hire one worker, and it costs the company $2,500 to lay off a worker. The cost to carry an item is $15 per unit per month. The stockout cost is estimated to be $40 per unit.

Develop a chase sales and operations plan for this firm. Develop the monthly production schedule, and show the labor workforce and inventory levels. Finally, compute the cost of the plan.

2. A company believes that its demand for the next six months is as follows:

Month	1	2	3	4	5	6	Total
Demand	6,000	8,000	10,000	6,000	9,000	12,000	51,000

The output per worker per month is 40 units. The per-worker hiring and layoff costs are $2,000 and $3,000, respectively. There is no beginning inventory, and the starting workforce is 200. It costs the company $20 to carry an item in inventory each month, and the stockout cost is estimated to be $50 per unit.

Develop a chase sales and operations plan for this firm. Develop the monthly production schedule and show the labor workforce and inventory levels. Finally, compute the cost of the plan.

3. Formulate a chase sales and operations plan for a company with the following predicted demand:

Month	1	2	3	4	5	6	Total
Demand	7,500	9,000	6,000	9,000	15,000	6,000	52,500

The beginning workforce is 125 employees. The monthly output per employee is 150 units. The costs to hire and lay off a worker are $2,500 and $4,000, respectively. The cost to carry an item in inventory for one month is estimated at $10, and the stockout cost is $25 per unit. Show the production schedule, the inventory levels, and the changes in workforce from period to period. Compute the plan's cost.

LEVEL SOP

4. A company has predicted the following demands for the next six months:

Month	1	2	3	4	5	6	Total
Demand	15,000	18,000	15,000	20,000	22,000	24,000	114,000

A single worker working for one month can produce 125 units. The beginning workforce is 50 workers. It costs the company $1,500 to hire one worker, and it costs the company $2,500 to lay off a worker. The cost to carry an item is $15 per unit per month. The stockout cost is estimated to be $40 per unit.

Develop a level sales and operations plan for this firm. Develop the monthly production schedule and show the labor workforce and inventory levels. Finally, compute the cost of the plan.

5. Formulate a level sales and operations plan for a company with the following predicted demand:

Month	1	2	3	4	5	6	Total
Demand	6,300	9,000	6,000	9,000	15,000	6,000	51,300

The beginning workforce is 125 employees. The monthly output per employee is 150 units. The costs to hire and lay off a worker are $2,500 and $4,000, respectively. The

cost to carry an item in inventory for one month is estimated at $10, and the stockout cost is $25 per unit. Show the production schedule, the inventory levels, and the changes in workforce from period to period. Compute the plan's cost.

6. A company believes that its demand for the next six months is as follows:

Month	1	2	3	4	5	6	Total
Demand	6,000	8,000	10,000	6,000	9,000	12,000	51,000

The output per worker per month is 100 units. The per-worker hiring and layoff costs are $2,000 and $3,000, respectively. There is no beginning inventory, and the starting workforce is 200. It costs the company $20 to carry an item in inventory each month, and the stockout cost is estimated to be $50 per unit.

Develop a level sales and operations plan for this firm. Develop the monthly production schedule and show the labor workforce and inventory levels. Finally, compute the cost of the plan.

Capacity Planning

MODELING CAPACITY

7. A process is designed to produce 500 units per hour with a scrap rate of 1 percent and inherent inefficiencies of 10 percent. With actual output at 425 units per hour, compute design capacity, available capacity, actual capacity, capacity utilization, efficiency, and output gap measure.

8. A process is designed to produce 2,000 units per hour. The process has a scrap rate of 2 percent and an 8 percent inherent inefficiency. Assuming that the actual output of the process is 1,750 units per hour, what are the process design capacity, available capacity, actual capacity, capacity utilization, efficiency, and output gap for this process?

9. Calculate the process design capacity, available capacity, actual capacity, capacity utilization, efficiency, and output gap for a process that has been designed to produce 200 units per hour with a scrap rate of 0.5 percent, inherent inefficiencies of 4 percent, and actual output of 180 units per hour.

ROUGH-CUT CAPACITY PLANNING

10. The demand for three products selected from a company's sales and operations plan are shown next, along with each product's standard hours. Assuming that the company has 27,500 labor hours available during the next planning horizon, determine whether the sales and operation plan is feasible.

Product	Units Demanded	Standard Hours (in hours/unit)
A	25,000	0.4
B	14,500	1.1
C	11,500	0.2

Product	Units Demanded	Standard Hours (in hours/unit)
A	8,000	1.2
B	21,000	1.5
C	7,000	0.3
D	30,000	0.95

11. Shown below are the planning period's demand and the standard hours required for four products from a company's sales and operations plan. Assume that the company has 65,000 hours of labor available during the planning period, and determine whether the sales and operations plan is feasible.

Product	Units Demanded	Standard Hours (in hours/unit)
A	32,500	0.60
B	23,000	0.80
C	40,000	0.20
D	15,000	1.15

12. Determine whether the following is a feasible sales and operations plan. Assume that the company has 75,000 labor hours available during the next planning period time horizon.

Material Requirements Management

MRP LOGIC

13. Item A has a gross requirement for 1,000 in week 5. There are currently 300 of the item on hand, with a scheduled receipt of 100 items in week 2. The order quantity is lot for lot, and there is a two-week lead time. Complete the MRP record for item A.

14. Item A has a gross requirement of 2,000 in week 6. Currently, 500 units of Item A are on hand, with a scheduled receipt of 500 items in week 3. The lead time for item A is three weeks with an order quantity of 500. Complete the MRP record for item A.

15. Complete the MRP record for the end item, item A, that has a gross requirement of 500 in week 3 and 1,500 in week 5. The lead time for this item is two weeks. Currently, there are 300 items on hand, with a scheduled receipt of 100 items in week 2. The item has a two-week lead time, and its order quantity is lot for lot.

CASE   Montclair State University

Montclair State University sued Oracle over an allegedly botched PeopleSoft ERP (enterprise resource planning) software project, saying that a series of missteps and delays could ultimately cost the school some $20 million more than originally planned. The school entered into contracts with Oracle for a PeopleSoft suite that was supposed to replace a 25-year-old set of legacy applications. Those pacts included about $4.3 million for software and support. The school and Oracle also agreed on a $15.75 million fixed-fee contract for implementation services. Under the latter agreement's terms, Oracle would undertake the project in a series of "pillars," each with a specific completion date. In turn, the school would pay out the fixed fee in a number of "milestone" payments, "each of which was tied to Oracle's satisfactory completion of a particular project deliverable." Dubbed the Bell Tower Initiative, the project was supposed to be done over a 25-month period, according to Montclair.

Oracle, though, "failed to deliver key implementation services, caused critical deadlines to be missed, refused to make available computer resources that it had promised, failed to deliver properly tested software, and overall, failed to manage properly the project," the complaint from Montclair alleges. In the end, Montclair suspended the project, fired Oracle, and began looking for a replacement systems integrator. Oracle asked the school for about $8 million more than the original $15.75 million fixed fee to complete the job. In addition, Oracle blamed the school for the project's woes while accepting no responsibility for any problems, the complaint adds. Oracle then threatened to pull its staffers off the project if a new agreement wasn't reached.

Oracle fired back against Montclair's complaint, claiming that Montclair was responsible for a problematic ERP software project and saying that school officials embarked on a "scorched-earth" litigation campaign to cover up their own shortcomings. Oracle's filing attacked Montclair officials on this basis while denying wrongdoing on Oracle's part. "When issues arose during the course of the project, it became clear that [the university's] leadership did not adequately understand the technology and the steps necessary to complete the project," the filing stated. "Instead of cooperating with Oracle and resolving issues through discussions and collaboration, [Montclair's] project leadership, motivated by their own agenda and fearful of being blamed for delays, escalated manageable differences into major disputes."

After two years, the lawsuit between Montclair and Oracle was settled out of court. Although details of the settlement have not been publicly disclosed, it appears that the implementation cost Montclair more than $10 million more than it had planned.

Questions:

1. What mistakes were made by Montclair University?

2. What mistakes were made by Oracle?

3. What would you recommend to officials at Montclair?

4. What improvements should Oracle make in the future?

Sources: Based on C. Kanaracus, "Oracle Sued by University for Alleged ERP Failure," *PC World*, May 23, 2011; and C. Kanaracus, "Oracle Says ERP Software Woes Are School's Own Fault," *CIO*, May 31, 2011.

11 Logistics

INTEGRATING

GLOBAL SC&O STRATEGY

INNOVATING

Supply Management

Operations Management

Customer Relationship Management

IMPACTING

Upstream Processes

Core Processes

Downstream Processes

IMPROVING

QUALITY MANAGEMENT, ANALYTICS, AND LOGISTICS

CHAPTER OUTLINE AND LEARNING OBJECTIVES

1 Understand the Strategic Importance of Logistics

- Discuss how SC&O managers reduce costs and how their savings benefit companies.
- Describe how SC&O managers manage the flow of materials and how management helps streamline certain delivery systems.
- Explain how and why SC&O managers must pay keen attention to access and what consequences they may face if they do not take this aspect of logistics into account.
- Understand why and how a company's sustainability plays a key role in its logistics and why and how sustainability benefits a company over time.

2 Understand and Apply Fundamental Logistics Trade-Offs

- Calculate cost-to-cost trade-offs and explain how trade-offs in transportation are managed.

- Explain why and how modal trade-offs help logisticians choose between different modes of transportation.
- Calculate cost-to-service trade-offs and apply them when dealing with increasing service levels.
- Apply the concept of landed costs, especially in the context of lean decision making.

3 List and Apply the Five Logistics Processes

- Contrast independent and dependent demand and explain the role of derived demand.
- List, define, and apply the five processes: (1) demand processing, (2) inventory management, (3) transportation, (4) warehousing, and (5) structural networking.
- Understand transportation methods and be able to ascertain and apply the correct method when the situation calls for it.
- Explain reverse logistics.

Amazon Faces Last Mile Supply Chain Problems

Amazon disrupted the retail industry by creating seemingly endless inventory selection for consumers through online selection and presence. However, as the war for consumers between Amazon and other retailers heats up, inexpensive and fast shipping has become the battleground. Amazon is pursuing same-day shipping while its competitors are trying to catch up. Amazon has Prime, which allows consumers free shipping for a small annual fee. Competitors are responding by also adding free shipping on many shipments.

The problem for Amazon, however, is not its competitors. The real problem is that shipping directly to a consumer's doorstep rather than to a retailer storefront creates a lot of variability. According to NBC News, 23 million Americans reported packages had been stolen from their homes, thus creating the need for reshipping. In addition, routing of direct-to-home deliveries changes so frequently that carriers can never rely on the same routes twice. This variability in delivering to a consumer's doorstep in what is commonly called the last mile supply chain drives up the costs of logistics for a company. Recently, Amazon reported making around $6.5 billion with prime memberships and other shipping revenues, but Amazon's cost of shipping was around $11.5 billion. Amazon lost $5 billion in shipping.

In this chapter, we will discuss many of the tools and approaches used by companies such as Amazon in improving their bottom lines. We will return to Amazon's logistics at the end of the chapter.

U NDERSTAND THE STRATEGIC IMPORTANCE OF LOGISTICS

logistics
The transportation and storage of goods and materials.

logistics management
From the Council of Supply Chain Management Professionals: "That part of supply chain management that plans, implements, and controls the efficient and effective forward and reverse flow and storage of goods, services, and related information between the point of origin and the point of consumption to meet customers' requirements."

Intuitively, we know that *logistics* deals with the details of getting things done, but it is much more than that. **Logistics** provides economic utility through providing "place" and "time." The Council of Supply Chain Management Professionals defines **logistics management** as "that part of supply chain management that plans, implements, and controls the efficient, effective forward and reverse flow and storage of goods, services, and related information between the point of origin and the point of consumption in order to meet customers' requirements." From a functional perspective, logistics managers generally plan, move, and store materials and goods.

For many years, companies looked at logistics as simply a cost-absorbing function. Today, it is seen as a strategically important function for many firms. The good news is that you can affect a firm's performance by correctly addressing logistical needs.

Managing Across Majors 11.1 Strategy majors, note that logistics has become an important strategic concern for many firms.

Transportation and logistics play an important role in a firm's success. Not until the U.S. government deregulated transportation industries and information technology allowed managers to share inventory and forecasting data seamlessly did executives begin to realize that logisticians belonged in the corporate suite.

Logistics can be a source of competitive advantage.

From a more strategic perspective, logistics creates a competitive advantage for the company in four major areas: (1) cost, (2) flow, (3) access, and (4) sustainability. We will discuss each area separately.

Cost

Walmart has reduced its shipping and driver turnover costs through creating efficient and effective logistics systems. It is important to note that next to the cost of goods, logistics costs are generally the highest costs that a manufacturer has to pay (often as high as 20 percent of operating costs).

In the past, managers reduced logistical costs to win over customers. Today, however, most companies have reduced their inventories, streamlined transportation, and created effective flows in their warehouses to attract customers. Efficient, low-cost logistics has become an order qualifier, making effectively run logistics essential for competitiveness.

Logisticians are SC&O professionals dedicated to analyzing and coordinating the transportation, storage, and distribution of supplies, materials, commodities, and finished goods. Companies still frequently task logisticians with reducing the costs for a company. Logisticians can employ many techniques, information systems, and tactics, and these are discussed in logistics specific courses. Executives love to trim costs from the logistics bill because a dollar saved goes directly to the bottom line. Logisticians have many responsibilities, but most executives see cost savings as the primary responsibility for logistics managers.

As shown in FIGURE 11.1, logisticians focused on reducing logistics costs in grocery management because logistics costs are a large portion of the total costs per case. Logisticians emphasize the following:

1. Reducing or controlling transportation costs
2. Redesigning distribution networks
3. Responding to rising freight costs
4. Improving service
5. Collaborating closely with their retailers so that significant costs are cut from grocery distribution[1]

FIGURE 11.2 shows a comparison of freight transport intensity for several countries as a percentage of gross domestic product (GDP) that the freight generates. Generally speaking, more

logisticians
Business professionals dedicated to analyzing and coordinating the transportation, storage, and distribution of supplies, materials, commodities, and finished goods.

[1]Based on P. Dawe, E. von Koeller, A. Pittman, and C. Asonye, "Time to Shift Gears—Top Trends in the CPG Supply Chain," Grocery Manufacturers Association, October 2015.

FIGURE 11.1 >

Logistics Managers Focus on Improvement in the Grocery Industry

Source: Based on http://www.gmaonline.org/file-manager/GMA-BCG_Time_To_Shift_Gears-Top_Trends_in_the_CPG_Supply_Chain.pdf.

economically advanced countries spend less as a percentage of GDP on logistics than less economically advanced countries because economically advanced countries invest in infrastructure that drives down logistics spending. This gives freight transportation in advanced countries more "bang for the buck." Advanced countries can invest in logistics infrastructure because this spending increases a nation's GDP.

Managing Across Majors 11.2   Finance and accounting majors, pay close attention to logistics costs because they affect a firm's cost structure and bottom line.

Flow

managing flow
Using logistics to regulate the speed of movement of goods through a supply chain.

Another strategic responsibility that falls on logisticians' shoulders is governing the flow of the supply chain, or **managing flow**. Because logistics is responsible for storing and transporting goods through the supply chain, logisticians can speed up or slow down the supply

FIGURE 11.2 >

Logistics Costs as a Percentage of Gross Domestic Product

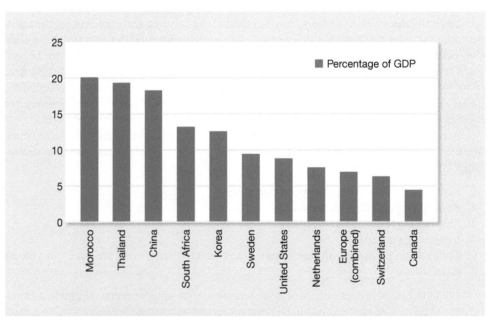

Source: Rantasila, K. and L. Ojala (2012), "Measurement of National-Level Logistics Costs and Performance," International Transport Forum Discussion Papers, No. 2012/04, OECD Publishing, Paris. DOI: http://dx.doi.org/10.1787/5k8zvv79pzkk-en.

Managing Flow for Fast Fashion

We discussed Zara from a strategic perspective in Chapter 2. We now discuss it from a logistics perspective. Zara, the Spanish fast-fashion retailer, uses logistics to ensure that the most recent fashion trends are on store shelves quickly. The secret to Zara's business strategy is the quick turnover of product lines within retail stores. In fact, Zara frequently stocks its shelves with fashion apparel that was displayed on fashion runways only three weeks earlier.

So how does Zara accomplish this fast-fashion supply chain? Zara has created a very cohesive logistics strategy between its factory operations and its retail stores. Zara creates clothing using just-in-time manufacturing and small batch sizes. Zara then ships these batches to retail stores to see what customers prefer. When Zara is informed about what is selling, not selling, or not available at retail stores, the factory produces what customers value most. The factory then uses its excess capacity and agile capabilities to manufacture the most popular styles.

Zara's commitment to a fast and steady tempo paced by order fulfilment to stores allows Zara to keep minimal inventory while still meeting customers' needs. Logisticians for Zara know that it delivers twice weekly from the factories in Bangladesh to the central distribution center in Spain. The shipments are then broken up and delivered to stores, usually in less than 24 hours to European stores and 40 hours to U.S. stores. The logistics costs of rapidly shipping inventory to stores are much more expensive than traditional, slower fashion shipping. However, Zara recoups the higher logistics costs by selling around 85 percent of its merchandise at full price, while those fashion retailers using slower supply chains sell only around 70 percent of their merchandise at full price. The fast flow necessary to accommodate fast fashion is facilitated by logistics.

Source: Based on https://www.forbes.com/sites/walterloeb/2015/03/30/zara-leads-in-fast-fashion/
#77ef445f5944https://www.tradegecko.com/blog/zara-supply-chain-its-secret-to-retail-success

chain as needed. Lean manufacturing strategies rely heavily on storage and transportation functions to ensure that materials and products truly do arrive "just in time." GLOBAL CONNECTIONS 11.1 discusses the issue of flow in more detail.

Access

As companies continue to expand into new markets, *access* becomes a strategic issue. For example, marketers may tell a company that there is significant demand for a product in Vietnam, but Vietnam's transportation infrastructure may be so inadequate that there is no way to reach this market. One of the strategic responsibilities of logisticians is to determine the accessibility of markets. Consumers in markets with poor infrastructure will have to bear the costs of difficult deliveries, so they must be prepared to understand the logistics costs and benefits of such markets. After the fall of the Soviet Union in 1991, many economists suggested that Russia was a prime market for Western goods. Because the 280 million citizens of the former Soviet states had been denied many of the market goods that Western Europe and the United States enjoyed, marketers expected a booming market. Logisticians would later tell companies, however, that Russia was not ready to be an export marketplace. Importing goods ran into too much red tape at the borders. In addition, the infrastructure was not efficient enough to import products cheaply. The efficient Russian railways were an exception, but Russian trains ran on a different gauge rail than the rest of the world. Therefore, every shipment going into Russia would have to be off-loaded onto a train equipped for the Russian rail. Even though there was a huge demand for these Western goods, the logistics made penetrating this market very difficult.

LOGISTICS ACCESS *Logistics access*, the ability of companies to deliver their product or service to a market affordably, does not apply only to countries with inadequate infrastructure. Business-to-business (B2B) and business-to-consumer (B2C) businesses must also consider logistics access.

B2C businesses frequently create logistics systems that do not consolidate orders or shipments, thus creating smaller, more-frequent shipments. This type of ordering drives up logistics costs, and managers must consider these costs when contemplating opening an online business.

ACCESS: NEARSHORING VERSUS OFFSHORING Companies must also consult logisticians when deciding whether to move their production facilities. Some companies relocate their production to the country that can offer the lowest manufacturing prices. This strategy is called offshoring. For example, in Guangdong, China's top exporting province, wages have greatly increased in recent years, and more than half the factories cannot find enough workers. As a result of these rising wages, factories that were once in China have now relocated to lower-cost production countries such as Vietnam. There is also some discussion about this production returning to the United States, in a process called nearshoring.

One aspect that managers must be acutely aware of when making offshoring decisions is the importance of logistics. When infrastructure is poorly developed or the type of business drives inefficient logistics, firms must be prepared to understand these consequences. For example, Nepal will probably never be a major offshoring manufacturer despite bordering both China and India and being a member of the World Trade Organization: Nepal has extremely difficult logistics hurdles to overcome. Nepal is landlocked, has one rail line to India, one railway to China, one international airport, and a very limited road system. In short, there is no inexpensive way to transport goods into or out of Nepal. Because offshoring relies on inexpensive transportation, logisticians would recommend that their company avoid offshoring to a country like Nepal.

landed cost
The total cost to get the product to the consumer.

Even when companies have good choices regarding offshoring locations, it pays to have logisticians involved in the decision. Logisticians help companies make decisions about which locations will offer the lowest **landed cost** (the total cost to get the product to the consumer) and the most reliable delivery. Logisticians offer companies great strategic value when executives make offshoring decisions. Important to deciding whether to offshore or to nearshore is the issue of managing supply chain disruptions. SC&O CURRENT EVENTS 11.1 tells of a few changes coming to logistics that may create technological disruptions.

Sustainability

Another area where logistics can help to improve competitiveness is in the area of logistics sustainability. *Logistics sustainability* initiatives are environmental initiatives and programs that save companies long-term costs, thus providing competitive advantage. Although logistics is very important for a company, it also affects the environment. The average 18-wheel commercial truck gets about 6 miles per gallon of diesel and emits about 50 grams of carbon dioxide per metric ton hauled per kilometer traveled. Many companies are doing their part to make sure that they increase the efficiency of their trucks to reduce both gas mileage and carbon emissions. In fact, the American Trucking Association, a lobbying group supporting truck transportation in the United States, suggests that all U.S. trucking companies should work with government to develop six specific recommendations:[2]

1. Enacting a national 65 mile per hour speed limit and limiting truck speeds to 65 miles per hour for trucks manufactured after 1992
2. Decreasing idling
3. Increasing fuel efficiency
4. Reducing congestion through highway improvements, if necessary by raising the fuels tax
5. Promoting the use of more productive truck combinations
6. Supporting national fuel economy standards for medium- and heavy-duty trucks

three cornerstones of sustainable logistics
(1) Society, (2) economy, and (3) environment.

All these initiatives are dedicated to increasing fuel efficiency while simultaneously improving both the truckers' profits and carbon emissions. FIGURE 11.3 shows the **three cornerstones of sustainable logistics**: (1) *society*, (2) *economy*, and (3) *environment*. The above recommendations address many of these concerns.

[2] For more information about these recommendations, go to http://www.truckline.com.

Coming Changes in Logistics

Logistics are changing very rapidly. Among the changes you will see are alternative forms of energy, driverless trucks, and the Hyperloop. With erratic fuel prices and social pressure to reduce carbon emissions, trucking companies are evaluating alternatives to the traditional diesel-powered engine. Trucking companies are currently exploring several different initiatives. The most frequent switch that has been happening is a switch from diesel to natural gas. Natural gas is a cleaner-burning energy source and is generally less expensive than diesel. Many companies whose fleet stays within a local area have switched to natural gas. BMW has also prototyped a tractor trailer that is 100 percent electric and that companies can use for local deliveries. Finally, a Utah-based company called Nikola has developed a truck powered entirely by a hydrogen fuel cell. The Nikola 1 truck has extended range, power equal to that of a diesel engine, and no emissions. As the search for cleaner and more efficient power sources continues, the trucking industry will also continue to see a shift toward cleaner engines.

One of the big issues that logistics companies face is that truck drivers, by law, are constrained on the number of hours that they must sleep each day. While autonomous passenger cars get a lot of press, the logistics industry is anticipating the advent of driverless trucks.

The American Trucking Association has declared that the shift to driverless trucks is inevitable. Driverless trucks will not need to sleep, change drivers, or have extra space used for driver sleepers. Driverless trucks will be able to move freight 24 hours a day without even the extra need for a cab. The Komatsu innovative autonomous haulage vehicle (IAHV) is a forerunner of what the future of autonomous trucking might be. The IAHV has no cab, thereby saving space for more haulage. The IAHV can drive a route back and forth with very little interaction with people. This saves companies the costs and variability of dealing with people and increases the amount of space utilized for hauling freight.

Elon Musk, the South African entrepreneur who founded Tesla and SpaceX, has recently put his entrepreneurial efforts behind building the Hyperloop. The Hyperloop is proposed to be a vacuum-sealed tube that uses magnetic levitation and Gaussian linear acceleration to propel pods within a tube at around 700 miles per hour. The technology proposes a high-speed; moderate, fixed-cost; and low variable-cost alternative for commuters and for freight. Musk suggests that the Hyperloop will be significantly cheaper to construct than high speed rail, have lower variable costs, and be more environmentally friendly.

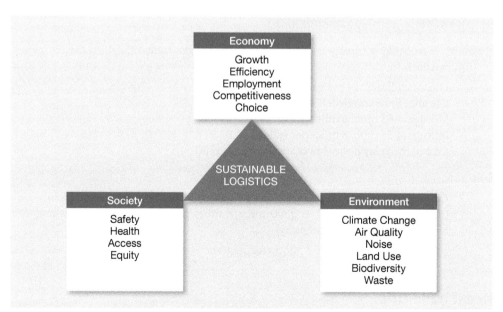

< FIGURE 11.3

The Three Cornerstones of Sustainable Logistics

Source: Based on The Three Cornerstones of Sustainable Logistics, http://www.greenlogistics.org.

FIGURE 11.4 >

Three Fundamental Logistics Trade-Offs

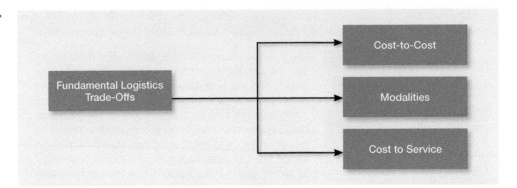

U NDERSTAND AND APPLY FUNDAMENTAL LOGISTICS TRADE-OFFS

Now that we understand how logistics adds strategic value to a company, we can discuss what logisticians do to add value. Fundamentally, logisticians, like all managers, are decision makers. One complication for logisticians is that every decision they make about one aspect of logistics influences all other areas of logistics. Logistics represents a system with fundamental trade-offs. Supply chain managers who do not recognize these trade-offs may very well create more problems than they initially intended to solve. Below, we discuss the **three fundamental logistics trade-offs**: (1) cost to cost, (2) modal, and (3) cost to service (**FIGURE 11.4**). Once we have covered these fundamental trade-offs, we can then see how logisticians calculate landed cost.

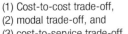

three fundamental logistics trade-offs
(1) Cost-to-cost trade-off,
(2) modal trade-off, and
(3) cost-to-service trade-off.

cost-to-cost trade-off
Trading off speed of delivery with saving fuel.

Cost-to-Cost Trade-Offs

In a **cost-to-cost trade-off**, a manager may be asked to slow down transportation to save fuel costs ("slow steaming" is quickly becoming a standard for ocean shipping liners). The reduced costs of slowing down the supply chain must be weighed against the increased cost of holding more inventories in warehouses, however. In other words, when the transportation system is slowed down to reduce costs, there is an increase in inventory carrying costs. Therefore, there is a cost-to-cost trade-off. To create the greatest value for their company, managers must understand these trade-offs. We demonstrate this in **SOLVED PROBLEM 11.1**.

---

f(x)   SOLVED PROBLEM 11.1 >

MyLab Operations Management Video

Cost-to-Cost Trade-Off Calculations

Problem: A trucking company is exploring the cost-to-cost trade-offs given the following information:

> Fuel cost (diesel): $4 per gallon
> Distance to be traveled: 800 miles
> Mileage at 65 mph: 6 miles per gallon
> Mileage at 55 mph: 8 miles per gallon
> Cost of the delay if the slower speed is used: $100

Solution:

> Cost at 65 mph = (800 miles/6 miles per gallon) × $4 per gallon = $533.33
> Cost at 55 mph = $100 + ([800 miles/8 miles per gallon] × $4 per gallon) = $500.00 (adding the cost of delay)

> Therefore, the slower speed should be used.

Modal Trade-Offs

Another fundamental trade-off that managers must understand is the one between and within the various modes of transportation, called a modal trade-off. For example, shipping freight on a train is much less expensive than shipping freight on a truck. However, trains are limited in where they can travel, have higher damage rates than trucks, and historically have had worse on-time service than trucks. If managers always made decisions based on costs, they could make mistakes that cost the company. Because they affect the entire logistical system, modal trade-offs are very important in logistics systems.

Cost-to-Service Trade-Offs

The **cost-to-service trade-off** suggests that improving service or service levels will cost additional money for the company. This trade-off is probably the most difficult one to conceptualize because the relationship between the value that service provides and the costs required to increase service is nonlinear. Instead, the relationship is based on the economic law of diminishing returns, which suggests that as you get closer to the maximum service level, the more difficult and more expensive it is to achieve each incremental improvement. For instance, a retailer may decide to carry enough Hershey's chocolate bars to ensure that 95 percent of the time, a customer looking for a Hershey's bar will find it. Sufficient inventory to have this 95 percent service level of chocolate may cost the retailer $30 million in inventory costs across all its stores. The nonlinear nature of the costs may mean that, if the retailer decides to carry enough chocolate so that 96 percent of the time the customer will find his or her chocolate in stock, it may cost the company $60 million. Cost-to-service trade-offs must be carefully considered because the nonlinear marginal costs make it a very tricky trade-off.

> **cost-to-service trade-off**
> Cost of improving service and service levels.

Generally, when evaluating cost-to-service trade-offs, managers attempt to establish a threshold level of service at a reasonable cost. This threshold service is the starting point in the process of deciding what a company's customer service policy should be.

This relationship is demonstrated in FIGURE 11.5 in terms of the customer's willingness to pay. The customer will not be willing to pay if the cost is high relative to the delivery time. Notice that the amount that the customer is willing to pay drops nonlinearly as the delivery time gets longer. Such is the fine line that logistics providers must tread. Sometimes logistics providers mask costs by using fuel surcharges.

Landed Cost

The guiding principles that generally help logistics managers integrate all the trade-offs in a meaningful way are encapsulated in landed cost analysis. To achieve the lowest landed costs, all logistics activities must be constructed as a system and must be well coordinated. If managers optimize only one area of logistics, the resulting trade-offs may increase the total cost of the system. For example, moving inventory by truckload (TL) shipments is usually less expensive on a per-unit basis than moving inventory by less-than-truckload (LTL) shipments. When a truckload of a product is ordered to reduce transportation costs, however, inventory holding costs

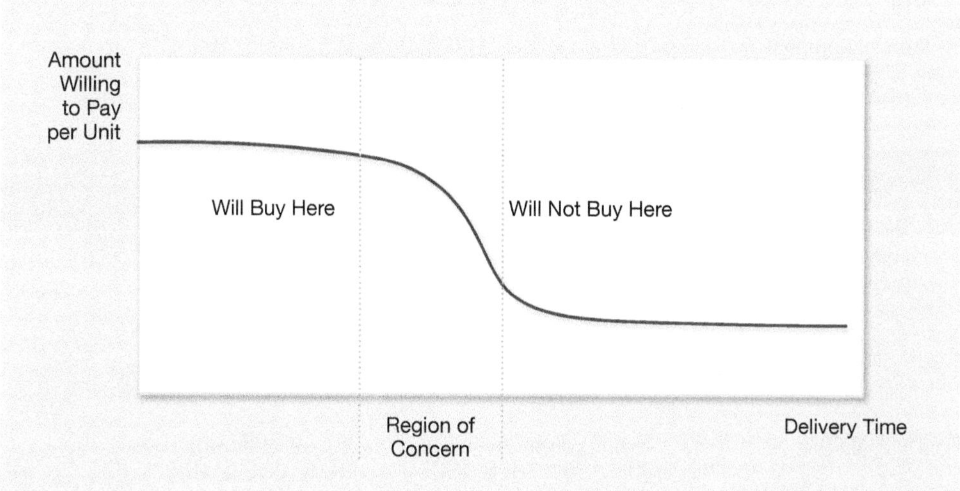

< FIGURE 11.5

Cost-to-Service Trade-Offs Considering Customer Willingness to Pay

increase, which may also increase the total logistics costs. Another example is *lean manufacturing*. One of the biggest strategic changes to supply chains in recent years is the implementation of lean inventory systems, or simply lean. Lean provides the ability to purchase minimal supplies to produce goods and the ability to minimize work-in-process inventories while simultaneously meeting production schedules. Lean created tremendous efficiencies by greatly reducing inventory costs and freeing up capital for other investments. It also improves product and process quality because defects are not "hidden" in extensive inventories.

However, lean operates under the assumption that holding inventory is relatively expensive when compared to transportation. This key logistics trade-off between inventory and transportation may be changing. Lean relies heavily on smaller transportation loads shipped using fast transportation. When lean started, interest rates on capital were high, and holding inventory was expensive in relation to transportation. As diesel fuel prices have increased and the transportation distance in the supply chain has been lengthened, transportation prices have increased. Simply put, the cost of holding inventory has fallen while transportation costs have risen. If transportation prices continue to rise and if inventory costs continue to fall, holding the minimal inventories prescribed by lean manufacturing may become more expensive than holding larger inventories.

The lean manufacturing example provides evidence for why considering landed cost instead of individual functional costs is so important. In the case of lean, changing these costs could create a major strategic shift for many companies. See **SOLVED PROBLEM 11.2**.

SOLVED PROBLEM 11.2 >

MyLab Operations Management
Video

Landed Cost Trade-Off Calculations

Problem: Your boss recently informed you that one of your major suppliers offered you a lower unit price by 1¢ (from $10 to $9.99) on the power cords for the most popular television model that you produce. You use 100,000 of these power cords annually. In exchange for this lower unit price, the supplier wants to be able to increase your order quantity from 5,000 units to 7,500 units to extend its manufacturing runs. Given the information in the following cost table, what should you do?

Cost	As-Is Ordering	Bulk Discount Ordering
Unit cost	$10.00	$9.99
Unit transport cost	$0.10	$0.10
Inventory carrying cost (ICC) (as a percentage)	25%	25%
Ordering cost	$40.00	$40.00
Annual demand	100,000	100,000
Order quantity	5,000	7,500

Solution: To perform this calculation, you need to understand how changing each individual cost affects the total costs of this purchase. The following table shows the Excel formulas for each individual cost and for calculating total costs.

	As-Is Ordering	Bulk Discount Ordering
Holding cost	= (0.5*As_Is_Order_Quantity) *As_Is_Unit_Cost*As_Is_ICC	= (0.5*Bulk_Order_Quantity) *Bulk_Unit_Cost*Bulk_ICC

Ordering cost	= (As_Is_Annual_Demand / As_Is_Order_Quantity) *As_Is_Order_Cost	= (Bulk_Annual_Demand / Bulk_Order_Quantity) *Bulk_Order_Cost
Transport cost	= As_Is_Transport_Cost *As_Is_Annual_Demand	= Bulk_Transport_Cost *Bulk_Annual_Demand
Cost of goods	= As_Is_Unit_Cost *As_Is_Annual_Demand	= Bulk_Unit_Cost *Bulk_Annual_Demand
Total landed cost	= As_Is_Hold_Cost+ As_Is_Ordering_Cost+ As_Is_Total_Transport_Cost +As_Is_COGs	= Bulk_Total_Holding_Cost +Bulk_Total_Order_Cost+ Bulk Total_Transport_Cost + Bulk_COGs

By doing these calculations, you can show your boss that, although the bulk discount would save $1,000 in cost of goods and $266.67 in ordering costs, it would also increase holding costs by $3,115.63. Therefore, it would be cheaper to stay with the price and ordering quantity that your company is currently using. Here is your proof:

	As-Is Ordering	Bulk Discount Ordering
Holding cost	$6,250.00	$9,365.63
Ordering cost	$800.00	$533.33
Transport cost	$10,000.00	$10,000.00
Cost of goods	$1,000,000.00	$999,000.00
Total landed cost	**$1,017,050.00**	**$1,018,898.96**
	Difference in costs	**($1,848.96)**

IST AND APPLY THE FIVE LOGISTICS PROCESSES

From a process perspective, most logisticians manage five main functions: (1) *demand processing*, (2) *inventory management*, (3) *transportation*, (4) *warehousing*, and (5) *structural networks* (FIGURE 11.6). Because these functions are interdependent, SC&O managers must understand how management of one area influences all functional areas. After discussing these functions in depth, we address the idea and benefits of reverse logistics.

Demand Processing

One of the primary purposes of all logistics systems is to satisfy customers. As a manager attempts to satisfy customers, it quickly becomes apparent that understanding demand and adapting capacity to meet demand are vital functions of logistics.

Managers generally discuss three types of demand: (1) independent demand, (2) dependent demand, and (3) derived demand. Independent and dependent demand have previously been introduced. **Independent demand** is the demand that the customers actually create

independent demand
Forecasted demand.

FIGURE 11.6 >

The Five Logistics Processes

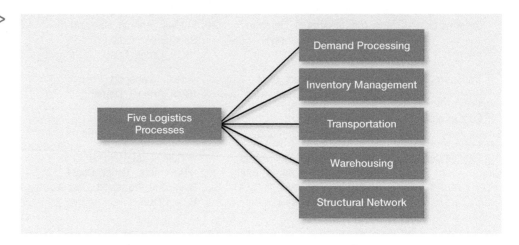

and is forecasted. It is the demand for the end product or service. Usually, managers are given information about this type of demand as historical data. Managers can then create a forecast for future independent demand.

Dependent demand is the demand created for production that is necessary to produce an end item and is calculated from the demand for a final product. If a customer tells a manufacturer that she wants to buy a chair, she creates dependent demand for four chair legs.

The third type of demand is derived demand. **Derived demand** (or imaginary demand) is created as managers conceptualize forecasts and guess at future demand; it exists only on paper. Derived demand is a major management issue and one that every logistician must understand.

When derived demand is introduced into logistics systems, the system capacity must expand to meet the imaginary needs of this demand, driving up costs and distorting the trade-offs between inventory, transportation, warehousing, and infrastructure. The goal of the logistician then is to remove as much derived demand as possible to be able to plan for the integration of the logistical system. One way to reduce derived demand is to share actual demand data, rather than forecasts, with everyone in the supply chain. Walmart has gone to the point of sharing cash register point-of-sale data with suppliers to ensure that they are receiving accurate demand. In addition, managers can be proactive by using statistical process control charts and other tools to make sure that inventory systems are not out of control. In short, managers must be aware of the importance of managing demand.

A second way that derived demand can be reduced is through reducing reliance on promotions and sales. Promotions and sales are effective marketing strategies that artificially raise demand, but the artificial spikes in demand that result ripple through the logistics systems. Logistics systems work best when demand is stable and predictable; promotions and sales create instability. Part of Walmart's logistics strategy has been to promote everyday low prices rather than sales. This strategy provides the system with the steady, stable demand needed to put consistent logistics systems in place.

The biggest logistics trade-off that has been realized due to demand management is the ability to trade information for inventory. SC&O managers realize this cost-to-service trade-off when they understand demand well enough to know when they can reduce inventory levels or when they can get rid of slow-moving items.

Let's return to the Hershey's chocolate bars mentioned earlier. Retailers often keep extra chocolate bars as safety stock in a back room of a retail store. When a company has hundreds of retail stores, this strategy creates a huge amount of extra chocolate bars that the company has to hold, thus increasing the potential for this chocolate to go past its shelf life and increasing the amount of money the company has to spend on chocolate bars. If the company realizes that demand for chocolate is steady with very little variability, it can remove the Hershey's bars from the retail back room and centralize the safety stock of Hershey's bars at a distribution center. Then the retail stores that need extra chocolate because their store has a spike in demand during finals week, for example, can still get to the safety stock in a reasonable time. The centralization of the chocolate inventory allows the company to reduce its inventory levels of

derived demand
Demand created as managers conceptualize forecasts and guess at future demand; it exists only on paper.

Hershey's bars greatly. In essence, the information that chocolate demand is steady translates into providing similar service levels to customers while simultaneously reducing costs.

Inventory Management

The next major logistics function that SC&O managers must understand is inventory management, the activities employed to order and maintain the optimum amount of each inventory item. One major difference between inventory management in logistics and traditional inventory management is that logisticians manage inventory throughout the value chain. Logistics managers oversee the inventory in manufacturing warehouses, in finished goods warehouses, en route, and in customer distribution centers. Operations managers are primarily concerned with the inventory to support production, but logisticians must be concerned with the inventory at every point of the supply chain because local inventory depends on the entire inventory in the supply chain (FIGURE 11.7).

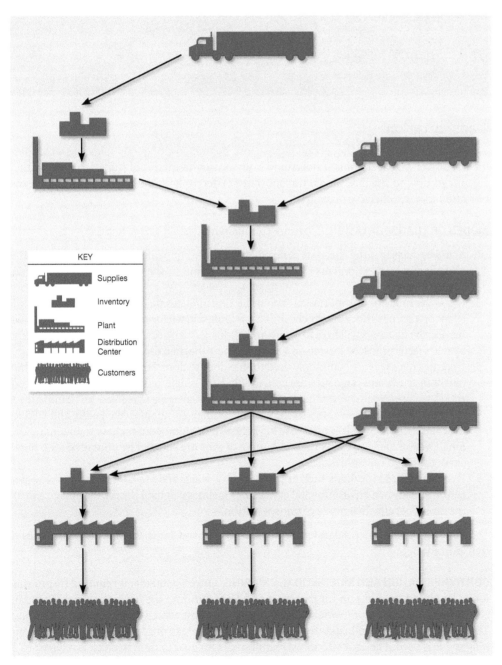

< FIGURE 11.7

Inventory Is Staged and Transported at Each Stage of the Supply Chain

KEY

Supplies

Inventory

Plant

Distribution Center

Customers

Pipelines are also a mode of transportation.

Transportation

Transportation is usually the second largest cost, behind cost of goods sold, that a company incurs. SC&O managers must understand how to use the modes of transportation to their advantage, how to use intermodal transportation effectively, and the global nature of transportation to be an effective manager.

MODES OF TRANSPORTATION There are five main modes of transportation:

1. *Maritime shipping* is the cheapest per tonnage of the nonpipeline carriers and is often used globally for large shipments. Most products arriving in the United States from China come on ships.
2. *Rail* is the mode of transportation within the United States that carries the most weight in terms of tons. It is also relatively cheap, but it is limited in where it can go. To get door-to-door service, the materials will have to be on- and off-loaded to trucks. To receive direct shipments by rail, a facility must be located on a railroad where the train can stop and be unloaded.
3. *Trucks and cargo vans* are commonly used to ship door to door. For example, most retail shipping is by truck, and cargo vans are used to ship large, single items. Although these methods are relatively inexpensive, routing both ways full and managing schedules can be difficult.
4. *Air* is the most expensive way to ship. Air is used by companies like FedEx and UPS for overnight shipments. It is also best for lightweight shipments such as semiconductors. Small, very expensive items such as human organs are shipped by **couriers**, who hand-carry the cargo on airlines.
5. *Pipelines* are used for fluids such as petroleum or water and are controversial due to perceived and known environmental concerns. Pipelines can haul the most tonnage and are the most cost effective mode of transportation.

TABLE 11.1 shows a comparison of considerations and costs for the various modes of transportation.

CONTAINERIZATION AND MULTIMODAL SHIPPING Once a container is removed from a ship, it can be placed onto a train for transport and later put onto the back of a truck. Standard containers have made worldwide shipping much more cost effective and safe than in the past. The use of containers eliminates the need to unload and reload product every time a new shipping mode is used. The ability to move seamlessly from boat to train to truck is referred to as multimodal shipping.

couriers
Companies hired to make expedited shipments.

multimodal shipping
A shipping method contracted with a single carrier or a non-asset-based integrator who works with subcarriers who do various types of shipping. Also known as intermodal shipping.

global trade agreements
The legal terms necessary to import goods.

North American Free Trade Agreement (NAFTA)
An agreement that created a trade bloc consisting of the United States, Canada, and Mexico as an effort to remove trade barriers among these three countries.

v TABLE 11.1

A Comparison of Different Transportation Modes					
	Maritime	**Railroads**	**Motor Carrier**	**Airlines**	**Pipeline**
Fixed costs	Container ship: $145 million	Locomotive: $2.3 million	Freightliner: $100,000	Boeing planes: $275 million	20″ pipeline: $1 million per mile
Variable costs	Low	Moderate	High	High	Very low
Speed	Average 25 mph*	Average 24 mph	Average 56 mph	Average 560 mph	Average 6 mph
Capacity	10,000 TEUs[†] or 480 million lbs.	25 million lbs on a 100-railcar train	45,000 lbs per trailer	12,000 lbs	1600 barrels of oil per mile or 490,000 lb per mile
Fuel economy	1,000 ton-miles per gallon	347 ton-miles per gallon	105 ton-miles per gallon	6.1 ton-miles per gallon	Not applicable (N/A)
Carbon footprint (grams per metric ton/km)	13 grams	17 grams	50 grams	550 grams	N/A[‡]

*Some shipping lines are slow steaming to conserve fuel, which increases fuel efficiency.
[†]Twenty-foot equivalent unit, which is an inexact measure of volume on a cargo ship.
[‡]Although there are no transport-related carbon dioxide emissions, Nacap estimates that 325.1 tons/km are released for the total construction of a 20-inch pipeline. Most of this carbon dioxide emission is from the production of the steel pipe.

Multimodal shipping (also commonly known as intermodal shipping) is contracted with a single carrier or a non-asset-based integrator who works with subcarriers who do various types of shipping. For example, when a shipper contracts with a sea carrier to move materials from China, the carrier might contract with rail and truck companies to complete the shipments. The original carrier with whom a shipper contracts is responsible for the safety of the shipment throughout the entire journey, from origin to destination.

GLOBALIZATION We have talked throughout about the importance of global supply chains and operations. In many cases, international logistics has been made easier as a result of global trade agreements. **Global trade agreements** are the legal terms necessary to import and export goods. Such agreements are made by trading partners' governments. Global trade agreements are important because they remove import tariffs on shipments, which can save firms millions of dollars.

One example of a trade agreement is the **North American Free Trade Agreement (NAFTA)**. This agreement created a trade bloc consisting of the United States, Canada, and Mexico as an effort to remove trade barriers among these three countries. Canada and Mexico are now the first- and third-largest export partners with the United States and are the top two purchasers of U.S.-made goods. **FIGURE 11.8** shows a map of the major trade agreements around the world.

Often, in international trade, **third-party logistics providers** are used to perform supply chain management functions. These companies provide all or part of the logistics function for another company. They can provide a number of logistics services, such as warehousing, transportation, and value-added logistics services. **Value-added logistics services** perform functions such as

A shipping container being loaded onto a seagoing vessel.

FIGURE 11.8 >

**Major World Trade
Agreements**

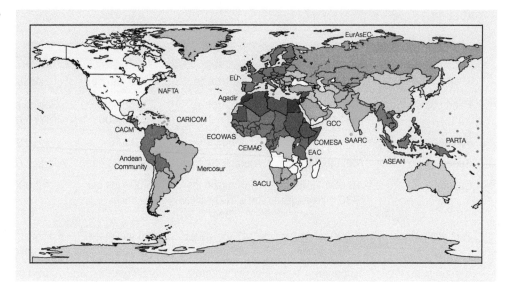

third-party logistics providers
Companies that provide all or part
of the logistics function for another
company.

value-added logistics services
Services that perform functions that
are not traditional logistics functions,
such as purchasing and production.

freight forwarder
An individual or company that
facilitates moving product from
producer to final destination.

purchasing and production that are not traditional logistics functions. We discuss value-added logistics services by one provider, DHL, in GLOBAL CONNECTIONS 11.2.

Despite global trade agreements, it is sometimes difficult to move materials through customs in many countries. U.S. companies have historically had trouble importing products into Japan because of arcane laws. For example, presuming that "the pen is mightier than the sword," Japanese customs declared that 200 pens made in the United States needed a special imports weapons license.[3]

To help navigate these difficult trade gauntlets, freight forwarders are used. A **freight forwarder** is an individual or company that facilitates moving product from producer to final destination. Freight forwarders handle a lot of the paperwork associated with shipping, including commercial invoices, export declarations, bills of lading, special fees, and whatever else is needed to complete shipments.

Warehousing

warehouse
A facility for storing inventory.

A **warehouse** is a facility for storing inventory. Warehouses are among the largest facilities in the world, sometimes covering more than a square mile. Warehouses are much more than just places to store inventory: They are often used to repackage and sort product.

DHL Adds Value in Brazil with an Automotive Competence Center

DHL Global Forwarding, the air and ocean freight specialist within Deutsche Post DHL, has opened a new automotive competence center in São Paulo, Brazil. The center bundles all the importing and distribution of international automotive supplies for the local automobile manufacturing market. Both first-tier suppliers and original equipment manufacturers have found the center to be of major importance, mainly because of the value-added activities (easing import) that DHL performs.

At the center, a team of 17 freight forwarders and customs brokers streamline the international automotive supply chain in collaboration with other countries and regions around the world so that local suppliers and manufacturers do not ever need to worry about the difficulty of importing parts. Instead, they can simply call the automotive competence center and be confident that their parts will arrive in a timely manner.

Source: Based on http://www.dp-dhl.com/en/media_relations/press_releases/2012/dhl_increases_presence_brazilian_automotive_market.html

[3] "Customs Officials Say Pens Need Weapons Import License," *Japan Today*, July 14, 2012.

Warehouses are among the largest facilities in the world.

SQUARE ROOT RULE Before we discuss the logistics of warehousing, let's first address one of the most important decisions an SC&O manager must make: how many warehouses to place in different locations. The square root law is generally considered in the structure function of logistics, but because it is so intertwined with the warehousing function, it is important to understand it in a warehousing context. The **square root rule** is

square root rule
A calculation for calculating safety stock inventory in warehouses, given the number of warehouses.

$$x_2 = x_1\sqrt{\frac{n_2}{n_1}}$$ (11.1)

where

n_1 = number of existing facilities
n_2 = number of future facilities
x_1 = total safety stock inventory of present facilities
x_1 = total safety stock inventory in future facilities

< SOLVED PROBLEM 11.3

MyLab Operations Management
Video

Warehousing Square Root Rule in Action

Problem: At present, a firm has 100,000 units of safety stock located in four facilities. It is considering expanding to 16 warehouses. What will be the change in safety stock inventory if each unit in inventory costs $1? It is expected that this investment will result in an additional $300,000 in revenue due to better inventory placement.

Solution: Use Equation 11.1:

$$x_2 = 100,000 \times \sqrt{\frac{16}{4}} = 200,000 \text{ units}$$

At $1 per unit, these units represent $200,000 more in inventory investment for inventory residing in future warehouses. So $300,000 (in increased revenue) − $100,000 (increase in costs) = $200,000 (total revenue increase before taxes) is potentially a good investment. Note that initially the inventory cost $100,000 and then increased to $200,000, which was a $100,000 increase in costs.

Now that we have established how many warehouses to build, the next task is to decide where these warehouses should be located. Several models are used in logistics to determine warehouse location. Two types of models that are both powerful and simple are the weighted center of gravity and the transportation method.

weighted center of gravity method
A method to identify a good (but not necessarily an optimal) location for the placement of a new facility.

WEIGHTED CENTER OF GRAVITY METHOD   The **weighted center of gravity method** is used to identify a good (but not necessarily an optimal) location for the placement of a new facility. This method assumes a gridlike (x, y) Cartesian coordinate plane. It is often an appropriate method because many cities and highway systems are structured in a gridlike manner. The weighted center of gravity method uses the following equations:

$$\text{weighted } x \text{ coordinate} = x^* = \frac{\sum_{i=1}^{I} Q_i \, x_i}{\sum_{i=1}^{I} Q_i} \tag{11.2}$$

$$\text{weighted } y \text{ coordinate} = y^* = \frac{\sum_{i=1}^{I} Q_i y_i}{\sum_{i=1}^{I} Q_i} \tag{11.3}$$

where:

$x^* =$ a best location on the x axis of the grid
$y^* =$ a best location on the y axis of the grid
$Q_i =$ the weighting factor or total quantity shipped from the "best" location
$x_i =$ the x position of demand for point i
$y_i =$ the y position of demand for point i

FIGURE 11.9 shows an x, y Cartesian grid for four different towns in a particular county. The purpose of the weighted center of gravity method is to find a "best" location for a distribution center to ship to these four towns. Realize that we used number of shipments here as our Q_i. In other situations, you might use other weights, such as population or average income multiplied by population. The solution is demonstrated in SOLVED PROBLEM 11.4.

FIGURE 11.9 >

***x, y* Grid for Current Demand Locations with Numbers of Shipments to Those Locations Annually**

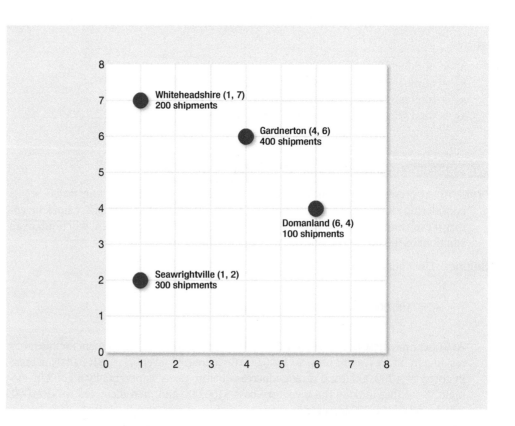

Weighted Center of Gravity in Action

Problem: Find the solution for the "best" location of a distribution center for the four towns in Figure 11.9 using the weighted center of gravity method.

Solution: Note that $Q_i = (200 + 400 + 100) = 1,000$ total shipments. Using Equations 11.2 and 11.3, we find

$$\text{weighted } x \text{ coordinate} = x^* = \frac{\sum_{i=1}^{I} Q_i x_i}{\sum_{i=1}^{I} Q_i}$$

$$= \frac{200 \times 1 + 400 \times 4 + 100 \times 6 + 300 \times 1}{1,000} = 2.7$$

$$\text{weighted } y \text{ coordinate} = y^* = \frac{\sum_{i=1}^{I} Q_i y_i}{\sum_{i=1}^{I} Q_i}$$

$$= \frac{200 \times 7 + 400 \times 6 + 100 \times 4 + 300 \times 2}{1,000} = 4.8$$

As shown in FIGURE 11.10, the new distribution center will be located in the area of (2.7, 4.8). The analysts should now start working with commercial real estate agents and brokers to secure the location.

< SOLVED PROBLEM 11.4

MyLab Operations Management
Video

Transportation Method

A linear programming tool used in scheduling shipments to different locations is the **transportation method**. This method uses the following components:

- *Sources:* A finite number of locations that can allocate resources, subject to capacity limitations
- *Destinations:* A finite number of locations that are demanding resources in specified quantities
- *Homogeneous resources:* The resources ordered being the same, regardless of destination or point of origin
- *Costs:* Known and constant shipping costs from each source to each destination

transportation method
An optimization technique for allocating shipments from sources to destinations.

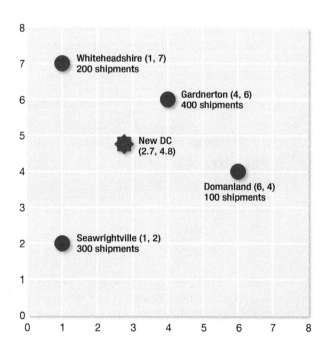

< FIGURE 11.10

Desired Location for the New Distribution Center at Point (2.7, 4.8)

The objective function for a transportation problem is

$$\text{minimize } TC = \sum_{i=1}^{I} \sum_{j=1}^{J} T_{ij} S_{ij} \tag{11.4}$$

subject to the following constraints:

$$\sum_{j=1}^{J} S_{ij} \leq C_i \text{ for all production facilities } i \tag{11.5}$$

$$\sum_{i=1}^{I} S_{ij} \geq D_j \text{ for all demand locations } j \tag{11.6}$$

$$S_{ij} \geq 0; \text{ nonnegativity constraint} \tag{11.7}$$

where

TC = total cost
T_{ij} = cost of shipping one unit from production facility i to destination j.
S_{ij} = quantity of units shipped from production facility i to destination j.
C_i = capacity at production facility i
D_j = demand at destination j

If you are not familiar with linear programming, these formulas can seem confusing, but their application is quite straightforward. In SOLVED PROBLEM 11.5, we solve a transportation method problem with three production sources and four demand destinations.

USING >
TECHNOLOGY 11.1

The Transportation Method in Action

f(x)   SOLVED PROBLEM 11.5

Problem: TABLE 11.2 shows three production locations (Atlanta, Denver, and Pittsburgh) and four demand destinations (St. Paul, Chicago, St. Louis, and Kansas City). The from/to matrix also gives the costs of shipping from each destination to each demand location. For example, it costs $1,100 per ton to ship from Atlanta to St. Paul. All the costs are given in Table 11.2.

TABLE 11.2 >

From/To Matrix with Costs

From \ To	St. Paul	Chicago	St. Louis	Kansas City
Atlanta	1,100	700	600	800
Denver	900	1,000	850	600
Pittsburgh	860	500	600	840

TABLE 11.3 shows the same table with the productive capacities (supply) for each plant and the demands for each destination. For example, Atlanta can produce 3,000 units, and St. Paul has a demand for 1,000 units.

TABLE 11.3 >

From/To Matrix with Costs, Productive Capacities, and Destination Demands

From \ To	St. Paul	Chicago	St. Louis	Kansas City	Supply
Atlanta	1,100	700	600	800	3,000
Denver	900	1,000	850	600	2,000
Pittsburgh	860	500	600	840	5,000
Demand	1,000	2,000	1,500	3,000	

Find the solution to this problem using Solver in Excel, which provides the lowest-cost solution. *Note:* Solver must be installed within your Excel package.

Solution: **FIGURE 11.11** shows the problem as it should be set up in Excel.

	A	B	C	D	E	F	G	H	I
1								*Excess*	
2	from\to	St Paul	Chicago	St Louis	Kansas City	*Supply*	*Shipped*	*Supply*	
3	Atlanta	0	0	0	0	3000	0	3000	
4	Denver	0	0	0	0	2000	0	2000	
5	Pittsburgh	0	0	0	0	5000	0	5000	
6	*Demand*	1000	2000	1500	3000				
7	*Shipped*	0	0	0	0				
8	*Cost =*	0							
9									

∧ FIGURE 11.11

Transportation Problem Formatting in Excel

We now need to establish an objective function and constraints. The objective function is assigned to cell B8 and is = 1100*B3+700*C3+600*D3+800*E3+900*B4+1000*C4+850*D4+600*E4+860*B5+500*C5+600*D5+840*E5. This function uses Equation 11.4 and sums the product of shipping costs and the amount shipped from the productive origin and the demand destination.

In addition, the shipped amounts are summed by rows. For example, cell G3 is summed as = (B3+C3+D3+E3). The result is the total amount shipped from Atlanta. Similar formulas must be written for Denver and Pittsburgh using their relative row numbers. Using a similar logic, the "shipped" amounts must be summed. For example, for St. Paul (cell B7), the formula is = (B3+B4+B5). Similar summations are made for Chicago, St. Louis, and Kansas City. The "Excess Supply" column is computed by subtracting column G from column F.

The constraints are given in **FIGURE 11.12** using Equations 11.5, 11.6, and 11.7. First, "Set Objective" refers to the cell where the objective function is found (B8). Because we are minimizing shipping costs, we choose the "Min" function.

∧FIGURE 11.12

Transportation Problem Constraints

(continued)

We minimize by "Changing Variable Cells" $B$3:$E$5. Those cells are highlighted in yellow in **FIGURE 11.13**. The first constraint is the nonnegativity constraint, which makes all the shipping amounts at least zero. Because the product of two negative numbers is positive, this constraint is needed; without it, you could have a solution that involves shipping an infinitely large negative amount, which is illogical.

The next constraint ($B$7:$E7 = $B$6:$E$6) ensures that no more will be shipped than is demanded. The final constraint ($G3:$G5 <= $F$3:$F$5) makes sure that the amount shipped does not exceed the amount available. Next, press Solve.

As shown in Figure 11.13, 1,000, 2,000, and 1,500 units will be shipped from Pittsburgh to St. Paul, Chicago, and St. Louis, respectively; 2,000 units will be shipped to Kansas City from Denver; and 1,000 units will be shipped to Kansas City from Atlanta. This strategy gives an optimal low cost of $4.76 million.

	A	B	C	D	E	F	G	H
1								*Excess*
2	from\to	St Paul	Chicago	St Louis	Kansas City	*Supply*	*Shipped*	*Supply*
3	Atlanta	0	0	0	1000	3000	1000	2000
4	Denver	0	0	0	2000	2000	2000	0
5	Pittsburgh	1000	2000	1500	0	5000	4500	500
6	*Demand*	1000	2000	1500	3000			
7	*Shipped*	1000	2000	1500	3000			
8	*Cost =*	4760000						

∧ **FIGURE 11.13**

Transportation Problem Solution

Configuring Logistics

We now turn to several ways of configuring logistic networks and warehouses, including consolidation warehousing, cross docking, break bulk facilities, and hub and spoke systems.

consolidation warehousing
Taking small shipments and combining them into more economical, larger shipments.

CONSOLIDATION WAREHOUSING As shown in **FIGURE 11.14**, **consolidation warehousing** takes small shipments and combines them into larger shipments that are more economical. This strategy is especially helpful when outgoing shipments are traveling a long distance or internationally.

cross docking
A warehousing approach whereby large shipments come in and are broken into smaller shipments to several locations.

CROSS DOCKING **Cross docking** occurs in warehousing when large shipments come in and are broken into smaller shipments to several locations. For example, a Frito-Lay's distributor may receive a large shipment of product from a centralized production facility. Because these products are often sold in convenience stores, it is not economical to drive an 18-wheel truck

FIGURE 11.14 >

Consolidation Warehousing Is Often Economical for Global Shipments

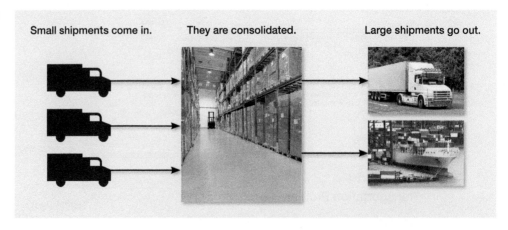

Small shipments come in. They are consolidated. Large shipments go out.

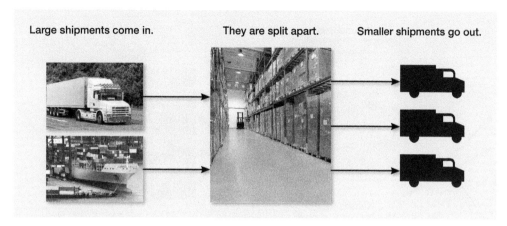

Large shipments come in.   They are split apart.   Smaller shipments go out.

Cross Docking Smaller Shipments to Several Locations

to several stores in an urban area. Instead the product is distributed to a number of delivery vans that bring product to the convenience stores (FIGURE 11.15).

BREAK BULK FACILITIES As shown in FIGURE 11.16, **break bulk facilities** are places where large shipments of the same items are broken out and separated to go to separate locations. For example, a large load of KitchenAid blenders may be shipped to a large regional warehouse for Target. These pallets are broken apart, and two blenders may be sent to restock a particular Target store.

break bulk facilities
Places where large shipments of the same items are broken out and separated to go to separate locations.

HUB AND SPOKE SYSTEMS A **hub and spoke system** is used to reduce the numbers of trucks or other carriers needed for shipping when there are networks of cities involved in the delivery. Due to the high cost of planes and maintenance, most airlines also use hub and spoke systems to operate economically. Hub and spoke systems use cross docking and break bulk facilities to be effective, as you can see in FIGURE 11.17.

Figure 11.17a shows a hubless system in which all possible routes from the six cities are possible. Shipments can go from any location to any location. There are a total of 20 possible routes, including long hauls from dispersed locations such as Seattle to Miami.

In Figure 11.17b, a centralized break bulk facility has been built in Kansas City, and the number of routes (and needed trucks) is reduced to only 10 (counting both ways). Reducing the number of trucks also reduces the routes by half and eliminates the long loads.

hub and spoke system
A method used to reduce the number of trucks or other carriers needed for shipping when networks of cities are involved in the delivery.

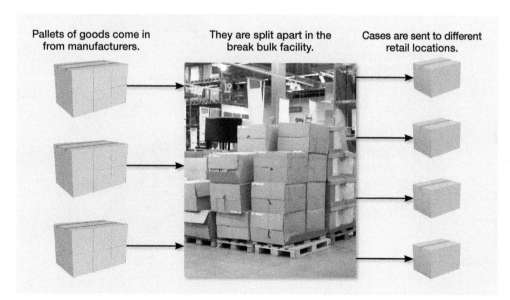

Pallets of goods come in from manufacturers.   They are split apart in the break bulk facility.   Cases are sent to different retail locations.

Break Bulk Facilities Are Needed When Large Shipments Need to Be Split Apart

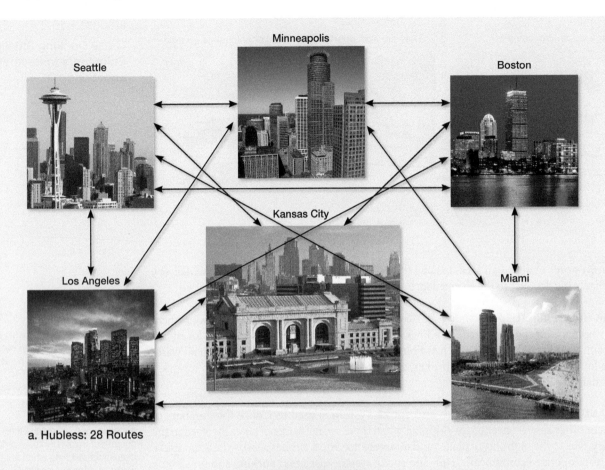

a. Hubless: 28 Routes

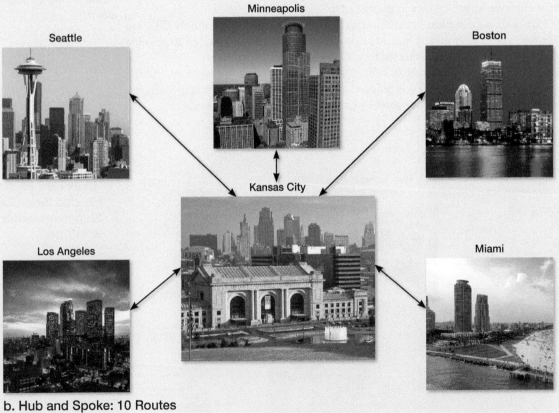

b. Hub and Spoke: 10 Routes

FIGURE 11.17 ∧

(a) Hubless and (b) Hub and Spoke Systems

Structural Network

The logistics structure of a supply chain has several dimensions, including (1) the extent of vertical integration, (2) flexibility, (3) cooperation, and (4) geographical dispersion.

Vertical integration is the extent to which the supply chain is outsourced versus being owned by the target firm. For example, does a supermarket chain buy eggs, or does it own an egg farm?

Flexibility is the supply chain's ability to respond to changes in customer needs or requirements. For example, can a logistics provider respond quickly with more trucks if there is a large set of orders from a customer?

Cooperation is the strength of integrated information and business models between logistics providers and customers. If information systems are integrated, the logistics network will be more responsive.

Geographical dispersion constrains the choice of logistics modes available, timing, and costs.

Reverse Logistics

A rapidly growing area in logistics is the management of reverse logistics. **Reverse logistics** occurs anytime you have to manage the reuse of products and materials, which often occurs with recycling. For example, you might be surprised that there are companies that specialize in moving hangers used in clothing and department stores back to the producers of the clothing in various parts of the world. Often, clothing is placed on hangers at the producer. As a result, hangers need to be shipped from clothing stores such as Zara back to production facilities. Reverse logistics is often associated with remanufacture and refurbishing of electronics products such as cell phones. Using supply chain language, reverse logistics involves moving product back upstream.

vertical integration
The extent to which the supply chain is outsourced versus being owned by the target firm.

flexibility
A supply chain's ability to respond to changes in customer needs or requirements.

cooperation
The strength of integrated information and business models between logistics providers and customers.

geographical dispersion
The extent to which a firm is spread out around the globe.

reverse logistics
Anytime you have to manage the reuse of products and materials.

In this chapter, we have talked about some of the approaches that world-class companies use to manage logistics. Recall the discussion of Amazon's last mile supply chain problems at the beginning of this chapter. Amazon is exploring technology solutions such as drone or robotic delivery, making the last mile delivery more predictable by employing Amazon lockers, which allow university bookstores to hold Amazon book shipments for students (driving more foot traffic to the bookstore), and working with key transportation partners already making last mile deliveries (Uber and Lyft, for example) to make the last mile supply chain less costly. Using Amazon Flex, the company pays private drivers $18 to $25 per hour to deliver packages as independent contractors. At the time of publication, Amazon Flex is already being implemented in large western U.S. cities such as Seattle, Las Vegas, Phoenix, and Dallas. In addition, Jeff Bezos, Amazon's founder, has alternatively considered either buying or replacing UPS. Amazon is also in discussion with smart home service providers to allow drivers to make deliveries in homes where no one is home. This could reduce theft, another high cost that Amazon incurs.

In short, Amazon realizes that its business model relies heavily on creating efficiency in the inefficient last mile. Amazon's largest cost is logistics, with the last mile making up 28 percent of logistics costs. Amazon is leveraging its innovative capabilities to solve the issues of last mile delivery in order to make its shipping more profitable.

Summary

In this chapter, we have introduced the important topic of logistics. We started by discussing the strategic importance of logistics in supply chains and operations. Many logistics decisions are difficult because they involve many different types of trade-offs involving cost parameters and service.

1. First, we discussed the strategic importance of logistics.
    a. Well-managed logistics results in savings going directly to the bottom line of the company.
    b. Well-managed logistics results in savings in cost with effective management of the flow of goods and materials.
    c. Logisticians understand the importance of access, especially in emerging economies.
    d. Logisticians are considering nearshoring as inventory costs lower and shipping costs increase.
    e. Well-managed logistics are good for the environment.

2. Logistics management involves trade-offs.
    a. Cost-to-cost trade-offs involve shipping decisions.
    b. Trade-offs are inherent in different shipping modes.
    c. Cost-to-service trade-offs help us determine appropriate service levels.
    d. Landed costs consider all these trade-offs to make better global decisions.

3. There are five logistic processes.
    a. Demand processing
    b. Inventory management
    c. Transportation
    d. Warehousing
    e. Structural networking

Throughout, we have emphasized the global nature of supply chains and operations. You now understand why professionals worry about logistics.

Key Terms

break bulk facilities   327
consolidation warehousing   326
cooperation   329
cost-to-cost trade-off   312
cost-to-service trade-off   313
couriers   318
cross docking   326
derived demand   316
flexibility   329
freight forwarder   320
geographical dispersion   329
global trade agreements   319

hub and spoke system   327
independent demand   315
landed cost   310
logisticians   307
logistics   306
logistics management   306
managing flow   308
multimodal shipping   319
North American Free Trade
    Agreement (NAFTA)   319
reverse logistics   329
square root rule   321

third-party logistics providers   319
three cornerstones of sustainable
    logistics   310
three fundamental logistics
    trade-offs   312
transportation method   323
value-added logistics
    services   319
vertical integration   329
warehouse   320
weighted center of gravity
    method   322

Integrative Learning Exercise

Select two companies from the Fortune 500 that are engaged in retailing or manufacturing. Research the logistics function for each of the companies you selected. How do these firms view their logistics function? Do they see it as a cost to be minimized or as a source of strategic importance? In what ways do the companies you identified seek to gain a competitive advantage through logistics?

Integrative Experiential Exercise

As part of a student team, visit a company that has a significant logistics function. Identify how this company manages its logistics function to achieve a competitive advantage. Be sure to address specifically the areas of cost, flow, access, and sustainability.

Discussion Questions

1. How does the Council of Supply Chain Management Professionals define logistics management?

2. What are the four major areas in which logistics can create a competitive advantage for a company?

3. What is meant by the term *logistics sustainability*? How are companies pursuing sustainability?

4. What are the major cornerstones of logistics sustainability? Why are they important?

5. What makes the cost-to-service trade-off the most difficult logistics trade-off to conceptualize?

6. What is the purpose of establishing a threshold service level in evaluating service trade-offs?

7. Should the concept of lean inventory systems always focus solely on minimizing inventory levels? Why or why not?

8. What is the difference between independent demand and dependent demand?

9. How does derived demand compromise the integrity and effectiveness of the logistics system?

10. What actions can be taken to reduce derived demand?

11. Discuss the information versus inventory trade-off in demand management.

12. What is consolidation warehousing? When (under what circumstances) is consolidation warehousing most helpful?

13. What is the purpose of employing a hub and spoke system?

14. List the five main modes of transportation. Of the non-pipeline carriers, which mode of transportation is cheapest per tonnage? Which mode carries the most weight within the United States?

15. What is reverse logistics, and why is it a rapidly growing area of logistics management?

Solved Problems

Fundamental Logistics Trade-Offs

COST-TO-COST TRADE-OFFS
SOLVED PROBLEM 11.1

1. A shipping company is evaluating the cost-to-cost trade-offs for the following situation:
   Diesel fuel cost of $4.25 per gallon
   Distance to be covered = 1,200 miles
   Miles per gallon at 70 mph = 6
   Miles per gallon at 60 mph = 7
   Cost of delay due to the slower mph = $200

   Solution:
   The cost at 70 mph is (1,200 miles/6 miles per gallon) × $4.25 per gallon = $850. The cost at 60 mph is (1200/7 miles per gallon) × $4.25 per gallon = $728.57. The difference in cost is $850 − $728.57 = $121.43, which is less than the cost of $200 due to the delay caused by the slower speed. Therefore, the slower speed should not be used.

LANDED COST
SOLVED PROBLEM 11.2

2. A major supplier has offered your company a lower price per unit for a component part that you use 200,000 units of annually. Currently, you order 10,000 units each time an order is placed, and you pay $25 per unit. Your ordering costs are estimated to be $75 per order regardless of the order size. Transportation costs are estimated to be $0.25 per unit. Your cost to hold a component part in inventory is estimated at 20 percent annually based on the cost of the purchased item. The supplier has offered you a cost of $23.50 per unit if you increase your purchasing quantity to 25,000. Should you continue with your current policy, or should you take the incentive offered by the supplier?

Solution:

A spreadsheet was developed as shown in Solved Problem 11.2 to summarize the costs. The results are as follows:

Inputs	As-Is Ordering	Bulk Discount Ordering
Unit cost	$25.00	$23.50
Unit transport cost	$0.25	$0.25
Inventory carrying cost, as a percentage	20%	20%
Ordering cost	$75.00	$75.00
Annual demand	200,000	200,000
Order quantity	10,000	25,000
Carrying cost	$25,000.00	$58,750.00
Ordering cost	$1,500.00	$600.00
Transport cost	$50,000.00	$50,000.00
Cost of goods	$5,000,000.00	$4,700,000.00
Total landed cost	$5,076,500.00	$4,809,350.00
Cost difference	−$267,150	

The total landed cost is $267,150 lower with the bulk ordering quantity of 25,000. It would be less expensive for the company to increase its order quantity size to 25,000.

The Five Logistics Processes

SQUARE ROOT RULE
SOLVED PROBLEM 11.3

3. A company currently carries 200,000 units of safety stock inventory located at nine facilities. The company believes that if it expands to 16 warehouses, it will realize an increase in revenue of $700,000 due to better customer service by reducing stockouts. If each unit in inventory costs $2, does the proposed plan make sense for the company?

Solution:

Using Equation 11.1, we find that $200,000 \times \sqrt{16/9} = 266,667$ units, which is an increase of 66,667 units $(266,667 - 200,000)$. At $2 per unit, this represents $133,334 more in inventory investment, for a safety stock inventory cost of $266,667 \times \$2 = 533,334$. With $700,000 in increased revenue expected from the expansion, the expansion is probably a good idea.

CENTER OF GRAVITY METHOD
SOLVED PROBLEM 11.4

4. Find the best location for a distribution center that will serve three locations at the following Cartesian coordinates:

City	x Coordinate	y Coordinate
City 1	7	3
City 2	2	4
City 3	4	6

The total quantity to be shipped from the distribution center to the cities is as follows:

City	Quantity to Be Shipped from the Distribution Center to the City
City 1	300
City 2	200
City 3	400

Solution:

Using the formulas for the weighted center of gravity, the best location for the distribution center is at Cartesian coordinates $(4.56, 4.56)$. $(x^*) = (2100 + 400 + 1600)/900 = 4.56$ and $(y^*) = (900 + 800 + 2400)/900 = 4.56$.

TRANSPORTATION METHOD
SOLVED PROBLEM 11.5

5. Large industrial motors are produced at three plants, in Boise, Richmond, and Lansing. The potential monthly production capacity at each of the plants is as follows:

Plants	Potential Monthly Supply
Boise	50
Richmond	75
Lansing	45

The monthly demands for the industrial motors for the following cities are as follows:

City	Monthly Demand
Salt Lake City	35
Chicago	60
Charlotte	45
Rochester	30

The per-unit shipping costs to transport the motors from each plant to the demand locations are given in the following cost matrix:

To From	Salt Lake City	Chicago	Charlotte	Rochester
Boise	375	550	800	675
Richmond	900	500	200	415
Lansing	650	250	390	300

Identify the optimal shipping plan that indicates the number of motors to be shipped from each plant to each demand location so that all demands are met and the lowest total shipping cost is achieved.

Solution:
The optimal shipping plan was determined using Excel's Solver. Boise should ship 35 motors to Salt Lake City and 15 to Chicago. Richmond should ship 45 motors to Charlotte and 30 to Rochester. Lansing should ship 45 motors to Chicago. The total cost of the optimal shipping plan is $54,075.

Quantity Shipped	Salt Lake City	Chicago	Charlotte	Rochester
Boise	35	15	0	0
Richmond	0	0	45	30
Lansing	0	45	0	0

Problems

Fundamental Logistics Trade-Offs

COST-TO-COST TRADE

1. You have been asked to evaluate the cost-to-cost trade-offs for the following situation:
   Diesel fuel cost of $5.00 per gallon
   Distance to be covered = 900 miles
   Miles per gallon at 75 mph = 6
   Miles per gallon at 55 mph = 8
   Cost of delay due to the slower mph = $500

2. A company would like to calculate a cost-to-cost trade-off analysis for the following scenario:
   Cost to ship by rail = $0.05 per unit per kilometer shipped
   Cost to ship by truck = $0.085 per unit per kilometer shipped
   Number of units to be shipped = 150,000
   Cost of delay due to slower shipping time if rail is used = $10,000
   Provide a cost-to-cost trade-off calculation for the rail-versus-truck alternative.

LANDED COST

3. A supplier to your company has offered you a reduced price per unit on a component if you agree to purchase the component in higher order quantities. Currently, you order 5,000 units each time an order is placed for the component, and you pay $10 per unit. Your ordering costs are estimated to be $150 per order regardless of the order size. Transportation costs are estimated to be $0.15 per unit. Your cost to hold a component part in inventory is estimated at 20 percent annually based on the cost of the purchased item. The supplier has offered you a cost of $9.50 per unit if you increase your purchasing quantity to 15,000. Currently, your company purchases 60,000 of these components annually, and this total demand is expected to remain constant for the foreseeable future. Should you continue with your current policy, or should you take the incentive offered by the supplier?

4. A supplier has offered your company a reduced price per unit for a component part you purchase if you will increase your purchase quantity from 20,000 to 40,000 units. Currently, you pay $30 per unit. The supplier has offered to reduce this cost to $28 per unit if you purchase the higher quantity. You purchase approximately 200,000 of the units annually. The cost to place an order is estimated to be $200 per order regardless of the order size. Transportation costs are estimated to be $0.20 per unit. Your cost to hold a component part in inventory is estimated at 20 percent annually based on the cost of the purchased item. Should you continue with your current policy, or should you take the incentive offered by the supplier?

The Five Logistics Processes

SQUARE ROOT RULE

5. Currently, a company has 50,000 units of safety stock for a product located in three warehouses. The company is contemplating expanding to nine warehouses. The company believes that this increased safety stock inventory investment with the new locations will result in an additional $600,000 in revenue due to improved customer service. Assuming that each unit in safety stock inventory costs $5, is the expansion to nine warehouses a potentially good idea?

6. A company currently has two stocking locations that hold a total of 8,000 units of safety stock inventory. If the company expands to six stocking locations, what would be the new safety stock inventory level for the company?

7. A company currently maintains inventory at eight stocking locations. The total safety stock inventory carried at these eight locations is 50,000 units. If the company decides to combine the eight locations into two, what will be the new safety stock inventory stocking level?

CENTER OF GRAVITY METHOD

8. A company must identify a location for a new distribution center. The distribution center will serve the five cities that have the following x and y Cartesian coordinates:

City	x Coordinate	y Coordinate	Annual Shipments to City from Proposed Distribution Center
City 1	9	3	5,000
City 2	12	6	8,000
City 3	6	11	4,000
City 4	9	12	9,000
City 5	5	8	15,000

Use the weighted center of gravity method to identify the location for the new distribution center.

9. A company must decide where to locate a new shipping facility. The facility will ship product weekly in the following amounts to four different cities:

City	Quantity
City 1	400
City 2	800
City 3	300
City 4	600

The cities are located at the following x, y Cartesian coordinates:

City	x Coordinate	y Coordinate
City 1	2	3
City 2	5	1
City 3	4	6
City 4	2	7

Use the weighted center of gravity method to identify the location for the new shipping facility.

10. A company must decide where to locate a new shipping facility. The facility will ship product weekly in the following amounts to three different cities:

City	Quantity
City 1	600
City 2	1,200
City 3	800

The cities are located at the following x, y Cartesian coordinates:

City	x Coordinate	y Coordinate
City 1	4	5
City 2	3	2
City 3	2	7

Use the weighted center of gravity method to identify the location for the new shipping facility.

TRANSPORTATION METHOD

11. A company produces a product at two manufacturing plants. The product is then shipped to warehouses in Fort Worth, Chicago, and Fresno. The cost of shipping from the plants to the warehouses is indicated in the following cost matrix. The amount that can be produced each week at the plants and the weekly demands at the warehouses are also shown. Determine the shipping schedule that minimizes the total cost of delivering the product from the plants to the warehouses. Ensure that each warehouse receives its weekly demand and that each plant does not exceed its weekly production supply.

Shipping Cost per Unit			
From/To	Fort Worth	Chicago	Fresno
Plant 1	55	70	80
Plant 2	45	50	20

Production Facility	Weekly Supply Capacity (in units)
Plant 1	4,000
Plant 2	2,000

Warehouse	Demand
Fort Worth	1,500
Chicago	3,500
Fresno	1,000

Determine the optimal shipping plan for the company.

12. A company holds inventory at warehouses in Amarillo, St. Louis, Knoxville, and Camden. Items are shipped from the warehouses to retail outlets in Louisville, Atlanta, Miami, Phoenix, and Los Angeles. The weekly demand at the retail outlets is as follows:

Retail Outlet	Weekly Demand
Louisville	175
Atlanta	250
Miami	100
Phoenix	350
Los Angeles	400

Each warehouse can process (ship) the following quantities each week:

Warehouse	Weekly Shipping Capacity
Amarillo	450
St. Louis	600
Knoxville	375
Camden	500

The per-unit shipping costs to ship from the warehouses to the retail outlets are given in the following cost matrix:

To From	Louisville	Atlanta	Miami	Phoenix	Los Angeles
Amarillo	2.50	3.00	5.35	4.15	6.35
St. Louis	1.25	3.50	5.25	11.20	7.40
Knoxville	1.75	3.00	3.20	7.80	8.35
Camden	4.25	3.25	4.75	15.70	11.15

Determine the shipping plan that satisfies the weekly demand requirements at the retail outlets for the minimum total shipping cost.

13. A manufacturing facility in Omaha must ship its product to customers in Bismarck, Little Rock, Toronto, Denver, Seattle, and Tulsa. The manufacturer can ship the product by rail, truck, or a combination of rail and truck. The weekly demands of each customer are shown. Production capacity is not an issue for the manufacturer, but there are limits on the amount of the product that can be shipped weekly by rail and truck, and those limits are also shown. Finally, a cost matrix, which indicates the per-unit shipping cost for each mode of transportation to each customer's city, is given in a from/to cost matrix. Using this information, identify the mode of transport and the amount to be shipped to each customer so that the manufacturing facility minimizes its overall shipping cost. *Hint:* Let the modes of transportation be the sources of supply.

Mode of Transport	Weekly Shipping Capacity
Rail	20,000
Truck	14,500

Customer	Weekly Demand
Bismarck	1,500
Little Rock	2,000
Toronto	9,000
Denver	7,500
Seattle	10,000
Tulsa	2,500

Per-Unit Shipping Cost By \ To	Bismarck	Little Rock	Toronto	Denver	Seattle	Tulsa
Rail	18	17	5	11	13	7
Truck	21	14	26	13	9	25

14. The cost to ship an item from four warehouses to five cities is shown in the following cost matrix:

From \ To	City 1	City 2	City 3	City 4	City 5
Warehouse 1	28	14	33	29	19
Warehouse 2	31	25	30	14	33
Warehouse 3	23	30	20	—	35
Warehouse 4	26	34	24	14	14

Warehouse	Weekly Shipping Capacity
Warehouse 1	20,000
Warehouse 2	15,000
Warehouse 3	25,000
Warehouse 4	10,000

City	Weekly Demand
City 1	7,000
City 2	12,500
City 3	17,500
City 4	10,000
City 5	18,000

Note: It is not possible to ship product from warehouse 3 to city 4. One way to ensure that no product gets shipped when there is an impossible shipping path is to assign a very high cost to the prohibited shipping route.

Assuming that the weekly city demands and the weekly warehouse capacities are as shown, determine the shipping plan that minimizes the overall shipping cost.

CASE

Brentward Logistics

Trudy Johnson had only recently graduated from the supply chain management program at her state university when she accepted a position as a logistics analyst with Brentward Logistics. Trudy was excited about her new position and believed that she brought a solid set of skills related to logistics and supply chain management to Brentward. Shortly after she started, she was assigned to a team that was confronted with two challenges: (1) Identify the best location for a warehouse that would be storing and shipping component parts to the five manufacturing plants that the company owned and operated, and (2) identify where a new warehouse should be located to increase shipping capacity while minimizing total costs for supplying finished manufactured items produced by the company to large industrial customers located around the United States.

Trudy quickly went to work collecting information that she believed could help the team analyze the two issues it faced. For the warehouse location problem, she collected information related to the locations of the existing plants that would be supplied by the new warehouse, as well as an estimate of the number of deliveries (measured in truckloads) that would take place each week from the new warehouse to the plants. This information is shown below with x and y as the Cartesian coordinates of the existing plants and daily shipments being the estimated weekly number of truck deliveries from the warehouse to the plants:

x	y	Daily Shipments Required
19	23	6
14	9	8
10	9	12
2	5	13
20	13	15
17	7	9
17	4	14
8	15	13
19	10	13
4	3	15
14	15	14
22	6	15
16	5	6

The team had previously identified two potential locations for the finished goods inventory warehouse. This warehouse would ship items to large industrial customers located in six U.S. cities. Currently, the company has three warehouses that could ship finished products to customers. The estimated weekly demands from the customers and the weekly shipping capacity from the warehouses are as follows:

Customer	Weekly Demand
Kansas City	125
Detroit	150
Los Angeles	75
Birmingham	50
Pittsburgh	80
Milwaukee	110

Current Warehouse	Weekly Shipping Capacity
St. Louis	200
Columbus	150
Denver	100

The current warehouses do not have sufficient capacity to meet the weekly demand, and it is not possible to expand the capacity of the existing warehouses. Consequently, a new warehouse must be built to meet customer needs. The team has identified two potential new warehouse locations: Dallas and Albuquerque. The projected capacity of the Albuquerque warehouse would be 150 units weekly. The Dallas warehouse has greater shipping options and could be built to a shipping capacity of 200 units weekly. Trudy collected the following actual costs per unit to ship from the existing warehouses to customers and the expected shipping costs for the proposed sites:

To From	Kansas City	Detroit	Los Angeles	Birmingham	Pittsburgh	Milwaukee
St. Louis	37	37	55	52	44	39
Columbus	44	39	56	43	38	44
Denver	46	47	41	46	54	58
Albuquerque	42	53	39	46	57	61
Dallas	36	42	43	42	50	54

Questions:

1. Only one warehouse can be built; assist Trudy in finding the best location.

2. What is the minimum transportation cost comparing the Albuquerque option to the Dallas option?

Part 4

Improving Supply Chain and Operations Management Performance

INTEGRATING

GLOBAL SC&O STRATEGY

INNOVATING

Supply Management

Operations Management

Customer Relationship Management

IMPACTING

Upstream Processes

Core Processes

Downstream Processes

IMPROVING

QUALITY MANAGEMENT, ANALYTICS, AND LOGISTICS

CHAPTER OUTLINE AND LEARNING OBJECTIVES

1 Understand Project Management
- Organize projects effectively.
- Select projects based on a qualifying matrix.
- Develop a project charter.

2 Utilize Project Planning Tools
- Estimate task times using beta distributions.

3 Plan and Control Projects Using PERT/CPM
- Find critical paths of projects, completion times, and slack.
- Perform probabilistic PERT.

4 Learn How to Manage Costs of Projects through Gantt Charts
- Expedite projects to ensure on-time completion.

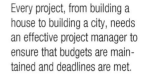

In this chapter, we introduce the important topic of project management. Projects are needed whenever large, time-consuming work needs to be done. One of the biggest projects in the history of the United States was Boston's Central Artery/Third Harbor Tunnel Project, or the Big Dig. Although from some perspectives the Big Dig was a marvel, it also illustrates many of the problems with large projects and project management. Even with its problems, it is an amazing project. Before the Big Dig, the highway entering Boston was a barrier between downtown Boston and Boston Harbor. To reconnect the downtown with the harbor, planners decided that a highway should be built under the city. What began as an audacious idea in 1982 took 25 years to complete.

The objective of the Big Dig was to burrow under Boston without interrupting traffic flow. It would have to be accomplished without letting the waters of Boston Harbor in and without the city and highway above collapsing. We will revisit this costly, time-consuming, and amazing project at the end of the chapter, after we discuss the fundamentals of project management.

Whether you work in a large company, a tiny start-up, or on your own, you will need to learn how to plan and manage projects. Creativity, strong communication and people skills, and the ability to solve problems are hallmarks of an effective project manager. A **project** is a one-time, temporary endeavor with a defined beginning and ending. Projects can be large or small, long term or short term, individual or team-based. There are many different types of projects, such as constructing a home or skyscraper, writing a term paper, or even taking a class. In many ways, life is a project. Skilled project management often determines whether projects succeed or fail.

project
A one-time, temporary endeavor with a defined beginning and end.

U NDERSTAND PROJECT MANAGEMENT

This chapter focuses on a project's logistics, challenges, and maintenance. In this section, we will introduce the ideas behind managing your projects and how the human element comes into play when managing projects. We will then present project plans sequentially, by first discussing project management and then walking you through the various phases of planning and updating a project. Managing projects is multifaceted, but as a manager, you are largely responsible for three things:

- Achieving the objective of the project (performance)
- Finishing the project on time (schedule)
- Completing the project within a budget (cost)

Every project, from building a house to building a city, needs an effective project manager to ensure that budgets are maintained and deadlines are met.

Project planning includes the following steps:

1. Charter the project with identifiable deliverables and metrics.
2. Create a work breakdown structure to identify tasks and precedence relationships.
3. Estimate task times using beta distributions.
4. Model the project using specific methods, including the program evaluation and review technique (PERT) and critical path method (CPM).
5. Find the critical path.
6. Establish a completion time with a high probability of success.
7. Install necessary controls to monitor the progress of the project.

Before we can begin discussing the logistics and challenges of managing projects, we must first review some relevant terms. **Project management** is the act of leading and directing people and other resources in a project. TABLE 12.1 shows activities performed in the management of a project. **Scope management** is the act of defining what the team needs to do to complete a project. A properly scoped project avoids **gold plating**, or unnecessary deliverables. The main tool for scoping a project is a *project charter*. (We will discuss charters in more depth later in the chapter.) Project managers lead their teams in completing these project phases. We distinguish project management from project planning, the act of forming a project plan. FIGURE 12.1 formally outlines the steps in planning projects. The project management activities are defined below.

- **Initiation** steps include scoping and chartering projects.
- **Planning** is developing a plan for the project. Planning steps include (1) developing a work breakdown structure (WBS), (2) defining tasks, (3) estimating task times, (4) developing a schedule, (5) estimating resources, and (6) expediting.
- **Execution** is performing the work necessary to complete the project, where managers and employees get their hands dirty.
- **Monitoring and controlling** a project is the process of reporting to see that the project plan is being followed. Part of this step is change control.
- **Change control** is the term applied to the process of managing changes to the project charter and plan.
- Finally, **closing a project** is celebrating successes; releasing resources, including people; and performing a project debrief.

The Human Element in Projects

In addition to the planning phases, managers must also consider the behavioral side of project management, which includes the role that the project leader plays in managing his or her team. Paul Hersey and Kenneth Blanchard, two well-known instructors in leadership, developed the **situational leadership model**, a graph (see FIGURE 12.2) that illustrates the correlation between

---

project management
The act of leading and directing the people and other resources in a project.

scope management
The act of defining what the team needs to do to complete a project.

gold plating
Adding unnecessary deliverables to a project.

initiation
Beginning project steps, including scoping and chartering projects.

planning
Developing a road map for the project.

execution
Performing the work necessary to complete the project.

monitoring and controlling
The process of reporting to see that the project plan is being followed.

change control
The process of managing changes to the project charter and plan.

closing a project
Celebrating successes; releasing resources, including people; and performing a project debrief.

situational leadership model
A graph by Hersey and Blanchard that illustrates the correlation between task behavior, relationship behavior, and leadership behavior.

∨ TABLE 12.1

Project Management Activities					
	Five Phases				
	Initiation	Planning	Executing	Monitoring and Controlling	Closing
Activities	1. Develop project charter.			5. Monitor and control project work.	
		3. Develop project management plan.	4. Direct and manage project execution.		7. Close project.
	2. Develop preliminary project scope statement.			6. Integrate change control.	

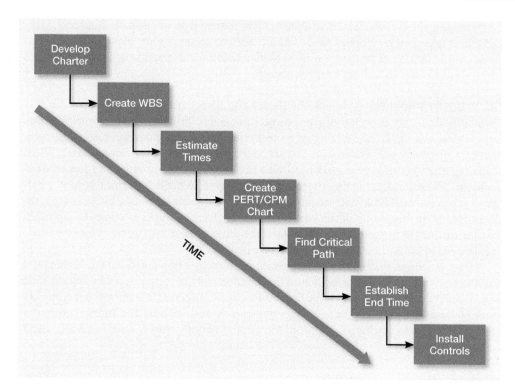

Project Planning Steps

task behavior, relationship behavior, and leadership behavior. If there is a low need for emotional support but a high need for guidance, the leader must engage in *telling*, providing and following up on directions. A manager's other roles are (1) selling or coaching, where the manager exhibits more emotional support; (2) participating; and (3) delegating. Many of these tasks center around the human element of project management, which we discuss next.

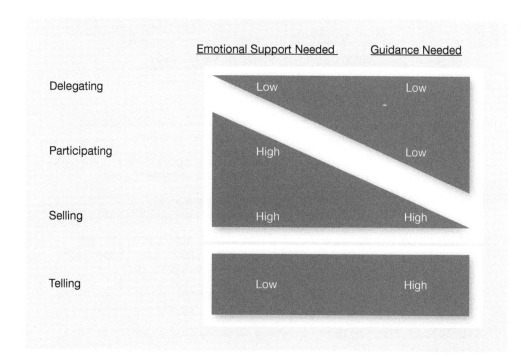

Situational Leadership Model

Managing the human element of a project is an essential part of its path to success. Managers must take their employees' needs and actions into account when planning and executing a project plan. We next discuss various human components that managers deal with and how they tackle any hurdles they may encounter.

THE STUDENT PROBLEM Although the Hersey and Blanchard project manager roles may seem fairly finite, we expect a lot from project managers. Project managers must manage communications, ensure the quality of project outcomes, manage human resources, communicate effectively, and understand cost accounting to keep the jobs within budget. When beginning a project task, managers must also understand human nature and the **student problem**. When considering the student problem, we ask, What is the typical student's barrier to achievement? The answer might be intuitive. How many term-long projects are actually started at the beginning of the term? If a class is given 10 weeks to complete a project, chances are that the majority of the class starts the project one or two weeks before the deadline. The end result is often a rushed, incomplete project.

When a manager plans projects, he or she must identify a task *start date*, task *duration*, and task *completion date*. Usually, the focus is on the duration and the completion date, but the start time should be a primary focus. If the duration estimate is correct, a team will not complete a task on the assigned date if the team does not start the task on time. Beginning a project in a timely manner and devoting the appropriate amount of time to the tasks at hand help avoid the student problem.

student problem
Procrastination in beginning project tasks.

....

Managing Across Majors 12.1 Human resources management majors, you play a key role in successful project management by assisting in selecting employees with the skills needed to complete projects.

....

MANAGING PROJECT TEAMS When managing a project, it is important to staff projects according to the scope of the project. Not all projects need teams; single individuals can perform simple projects. As a manager, you can also outsource project work when you cannot find the capacity or the needed expertise within your firm. TABLE 12.2 shows several different types of teams. You will also make choices about your teams based on the nature or scope of the project you are undertaking.

TABLE 12.2 >

Types of Teams		
Type of Team	**Scope**	**Nature of the Project**
Process improvement team	Local or single department	Improving existing projects and improving customer service.
Cross-functional team	Multiple departments	The project involves a variety of areas of expertise and has big impact.
Tiger team	Organization-wide	Specialists are assigned full-time to a project that needs to be completed quickly.
Natural work group	Customer- or region-centered	People who normally work together are bound by a need to improve work in their area.
Self-directed work team	Narrow or broad	A team of peers works together to make needed improvements without a specified leader or top-down guidance.
Virtual team	Narrow or broad	People are dispersed around the country or world and work together over the Internet.

Source: S. Foster, *Managing Quality: Integrating the Supply Chain* (Upper Saddle River, NJ: Pearson, 2010), p. 379.

When forming teams, it is helpful to ensure that you fill all the roles listed in TABLE 12.3 with at least one person. Note that a single individual can perform a variety of roles simultaneously.

The way that you form a team depends to an extent on the objectives of the project. Regardless of the type of team you employ, the team will go through different phases of development over time, as listed in FIGURE 12.3.

Understanding the basics of team management helps you understand what you should expect when participating in teams. Successful teams will encounter these stages as they proceed through a project.

ORGANIZING PROJECT TEAMS Organizing projects can be done in many ways. We will focus on just three: (1) pure projects, (3) matrix organizations, and (3) functional project organizations.

Pure projects are just as they sound. If your manager assigns you, an employee, to a project, you will be taken out of your functional duties and assigned to that project full-time. Because you are fully committed to your project, this setup is best for completing projects that are of strategic importance to an organization. If you work on a pure project team, you may get visibility you wouldn't achieve otherwise. On the other hand, this way of organizing a project does take you out of your functional responsibilities, which could result in losses of other career opportunities. For example, a government organization recently created an organization-wide information system. Employees from various departments were assigned to the 18-month project full-time. This project was of a scope that was broad enough that

pure project
A project to which an employee is assigned full-time.

∨ TABLE 12.3

Belbin's Team Roles			
	Team Role	**Strengths**	**Allowable Weaknesses**
Action-Oriented Roles	Shaper	• Challenging, dynamic, thrives on pressure • The drive and courage to overcome obstacles	• Can be prone to provocation • May sometimes offend people's feelings
	Implementer (Company Worker)	• Disciplined, reliable, conservative, and efficient • Turns ideas into practical actions	• Can be a bit inflexible and slow to respond to new possibilities
	Completer Finisher	• Painstaking, conscientious, anxious • Searches out errors and omissions • Delivers on time	• Can be inclined to worry unduly • Reluctant to delegate
People-Oriented Roles	Coordinator (Chairperson)	• Mature, confident, a good chairperson • Clarifies goals, promotes decision making, delegates well	• Can be seen as manipulative • Might offload their own share of the work
	Team Worker	• Cooperative, mild, perceptive, and diplomatic • Listens, builds, averts friction	• Can be indecisive in crunch situations • Tends to avoid confrontation
	Resource Investigator	• Extrovert, enthusiastic, communicative • Explores opportunities • Develops contacts	• Might be overoptimistic • Can lose interest once the initial enthusiasm has passed
Cerebral Roles	Plant (or facility level)	• Creative, imaginative, unorthodox • Solves difficult problems	• Might ignore incidentals • May be too preoccupied to communicate effectively
	Monitor Evaluator	• Sober, strategic, and discerning • Sees all options • Judges accurately	• Sometimes lacks the drive and ability to inspire others • Can be overly critical
	Specialist	• Single-minded, self-starting, dedicated • Provides knowledge and skills in rare supply	• Can only contribute on a narrow front • Tends to dwell on the technicalities

Source: Meredith Belbin, *Team Roles at Work* (Oxford: Butterworth-Heinemann, 2010).

FIGURE 12.3 >

**Project Team Stages
of Development**

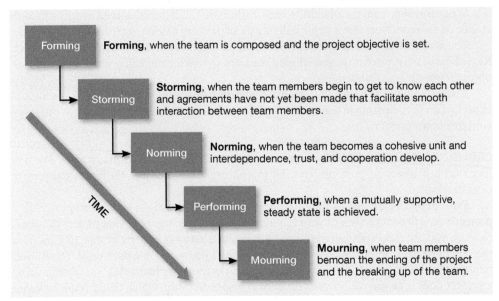

Source: Based on Bruce W. Tuckman, "Developmental Sequence in Small Groups," *Psychological Bulletin* 63, no. 6 (1965): 384.

it could involve many different departments. It was also of such strategic importance to the future of the organization that it justified such a high level of commitment.

The **functional project organization** is just the opposite of the pure project team. In this organizational form, each employee stays in a functional area, and certain project tasks are assigned to the employees through their functional leader. As such, one employee may never meet with a team or be part of a team. The employee may be assigned certain tasks that he or she delivers to the boss, who in turn delivers that output to the team manager. For example, when exploring for oil, several different departments in an oil company are assigned tasks. Purchasing buys equipment, accounting pays bills, exploration does the geological work, and production starts the pumping of the oil. There is never a team per se, but individuals in different departments perform tasks that lead to the furthering of the project.

FIGURE 12.4 shows an outline of a **matrix team structure**, the most common team organization. In this setup, the team member maintains a functional position in the company but is also assigned to a project team, which keeps the team member in the flow of the normal department and allows participation as part of a project team. In theory, when a manager adds someone to a team, some of the prior work burden should be taken away to equalize that employee's responsibilities. When such reassignment does not happen, however, the team member will be working more hours. As an example, a team was created to work on a new textbook for supply chain and operations management. The team included an executive editor, a style editor, artists, and an author. The people all worked on multiple projects simultaneously but were assigned the textbook in addition to other duties.

Qualifying Projects

Projects are qualified prior to their initiation. When companies qualify projects, they evaluate potential projects to prioritize and determine which project or projects to embark on first. In this section, we will discuss qualifying and chartering projects. **Qualifying projects** is the act of justifying a project financially and strategically. **Project chartering** is the act of creating a document outlining the deliverables of a project. These concepts are discussed more in the coming pages.

RISK/RETURN MATRIX Before beginning a project, managers must prioritize project tasks and time lines. They must then compile and present their project plan in a direct and cohesive manner.

functional project organization
An organizational form in which employees stay in a functional area and certain project tasks are assigned to them through their functional manager.

matrix team structure
A setup in which an employee works part-time on a project team and continues to perform fundamental job assignments.

qualifying projects
The act of justifying a project financially and strategically.

project chartering
The act of creating a document outlining the deliverables of a project.

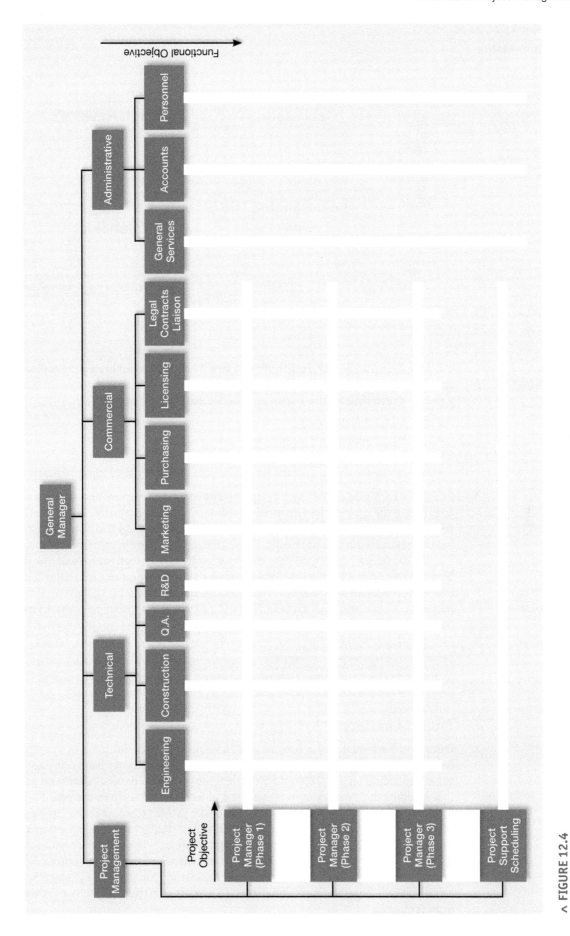

∧ FIGURE 12.4
Matrix Team Organization

FIGURE 12.5 >

Risk/Return Matrix

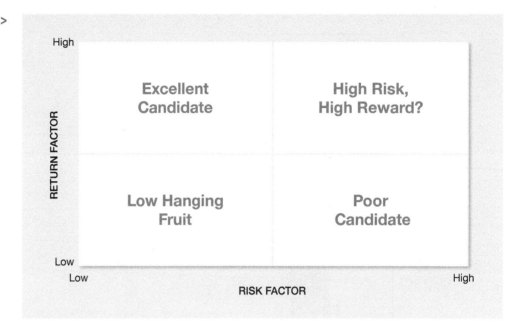

FIGURE 12.5 >
Risk/Return Matrix

risk/return matrix
A tool for prioritizing potential projects.

Managers use the **risk/return matrix** (see FIGURE 12.5) when evaluating projects. In evaluating risk, an estimate is made of the difficulty of completing the project in a reasonable amount of time with available resources. Other issues are raised, such as:

- The availability of data
- Managerial support for the project
- Time and resources required
- A subjective assessment of the probability of completing the project satisfactorily

The return side of the matrix requires assessing the financial and strategic benefits of completing the project. The financial benefits are usually evaluated in terms of the dollar return associated with successful project completion. Managers define strategic benefits based on how the project will position the company for future growth and competitiveness.

When comparing projects, it is clear that projects with high return and low risk are the best candidates for adoption. Projects with low risk and modest returns that will not require too many resources are often referred to as *low-hanging fruit* because they are simple and of minimal cost to complete. On the other hand, risky projects with high paybacks may have to be evaluated carefully before embarking.

....

Managing Across Majors 12.2 Accounting and finance majors, return on investment, payback period, and other financial measures are commonly used to justify projects.

....

Project Charters

project charter
A document that outlines the primary deliverables, the objective, and the parameters of a project.

Once you have qualified a project and have specified the purpose of your project, an important first step is to develop a *project charter*, which can range from one page to several pages depending on the scope and breadth of the project. A **project charter** is a document that outlines the primary deliverables, the objective, and the parameters of a project. It includes resources allocated, the members of the project team, the measurable outcomes of the project, other expected benefits of the project, budget allocation for the project, and signatures from top management approving the project. The charter provides the mechanism for providing discipline for a project and helps guard against **scope creep**, which occurs when the goals for a project expand the farther you get into a project. Scope creep can result in delays in completing projects and cost overruns. FIGURE 12.6 shows a sample project charter.

scope creep
Allowing the deliverables of a project to expand over time.

Project Name	Filling Line Automated Testing (FLAT)
Executive Sponsor	Bill Evans—Engineering Department Manager
Project Manager	Susan James—Project Engineer (Electronics and System Programming)
Primary Stakeholder(s)	Muhammed Parva—Quality Mgr and Sarah Johnson—Business Unit Ldr & Operations Mgr

Project Description / Statement of Work

The juice bottles are not being filled to the correct level. Customers are complaining about the shortage of juice. Operator visual inspection is no longer meeting quality metrics. Installing inspection equipment on the Bottle Filling line will eliminate the need for visual inspection, improve performance metrics, and enable inspection section of line to run at full speed.

Business Case / Statement of Need (Why is this project important now?)

• Customer complaints about quality have increased.
• Customer demand has increased, so production needs to run faster.
• Previous process improvements have reduced the number of line operators, so inspections are less frequent.

Customers	Customer Needs / Requirements
Business Unit Leader and Sales Associates	Avoid rework, run to capacity, and fulfill demand
Purchasing Customer	Wants bottle filled to correct level and no stockouts

Project Definition

Project Goals	Improve quality and other performance metrics. Portion of Bottle Filling line is capable of running at full capacity.
Project Scope	Tester will be installed and configured for only Bottle Filling line. Only resolve issue of underfilled bottles. Inspection section must be able to function at max line speed. Other issues related to running at full speed will not be addressed at this time.
Project Deliverables	Automated inspecting equipment installed on line, including all computer system programming. Documented training on equipment and revised Standard Work procedures for operators.

Project Constraints / Risks (Elements that may restrict or place control over a project, project team, or project action)

This is the first automated quality inspection in facility. No previous example of what to expect for results or issues.
The filling line could be down longer than planned, thus affecting demand.
Employee morale may reduce due to installation of another automated component of the filling line.

Implementation Plan / Milestones (Due dates and durations)

Phase 1: Inspection equipment researched and ordered: Start June 1 (3 weeks)
        Filling line should be prepped during this time.
Phase 2: Inspection equipment configured and installed: Start June 21 (2 weeks)
        Milestone: Have tester installed at end of 2 weeks. Line should be able to run, even if tester is not fully operational.
Phase 3: Troubleshoot and adjust inspection equipment: Start July 5 (2 weeks)
        Milestone: Testing equipment should be fully operational. System functions properly at full line capacity.

Communication Plan (What needs to be communicated? When is communication needed? To whom? How?)

Weekly updates to Engineering Manager.
Updates to all Stakeholders at the end of each phase.

Change Management / Issue Management (How decisions will be made? How changes will be made?)

Engineering Manager to be informed of all issues and changes.
Issues and changes to be discussed between project lead and appropriate stakeholder.

Project Team Roles and Responsibilities

Team members	Roles	Responsibilities
James Naybors	Service Maintenance	Support with equipment installation and line maintenance.
Jon Quest	Line Operator	Rewrite Standard Work and verify line is operating properly.

Stakeholder Roles and Responsibilities

Stakeholders	Roles	Responsibilities
Bill Evans	Engineering Manager	Expense and equipment changes approval.
Muhammed Parva	Quality Manager	Bottles must meet Bottle Filling level metrics.
Angie Jolley	BUL & Operations Manager	Filling line runs properly and demand is met.

Sign-off

Sponsor _____ Date_____
(Name)

∧ FIGURE 12.6

Project Charter

SOLVED PROBLEM 12.1 > **Project Charters in Action**

Problem: An example of scope creep occurred when an insurance firm entered into a project automating the manual processing of insurance applications. At first, underwriting managers approved the project focusing on underwriting loan applications. As the system developers generated prototypes of screens for the new system, however, managers became aware of additional functionality that could be built into the system, such as digital document capture and claims processing. As a result, the underwriting managers began to ask for this additional system functionality. Because this additional functionality had not been budgeted for this project, the developers were unsure about what to do.

Solution: Because the developers had written a charter laying out the original budget and deliverables for the project, they were able to go to the user managers and show them the original charter with time lines and budgets, providing a basis for negotiating whether to add the new deliverables or not. The developers could add the additional functionality, but project managers and leaders would have to revise the charter and provide new deliverables, time lines, and budgets and have them approved by top management. As a result of the existing charter, the developers and management decided to focus on the original scope of the project. The additional claims and digital document capture would be added in a separate, future project.

Ⓤ TILIZE PROJECT PLANNING TOOLS

milestones
Phases in a project.

work breakdown structure (WBS)
A brainstorming tool used to plan projects.

Key phases in a project time line are often referred to as **milestones**, which are the building blocks of a project plan and help determine if a project is on track. To capture these milestones in planning, managers use a **work breakdown structure (WBS)**, a brainstorming tool used to plan projects.

As FIGURE 12.7 shows, we start a WBS by identifying the final objective of the project. In our example, the project is a software product release. Project planners often use sticky notes to make a WBS. Once they identify the final objective, the next level of planning includes the milestones. In the top row of Figure 12.7, the project milestones are defining project management, identifying product requirements, completing detailed design, product development, and integration and testing. The project planner then brainstorms the tasks and subtasks that are required for completing the milestones.

Work breakdown structures provide a standard method for determining the required tasks for completing a project. It is best to start with a blank sheet of paper and involve the project team members in brainstorming the milestones and tasks. Once a manager defines

task precedence
Determining which tasks precede and follow other tasks.

the tasks, he or she then has to determine the **task precedence**, or the sequence of tasks to complete the project. GLOBAL CONNECTIONS 12.1 shows how these project management planning concepts were used in large projects such as the Panama Canal makeover.

Estimating Task Completion Times

One benefit of determining the WBS is that you have now broken your project into tasks, which makes your planning much more finite. When managing your course work, it is easier to determine the time it will take to complete a chapter assignment than it is to determine exactly how long it will take you to finish a term research paper. We use this same rationale in planning projects.

Arbitrary dates are often set for completion of projects. In one company, every major project had a completion date of January 1. Of course, the irony was that the company was not even open on New Year's Day. Completing projects on New Year's Day only highlighted the arbitrary nature of how this firm assigned project completion dates.

We have already discussed charters and WBS; the following section discusses how to estimate task times with beta distributions. Because it is easier to plan for completion at the

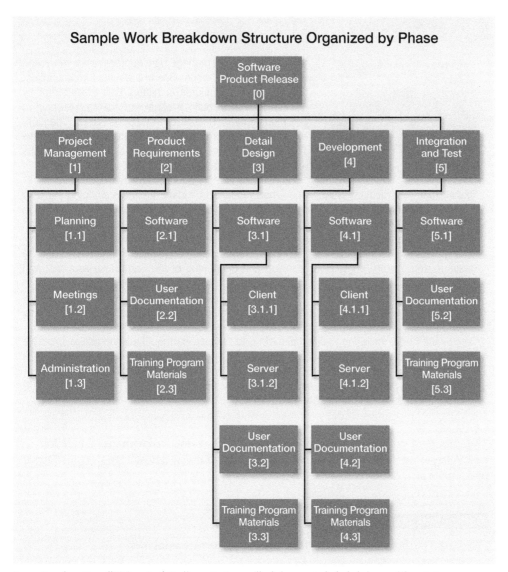

Sample Work Breakdown Structure Organized by Phase

Source: Based on Cornell University, http://www2.cit.cornell.edu/computer/robohelp/cpmm/Phase3_Process_Descriptions.htm.

task level, managers ask the project planning team members for three task completion time estimates:

t_o = **optimistic completion time**: the time to complete the task given optimal conditions

t_m = **most likely completion time**: the completion time that is the most probable

t_p = **pessimistic completion time**: the longest completion time if everything that can go wrong does go wrong (the Murphy's law time)

The estimated task time is then computed using the formula

$$t_e = \frac{t_o + 4t_m + t_p}{6} \tag{12.1}$$

where t_e = expected task completion time. In **SOLVED PROBLEM 12.2**, we demonstrate computing task times.

While we are discussing task completion times, we will also introduce the formula for computing task variance, which helps compute project times with a high probability of completion. The formula for estimating task variance (s_t^2) is:

$$s_t^2 = \left(\frac{t_p - t_o}{6}\right)^2 \tag{12.2}$$

optimistic completion time
The shortest time for completing a task.

most likely completion time
The best estimate of task completion time.

pessimistic completion time
The longest foreseeable task completion time.

GLOBAL >
CONNECTIONS 12.1

The Panama Canal Gets a Makeover

Modern project management approaches have worked throughout the world. One of the most famous project management failures in history was the attempt by the French to build a canal in Panama, resulting in thousands of deaths in the 1880s. Later, Theodore Roosevelt approved the completion of the first Panama Canal. The Panama Canal served the Americas for many years until another project was launched in 2006 and completed in 2016. The growth of international trade—particularly from China—had resulted in a need for more shipping capacity through the Panama Canal and for the locks to handle larger Panamax ships.

The $5.25 billion project was very risky, with literally the wealth and future of a nation held in the balance. The project was awarded to a Spanish firm named Sacyr Vallehermoso. The dimensions of the project were breathtaking: deeper and wider entrances at both the western and eastern entrances; widening and deepening of the Gatun lake sections; and new, larger locks to handle the bigger ships. The canal is fifty miles long and required an incredible amount of concrete.

There were concerns that the Spanish firm managing the project (also the low bidder by over $1 billion) was scrimping on concrete and steel reinforcement. The engineering problems were huge, including Pacific tides of up to 19 feet, earthquake vulnerability, unstable soil, and Panamanian rainstorms.

After many technical and political problems, on June 9, 2016, the Chinese Neopanamax ship, the *Baroque Valletta*, passed through the canal. In March 2017, more than 1,100 vessels transited the Panama Canal.

The amount of variance is reflective of the uncertainty associated with the completion of the task. A larger variance is associated with more uncertainty. **SOLVED PROBLEM 12.3** illustrates how to compute task variance.

 SOLVED PROBLEM 12.2 > | **Computing Task Times**

MyLab Operations Management
Video

Problem: The three time estimates for a task in a project are as follows:

t_o = optimistic completion time = 3 weeks
t_m = most likely completion time = 6 weeks
t_p = pessimistic completion time = 15 weeks

Compute the expected time for this task.

Solution: The expected task completion time was computed using Equation 12.1 as

$$t_e = \frac{t_o + 4t_m + t_p}{6} = \frac{3 + 4(6) + 15}{6} = 7 \text{ weeks}$$

This estimated time of seven weeks was then used for planning the project. Note that this estimate is the task completion time, not the completion time for the entire project. We will introduce how to compute project completion time later in this chapter.

 SOLVED PROBLEM 12.3 > | **Computing Task Variance**

MyLab Operations Management
Video

Problem: Using the data from Solved Problem 12.2, compute task variance.

t_o = optimistic completion time = 3 weeks
t_m = most likely completion time = 6 weeks
t_p = pessimistic completion time = 15 weeks

Compute task variance.

Solution: Using Equation 12.2, we compute the task variance as

$$s_t^2 = \left(\frac{15 - 3}{6}\right)^2 = (2)^2 = 4 \text{ weeks}$$

Note that s_t^2 is an estimate of variance.

. . . .

If we combine Solved Problems 12.2 and 12.3, the expected completion time for the task is seven weeks with a variance of four weeks. Notice that the task standard deviation (s_t) is 2 weeks (the square root of the variance). These calculations are then demonstrated in **SOLVED PROBLEM 12.4** and in Excel in **USING TECHNOLOGY 12.1**.

. . . .

| Putting It Together: Task Times and Variances |

< SOLVED PROBLEM 12.4

MyLab Operations Management Video

Problem: The following table shows (1) optimistic, (2) most likely, and (3) pessimistic times. Using this data, compute the expected completion time and variance for each task.

Task	t_o	t_m	t_p
A	1	3	5
B	2	6	10
C	3	5	13
D	3	3	3
E	12	15	24
F	7	9	11
G	3	4	5
H	8	8	8
I	14	16	32

Solution: Using Equations 12.1 and 12.2, we find the following:

Task	t_o	t_m	t_p	t_e	s_t^2
A	1	3	5	$\dfrac{1 + (4 \times 3) + 5}{6} = 3.00$	$\left(\dfrac{5 - 1}{6}\right)^2 = 0.44$
B	2	6	10	$\dfrac{2 + (4 \times 6) + 10}{6} = 6.00$	$\left(\dfrac{10 - 2}{6}\right)^2 = 1.78$
C	3	5	13	$\dfrac{3 + (4 \times 5) + 13}{6} = 6.00$	$\left(\dfrac{13 - 3}{6}\right)^2 = 2.78$
D	3	3	3	$\dfrac{3 + (4 \times 3) + 3}{6} = 3.00$	$\left(\dfrac{3 - 3}{6}\right)^2 = 0.00$
E	12	15	24	$\dfrac{12 + (4 \times 15) + 24}{6} = 16.00$	$\left(\dfrac{24 - 12}{6}\right)^2 = 4.00$
F	7	9	11	$\dfrac{7 + (4 \times 9) + 11}{6} = 9.00$	$\left(\dfrac{11 - 7}{6}\right)^2 = 0.44$
G	3	4	5	$\dfrac{3 + (4 \times 4) + 5}{6} = 4.00$	$\left(\dfrac{5 - 3}{6}\right)^2 = 0.11$
H	8	8	8	$\dfrac{8 + (4 \times 8) + 8}{6} = 8.00$	$\left(\dfrac{8 - 8}{6}\right)^2 = 0.00$
I	14	16	32	$\dfrac{14 + (4 \times 16) + 32}{6} = 18.33$	$\left(\dfrac{32 - 14}{6}\right)^2 = 9.00$

Computing Beta Distribution Times Using Excel

The beta distribution task mean times and task variances can easily be computed in Excel. Using the data from Solved Problem 12.4, we use Equations 12.1 and 12.2 to compute expected task times (t_e) and task variances (s_t^2). The formulas used are shown in **FIGURE 12.8**.

	A	B	C	D	E	F	G	H	I
1	**Task**	t_o	t_m	t_p	t_e	s_t^2			
2	A	1.00	3.00	5.00	3.00	0.44			
3	B	2.00	6.00	10.00	6.00	1.78			
4	C	3.00	5.00	13.00	6.00	2.78			
5	D	3.00	3.00	3.00	3.00	0.00			
6	E	12.00	15.00	24.00	16.00	4.00			
7	F	7.00	9.00	11.00	9.00	0.44		=((D9-B9)/6)^2	
8	G	3.00	4.00	5.00	4.00	0.11			
9	H	8.00	8.00	8.00	8.00	0.00			
10	I	14.00	16.00	32.00	18.33	9.00			
11									
12				=(B10+4*C10+D10)/6					
13									

∧ FIGURE 12.8

Computing Beta Distribution Task and Variances in Excel

Managing Multiple Projects

Often, individuals must manage multiple projects within an organization simultaneously, which can make coordination difficult. To keep things organized, managers must phase the implementation of multiple projects. Also, there needs to be a centralized document to help keep individuals from being assigned to too many or too few projects. The **multiple project assignment matrix** in FIGURE 12.9 is a management tool to aid company-wide coordination of multiple projects. Note that the matrix identifies participants with varying levels of responsibility as well as project managers, which helps balance work assignments in a project-oriented environment and aids in ensuring that the best talent is prioritized to the most important projects.

multiple project assignment matrix
A tool for monitoring who is assigned to multiple projects.

FIGURE 12.9 >

A Project Assignment Matrix for Multiple Projects

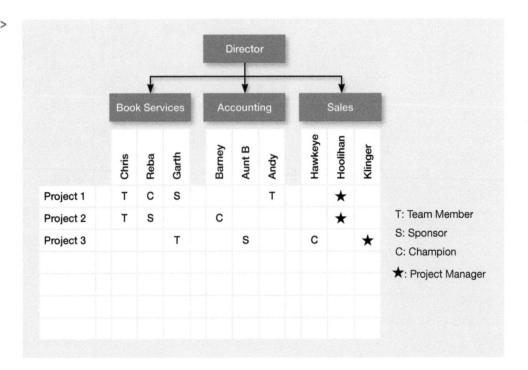

ⓟ LAN AND CONTROL PROJECTS USING PERT/CPM

Now that we have learned how to develop charters, defined project tasks using WBSs, and calculated task times and variances using beta distributions, we are ready to develop a project plan using PERT/CPM: **program evaluation and review technique (PERT), critical path method (CPM)**.

The U.S. Navy Speech Project office first introduced PERT in 1957 to help plan the production of Polaris nuclear submarines. Around the same time, DuPont Corporation first used the critical path method when it began shutting down its chemical plants. Although the two techniques were developed separately, today they are taught and used in conjunction because they dovetail so well.

The objectives of PERT/CPM are as follows:

- Help map out a plan of the project to understand more clearly where the project team is going visually.
- Determine how long it should take to complete the project.
- Go through the mental exercise of visualizing what will need to be done to complete the project.
- Find out which tasks require tight control and which can be delegated more easily.
- Find out which tasks are most critical to completing the project on time.

The steps in PERT/CPM are as follows:

1. Clearly identify all tasks for a project.
2. Identify the precedence relationships of the tasks.
3. Draw a network diagram of the tasks with precedence relationships.
4. Calculate the time required to complete the tasks. Many times, we will simply provide these times in examples. Otherwise, managers calculate task times using the beta distributions discussed earlier in the chapter.
5. Using the task times, compute early start, late start, early finish, and late finish times for each task.
6. Using the times calculated in step 5, find the critical paths.
7. Revise project plans as necessary.

Using the tasks and expected times we calculated from Solved Problem 12.4, we now add precedence:

Task	t_e	Preceding Tasks
A	3.00	None
B	6.00	A
C	6.00	A
D	3.00	B
E	16.00	B, C
F	9.00	D
G	4.00	E
H	8.00	G
I	18.33	F, H

Some tasks must be completed before other tasks can be started. Note that in the table above, task B (column 1) cannot be started until task A (column 3) is done. Given these tasks and predecessors, we are ready to draw a network diagram of this project. The **activity-on-node (AON) network** in FIGURE 12.10 shows the tasks in order. An AON network signifies that activities are labeled on the network nodes. We practice drawing another AON PERT diagram in SOLVED PROBLEM 12.5.

program evaluation and review technique (PERT)
A method for planning and controlling projects using networks.

critical path method (CPM)
A method for planning projects that uses shortest paths.

activity-on-node (AON) network
A project network in which activities are labeled on the network nodes.

FIGURE 12.10 >

FIGURE 12.10 >

Activity-on-Node Network Diagram of Project Management

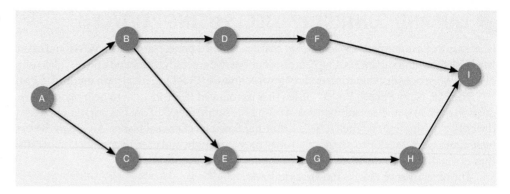

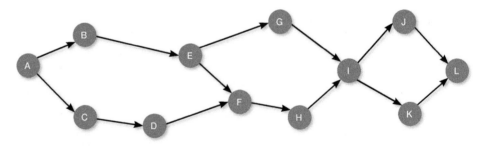

f(x)   **SOLVED PROBLEM 12.5 >**

MyLab Operations Management Video

Drawing AON Networks

Problem: The following table gives tasks (A–L), task times, and preceding tasks for a project at the Hoosier Company. Ignoring the task times for now, draw an activity-on-node (AON) diagram.

Task	t_e (in weeks)	Preceding Tasks
A	4	None
B	5	A
C	3	A
D	4	C
E	6	B
F	4	D, E
G	5	E
H	18	F
I	3	G, H
J	4	I
K	7	I
L	1	J, K

Solution: The network diagram shown here maintains these precedence relationships.

Finding the Critical Path

By identifying and prioritizing tasks and completing our task network, we have covered much of the PERT aspect of project management. We will now turn to computing the critical path. The **critical path** has two definitions:

critical path
The path in a PERT diagram with no slack.

1. The longest path through the PERT network
2. The path in the PERT network with no slack

From a managerial point of view, the second definition is the most profound. **Slack** is the amount of time that a task can be delayed without delaying the entire project. To demonstrate the critical path method, we return to the tasks, task times, and precedence relationships we introduced earlier in this chapter:

slack
The difference between the latest possible completion time and the shortest possible completion time.

Task	t_e (in weeks)	Preceding Tasks
A	3.00	None
B	6.00	A
C	6.00	A
D	3.00	B
E	16.00	B, C
F	9.00	D
G	4.00	E
H	8.00	G
I	18.33	F, H

Because we have already drawn the network, we will use the same AON network diagram. This time, though, we will use the node convention shown in FIGURE 12.11.

Computing Early Times

To compute a critical path, we must first compute early times. As we already showed, early times consist of early start and early finish times. The early start (ES) time is the earliest time you can possibly start a task, based on the precedence relationships. First, we start by working from left to right in the network with the first node (task A). This process of working from left to right is sometimes referred to as the *forward pass*. Because task A is the first task in the network, the earliest start time is 0. If we start at time 0 and the task duration is three weeks, the earliest finish time is week 3 (i.e., the last second of week 3). We have an exploded view of the nodes for tasks A and B in FIGURE 12.12. As you can see, the early start time for B is (the end of) week 3, and the early finish time for task B is week 9. This same logic is followed in computing the rest of the early start and early finish times throughout the rest of the PERT network (FIGURE 12.13).

The early finish (EF) time for any task is computed as

$$EF = ES + t_e \tag{12.3}$$

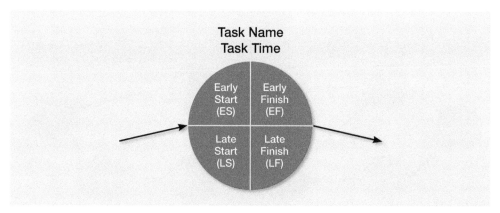

Task Name
Task Time

Early Start (ES)	Early Finish (EF)
Late Start (LS)	Late Finish (LF)

< **FIGURE 12.11**

Exploded View of the Critical Path Method Node with Early and Late Times

FIGURE 12.12 >

Early Start and Finish
Times for Tasks A and B

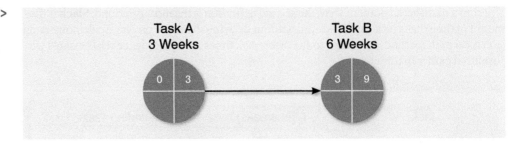

where the early start (ES) time for a particular task is equal to the largest EF time of the prior tasks. Because task C follows task A, its ES time is 3; using Equation 12.3, its EF time is 9 (the EF time is the earliest you can possibly finish any task, based on the precedence relationships). Because task D follows task B, its ES time is 9, and its EF time is 9 + 3 = 12. Task E follows both tasks B and C, which both have an EF time of 9, so the ES time for task E is 9, and the EF time is 9 + 16 = 25. The rest of the network follows the exact same logic. You will notice, however, that task I follows both tasks F and H. Task F has an EF time of 21, and task H has an EF time of 37. Note that both tasks F and H must be completed prior to starting task I. Therefore, the ES time for task I is 37, and its EF time is 37 + 18.33 = week 55.33. The expected completion time for this project is 55.33 weeks.

Computing Late Times

Now that we have computed the early times, we must compute late times. To compute late start (LS) and late finish (LF) times for the project, (LS and LF are the latest you can either start or finish a task, based on the precedence relationships) we perform the *backward pass* from right to left. The LF time for any task is the smallest LS time for the follower tasks. By convention, we will use the EF time as the LF time for the final node in the network. The formula for computing the LS time is

$$LS = LF - t_e \qquad (12.4)$$

Because task I is the follower task for tasks F and H, the LF times for tasks F and H equal 37. The LS time for task H is 37 − 8 = 29. By the same token, the LF time for task F is 37, and the LS time is 37 − 9 = 28. The same logic is followed during the backward pass through the network. Note that we have to choose the LF time for task B that precedes both tasks E and D. Thinking logically, task B has to be completed before either task D or task E can be started. Because the latest time that task E can be started without delaying the project is week 9, the latest time that task B can be finished is also week 9. Therefore, the LF time for task B is week 9 (**FIGURE 12.14**).

Computing Slack and the Critical Path

For some tasks, the ES and LS times are the same. For other tasks, such as task D in our example, they are not the same. A project task has slack when the late start times are later than the early start times. The formula for computing slack is

$$slack = LS - ES = LF - EF \qquad (12.5)$$

FIGURE 12.13 >

Early Start and Finish
Times for the Whole
Network

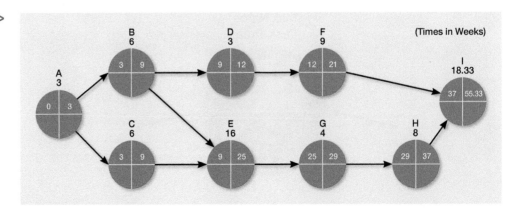

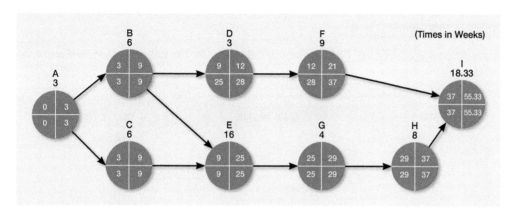

< **FIGURE 12.14**

Late Finish and Late Start Calculations

Therefore, the slack times for the problem we have been working on are as follows:

Task	Late Finish (LF) Time	Early Finish (EF) Time	Slack
A	3	3	0
B	9	9	0
C	9	9	0
D	28	12	16
E	25	25	0
F	37	21	16
G	29	29	0
H	37	37	0
I	55.33	55.33	0

To repeat, a critical path is made up of **critical tasks**. Because tasks A, B, C, E, G, H, and I have no slack, we say that they are critical. These tasks, with their connecting arcs, show us the critical path(s). As you see in **FIGURE 12.15**, A–B–E–G–H–I and A–C–E–G–H–I are both critical paths. Any delay in these tasks will delay the entire project completion time. The expected project completion time (T_e) is computed as

critical tasks
Tasks on the critical path with no slack.

$$T_e = \text{(sum of expected completion times for critical path tasks)} \qquad (12.6)$$

In Solved Problem 12.6, we provide another example of the work we have been doing here.

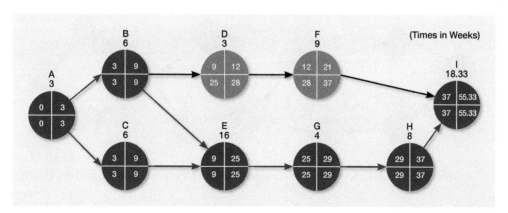

< **FIGURE 12.15**

The Critical Paths in Purple

f(x) **SOLVED PROBLEM 12.6 >**

MyLab Operations Management
Video

Finding the Critical Path

Problem: In Solved Problem 12.5, we drew a PERT chart for the following Hoosier Company data:

Task	t_e (in weeks)	Preceding Tasks
A	4	None
B	5	A
C	3	A
D	4	C
E	6	B
F	4	D, E
G	5	E
H	18	F
I	3	G, H
J	4	I
K	7	I
L	1	J, K

Solution: We now calculate the early times using Equation 12.3 and remembering that the *first task starts at time 0*. By using the forward pass to compute ES and EF times, we find the following:

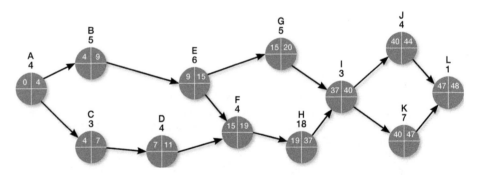

The expected completion time for the project is 48 weeks. Using Equation 12.4 and performing a backward pass to compute the LS and LF times, we find the following:

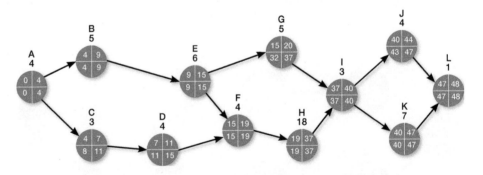

Using Equation 12.5, we can now compute the slack for each task to find the critical path.

Task	Late Finish (LF) Time	Early Finish (EF) Time	Slack
A	4	4	0
B	9	9	0
C	11	7	4
D	15	11	4
E	15	15	0
F	19	19	0
G	37	20	17
H	37	37	0
I	40	40	0
J	47	44	3
K	47	47	0
L	48	48	0

As you can now see, the critical tasks are A, B, E, F, H, I, K, and L. The critical path is as follows:

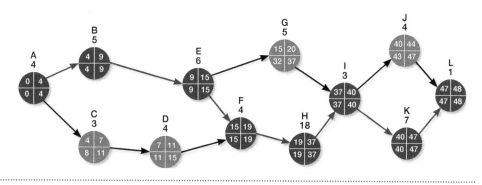

TABLE 12.4 contains a summary of the rules and formulas we have used for computing task times and slack for each of the tasks. Use this table as a quick guide to solving these problems. Companies apply these project management tools to many situations.

Using PERT/CPM in Delegation Decisions

One useful aspect of PERT/CPM is helping project managers identify when to delegate and where to control project progress more diligently. Tasks that have large amounts of slack can get somewhat behind without delaying the entire project. The people responsible for the completion of various tasks may also perform less oversight and request less reporting and updating. By the same token, they monitor critical tasks more carefully to avoid delaying the project. These project management tools are widely applicable. SC&O CURRENT EVENTS 12.1 shows how they were applied in lawyer's offices.

Probabilistic PERT

Now that we have demonstrated some of the basics of PERT/CPM, we can combine it with probability theory to give us a more applicable use of the PERT/CPM data. We refer to this application as **probabilistic PERT**.

probabilistic PERT
A method for computing the probability of completing a project in a given period of time.

∨ TABLE 12.4

PERT/CPM Rules		
Forward Pass Rules for PERT/CPM Early Times	**Backward Pass Rules for PERT/CPM Late Times**	**To Find the Critical Path**
Work from the left.	Work from the right.	Compute slack times for each task where slack $= LS - ES = LF - EF$.
The early start (ES) time for the first task is 0.	Generally, we use the EF time for the last task as the LF time for that same task. (Other LF times could be specified by management to give some additional slack time to the project for unforeseen circumstances.)	The critical path is the path from beginning to end with no slack.
For subsequent tasks, the ES time is the largest EF time for the previous task(s).	For the prior tasks, as you work backward, use the smallest LS time from the follower task(s) as the LF time for the predecessor task.	Any network may have more than one critical path.
The EF time for each task $= ES = t_e$.	The LS time for each task $= LF = t_e$ for that same task.	

In Figure 12.13, we computed an expected completion time of 55.33 weeks. Did you stop to think about what that really means? What do you suppose the probability is of completing the project in 55.33 weeks or less? Project managers use means to determine such probabilities, as illustrated in FIGURE 12.16. An expected value is a mean or average. Assuming that our project completion times are normally distributed, we see that the probability for completing the project in 55.33 weeks or less is 50 percent.

SC&O CURRENT >
EVENTS 12.1

Attorneys Learn to Manage Their Projects

Managers in any company can use the project management tools discussed in this chapter in many situations and in creative ways. Here we see how project management was used by a law firm to improve how its attorneys managed cases.

When you think about it, major court cases are projects. Each one is unique, and each consists of tasks that need to be performed flawlessly for positive outcomes. The chairperson of a large Chicago law firm stated the following: "We work on small, medium and large projects, some litigation, some transactional, some we answer questions."

When a law firm began to implement project management techniques, some of the managers were skeptical. It was apparent that each case was unique and that a one-size-fits-all approach would be spurned by attorneys, who tended to be very independent.

After implementing project management in cases, it became clear that performance was improved, resulting in a better use of an attorney's time. According to a project management expert, "From a law firm perspective, this type of process is enormously effective when operating on an alternative fee arrangement because, if they are going to be profitable, they cannot operate the way they have in the past."*

Source: Based on P. Woldlow, "Lawyers Are Ignoring a Vital Business Development Tool," *The American Lawyer*, Feb 28, 2017.

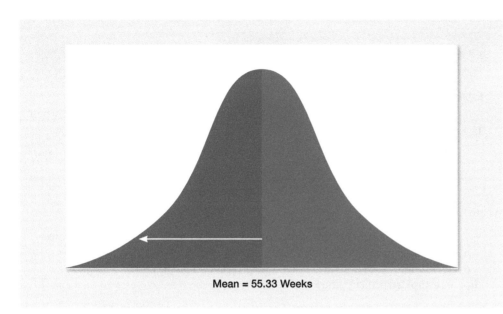

The Probability of
Project Completion
in 55.33 Weeks Is 50
Percent

Mean = 55.33 Weeks

If we want to establish a completion time for the project that provides a greater chance of success, we need to move the completion time farther out into the future, as shown in FIGURE 12.17. Here we see that one key to completing a project successfully comes from having a later due date. Before changing the date, however, managers must determine what is a helpful due date and what is excessive in terms of wasting time, labor, and money.

To solve these problems, we recall Equations 12.1 and 12.2 from the beta distributions, which we reprise in TABLE 12.5. To get the variance σ_p^2 for the entire project (note that the subscript p stands for "project"), add the variances for all critical tasks. Then calculate the standard deviation σ_p of the project by taking the square root of the project variance. Here are the equations:

$$\text{project variance } \sigma_p^2 = \sum \text{critical path variances} \qquad (12.7)$$

$$\text{project standard deviation} = \sqrt{\sigma_p^2} \qquad (12.8)$$

$$\text{needed time to complete a project} = T_{p,est} = \mu_p + z\sigma_p \qquad (12.9)$$

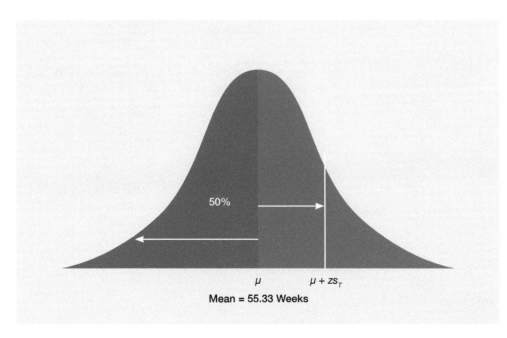

Adding Additional
Time to Increase
the Probability of
Finishing the Project
Successfully

50%

μ $\mu + zs_T$

Mean = 55.33 Weeks

TABLE 12.5 >

Beta Distribution Formulas	
Formula Number and Definition	**Formula**
Expected task time (Equation 12.1)	$t_e = \dfrac{t_o + 4t_m + t_p}{6}$
Task variance (Equation 12.2)	$s_t^2 = \left(\dfrac{t_p - t_o}{6}\right)^2$

where

z = number of standard deviations to provide additional slack time to the project
μ_p = average project completion time
σ_p = estimated standard deviation of the project completion time
$T_{est.p}$ = estimated project time

To demonstrate how to solve these equations, let's turn to Solved Problem 12.7.

 SOLVED PROBLEM 12.7 >

MyLab Operations Management
Video

Computing Required Project Completion Times

Problem: Based on the information we have learned and computed so far, we can now compute critical paths and determine the expected time to complete a project. We recently learned, however, that we only have a 50 percent chance of completing our example project within 55.33 weeks. Our boss has asked us to find a completion time that would give us a 95 percent chance of success.

Task	t_o	t_m	t_p	Preceding Task	t_e	s_e
A	1	3	5	None	$\dfrac{1 + (4 \times 3) + 5}{6} = 3.00$	$\left(\dfrac{5 - 1}{6}\right)^2 = 0.44$
B	2	6	10	A	$\dfrac{2 + (4 \times 6) + 10}{6} = 6.00$	$\left(\dfrac{10 - 2}{6}\right)^2 = 1.78$
C	3	5	13	A	$\dfrac{3 + (4 \times 5) + 13}{6} = 6.00$	$\left(\dfrac{13 - 3}{6}\right)^2 = 2.78$
D	3	3	3	B	$\dfrac{3 + (4 \times 3) + 3}{6} = 3.00$	$\left(\dfrac{3 - 3}{6}\right)^2 = 0.00$
E	12	15	24	B, C	$\dfrac{12 + (4 \times 15) + 24}{6} = 16.00$	$\left(\dfrac{24 - 12}{6}\right)^2 = 4.00$
F	7	9	11	D	$\dfrac{7 + (4 \times 9) + 11}{6} = 9.00$	$\left(\dfrac{11 - 7}{6}\right)^2 = 0.44$
G	3	4	5	E	$\dfrac{3 + (4 \times 4) + 5}{6} = 4.00$	$\left(\dfrac{5 - 3}{6}\right)^2 = 0.11$
H	8	8	8	G	$\dfrac{8 + (4 \times 8) + 8}{6} = 8.00$	$\left(\dfrac{8 - 8}{6}\right)^2 = 0.00$
I	14	16	32	F, H	$\dfrac{14 + (4 \times 16) + 32}{6} = 18.33$	$\left(\dfrac{32 - 14}{6}\right)^2 = 9.00$

Note: Critical tasks are in bold face type.

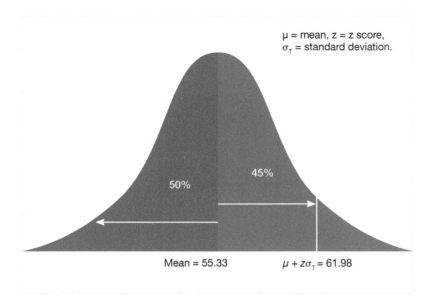

μ = mean, z = z score, σ_T = standard deviation.

45%

50%

Mean = 55.33 $\mu + z\sigma_T = 61.98$

Solution: To find our desired completion time, we will add the variances along the critical path A–C–E–G–H–I. Note that we chose the path with task C over the path with task B because it has a larger variance, which will give us a more conservative estimate. The sum of the task variances is $0.44 + 2.78 + 4 + 0.11 + 0 + 9 = 16.33$. Therefore, the project variance is 16.33. Using Equation 12.8, we find the project standard deviation to be $\sqrt{16.33} = 4.04$. The z value associated with 95 percent from Table A.2 in Appendix A (normal distribution z table) is 1.645. Using Equation 12.9, we see that the completion time that will give us a 95 percent chance of success is $55.33 + 1.645(4.04) = 61.98$ weeks (see Figure 12.17).

< SOLVED PROBLEM 12.8

MyLab Operations Management Video

The Other Side of the Coin: Determining the Probability of Completing a Project in a Given Time

Problem: Suppose that your boss's manager came to your boss asking if she thinks that you can complete the project that we analyzed in Solved Problem 12.7 in 45 weeks. What is the probability of completing the project within 45 weeks?

Solution: Revising Equation 12.9, we get

$$z = \frac{T_{p,est} - \mu_p}{\sigma_p} \qquad (12.10)$$

Using the data from Solved Problem 12.7, we find

$$z = \frac{45 - 55.33}{4.04} = -2.56$$

From Table A.2, we find that $z = -2.56$ results in a probability of 0.4948. Using the following distribution, we can see that the prognosis is not good.

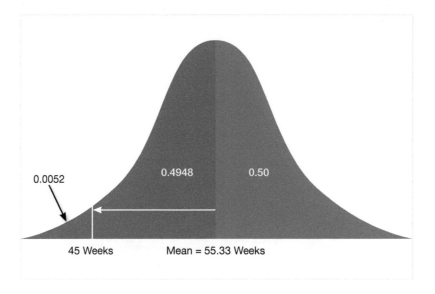

45 Weeks   Mean = 55.33 Weeks

The probability of completing the project within 45 weeks is only 0.0052, or about one-half of 1 percent. This example illustrates the fallacy of setting arbitrary completion dates for projects.

LIMITATIONS OF PERT/CPM Even though PERT and CPM are widely used in project planning, these methods have some limitations:

- For PERT/CPM to be useful, you must clearly identify independent tasks.
- Precedence relationships must be clearly specified and tied together as networks, which requires getting agreement on precedence relationships.
- Time estimates are subject to error.
- Focusing too much on a critical path may lead to ignoring other noncritical paths.

 EARN HOW TO MANAGE COSTS OF PROJECTS THROUGH GANTT CHARTS

Gantt chart
A bar chart project management tool.

Gantt charts are named for Henry Gantt (1861–1919). Gantt charts were early project management tools that were used in the construction of the Hoover Dam and the interstate highway system in the United States.

The Gantt chart in FIGURE 12.18 is a simple bar chart. As you can see, the bars relate to the completion of tasks, and their length relates to the length of time required to complete a task. The bars are shaded relative to the amount of work completed for a particular task. In Figure 12.18, the first task is completed, and the second task is about 20 percent completed. The arrowhead at the top indicates the current date for the project, which makes it easy to see that the second task is behind schedule.

A traditional criticism was that Gantt charts did not show precedence relationships the way that a PERT/CPM chart does, but that is no longer the case. Many software packages, such as MS Project (FIGURE 12.19), provide Gantt charts with arrows that indicate precedence relationships.

Managing Costs and Expediting Projects

We now turn our attention to the management of costs in project management. First, we discuss the *S*-curve pattern of expenditures during a project. Next, we demonstrate the important method of crashing or expediting projects.

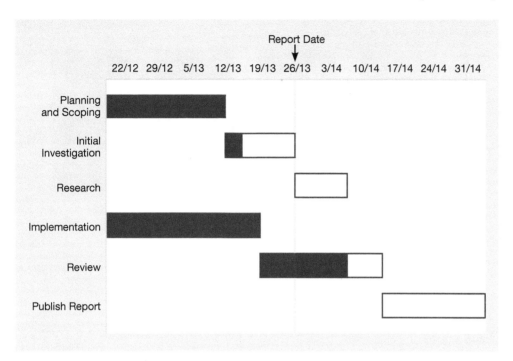

< FIGURE 12.18

Simple Gantt Chart

THE _S_ CURVE The _S_ curve in FIGURE 12.20 shows conceptually how cumulative costs are incurred during a project over time. Managers use the _S_ curve to help track their spending over the course of a project. A variety of project costs, such as labor, materials, and equipment, follow this pattern. As the curve shows, managers do not spend money in a straight-line manner. The early expenditures, typically spent during the concept and planning phases, are low. As projects move into implementation, the rate of spending increases. Finally, in the late stages of the project, the rate of spending once again flattens to zero. Teams use this information

_S_ curve
A graph that shows conceptually how cumulative costs are incurred during a project over time.

∧FIGURE 12.19

MS Project Gantt Chart with Precedence Relationships

FIGURE 12.20 >

The *S* Curve of Project Costs

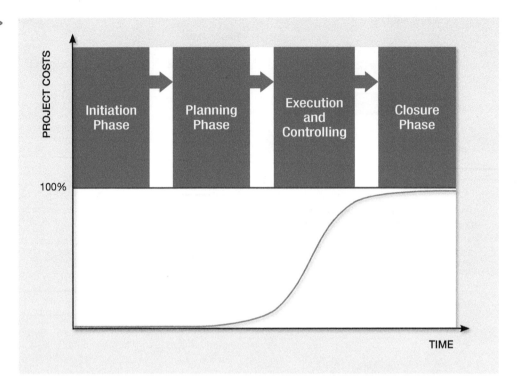

to gauge spending as the project progresses. For example, if a project is one-third of the way through and has spent one-third of the budget, it could be headed for trouble.

Expediting or Crashing Tasks

In Solved Problem 12.8, we discussed increasing the completion time of a project to find a realistic completion time. If increasing the completion time of the project is not an option, managers can use another method to increase the probability of on-time completion, called expediting, or crashing, a project task or set of tasks. **Expediting or crashing**, calls for managers to apply more resources to a project task to reduce its expected completion time. Remember that the expected completion time is usually longer than its optimistic completion time, which means that there may be some opportunity to reduce the task completion time. Reducing the time, however, may require more money or resources.

Despite extra costs, managers find that there can be a business case for spending the extra money to expedite, such as a new market opportunity, a penalty for missing a deadline, or specific performance needs of your supply chain associates. Many of these delay-related costs are indirect project costs. As is shown in FIGURE 12.21, lengthening the project time can result in increased indirect costs. Companies can use the extra resources needed to expend more on overtime, equipment, facilities, or contract labor to expedite tasks and projects.

expediting or crashing
Applying more resources to a project task to reduce its expected completion time.

FIGURE 12.21 >

A Possible Case for Crashing

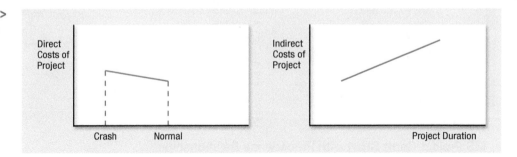

Crashing is fairly straightforward:

1. Identify critical path tasks.
2. Find critical tasks where crashing is possible. Team members cannot crash just any task. If there is more than one critical path, focus on tasks that occupy all the critical paths, if any exist.
3. Compute the average *periodic cost* of crashing. If the project planning was done on a weekly basis, the periodic cost of crashing is a single week. Planning on a daily basis means that the periodic cost of crashing is a single day.
4. Crash the lowest cost critical task by *one period*.
5. Recalculate the entire PERT network to see if the critical path has changed.
6. Repeat steps 1 through 5 until time reduction goals are acheived or no additional crashing can be done. See **SOLVED PROBLEM 12.9**.

....

Crashing Projects

< SOLVED PROBLEM 12.9

Problem: Use the information below to expedite the project by one week. Activities and crash costs are given.

MyLab Operations Management Video

Activity	Normal Task Time (t_e)	Crash Time	Weekly Crash Costs ($)	Critical Task
A	2	2	—	Yes
B	13	9	450	No
C	8	6	375	Yes
D	4	2	650	Yes
E	7	6	1,000	No
F	5	3	350	No
G	3	2	500	Yes

Solution: The following table contains a sorting of the critical tasks. Because we cannot crash task A, we pass on it. The first task we can crash is C because it has the lowest crash cost. After crashing one week, it is typical to resolve the PERT/CPM network to find out what critical task should be considered next.

Activity	Normal Task Time (t_e)	Crash Time	Weekly Crash Costs ($)	Critical Task
A	2	2	0	Yes
C	8	6	375	Yes
G	3	2	500	Yes
D	4	2	650	Yes

Early in the chapter, we talked about the Big Dig and the complications that a project of such magnitude entails. The life of a project manager can be frustrating, but it can also require a great deal of creativity, problem-solving acumen, and energy. Among the problems in the Big Dig were legions of dips and a tunnel collapse that resulted in the death of Milena Del Valle. After the collapse, the tunnel project was shut down for months by then-governor Mitt Romney until a new fastening system was installed.

There were also several design changes to find the best way to cross Boston's Charles River. Delays frustrated Congress, and the spigots of money were slowed. The original cost estimate for the project was $2.8 billion, but the final cost was close to $15 billion.

Even with the construction problems, citizens can now walk from the city center to the waterfront with few problems, and there is open space in the heart of the city. Boston is a better city because of this project. The following are some of the marvels of the Big Dig:

- Five miles of slurry walls
- The widest cabled bridge in the world using an asymmetrical hybrid design
- Changes in soil management to bolster Boston's soft soil
- The most advanced traffic management system in the world

Summary

In this chapter, we introduced some of the key concepts relative to managing projects. We talked about how projects are organized and provided a path to plan projects adequately. The following are some key concepts:

1. The five phases for projects are initiation, planning, execution, monitoring, and closing.
2. The human element is important in managing projects.
   a. The student problem in project management involves procrastinating starting times.
   b. There are several different types of project teams, including process improvement teams, cross-functional teams, tiger teams, natural work groups, self-directed work teams, and virtual teams.
   c. Teams go through stages of forming, storming, norming, performing, and mourning.
   d. Project organizational forms include pure projects, functional project organization, and matrix team structure. Matrix is the most common.
   e. Project charters are important tools for avoiding scope creep.
   f. Risk/return matrices are used to qualify projects.
3. Work breakdown structures are used to identify task times and milestones.
4. PERT/CPM is an excellent method for determining which tasks are critical as well as the completion time for a project.
   a. By creating reasonable completion dates, probabilistic PERT allows you to determine completion times that will give your team a higher chance of success.

b. At the beginning of the chapter, we discussed how project teams are evaluated based on performance, schedule, and cost. It is amazing how these simple tools can provide structure to complete projects successfully. In the end, however, success still lies in the hands of the individuals on the project team. As you apply your talent and creativity to solve novel and difficult problems, you can manage toward project success.

Key Terms

activity-on-node (AON) network   355
change control   342
closing a project   342
crashing   368
critical path   356
critical path method (CPM)   355
critical tasks   359
execution   342
expediting or crashing   368
functional project organization   346
Gantt charts   366
gold plating   342
initiation   342

matrix team structure   346
milestones   350
monitoring and controlling   342
most likely completion time   351
multiple project assignment matrix   354
optimistic completion time   351
pessimistic completion time   351
planning   342
probabilistic PERT   361
program evaluation and review
    technique (PERT)   355
project   341
project charter   348

project chartering   346
project management   342
pure projects   345
qualifying projects   346
risk/return matrix   348
scope creep   348
scope management   342
S curve   367
situational leadership model   342
slack   357
student problem   344
task precedence   350
work breakdown structure (WBS)   350

Integrative Learning Exercise

With a team composed of fellow students, identify a project in which you could be involved. For the project, develop the set of tasks that must be completed, task times, resources required, and objective of the project. Develop a network diagram of the project. Incorporate your time estimates, and identify the project's estimated completion time and the critical path. Also identify the time estimate for which you believe you have a 90 percent chance of success.

Integrative Experiential Exercise

As part of a team, visit an organization and ask employees about a recent project they have undertaken. Inquire about the overall purpose of the project and the objective in completing it, the project's scope, the resources available to complete the project, the time required, and the roles and responsibilities of various managers assigned to the project. Also ask about various project management tools employed to schedule activities, assign resources, and manage the time and costs of the project. What challenges did the company have to overcome to complete the project? Prepare a report that describes your findings.

Discussion Questions

1. Discuss the three primary responsibilities of a project manager.

2. What is meant by the behavioral side of project management?

3. What is the student problem, and how does it relate to project management?

4. Briefly describe four different types of teams. How is the choice of team related to the scope of the project?

5. Outline the different phases of development that teams go through in a project.

6. Discuss possible sources or reasons why conflict can arise in teams.

7. In what ways does the functional project organization differ from the pure project organization?

8. Why do you think the matrix team structure is the most common team organization in project management?

9. What is scope creep? How is scope creep detrimental to a project?

10. What does PERT stand for in project management? What does CPM stand for in project management? What is the purpose of these techniques in project management?

11. What are the major categories of the costs of a project? How are these costs best controlled?

12. What role does the beta distribution play in calculating expected task times and task variances in project management?

13. What does the S curve describe in project management?

14. What is a multiple project assignment matrix? When would it be used?

15. Why do project teams expedite project tasks? How is task expediting accomplished?

Solved Problems

Project Planning Tools

COMPUTING EXPECTED TASK TIME
SOLVED PROBLEM 12.1

1. Assume that a task in a project has the following three time estimates:

optimistic completion time $= t_o = 12$ weeks
most likely completion time $= t_m = 16$ weeks
pessimistic completion time $= t_p = 23$ weeks

Compute the estimated task completion time for this task.

Solution:
Using Equation 12.1, the estimated task completion time is

$$t_e = \frac{t_o + 4t_m + t_p}{6} = \frac{12 + 4(16) + 23}{6} = 16.5 \text{ weeks}$$

COMPUTING TASK VARIANCE
SOLVED PROBLEM 12.2

2. Assume that a task in a project had the following three time estimates:

optimistic completion time $= t_o = 12$ weeks
most likely completion time $= t_m = 16$ weeks
pessimistic completion time $= t_p = 23$ weeks

Compute the task activity time variance.

Solution:
Using Equation 12.2, the estimated task variance is

$$s_t^2 = \left(\frac{t_p - t_o}{6}\right)^2 = \left(\frac{23 - 12}{6}\right)^2 = 3.36 \text{ weeks}$$

PUTTING TOGETHER TASK TIMES AND VARIANCES
SOLVED PROBLEM 12.3

3. The following table shows the optimistic, most likely, and pessimistic times (in weeks) for tasks that are part of a project. Use the information given to compute the expected completion time and variance for each task.

Task	t_o	t_m	t_p
A	2	6	10
B	5	7	9
C	8	11	16
D	12	18	22
E	7	9	11
F	14	16	32
G	8	9	10

Solution:
Using Equation 12.1 to compute the expected task time and Equation 12.2 to compute the task variance, we find the following:

Task	t_o	t_m	t_p	t_e	t_e	s_e^2	s_e^2
A	2	6	10	$\frac{2 + (4 \times 6) + 10}{6} =$	6.00	$\left(\frac{10 - 2}{6}\right)^2 =$	1.78
B	5	7	9	$\frac{5 + (4 \times 7) + 9}{6} =$	7.00	$\left(\frac{9 - 5}{6}\right)^2 =$	0.44
C	8	11	16	$\frac{8 + (4 \times 11) + 16}{6} =$	11.33	$\left(\frac{16 - 8}{6}\right)^2 =$	1.78
D	12	18	22	$\frac{12 + (4 \times 18) + 22}{6} =$	17.67	$\left(\frac{22 - 12}{6}\right)^2 =$	2.78
E	7	9	11	$\frac{7 + (4 \times 9) + 11}{6} =$	9.00	$\left(\frac{11 - 7}{6}\right)^2 =$	0.44
F	14	16	32	$\frac{14 + (4 \times 16) + 32}{6} =$	18.33	$\left(\frac{32 - 14}{6}\right)^2 =$	9.00
G	8	9	10	$\frac{8 + (4 \times 9) + 10}{6} =$	9.00	$\left(\frac{10 - 8}{6}\right)^2 =$	0.11

PERT/CPM

DRAWING AON NETWORKS
SOLVED PROBLEM 12.4

4. The following table provides the list of tasks and immediate preceding tasks for a project. Draw the activity-on-
node (AON) diagram for this project.

Task	Preceding Tasks
A	None
B	A
C	B
D	B
E	C
F	D, E
G	F

Solution:
The AON diagram is as follows:

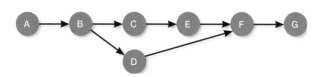

SOLVED PROBLEM 12.5

5. The following table shows a list of tasks, task times (in
weeks), and preceding tasks for a project. Use the information to find the project's critical path.

Activity	t_e	Preceding Tasks
A	4	None
B	5	A
C	4	A
D	9	B
E	7	B
F	4	C
G	5	C
H	9	G
I	7	D, H
J	3	I

Solution:
The activity-on-node diagram is as follows:

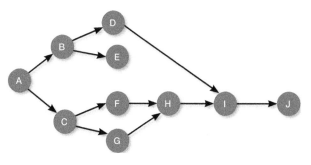

Assuming that the first task starts at time 0, the forward
pass is used to compute the ES and EF times shown in the
following table.

Activity	ES	EF
A	0	4
B	4	9
C	4	8
D	9	18
E	9	16
F	8	12
G	8	13
H	13	22
I	22	29
J	29	32

Using Equation 12.4 and performing the backward pass,
we find the LS and LF times as follows:

Activity	LS	LF
A	0	4
B	8	13
C	4	8
D	13	22
E	25	32
F	9	13
G	8	13
H	13	22
I	22	29
J	29	32

The slack can be computed using Equation 12.5:

Activity	ES	EF	LS	LF	Slack
A	0	4	0	4	0
B	4	9	8	13	4
C	4	8	4	8	0
D	9	18	13	22	4
E	9	16	25	32	16
F	8	12	9	13	1
G	8	13	8	13	0
H	13	22	13	22	0
I	22	29	22	29	0
J	29	32	29	32	0

The activities with 0 slack are the critical path activities and make up the critical path. In this example, the critical path is A → C → G → H → I → J. The expected completion time for the project is 32 weeks.

COMPUTING REQUIRED PROJECT COMPLETION TIMES
SOLVED PROBLEM 12.6

6. A project consists of the following activities (times are in weeks). What is the completion time for the project that would provide a 90 percent chance of completing the project successfully within that time?

Activity	Preceding Task	t_o	t_m	t_p
A		2	4	6
B		3	5	7
C	A	1	4	7
D	B	5	9	13
E	C, D	2	7	12
F	E	3	4	5

Solution:
Draw the network diagram, calculate the expected activity times, and solve for the critical path.

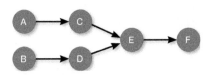

The expected activity times are as follows:

Activity	Preceding Task	$a =$ optimistic time	$m =$ most likely time	$b =$ pessimistic time	$t_e =$ expected time
A		2	4	6	4
B		3	5	7	5
C	A	1	4	7	4
D	B	5	9	13	9
E	C, D	2	7	12	7
F	E	3	4	5	4

Solving for the critical path produces the following:

Activity	Preceding Task	$a =$ optimistic time	$m =$ most likely time	$b =$ pessimistic time	$t_e =$ expected time	$ES =$ early start	$EF =$ early finish	$LS =$ late start	$LF =$ late finish	Slack
A		2	4	6	4	0	4	6	10	6
B		3	5	7	5	0	5	0	5	0
C	A	1	4	7	4	4	8	10	14	6
D	B	5	9	13	9	5	14	5	14	0
E	C, D	2	7	12	7	14	21	14	21	0
F	E	3	4	5	4	21	25	21	25	0

The critical path consists of activities B, D, E, and F.

The variance for each activity on the critical path is as follows. Recall that the variance is $[(t_p - t_o)/6]^2$.

Activity	Preceding Task	$a =$ optimistic time	$m =$ most likely time	$b =$ pessimistic time	$t_e =$ expected time	Slack	Variance
A		2	4	6	4	6	0.444
B		3	5	7	5	0	0.444
C	A	1	4	7	4	6	1
D	B	5	9	13	9	0	1.778
E	C, D	2	7	12	7	0	2.778
F	E	3	4	5	4	0	0.111

The sum of the variances for the critical path activities equals $0.444 + 1.778 + 2.778 + 0.111 + 5.111$, which makes the standard deviation of the project equal to 2.26. The z value associated with a 90 percent probability is found from the normal *distribution z table* to be 1.28.

The completion time that will provide a 90 percent chance of success is $25 + (1.28 \times 2.26) = 27.89$ weeks.

DETERMINING THE PROBABILITY OF COMPLETING A PROJECT IN A GIVEN TIME
SOLVED PROBLEM 12.7

7. A project consists of the following activities (times are in weeks). What is the probability of completing the project within 27 weeks?

Activity	Preceding Task	t_o	t_m	t_p
A		2	4	6
B		3	5	7
C	A	1	4	7
D	B	5	9	13
E	C, D	2	7	12
F	E	3	4	5

Solution:

Draw the network diagram, calculate the expected activity times, and solve for the critical path.

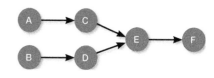

The expected activity times are as follows:

Activity	Preceding Task	$a =$ optimistic time	$m =$ most likely time	$b =$ pessimistic time	$t_e =$ expected time
A		2	4	6	4
B		3	5	7	5
C	A	1	4	7	4
D	B	5	9	13	9
E	C, D	2	7	12	7
F	E	3	4	5	4

Solving for the critical path produces the following:

Activity	Preceding Task	$a =$ optimistic time	$m =$ most likely time	$b =$ pessimistic time	$t_e =$ expected time	$ES =$ early start	$EF =$ early finish	$LS =$ late start	$LF =$ late finish	Slack
A		2	4	6	4	0	4	6	10	6
B		3	5	7	5	0	5	0	5	0
C	A	1	4	7	4	4	8	10	14	6
D	B	5	9	13	9	5	14	5	14	0
E	C, D	2	7	12	7	14	21	14	21	0
F	E	3	4	5	4	21	25	21	25	0

The critical path consists of activities B, D, E, and F.
   The variance for each activity on the critical path is (recall that the variance is $[(t_p - t_o)/6]^2$).

Activity	Preceding Task	$a =$ optimistic time	$m =$ most likely time	$b =$ pessimistic time	$t_e =$ expected time	Slack	Variance
A		2	4	6	4	6	0.444
B		3	5	7	5	0	0.444
C	A	1	4	7	4	6	1
D	B	5	9	13	9	0	1.778
E	C, D	2	7	12	7	0	2.778
F	E	3	4	5	4	0	0.111

The sum of the variances for the critical path activities equals $0.444 + 1.778 + 2.778 + 0.111 = 5.111$, which makes the standard deviation of the project equal to 2.26. The z value associated with 27 weeks is $z = (27 - 25)/2.26 = 0.885$, rounded to 0.89. Using the standard normal z table (Table A.2), we find that the probability associated with a z value equal to 0.89 is 0.813 ($= .5 + .313$). Thus, there is an 81.3 percent probability of completing the project within 27 weeks.

Gantt Charts with Precedence
EXPEDITING OR CRASHING TASKS
SOLVED PROBLEM 12.8

8. Use the following information to expedite the project by two weeks. The project activities and crash costs are given.

Activity	Normal Task Time (t_e)	Crash Time	Weekly Crash Costs	Critical Task
A	4	4	—	Yes
B	8	6	150	No
C	12	8	300	Yes
D	5	4	500	Yes
E	9	7	450	Yes
F	3	2	650	Yes
G	10	9	900	Yes

Solution:
We are unable to reduce the time required to complete task A. Task B is not on the critical path, so reducing its time will not shorten the overall project completion time. Task C is on the critical path, and its weekly crashing cost is less than the weekly cost of any other critical path activities. Therefore, we expedite task C by two weeks (note that it could be expedited by four weeks). The critical path has not changed, but now the project's total time has been reduced by two weeks at a cost of $600.

Problems

Project Planning Tools

ESTIMATING TASK COMPLETION TIMES

1. Three time estimates for a task in a project are as follows:
   optimistic completion time = 4 weeks
   most likely completion time = 9 weeks
   pessimistic completion time = 15 weeks

   Calculate the expected task completion time.

2. Suppose that a task in a project has the following time estimates:
   t_o = optimistic completion time = 6 weeks
   t_m = most likely completion time = 8 weeks
   t_p = pessimistic completion time = 11 weeks

   Compute the expected task completion time.

3. A project has a task with the following task time estimates:
   pessimistic completion time = 18 weeks
   most likely completion time = 15 weeks
   optimistic completion time = 7 weeks

   What is the estimated completion time for the task?

ESTIMATING TASK VARIANCE

4. Three time estimates for a task in a project are as follows:
   optimistic completion time = 4 weeks
   most likely completion time = 9 weeks
   pessimistic completion time = 15 weeks

   Calculate the expected task variance.

5. Suppose that a task in a project has the following time estimates:
   t_o = optimistic completion time = 6 weeks
   t_m = most likely completion time = 8 weeks
   t_p = pessimistic completion time = 11 weeks

   Compute the expected task variance.

6. A project has a task with the following task time estimates:
   pessimistic completion time = 18 weeks
   most likely completion time = 15 weeks
   optimistic completion time = 7 weeks

   What is the variance for the task?

ESTIMATING TASK COMPLETION TIMES AND VARIANCE

7. The optimistic, most likely, and pessimistic times for the tasks making up a project are shown in the following table. Use the data to compute the expected completion time and variance for each task.

Task	t_o	t_m	t_p
A	4	7	11
B	6	10	14
C	2	4	7
D	10	18	22

E	12	17	30
F	14	16	23
G	5	9	10

8. The optimistic, most likely, and pessimistic times for the tasks comprising a project are shown in the following table. Use the data to compute the expected completion time and variance for each task.

Task	t_o	t_m	t_p
A	3	8	13
B	5	11	16
C	1	5	9
D	9	19	24
E	11	18	32
F	13	17	25
G	4	10	12

9. The optimistic, most likely, and pessimistic times for the tasks comprising a project are shown in the following table. Use the data to compute the expected completion time and variance for each task.

Task	t_o	t_m	t_p
A	6	9	12
B	3	10	16
C	4	5	9
D	8	16	24
E	14	21	27

PERT/CPM

10. The following table lists the tasks and preceding tasks for a project. Draw the activity-on-node diagram for this project.

Task	Preceding Tasks
A	None
B	A
C	B
D	B
E	C, D

11. The following table lists the tasks and preceding tasks for a project. Draw the activity-on-node diagram for this project.

Task	Preceding Tasks
A	None
B	A
C	A
D	B
E	C
F	D, E

12. The following table lists the tasks and preceding tasks for a project. Draw the activity-on-node diagram for this project.

Task	Preceding Tasks
A	None
B	None
C	A
D	B
E	C, D
F	E
G	F

FINDING THE CRITICAL PATH

13. Find the critical path for a project with the following task times (task times are in weeks):

Task	Preceding Tasks	t_o	t_m	t_p
A	None	4	6	8
B	A	9	11	14
C	B	6	10	12
D	B	5	8	9
E	C, D	3	6	9

14. The following data describe the tasks and their relationships in a project. Use the data to identify the project's critical path.

Task	Preceding Tasks	t_o	t_m	t_p
A	None	5	9	11
B	A	3	6	12
C	A	8	9	14
D	B	2	4	6
E	C	7	12	15
F	D, E	10	14	20

15. A project consists of the following tasks, with task times in weeks. Use the data provided to identify the project's critical path.

Task	Preceding Tasks	t_o	t_m	t_p
A	None	8	9	10
B	None	5	9	12
C	A	3	5	7
D	B	8	14	19
E	C, D	7	12	16
F	E	10	14	18
G	F	6	10	15

16. The following information relates to a project for the Hawking Company. Use the data provided to solve for the critical path of the project.

Task	Preceding Tasks	t_o	t_m	t_p
A	None	4	5	6
B	A	3	8	11
C	B	5	9	14
D	B	8	10	13
E	C	7	8	9
F	D	12	15	18
G	E, F	6	9	11
H	G	8	14	20
I	H	6	11	17

PROBABILISTIC PERT

17. The following information relates to a project:

Task	Preceding Tasks	t_o	t_m	t_p
A	None	4	6	8
B	A	5	7	9
C	A	3	6	9
D	B	7	11	15
E	C	4	9	14
F	D, E	5	6	7

Use the information to solve for the critical path and then to determine the completion time that would provide a 90 percent chance of success. (*Note:* Task times are in weeks.)

18. The following information relates to a project:

Task	Preceding Tasks	t_o	t_m	t_p
A	None	4	6	8
B	A	5	7	9
C	A	3	6	9
D	B	7	11	15
E	C	4	9	14
F	D, E	5	6	7

Use the information to solve for the critical path and then to determine the probability that the project could be completed within 33 weeks. (*Note:* Task times are in weeks.)

19. The following information relates to a project:

Task	Preceding Tasks	t_o	t_m	t_p
A	None	8	9	10
B	None	5	9	12
C	A	3	5	7
D	B	8	14	19
E	C, D	7	12	16
F	E	10	14	18
G	F	6	10	15

What is the project's completion time for which we are 95 percent sure of success? (*Note:* Task times are in weeks.)

20. The following information relates to a project:

Task	Preceding Tasks	t_o	t_m	t_p
A	None	8	9	10
B	None	5	9	12
C	A	3	5	7
D	B	8	14	19
E	C, D	7	12	16
F	E	10	14	18
G	F	6	10	15

What is the probability that the project can be completed within 60 weeks? What is the probability that the project will take longer than 60 weeks? (*Note:* Task times are in weeks.)

Gantt with Precedence

EXPEDITING (OR CRASHING) TASKS

21. Use the following project information to expedite the project by one week. Times are shown in weeks.

Activity	Normal Task Time	Crash Time	Weekly Crash Costs	Critical Task
A	5	5	—	Yes
B	6	5	500	Yes
C	4	2	250	No
D	8	7	800	Yes
E	3	3	—	Yes

22. Use the following information to expedite the project by two weeks. Project times are in weeks.

Activity	Normal Task Time	Crash Time	Weekly Crash Costs	Critical Task
A	9	7	200	No
B	7	6	300	Yes
C	5	4	100	No
D	14	12	400	Yes
E	12	10	250	Yes
F	10	10	—	Yes
G	8	7	600	Yes

23. The following information relates to a company's project. Times are in days. How should the company crash the project to expedite it by three days?

Activity	Normal Task Time	Crash Time	Daily Crash Costs	Critical Task
A	7	7	—	No
B	12	10	1,000	No
C	6	5	600	Yes
D	8	5	1,400	Yes
E	12	10	1,200	Yes
F	3	1	800	Yes

Getting the Ducks in a Row for Project Management

Roberta Rodriguez has been assigned the responsibility of managing the new layout design for her company's production facility in Tennessee. This redesign involves an analysis of the existing layout, identifying and analyzing improved layout solutions, selecting new equipment, designing the new layout, modifying the existing plant, and implementing the new production process. The company would like to complete the project as expeditiously as possible because the demand for its products is strong and because no production capacity will be available at Roberta's plant during the modification. Roberta has been meeting with plant management and engineers, and the following tasks and estimated task times required to complete the changeover have been identified:

Activity Description	Activity Label	Predecessor	Optimistic Time (days)	Most Likely Time (days)	Pessimistic Time (days)
Analyze current layout	A	—	5	7	15
Investigate alternative layouts	B	—	10	15	30
Analyze proposed layouts and identify solution	C	B	10	30	45
Identify and approve equipment vendors	D	C	5	7	9
Source equipment	E	D	45	60	90
Break down existing layout	F	C	5	10	15
Update plant power infrastructure	G	F	3	8	12
Install new equipment	H	G	5	9	16
Train workers on new layout and equipment	I	H	8	12	20
Test layout	J	I	3	5	9
Revise layout as needed	K	J	2	4	6
Implement standard operating procedures	L	K	2	3	4

Questions:

1. Draw the network diagram for the project.

2. Compute the expected activity times and activity time variances for each task.

3. Identify the project's critical path.

4. For what project duration could Roberta be 90 percent certain of completing the layout redesign project?

5. Which tasks, if any, would you recommend crashing?

13 Supply Chain Quality Management

CHAPTER OUTLINE AND LEARNING OBJECTIVES

1 Understand the Importance of Product Quality Dimensions
- Articulate dimensions of quality clearly.

2 Discuss the Basics of Quality Management as Espoused by Deming, Juran, Crosby, and Ishikawa
- Reconcile differences between various quality experts.

3 Understand Supply Chain Quality Management
- Explain the importance of forming collaborative relationships with international suppliers.
- Understand and apply ISO 9000 and industry-specific standards.

4 Understand and Apply Quality in Services
- Apply various service quality dimensions and understand their effects.
- Understand and apply SERVQUAL.
- Acknowledge the importance of customer-driven excellence in the service industry and know when to use it effectively.

5 Understand and Apply Quality Tools and Approaches
- Discuss and apply the seven basic quality tools.
- Discuss and apply the seven managerial tools.
- Describe merits of the Malcolm Baldrige National Quality Award.
- Understand the importance of and apply benchmarking techniques.

Chipotle "Crashes" Because of Quality Problems

Quality is a major strategic imperative for firms today. Consider the case of Chipotle.

Steve Ells, a former sous-chef at a posh San Francisco restaurant and student at the Culinary Institute of America, founded Chipotle, a purveyor of cannon-sized burritos and Mexican food. Its menu consists of Tex-Mex burritos, burrito bowls, tacos, chips, guacamole, and drinks. Chipotle positioned itself as a forward-thinking, animal-friendly, environment-friendly, millennial-understanding, storytelling restaurant chain. The food and the story were equally good. Its advertising was largely word-or-mouth and viral.

In 2015, five cases of *E. coli* broke out in Seattle, Washington. Next, customers contracted norovirus from Chipotle food in California and Massachusetts. Chipotle's stock price dropped from a high of $750 per share to under $400. This was followed by a devastating $28 million loss. It was obvious that Chipotle's food was unsafe and that the company's supply chain quality practices needed to improve as in-store sales dropped by 20 percent. In this chapter, we will discuss supply chain quality basics to help your firms avoid such problems. We will return to Chipotle at the end of the chapter.

In this chapter, we will discuss the fundamentals of managing quality in the supply chain. They are core ideas, tools, and philosophies that firms follow to enhance competitiveness and customer satisfaction.

You hear news stories about quality mishaps, some perceived and others real. IRS employees give incorrect tax advice. Delta and United cancel flights due to computer problems. VW/Audi misrepresents emissions data. Samsung phones burst into flames due to defective batteries. Government computers are hacked due to outdated security. Public schools come under fire for poor outcomes. The list goes on and on. The costs incurred from finding and fixing these problems run into the billions of dollars, and consumers are left to wonder which products or services they can trust.

Quality in products and services is a leading concern of chief executive officers and supply chain and operations (SC&O) executives around the world. Quality problems can cause firms to lose customers and can land companies on the front pages of the world's newspapers or ridiculed in online reviews. As a result, to be an effective manager, you need to understand the fundamentals of quality management. This chapter covers many of the concepts, principles, and tools that you will encounter in your professional life, regardless of your major or field of study. Chapter 14 introduces statistical quality control, and Chapter 15 introduces lean management and Six Sigma principles. In these three chapters, we discuss quality management, review quality tools, and teach you principles that are used throughout the world to improve competitiveness.

UNDERSTAND THE IMPORTANCE OF PRODUCT QUALITY DIMENSIONS

In this chapter, we will study the basics of supply chain quality management, an important subject for SC&O managers. Think about how you evaluate the quality of a car, a dinner, a computer, a class at your university, or a guitar. Experts in quality management do not necessarily talk about "improving quality" very much because the term *quality* is very subjective and means different things to different people. This subjective nature of the word *quality* is difficult to communicate but is inherently understood by us all. Although we may not be able to define and measure quality concretely, we can still recognize it.

The American Society for Quality defines quality as follows:

> **Quality:** A subjective term for which each person or sector has its own definition. In technical usage, quality can have two meanings: 1. the characteristics of a product or service that bear on its ability to satisfy stated or implied needs; 2. a product or service free of deficiencies.

Instead of belaboring a universal definition of quality, David Garvin, a Harvard professor and quality expert, has identified product quality dimensions for manufactured products. **Garvin's eight dimensions of quality** are found in TABLE 13.1. Understanding these dimensions of quality will help you communicate more clearly about quality. Even though the statement "We need to improve quality" is unclear, when you discuss reliability, people generally understand that you are discussing the failure rate of products. Thus, dimensions of quality are useful because they are much more clearly communicated.

quality
(1) The characteristics of a product or service that bear on its ability to satisfy stated or implied needs. (2) A product or service free of deficiencies.

Garvin's eight dimensions of quality
Performance, features, reliability, conformance, durability, serviceability, aesthetics, and perceived quality.

< TABLE 13.1

Garvin's Dimensions of Product Quality

Quality Dimension	Definition	Application
Performance	The efficiency with which a product achieves its intended purpose	A product's carbon footprint, distortion level of a speaker, ability of a pair of skis to "shred the gnar" effortlessly
Features	Product attributes that supplement the product's basic functionality	Self-cleaning oven, keyless entry to an auto, Bluetooth on a computer, 4G on an iPad
Reliability	Propensity for a product to function over its useful life	Long-life lightbulbs, Steelcase desks that last nearly forever, everlasting love
Conformance	The extent to which products meet specifications	Airplanes that meet demanding federal requirements, mating parts that fit together well, on-time delivery
Durability	The degree to which a product tolerates stress or trauma without failing	Fisher-Price toys, Corelle nonbreaking dishes, products made with titanium alloys
Serviceability	Ease of repair for products	No-questions-asked guarantees, on-site repair, 100,000-mile bumper-to-bumper warrantees
Aesthetics	Subjective sensory attributes of a product such as taste, feel, sound, look, and smell	Cashmere socks, gold-plated faucets, plasma televisions, down-filled silk comforters
Perceived quality	Quality assessment based on customer opinion	Most luxury goods, products that have strong reputations for reliability

Based on Garvin, D., "What Does Product Quality Really Mean?," *Sloan Management Review* (Fall 1984): 25–43.

D ISCUSS THE BASICS OF QUALITY MANAGEMENT AS ESPOUSED BY DEMING, JURAN, CROSBY, AND ISHIKAWA

To understand quality management, we must first lay its foundations. Historically, firms and individuals made money by harvesting resources, such as lumber or minerals. In recent decades, however, industries and firms created great amounts of wealth by simply learning how to produce things more effectively. In this section, we discuss the people who led to this better way of making and delivering products and services: W. Edwards Deming, Joseph Juran, Philip Crosby, and Kaoru Ishikawa. These leading quality thinkers have fundamentally changed the world economy.

W. Edwards Deming

statistical thinking
Deming's concept of looking at problems through the lens of data.

system for quality improvement
A system in which all the variables (e.g., processes, tools, equipment, and people) interact to create a quality result.

plan, do, check, act (PDCA) cycle
Deming's improvement cycle based on the scientific method.

Dr. W. Edwards Deming gained credibility as a quality leader due to the influence he had on Japanese and U.S. firms. He is best known for **statistical thinking**, or looking at quality problems from a data-driven perspective. He also proposed focusing on the **system for quality improvement**, a system in which all the variables interact to create a quality result (e.g., processes, tools, equipment, or people). After World War II, the U.S. Secretary of War sent Deming to Japan to work on a population census. During this time, the Japanese Union of Scientists and Engineers invited him to provide lectures on statistical quality control. These lectures were condensed into a book titled *Elementary Principles of the Statistical Control of Quality*. The sales of this book were used to fund the Japanese Deming Prize for Quality.

The process for improvement espoused by Deming was the **plan, do, check, act (PDCA) cycle** (also referred to as plan, do, study, act). As shown in FIGURE 13.1, PDCA is a continual cycle for improvement. During the *plan phase*, managers identify problems, assess root causes, and propose new and better methods for processing. During the *do phase*, managers perform a trial experiment to test their improvements. During the *check phase*, managers review their implementation to see if they achieved the desired results and make adjustments as necessary.

FIGURE 13.1 >

Deming's Plan-Do-Check-Act (PDCA) Cycle

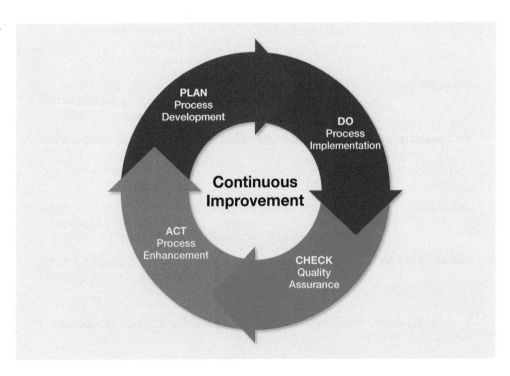

Deming's 14 Points for Management

1. Create constancy of purpose toward improvement of product and service, with the aim to become competitive and stay in business, and to provide jobs.
2. Adopt the new philosophy. We are in a new economic age. Western management must awaken to the challenge, must learn their responsibilities, and must take on leadership for change.
3. Cease dependence on inspection to achieve quality. Eliminate the need for massive inspection by building quality into the product in the first place.
4. End the practice of awarding business on the basis of price tag. Instead, minimize total cost. Move toward a single supplier for any one item, on a long-term relationship of loyalty and trust.
5. Improve constantly and forever the system of production and service, to improve quality and productivity, and thus constantly decrease costs.
6. Institute training on the job.
7. Institute leadership. The aim of supervision should be to help people and machines and gadgets do a better job. Supervision of management is in need of overhaul, as well as supervision of production workers.
8. Drive out fear so that everyone may work effectively for the company.
9. Break down barriers between departments. People in research, design, sales, and production must work as a team to foresee problems of production and in use that may be encountered with the product or service.
10. Eliminate slogans, exhortations, and targets for the workforce asking for zero defects and new levels of productivity. Such exhortations only create adversarial relationships as the bulk of the causes of low quality and low productivity belong to the system and thus lie beyond the power of the workforce.
11. a. Eliminate work standards (quotas) on the factory floor. Substitute leadership.
    b. Eliminate management by objective. Eliminate management by numbers, numerical goals. Substitute leadership.
12. a. Remove barriers that rob the hourly worker of his or her right to pride of workmanship. The responsibility of supervisors must be changed from sheer numbers to quality.
    b. Remove barriers that rob people in management and in engineering of their right to pride of workmanship.
13. Institute a vigorous program of education and self-improvement.
14. Put everybody in the company to work to accomplish the transformation. The transformation is everybody's job.

Source: Deming, W. Edwards, *Out of the Crisis*, 14 Points, pages 23–24, © 2000 Massachusetts Institute of Technology, by permission of The MIT Press.

Finally, during the *act phase*, they make the improvements permanent. The PDCA cycle is the basis for continuous improvement. For example, the Health Survey of England, an independent work-health regulator in Great Britain, has based all its health and safety activities on continuous improvement by using the PDCA cycle.

Another major contribution from Deming was **Deming's 14 points for management**, listed in TABLE 13.2. These points provide an overview of modern quality management thinking. Deming synthesized these points as a result of years of experience with the world's leading firms.

Deming's 14 points for management
The underpinnings for modern quality thinking.

Joseph Juran

Along with Deming, Joseph Juran helped change the thinking about quality management around the world. Whereas Deming was more statistically oriented, Juran was much more strategic in his approach to quality. He proposed three basic processes that are essential for managing to improve quality known now as **Juran's trilogy**. The interrelated points of the trilogy are *planning*, *control*, and *improvement*. Juran discussed these points as follows:[1]

Juran's trilogy
Juran's interrelated points of planning, control, and improvement.

[1] J. M. Juran, *Juran on Planning for Quality* (Boston: Free Press, 1988).

It all begins with quality planning. The purpose of quality is to provide the operating forces with the means of producing products that meet the customer's needs, products such as invoices, polyethylene film, sales contracts, service calls, and new designs for goods. Once planning is complete, the plan is turned over to the operating forces. Control includes putting out the fires, such as sporadic spikes.[2]

Juran emphasized the differences between **big Q quality** and **little q quality**.[3] *Little q quality* considerations were primarily tactical in nature. *Big Q quality* issues were strategic. Big Q and little q quality are shown in TABLE 13.3.

big Q quality
Strategic quality issues.

little q quality
Tactical quality issues.

....

Managing Across Majors 13.1 Strategy majors, Joseph Juran's approach to quality management mostly focuses on strategic planning to improve quality.

....

TABLE 13.3 >

Juran's Little q and Big Q Qualities		
Topic	**Content of Little q**	**Content of Big Q**
Products	Manufactured goods	All products, goods, and services, whether for sale or not
Processes	Processes directly related to manufacture of goods	All process manufacturing support: business, and so on
Industries	Manufacturing	All industries, manufacturing, service, government, and so on, whether for profit or not
Quality viewed as:	A technological problem	A business problem
Customers	Clients who buy the products	All who are affected, external and internal
How to think about quality	Based on culture of functional departments	Based on the universal trilogy (Juran's trilogy involves *planning*, *control*, and *improvement*)
Quality goals are included:	Among factory goals	In company business plan
Cost of poor quality	Costs associated with deficient manufactured goods	All costs that would disappear if everything were perfect
Evaluation of quality is based mainly on:	Conformance to factory specifications, procedures, standards	Responsiveness to customer needs
Improvement is directed at:	Departmental performance	Company performance
Training in managing for quality is:	Concentrated in the quality department	Company-wide
Coordination is by:	The quality managers	A quality council of upper managers

Source: J. Juran, *Juran on Leadership for Quality* (New York, NY: The Free Press, 1989), pp. 47–48.

[2]J. M. Juran, *Juran on Planning for Quality* (Boston: Free Press, 1988), p. 11.

[3]J. M. Juran, *Juran's Quality Handbook* (New York: McGraw-Hill, 1998).

Philip Crosby

Philip Crosby was the well-known author of *Quality Is Free* and the DRIFT principle ("*do it right the first time*"). Crosby was probably the most successful quality consultant of all time. Although he began his career as a podiatrist, he later joined International Telephone and Telegraph as the director of quality. Subsequently, he founded Philip Crosby and Associates.

The primary thesis of his book is that quality, as a managed process, can be a source of improved financial performance for any firm. He specified an approach known as **Crosby's 14 steps** for quality improvement.

Crosby's 14 steps
The steps Crosby suggests for guiding quality improvement.

Managing Across Majors 13.2 Human resources and organizational behavior majors, Philip Crosby emphasizes human resources and organizational behavior factors in improving quality.

Kaoru Ishikawa

Dr. Ichiro Ishikawa was the distinguished founder of the Japanese Union of Scientists and Engineers (JUSE). His son, Kaoru Ishikawa, went on to lead JUSE and became the foremost Japanese leader in the quality movement. Kaoru Ishikawa developed the seven basic tools of quality that work well within the Deming and Juran frameworks.[4] These tools will be presented later in this chapter.

As the developer of the seven basic tools of quality, Kaoru Ishikawa is credited with *democratizing statistics*; that is, the tools are designed so that workers can achieve the effect of statistical analysis without advanced statistical training. He is also credited with coining the phrase *company-wide quality control*.

The resources these quality leaders have provided are guideposts for all industries worldwide. Companies from General Electric to General Motors to Toyota have applied the philosophies and concepts of these quality leaders to improve their production methods. Managers use these ideas as a springboard, taking them to the next level by implementing the concepts and tools you will learn in this chapter.

UNDERSTAND SUPPLY CHAIN QUALITY MANAGEMENT

Now that we have defined the various dimensions of quality and discussed the basics of quality thought, we can put quality into a supply chain context. Because competition is between supply chains, a firm's product quality conformance is only as good as the conformance of its weakest supplier. Coordination, collaboration, and development are needed for firms to ensure quality for the customer. To provide customers with the best-quality goods and services in the most effective manner, we adopt the following definition of supply chain quality management:

> **Supply chain quality management (SCQM)** is defined as a systems-based approach to performance improvement that leverages opportunities created by upstream and downstream linkages with suppliers and customers.[5]

supply chain quality management (SCQM)
A systems-based approach to performance improvement that leverages opportunities created by upstream and downstream linkages with suppliers and customers.

A lot of the quality problems you hear about in the press relate to supplier issues. Although some issues stem from poor quality products from local suppliers (such as Toyota's accelerator issue), international suppliers present their own set of problems. In GLOBAL CONNECTIONS 13.1, we discuss how firms have struggled with international suppliers and what tools they use to circumvent and solve supply issues.

[4]K. Ishikawa, *Guide to Quality Control* (White Plains, NY: Asian Productivity Organization, 1968).
[5]S. T. Foster, "Towards an Understanding of Supply Chain Quality Management," *Journal of Operations Management* 26, no. 4 (2008): 461–7.

Managing International Suppliers

Supply chain quality problems have filled the front pages of the popular press and online news reports in recent years. When a firm chooses to outsource internationally, order times can fluctuate, there is loss of control, and communication can be poor. A volcano in Iceland can ground airlines in Europe. A tsunami can cause disruptions in supplies coming from Japan. Bureaucratic snafus in India can create headaches for supply chain partners around the world.

China has become a leading manufacturing powerhouse since the 1990s. With liberalization of the Chinese economy under Deng Xiaoping and subsequent leaders, China entered the world economy with an open door policy, which was an attempt to alleviate poverty in this populous country. Deng's effort was rewarded with admission to the World Trade Organization (WTO), and a quick walk down the aisle of any store will reveal that many of the products that we use in our daily lives are made in China.

China is constantly dealing with the tension between internal actors who want protectionism and those who want to increase international trade. Setting that issue aside, what do you think about the quality of Chinese products? Admittedly, their product quality results have been mixed.

The U.S. Consumer Product Safety Commission ordered a recall of some toys made by Fisher-Price due to high levels of leaded paint. The Chinese government quickly responded by calling this move protectionist and blaming Mattel and Fisher-Price for the dire quality mistake. The Fisher-Price lead scare came on the heels of successive warnings on products from China involving toothpaste, pet food, tires, eels, seafood, and medicines. Other products, such as Chinese chopsticks, soybeans, blankets, clothing, bottled water, and canned fruit, have all come under condemnation. These problems and others led *Business Week* to wonder aloud with its cover page question, "Can China Be Fixed?"

The Chinese government has dealt with quality issues in a variety of conflicting ways:

- The government admitted to "widespread quality-control issues."
- The government has complained about unfair treatment in the world press and ruminated about other countries using the quality issue as a protectionist canard.
- Internally, China has executed two businesspeople over tainted melamine milk and executed a food and drug government official for accepting bribes and allowing unsafe medicines to be exported.
- In a proverbial shot across the bow at the European Union, Chinese provincial officials slammed foreign luxury brands such as Hermes, Hugo Boss, Tommy Hilfiger, Versace, Dolce and Gabanna, and Zara. In a statement from the Zheijang Administration of Industry and Commerce, they said, "International designer clothes, blindly worshipped by Chinese consumers and enjoying super-national treatment . . . have once again proven unsuitable for China."*

Although these responses from China have been contradictory and confusing to some supply chain partners, it has been predicted that within a very few years, China will consistently compete at a world-class quality level. Just one example of outstanding production quality is the production of Apple products by Foxconn, a Taiwanese firm with plants in China.

*Based on S. Canaves, "China Slams Luxury Goods' Quality," *The Wall Street Journal*, March 17, 2010.

Managing Across Majors 13.3 International business students, global supply chain quality is a hot topic as firms struggle with managing supplier quality.

Now that we have discussed the issues that U.S. firms have had with global manufacturers, let's turn to ways managers have found to alleviate some of the risks that come with using foreign-made products.

Forming Collaborative Relationships

As discussed in Chapter 6, when purchasing managers procure a product or service that is critical in nature, meaning that it is important to the production of the end product, they should work toward alliance-based relationships with a limited number of suppliers. These **collaborative supplier relationships** comprise several quality dimensions:

- Long-term relationships with few suppliers
- Selecting and rewarding suppliers based on quality considerations
- Training and developing suppliers
- Involving suppliers in design and troubleshooting

Inspired by lean purchasing approaches learned from Japanese industry, collaborative relationships have emerged that treat suppliers as de facto subsidiaries of the customer organization. We say "de facto subsidiaries" because as information is shared and communications are improved, the relationship begins to resemble that between a parent and a subsidiary instead of between separate firms.

It is difficult to accomplish a collaborative relationship if a firm has many suppliers. First, it is cost prohibitive because it takes a lot of money to develop and to train suppliers. Second, suppliers add variation to the process. For example, materials from different suppliers such as rolls of sheet metal, although they meet the same specifications, will have different properties, thus creating difficult-to-handle variation. And it is difficult to communicate effectively or to link enterprise systems to suppliers.

ISO 9000 and Industry-Specific Standards

ISO 9000 is the most significant quality standard in the world. The standard is administered by the International Organization for Standardization (ISO) of Geneva, Switzerland (the Greek symbol *isos* means "equal"). ISO 9000 is not a prescription for running a business or a firm, but its requirements provide a recognized international quality standard that businesses can follow. It also makes a statement to customers that a firm has a quality system in place and shows that a firm's quality system has been audited by an outside firm (an ISO registrar).

The focus for ISO 9000 is for companies to document their quality systems in a series of manuals to facilitate global trade through supplier conformance. ISO 9000 registration shows that a company has a quality system in place and is adhering to it. There are hundreds of thousands of firms internationally that are ISO 9000–registered. If you go to work for a major or even a small company, it too will likely be ISO 9000–registered.

Through ISO 9000, firms document their quality management system using a variety of established standard operating procedures. Steps include how to develop, design, implement, and maintain quality-related documentation. Sections of ISO 9000 are shown in TABLE 13.4.[6]

The ISO process includes choosing a registrar that is recognized by your customers. The registrar can assist in developing procedures and performing an audit to ensure that companies follow those procedures. After achieving registration, the company will perform audits at regular intervals to ensure that firms are following the ISO 9000 standard.

Industry-specific standards are adaptations of the ISO 9000 standard to specific industries and situations. Some of these standards are major. For example, ISO/TS 16949 is a standard for the global auto industry. ISO 14000 is a global environmental standard. Some of the standards are quite arcane, such as ISO 261, the "standard for general purpose metric screw threads."

[6]Reprinted by permission from the International Organization for Standardization. This material is being adapted from ISO 9001—Page 5 (100 words/1000) from http://www.iso.org/iso/pub100304.pdf.

collaborative supplier relationships
Working with suppliers to provide value to customers.

ISO 9000
A global standard for quality.

ISO 9000 is an important global standard for quality.

TABLE 13.4 >

ISO 9000 Standards

ISO 9000—Quality management systems: Fundamentals and Vocabulary

ISO 9001—Quality management systems: Requirements. This specifies the requirements of a quality management system. These requirements are used for internal implementation, contractual purposes, or third-party registrations.

ISO 9001consists of five clauses:
- Clause 4: Quality management system
- Clause 5: Management system
- Clause 6: Resource management
- Clause 7: Product realization
- Clause 8: Measurement, analysis, and improvement

ISO 9004—Quality management: guidelines for performance improvement. This broader document provides guidelines for objectives that are not included in ISO 9001. These include continual improvement and enhancing overall performance.

Source: Based on ISO 9000 Standards from https://www.iso.org/obp/ui/#iso:std:iso:9001:ed-4:v1: en:sec:4

U NDERSTAND AND APPLY QUALITY IN SERVICES

In Chapter 4, we discussed designing services that are world-class and providing the utmost satisfaction to customers. Quality in services and products (manufacturing) are not mutually exclusive. All manufacturers have a service element to their business, and all service providers create tangibles. Therefore, service quality is very important to you no matter what type of business you go into. First, we will define service quality, and then we will talk about service quality concepts and tools.

Managers always need to remember to mind the service "gap" when anticipating and analyzing customer expectations.

Parasuraman, Zeithamel, and Berry's Dimensions of Service Quality			< TABLE 13.5
Quality Dimensions	**Definition**	**Application**	
Tangibles	Physical appearance and appropriateness of service facility and other related material attributes	Clean hotel rooms, attractive stage setting at a concert, well-designed classrooms, appealing brochures	
Service reliability	The ability of the service provider to perform her job dependably and accurately	Trusted doctors, authors who write books with few errors, truly funny clowns	
Responsiveness	The willingness of a service provider to be prompt and helpful	Short waiting times in doctor's offices, fast service at the department of motor vehicles, quick and friendly service at a restaurant	
Assurance	The ability of service providers to inspire trust and confidence	A reassuring president during a crisis, a favorite professor who helped you succeed in a difficult class	
Empathy	Caring and individualized attention	The dentist who assures you about upcoming dental work, a beloved teacher, the funny clown who shakes a child's hand	

Source: Reprinted by permission from A. Parasuraman, V. Zeithamel, and L. Berry, "A Conceptual Model of Service Quality" (Report No. 84-106), Marketing Science Institute, 1984.

Service Quality Dimensions

Service quality is somewhat more difficult to define than product quality. Although service and manufacturing share many attributes, services often are harder to manage in terms of quality because of provider–customer interactions. For example, you probably would not care if the worker who produced your backpack was in a foul mood during production as long as the backpack is made correctly, but it would be hard to have a good time in a restaurant if your server is in a bad mood, despite great food and decor. Parasuraman, Zeithamel, and Berry (PZ&B), three marketing professors, published a widely recognized set of service quality dimensions, which have been applied in many firms. TABLE 13.5 shows the PZ&B dimensions.

The Ritz-Carlton in Dubai is an excellent example of a firm that focuses its resources on high-quality service. Remember that the outstanding service provided by Ritz-Carlton does not just happen because of good intentions. It is the result of philosophies, policies, procedures, service design, and excellent execution through its employees. SC&O CURRENT EVENTS 13.1 discusses service quality at the Ritz-Carlton.

SERVQUAL

When you ride the subway in London, signs warn you to "mind the gap," the space between the platform and the train. In this section, we discuss how to "mind the quality gap." In Chapter 5, we discussed customer relationship management and talked about B2B and B2C relationships. Sometimes, you may need to evaluate whether or not you are adequately satisfying your customers. **SERVQUAL** is a set of companion surveys used to perform gap analysis in service firms. It is based on the notion that customers are more satisfied when their perceptions

SERVQUAL
A set of companion surveys used to perform gap analysis in service firms and based on the notion that customers are more satisfied when their perceptions of a service are closely aligned with the service design of the service provider.

Excellent Service at the Ritz-Carlton

The Ritz-Carlton Hotel Company manages 80 luxury hotels in North America, Europe, Asia, Australia, the Middle East, Africa, and the Caribbean and competes against nearly 10 hotel groups in the "luxury" and "upscale, deluxe" categories in the industry. More than 85 percent of the company's employees, known as "The Ladies and Gentlemen of The Ritz-Carlton," are frontline workers in hotels. Through extensive training programs and by offering opportunities for professional development, the company encourages personnel to advance in the organization.

Highlights

- In an independent survey, 99 percent of guests said they were satisfied with their overall experience; more than 80 percent were "extremely satisfied."
- First-year managers and employees receive 250 to 310 hours of training.
- Any employee can spend up to $2,000 to correct a problem or handle a complaint immediately.
- Pretax return on investment and earnings (before income taxes, depreciation, and amortization) nearly doubled since 1995.
- From a field of 3,528 nominees, the Ritz-Carlton was selected "Overall Best Practices Champion" from a study by Cornell School of Hotel Administration and McGill University.

Managers raised the goals for customer satisfaction to the "top of the box"; earning ratings of "very satisfied" or "extremely satisfied" became a top priority as well as a key element of the hotel's strategy to achieve 100 percent customer loyalty. In its operations, the company set the target of "defect-free" experiences for guests, implementing a measurement system to chart progress toward elimination of all customer problems, no matter how minor. Management took actions to realize other major opportunities for improvement. It revamped its strategic planning process to make it more systematic, and it refined its total quality management system, with the aim of achieving fuller and deeper integration into the organization. One output of this reassessment is the *Greenbook*, Ritz-Carlton's handbook of quality processes and tools, a reference that is distributed to all employees, who can refer to it at any time.

To help set a clear direction for continuous improvement and to align actions at all business and operational levels, the Ritz-Carlton has developed its pyramid concept. Positioned at the top is the company's mission: "To be the premier worldwide provider of luxury travel and hospitality products and services." Levels below that consist of the Ritz-Carlton 10-year mission (product and profit dominance), 5-year mission (broken down into 14 "vital few objectives"), tactics for improving key processes, and strategies and action plans for sharpening customer and market focus. The foundations for these tiers are the company's total quality management system and methods.

Source: Based on NIST, Criteria for Performance Excellence (Gaithersburg, MD: NIST, 2017).

gap
A difference between current quality and desired quality.

gap analysis
Quality management using Parasuraman, Zeithamel, and Berry's SERVQUAL tool.

expectation-perception gap
The difference between what customers expect and what they receive from a service provider.

SERVQUAL expectations survey
An instrument to measure customer expectations of a service.

SERVQUAL perceptions survey
An instrument to measure customer perceptions of a service.

of a service are closely aligned with the service design of the service provider. A misalignment between provider and customer perceptions of service quality is called a **gap**. Therefore, SERVQUAL analysis is often referred to as **gap analysis.**

FIGURE 13.2 illustrates the **expectation-perception gap**, the gap that occurs when the service that the customer expects is different from his or her perception of the service that he or she receives. To determine if this gap exists, a **SERVQUAL expectations survey** is administered to potential customers to see what the customers really desire in the areas of tangibles, reliability, responsiveness, assurance, and empathy (recall the PZ&B dimensions from earlier in the chapter). Next, the service organization's customers are administered a **SERVQUAL perceptions survey**. Based on the findings, managers estimate the differences

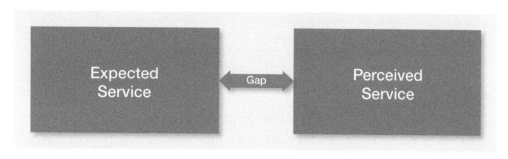

The Expectation-Perception Gap

to determine if there is a gap in perceptions by the customer. If differences are found, managers must then develop plans to close the gap.

SERVQUAL "Minding the Gap" Exercise

< SOLVED PROBLEM 13.1

MyLab Operations Management Video

A dentist's office administered SERVQUAL surveys to customers and potential customers. The dentists wanted to know if they were performing well in the area of service. One hundred surveys were administered to customers before and after they were treated. In cases in which the patients were in too much pain to fill out the perceptions survey after a procedure, they were asked to fill out a survey on the follow-up visit. On the basis of the 100 responses, the following averages were computed for each item (based on a seven-point scale):

PZ&B Service Dimensions	Expectations	Perceptions
Tangibles	6.65	6.425
Reliability	3.4	6.02
Responsiveness	5.525	2.4
Assurance	4.5	3.275
Empathy	2.9	5.86

The differences are as follows:

Tangibles $= 6.65 - 6.425 = 0.225$
Reliability $= 3.4 - 6.02 = -2.62$
Responsiveness $= 5.525 - 2.4 = 3.125$
Assurance $= 4.5 - 3.275 = 1.225$
Empathy $= 2.9 - 5.86 = -2.96$

The biggest gap between expectations and perceptions is in the area of *responsiveness*. The dental group should focus its improvement efforts in this area by implementing training to teach employees how to be more responsive to customer needs.

Customer-Driven Excellence

A mantra for SC&O management is "**customer-driven excellence**," which focuses on the customer having the final say about the quality of the goods and services received. The focus of company systems must be to satisfy and delight the customer. According to the U.S. National Institute of Standards and Technology (NIST):

> Performance and quality are judged by an organization's *customers*. Thus, your organization must take into account all product features and characteristics and all modes of *customer* access and support that contribute value to your *customers*. Such behavior

customer-driven excellence
A quality management approach based on understanding customers and striving to satisfy their needs.

leads to *customer* acquisition, satisfaction, preference, and loyalty; to positive referrals; and ultimately to business expansion. *Customer*-driven excellence has both current and future components: understanding today's *customer* desires and anticipating future *customer* desires and marketplace potential.

Value and satisfaction may be influenced by many factors throughout your *customers'* overall experience with your organization. These factors include your organization's *customer* relationships, which help to build trust, confidence, and loyalty.

Customer-driven excellence means much more than reducing defects and errors, merely meeting specifications, or reducing complaints. Nevertheless, these factors contribute to your *customers'* view of your organization and thus also are important parts of *customer-driven* excellence. In addition, your organization's success in recovering from defects, service errors, and mistakes is crucial to retaining *customers* and engaging customers for the long term.

A *customer-driven* organization addresses not only the product and service characteristics that meet basic *customer* requirements but also those features that differentiate it from its competitors. Such differentiation may be based upon innovative offerings, combinations of product and service offerings, customization of offerings, multiple access mechanisms, rapid response, or special relationships.

Customer-driven excellence is thus a strategic concept. It is directed toward *customer* retention and loyalty, market share gain, and growth. It demands constant sensitivity to changing and emerging *customer* and market requirements and to the factors that drive customer engagement. It demands close attention to the voice of the customer. It demands anticipating changes in the marketplace. It demands a customer-focused culture. Therefore, *customer-driven excellence* demands organizational agility.[7]

Customer-driven quality is a concept that recognizes the importance that the customer plays in supply chain quality management. Firms such as the Ritz-Carlton have come to recognize that the customer should be central to process and service design.

NDERSTAND AND APPLY QUALITY TOOLS AND APPROACHES

This section discusses the many tools and approaches to improving quality. These tools include the seven basic tools of quality, the seven managerial tools, the Malcolm Baldrige National Quality Award (MBNQA), benchmarking, and supply chain quality improvement approaches.

Seven Basic Quality Tools

seven basic tools
The basic tools of quality improvement.

Some tools are more strategic in nature, but the **seven basic tools** (see **FIGURE 13.3**) are tactical tools that managers use to improve processes. These tools are the result of work by Kaoru Ishikawa, who was introduced earlier in this chapter. They are (1) process maps, (2) check sheets, (3) histograms, (4) scatter plots, (5) run charts, (6) fishbone diagrams, and (7) Pareto charts. Although simple, these tools can be very powerful approaches for analyzing data to guide improvement. We will briefly introduce each of the tools. Figure 13.3 shows the tools in their logical order of implementation.

process maps
Flowcharts used to improve a process.

PROCESS MAPS We introduced **process maps**, or pictures of a process, in Chapter 3. They include symbols to help define steps, decisions, and flows. When working on quality improvement projects, managers commonly first develop a process map of a process as it currently exists.

As shown in **FIGURE 13.4**, after brainstorming, managers then develop a "proposed" process map with improvements. Another development in process mapping is the suppliers-inputs-process-outputs-customer (SIPOC) diagram. **SC&O CURRENT EVENTS 13.2** talks about how one firm has implemented extended process maps.

[7]National Institute of Standards and Technology, *Criteria for Performance Excellence* (Gaithersburg, MD: NIST, 2017).

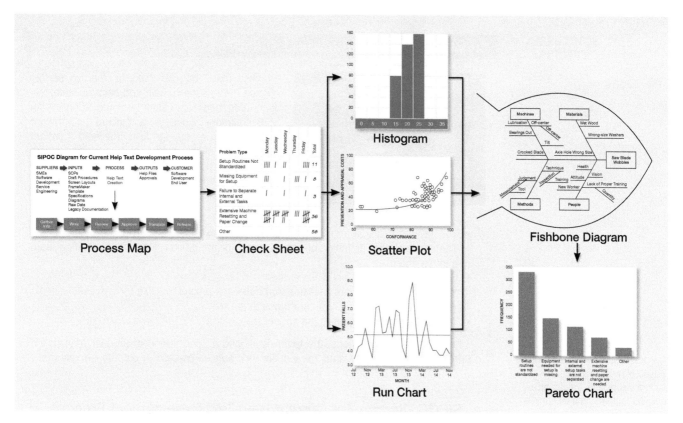

The Seven Basic Tools of Quality

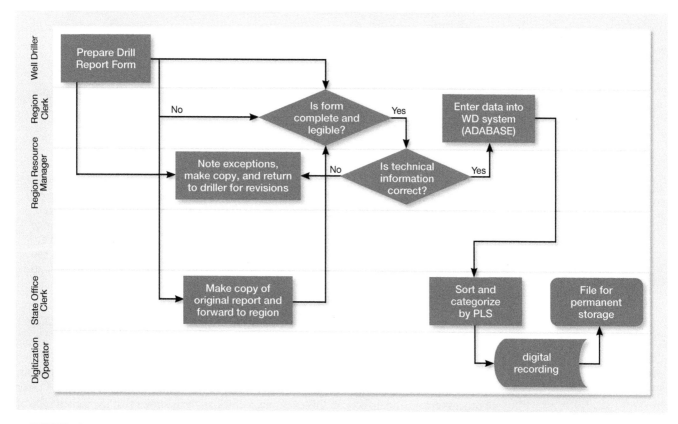

A Current Process Map

SC&O CURRENT >
EVENTS 13.2

Supply Chain Process Maps in Action

Process maps can be used to improve performance in the supply chain and help facilitate collaboration between customers and suppliers in B2B situations. Recently, a team of six software developers in a software firm chartered a project with a goal of minimizing or eliminating defects in electronic documentation before delivery to the software-testing phase.

The project met several important improvement criteria:

- The savings available from a reduction in rework exceeded $60,000.
- There was a clear definition of the customer for the project: the software testing team and the end user.
- Clear definitions of defect types existed.
- Measures for errors were available that made the project feasible.
- The project was of strategic importance to the firm.
- Top management supported the project fully.

SIPOC diagram
A type of process map that includes suppliers, inputs, processing, outputs, and customers.

In addition to other steps, the team developed a special kind of process map called a **SIPOC diagram**, which stands for *supplier → inputs → process → outputs → customer*.

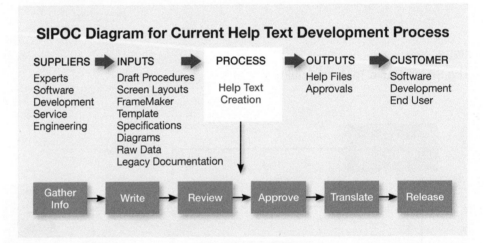

A SIPOC Diagram

As a result of this study, the team decided to monitor the reports of errors documented during software testing. If testing identified any errors in the electronic documentation, the software-testing group would notify the team leader. The team leader set up a series of run charts to track reported errors. The expectation was that in the beginning of the new process, the team might discover some errors. If the new process worked, however, the team expected to see the number of errors decrease significantly, ultimately to zero. The team leader continued to monitor any errors and pay attention to any trends or shifts that became evident. If the number of errors began to increase once more, the team would then investigate the cause.

Source: Based on J. Finan, "Chronicle of a Six Sigma Project," *Quality SIG Newsletter*, June 2003, 3.

check sheets
A tool of quality used to tally defects and problems by occurrence.

CHECK SHEETS **Check sheets** are used to form histograms and perform Pareto analysis, both of which we discuss below. In the check sheet in FIGURE 13.5, the operator keeps track of process errors and defects. In this example, a quick analysis shows that the fourth type of error occurs the most often. Based on these findings, managers can implement a project that will find a way to eliminate the causes for this defect.

Copier Problem Check Sheet

Problem Type	Monday	Tuesday	Wednesday	Thursday	Friday	Total
Setup Routines Not Standardized	IIII	I	II		IIII	11
Missing Equipment for Setup	III		I	III	I	8
Failure to Separate Internal and External Tasks	I		I		I	3
Extensive Machine Resetting and Paper Change	HHt HHt	HHt I	HHt II	III	HHt HHt	36
Other						58

HISTOGRAMS Histograms are graphical representations of data in bar charts. FIGURE 13.6 shows a frequency histogram. There are some rules relative to histograms:

histogram
A bar graph.

- The width of the histogram bars must be consistent (i.e., class widths have the same ranges).
- The classes must be *mutually exclusive* and *all-inclusive*.

The information in TABLE 13.6 is helpful in developing histograms.

SCATTER PLOTS Managers use **scatter plots** to study the relationships between variables. In quality management, firms sometimes use what are referred to as indicator variables, which are predictive of other phenomena. For example, a restaurant's customer retention results in higher profitability. In hospitals, the postoperative infection rate relates to adherence to proper procedures.

scatter plot
A tool of quality used to study the relationship between variables.

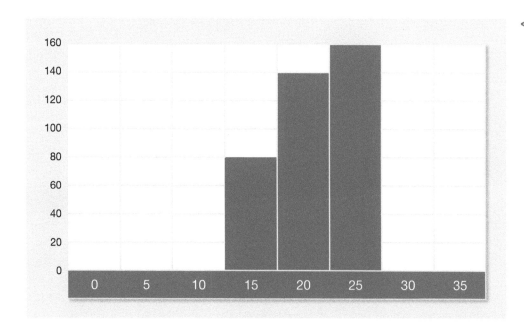

Number of Classes in a Histogram	
Number of Observations	Number of Classes
9 to 16	4
17 to 32	5
33 to 64	6
65 to 128	7
129 to 256	8

In essence, the scatter plot gives us a sense of the relationships between variables without having to perform regression and correlation analysis. In FIGURE 13.7, the scatter plot shows a positive relationship between conformance quality and prevention-related costs. This positive relationship means that more emphasis on preventing errors has resulted in better conformance. Close inspection of the plot also reveals that conformance and prevention are related in a nonlinear fashion.

run chart
Chart used to plot time series data.

RUN CHARTS **Run charts** are used to plot time series data. Managers use run charts to identify data trends. A review of FIGURE 13.8 shows that the data are trending downward in the final periods.

fishbone diagram
A tool of quality used to identify the causes of problems.

FISHBONE DIAGRAM FIGURE 13.9 shows a fishbone diagram. The **fishbone diagram** (also called a cause-and-effect or Ishikawa diagram) is a good brainstorming tool for identifying underlying causes to problems. The head of the fish contains the ultimate issue to be addressed. In Figure 13.9, the issue is wobbly saw blades. The bones of the fish contain causes or subcauses. On studying the diagram, you can see that the head was a symptom, not the main problem. By continually brainstorming and asking "Why?," managers and their teams can understand underlying causes. Asking "Why?" up to five times is sometimes referred to as the "five whys."

FIGURE 13.7 >

A Scatter Plot

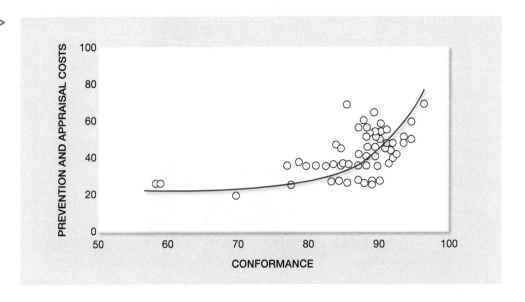

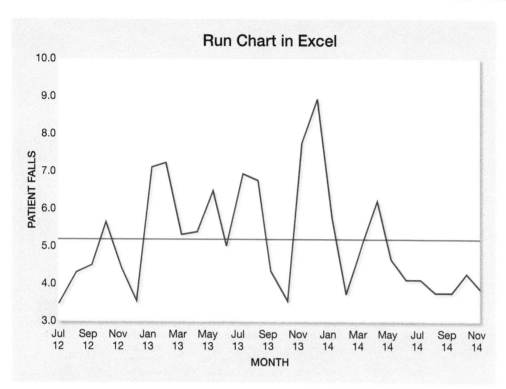

PARETO CHARTS Managers use Pareto analysis to identify and prioritize problems they need to solve. FIGURE 13.10 is based on **Pareto's law**. Vilfredo Pareto (1848–1923) was an Italian economist and mathematician who modeled income distribution during his lifetime in Italy. He found that most of the income was held by a relatively few people, a finding that is known as the 80/20 rule.

In quality management, the 80/20 rule states that roughly 80 percent of quality problems have a small number of the same causes. If a firm can eliminate those few causes, it can drive major improvements in the quality of products and services. For example, think of your local grocers. Some have better produce but a poor meat section. Some have better meats but wilting produce. If the grocery manager administers a questionnaire to customers asking about "quality of stock," the most egregious problems will get by far the most responses. Improving in that major area can help the grocers improve their customer satisfaction with their offerings.

Pareto's law
The 80/20 rule.

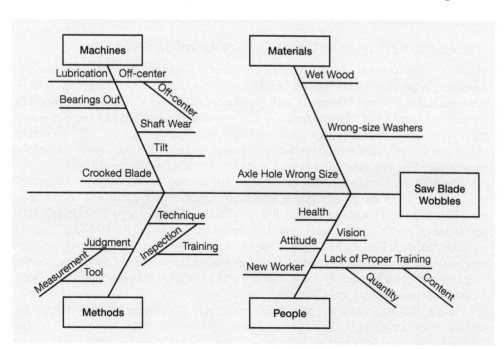

< FIGURE 13.9

A Fishbone Diagram

FIGURE 13.10 >

A Pareto Chart

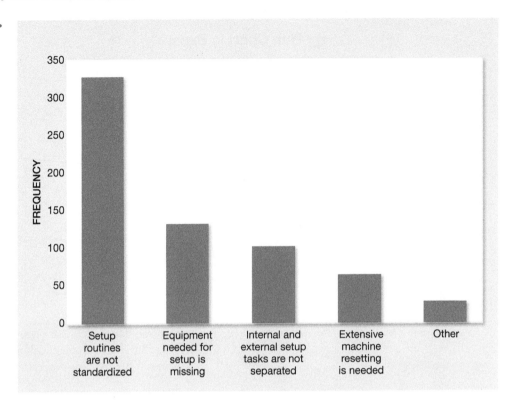

This simple rule often occurs in the real world. For example, 20 percent of stock makes up 80 percent of the stock market's value, 20 percent of students consume 80 percent of your professor's office hours, and 80 percent of defects emanate from a relatively few number of causes.

THE SEVEN MANAGERIAL TOOLS The basic seven tools of quality are not the only quality tools you will use. Dozens of tools are used in different situations. The **seven managerial quality tools** are (1) affinity diagrams, (2) interrelationship digraphs, (3) tree diagrams, (4) prioritization matrices, (5) matrix diagrams, (6) process decision program charts, and (7) activity network diagrams. These tools were developed by a research committee of the Japanese Society for Quality Control Technique Development and are focused on helping managerial decision making when qualitative data are analyzed. Although such tools are outside the scope of our discussion, be aware that managers use these and other tools to improve functionality and ultimately customer service.

seven managerial quality tools
(1) Affinity diagrams, (2) interrelationship digraphs, (3) tree diagrams, (4) prioritization matrices, (5) matrix diagrams, (6) process decision program charts, and (7) activity network diagrams.

The Malcolm Baldrige National Quality Award (MBNQA)

Smart and effective firms assess their quality systems to determine where improvements can be made. The best-known mechanism for self-assessment combined with external assessment is the **Malcolm Baldrige National Quality Award Criteria for Performance Excellence** (hereafter referred to as "the criteria"). The Baldrige Award was created by the U.S. government as a means for increasing national competitiveness. FIGURE 13.11 shows the categories for the criteria for the Malcolm Baldrige National Quality Award (MBNQA). Organizations assess themselves with categories found in the criteria when striving to win the MBNQA.

Malcolm Baldrige National Quality Award Criteria for Performance Excellence
The guiding document to the Baldrige Award Program.

The MBNQA is open to small (fewer than 500 employees) and large (more than 500 employees) firms in the manufacturing, healthcare, education, for-profit, and nonprofit sectors. Although there is a Senate Quality Recognition that is based on the MBNQA criteria for governmental entities, government organizations are excluded from the MBNQA.

The model in Figure 13.11 consists of seven interrelated categories that compose the organizational system for performance. The categories are (1) leadership; (2) strategic planning; (3) customer focus; (4) measurement, analysis, and knowledge management; (5) workforce focus; (6) operations focus; and (7) results.

After a firm documents its approaches, deployment, improvements, and results in each of these seven categories, the Baldrige Board of Examiners reviews its application. If the firm is judged to be one of the best of the best, it receives the MBNQA. The Board of Examiners

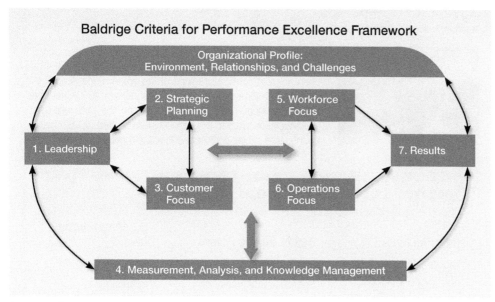

Source: Based on NIST, 2011.

provides an examiner feedback report that provides losing firms with an excellent guide for improvement. Many firms, from Xerox to Pal's Sudden Service, have benefited from using the Baldrige criteria. For example, Nestlé/Purina Pet Foods sales grew between 7 and 15 percent and achieved number one with consumers on the University of Michigan's Customer Satisfaction Index while using the Baldrige criteria. GLOBAL CONNECTIONS 13.2 discusses other award programs around the world that grew out of the Baldrige Award program.

Benchmarking

One of the more strategic approaches to finding ways to improve is benchmarking. A **benchmark** is an exemplar firm that others revere as a role model. Benchmarks include Baldrige Award winners, and firms that are outstanding in some way but do not have to be excellent in all areas and instead need excel in only one area. Examples include the Ritz-Carlton in customer data gathering, IBM in product design, Motorola in design for Six Sigma, Federal Express in service, and McDonald's in consistency of service and product.

TABLE 13.7 shows the six basic types of benchmarking. Robert Camp, the manager who developed benchmarking at Xerox, argues that the most important type of benchmarking is process benchmarking, which allows firms to visit other firms and study each other's processes to guide improvement. The firm that is best known for benchmarking is Xerox. Firms such as IBM have also used benchmarking to improve processes. Managers should use benchmarking whenever they want to go outside the box to see how others perform work. A major drawback of benchmarking is that firms have to make sure that they have something to offer other firms when they approach them to benchmark.

benchmark
An exemplar. In the context of business quality improvement, a firm against which other firms measure themselves.

< TABLE 13.7

Types of Benchmarking	
Benchmarking Type	**Application**
Process	Comparing processes such as how another company performs receiving or purchasing
Financial	Comparing business results and accounting information
Performance	Comparing cost structures, speed, quality levels, and so on
Product	Comparing product attributes and functionality
Strategic	Comparing firm competitiveness along several dimensions
Functional	Comparing or learning how another firm performs a particular function such as running call centers

Global Quality Awards

The Baldrige Award (recently presented by Vice President Joseph Biden) has been such a success in the United States that it has been adapted for other regions of the world. For example, the European Federations for Quality Management (EFQM) created a European Quality Award (EQA). In addition, the Japanese Quality Association created the Japan Quality Award (JQA). The following table shows a comparison of the three award categories.

Comparison of the Baldrige Award, Japan Quality Award, and European Quality Award

Baldrige Award	Japan Quality Award	European Quality Award
Leadership	Leadership of Senior Leaders	Leadership
Strategic Planning	Social Responsibility of Management	People
Customer Focus	Understanding and Responding to Customer and Market Needs	Strategy
Measurement, Analysis, and Knowledge Management	Strategic Planning and Deployment	Partnership and Resources
Workforce Focus	Improving Employee and Organizational Capacities	Processes, Products, and Services
Operations Focus	Customer Value Creating Process	People Results
Results	Information and Management Activity Results	Customer Results
		Society Results
		Business Results

The JQA has been successful in helping to promote quality management principles, organization, and management for Japanese firms. It is very similar to the Baldrige Award.

The EFQM has also been very successful. Many firms, such as Super Hotel Small Business (Service), Bankyo Pharmaceutical Small Business, Musashino Small Business, Cisco Systems, GK Enterprise, Public Sector Big Business, and other firms, have been identified as role models of quality for other European firms.

One company that won the EQA was the BMW plant at Regensburg, Germany. According to Andreas Wendt, general director of the Regensburg plant, "Through the EFQM assessment we receive objective, valuable and helpful suggestions about our strengths and—even more important— potential. We use it in strategy and target processes to decide about 'doing the right things.'"[8] As a result of the EQA:

- Plant Regensburg achieved higher flexibility.
- Labor productivity exceeded standards by 82 percent.
- Employee satisfaction was measured at 99 percent.
- Customer results are trending upward.
- Annual financial targets were achieved.

As you can see, the Baldrige Award has had a worldwide effect, with others having adapted the criteria to their regions of the world.

[8]Anon, Process and Results: BMW Plant Regensberg, http://www.efqm.org/success-stories/process-and-results, 2017.

In the beginning of the chapter, we discussed quality problems at Chipotle. With sales down, a free-falling stock price, and lost customer trust, the company understood that it needed to refocus its efforts on improving quality. Following are some of the supply chain quality measures undertaken at Chipotle to regain customer trust:

- Increased spending on pork and beef to ensure better quality
- Implemented scanning and food traceability to identify problem sources when they occur
- Changed suppliers (which did result in a temporary lack of supply of Carnitas)
- Invested in technology, training, and food inspections in the supply chain and in stores
- Implemented an iTunes series called Rad Lands to help kids make healthier food choices
- Changed the company mission statement to focus more on fresh and local food sourcing
- Improved food-handling standards
- Renewed its focus on the customer experience

As a result of these changes, Chipotle has regained the number one spot in a quick service restaurant study of food quality, although their lead did drop to 53 percent, down from a high of 59 percent. Their in-store sales have increased by 15 percent. Also, they have regained the number one spot in Mexican food sales in the United States. While the future is always uncertain, supply chain quality practices are important to the future of companies such as Chipotle.

Summary

In this chapter, we have discussed many of the fundamentals of supply chain quality management. Quality management is important for organizations. Every week, we read in the news about new quality problems that beset society and even cause injury to people.

1. Besides discussing many current events relative to quality, we defined quality dimensions using Garvin and Parasuraman, Zeithamel, and Berry.
2. Many of the key leaders in the quality movement were introduced.
   a. These leaders include Deming, Juran, Crosby, and Ishikawa.
   b. These individuals have helped change the world economy by instructing us in how to improve our organizations and firms.

3. Supply chain quality management (SCQM) was defined, and we discussed how companies approach quality from a collaborative point of view.
   a. Some of the approaches discussed were ISO 9000, collaborative supplier relationships, and industry-specific standards.
4. We then turned our focus to services.
   a. We should remember that all firms have a service component. By the same token, the firms that we view as service firms also have a nonservice component.
   b. Customer-driven excellence and SERVQUAL provide ways to understand how to manage customer interaction. Remember to "mind the gap."
5. Some of the strategic approaches to quality improvement include the Malcolm Baldrige Award criteria and benchmarking.
   a. We then moved to more tactical tools that are often used in improving quality, such as the seven basic and the seven managerial tools.

Key Terms

benchmark   401
big Q quality   386
check sheets   396
collaborative supplier relationships   389
Crosby's 14 steps   387
customer-driven excellence   393
Deming's 14 points for management   385
expectation-perception gap   392
fishbone diagram   398
gap   392
gap analysis   392

Garvin's eight dimensions of quality   383
histograms   397
ISO 9000   389
Juran's trilogy   385
little q quality   386
Malcolm Baldrige National Quality Award Criteria for Performance Excellence   400
Pareto's law   399
plan, do, check, act (PDCA) cycle   384
process maps   394

quality   383
run chart   398
scatter plots   397
SERVQUAL   391
SERVQUAL expectations survey   392
SERVQUAL perceptions survey   392
seven basic tools   394
seven managerial quality tools   400
SIPOC diagram   396
statistical thinking   384
supply chain quality management (SCQM)   387
system for quality improvement   384

Integrative Learning Exercise

In this chapter, we discussed benchmarking and ISO 9000. They are very different approaches to driving improvement in a firm. With a team, reflect on these approaches and try to determine under which conditions you might choose one approach over the other. Consider the following questions to get started:

1. Which approach is better for an early-stage start-up business?
2. Which approach is better for a more mature company?
3. How would these approaches be useful for a firm that is globalizing?

Integrative Experiential Exercise

Hundreds of thousands of firms have implemented ISO 9000. Visit a company near your campus and interview a quality manager. Find answers to the following questions:

1. How long have you been ISO-registered?
2. How often are you audited?
3. How has ISO influenced the way that you do business?

4. Is ISO a good model for improvement, or is it too bureaucratic (lots of paperwork)?
5. How has ISO influenced how you interact with your suppliers?

Report your findings to the class. See if you can identify common themes from different members of the class.

Discussion Questions

1. Why do you think Chipotle has come to the point where it is now in crisis due to the *E. coli* outbreak?

2. What has Chipotle done to improve or worsen its situation since this book was published? Support your answer with references.

3. Refer again to Table 13.1. Why do you think that Chipotle has gotten so much bad press? What additional steps should it take to improve?

4. How do the dimensions of quality help communicate effectively about organizational improvement?

5. Do you agree with the PZ&B service quality dimensions? Can you think of other dimensions in services?

6. Might any of Deming's 14 points be debatable in certain circumstances?

7. Notice that Deming's point 10 mentions eliminating slogans such as "zero defect." However, Crosby's ninth step is to hold a "zero defects day." These points are in disagreement. Who is correct? Why?

8. Joseph Juran's approach is more strategy-based than other approaches. Is it a better approach than Deming's? Why or why not?

9. How does the definition of supply chain quality management differ from the American Society for Quality's definition of quality? Is it helpful to have a definition for supply chain quality management? Why or why not?

10. What is your feeling about the quality of products from China? In your opinion, what steps should the Chinese government take to ameliorate this problem?

11. In your mind, who is more at fault for the leaded paint in Fisher-Price toys? Is it Mattel/Fisher-Price, the supplier, or someone else? Is it fair that this problem is seen as a "China" problem by some?

12. ISO 9000 refers to a quality management system. What is a quality management system?

13. Is ISO 9000 a good model for improvement, or is it responsible for the "bureaucratization of quality"? Explain.

14. How does customer contact make service quality difficult to manage? Give examples.

15. Do you agree with the NIST definition of *customer-driven excellence* in the chapter? Can an overemphasis on customer-driven excellence make a company too reactive instead of proactive? Explain.

Solved Problems

Quality in Services

SERVQUAL
SOLVED PROBLEM 13.1

1. A tavern owner recently performed a gap analysis with the SERVQUAL model. The survey was limited to the five PZ&B service quality dimensions. After administering 50 expectations surveys to potential customers and 50 surveys to customers (the tavern offered free desserts to anyone who would fill out a survey), the owner found the following:

PZ&B Service Dimensions	Expectations	Perceptions
Tangibles	5.4	5.2
Reliability	6.8	3.4
Responsiveness	5.5	5.4
Assurance	3.2	5.3
Empathy	6.5	5.4

Help the restaurant managers find out where to place emphasis for improvement.

Solution:
To find the answer, we will perform simple differencing.
  Tangibles: $5.4 - 5.2 = 0.2$
  Reliability: $6.8 - 3.4 = 3.4$
  Responsiveness: $5.5 - 5.4 = 0.1$
  Assurance: $3.2 - 5.3 = -2.1$
  Empathy: $6.5 - 5.4 = 1.1$
It appears that the owner should first emphasize service reliability in its improvement efforts.

Problems

Quality in Services

SERVQUAL

1. An owner of a Bronze's Gym recently performed a gap analysis with the SERVQUAL model. The survey was limited to the five PZ&B service quality dimensions. After administering 75 expectations surveys to potential customers and 75 surveys to customers, the owner computed the following means:

PZ&B Service Dimensions	Expectations	Perceptions
Tangibles	6.7	5.4
Reliability	6.2	3.2
Responsiveness	4.5	4.3
Assurance	1.3	5.4
Empathy	6.8	6.2

Compute simple differences and make recommendations to management.

Quality Tools and Approaches

SEVEN BASIC QUALITY TOOLS

2. Develop a process map for the following processes:
   a. Buying a car
   b. Completing a research paper for a class
   c. Developing a new course at a university (interview a professor for these steps)

3. For each of the processes in Problem 2, perform a value analysis to determine which steps are value-added and which are wasteful steps.

4. Refer to the data in the following check sheet:

Check Sheet

Problem Type	Monday	Tuesday	Wednesday	Thursday	Friday	Total
Setup Routines Not Standardized	⊦⊦⊦ ⊦⊦⊦ |||	⊦⊦⊦ ||	||||		⊦⊦⊦		⊦⊦⊦	
Missing Equipment for Setup			⊦⊦⊦ ⊦⊦⊦ ⊦⊦⊦			
Failure to Separate Internal and External Tasks											
Extensive Machine Resetting and Paper Change			|||				|||	
Other							

What do you recommend?

5. Develop a histogram for the following array of data:

Employee	Hours of Overtime	Days Absent
1	243	0
2	126	3
3	86	1
4	424	9
5	236	3
6	128	3
7	0	3
8	126	2
9	324	6
10	118	4
11	62	0
12	128	3
13	460	8
14	135	1
15	118	1
16	260	2
17	0	1
18	126	1
19	234	2
20	246	3
21	120	1
22	80	0
23	112	1
24	237	3
25	129	2
26	24	1
27	36	0
28	128	2
29	246	5
30	326	9

6. For the data in Problem 5, create a scatter plot to see if there is a relationship between overtime hours and days absent.

7. For the following data, develop a Pareto chart. The letters A, B, C, and D are problems that occur in a process. Which cause should you focus on first?

B	B
A	C
B	A
B	A
B	A
B	C
B	A
D	C
B	B
A	A
A	B
B	B
D	B
C	E
A	F

B	E
C	A
D	B
A	A
A	B
A	B
B	B
C	B
B	B
C	A
A	B
B	D
A	C
C	B
A	E

8. Create a fishbone diagram to help determine the underlying causes for doing poorly in a supply chain and operations class at your university.

CASE — Corporate Universities: Teaching the Tools of Quality

Although most of us are familiar with major public universities like Michigan, Ohio State, Florida State, and the University of California at Los Angeles (UCLA), we are typically unfamiliar with corporate universities such as Motorola Solutions, Intel University, and the AT&T Learning Center. Corporate universities are a fairly new concept, created to serve the needs of a particular company's employees and other stakeholders.

The term *corporate university* has been adopted by firms that have significantly upgraded their training and development activities by creating learning centers within their corporations. These learning centers are typically designed to prioritize a firm's training initiatives and to share quickly with a firm's employees the skills, techniques, and best practices that are necessary to remain competitive. For example, when a new quality tool or technique is developed, it is often the responsibility of a firm's corporate university to develop a plan to equip the firm's employees with the skills necessary to incorporate the new tool or techniques into their work areas quickly.

The following is a brief description of two corporate universities. After reading these descriptions, ask yourself the following rhetorical question: Are these corporations well-equipped to teach their employees the tools of quality?

Motorola Solutions: Motorola Solutions began in 1981 as the Motorola Training and Education Center. During the 1980s, the purpose of the university was to help Motorola strengthen its training efforts and build a quality-focused corporate culture. Through the years, the university has grown in both size and stature, and now has a staff of more than 400 employees and seven facilities around the world. The stated objectives of Motorola Solutions are as follows:

- To provide training and education to all Motorola employees.
- To prepare Motorola employees to be best in class in their industries.
- To serve as a catalyst for change and continuous improvement to position Motorola Corporation for the future.
- To provide added value to Motorola in the marketing and distribution of products throughout the world.

To accomplish these objectives, Motorola Solutions does many things. For example, each of the company's employees is required to take a minimum of 40 hours a year of job-relevant training and education. The university also provides its employees consulting services in a number of areas, including benchmarking, cycle-time reduction, quality improvement processes, and statistical tools and problem-solving techniques.

One unique aspect of Motorola Solutions is that it reaches beyond the Motorola Corporation. The university provides training and certification programs for Motorola suppliers and also provides consulting services and training for other corporations on a fee basis.

Sears University: Sears University was established in 1994 with the ambitious goal of becoming an intricate part of the company's turnaround efforts. The university was opened with the idea of offering a wide selection of formal training and self-study courses for Sears' employees. In its first year of operation, approximately 10,000 of the company's employees participated in formal programs ranging from one day to one week in duration. Another 4,000 employees completed self-study courses each month.

In addition to offering training programs in areas such as merchandising, operations, customer service, and human resources management, Sears University also provides the company's employees programs designed to help them function as change agents and strategic leaders within the corporation. For example, participants in financial management training programs use computer-based simulations to model the effect of various financial strategies on business unit performance. Particular attention is paid to trying to help employees see the company's operations from the customer's perspective. The courses are taught by seasoned line managers along with professional facilitators and Sears University personnel.

Questions:

1. Are corporate universities a good idea? If so, why or why not?

2. In what ways can a corporate university do a better job of teaching a firm's employees the tools of quality than can traditional training programs?

14 Statistical Process Control

INTEGRATING	GLOBAL SC&O STRATEGY
INNOVATING	Supply Management / Operations Management / Customer Relationship Management
IMPACTING	Upstream Processes / Core Processes / Downstream Processes
IMPROVING	QUALITY MANAGEMENT, ANALYTICS, AND LOGISTICS

CHAPTER OUTLINE AND LEARNING OBJECTIVES

1 Articulate the Purposes of Statistical Quality Control and Statistical Thinking

- Communicate different types of variation that affect processes.

2 Understand Process Stability

- Understand the basics of sampling and inspection methods.
- Understand and describe different sample types.
- Apply various inspection methods throughout different stages of the supply chain.

3 Explain and Use Variables and Attributes Process Control Charts

- Walk through the generalized procedure for applying control charts.
- Understand how managers use variables and attributes control charts.

4 Apply Control Charts

- Interpret a control chart and apply your findings.
- Understand how to use corrective action effectively.

5 Perform Process Capability Analysis

- Compute and interpret Cpk.

Statistics Makes Water Taste Better!

Sales of bottled water have skyrocketed in North America. In 1976, the average person drank less than 2 gallons of bottled water per year. That amount is now more than 30 gallons per year. It is rare to have a meeting without several people drinking bottled water. People see bottled water as refreshing, healthy, and nonfattening.

Nestlé entered the bottled water market by bringing Perrier to the United States in 1976. Its product line has now expanded to include the Pure Life brand of bottled water. The water for Pure Life comes from well and municipal water sources. Because so many people drink bottled water, Nestlé works hard to ensure that the water received by clients is safe. A quality problem could result in lawsuits, recalls, and bad press. As a result, Nestlé uses a 14-step quality process to bottle Pure Life water.

Quality control inspections occur during various process steps. In this chapter, we introduce methods used by Nestlé, and many other firms, to ensure process and product quality through the use of statistics. We will return to this example later in the chapter to demonstrate how these statistical tools are used.

---

statistical process control
The application of statistical concepts to the production process to determine if a process displays *stability*.

stability
Only random variation is present in the process.

To ensure high levels of quality for products and services, a firm needs more than good concepts and theories. It also needs science. This science takes the form of **statistical process control**, the application of statistical concepts to the production process to determine if your processes display *stability*. When a process has **stability**, it exhibits only random variation.

This chapter introduces the basics of statistical quality control as used by many firms around the world. It is an important topic because statistical quality control is used to monitor processes, and managers are responsible for processes and their performance. You need to be familiar with these tools to be an effective process manager. This chapter will discuss statistical quality control in general, charts for variables, charts for attributes, and process capability.

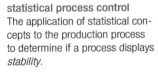

RTICULATE THE PURPOSES OF STATISTICAL QUALITY CONTROL AND STATISTICAL THINKING

Statistical thinking is based on three main concepts:

1. A system of production focuses on the interconnectedness of processes and variables.
2. Variation is everywhere.
3. Firms need to understand variation to reduce it.

As is stated above, all processes exhibit variation. There is some variation that managers can manage and other variation that they cannot manage. If there is too much variation, parts will not fit correctly, products will not function properly, and a firm will gain a reputation for poor quality.

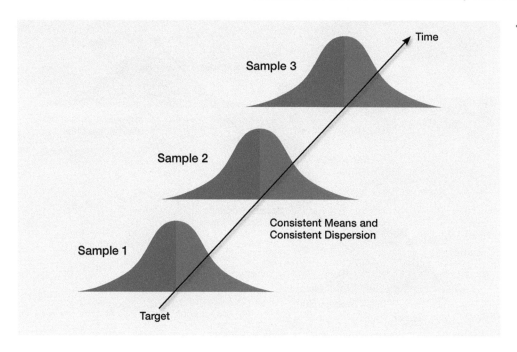

Random Variation

Two types of process variation commonly occur: random and nonrandom variation. Random variation is uncontrollable, and nonrandom variation has a cause that can be identified. This chapter discusses the statistical tools that determine whether or not variation is random.

Random variation centers on a mean and occurs with a somewhat consistent amount of dispersion. This type of variation cannot be controlled. Hence, we refer to it as **common cause variation**. The amount of random variation in a process may be either large or small. When the variation is large, processes may not meet specifications on a consistent basis. For example, various minerals occur in bottled water, and there are national standards for acceptable levels (usually stated in parts per million) of minerals, such as lead. Although we do not like to think of lead in our drinking water, some trace amounts occur naturally in all water without negative health effects. These trace amounts vary randomly and slightly, but if too much lead is in the water, statistical analysis will identify these levels as a nonrandom variation.

The statistical tools discussed in this chapter are *not* designed to detect random variation. FIGURE 14.1 shows normal distributions resulting from a variety of samples taken from the same population over time. We find a consistency in the amount of dispersion and the **mean** of the process, which is a measure of central tendency that is the arithmetic average. That not all observations within the distributions fall exactly on the target line shows that there is variation. **Dispersion** is a measure of the width of a distribution. The dispersion of the distribution is wide if there is a lot of variation, and it is narrow if variation is small. The consistency of the variation, however, shows that only random causes of variation are present within the process. So when we gather samples from the process in the future, we can expect that the distributions associated with such samples will also take the same form.

Nonrandom variation, or **special cause variation**, results from a specific event, which may be a shift in a process mean or an unexpected occurrence. For example, a warehouse manager might receive flawed materials from a supplier, there might be a change in work shift, an employee might come to work under the influence of drugs and make errors, or the machine may break down or not function properly. FIGURE 14.2 shows distributions resulting from a number of samples taken from the same population over time where nonrandom variation is exhibited. Notice that from one sample to the next, the dispersion and average of the process change. When we compare this figure to random variation in Figure 14.1, it is clear that nonrandom variation results in a process that is not repeatable.

random variation or **common cause variation**
Variation that centers on a mean and occurs with a somewhat consistent amount of dispersion.

mean
Arithmetic average.

dispersion
The width of a distribution.

nonrandom variation or **special cause variation**
Variation that results from a specific event, which may be a shift in a process mean or an unexpected occurrence.

FIGURE 14.2 >
Nonrandom Variation

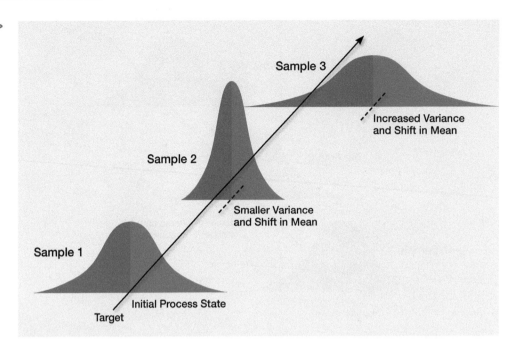

Managing Across Majors 14.1 Marketing majors, you will need to communicate key product characteristics to supply chain and operations (SC&O) managers so that they can determine what variables are most important to inspect when using statistical quality control.

NDERSTAND PROCESS STABILITY

process charts
Graphs designed to signal process workers when nonrandom variation occurs in a process.

If a process has process stability, its variation is random and does not have a special or assignable cause. To determine process stability, we use process charts. **Process charts** (see FIGURE 14.3) are graphs designed to signal process workers when nonrandom variation occurs in a process.

FIGURE 14.3 >
Process Control Chart

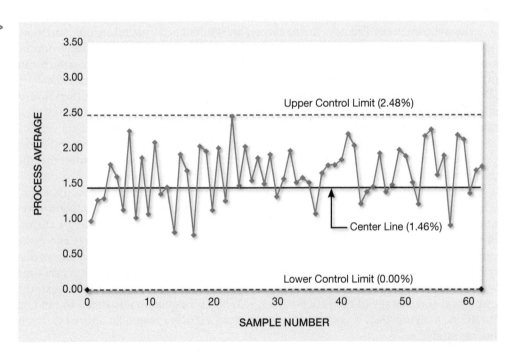

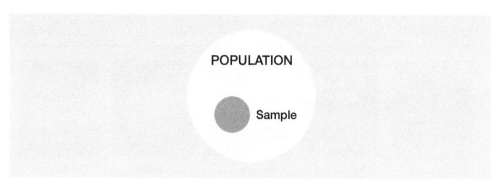

Sampling and Inspection

To ensure that processes are stable, data are gathered in samples. As shown in FIGURE 14.4, a **sample** is a part representing a whole. For the most part, managers prefer collecting samples over performing 100 percent inspection because samples are cheaper, take less time to collect, are less intrusive, and allow the user to frame the sample. For example, when sampling bottled water for lead, it is not feasible to open every bottle and test everything because there would then be nothing left to sell. As a result, sampling is used to determine if too much lead is present. Below, we discuss sampling methods and different approaches to inspection.

sample
A part representing a whole.

Types of Samples

For quality control purposes, we will focus on two types of samples: random samples and systematic samples. Each type has its own advantages and disadvantages.

RANDOM SAMPLES Randomization is useful because it ensures independence between observations. To **randomize** means to sample so that every piece of product has an equal chance of being selected for inspection. For example, if 1,000 products are produced in a single day, each product has a 1/1,000 chance of being selected for inspection on that day. **Random samples** are often the preferred form of sampling and yet often the most difficult to achieve. This is especially true in continuous processes where products are made by the same machines, workers, and processes in sequence. In such cases, there is no statistical independence between products being made because the process results in ordered products that can be subject to machine drift (going out of adjustment slowly over time). For example, if a company has multiple lines producing window frames, saw blades cutting the frames can wear out over time and cause some sequential changes in the lengths of window frames. Random sampling overcomes this problem of process drift in the lengths of the window frames by taking out the effect of time.

randomize
To make random.

random samples
To gather samples so that every piece of product has an equal chance of being selected for inspection.

SYSTEMATIC SAMPLES When taking random samples is not possible, managers use **systematic samples**, which have some of the benefits of random samples without the difficulty of randomizing. Samples can be systematic according to *time* or *sequence*. If a sample is systematic according to time, a product is inspected at regular intervals of time, say, every 15 minutes. Systematic samples are much more convenient than random samples. If a systematic sample is performed according to sequence, one product may be inspected every tenth iteration. Most firms using continuous or mass assembly processes use systematic samples.

systematic samples
Samples ordered by time or sequence.

Inspection Methods

Although sampling does have its benefits, 100 percent inspection can be effective in instances in which the cost of inspection is low and the process for inspection is simple. One hundred percent samples are also known as *screening samples, sorting samples, rectifying samples,* or *detailing samples.* Such samples have been most common when past shipments have been rejected. As shown in FIGURE 14.5, different types of samples are often used at different stages of the supply chain.

Another example of 100 percent inspection may be used when performing **in-process inspection**. Many firms with continuous and mass assembly processes, such as Ford, have asked their employees to inspect their own work as the work is being performed. The result

in-process inspection
Quality inspection performed during the production process.

FIGURE 14.5 >

**Different Types of
Samples throughout
the Supply Chain**

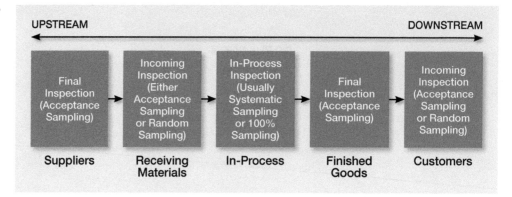

can be 100 percent inspection at every stage of the process! We should clarify that in-process inspection can also be performed on a sampling basis. Because sampling is so important, let's look at some different types of samples.

In cases in which quality testing is destructive, 100 percent inspection would be impossible and would literally drive the company out of business. In some processes, chemicals are used in testing, or damaging pull tests are applied to cables. These destructive tests ruin the sample but are useful to show that a good product is being made when performed on a sampling basis. **SC&O CURRENT EVENTS 14.1** talks about the use of statistical quality control in the production of medications.

**SC&O CURRENT >
EVENTS 14.1**

Using Statistical Methods in Drug Making

Pharmaceutical companies often hesitate to invest heavily in large-scale quality control efforts before a drug is approved for marketing because failure in the clinic means product failure. The time from inception to clinical approval may span 12 to 15 years, and 60 percent to 75 percent of the product's patent life may have expired by the time final approval has been received. A number of factors are converging to increase the need for sophisticated statistics and sampling-driven approaches to quality and process understanding in the pharmaceuticals industry, including the following:

- *Economic pressures:* Many companies, faced with expensive product supply chains, major patent expirations, and downward pressure on prices, need to cut production costs, improve yields and productivity, and generate bottom-line savings that can be used to drive growth and innovation. Statistical sampling methods are critical to these efforts.
- *Regulatory trends:* Recent regulatory guidelines from the U.S. Food and Drug Administration, the European Medicines Agency, and the International Conference on Harmonization encourage scientific approaches to quality and compliance. Implementing the concepts embodied in the guidelines requires statistically rigorous methods.
- *Inherent characteristics of pharmaceutical manufacturing:* Many of these inherent characteristics and the challenges they represent call for the increased use of statistical sampling methods. For example, in most other manufacturing industries, product specifications are clearly tied to product performance. In pharmaceuticals, however, it is difficult to connect tightly, say, tablet dissolution to drug efficacy and safety over a vast array of potential product users, each with differing body sizes, ages, lifestyles, genetics, and chemistries. It is made more complex because pharmaceutical companies must maintain quality in a many-step production process that creates a complex molecular structure that must be free of serious impurities or contaminants.

As these trends continue and become magnified, statistical understanding will become more and more important. The tools in this chapter are key to this understanding.

PLANNING FOR INSPECTION To sample effectively without overreaching or managing the product, sampling plans are used. These plans force production workers to answer questions about what type of *sampling plan* they will use, who will perform the inspection, who will use in-process inspection, what the sample size will be, what the critical attributes to be inspected are, and where inspection should be performed.

INSPECTION RATIOS Certain rules for inspection help managers prioritize where inspection should be performed. To prioritize where in the process inspection should occur first, many firms compute the *ratio between the cost of inspection and the cost of failure* resulting from a particular step in the process. The **inspection ratio** is computed by (see **SOLVED PROBLEM 14.1**)

$$IR = \frac{C_i}{C_f} \tag{14.1}$$

where

IR = inspection ratio
C_i = cost of a single inspection
C_f = cost of failure of the product

inspection ratio
The ratio between the cost of inspection and the cost of failure resulting from a particular step in the process.

···

Computing Inspection Ratios

SOLVED PROBLEM 14.1 f(x)

MyLab Operations Management
Video

Problem: The cost of inspection for three different product characteristics A, B, and C is $8, $5, and $7, respectively. The cost of failure if any of them breaks down is $125 (full replacement cost of the product). Prioritize where we should inspect first.

Solution: Because the cost of replacement is the same for them all, the solution is straightforward. For instructional purposes, however, we will demonstrate the solution. Using Equation 14.1, we obtain the following:

Product Characteristic	C_i	C_f	$IR = \dfrac{C_i}{C_f}$
A	8	125	$0.064 = \dfrac{8}{125}$
B	5	125	$0.040 = \dfrac{5}{125}$
C	7	125	$0.056 = \dfrac{7}{125}$

Reviewing these results, it appears that we would prioritize inspection of B as most important, C as second most important, and A as least important. If we inspect all three, the cumulative cost of inspection is $8 + $5 + $7 = $20, which is 16 percent of the cost of the final product ($125), making 100 percent inspection very expensive.

···
···

Managing Across Majors 14.2 Finance and accounting majors, you will need to assist in studying the economics of inspection so that firms get their biggest "bang for the buck" out of inspection.
···

 # XPLAIN AND USE VARIABLES AND ATTRIBUTES PROCESS CONTROL CHARTS

Before discussing process charts, we must first differentiate between variables and attributes. A **variable** is a continuous measurement, such as weight, height, or volume. An **attribute** is an either-or situation, such as whether a motor starts or does not start.

variable
A continuous measurement such as weight, height, or volume.

attribute
An either-or situation, such as whether a defect is present or it isn't.

TABLE 14.1 >

Variables and Attributes	
Variables	**Attributes**
X (process population average)	p (proportion defective)
$\bar{x}$ (mean or average)	np (number defective or number nonconforming)
R (range) MR (moving range)	c (number nonconforming in a consistent sample space)
s (standard deviation)	u (number of defects per unit)

TABLE 14.1 shows the most common types of variable and attribute charts. The variables charts are X, $\bar{x}$, R, MR, and s charts. The attributes charts are p, np, c, and u charts. In the following pages, we will introduce $\bar{x}$, R, and p charts as examples of control charts.

Statistical process control charts are tools for monitoring process variation. FIGURE 14.6 shows a control chart. It has an upper limit, a center line, and a lower limit.

There are four central requirements for properly using process charts (TABLE 14.2). We will discuss each of these requirements in the following sections.

Understanding Control Charts

Before we show you how to establish control charts, it is important first to understand what control charts are and how they work. An $\bar{x}$ chart monitors average measurements. For example, suppose that you were a producer of 8.5-by-11-inch notebook paper. Because the width of paper is measured in inches, a variables $\bar{x}$ chart is appropriate. If the width of the paper is a key critical characteristic, we might inspect a sample of sheets to see whether the sheets are indeed 8.5 inches wide.

FIGURE 14.6 >

Sample Control Chart

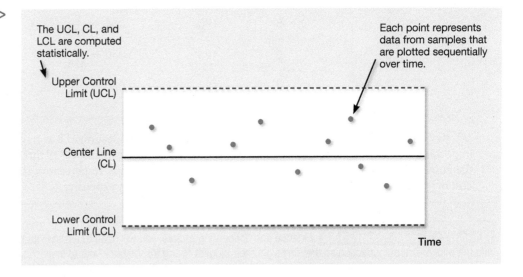

TABLE 14.2 >

Central Requirements for Using Control Charts
1. You must understand the generalized procedure for implementing process charts.
2. You must know how to interpret process charts.
3. You need to know when different process charts are used.
4. You need to know how to compute limits for the different types of process charts.

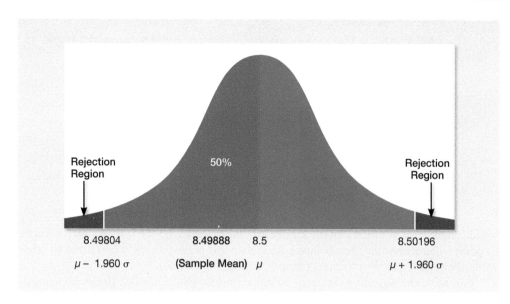

To demonstrate how a control chart works, we could use a hypothesis test instead of a control chart to determine whether the paper is really 8.5 inches wide. Therefore, the null hypothesis is

$$H_0: \mu = 8.5 \text{ inches}$$

The alternative hypothesis is

$$H_1: \mu \neq 8.5 \text{ inches}$$

If we performed the hypothesis test, we would establish a distribution with the following 95 percent ($z = 1.96$) rejection limits. If the standard error of the sample distribution ($n = 10$) is 0.001 inch, the rejection limits are $8.5 \pm 1.96(0.001) = \{8.50196, 8.49804\}$. FIGURE 14.7 shows the distribution with its rejection regions.

Next, to test this hypothesis, we draw a sample of $n = 10$ sheets of paper and measure the sheets. The measurements are shown in the following table:

Sheet Number	Measurements
1	8.5001
2	8.4988
3	8.5123
4	8.4689
5	8.4667
6	8.4996
7	8.5021
8	8.4956
9	8.5123
10	8.5324
Mean =	**8.4988**

Because 8.49888 does not fall in either of the rejection regions shown in Figure 14.7, we fail to reject the null hypothesis and conclude that the sheets do not differ significantly from an average of 8.5 inches.

This example illustrates a basic hypothesis test. Now let's use a process control chart to monitor this paper production process. With process charts, we place the distribution on its side, as shown in FIGURE 14.8. We draw a center line and upper and lower rejection lines, which

FIGURE 14.8 >

Process Chart

we call *control limits*. We then plot the sample average (8.49888) on the control chart. Because the point falls between the control limits, we conclude that the process is in control. In other words, the variation in the process is random (common variation).

Notice that the preceding example was based on a sample of $n = 10$. Using this value of n means that the distribution we drew was a sampling distribution (not a population distribution). Therefore, we can invoke the **central limit theorem**, which states that when we plot the sample means, the sampling distribution approximates a normal distribution.

As you will see later, simplified formulas can be used to compute control limits. These control limits are only approximations. These formulas use tables to simplify computations because often there are not enough data to compute standard deviations with much confidence.

central limit theorem
Rule stating that sampling distributions generally are normally distributed.

A Generalized Procedure for Developing Process Charts

With this understanding of process control charts, we can now introduce a generalized procedure for developing control charts. The process for developing a process chart is the same for almost all charts. The only differences are in the actual statistical computations. TABLE 14.3 contains the steps used in developing process control charts.

Variables Control Charts

We now turn our attention to charts for variables. The charts are useful in monitoring for nonrandom activity relative to mean and dispersion. These charts are kept on paper in many plants; in others, they are on computers.

BACKGROUND ON VARIABLES CONTROL CHARTS In step 3 of Table 14.3, the first determination is whether variables or attributes are being measured. Remember that a variable is a continuously measured product or process characteristic such as time, width, height, or weight. We will first discuss variables control charts such as $\bar{x}$ and R charts. Later, an attribute chart will be presented.

TABLE 14.3 >

Developing Process Charts

1. Identify *critical operations* in the process where inspection might be needed. Such operations are those in which, if the operation is performed improperly, the form, fit, or function of the product will be negatively affected.
2. Identify *critical product characteristics*. They are the aspects of the product that will result in either good or poor functioning of the product.
3. Determine whether the critical product characteristic is a variable or an attribute.
4. Select the appropriate *process control chart* from among the many types of control charts. This decision process and the types of charts available are discussed later in the chapter.
5. Establish the *control limits* and use the chart to *continually monitor and improve the process*.
6. *Update the limits* when changes have been made to the process.

Source: S. Thomas Foster, *Managing Quality: Integrating Tile Supply Chain*, 5th Ed., © 2012. Reprinted and Electronically Reproduced by Permission of Pearson Education, Inc., Upper Saddle River, New Jersey.

x̄ AND R CHARTS Two variables charts go hand in hand: x̄ and R charts. An x̄ chart was developed in the prior example. When monitoring a measurement for a particular product in a process, there are two primary variables of interest: the mean of the process and the dispersion of the process. The x̄ chart aids in monitoring the process mean or average. The R chart is used in monitoring process dispersion. An x is a measurement in a sample. The bar above the x represents an average of several measurements that make up a sample. R stands for the range (from the largest number to the smallest number) in a sample.

The **x̄ chart** is a process control chart used to monitor the average of the characteristic being measured. To set up an x̄ chart, select samples from the process for the characteristic being measured. For example, on one process, workers decided to draw a systematic sample of five pieces of product every hour to measure. Next, find the average value of each sample by dividing the sums of the measurements by the sample size and plot the value on the process control x̄ chart. We will demonstrate in a later example.

The **R chart** is used to monitor the dispersion of the process. It is used in conjunction with the x̄ chart when the process characteristic is a variable. To develop an R chart, collect samples from the process, usually of three to six items. Next, compute the range R by taking the difference of the high value in the sample minus the low value. Then, plot the R values on the R chart.

A standard process chart form is shown in FIGURE 14.9. This form has spaces for measurements and totals. In the example in FIGURE 14.10, our control chart form is filled out with

x̄ chart
A process control chart used to monitor the average of the characteristic being measured.

R chart
A process control chart used to monitor the dispersion of the process.

∧ **FIGURE 14.9**

x̄ and R Chart

	1	2	3	4	5	6	7	8	9	10	11	12	13	14	15	16	17	18	19	20	21	22	23	24	25
1	24	29	38	24	33	28	30	19	24	26	25	28	31	30	26	24	25	26	27	28	24	18	29	20	14
2	27	30	42	28	36	28	28	26	27	27	26	24	26	31	25	36	35	30	31	33	24	42	30	36	25
3	28	29	36	27	31	28	27	23	33	38	27	29	38	33	24	24	25	28	29	30	32	36	31	34	36
4	33	31	35	32	28	28	26	22	28	26	28	30	24	32	36	36	35	32	33	34	32	30	28	32	35
5																									
Sum	112	119	151	111	128	112	111	90	112	117	106	111	119	126	111	120	120	116	120	125	112	126	118	122	110
Average, $\bar{x}$	28	29.75	37.75	27.75	32	28	27.75	22.5	28	29.25	26.5	27.75	29.75	31.5	27.75	30	30	29	30	31.25	28	31.5	29.5	30.5	27.5
Range, R	9	2	7	8	8	0	4	7	9	12	3	6	14	3	12	12	10	6	6	6	8	24	3	16	22
Notes																									

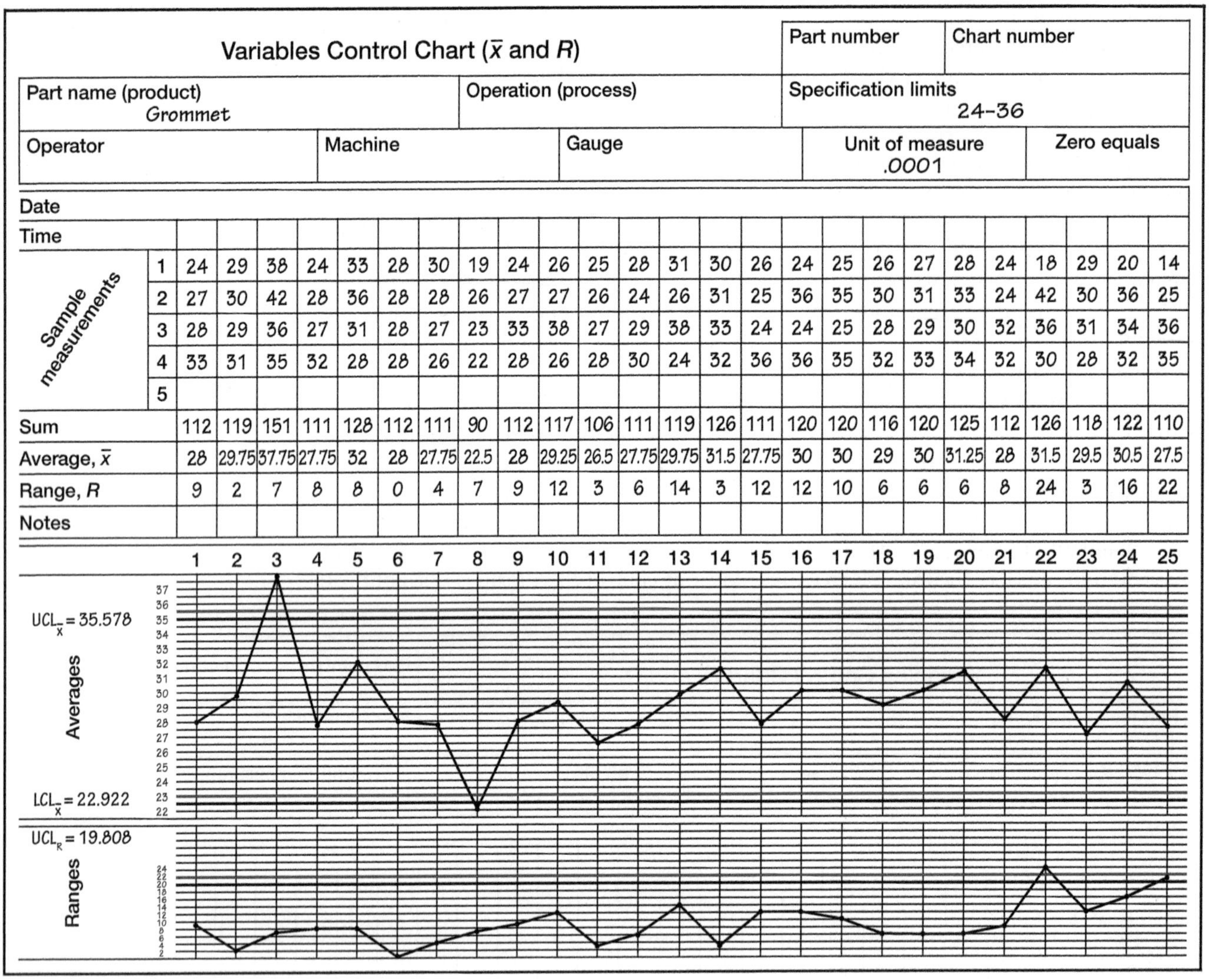

^ **FIGURE 14.10**
Completed $\bar{x}$ and R Charts

measurements from a process. There are $k = 25$ samples of size $n = 4$. A sample size (n) is the number of measurements in a sample; k is the number of samples of size n. For each of the samples, totals, ranges, and averages are computed. The range is the difference between the largest measurement and the smallest measurement in a particular sample.

Now that we have measurements, we need to compute a center line and control limits for our $\bar{x}$ and R charts. The center line is the process average. The upper and lower control limits are usually located three standard deviations from the center line. The formulas for computing these lines are given in **FIGURE 14.11** and are

$$UCL_{\bar{x}} = \bar{\bar{x}} + A_2(\bar{R}) \quad (14.2)$$

$$LCL_{\bar{x}} = \bar{\bar{x}} - A_2(\bar{R}) \quad (14.3)$$

where

UCL = upper control limit
LCL = lower control limit
$\bar{\bar{x}}$ = the grand mean (overall average)
A_2 = constant from Figure 14.11 (based on sample size, n)
$\bar{R}$ = average range within the samples

< FIGURE 14.11

$\bar{x}$ and R Chart
Calculation Worksheet

Control Limits

Subgroups included _____   _____

$$\bar{R} = \frac{\Sigma R}{k} = \text{———} = \quad \text{———}$$

$$\bar{\bar{x}} = \frac{\Sigma \bar{x}}{k} = \text{———} = \quad \text{———}$$

or

$\bar{x}$ (Midspec or std) $=$

$A_2\bar{R} = \quad$ x $=$

$UCL_{\bar{x}} = \bar{\bar{x}} + A_2\bar{R}$ $=$

$LCL_{\bar{x}} = \bar{\bar{x}} - A_2\bar{R}$ $=$

$UCL_R = D_4\bar{R} = \quad\quad$ x $=$

Factors for Control Limits

n	A_2	D_4
2	1.880	3.268
3	1.023	2.574
4	0.729	2.282
5	0.577	2.114
6	0.483	2.004

The formulas for the R chart are

$$LCL_R = D_3(\bar{R}) \tag{14.4}$$

$$UCL_R = D_4(\bar{R}) \tag{14.5}$$

where

D_3 = R chart lower control limit constant from Table A-3 in the appendix (based on sample size, n)

D_4 = R chart upper control limit constant from Figure 14.11 (based on sample size, n)

These formulas are also contained in **FIGURE 14.12** for the example in Figure 14.10. Notice that the A_2 and D_4 table values come from the Factor for Control Limits table in the lower left corner of Figure 14.12. These table values provide estimates for the three standard deviation limits for the $\bar{x}$ and R charts (when combined with $\bar{R}$, the mean of the R values).

Note that the lower limit of R is zero for sample sizes less than or equal to 6. For sample sizes greater than 6, D_3 values must be used from Table A-3 in the appendix. Notice that we have superimposed the control limits computed in Figure 14.12 on the charts in Figure 14.10. See **SOLVED PROBLEM 14.2** to learn to calculate control limits. As we explain later, the formulas used in computing control limits are used to approximate three standard deviation limits and simplify mathematical computations.

FIGURE 14.12 >

Calculation Worksheet
with Data from
Figure 14.11

Control Limits
Subgroups included

$$\bar{R} = \frac{\Sigma R}{k} = \frac{217}{25} = 8.68$$

$$\bar{\bar{x}} = \frac{\Sigma \bar{x}}{k} = \frac{731.25}{25} = 29.25$$

or

$\bar{x}$ (Midspec or std)   =

$A_2\bar{R} = 0.729 \times 8.68 = 6.328$

$UCL_{\bar{x}} = \bar{\bar{X}} + A_2\bar{R} = 29.25 + 6.328 = 35.578$

$LCL_{\bar{x}} = \bar{\bar{X}} - A_2\bar{R} = 29.25 - 6.328 = 22.922$

$UCL_R = D_4\bar{R} = 2.282 \times 8.68 = 19.808$

Factors for Control Limits

n	A_2	D_4
2	1.880	3.268
3	1.023	2.574
4	0.729	2.282
5	0.577	2.114
6	0.483	2.004

---

f(x) SOLVED PROBLEM 14.2 > ┃ **Developing $\bar{x}$ Charts** ┃

MyLab Operations Management
Video

Problem: Four samples ($k = 4$) of size four ($n = 4$) were taken with the following data. Compute an $\bar{x}$ chart to see if the process is stable (exhibits only random variation).

Sample	Obs1	Obs2	Obs3	Obs4
1	7	6	6	7
2	9	7	5	8
3	8	7	5	5
4	7	8	6	9

Solution: To begin our analysis, we compute means using Equations 14.2 and 14.3.

Sample	Obs1	Obs2	Obs3	Obs4	Means
1	7	6	6	7	6.5
2	9	7	5	8	7.25
3	8	7	5	5	6.25
4	7	8	6	9	7.5
					$\bar{\bar{x}}$ = Grand mean = 6.875

As we can see, $\bar{\bar{x}} = 6.875$. The grand mean is found by finding the sample averages and then taking the average of the sample averages. From the table in Figure 14.12, the A_2 value is 0.729. We also need to compute $\bar{R}$ (the average range), which we can do by subtracting the minimum value for each sample from its associated maximum and then computing the average of the ranges. The $\bar{R}$ value is 2.75.

Sample	Obs1	Obs2	Obs3	Obs4	Max	Min	R
1	7	6	6	7	7	6	1
2	9	7	5	8	9	5	4
3	8	7	5	5	8	5	3
4	7	8	6	9	9	6	3
						$\bar{R} =$	2.75

Substituting into Equations 14.2 and 14.3, we get

$$UCL = 6.875 + (0.729 \times 2.75) = 8.88$$
$$LCL = 6.875 - (0.729 \times 2.75) = 4.87$$

The control chart is as follows. We plot each of the sample means in sequence (6.5, 7.25, 6.25, 7.5).

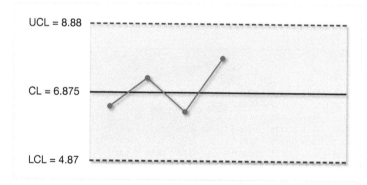

It appears that the process is in control because all the points are between the upper and lower control limits, which means that the variation in the process is random and the process is stable. **SOLVED PROBLEM 14.3** shows how to use Excel to develop $\bar{x}$ charts.

Using Excel to Develop $\bar{x}$ Control Charts

< USING
TECHNOLOGY 14.1

Problem: The following are the results of 20 samples ($k = 20$) of size 6 ($n = 6$) for a continuous measurement. Develop a control chart in Excel using these data.

Solution: First, compute the sample averages for each sample. The resulting spreadsheet is as follows:

< SOLVED PROBLEM 14.3

MyLab Operations Management
Video

Excel Window 1

	A	B	C	D	E	F	G	H	I	J	K	L	M	N
1														
2														
3	Sample	Obs 1	Obs 2	Obs 3	Obs 4	Obs 5	Obs 6	Means						
4	1	14.88	14.64	15.12	15.60	15.36	15.072	15.112						
5	2	14.88	14.88	14.88	15.12	15.36	14.976	15.016						
6	3	15.12	14.16	14.88	15.36	15.12	13.728	14.728						
7	4	12.72	12.24	12.72	12.24	12.72	13.848	12.748						
8	5	14.64	15.84	15.12	14.88	15.36	15.024	15.144						
9	6	14.88	14.88	14.88	14.88	14.88	14.592	14.832						
10	7	13.92	13.68	14.16	17.28	12.48	14.616	14.356						
11	8	15.12	14.16	14.88	15.36	15.12	14.928	14.928						
12	9	15.12	14.16	14.88	15.36	15.12	16.176	15.136						
13	10	17.76	17.76	17.04	17.52	17.04	16.2	17.22						
14	11	14.88	15.12	14.88	15.12	14.88	14.952	14.972						
15	12	15.36	15.12	14.88	14.64	14.64	14.976	14.936						
16	13	15.12	15.36	14.88	15.12	14.64	14.832	14.992						
17	14	14.64	14.64	14.64	14.64	14.64	14.808	14.668						
18	15	15.12	15.36	14.64	15.12	14.64	15.024	14.984						
19	16	15.36	14.88	15.36	14.88	14.88	15.096	15.076						
20	17	14.88	15.36	15.12	15.36	14.88	15.12	15.12						
21	18	14.64	14.88	15.12	15.36	15.60	14.904	15.084						
22	19	14.88	14.64	14.64	14.64	14.64	14.952	14.732						
23	20	15.36	15.12	14.88	15.60	15.12	15.216	15.216						
24														
25														
26														
27														
28														

The second Excel window shows the formulas for the various calculations needed to develop the control charts. Sample formulas are given for every calculation in the spreadsheet. You can enter these formulas and then copy the formulas into the other cells for conditional formatting to occur.

Excel Window 2

	A	B	C	D	E	F	G	H	I	J	K	L	M	N
1														
2														
3	Sample	Obs 1	Obs 2	Obs 3	Obs 4	Obs 5	Obs 6	Means	CL	UCL	LCL	Max	Min	R
4	1	14.88	14.64	15.12	15.60	15.36	15.07	15.11	14.95	15.46	14.44	15.60	14.64	0.96
5	2	14.88	14.88	14.88	15.12					15.46				
6	3	15.12	14.16	14.88	15.36					15.46				
7	4	12.72	12.24	12.72	12.24	12.72	13.85	12.75	14.95	15.46	14.44	13.85	12.24	1.61
8	5	14.64	15.84	15.12	14.88	15.36	15.02	15.14	14.95	15.46	14.44	15.84	14.64	1.20
9	6	14.88	14.88	14.88	14.88	14.88	14.59	14.83	14.95	15.46	14.44	14.88	14.59	0.29
10	7	13.92	13.68	14.16				14.36	14.95	15.46	14.44	17.28	12.48	4.80
11	8	15.12	14.16	14.88			14.93					15.36	14.16	1.20
12	9	15.12	14.16	14.88	15.36	15.12	16.18	15.14				16.18	14.16	2.02
13	10	17.76	17.76	17.04	17.52	17.04	16.20	17.22	14.95	15.46	14.4.	17.76	16.20	1.56
14	11	14.88	15.12	14.88	15.12	14.88	14.95	14.97	14.95	15.46	14.44	15.12	14.88	0.24
15	12	15.36	15.12	14.88	14.64	14.64	14.98	14.94	14.95	15.46	14.44	15.36	14.64	0.72
16	13	15.12	15.36	14.88	15.12	14.64	14.83	14.99	14.95	15.46	14.44	15.36	14.64	0.72
17	14	14.64	14.64	14.64	14.64	14.64	14.81	14.67	14.95				14.64	0.17
18	15	15.12	15.36	14.64	15.12	14.64	15.02	14.98	14.95				14.64	0.72
19	16	15.36	14.88	15.36	14.88	14.88	15.10	15.08	14.95	15.46	14.44	15.36	14.88	0.48
20	17	14.88	15.36	15.12	15.36	14.88	15.12	15.12	14.95	15.46				0.48
21	18	14.64	14.88	15.12	15.36	15.60	14.90	15.08	14.95	15.46				0.96
22	19	14.88	14.64	14.64	14.64	14.64	14.95	14.73	14.95	15.46	14.44	14.95	14.64	0.31
23	20	15.36	15.12	14.88	15.60	15.12	15.22	15.22	14.95	15.46	14.44	15.60	14.88	0.72
24							Grand mean =	14.95					R-bar =	1.06
25							A2 =	0.483						
26														
27														
28														

Callouts:
- Center line (CL)=$H$24
- Upper control limit (UCL) =$H$24+$H$25*$N$24
- Lower control limit (LCL) =$H$24−$H$25*$N$24
- Mean for sample 5 =AVERAGE(B8:G8)
- Max for sample 11 =MAX(B14:G14)
- Min for sample 12 =MIN(B15:G15)
- Range for sample 15 =L18−M18
- The grand mean is computed as =AVERAGE(H4:H23)
- The A2 value comes from Figure 14.12 where n=6.
- R-bar =AVERAGE(N4:N23)

Next, to print the control chart in Excel, highlight columns H through K (including the column headings), click on the Insert tab, click on "Line" graph, and select the two-dimensional formatting that you prefer. You may need to limit the vertical scale by clicking on the chart and setting maximum and minimum values to 12 and 18, respectively. The following $\bar{x}$ chart will result:

	A	B	C	D	E	F	G	H	I	J	K	L	M	N
1														
2														
3	Sample	Obs 1	Obs 2	Obs 3	Obs 4	Obs 5	Obs 6	Means	CL	UCL	LCL	Max	Min	R
4	1	14.88	14.64	15.12	15.60	15.36	15.07	15.11	14.95	15.46	14.44	15.60	14.64	0.96
5	2	14.88	14.88	14.88	15.12	15.36	14.98	15.02	14.95	15.46	14.44	15.36	14.88	0.48
6	3	15.12	14.16	14.88	15.36	15.12	13.73	14.73	14.95	15.46	14.44	15.36	13.73	1.63
7	4	12.72	12.24	12.72	12.24	12.72	13.85	12.75	14.95	15.46	14.44	13.85	12.24	1.61
8	5	14.64	15.84	15.12	14.88	15.36	15.02	15.14	14.95	15.46	14.44	15.84	14.64	1.20
9	6	14.88	14.88	14.88	14.88	14.88	14.59	14.83	14.95	15.46	14.44	14.88	14.59	0.29
10	7	13.92	13.68	14.16	17.28	12.48	14.62	14.36	14.95	15.46	14.44	17.28	12.48	4.80
11	8	15.12	14.16	14.88	15.36	15.12	14.93	14.93	14.95	15.46	14.44	15.36	14.16	1.20
12								16.18	15.14	14.95	15.46	14.44	16.18	14.16	2.02
13								16.20	17.22	14.95	15.46	14.44	17.76	16.20	1.56
14								14.95	14.97	14.95	15.46	14.44	15.12	14.88	0.24
15								14.98	14.94	14.95	15.46	14.44	15.36	14.64	0.72
16								14.83	14.99	14.95	15.46	14.44	15.36	14.64	0.72
17								14.81	14.67	14.95	15.46	14.44	14.81	14.64	0.17
18								15.02	14.98	14.95	15.46	14.44	15.36	14.64	0.72
19								15.10	15.08	14.95	15.46	14.44	15.36	14.88	0.48
20								15.12	15.12	14.95	15.46	14.44	15.36	14.88	0.48
21								14.90	15.08	14.95	15.46	14.44	15.60	14.64	0.96
22								14.95	14.73	14.95	15.46	14.44	14.95	14.64	0.31
23								15.22	15.22	14.95	15.46	14.44	15.60	14.88	0.72
24								mean =	14.95					R-bar =	1.06
25								A2 =	0.483						
26														
27														
28														

x-bar Chart

18.00
17.00
16.00
15.00
14.00
13.00
12.00
1 2 3 4 5 6 7 8 9 10 11 12 13 14 15 16 17 18 19 20
Means — CL — UCL — LCL

Excel Window 3 with the Completed Control Chart

Reviewing the chart, it appears that samples 4, 7, and 10 are out of control. That means that the process is not random and that you should investigate to find assignable causes of variation. Now, try to do it on your own!

Developing R Charts

< SOLVED PROBLEM 14.4

MyLab Operations Management
Video

Problem: Go back to the data in Solved Problem 14.2 and develop an R chart to see if the dispersion is stable. Here are the data again:

Sample	Obs1	Obs2	Obs3	Obs4
1	7	6	6	7
2	9	7	5	8
3	8	7	5	5
4	7	8	6	9

Solution: The calculations are listed in the following table:

Sample	Obs1	Obs2	Obs3	Obs4	Max	Min	Range (Max – Min)	CL	UCL	LCL
1	7	6	6	7	7	6	1	2.75	6.2755	0
2	9	7	5	8	9	5	4	2.75	6.2755	0
3	8	7	5	5	8	5	3	2.75	6.2755	0
4	7	8	6	9	9	6	3	2.75	6.2755	0
						$\bar{R} =$	2.75			
						$D_4 =$	2.282			

The center line for the R chart is the average range $= (1 + 4 + 3 + 3)/4 = 2.75$. Therefore, the center line of our control chart (CL) $= 2.75$. Because the sample size is 6 or less, the lower control limit (LCL) $= 0$. The upper control limit is computed using Equation 14.5. The value of D_4 is found in Figure 14.12 where $n = 4$, and the value of $D_4 = 2.282$. Thus, the upper control limit is $2.282 \times 2.75 = 6.2755$. The following control chart results from this analysis:

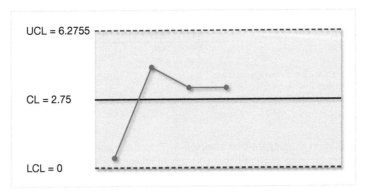

We plotted the ranges (1, 4, 3, 3) in sequence in the graph. The dispersion of the process appears to be stable. All of the points are between the upper and lower control limits. There is no reason to conclude that the dispersion (R chart) is out of control.

SOLVED PROBLEM 14.5 shows how to use Excel to develop R charts. **SC&O CURRENT EVENTS 14.2** shows how control charts were used in a human resources department.

USING >
TECHNOLOGY 14.2

 SOLVED PROBLEM 14.5 >

MyLab Operations Management
Video

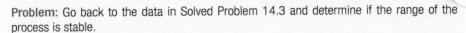

Developing *R* Charts in Excel

Problem: Go back to the data in Solved Problem 14.3 and determine if the range of the process is stable.

Solution: The raw process data for the 20 samples was given in Solved Problem 14.3. We will move straight to the calculations in **FIGURE 14.13**. Calculations are shown for the center line (CL), upper control limit (UCL), and lower control limit (LCL).

The control limits were computed using Equations 14.4 and 14.5. The formatting for these formulas in Excel is given in Figure 14.13. The control chart is shown in **FIGURE 14.14**.

< FIGURE 14.13

Excel Window 1

	A	B	C	D	E	F	G	H	I	J	K	L	M	N
1														
2														
3	Sample	Obs 1	Obs 2	Obs 3	Obs 4	Obs 5	Obs 6	Max	Min	R	CL	LCL	UCL	
4	1	14.88	14.64	15.12	15.60	15.36	15.07	15.60	14.64	0.96	1.06	0.00	2.13	
5	2	14.88	14.88					15.36	14.88	0.48	1.06	0.00	2.13	
6	3	15.12	14.16					15.36	13.73	1.63	1.06	0.00	2.13	
7	4	12.72	12.24	12.72	12.24	12.72	13.85	13.85	12.24	1.61	1.06	0.00	2.13	
8	5	14.64	15.84	15.12					14.64	1.20	1.06	0.00	2.13	
9	6	14.88	14.88	14.88					14.59	0.29	1.06	0.00	2.13	
10	7	13.92	13.68	14.16	17.28	12.48	14.62	17.28	12.48	4.80				
11	8	15.12	14.16	14.88	15.36	15.12	14.93	15.36	14.16	1.20				
12	9	15.12	14.16	14.88	15.36	1				2.02				
13	10	17.76	17.76	17.04	17.52	1				1.56	1.06	0.00	2.13	
14	11	14.88	15.12	14.88	15.12	14.88	14.95	15.12	14.88	0.24	1.06	0.00	2.13	
15	12	15.36	15.12	14.88	14.64	14.64	14.98	15.36	14.64	0.72	1.06	0.00	2.13	
16	13	15.12	15.36	14.88	15.12	14.64	14.83	15.36	14.64	0.72	1.06	0.00	2.13	
17	14	14.64	14.64	14.64	14.64	14.64	14.81	14.81	14.64	0.17	1.06	0.00	2.13	
18	15	15.12	15.36	14.64	15.12	14.64	15.02	15.36	14.64	0.72	1.06	0.00	2.13	
19	16	15.36	14.88	15.36	14.88	14.88	15.10	15.36	14.88	0.48	1.06	0.00	2.13	
20	17	14.88	15.36	15.12	15.36	14.88	15.12	15.36	14.88	0.48	1.06	0.00	2.13	
21	18	14.64	14.88	15.12						0.96	1.06	0.00	2.13	
22	19	14.88	14.64	14.64						0.31	1.06	0.00	2.13	
23	20	15.36	15.12	14.88	15.60	15.12	15.22	15.60	14.88	0.72	1.06	0.00	2.13	
24										R-bar =	1.06			
25							D3 =	0						
26							D4 =	2.004						
27														
28														

Callouts:
- Center line (CL)=$J$24
- The maximum value for sample 1 =MAX(B4:G4)
- The minimum value for sample 3 =MIN(B6:G6)
- The upper control limit =$H$26*$J$24
- The range for sample 7 =H10−I10
- The R-bar is the average of the above column =AVERAGE(J4:J23)
- D_3 is zero since the sample size is 6 or less. D_4 is drawn from the table in the lower right-hand corner of Figure 14.12 where n=6.
- The lower control limit for sample 20 is D_3*R-bar =$H$25*$J$23

As you can see, the process is out of control in sample 7, where the range (R) is 4.8. Investigate for an assignable cause of variation. On further inspection, you can see that the ranges for samples 11 through 20 all fall below the mean in what is called a run, or a non-random event. We will discuss runs more in the next section.

< FIGURE 14.14

Excel Window 2 with the Control Chart

	A	B	C	D	E	F	G	H	I	J	K	L	M	N
1														
2														
3	Sample	Obs 1	Obs 2	Obs 3	Obs 4	Obs 5	Obs 6	Max	Min	R	CL	LCL	UCL	
4	1	14.88	14.64	15.12	15.60	15.36	15.07	15.60	14.64	0.96	1.06	0.00	2.13	
5	2	14.88	14.88	14.88	15.12	15.36	14.98	15.36	14.88	0.48	1.06	0.00	2.13	
6	3	15.12	14.16	14.88	15.36	15.12	13.73	15.36	13.73	1.63	1.06	0.00	2.13	
7	4	12.72	12.24	12.72	12.24	12.72	13.85	13.85	12.24	1.61	1.06	0.00	2.13	
8	5	14.64	15.84	15.12	14.88	15.36	15.02	15.84	14.64	1.20	1.06	0.00	2.13	
9	6	14.88	14.88	14.88	14.88	14.88	14.59	14.88	14.59	0.29	1.06	0.00	2.13	
10	7	13.92	13.68	14.16	17.28	12.48	14.62	17.28	12.48	4.80	1.06	0.00	2.13	
11	8	15.12	14.16	14.88	15.36	15.12	14.93	15.36	14.16	1.20	1.06	0.00	2.13	
12	9	15.12	14.16	14.88	15.36	15.12	16.18	16.18	14.16	2.02	1.06	0.00	2.13	
13	10	17.76	17.76	17.04	17.52	17.04	16.20	17.76	16.20	1.56	1.06	0.00	2.13	
14	11	14.88	15.12	14.88	15.12	14.88	14.95	15.12	14.88	0.24	1.06	0.00	2.13	
15	12	15.36	15.12	14.88	14.64	14.64	14.98	15.36	14.64	0.72	1.06	0.00	2.13	
16	13								14.64	0.72	1.06	0.00	2.13	
17	14								14.64	0.17	1.06	0.00	2.13	
18	15								14.64	0.72	1.06	0.00	2.13	
19	16								14.88	0.48	1.06	0.00	2.13	
20	17								14.88	0.48	1.06	0.00	2.13	
21	18								14.64	0.96	1.06	0.00	2.13	
22	19								14.64	0.31	1.06	0.00	2.13	
23	20								14.88	0.72	1.06	0.00	2.13	
24										R-bar =	1.06			
25														
26														
27														
28														

Control chart (rows 16–26): vertical axis 0.00 to 5.00; horizontal axis samples 1–20. Series: R, CL, LCL, UCL.

Using x̄ Charts in a Human Resources Department

Control charts are used frequently in manufacturing firms, but they can also be applied to service and administrative processes. One example is the application of $\bar{x}$ and R charts in a human resources (HR) department. The HR department in question identified a project to reduce the amount of time required to fill exempt employee openings. First, a team put together a project charter and then gathered historical data and plotted the data in a run chart. Next, they mapped the process into the following simple six-step process, with $\bar{x}$ and R values, for selecting and hiring employees.

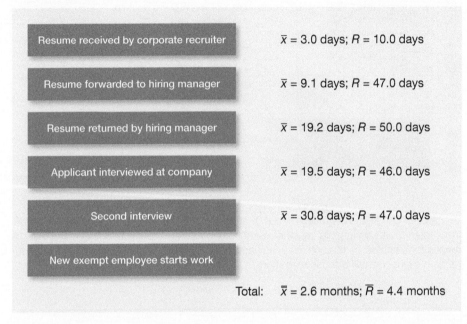

Resume received by corporate recruiter	$\bar{x}$ = 3.0 days; R = 10.0 days
Resume forwarded to hiring manager	$\bar{x}$ = 9.1 days; R = 47.0 days
Resume returned by hiring manager	$\bar{x}$ = 19.2 days; R = 50.0 days
Applicant interviewed at company	$\bar{x}$ = 19.5 days; R = 46.0 days
Second interview	$\bar{x}$ = 30.8 days; R = 47.0 days
New exempt employee starts work	

Total: $\bar{\bar{x}}$ = 2.6 months; $\bar{R}$ = 4.4 months

By studying the process with the use of control charts coupled with the other seven basic tools, the team was able to reduce the total process time from 4.4 months to 2 months, thereby reducing the time by 50 percent. Further process monitoring showed that the improved time persisted.

Source: Based on J. Leonard, "Statistical Methods Applied to a Non-Manufacturing Process," 2012, http://www.jimleonardpi.com/case-studies/case-study-statistical-methods-applied-to-a-non-manufacturing-process/.

Attributes Control Charts

Attributes control charts deal with binomial or Poisson processes that are not continuous measurements. We will now think in terms of *defects* and *defectives* rather than diameters and widths.

defect
An irregularity or problem with a larger unit.

defective unit
A unit that, as a whole, is not acceptable or does not meet performance requirements.

DEFECTS A **defect** is an irregularity or problem with a larger unit. The larger unit may contain many defects. For example, a piece of glass may contain several bubbles or scratches. Some of them may be detectable only with a magnifying glass. Defects are countable, such as six flaws within a particular pane of glass. A **defective unit** is a unit that, as a whole, is not acceptable or does not meet performance requirements. For example, a window with too many bubbles or scratches may be deemed defective. Defectives are monitored using p charts. Defects are monitored using c and u charts, which will not be covered here.[1] GLOBAL CONNECTIONS 14.1 discusses attributes in the international airline industry.

[1]For a more in-depth discussion of a wider variety of control charts, see S. T. Foster, *Managing Quality: Integrating the Supply Chain* (Upper Saddle River, NJ: Pearson, 2013).

Airline Quality

Attributes are everywhere. Reports about the airline industry that include statistics relative to customer satisfaction are usually full of attributes: either the bag is lost or it isn't, either the flight was on time or it wasn't.

An Airline Quality Rating report compiled information on 18 airlines based on factors such as on-time arrivals, denied boardings, mishandled baggage, and customer complaints, all of which are attributes. The industry rate of mishandled bags per 1,000 passengers dropped from 3.62 to 3.24 bags. Alaska Air had the lowest number of complaints, with 0.5 complaints per 100,000 passengers. The average on-time arrival percentage for all airlines was 80 percent.

Here are the 2016 Airline Quality Rating rankings:

1. Virgin America
2. JetBlue
3. Delta
4. Hawaiian
5. Alaska
6. Southwest
7. SkyWest
8. United
9. ExpressJet
10. American
11. Frontier
12. Envoy
13. Spirit

These numbers are very important to the industry. Companies can use and plot these metrics to improve.

Source: Based on Air Quality Rating Report, 2016.

p CHARTS FOR PROPORTION DEFECTIVE The **p chart** is a process chart used to graph the proportion of items in a sample that are defective (nonconforming to requirements). These charts are effectively used to determine when there has been a shift in the proportion defective for a particular product or service. Typical applications of the p chart include late deliveries, incomplete orders, calls not getting dial tones, accounting transaction errors, clerical errors on written forms, and parts that do not mate properly. The subgroup size on a p chart is typically between 50 and 100 units.

Although subgroups may be of different sizes for a p chart, it is best to hold subgroup sizes constant. Usually, at least 25 subgroups are used to establish a p chart. The formulas for the p chart are:

$$\text{Control limits for } p = \bar{p} \pm 3\sqrt{\frac{(\bar{p})1 - \bar{p}}{n}} \qquad (14.6)$$

where

p = the proportion defective in a particular sample
$\bar{p}$ = the average proportion defective among all samples
n = the sample size

Note that these control limits are $z = 3$ standard deviations from the mean, which captures 99.7 percent of the random variation.

p chart
A process chart used to graph the proportion of items in a sample that are defective (nonconforming to specification).

SC&O CURRENT >
EVENTS 14.3

Using *p* Charts at Biocompatibles, PLC

Biocompatibles design engineers developed a coating material that mimicked the properties of a human cell. An application of the new technology was a coating for contact lenses. The company was excited about the new development and wished to get the coated lenses to market.

Production of the contact lenses required a molding process that initially resulted in many defects, including scratches, rough edges, holes, water spots, and bubbles. These attributes were plotted using *p* charts while experimenting continued to improve the process. At times process changes resulted in improvement in the proportion defective, and other times in worsening the process. The charts were used to monitor the process and to determine which process changes were effective in reducing defects. As a result of the experimentation—coupled with the skilled use of *p* charts—sale of the contact lenses increased from 200,000 units per month to 1.6 million units per month.

One of the goals of the control chart user is to reduce variation. Over time, as processes are improved, control limits are recomputed to show improvements in stability. The process is improving as upper and lower control limits get closer and closer together.

Source: Based on J. Leonard, "Process Improvement in Dry Cast Molding," Case Study, 2013, http://www .jimleonardpi.com/case-studies/case-study-dry-cast-molding-rejects/.

The generic process for developing a *p* chart is the same as for the previous charts we have created in this chapter. Only the statistic of interest and the formula have changed. The *p* chart is demonstrated in **SOLVED PROBLEM 14.6**, and **SC&O CURRENT EVENTS 14.3** discusses the use of *p* charts in the production of contact lenses.

f(x)   **SOLVED PROBLEM 14.6 >**   **Developing *p* Charts**

Problem: An inspector visually inspects 10 samples of 300 windowpanes for defects. Using trained judgment, the inspector will either accept or reject windows based on whether or not they are flawless. The following are the results of recent inspections.

Sample Number	Defectives (out of 300 per sample)
1	11
2	12
3	14
4	10
5	3
6	26
7	14
8	12
9	15
10	10

Solution: The following table shows the resulting proportions defective for each sample. These proportions are found by dividing the defectives by 300. For example, for sample 1, $11/300 = 0.037$. The $\bar{p}$ value is found by summing the p values for each sample and dividing by the number of samples ($k = 10$). In this problem, $n = 300$.

Sample Number	Defectives (out of 300 per sample)	p (proportion defective)
1	11	0.037
2	12	0.040
3	14	0.047
4	10	0.033
5	3	0.010
6	26	0.087
7	14	0.047
8	12	0.040
9	15	0.050
10	10	0.033
	$\bar{p} =$	**0.042**

Using Equation 14.6, the control limits are

$$UCL_p = 0.042 + 3\sqrt{\frac{0.042(1 - 0.042)}{300}} = 0.0767$$

$$UCL_p = 0.042 - 3\sqrt{\frac{0.042(1 - 0.042)}{300}} = 0.0073$$

$$CL = 0.042$$

The resulting control chart is as shown below. Note that we plotted each of the 10 sample proportions in sequence.

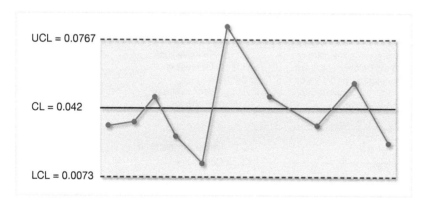

The sixth point on the graph is above the upper control limit. Investigate for an assignable cause of variation. Also, the erratic jump between the fifth and sixth points is more than four standard deviations. Investigate. The process is not in statistical control.

 **PPLY CONTROL CHARTS**

Now that you have learned how to develop control charts, it is important to learn how to interpret them. We cover a number of topics in the next section, including interpretation, corrective action, process tampering, and control charts in services.

Interpreting Control Charts

Until now, we have discussed nonrandom events with a single out-of-control point. However, a control chart can signal special cause situations in other ways. FIGURE 14.15 shows several different signals for concern that are sent by a control chart, as in the second and third boxes of the first row. When a point is found to be outside the control limits, we call it an "out-of-control situation." When a process is out of control, variation is probably no longer random. If there are three standard deviation limits, the chance of a sample average or range being out of control when the process is stable is less than 1 percent. Because this probability is so small, we conclude that it was a nonrandom event and search for an assignable cause of variability.

FIGURE 14.15 >

Control Chart Evidence for Investigation

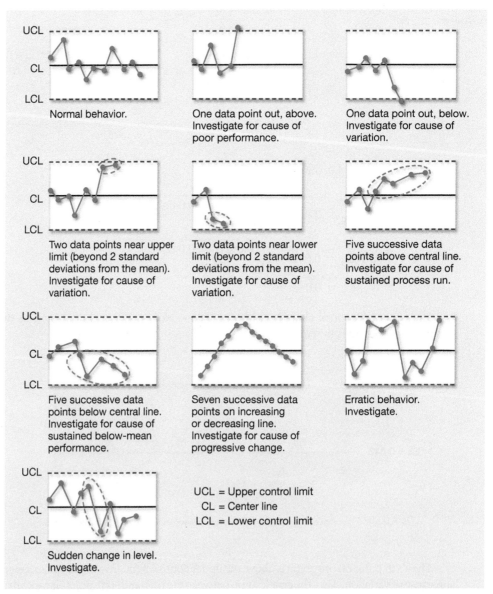

Source: S. Thomas Foster, *Managing Quality: Integrating Tile Supply Chain,* 5th Ed., © 2012. Reprinted and Electronically Reproduced by Permission of Pearson Education, Inc., Upper Saddle River, New Jersey.

Figure 14.15 presents examples where nonrandom situations occur. These nonrandom events in a process signal that the process is an **out-of-control process** or is experiencing nonrandom variation. You do not need to have a single out-of-control situation to determine that a process is no longer random. Two points in succession farther than two standard deviations from the mean likely will be a nonrandom event because the chances of this happening at random are very low. Five points in succession (either all above or all below the center line) is called a **process run**, which occurs when the process mean or dispersion has shifted. Seven points that are all either increasing or decreasing result in **process drift**. Process drift usually means that either materials or machines are drifting out of alignment. An example is a drill bit that is wearing out rapidly in a machine shop. Large jumps of more than three or four standard deviations result in *erratic behavior*. In all these cases, process charts help us understand when the process is or is not in control.

If a process loses control and becomes nonrandom, the process should be stopped immediately. Often, this situation can result in the stoppage of several workstations. The team of workers who are to address the problem should use a structured problem-solving process using brainstorming and cause-and-effect tools such as those discussed in Chapter 13 to identify the root cause of the out-of-control situation. Typically, the cause is somewhere in the interaction among processes, materials, machinery, and/or labor. Once the assignable cause of variation has been discovered, corrective action can be taken to eliminate the cause. The process is then restarted, and people return to work.

The cause of the problem should be documented and discussed later during the weekly departmental meeting. All workers should know why a problem in the process occurred. They should understand the causes and the corrective actions that were taken to solve the problem. **SOLVED PROBLEM 14.7** gives you some practice in interpreting control charts.

out-of-control process
A process that exhibits nonrandom variation.

process run
Five points in sequence, either above or below the mean.

process drift
Seven points in succession, all increasing or decreasing in a process chart.

Interpreting Control Charts

SOLVED PROBLEM 14.7

Problem: Interpret the following charts to determine if the processes are stable.

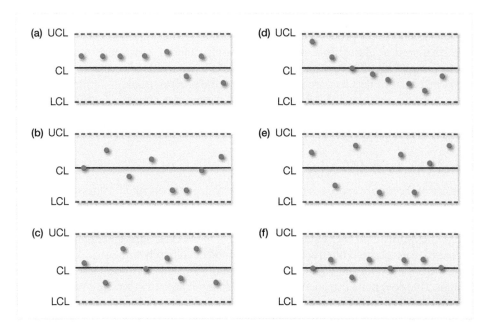

Solution: Control chart (a) has a run in the first five points. Control chart (b) has two points that are over two standard deviations below the mean. Control chart (c) appears to be stable, exhibiting only random variation. Control chart (d) has process drift, with seven points all decreasing. Control chart (e) is erratic, with several four standard deviation jumps above and below the mean. Control chart (f) is stable, but it looks too good. This process might have changed, and limits may need to be recalculated. Compare control chart (f) with control chart (c). Control chart (c) is more what you would expect from a random process.

FIGURE 14.16 >

Process Tampering

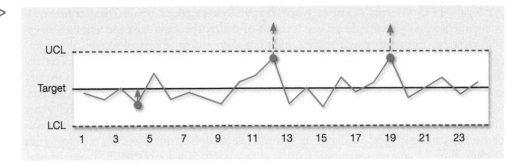

Corrective Action

corrective action
Eight steps taken when a process chart is out of control.

When a process is out of control, **corrective action** is needed. Corrective action steps are similar to continuous improvement processes:

1. Carefully identify the quality problem.
2. Form the correct team to evaluate and solve the problem.
3. Use structured brainstorming along with fishbone diagrams or affinity diagrams to identify causes of problems.
4. Brainstorm to identify potential solutions to problems.
5. Eliminate the cause.
6. Restart the process.
7. Document the problem, root causes, and solutions.
8. Communicate the results of the process to all personnel so that this process becomes reinforced and ingrained in the organization.

Tampering with the Process

process tampering
Adjusting a process when it exhibits only random variation.

One of the cardinal rules of process charts is that you should never tamper with the process or make adjustments to the process any time it deviates from the target because random effects are just that, *random*. Adjusting a process when only random variation is present is called **process tampering**. Effects cannot be controlled; if we make adjustments to a random process, we actually inject a nonrandom event into the process. FIGURE 14.16 shows a random process. Suppose that we had decided to adjust the process after the fourth observation. Samples 12 and 19 would then have fallen above the upper control limit. Our nonrandom tampering after sample 4 would have worsened the process.

Control Charts and Services

The choice of the proper approach to quality control depends on your business needs. Sometimes people attempt to use control charts in inappropriate situations with disastrous results.

Control charts are sometimes difficult to use in services because of the subjectivity of services, in other words, customer-induced variation. Although cycle times and response times can be measured, control charts often are simply not a good fit culturally with services situations. As a result, there is an opportunity for the development of new statistical tools for services that are a better fit. That does not mean control charts should never be used in services. We are just proposing that they be used in a manner that is productive and that fits with the culture you work in.

ERFORM PROCESS CAPABILITY ANALYSIS

process capability
The ability of a process to produce a product that meets specification.

Once a process is stable, the next area of emphasis is to ensure that the process is *capable*. **Process capability** refers to the ability of a process to produce a product that meets specification. A highly capable process produces high volumes with few or no defects and is the result of optimizing the interactions between people, machines, raw materials, procedures, and measurement systems. World-class levels of process capability are measured by parts per million defect levels, which means that for every 1 million pieces produced, only a small number (fewer than 100) are defective.

Now that we have defined process capability, we can discuss how to determine whether a process is capable and whether individual products meet specifications. Performing process capability studies has two purposes:

1. To determine whether a process consistently results in products that meet specifications
2. To determine whether a process is in need of monitoring through the use of permanent process control charts

Process capability studies help process managers understand whether the range, over which natural variation of a process occurs, is the result of the system of common (or random) causes. There are five steps in performing process capability studies:

1. Select a critical operation. Operations may be bottlenecks, costly steps of the process, or places in the process where problems have occurred in the past.
2. Take k samples of size n, where x is an individual observation.

   - where $19 < k < 26$.
   - If x is an attribute, $n > 50$ (as in the case of a binomial).
   - Or, if x is a measurement, $1 < n < 11$.
   (*Note:* Small sample sizes can lead to erroneous conclusions.)

3. Use a *trial control chart* to see whether the process is stable.
4. Compare process natural tolerance limits with specification limits. Note that natural tolerance limits are three standard deviation limits for the population distribution. This can be compared with the specification limits.
5. Compute capability indexes: A **capability index (Cpk)** is a comparative measure of the extent to which individual products meet specification. To compute capability indexes, compute an upper capability index (Cp_u), a lower capability index (Cp_l), and a capability index (Cp_k). The formulas used to compute these indexes are as follows:

capability index (Cpk)
A comparative measure of the extent to which individual products meet specification.

$$CP_u = \frac{USL - \mu}{3\hat{\sigma}} \qquad (14.7)$$

$$CP_l = \frac{\mu - LSL}{3\hat{\sigma}} \qquad (14.8)$$

$$CP_k = \min\{CP_u, CP_l\} \qquad (14.9)$$

where

  USL = upper specification limit
  LSL = lower specification limit
  μ = process mean
  $\hat{\sigma}$ = estimated process standard deviation

6. Make a decision concerning whether the process is capable.

Although different firms use different benchmarks for what Cp_k value is preferred, the generally accepted benchmarks for process capability are 1.25, 1.33, and 2.0. We will say that processes that achieve capability indexes (Cp_k) of 1.25 are capable, 1.33 are highly capable, and 2.0 are world-class capable (Six Sigma). Capability analysis calculations are demonstrated in **SOLVED PROBLEM 14.8.**

....

Capability Analysis

< SOLVED PROBLEM 14.8

Problem: For a personal computer, an important component is specified to be between 30 and 40 millimeters. Thirty samples of components yield a grand mean (μ) of 33 millimeters, with an estimated standard deviation ($\hat{\sigma}$) of 1.2. Calculate the process capability index by following the steps previously outlined.

Solution: We calculate the indexes using Equations 14.7 through 14.9:

$$CP_u = \frac{40 - 33}{(3)(1.2)} = 1.94$$

$$CP_l = \frac{33 - 30}{(3)(1.2)} = 0.83$$

$$CP_k = \min\{1.94, 0.83\} = 0.83$$

The process capability in this case is poor because 0.83 is below 1.25, which is the minimum acceptable standard for capability.

Once a firm establishes that its processes are stable (process control charts) and its products are capable (Cp$_k$), it is poised for success. These statistical analysis tools provide a basis for determining if products and processes function properly.

Nestlé Pure Life Water Revisited

Recall from the chapter-opening vignette that Nestlé has a 14-step process to ensure that the water it sells is safe to drink. To ensure water safety, Nestlé employs at least three types of inspection strategies: visual inspection of bottles, statistical inspection of the water, and inspection by external agencies such as the National Sanitation Foundation.

The bottling process is subject to Food and Drug Administration standards, but Nestlé has adopted internal standards that exceed federal standards. Among the minerals it tests for regularly are calcium, sodium, potassium, fluoride, magnesium, chloride, arsenic, and lead.

A review of the Pure Life water bottling process highlights the importance of statistical quality control. The first step of the process is source receiving and inspection. At this stage, Nestlé uses weekly systematic samples to determine the microbiology and general chemistry of the water. Next, Nestlé workers closely monitor the storage tanks for cleanliness and temperature. This includes monitoring process averages. Afterward, the filtration process is monitored hourly and is tested daily. Then, sequential samples are taken hourly to test for impurities in the process. Ozone disinfection is monitored on an hourly basis. During bottling control, the process is monitored and tested continuously. Later, packaging is inspected using attributes charts, and packaging materials not meeting internal standards are rejected. During the final steps, a quality assurance department and a national testing laboratory statistically analyze product to ensure its conformance to standards.

Although you may be surprised that so much statistical sampling and analysis goes into a single bottle of water, Nestlé's attention to detail means higher sales numbers. Given this attention to purity, Pure Life has become the largest-selling bottled water brand in the world, with a 22 percent market share. In addition, quality assurance has allowed Nestlé to expand this product line to include flavored waters under the name Pure Life Splash, despite strong competition from Coca Cola and Pepsi.

Source: Based on Nestlé Bottled Water Quality Report, Nestlé Waters North America, 2015, http://www .nestle-watersna.com/asset-library/documents/pl_eng.pdf.

Summary

In this chapter, we introduced process control charting. This discussion builds on the work we began in Chapter 13 and leads into improving processes with lean and Six Sigma in Chapter 15.

1. Statistical process control is essential to managing processes.
2. Processes are stable if they exhibit only random variation.
   a. Control charts are used to test if processes exhibit common or special causes of variation.
   b. Inspection ratios are used to prioritize inspection.
3. Variables and attributes control charts measure different things.
   a. We introduced $\bar{x}$, R, and p charts. The formulas used in this chapter are given in TABLE 14.4.
   b. The process for developing different types of charts is the same depending on the statistic of interest. We introduced a generalized procedure for developing control charts.
4. Process capability analysis (Cp_k) is used to determine if individual products meet specification.
   a. Processes are functioning properly when they are both stable (quality control) and capable (Cp_k analysis).

Summary of Chapter Formulas

< TABLE 14.4

Formula	Equation Number	Application
$IR = \dfrac{C_i}{C_f}$	14.1	A ratio to determine where we should inspect first
$UCL = \bar{\bar{x}} + A_2(\bar{R})$	14.2	Upper control limit for an $\bar{x}$ chart
$LCL = \bar{\bar{x}} - A_2(\bar{R})$	14.3	Lower control limit for an $\bar{x}$ chart
$LCL = D_3(\bar{R})$	14.4	Lower control limit for an R chart
$UCL = D_4(\bar{R})$	14.5	Upper control limit for an R chart
Control limits for $p = \bar{p} \pm 3\sqrt{\dfrac{(\bar{p})1 - \bar{p}}{n}}$	14.6	Upper and lower control limits for a p chart
$CP_u = \dfrac{USL - \mu}{3\sigma}$	14.7	Upper capability index
$CP_l = \dfrac{\mu - LSL}{3\sigma}$	14.8	Lower capability index
$CP_k = \min\{CP_u, CP_l\}$	14.9	Capability index

Key Terms

attribute   415
capability index (Cp$_k$)   435
central limit theorem   418
common cause variation   411
corrective action   434
defect   428
defective unit   428
dispersion   411
in-process inspection   413
inspection ratio   415

mean   411
nonrandom variation   411
out-of-control process   433
p chart   429
process capability   434
process charts   412
process drift   433
process run   433
process tampering   434
randomize   413

random samples   413
random variation   411
R chart   419
sample   413
special cause variation   411
stability   410
statistical process control   410
systematic samples   413
variable   415
$\bar{x}$ chart   419

Integrative Learning Exercise

With a team of fellow students, develop a procedure for identifying, measuring, monitoring, and improving a process characteristic of your choosing. You should identify a process, discuss the ways in which you will identify the process or product to be monitored, determine whether you will be measuring an attribute or a variable characteristic, describe how data will be collected, choose which control chart(s) you will be using to determine whether the process is stable or not, describe corrective actions to take when a process is deemed not to be stable, and describe how you will determine whether a process is capable of producing within stated specifications.

Integrative Experiential Exercise

With a team of fellow students, visit a company or organization that employs statistical process control. Have the company walk you through its process for identifying which process or products are monitored and what sampling plans are used to collect data. Have the company describe for you the types of control charts used and the people who collect the data and construct the control charts. Describe the action plans that the company has in place if it is determined that a process has lost statistical control. Ask the company to describe the challenges it faces in performing statistical process control. What costs has the company incurred and what benefits has it experienced as part of its statistical process control efforts?

Discussion Questions

1. Briefly describe statistical process control.
2. Briefly describe the three main concepts on which statistical thinking is based.
3. Briefly describe what is meant by random variation in statistical process control.
4. Briefly describe what is meant by nonrandom variation in statistical process control.
5. What is meant by process stability in statistical process control?
6. Why are samples preferred to 100 percent inspection to ensure that processes are stable?
7. What is meant by a random sample?
8. Provide an example of systematic sampling in statistical process control. Why might systematic sampling be preferred to taking random samples?
9. What is an inspection ratio, and what role does it play in statistical process control?
10. What distinguishes a variable from an attribute? Provide an example of both a variable and an attribute characteristic.
11. What are statistical process control charts used for? What do they consist of?
12. When a process is judged to be out of control, what action steps should be taken?
13. Why is it a bad idea to make adjustments to a process every time the process deviates from the target?
14. Is there a difference between a defect and a defective? Briefly explain the two terms as they relate to statistical process control.
15. What is meant by process capability?

Solved Problems

Process Stability

INSPECTION RATIOS
SOLVED PROBLEM 14.1

1. The costs of inspection for three different product attributes A, B, and C are $10, $7, and $15, respectively. The cost of failure if any of these fail is $250 (the full replacement cost of the product). Develop a priority for where the company should inspect.

Solution:
The solution is as follows, using Equation 14.1:

Product Attribute	Cost of Inspection	Cost of Failure	Inspection Ratio
A	$10	$250	0.04
B	$ 7	$250	0.028
C	$15	$250	0.06

Based on the inspection ratio, we would prioritize inspection with B first, followed by A, and finally C. If all three are inspected, the cumulative cost would be

$10 + $7 + $15 = 32$, which is ($32/$250) = 12.8 percent of the cost of the final product.

Variables and Attributes Process Control Charts

$\bar{X}$ CHARTS
SOLVED PROBLEM 14.2

2. Four samples ($k = 4$) of size five ($n = 5$) were taken with the following data:

Sample	Obs1	Obs2	Obs3	Obs4	Obs5
1	5	6	3	5	4
2	3	4	6	4	4
3	6	5	5	4	6
4	5	5	4	5	5

Develop an $\bar{x}$ chart to determine whether the process is stable or not.

Solution:
To begin the analysis, we compute means for each sample and an overall grand mean using Equations 14.2 and 14.4.

Sample	Obs1	Obs2	Obs3	Obs4	Obs5	Means
1	5	6	3	5	4	4.6
2	3	4	6	4	4	4.2
3	6	5	5	4	6	5.2
4	5	5	4	5	5	4.8
					Grand mean =	4.7

The range for each sample must also be computed as follows:

Sample	Obs1	Obs2	Obs3	Obs4	Obs5	Max	Min	Range
1	5	6	3	5	4	6	3	3
2	3	4	6	4	4	6	3	3
3	6	5	5	4	6	6	4	2
4	5	5	4	5	5	5	4	1

The average of the sample ranges is $\bar{R} = 2.25$. The value of A_2 from Figure 14.12 is 0.577. Substituting the values into Equations 14.2 and 14.3 yields

$$UCL = 4.7 + 0.577 \times 2.25 = 5.998$$
$$LCL = 4.7 - 0.577 \times 2.25 = 3.402$$

The control chart is shown below:

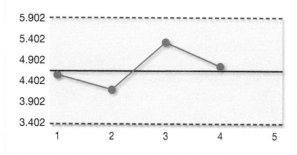

In respect to the mean, it appears that the process is in control.

SOLVED PROBLEM 14.3

3. A company decides to monitor its bottle-filling process by randomly selecting 20 samples ($k = 20$) of size 4 ($n = 4$). The amount of fluid in ounces for each sample bottle is measured. The sampled observations are as follows:

Sample	Obs1	Obs2	Obs3	Obs4
1	16.02	16.04	16.01	15.96
2	15.99	16.03	16.02	15.93
3	15.97	15.96	15.94	15.98
4	16.01	15.99	16.05	16.00
5	16.01	15.97	16.00	16.00
6	16.04	16.02	16.03	16.04
7	16.01	15.95	16.01	16.02
8	15.97	15.99	16.00	16.01
9	16.00	16.00	16.01	16.02
10	16.01	16.02	16.01	16.02
11	15.96	15.98	16.03	16.02
12	16.04	15.97	16.01	15.98
13	15.96	15.98	16.01	15.97
14	15.96	16.00	15.95	16.06
15	15.98	16.00	15.95	16.07
16	16.04	16.00	16.04	15.95
17	15.99	16.04	16.00	16.11
18	16.06	16.07	16.06	16.05
19	16.04	15.95	16.04	15.97
20	15.98	15.99	15.97	15.95

Find control limits for an $\bar{x}$ chart.

Solution:
For each sample, the sample mean (average) and sample range are calculated using Excel. The A_2 factor is 0.729 for samples of size $n = 4$. The upper and lower control limits and the center line are calculated using Equations 14.2 and 14.3. The results are as follows:

Sample	Obs1	Obs2	Obs3	Obs4	Means	Max	Min	Range
1	16.02	16.04	16.01	15.96	16.0075	16.04	15.96	0.08
2	15.99	16.03	16.02	15.93	15.9925	16.03	15.93	0.10
3	15.97	15.96	15.94	15.98	15.9625	15.98	15.94	0.04
4	16.01	15.99	16.05	16.00	16.0125	16.05	15.99	0.06
5	16.01	15.97	16.00	16.00	15.9950	16.01	15.97	0.04
6	16.04	16.02	16.03	16.04	16.0325	16.04	16.02	0.02
7	16.01	15.95	16.01	16.02	15.9975	16.02	15.95	0.07
8	15.97	15.99	16.00	16.01	15.9925	16.01	15.97	0.04
9	16.00	16.00	16.01	16.02	16.0075	16.02	16.00	0.02
10	16.01	16.02	16.01	16.02	16.0150	16.02	16.01	0.01
11	15.96	15.98	16.03	16.02	15.9975	16.03	15.96	0.07
12	16.04	15.97	16.01	15.98	16.0000	16.04	15.97	0.07
13	15.96	15.98	16.01	15.97	15.9800	16.01	15.96	0.05
14	15.96	16.00	15.95	16.06	15.9925	16.06	15.95	0.11
15	15.98	16.00	15.95	16.07	16.0000	16.07	15.95	0.12
16	16.04	16.00	16.04	15.95	16.0075	16.04	15.95	0.09
17	15.99	16.04	16.00	16.11	16.0350	16.11	15.99	0.12
18	16.06	16.07	16.06	16.05	16.0600	16.07	16.05	0.02
19	16.04	15.95	16.04	15.97	16.0000	16.04	15.95	0.09
20	15.98	15.99	15.97	15.95	15.9725	15.99	15.95	0.04
		$n = 4$		Grand mean =	16.0030		$\bar{R} =$	0.063

n	A_2
2	1.880
3	1.023
4	0.729
5	0.577
6	0.483

UCL	16.049
LCL	15.957

The UCL $= 16.003 + 0.729 \times 0.063 = 16.049$. The LCL $= 16.003 - 0.729 \times 0.063 = 15.957$. The control chart is shown below:

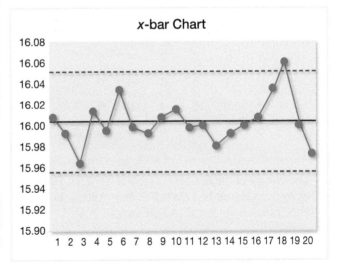

Upon reviewing the control chart, we see that sample 17 is very close to the UCL and that sample 18 has its sample mean above the upper control chart limit. The company should investigate for a potential assignable cause of variation.

DEVELOPING *R* CHARTS
SOLVED PROBLEM 14.4

4. Four samples (*k* = 4) of size five (*n* = 5) were taken with the following data:

Sample	Obs1	Obs2	Obs3	Obs4	Obs5
1	5	6	3	5	4
2	3	4	6	4	4
3	6	5	5	4	6
4	5	5	4	5	5

Develop an R chart to determine if the dispersion of the process is stable or not.

Solution:
The calculations are as follows:

Sample	Obs1	Obs2	Obs3	Obs4	Obs5	Max	Min	Range
1	5	6	3	5	4	6	3	3
2	3	4	6	4	4	6	3	3
3	6	5	5	4	6	6	4	2
4	5	5	4	5	5	5	4	1

D_4 = 2.114; D_3 = 0 $\bar{R}$ 2.25

The UCL for the R chart is computed as $D_4 \times \bar{R}$ = 2.114 × 2.25 = 4.757. The center line is the average of the sample ranges, and it equals 2.25. The control chart is shown below:

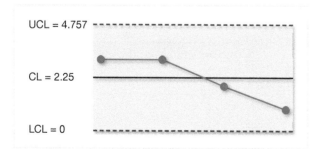

The dispersion of the process appears to be stable.

DEVELOPING *R* CHARTS IN EXCEL
SOLVED PROBLEM 14.5

5. A company decides to monitor its bottle-filling process by randomly selecting 20 samples (*k* = 20) of size 4 (*n* = 4). The amount of fluid, in ounces, for each samples bottle is measured. The sampled observations are as follows:

Sample	Obs1	Obs2	Obs3	Obs4
1	16.02	16.04	16.01	15.96
2	15.99	16.03	16.02	15.93
3	15.97	15.96	15.94	15.98
4	16.01	15.99	16.05	16.00
5	16.01	15.97	16.00	16.00
6	16.04	16.02	16.03	16.04
7	16.01	15.95	16.01	16.02
8	15.97	15.99	16.00	16.01
9	16.00	16.00	16.01	16.02
10	16.01	16.02	16.01	16.02
11	15.96	15.98	16.03	16.02
12	16.04	15.97	16.01	15.98
13	15.96	15.98	16.01	15.97
14	15.96	16.00	15.95	16.06
15	15.98	16.00	15.95	16.07
16	16.04	16.00	16.04	15.95
17	15.99	16.04	16.00	16.11
18	16.06	16.07	16.06	16.05
19	16.04	15.95	16.04	15.97
20	15.98	15.99	15.97	15.95

Use the sampled data to determine whether the range of the process is stable.

Solution:

The calculations, made in Excel, are as follows:

Sample	Obs1	Obs2	Obs3	Obs4	Max	Min	Range
1	16.02	16.04	16.01	15.96	16.04	15.96	0.08
2	15.99	16.03	16.02	15.93	16.03	15.93	0.10
3	15.97	15.96	15.94	15.98	15.98	15.94	0.04
4	16.01	15.99	16.05	16.00	16.05	15.99	0.06
5	16.01	15.97	16.00	16.00	16.01	15.97	0.04
6	16.04	16.02	16.03	16.04	16.04	16.02	0.02
7	16.01	15.95	16.01	16.02	16.02	15.95	0.07
8	15.97	15.99	16.00	16.01	16.01	15.97	0.04
9	16.00	16.00	16.01	16.02	16.02	16.00	0.02
10	16.01	16.02	16.01	16.02	16.02	16.01	0.01
11	15.96	15.98	16.03	16.02	16.03	15.96	0.07
12	16.04	15.97	16.01	15.98	16.04	15.97	0.07
13	15.96	15.98	16.01	15.97	16.01	15.96	0.05
14	15.96	16.00	15.95	16.06	16.06	15.95	0.11
15	15.98	16.00	15.95	16.07	16.07	15.95	0.12
16	16.04	16.00	16.04	15.95	16.04	15.95	0.09
17	15.99	16.04	16.00	16.11	16.11	15.99	0.12
18	16.06	16.07	16.06	16.05	16.07	16.05	0.02
19	16.04	15.95	16.04	15.97	16.04	15.95	0.09
20	15.98	15.99	15.97	15.95	15.99	15.95	0.04
$D_4 = 2.282; D_3 = 0$						$\bar{R} =$	0.063

UCL	0.144
LCL	0.000

The LCL is 0, and the UCL $= D_4 \times \bar{R} = 2.282 \times 0.063 = 0.144$. The control chart is shown below:

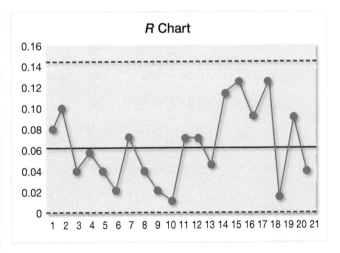

The process appears to be in statistical control with respect to the dispersion.

INTERPRETING CONTROL CHARTS
SOLVED PROBLEM 14.6

6. Interpret the following control charts to determine if the processes are stable.

a

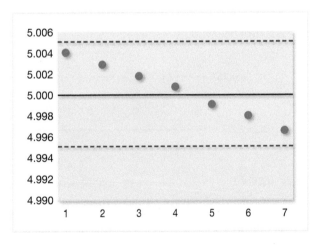

b

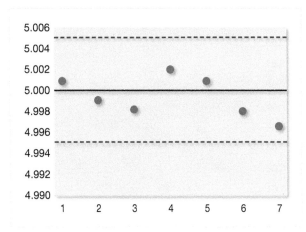

c

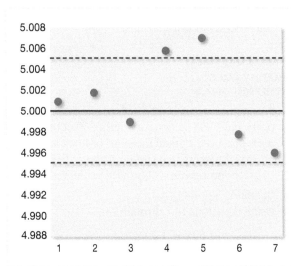

d

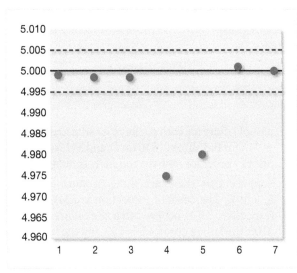

Solution:

a. The control chart displays a loss of statistical control. The process is not stable. Note the declining values for the measurements, which is an indication of a process drift.

b. The process appears to be in control.

c. The process is out of control. Samples 4 and 5 are above the upper control limit.

d. The process is out of control. Samples 4 and 5 are below the lower control limit. Furthermore, the first five samples are all below the center line, indicating a process run.

Applying Control Charts

P CHARTS
SOLVED PROBLEM 14.7

7. A company randomly samples 100 items and classifies the sampled items as either good or bad (bad items are considered to be defective). The following 15 samples, with each sample consisting of 100 items, show the number of bad items in each sample. Use the information to develop a *p* chart for the process.

Sample	n = Sample Size	Defectives
1	100	3
2	100	5
3	100	2
4	100	4
5	100	3
6	100	1
7	100	4
8	100	2
9	100	4
10	100	5
11	100	2
12	100	3
13	100	2
14	100	3
15	100	2

Solution:
The proportion defective for each sample is calculated. The calculations are as follows:

Sample	$n =$ Sample Size	Defectives	Proportion Defective (p)
1	100	3	0.03
2	100	5	0.05
3	100	2	0.02
4	100	4	0.04
5	100	3	0.03
6	100	1	0.01
7	100	4	0.04
8	100	2	0.02
9	100	4	0.04
10	100	5	0.05
11	100	2	0.02
12	100	3	0.03
13	100	2	0.02
14	100	3	0.03
15	100	2	0.02
		$\bar{p} =$	0.03

The UCL $= 0.03 + 3\sqrt{(0.03 \times (1 - 0.03))/100} = 0.03 + 0.0512 = 0.0812$.

The LCL $= 0.03 - 3\sqrt{(0.03 \times (1 - 0.03))/100} = 0.03 - 0.0512 = -0.0212 \rightarrow 0.00$.

Whenever the LCL is less than zero, it is set equal to 0.00. The resulting control chart is shown next:

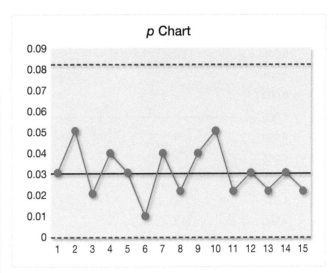

p Chart

The process appears to be stable. The last five sampled points may provide cause for concern, however, because they are all at or below the center line. It may constitute a run that signals that the process has lost statistical control.

Process Capability

CAPABILITY ANALYSIS
SOLVED PROBLEM 14.8

8. A component part is specified to have a diameter between 0.995 and 1.005 inches. A sample of 30 of the component parts produced a grand mean (μ) of 1.002 inches, with an estimated process standard deviation of 0.0025 inch. Calculate the process capability index for this component part.

Solution:
Using Equations 14.7 through 14.9,

$$CP_u = \frac{1.005 - 1.002}{3 \times 0.0025} = 0.40$$

$$CP_l = \frac{1.002 - 0.995}{3 \times 0.0025} = 0.9333$$

$$CP_k = \min(0.40, 0.9333) = 0.40$$

The process is not capable of producing to the required specifications consistently. The process capability is poor in this instance.

Problems

Process Stability

INSPECTION RATIOS

1. The costs of inspection for four product attributes A, B, C, and D are $15, $5, $20, and $10, respectively. The cost of failure if any of these attributes fails is $200 (i.e., full replacement cost of the product). Prioritize where the company should inspect.

2. The costs of inspection for five product attributes A, B, C, D, and E are $10, $5, $4, $2, and $12, respectively. The cost of failure for each attribute is estimated to be $25 for A, $15 for B, $30 for C, $10 for D, and $42 for E. Develop a priority order for how the company should inspect.

3. Suppose that there are three product attributes: A, B, and C. The costs of inspection are $10, $5, and $8, respectively. It is believed that the failure cost for A is $100, the failure cost for B is $50, and the failure cost for C is $90. In what order should the company inspect the product attributes?

Variables and Attributes Process Control Charts

$\bar{x}$ CHARTS

4. A company selects five samples ($k = 5$) of size four ($n = 4$) used in a production process and measures the diameter of each part. The following results are shown:

Sample	Obs1	Obs2	Obs3	Obs4
1	5	6	3	5
2	3	4	6	4
3	6	5	5	4
4	5	5	4	5
5	4	4	6	5

Develop an $\bar{x}$ chart to determine if the process is stable or not.

5. Four samples ($k = 4$) are taken from a process, with each sample consisting of six observations ($n = 6$). The length in centimeters of each sampled item was measured, with the following results:

Sample	Obs1	Obs2	Obs3	Obs4	Obs5	Obs6
1	24.36	24.70	25.66	25.46	24.66	25.00
2	24.82	24.66	25.08	25.21	26.29	24.85
3	24.24	25.73	24.92	25.31	23.91	25.14
4	26.26	25.50	24.82	25.56	23.74	25.94

Develop an $\bar{x}$ chart to determine if the process is stable or not.

6. Four samples ($k = 4$) are taken from a process, with each sample consisting of five observations ($n = 5$). The sampled items are subjected to a stress test, and the amount of pressure, measured in pounds per square inch, required to crack each item was computed. The results are as follows:

Sample	Obs1	Obs2	Obs3	Obs4	Obs5
1	125.99	118.14	125.82	131.21	122.41
2	115.47	115.56	114.80	120.80	123.13
3	139.48	117.53	130.86	120.49	108.22
4	125.50	141.03	121.64	108.45	109.18

Develop an $\bar{x}$ chart to determine if the process is stable or not.

7. A lumber company makes plywood for commercial construction. A key quality measure is the thickness of the plywood. Every two hours, five pieces of plywood ($n = 5$) are selected, and the thicknesses are measured. The data (in inches) for the first 20 samples are as follows:

Two-Hour Period	Plywood 1	Plywood 2	Plywood 3	Plywood 4	Plywood 5
1	0.642	0.612	0.659	0.691	0.689
2	0.705	0.584	0.644	0.685	0.618
3	0.630	0.599	0.594	0.621	0.628
4	0.586	0.634	0.639	0.656	0.640
5	0.641	0.640	0.693	0.649	0.646
6	0.636	0.713	0.678	0.725	0.631
7	0.703	0.602	0.668	0.679	0.711
8	0.649	0.635	0.672	0.640	0.675
9	0.607	0.625	0.604	0.640	0.650
10	0.652	0.641	0.720	0.597	0.629
11	0.572	0.696	0.612	0.631	0.675
12	0.666	0.679	0.670	0.609	0.617
13	0.673	0.662	0.622	0.644	0.656
14	0.669	0.656	0.623	0.710	0.667
15	0.654	0.677	0.678	0.632	0.623
16	0.686	0.614	0.603	0.674	0.671
17	0.720	0.696	0.692	0.655	0.652
18	0.666	0.651	0.619	0.596	0.677
19	0.665	0.671	0.658	0.620	0.690
20	0.642	0.625	0.626	0.638	0.637

Use Excel to develop an $\bar{x}$ chart to determine if the process is stable or not.

8. The service manager for a bicycle sales and service shop wants to study the length of time required to replace the gears on road bikes. The manager has implemented a quality improvement program to standardize the process for replacing bike gears. As part of the improvement program, four bikes needing gear replacements are randomly selected each day for 20 days. The time required, in minutes, to replace the gears for each bike is measured. The results are as follows:

Day	Bike 1	Bike 2	Bike 3	Bike 4
1	16.26	22.95	26.12	10.92
2	33.97	18.80	20.67	20.04
3	17.74	28.60	19.96	10.98
4	27.22	22.02	25.32	21.93
5	30.67	14.65	18.29	21.70
6	20.44	9.48	32.87	17.69
7	19.88	16.96	11.79	27.61
8	18.13	22.06	21.22	20.33
9	21.82	32.25	16.50	20.11
10	25.18	23.24	19.97	17.83
11	18.49	13.66	27.44	20.87
12	23.22	17.36	22.25	24.19
13	23.97	21.79	23.14	35.88
14	18.53	25.38	13.31	29.83
15	20.66	26.50	20.42	18.76
16	21.32	28.41	29.75	19.91
17	22.92	18.58	18.16	15.60
18	20.65	20.85	23.50	22.74
19	22.15	21.73	21.28	24.94
20	20.17	19.15	22.87	25.89

6	7.02	7.18	8.64	8.08
7	7.78	7.02	6.54	7.91
8	7.18	7.07	6.76	7.81
9	7.16	8.52	7.25	8.69
10	7.64	7.86	6.79	6.68
11	7.21	7.28	7.91	7.99
12	7.25	7.36	6.91	6.83
13	6.64	6.37	7.80	6.96
14	6.38	7.14	6.40	7.32
15	7.37	7.58	7.58	7.32
16	7.63	8.11	7.42	7.42
17	8.04	7.48	6.88	7.62
18	6.59	8.98	8.16	7.16
19	6.42	6.86	7.04	6.35
20	7.88	7.20	8.10	7.12
21	7.25	7.38	7.31	7.81
22	6.89	7.34	6.64	7.81
23	8.04	7.22	8.04	6.48
24	7.63	7.20	6.94	6.85
25	7.44	7.98	7.18	7.61
26	6.92	9.29	8.11	6.83
27	8.22	7.31	7.28	8.72
28	7.82	6.78	8.59	7.92
29	7.70	7.63	7.51	8.57
30	6.30	8.14	8.17	7.85

Use Excel to develop an $\bar{x}$ chart to determine if the process is stable or not.

9. A chocolate company makes candy bars to be used by elementary schools for fund-raising. One of the important quality characteristics is the weight of the bar. To monitor the weight of each bar, the production team wants to use process control charts. Data for 30 samples of four bars each are as follows:

Sample	Candy Bar 1	Candy Bar 2	Candy Bar 3	Candy Bar 4
1	8.30	8.50	6.85	7.86
2	7.30	7.39	8.17	7.43
3	7.60	7.49	7.34	7.75
4	7.08	6.56	7.97	7.45
5	6.82	6.70	8.41	7.91

Use Excel to develop an $\bar{x}$ chart to determine if the process is stable or not.

R CHARTS

10. A company selects five samples ($k = 5$) of size four ($n = 4$) used in a production process and measures the diameter of each part. The following results are shown:

Sample	Obs1	Obs2	Obs3	Obs4
1	5	6	3	5
2	3	4	6	4
3	6	5	5	4
4	5	5	4	5
5	4	4	6	5

Develop an R chart to determine if the dispersion is stable or not.

11. Four samples ($k = 4$) are taken from a process, with each sample consisting of six observations ($n = 6$). The length in centimeters of each sampled item was measured, with the following results:

Sample	Obs1	Obs2	Obs3	Obs4	Obs5	Obs6
1	24.36	24.70	25.66	25.46	24.66	25.00
2	24.82	24.66	25.08	25.21	26.29	24.85
3	24.24	25.73	24.92	25.31	23.91	25.14
4	26.26	25.50	24.82	25.56	23.74	25.94

Develop an R chart to determine if the dispersion is stable or not.

12. Four samples ($k = 4$) are taken from a process, with each sample consisting of five observations ($n = 5$). The sampled items are subjected to a stress test, and the amount of pressure, measured in pounds per square inch, required to crack each item is computed. The results are as follows:

Sample	Obs1	Obs2	Obs3	Obs4	Obs5
1	125.99	118.14	125.82	131.21	122.41
2	115.47	115.56	114.80	120.80	123.13
3	139.48	117.53	130.86	120.49	108.22
4	125.50	141.03	121.64	108.45	109.18

Develop an R chart to determine if the dispersion is stable or not.

13. A lumber company makes plywood for commercial construction. A key quality measure is the thickness of the plywood. Every two hours, five pieces of plywood ($n = 5$) are selected, and the thicknesses are measured. The data (in inches) for the first 20 samples are as follows:

Two-Hour Period	Plywood 1	Plywood 2	Plywood 3	Plywood 4	Plywood 5
1	0.642	0.612	0.659	0.691	0.689
2	0.705	0.584	0.644	0.685	0.618
3	0.630	0.599	0.594	0.621	0.628
4	0.586	0.634	0.639	0.656	0.640
5	0.641	0.640	0.693	0.649	0.646
6	0.636	0.713	0.678	0.725	0.631
7	0.703	0.602	0.668	0.679	0.711
8	0.649	0.635	0.672	0.640	0.675
9	0.607	0.625	0.604	0.640	0.650
10	0.652	0.641	0.720	0.597	0.629
11	0.572	0.696	0.612	0.631	0.675
12	0.666	0.679	0.670	0.609	0.617
13	0.673	0.662	0.622	0.644	0.656
14	0.669	0.656	0.623	0.710	0.667
15	0.654	0.677	0.678	0.632	0.623
16	0.686	0.614	0.603	0.674	0.671
17	0.720	0.696	0.692	0.655	0.652
18	0.666	0.651	0.619	0.596	0.677
19	0.665	0.671	0.658	0.620	0.690
20	0.642	0.625	0.626	0.638	0.637

Use Excel to develop an R chart to determine if the range of the process is stable or not.

14. The service manager for a bicycle sales and service shop wants to study the length of time required to replace the gears on road bikes. The manager has implemented a quality improvement program to standardize the process for replacing bike gears. As part of the improvement program, four bikes needing gear replacements are randomly selected each day for 20 days. The time required, in minutes, to replace the gears for each bike is measured. The results are as follows:

Day	Bike 1	Bike 2	Bike 3	Bike 4
1	16.26	22.95	26.12	10.92
2	33.97	18.80	20.67	20.04
3	17.74	28.60	19.96	10.98
4	27.22	22.02	25.32	21.93
5	30.67	14.65	18.29	21.70
6	20.44	9.48	32.87	17.69
7	19.88	16.96	11.79	27.61
8	18.13	22.06	21.22	20.33
9	21.82	32.25	16.50	20.11
10	25.18	23.24	19.97	17.83
11	18.49	13.66	27.44	20.87
12	23.22	17.36	22.25	24.19

13	23.97	21.79	23.14	35.88
14	18.53	25.38	13.31	29.83
15	20.66	26.50	20.42	18.76
16	21.32	28.41	29.75	19.91
17	22.92	18.58	18.16	15.60
18	20.65	20.85	23.50	22.74
19	22.15	21.73	21.28	24.94
20	20.17	19.15	22.87	25.89

23	8.04	7.22	8.04	6.48
24	7.63	7.20	6.94	6.85
25	7.44	7.98	7.18	7.61
26	6.92	9.29	8.11	6.83
27	8.22	7.31	7.28	8.72
28	7.82	6.78	8.59	7.92
29	7.70	7.63	7.51	8.57
30	6.30	8.14	8.17	7.85

Use Excel to develop an R chart to determine if the range of the process is stable or not.

Use Excel to develop an R chart to determine if the range of the process is stable or not.

15. A chocolate company makes candy bars to be used by elementary schools for fund-raising. One of the important quality characteristics is the weight of the bar. To monitor the weight of each bar, the production team wants to use process control charts. Data for 30 samples of 4 bars each are as follows:

p CHARTS

16. A company randomly selects 50 shipping records every day to determine the number of orders that are shipped late. The following are the most recent 20 days of samples. The company wants to use the sampled data to develop a p chart to monitor the proportion of late shipments.

Sample	Candy Bar 1	Candy Bar 2	Candy Bar 3	Candy Bar 4
1	8.30	8.50	6.85	7.86
2	7.30	7.39	8.17	7.43
3	7.60	7.49	7.34	7.75
4	7.08	6.56	7.97	7.45
5	6.82	6.70	8.41	7.91
6	7.02	7.18	8.64	8.08
7	7.78	7.02	6.54	7.91
8	7.18	7.07	6.76	7.81
9	7.16	8.52	7.25	8.69
10	7.64	7.86	6.79	6.68
11	7.21	7.28	7.91	7.99
12	7.25	7.36	6.91	6.83
13	6.64	6.37	7.80	6.96
14	6.38	7.14	6.40	7.32
15	7.37	7.58	7.58	7.32
16	7.63	8.11	7.42	7.42
17	8.04	7.48	6.88	7.62
18	6.59	8.98	8.16	7.16
19	6.42	6.86	7.04	6.35
20	7.88	7.20	8.10	7.12
21	7.25	7.38	7.31	7.81
22	6.89	7.34	6.64	7.81

Sample	n = Sample Size	Number of Late Shipments
1	50	3
2	50	5
3	50	2
4	50	4
5	50	6
6	50	4
7	50	4
8	50	2
9	50	4
10	50	5
11	50	2
12	50	3
13	50	5
14	50	3
15	50	6
16	50	4
17	50	5
18	50	4
19	50	5
20	50	2

Using the data above, develop a p chart to monitor this process. Does the process appear to be in control?

17. A credit card processor has randomly sampled 100 credit card bills every week for 15 weeks. A credit card bill is considered defective if it has an error that requires that it be reprocessed. The number of credit card bills requiring reprocessing each week for the sampled credit card bills is as follows:

Sample	n = Sample Size	Number of Credit Card Bills Reprocessed
1	100	8
2	100	10
3	100	9
4	100	12
5	100	8
6	100	9
7	100	12
8	100	9
9	100	11
10	100	10
11	100	7
12	100	11
13	100	8
14	100	8
15	100	6

The company wants to use the sampled information to develop a p chart to monitor the reprocessing operation. Construct a p chart using the sampled data and comment on whether the process appears to be in control or not.

18. A company samples 200 items per eight-hour shift and identifies the number of defective items produced. The results of the most recent 15 samples are to be used to develop a p chart to monitor the proportion defective for the process. The sampled data are as follows:

Sample	n = Sample Size	Number of Defectives
1	200	96
2	200	120
3	200	108
4	200	144
5	200	96
6	200	108
7	200	144
8	200	108
9	200	132
10	200	120
11	200	84
12	200	132
13	200	96
14	200	96
15	200	72

Develop a p chart and comment on whether it appears that the company's process is in control.

19. An accounting firm monitors its tax advisory service by sampling 200 tax records and auditing the returns to determine whether there is an error that requires an amended return be filed. The firm wants to use the following data to develop a p chart to monitor the proportion of defective returns (a return is considered defective if an amended return had to be filed). Use the data to develop a p chart. Does the process appear to be in control? Justify your answer.

Sample	n = Sample Size	Amended Returns
1	200	11
2	200	16
3	200	9
4	200	9
5	200	19
6	200	20
7	200	20
8	200	20
9	200	17
10	200	21
11	200	11
12	200	7
13	200	10
14	200	14
15	200	3

Applying Control Charts

INTERPRETING CONTROL CHARTS

20. Based on the following control chart, does the process appear to be in statistical control? Justify your decision.

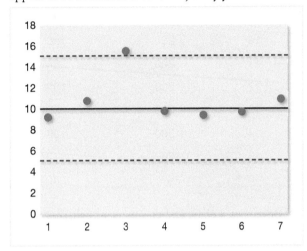

21. Output from a process was used to produce the following control chart:

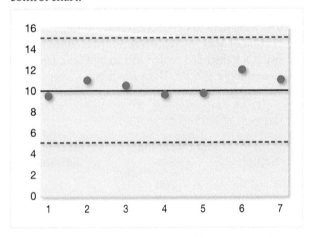

Based on the chart produced, would you conclude that the process is in control or not? Justify your answer.

22. What conclusion would you reach concerning whether the following process is in control or not? Be sure to justify your answer.

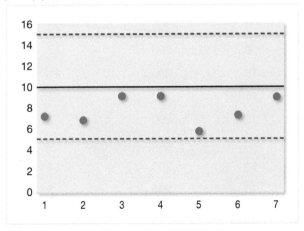

23. Sampled output from a process produced the following control chart:

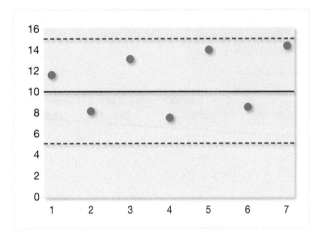

Based on the control chart, would you conclude that the process is stable? Justify your answer.

Process Capability

24. A machine is designed to fill bottles to between 16.01 and 15.98 ounces. Thirty samples of bottles filled by the machine were randomly selected from the process. The sample bottles yielded a grand mean ($\bar{\bar{x}}$) of 15.99 and a standard deviation of 0.0025. Calculate the process capability index for the bottle-filling machine and comment on its capability.

25. To fit correctly, a metal bar must be cut to be between 45 and 50 centimeters in length. A random sample of 40 metal bars was selected, and the bars were measured. The sampled bars yielded a grand mean of 48.2 centimeters with a standard deviation of 0.4. Based on these results, is the process capable of producing the metal bars within the specifications?

26. Cereal boxes are to be filled to between 11.9 and 12.2 ounces. The boxes are automatically filled by a machine. Thirty sampled boxes are randomly selected, and a grand mean of 12.1 ounces and a standard deviation of 0.05 ounce are calculated. Based on these results, what can you conclude about the capability of the cereal-filling machine?

Poor software design in a radiation machine, known as the Therac-25, contributed to the deaths of three cancer patients. The Therac-25 was built by Atomic Energy of Canada, Ltd., which was a Crown corporation of the government of Canada. According to Nancy Levenson, a professor at the Massachusetts Institute of Technology (MIT), the design flaws included the inability of the software to handle some of the data it was given and the delivery of hard-to-decipher user messages.

When the Patient Protection and Affordable Care Act was launched, people were unable to get onto the website launched by the federal government in the United States to register for insurance. At the same time, because of the requirements of the law, people were losing their existing policies, resulting in a loss of trust in the new law.

During Operation Desert Storm, an Iraqi missile hit a U.S. Army barracks in Saudi Arabia, killing 28 Americans. The approach of the missile should have been noticed by a Patriot missile battery. A subsequent government investigation found a flaw in the Patriot's weapons-control software, however, that prevented the system from properly tracking the incoming missile.

The types of errors are likely to mount as software becomes more complex. In addition, the software systems are tied across networks. Software is one of the most sophisticated products the human mind can create.

Questions:

1. What type of inspection would be helpful in monitoring and ensuring software quality?

2. What type of inspection plan would you recommend?

Lean and Six Sigma Management and Leading Change

INTEGRATING	GLOBAL SC&O STRATEGY
INNOVATING	Supply Management	Operations Management	Customer Relationship Management
IMPACTING	Upstream Processes	Core Processes	Downstream Processes
IMPROVING	QUALITY MANAGEMENT, ANALYTICS, AND LOGISTICS

CHAPTER OUTLINE AND LEARNING OBJECTIVES

1 Define Six Sigma and Explain Its Various Roles
- Describe the steps managers take when using Six Sigma.
- Develop a Six Sigma business case.

2 Understand and Use Lean
- Distinguish between lean philosophy and systems.

3 Apply Lean Practices
- Find ways to reduce waste in production and service environments.

4 Familiarize Yourself with Change Management
- Be ready to implement changes on every level as a manager and an employee.

Six Sigma at Landscape Structures

Many healthcare providers have adopted lean and Six Sigma quality improvement approaches to improve patient satisfaction and process performance. One such hospital is the Charleston Area Medical Center Health System (CAMCHS) in West Virginia. CAMCHS has ranked in the top 5 percent nationally for inpatient quality service. To accomplish such high levels of satisfaction, the hospital implemented a learning culture and continuous performance review process. This process is based on the define, measure, analyze, improve, and control (DMAIC) approach discussed in this chapter. The approach required the participation of employees throughout CAMCHS and resulted in the saving of almost 1,800 lives.

You may be a little surprised that we start a chapter on lean and Six Sigma by discussing a hospital, but you will find that the tools discussed in this chapter are used by many different types of firms. When you interview for jobs, it will be very helpful for you to be familiar with lean and Six Sigma. We will return to CAMCHS at the end of the chapter.

Lean management and Six Sigma principles focus on renewal and renovation, which occur as a result of ridding the work world of anything wasteful. In our own lives, we may compare this ridding process to exercising, eating better, and getting rid of fat. In a more esoteric way, we can think of making our lives lean as getting rid of all the extra baggage, nonsense, and unnecessary problems that clutter our lives.

In business, **lean management** practices reduce waste methodically to optimize processes. **Six Sigma** is a well-thought-out approach to improving product and process through an emphasis on system and product design. **Lean/Six Sigma** involves a marriage of these two approaches to guide improvement and change in organizations.

In this chapter, we discuss both lean and Six Sigma approaches. We end the chapter by focusing on **change management**, which is the process of transitioning an organization from an existing state to a desired state through skilled management of transitioning processes.

lean management
Reducing waste in a methodical manner to optimize processes.

Six Sigma
An approach to improving product and process through an emphasis on system and product design.

lean/Six Sigma
Combining waste reduction with quality management to guide improvement and change in organizations.

change management
The process of guiding improvement in an organization.

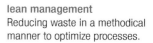

DEFINE SIX SIGMA AND EXPLAIN ITS VARIOUS ROLES

The *sigma* in Six Sigma refers to the Greek symbol σ, which designates a standard deviation in statistics. The *six* refers to the number of standard deviations from a specification limit to the mean of a highly capable process. Six Sigma began at Motorola in 1982. That year, Motorola's chief executive officer requested that costs be cut in half. He then repeated the same request the following year. These efforts pointed out that Motorola needed to improve its product designs and analytical techniques to achieve these goals. Motorola emphasized designing products to achieve Six Sigma.

FIGURE 15.1 illustrates how a company like Motorola approaches Six Sigma. In Figure 15.1a, the distribution shows a typical product design with plus-or-minus three-standard-deviation specifications (or tolerances). In such a product design, about 0.5 percent of products will not meet specification. As shown in Figure 15.1b, if the tolerances are plus or minus six standard

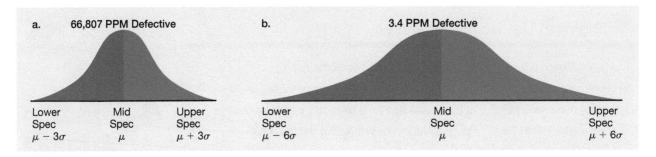

^ FIGURE 15.1

Comparison of Three and Six Sigma

deviations, the probability of producing a bad part is very low (about 3.4 parts per million); notice how in Figure 15.1b the mean or dispersion of the process could change significantly, and the product would still meet specifications. TABLE 15.1 shows the number of defective parts per million that are produced between the Six Sigma levels. Using this definition, Six Sigma translates into more robust designs, radically lower defect levels, and lowered costs of poor quality.

Since the early days of improving the robustness of design at Motorola, Six Sigma has morphed into an organization-wide program for improvement involving hierarchical training, organizational learning, and pay for learning. None of the analytical tools used in Six Sigma efforts is new. What is new is how they are packaged and deployed within a company.

Some argue that Six Sigma is an advanced quality improvement approach designed to help tackle the most difficult quality problems. As you can see in the pyramid in FIGURE 15.2, managers use the seven basic tools of quality, such as fishbone diagrams and Pareto analysis, to handle 90 percent of quality problems. Most of the next 10 percent requires advanced training and analytical techniques found in Six Sigma. Beyond that, few problems require expertise that may not be found within the company. Care should be taken in determining what projects should be undertaken by Six Sigma specialists.

Six Sigma is based on the following equation:

$$y = f(x) \qquad (15.1)$$

where y (the dependent variable) is a function of x (an independent variable). To Six Sigma practitioners, Equation 15.1 means that an output is a function of inputs and processes, where

y = the output (key business objectives and measures)
f = the function (interrelationships to be controlled and managed)
x = the controllable and noncontrollable variables that affect y

For example, the profitability of a company (y) is affected by several variables (x's), including customer retention, inventory turnovers, rolled throughput yield, and production costs.

TABLE 15.1 >

Sigma Levels and Defects	
Sigma Level	Long-Term Defects (in parts per million)
1	691,462
2	308,538
3	66,807
4	6,210
5	233
6	3.4

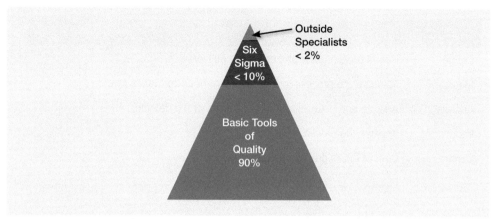

Customer satisfaction with a call center (y) is a function of several variables (x's), such as time to answer the phone, friendliness of the phone workers, and knowledgeable phone workers. If the objective is to improve profits, focus on these x variables on a project-by-project basis and improve performance. Using our call center example, if phone employees are poorly trained, training will help their performance. In this scenario, it is management's job to identify and prioritize projects to achieve the goal of higher profits. The job of employees is to obtain the training and expertise required to meet these objectives.

Six Sigma evolved from a single firm's approach to reducing costs and improving products and processes to much more. It now involves planning, organizing, training, human resources planning, and pay for knowledge. Six Sigma requires both organizational and individual cooperation to achieve a goal. At General Electric, management made it clear that participation in Six Sigma was a prerequisite for advancement within the company.

Six Sigma Roles

Several roles are available for different people in a Six Sigma organization. We will focus on four roles typically seen in organizations who adopt Six Sigma: **champions**, **master black belts**, **black belts**, and **green belts**. These roles are shown in TABLE 15.2.

champion
A senior manager who provides leadership in a Six Sigma project.

master black belt
Mentors who are experienced black belts who train in Six Sigma projects.

black belt
Specially trained individuals who perform Six Sigma projects.

green belt
A person trained in basic quality tools.

Six Sigma Roles	
Title	**Application**
Champion	Champions are senior management officials who guide Six Sigma projects by providing leadership, helping identify and approve projects, and providing funding.
Master black belt	In some firms, experienced black belts are designated master black belts. In these cases, master black belts serve as mentors and trainers for new black belts, which brings the training in-house and can reduce costs.
Black belt	The black belt is the key to lean/Six Sigma. Black belts are specially trained individuals. The training usually lasts four to six months. After completing the training, these individuals are committed full-time to completing Six Sigma cost-reduction projects.
Green belt	Green belts are trained in basic quality tools and work in teams to improve quality. Green belts are assigned part-time to work on process and design improvement. In some cases, the results of green belt activities are the same as black belts. In other organizations, green belts are involved in less critical projects.

< TABLE 15.2

TABLE 15.3 >

DMAIC Definitions	
Define	Define project goals and customer deliverables.
Measure	Measure the process to establish current performance levels.
Analyze	Analyze and determine the root causes of the defects.
Improve	Improve the process by eliminating defects.
Control	Control future process performance.

Managing Across Majors 15.1 Human resources management majors, you need to be involved in identifying candidates to become black belts and green belts. As human resources managers in many organizations, you will use this training in the development of future managers.

DMAIC

DMAIC
An acronym used in Six Sigma that stands for define, measure, analyze, improve, and control.

Six Sigma is organized into five phases, as defined in TABLE 15.3. The acronym **DMAIC** stands for define, measure, analyze, improve, and control. The DMAIC process is based on the scientific process that involves defining a problem, gathering data, analyzing data, designing and implementing improvements, and monitoring the process to see that the improvements are sustained.

FIGURE 15.3 shows activities performed during each of the five stages of the DMAIC process. These stages are used consistently in Six Sigma projects to provide a standard method for improvement. SC&O CURRENT EVENTS 15.1 discusses how waste reduction and continuous improvement have improved performance in a textile company.

Business Cases

An important step during the define phase is developing the business case. This process involves identifying possible projects, writing business cases for each project, stratifying the business case into problem and objective statements, and choosing the best business case. A Six Sigma black belt typically develops the business case in conjunction with the project champion. Below is a sample **business case**, a short statement outlining the objectives, measurables, and justification for the project.

business case
A document designed to justify a Six Sigma project.

Business Case: During the four-week period from January 1, 2018, to February 1, 2018, the rolled throughput yield for plant number 3 in region 4 was at 57 percent of

FIGURE 15.3 >

DMAIC Activities

Define	Measure	Analyze	Improve	Control
• Develop a business case	• Select process outcomes	• Define performance objectives	• Perform off-line experiments	• Establish process controls and control plans
• Evaluate potential projects	• Verify measurements	• Identify independent variables	• Implement changes	• Monitor processes
• Perform payback/risk analysis		• Analyze sources of variation	• Perform post-implementation review	
• Define the project				

Quality Improvement at the Momentum Group

The Momentum Group of Irvine, California, is a leader in the commercial interiors industry. Starting over thirty years ago in textiles, it now produces fabrics for interior design and furniture. Momentum has achieved outstanding results by focusing on the reduction of waste in its operations, which has resulted in the following:

- It has reduced sample production time by 50 percent.
- It has improved sample yield by 20 percent per yard.
- It has worked with suppliers to reduce defects and installed high intensity lights to improve the inspection of incoming fabrics.
- It has reduced employee turnover, which can result in waste.
- It has focused on sustainability and reduced waste in operations.

capacity, resulting in an annualized cost of poor quality of $5.6 million. This gap of rolled throughput yield mandates a business objective to improve throughput by 50 percent, from 57 percent of design capacity to 85 percent by February 1, 2019, representing $3 million in savings. This project will increase the throughput for plant 3 in region 4 to meet the year's 2018 corporate goal of increasing sales in region 4 by $10 million.

After writing the business case, the black belt performs a risk and return analysis. A sample risk and return analysis is shown in **FIGURE 15.4**. According to this analysis, a black belt analyzed a project on 100-point scales for both risk and reward. With a score of 40/100, the project was fairly low risk. With a score of 45/100 for return, however, the return was also modest. This point is plotted on the two-dimensional matrix in Figure 15.4. As a result, this project is viewed as *low-hanging fruit:* low risk but modest return. If another potential project is evaluated to have the same or lower risk with a higher return, the second project will be chosen instead. **SC&O CURRENT EVENTS 15.2** shows how Six Sigma was implemented by Metalor Technologies.

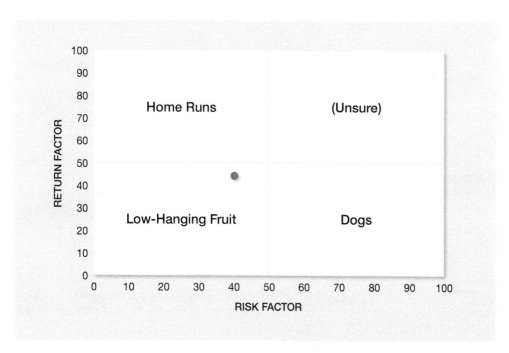

< FIGURE 15.4

Risk and Return Evaluation

Six Sigma at Metalor Technologies

Metalor Technologies produces metallurgic products in 15 countries. The company was successful in using Six Sigma to improve its silver powder production process. The company's process to produce silver powder, which is used in other products such as switches and polysilicon wafers, is shown below.

The silver powder production process is very scientific and requires strict dimensioning of density and surface area. If these dimensions are not correct, the silver powder will not extrude properly onto the products for which it is used. Density and surface area are very hard to control, however.

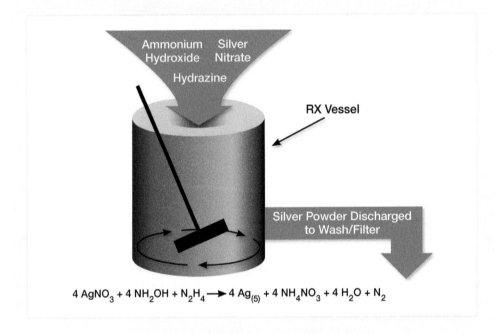

$$4\ AgNO_3 + 4\ NH_2OH + N_2H_4 \longrightarrow 4\ Ag_{(5)} + 4\ NH_4NO_3 + 4\ H_2O + N_2$$

Using Six Sigma experimentation, Metalor set out to determine how density and surface area (y variables) are affected by three key inputs: reaction temperature, ammonium, and stir rate (x variables). Metalor created an experiment with two phases.

1. Understand how variation in ammonium, stir rate, and temperature affected surface area and density in the silver powder production process.
2. Given a surface area specification of 0.3 to 0.6 cm^2/g and a density less than 14 g/cm^3, it was necessary to determine the settings of the three variables to achieve these goals. To meet these criteria, Metalor created models for each x variable that would effectively predict the density and surface outcomes.

Even though Metalor had been producing silver powder for many years, it was not until after the completion of this project that the company was able to understand how variables interacted to make a conforming product. It was now able to satisfy its customers better and produce this product with a more robust process.

Source: Based on L. Johnson and K. McNeilly, "Results May Not Vary," *Quality Progress*, May 2011, 42–48.

Managing Across Majors 15.2 Finance and accounting majors, you will provide key inputs into lean/Six Sigma business cases to validate numbers and to analyze the reasonableness of savings projections.

NDERSTAND AND USE LEAN

When firms began to implement Six Sigma, many saw that the processes had elements in common with lean manufacturing. Rather than having two competing models for improvement, they combined Six Sigma with lean practices, a combination called lean/Six Sigma. In this section, we elaborate on the basics of lean production. With lean manufacturing, the focus of Six Sigma becomes more oriented toward reducing wastefulness in organizations.

....

Managing Across Majors 15.3 Students focusing on services management, SC&O Current Events 15.1 showed how lean/Six Sigma principles and tools are applied in an interior design. Take care in applying lean principles in services, however, because services are so heterogeneous.

....

Lean Solutions

Lean/Six Sigma has been applied in many organizations. As you can see in TABLE 15.4, many types of problems are commonly addressed by black belts and teams involved in organizational improvement. Companies seeking to improve on-time delivery, reduce

< TABLE 15.4

Situations in Which Managers Use Lean Tactics

Problem Number	Class of Problem
1	Late deliveries
2	Too little process capacity
3	Too many defects in products
4	Process percentage up time too low
5	The process is too slow
6	The process has too many failures
7	Process lead times are too slow
8	While the sum of the step times meets the pace of the downstream demand, the process, as a whole, does not meet demand
9	Evidence of bullwhip effect
10	Not enough product standardization
11	Scheduling is highly inaccurate
12	Measurement systems are not accurate
13	Performance does not match specifications
14	Maintenance is too slow
15	The process does not produce good products ever
16	Resources are overutilized
17	Too much inventory
18	Too much waste in process
19	Forecasting does not reflect reality
20	High order backlogs
21	Cash flow is poor due to poor accounting practices
22	Too many receivables
23	Too many payables
24	Process cycle times are not realistic
25	Products are not reliable

Source: Based on I. Wedgwood, *Lean Sigma: A Practitioner's Guide*, Upper Saddle River, NJ: Prentice Hall, 2006.

FIGURE 15.5 >

Inventory Is Just
the Tip of the Lean
Iceberg

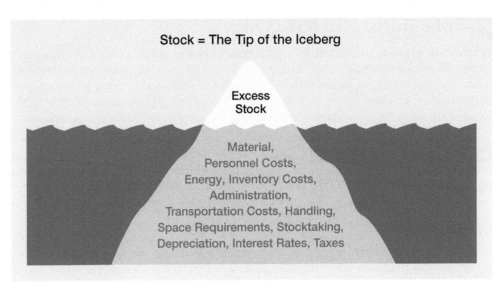

defects, improve service, and solve many other problems turn to Six Sigma methods for help. Note that all problems listed have to do with waste in supply chain and operations (SC&O). They are the types of problems addressed by black belts, teams, and champions in world-class organizations such as 3M, Caterpillar, General Electric, and Whirlpool that have adopted lean/Six Sigma principles and tools. For example, the GE corporate website states:

> Globalization and instant access to information, products and services continue to change the way our customers conduct business. Today's competitive environment leaves no room for error. We must delight our customers and relentlessly look for new ways to exceed their expectations. This is why Six Sigma Quality has become a part of our culture.

Lean Viewpoints

Two views emerge pertaining to lean manufacturing. The first is a philosophical view of waste reduction. This view asserts that anything in the process that does not add value for the customer should be eliminated. Given this view, quality problems cause scrap and rework and are wasteful. FIGURE 15.5 demonstrates waste. Although excess stock may be visible, many other wasteful practices lie beneath the surface. It takes attention to detail and study to reduce these problems.

The second view of lean is a systems view about a group of techniques or systems focused on optimizing quality processes. An example of this view is the lean production system refined by the Toyota Motor Company and spread to the rest of the world. For our purposes, we combine the philosophical and systems views to define a lean system as a *productive system whose focus is on optimizing processes through the philosophy of waste reduction.*

Lean Philosophy

Philosophy is an important element in improving organizational performance. Words and definitions help us communicate on a cerebral level. Philosophies, once internalized, help individuals and organizations to communicate on a feelings-based level. For Toyota Motor Company, the focus was on the continual reduction of waste. **Shigeo Shingo**, the industrial engineer who was fundamental in helping Toyota reduce waste, identified a group of seven wastes that workers could address in improvement processes (TABLE 15.5). The reduction of these seven wastes is at the core of lean principles. GLOBAL CONNECTIONS 15.1 provides more information about Shigeo Shingo.

Shigeo Shingo
Creator of an approach to quality management that includes identifying a group of seven wastes.

Shingo's Seven Wastes	< TABLE 15.5
1.	Overproduction
2.	Waiting
3.	Transportation
4.	Processing itself
5.	Inventories
6.	Motion
7.	Making defective products

Understanding Shingo's Work at Toyota

When referring to Shigeo Shingo, Norman Bodek, president of Productivity, Inc., stated:

> If I could give a Nobel [P]rize for exceptional contributions to world economy, prosperity, and productivity, I wouldn't have much difficulty selecting a winner—Shigeo Shingo's life work has contributed to the well-being of everyone in the world. Along with Taiichi Ohno, former vice president of Toyota Motors, Mr. Shingo has helped revolutionize the way we manufacture goods. His improvement principles vastly reduce the cost of manufacturing. They make the manufacturing process more responsive while opening the way to new and innovative products, substantially reduce defects and improve quality, and give us a strategy for continuous improvement through the creative involvement of all employees.

Shingo's approach emphasizes production rather than primarily management. His motto (actually one of very many) is that "those who are not dissatisfied will never make any progress." He believed that progress is achieved by careful thought, pursuit of goals, planning, and implementation of solutions.

While at Mitsubishi Heavy Industries in Nagasaki, Shingo was responsible for reducing the time for hull assembly of 65,000-ton supertankers from four months to two months, establishing a world record in shipbuilding, and the system spread to every shipyard in Japan. He then left the Japan Management Association and established the Institute of Management Improvement, with himself as president. Subsequently, he started industrial engineering and plant-improvement training at Matsushita Electric Industrial Company. As previously, training was done on a large scale, with some 7,000 persons trained.

Later, Shigeo Shingo extended the ideas of quality control to develop the mistake-proofing, or the "Defects = 0," concept. Subsequently, the approach was applied successfully at various plants, with records of over two years totally defect-free operation being established. Shingo's work laid the groundwork for process restructuring and waste reduction at Toyota in Japan and has been fundamental to lean. Those who practice lean/Six Sigma carefully study Shingo's writings.

Source: Based on S. Shingo, *Fundamental Practices of Lean Manufacturing*, Cambridge MA: Productivity Press, 2017).

APPLY LEAN PRACTICES

Lean manufacturing does not simply target the production line; it also focuses on streamlining how workers do their jobs. The purpose of a lean approach is to reduce waste, or *muda*, the Japanese term. Keep this goal in mind as you read through this section on the specific practices and techniques that lean companies use, be it on the production line, within the workforce, or as a company-wide approach. The end result of each one is less muda and more efficiency.

Practicing Lean Production

Companies use a variety of tactics to streamline their production systems. One of the overarching tools of lean manufacturing is **kaizen**, or continual improvement. Kaizen is a process of constantly focusing attention on fine details in production so that daily improvement is made. These improvements are often team based and use the *plan, do, check, act* (PDCA) cycle. **Rapid kaizen** is used in many organizations as a short-term, often as a one- or two-day, improvement event where a team focuses on solving a particular problem. Managers can use kaizen in their overall approach or on a specific task.

KANBAN AND PULL PRODUCTION   When a manufacturer uses **pull production**, parts and components are not released from one work area to the next until the receiving work area has requested them. The result is a "chain of customers," where the final link in the chain is the purchasing customer. This approach simplifies shop-floor control and allows work to move without sophisticated scheduling software or forecasts. A **kanban** (card system) is a method for controlling the flow of materials through a process.

As shown in **FIGURE 15.6**, the kanban card is a communication device so that inventory can be *pulled* through a process only when it is needed. The idea behind kanban is that no material should be released until it is needed by the customer. When a kanban is released, the card is physically moved from a workstation and is attached to incoming materials. Those materials are then transported to the destined workstation. That is, if you are at workstation 2, workstation 1 cannot release its finished work to you until you request it with a kanban. Once a kanban is released from workstation 2 to workstation 1, the materials are transported, and workstation 1 can then release a kanban to the warehouse for more raw materials (see **FIGURE 15.7**).

TABLE 15.6 lists various types of kanbans. The choice of kanban depends on the circumstances surrounding the request for parts, subassemblies, or components needed at any stage of production. For example, if you need a component or part to be produced, a **production kanban** is used. These kanbans are often referred to as "make cards." If something is at another workstation, a **withdrawal kanban** is used. It is often referred to as a "move card."

kaizen
Continual improvement.

rapid kaizen
Fast improvement focusing on a finite problem.

pull production
The process of not releasing materials until the next stage in production or consumption is ready.

kanban
A card system for controlling the flow of materials through a process.

production kanban
A card that orders the production of a part or component.

withdrawal kanban
A card that orders the transportation of a part or component.

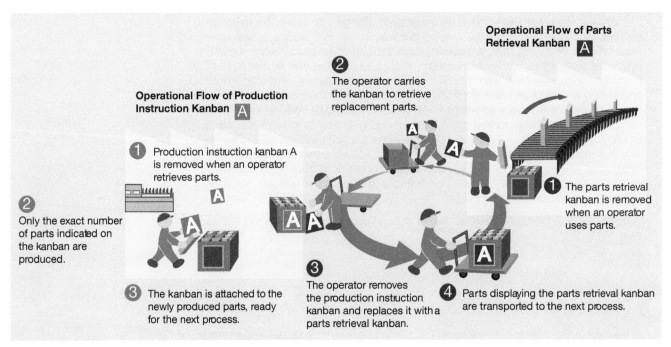

Source: Reprinted by permission from Toyota Motor Sales, U.S.A., Inc.

∧ **FIGURE 15.6**

Conceptual Diagram of a Kanban System

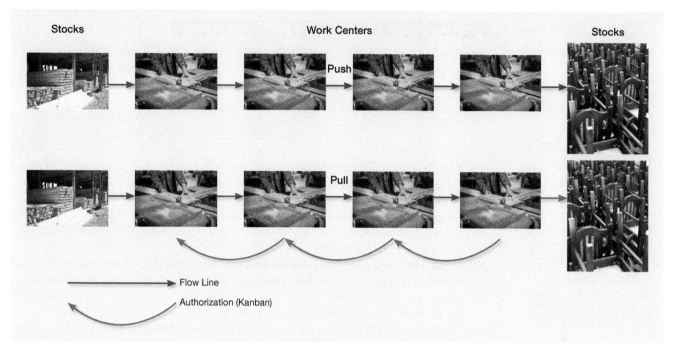

∧ FIGURE 15.7

Push versus Pull Processes: For Pull, Product Cannot Move Downstream until the Next Stage of Production Requests or Authorizes That Movement

We can compute the preferred number of kanban cards in a system as follows:

$$C = \frac{B + (D \times L)}{S}$$ (15.2)

where:

C = the number of kanban cards
S = the standard container size
D = the average daily demand
L = the lead time (in days) to replenish one kanban
C = safety stock

Note that this equation assumes that the bins and cards are separable. If this is not the case, one more card may be needed. The application of Equation 15.2 is demonstrated in **SOLVED PROBLEM 15.1**.

Types of Kanbans	
Type of Kanban	**Application**
Withdrawal	This "move" card is used to transport parts from one location to another.
Production	This "make" card is a work order that initiates the production of parts needed in production. It often contains bill of materials information for incoming parts or components.
Throughput	This card is a combination move and make card that allows materials to be pulled from inventory and placed into a production process to save a step in ordering materials.
Supplier	This kanban is a requisition that goes directly to a supplier.
Emergency	When defective parts are received, an emergency kanban is used to expedite the receipt of other parts.
Express	Express kanbans are used when an expedited order is needed in the event of unexpected stockouts.

< TABLE 15.6

SOLVED PROBLEM 15.1 >

MyLab Operations Management Video

Determining the Number of Kanban Cards Needed

Problem: In a production plant, 500 parts per day are needed. A standard container holds 50 parts. It takes 0.25 day to receive the parts once the move card is released. There is no safety stock. Compute the number of kanban cards needed.

Solution: Using Equation 15.2, we find

$$C = \frac{0 + 500 \times 0.25}{50} = 2.5$$

Round up to three cards needed to maintain production. It should be noted that rounding up makes the system more forgiving because the necessary cards should always be available.

---

heijunka

The practice of "producing a little bit of everything, every day," which is attained by making setup times short.

HEIJUNKA Heijunka is also known as uniform plant loading, mix-model assembly, or uniform plant scheduling. It involves "producing a little bit of everything, every day" and is attained by making setup times short.

For example, Gibson makes three types of Les Paul guitars: standard, deluxe, and custom (**FIGURE 15.8**). Standards are the least expensive, and customs are the most expensive. The monthly demands are for 20,000 standards, 8,000 deluxes, and 2,000 customs. For simplicity, suppose that we say that setup times are long, the production times are equal for all three products (1,000 a day), you cannot sell a product until its production run is complete, and there are 30 days in a month. Thus, all the products are made in large batches. That is, we will produce standards for 20 days and then sell them for the coming month, deluxes for 8 days, and customs for 2 days, month after month. The result is larger lot sizes. If we sell our products at a steady rate—20,000/30 = 667 standards per day, 8,000/30 = 267 deluxes per day, and 2,000/30 = 67 customs per day—average inventory for standards under the poor plan will be 20,000/2 = 10,000. (To find the average inventory, divide the full quantity by 2.) Under the better plan, this average inventory for standards drops to around 2,500. Under the best plan with daily production, the average inventory drops to less than 400 (around 667/2 = 333.5). Realize the cost savings that are available as the money needed to finance this inventory is reduced!

To achieve uniform loads, small lot production is necessary. The final goal of small lot production is a *lot size of one*, which means that a single line can produce a family of products with minimal changeover. To achieve small lot production, setup times must be minimized.

FIGURE 15.8 >

Heijunka in Action

Monthly Demand for Three Products:

Standard (S):	20,000
Deluxe (D):	8,000
Custom (C):	2,000
Sum:	30,000

SSSSSSSSSSSSSSSSSSSSDDDDDDDDCC — poor

CDDSSSSSDDSSSSSCDDSSSSSDDSSSSS — better

CDSSDSSDSSDSSSS ~ 67 times per day — best (based on 30 days)

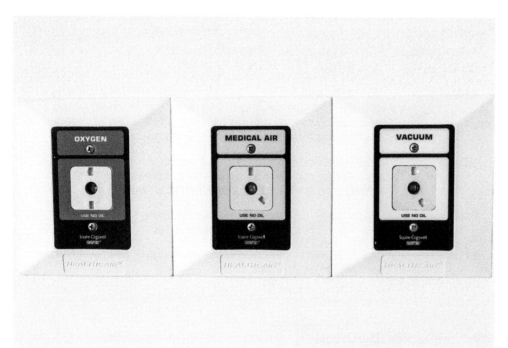

An example of a poka yoke.

POKA YOKES *Poka yokes* (pronounced: "poh-kah-yoh-kehs") are system fail-safes that prevent problems from occurring. A simple example of a poka yoke is the restrictor in your gas tank that will not allow you to put the wrong type of fuel in your tank. Shown above are gas outlets in a hospital. They are considered poka yokes because the outlets are different for the different gases, keeping medical workers from giving a patient the wrong type of gas. This is a commonly used safety poka yoke.

QUICK SETUPS Shown here is a high-tech sheet metal die. These types of dies are used in stamping shapes from sheet metal. Although dies are used in making anything from plastic products to all metal products, a die like this one may have been used in stamping out the oil pan of your automobile; dies like this are used to stamp out many steel components. Dies are very expensive to make and can take very long to install when changing over machines from one design to another. Shigeo Shingo at Toyota developed a method for reducing setup times by reducing the time it took to exchange a die, a major component in setup times. The process he developed was the **single minute exchange of die (SMED) system**. The SMED system follows a learning process outlined in TABLE 15.7. Inherent in the SMED system is an evolutionary learning process starting with an outside exchange of die and eventually progressing to a one-touch exchange of die. Table 15.7 shows the various steps involved in this approach. Notice how fine attention is given to learning how to reduce the time it takes to perform changeovers and setup times. SMED principles have also been used in the production of plastic items such as sprinkler heads, porcelain sinks, and virtually any other type of production involving large setup times.

single minute exchange of die (SMED) system Shingo's single minute exchange of die.

SMED is used in quick-changing dies.

Lean Workforce Practices

Lean firms gain complete organizational commitment to improvement. By deploying lean practices throughout the organization, employees and managers become responsible for the aspects of quality that they influence in a day's work. Included in this discussion are vertical deployment and horizontal deployment of

TABLE 15.7 >

A SMED System for Exchanging Dies

Die Exchange	Application
OED	Outside exchange of die is the traditional long setup time requiring preparation of jigs, dies, and fixtures outside the machine. It could take from hours to days to complete, depending on the operation. OED requires making die changes while the machine is stopped.
IED	Inside exchange of die can be performed while the machine is operating. It may involve movable dies where materials can be attached while the die is installed, thus reducing setup times.
SMED	Single minute exchange of die involves reducing setups to a single movement. The standard is 10 minutes or less.
OTED	One-touch exchange of die involves simplifying or automating the die exchange to less than one minute.

horizontal deployment
The extent that all departments are *involved* in improvement.

vertical deployment
The extent that all *levels* of management and workers are actively involved in achieving lean practices.

visibility
The philosophy that problems and defects should be easy to see and identify.

jidoka
A lean method that gives employees the authority to stop the production line when a problem has occurred, which triggers a machine stop.

process management. **Horizontal deployment** means that all departments are involved in improvement. **Vertical deployment** means that all levels of management and workers are actively involved in achieving lean practices.

A lean workforce is just as important as lean processes. Without a focus on efficient workforces to implement the lean manufacturing process, companies cannot decrease muda. Some practices that companies implement within the workforce are discussed next.

VISIBILITY   An important aspect of the lean approach is **visibility**, the philosophy that problems and defects should be easy to see and identify. When problems exist in business, the first reflex is often to hide the problems as though they do not exist. The lean approach is the opposite. In the lean approach, problems must be made visible before they can be addressed.

Among the approaches to achieving visibility is inventory reduction. Excess work-in-process inventory has the effect of hiding problems. Therefore, it is eliminated. There are various visibility techniques, such as jidoka and andon. **Jidoka**, or a line stop, gives employees the

When a line is stopped (jidoka), a warning light will go off (andon).

authority to stop the production line when a problem has occurred that triggers a machine stop. This employee interaction with automation is often referred to as autonomation. Jidoka involves a five-step process:

1. Detect the problem.
2. Stop production.
3. Find the root cause of the problem.
4. Correct the problem.
5. Train others based on the learning that has taken place.

Andon are warning lights and alarms used to warn workers, management, and maintenance when there is a quality or process problem. Whenever a defect occurs on the line, the line is stopped, halting production in several workstations, not just one workstation. As a result of the stoppage, workers from the production line all converge on the process where the warning light went off. Teams are used to identify and eliminate the fundamental causes of the defect. Once the cause is discovered and fixed, work resumes as normal. This lean process adds to visibility by stopping *all* the steps in the process when one step has a problem.

QUALITY CIRCLES **Quality circles** are natural work teams made up of workers who are empowered to improve work processes. They are used by lean companies to involve employees in improving processes and process capability. Using quality circles, employees brainstorm quality improvement methods and identify causes of quality problems using quality tools. Recall in Chapter 13 that we discussed the seven basic tools of quality. Members of quality circles often apply tools such as Ishikawa diagrams and process maps to solve problems. For example, the Boise Parks and Recreation Department used affinity diagrams to solve the problem of identifying a mission for the city zoo. Managers apply these tools in a variety of situations.

andon
Warning lights and alarms used to warn workers, management, and maintenance when there is a quality or process problem.

quality circles
Natural work teams made up of workers who are empowered to improve work processes.

flexibility
The ability to perform a variety of tasks or make a variety of products.

five S's
A lean approach to simplifying the working environment.

Tools in standard locations as part of the 5 S's.

Systemwide Solutions

Lean companies tend to use flexible equipment and workers. Firms can achieve **flexibility** by adopting general-purpose machinery and by cross-training employees. For example, it is preferable to have two machines that can process 50 units per hour rather than one machine that can produce 100 units per hour. The smaller machines offer more flexibility and will be easier to relocate and redeploy. Other systemwide solutions include adopting the five S's and employing value analysis.

THE FIVE S's AND TOTAL PRODUCTIVE MAINTENANCE Many lean firms have adopted the five S's in an effort to improve operations. The **five S's** are steps in a sequential process that companies follow to "clean up their acts." The five S's are:

1. *Seiri:* Organizing by getting rid of the unnecessary. Unnecessary items may include old files, forms, tools, or other materials that have not been used within the past two or three years.
2. *Seiton:* Neatness that is achieved by straightening offices and work areas.
3. *Seiso:* Cleaning plant and equipment to eliminate dirt that can hide or obscure problems.
4. *Seiketsu:* Standardizing locations for tools, files, equipment, and all other materials. This step often involves color coding and labeling areas so that materials are always found in a standard location. An example of seiketsu is a tool drawer where each tool is located in a fixed location and cutouts make it easy to see if tools are missing.
5. *Shetsuke:* Discipline in maintaining the prior four S's.

Lean manufacturers are known for their approach to maintenance of equipment and machines. The maintenance technique followed in lean companies is preventive maintenance. The idea behind preventive maintenance is that the worst condition that a machine should ever be in is on the day you purchase the machine. By maintaining scheduled maintenance and improvement to equipment, machinery can actually improve with age.

In the 1980s, the Toyota Kamigo Plant 9 in Japan won the Deming Prize with aged equipment. The key to its success was that the equipment was maintained very well with preventive and heavy unscheduled maintenance. The people who operated the machinery also handled regular cleaning, fluid changing, and light maintenance on a regularly scheduled basis.

value analysis and value engineering
Mapping processes to identify non-value-adding steps.

VALUE ANALYSIS AND VALUE ENGINEERING **Value analysis and value engineering** involve mapping processes to identify non-value-adding steps. These steps add to cost without improving the life of the customer. As a result, these steps are eliminated, thereby removing waste from the process.

Part of making processes lean is to make sure that processes are evaluated from a value-analysis perspective prior to automation. The main theme is do not automate a process and further institutionalize it if that process is unnecessary.

Lean Supply Chain Management

The concepts of lean management can be applied to SC&O management. For example, when Simplot Corporation was working with Union Pacific to improve on-time delivery, the companies worked together in a team to apply lean thinking to the processes of providing information to Union Pacific so that the logistics provider could plan better. The use of lean management principles led to an improvement of 30 percent in on-time deliveries.

single sourcing
The process of reducing the number of suppliers for a single part to a single supplier.

SINGLE SOURCING Lean companies use **single sourcing** to supplier management to reduce variation and to be able to develop suppliers adequately. Single sourcing is the practice of reducing the number of suppliers to a single supplier for a single purchased item or component of production.

N = 2 technique
Lean acceptance sampling in which the first and last pieces in a shipment are inspected. If supplier documentation shows that the process is stable and capable, the shipment will conform to requirements.

$N = 2$ TECHNIQUE The **$N = 2$ technique** is an alternative to acceptance sampling. In traditional acceptance sampling, when a company receives a shipment from its suppliers, the shipment is sampled and a determination is made about whether the shipment should be accepted or rejected. Usually, an acceptance sampling plan involves rules such as this: If 4 or fewer defects occur, accept the lot, and if there are more than four defects, reject the lot.

The $N = 2$ technique involves developing and maintaining a close relationship with suppliers so that it is known whether the supplier's processes are in statistical control. If the supplier's processes are in control and capable, and if the first and last pieces in the lot meet specification, it is concluded that the entire lot of materials will meet specification. Therefore, only a sample size of two (the first and last pieces) is needed for acceptance inspection.

Lean management in supply chain management is used to mitigate risk. For example, there is risk of delayed shipments resulting in dissatisfied customers. Unstable supply chains can result in supply chain disruptions. Poor quality from suppliers up the supply chain can result in poor performance. These issues can result in too much stock, excess capacity, the need for alternative suppliers (which can lead to variation), and supply chains that are unable to respond to changing customer requirements.

F AMILIARIZE YOURSELF WITH CHANGE MANAGEMENT

As a result of taking this course, you can become an agent for change in any organization that you join. Six Sigma, lean, and supply chain management are only some of the more leading-edge methods for managing organizations and improving them.

Managing change involves moving from an existing state to a more desired state of being. Strategic change often follows an S-shaped pattern where new changes are launched, flourish, and then stabilize.

A variety of changes may be needed by your organization. They may be related to mission, or they may be strategic, operational, cultural, technological, or organizational in nature. Six Sigma and lean principles not only address operational change but can also lead to cultural change.

To manage change effectively, the needs of workers, managers, and stakeholders should be aligned. To lead and implement change, managers must establish an organizational structure. They need to set up communication systems to inform employees about the change as it is in process. Firms must not overlook training, and managers must set adequate budgets to see the change to fruition. Finally, organizations as a whole must overcome fear of change through counseling and guidance.

At the beginning of the chapter, we discussed the Charleston Area Medical Center Health System (CAMCHS) in West Virginia.[1] By focusing on lean/Six Sigma and continuous improvement, CAMCHS has achieved fantastic results:

- Outpatient satisfaction is in the top 10 percent nationally.
- Almost 1,800 lives have been saved through the creation of a Sepsis Performance Improvement Team.
- The hospital has received the Distinguished Hospital Award from Healthgrades, a service that rates hospitals.
- The hospital is in the top 10 percent for patient safety.
- According to a national database, the hospital is in the top 10 percent for best care and lowest mortality.
- It is a leader in avoiding unnecessary readmissions.

CAMCHS leadership created a vision of providing the best in patient care. Through lean/Six Sigma, the hospital is achieving this objective.

[1]Profiles of Baldrige Winners, *Charleston Area Medical Center Health System*, www.nist.gov, 2017.

Summary

In the chapter, we introduced Six Sigma, lean, and change management, three methods that have been implemented in thousands of organizations around the world. You will likely hear these topics discussed as you interview for jobs.

1. We emphasized Six Sigma leadership and definition.
   a. The process for implementing Six Sigma is DMAIC: define, measure, analyze, improve, and control. You should familiarize yourself with each of these steps.
2. Lean management is based on the concept of continual pursuit of waste reduction. This waste reduction can be achieved through different approaches, such as heijunka, kanban, and kaizen. With this chapter, you are now armed with a basic knowledge of these approaches.

3. Change management involves a pattern of growth that follows an *S* curve and is continual. The growth occurs as you move from a current state to a desired state and involves changes in operations and culture.

Key Terms

andon 467	jidoka 466	Shigeo Shingo 460
black belt 455	kaizen 462	single minute exchange of die (SMED)
business case 456	kanban 462	system 465
champion 455	lean management 453	single sourcing 468
change management 453	lean/Six Sigma 453	Six Sigma 453
DMAIC 456	master black belt 455	value analysis and value
five S's 467	$N = 2$ technique 468	engineering 468
flexibility 467	production kanban 462	vertical deployment 466
green belt 455	pull production 462	visibility 466
heijunka 464	quality circles 467	withdrawal kanban 462
horizontal deployment 466	rapid kaizen 462	

Integrative Learning Exercise

Successful businesses and organizations continually look for ways to improve operations and business processes. Working with a team of fellow students, describe how lean/Six Sigma techniques can be used to identify problems, solve problems, and improve operations. Discuss the design, measure, analyze, improve, and control activities as they relate to continuous improvement. What types of employees would be involved in your lean/Six Sigma efforts? Describe the challenges you might face leading the change.

Integrative Experiential Exercise

With a team of fellow students, visit a company that has recently or is currently engaged in a lean/Six Sigma project. Ask the company to take you through its process for continuous improvement. What challenges did the company face? How were the challenges overcome? What opportunities did the company uncover? What specific tools and techniques were used to bring about continuous improvement? How has the company quantified the benefits of its improvement activities?

Discussion Questions

1. Within an organization, what is meant by change management?

2. How can combining Six Sigma and lean techniques help an organization identify and solve problems?

3. Briefly describe what is meant by the term *Six Sigma*. How is it related to product design?

4. Briefly compare and contrast the roles and responsibilities of black belts and green belts in a Six Sigma organization.

5. What is DMAIC? How is it related to the Six Sigma process?

6. What is meant by the term *muda*? Why is reducing muda a focus of lean/Six Sigma management?

7. Briefly describe the two views of lean management that are common in business literature.

8. How do Shingo's seven wastes help firms to improve processes?

9. What is a *kanban*? How is it related to inventory movement through a process?

10. List and briefly define the different types of kanbans that can be found in a production process.

11. What is meant by the term *jidoka*? Briefly outline the steps involved in its implementation.

12. Why is visibility an important component of the lean approach?

13. What is pull production? How does it help to accomplish the objectives of lean?

14. What is SMED? How is SMED related to small lot production?

15. How is the $N = 2$ technique different from traditional acceptance sampling?

Solved Problem

Lean Practices

NUMBER OF KANBANS 15.1
SOLVED PROBLEM

1. A company requires that 1,000 parts per day be produced to meet demand. A standard container holds 100 parts. It takes 0.5 day to receive the parts once the move card is released. Assuming that there is no safety stock, compute the number of kanban cards needed.

Solution:

Using Equation 15.2, we find that $C = ([0 + (1,000 \times 0.5)])/100 = 5$. Therefore, five cards are needed to maintain production.

Problems

Lean Practices

NUMBER OF KANBANS

2. A company produces 200 parts per day to meet daily demand. A standard container of the parts holds 25 items. It takes 0.1 day to receive the parts once the card is released. Assuming that the company has no safety stock for this part, determine the number of kanban cards needed to maintain production.

3. A company produces 500 parts per day to meet its demand. A standard container of the parts holds 100 items. It takes 0.25 day to receive the parts once a card is released. If the company wants a safety stock of 100 parts, how many kanban cards are needed?

4. Currently, a company produces 1,500 parts per day to meet demand. A standard container of the parts under consideration holds 250 items. It takes 0.75 day to receive the parts once a card is released. If the company wants a safety stock of 500 of these parts, how many kanban cards are needed?

CASE

Automotive Resources

Susan Gonzalez was puzzled. Her company, Automotive Resources, had established a favorable reputation as a supplier of parts and components to automobile assembly plants in the United States, Canada, and Mexico. She has been with the company for nearly 20 years and has watched it grow from a small company with only one plant, producing a limited number of products, to a company with five production facilities in a three-state region now supplying a variety of components for the small car, small truck, and SUV market.

Susan, now the company's vice president of production and lean operations, was facing a growing challenge. The economic downturn was threatening not only the firm's profitability but its very survival. Customers were beginning to complain about late deliveries and quality problems with parts supplied by Automotive Resources. Customers were also less willing to accept price increases now than in the past. Employees of Automotive Resources were grumbling about unpredictable work schedules, declining worker benefits, and hourly wages, which had been decreasing since the start of the downturn. Susan, who over her career at Automotive Resources had attended a variety of professional development programs focused on manager-employee relations, quality improvement, supplier-customer relationship management, lean operations, Six Sigma principles, and kaizen, knew that something significant needed to be done to put her company in a better position in the current economy. Recently, she had been hearing more and more companies and consultants talk about sustainability and its relationship to the supply chain. She also knew that any program she implemented would have to have input from management and employees. Her customers would need to be convinced that she could supply cost-competitive, quality parts with faster response times. She also understood that her customers were now concerned about how her company was engaged in enhancing its efforts in sustainability. Susan knew that she needed to develop a program that could help address the many issues she faced. Which program would that be, and how could it be structured? If only she had a blueprint to follow.

Questions:

1. Briefly describe the problems facing Automotive Resources.

2. What options do you think are available to Susan?

3. What attributes of lean management, kaizen, and Six Sigma management might be applicable to the challenges that Susan faces?

4. How can Susan and the Automotive Resources management team lead the change needed to improve the company's competitive position?

Appendix

∨ TABLE A.1

L_q Values for Queuing Model III (Multiserver System)									
				Number of Servers (M)					
λ/μ	1	2	3	4	5	6	7	8	9	10
0.10	0.0111									
0.15	0.0264	0.0008								
0.20	0.0500	0.0020								
0.25	0.0833	0.0039								
0.30	0.1285	0.0069								
0.35	0.1884	0.0110								
0.40	0.2666	0.0166								
0.45	0.3681	0.0239	0.0019							
0.50	0.5000	0.0333	0.0030							
0.55	0.6722	0.0449	0.0043							
0.60	0.9000	0.0593	0.0061							
0.65	1.2071	0.0767	0.0084							
0.70	1.6333	0.0976	0.0112							
0.75	2.2500	0.1227	0.0147							
0.80	3.2000	0.1523	0.0189							
0.85	4.8166	0.1873	0.0239	0.0031						
0.90	8.1000	0.2285	0.0300	0.0041						
0.95	18.0500	0.2767	0.0371	0.0053						
1.00		0.3333	0.0454	0.0067						
1.50		1.9286	0.2368	0.0448	0.0086					
2.00			0.0888	0.1730	0.3980	0.0090				
2.50			3.5112	0.5331	0.1304	0.0339	0.0086			
3.00				1.5282	0.3541	0.0991	0.0282	0.0077		
3.50				5.1650	0.8816	0.2485	0.0762	0.0232		
4.00					2.2164	0.5694	0.1801	0.0590	0.0189	
4.50					6.8624	1.2650	0.3910	0.1336	0.0460	0.0155
5.00						2.9375	0.8102	0.2785	0.1006	0.0361
5.50						8.5902	1.6736	0.5527	0.2039	0.0767
6.00							3.6878	1.0707	0.3918	0.1518
6.50							10.3406	2.1019	0.7298	0.2855
7.00								4.4471	1.3471	0.5172
7.50								12.1088	2.5457	0.9198
8.00									5.2264	1.6364
8.50									13.8914	3.0025
9.00										6.0183
9.50										15.6861
10.00										

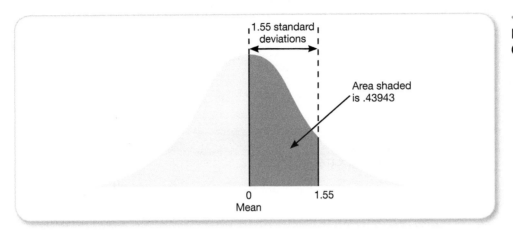

< FIGURE A.1

Normal Distribution Curve

∨ TABLE A.2

Normal z Curve Areas									
z	.00	.01	.02	.03	.04	.05	.06	.07	.08	.09
0.0	.00000	.00399	.00798	.01197	.01595	.01994	.02392	.02790	.03188	.03586
0.1	.03983	.04380	.04776	.05172	.05567	.05962	.06356	.06749	.07142	.07535
0.2	.07926	.08317	.08706	.09095	.09483	.09871	.10257	.10642	.11026	.11409
0.3	.11791	.12172	.12552	.12930	.13307	.13683	.14058	.14431	.14803	.15173
0.4	.15542	.15910	.16276	.16640	.17003	.17364	.17724	.18082	.18439	.18793
0.5	.19146	.19497	.19847	.20194	.20540	.20884	.21226	.21566	.21904	.22240
0.6	.22575	.22907	.23237	.23565	.23891	.24215	.24537	.24857	.25175	.25490
0.7	.25804	.26115	.26424	.26730	.27035	.27337	.27637	.27935	.28230	.28524
0.8	.28814	.29103	.29389	.29673	.29955	.30234	.30511	.30785	.31057	.31327
0.9	.31594	.31859	.32121	.32381	.32639	.32894	.33147	.33398	.33646	.33891
1.0	.34134	.34375	.34614	.34850	.35083	.35314	.35543	.35769	.35993	.36214
1.1	.36433	.36650	.36864	.37076	.37286	.37493	.37698	.37900	.38100	.38298
1.2	.38493	.38686	.38877	.39065	.39251	.39435	.39617	.39796	.39973	.40147
1.3	.40320	.40490	.40658	.40824	.40988	.41149	.41309	.41466	.41621	.41174
1.4	.41924	.42073	.42220	.42364	.42507	.42647	.42786	.42922	.43056	.43189
1.5	.43319	.43448	.43574	.43699	.43822	.43943	.44062	.44179	.44295	.44408
1.6	.44520	.44630	.44738	.44845	.44950	.45053	.45154	.45254	.45352	.45449
1.7	.45543	.45637	.45728	.45818	.45907	.45994	.46080	.46164	.46246	.46327
1.8	.46407	.46485	.46562	.46638	.46712	.46784	.46856	.46926	.46995	.47062
1.9	.47128	.47193	.47257	.47320	.47381	.47441	.47500	.47558	.47615	.47670
2.0	.47725	.47778	.47831	.47882	.47932	.47982	.48030	.48077	.48124	.48169
2.1	.48214	.48257	.48300	.48341	.48382	.48422	.48461	.48500	.48537	.48574
2.2	.48610	.48645	.48679	.48713	.48745	.48778	.48809	.48840	.48870	.48899
2.3	.48928	.48956	.48983	.49010	.49036	.49061	.49086	.49111	.49134	.49158
2.4	.49180	.49202	.49224	.49245	.49266	.49286	.49305	.49324	.49343	.49361
2.5	.49379	.49396	.49413	.49430	.49446	.49461	.49477	.49492	.49506	.49520
2.6	.49534	.49547	.49560	.49573	.49585	.49598	.49609	.49621	.49632	.49643
2.7	.49653	.49664	.49674	.49683	.49693	.49702	.49711	.49720	.49728	.49736
2.8	.49744	.49752	.49760	.49767	.49774	.49781	.49788	.49795	.49801	.49807
2.9	.49813	.49819	.49825	.49831	.49836	.49841	.49846	.49851	.49856	.49861
3.0	.49865	.49869	.49874	.49878	.49882	.49886	.49889	.49893	.49897	.49000
3.1	.49903	.49906	.49910	.49913	.49916	.49918	.49921	.49924	.49926	.49929

∨ TABLE A.3

Factors for Determining Control Limits for $\bar{x}$ and R Charts

Number of Observations in Subgroup n	Factor for $\bar{x}$ Chart A_2	Factors for R Chart	
		Lower Control Limit D_3	Upper Control Limit D_4
2	1.88	0	3.27
3	1.02	0	2.57
4	0.73	0	2.28
5	0.58	0	2.11
6	0.48	0	2.00
7	0.42	0.08	1.92
8	0.37	0.14	1.86
9	0.34	0.18	1.82
10	0.31	0.22	1.78
11	0.29	0.26	1.74
12	0.27	0.28	1.72
13	0.25	0.31	1.69
14	0.24	0.33	1.67
15	0.22	0.35	1.65
16	0.21	0.36	1.64
17	0.20	0.38	1.62
18	0.19	0.39	1.61
19	0.19	0.40	1.60
20	0.18	0.41	1.59

Glossary

ABC analysis A method for categorizing inventory based on a criterion such as usage or value.

acquisition Finding new customers.

acquisition costs Includes all costs related to identifying, selecting, ordering, receiving, and paying for a purchased item.

activity-on-node (AON) network A project network in which activities are labeled on the network nodes.

adaptability The capability to adjust a supply chain's design (i.e., the supply network, manufacturing capabilities, and distribution network) to meet major structural shifts in the market.

advertising and promotion Different methods for managing demand.

aggregate capacity plan A quick analysis to make sure that capacity exists at the aggregate level to produce the units projected in the sales and operations plan.

aggregation Creating a high-level overview of planning, which involves groups or families of products and is usually done at a divisional level.

agility The ability of a supply chain to respond quickly to short-term changes in demand or supply.

alignment Consistency among strategic, supply chain, and operational decisions.

analytics Quantitative process used to aid SC&O decision making.

andon Warning lights and alarms used to warn workers, management, and maintenance when there is a quality or process problem.

applied research Practical exploration that often has a profit motive.

arm's-length relationship A transactional relationship.

assembly line A process type that produces a high volume of products with very little variety.

attribute An either-or situation, such as whether a defect is present or it isn't (binary).

back office A service definition of processes that are buffered from the customer.

back orders Orders that are held in abeyance until more stock arrives.

balance delay The proportion of time that the resources in the process are not used.

basic research Theoretical exploration that is generally not profit motivated.

batch production A process type that emphasizes making like products in mid to large quantities.

bathtub-shaped hazard function A model that shows that products fail either early or late in their useful life.

benchmark An exemplar. In the context of business quality improvement, a firm against which other firms measure themselves.

best operating level The rate of capacity utilization that minimizes average product cost.

bias The tendency to forecast either too high or too low.

bidirectional flows Flows that go both upstream and downstream.

big Q quality Strategic quality issues.

bill of materials (BOM) A data file that shows how a product is manufactured, including what components are used in the manufacture of the finished product, the quantities needed, lead times for each stage of production, and the order of assembly.

black belt Specially trained individuals who perform Six Sigma projects.

bottleneck A department, step, or machine in a process that constrains throughput.

bottleneck item A purchased item with few alternate sources of supply, typically due to complex specifications requiring complex manufacturing or service processes, new technologies, or untested processes.

break bulk facilities Places where large shipments of the same items are broken out and separated to go to separate locations.

break-even analysis The process of considering fixed costs, variable costs, and expected revenues to determine the viability of an investment.

buffers Inventories that are kept at the intersection of differing stages of production to maintain continuity of processing.

bullwhip effect Increasing upstream supply chain variation resulting from forecasts in a supply chain or distribution channel.

business case A document designed to justify a Six Sigma project.

business plan A document that provides guidance for each of the operational subplans in areas such as finance, human resources, marketing, and SC&O management.

business to business (B2B) Business transacted between two commercial firms.

business to consumer (B2C) Business transacted between a business and a consumer.

business-to-business integration (B2Bi) Using third-party facilitators who format planning information in a way that even a small company with limited resources can access and use via the Internet.

capabilities The network of people, knowledge, information systems, tools, and business processes that create value for customers.

capability index (Cpk) A comparative measure of the extent to which individual products meet specification.

capacity loading analysis A method for planning capacity on a daily basis.

capacity utilization A measure of what proportion of design capacity is actually being used during a time period.

capital spend Includes all spending for buildings, large equipment, and anything that will be depreciated.

catchball Strategic back-and-forth dialogue between successive levels of managers and their teams in Hoshin Kanri.

causal models Forecasting methods using regression.

cellular manufacturing U-shaped production lines that have combined various types of flexible pieces of equipment so that low-volume production can happen more efficiently than it can in a job shop.

central limit theorem Rule stating that sampling distributions generally are normally distributed.

champion A senior manager who provides leadership in a Six Sigma project.

change control The process of managing changes to the project charter and plan.

change management The process of guiding improvement in an organization.

channel management Using differing marketing channels to complement each other to level demand.

chase SOP A planning strategy in which the exact amount demanded is produced each month.

check sheets A tool of quality used to tally defects and problems by occurrence.

churn The loss and replacement of customers.

closing a project Celebrating successes; releasing resources, including people; and performing a project debrief.

collaboration Working together and integrating processes between the buyer and supplier, which requires sharing information, knowledge, and expertise and making specific investments in the buyer-supplier relationship.

collaborative planning, forecasting, and replenishment (CPFR) A method for moderating the impacts of the bullwhip effect by sharing planning and scheduling information.

collaborative relationship A buyer-supplier relationship marked by long-term cooperation.

collaborative supplier relationships Working with suppliers to provide value to customers.

complementary products Goods that use similar technologies that can coexist in a family of products, such as ATVs and snowmobiles.

complementary relationship A relationship that occurs when companies understand that their core competencies need another firm's competencies in order to maintain world-class service.

complex specification A description that details the exact quantities of all purchased raw materials and the precise manner in which an item should be made.

component reliability The propensity for a part not to fail over a given time.

concurrent engineering Team-based design in which the differing tasks of design are performed simultaneously.

consignment inventory Stock that is owned by the supplier but is in the physical possession of the buyer.

consolidation warehousing Taking small shipments and combining them into more economical, larger shipments.

continuous design The process of designing products that are enhancements to existing products.

continuous review systems Inventory models used in monitoring inventory levels for items held in stock until the items reach a predetermined level known as a reorder point (R). Also known as perpetual systems.

continuous-flow process A specialized process in which products flow from one place to another with very little human interaction, such as petroleum refining.

cooperation The strength of integrated information and business models between logistics providers and customers.

coproduction Customer participation in the service creation process.

core competencies Abilities that companies compete on that are difficult for competitors to replicate.

corrective action Eight steps taken when a process chart is out of control.

cost analysis Strategic study of cost structures.

cost strategy A generic strategy that focuses on reducing cost.

cost-to-cost trade-off Trading off speed of delivery with saving fuel.

cost-to-service trade-off Cost of improving service and service levels.

counterseasonal products A means to level capacity demands during differing times of year.

couriers Companies hired to make expedited shipments.

critical fractile The optimal capacity level in newsvendor analysis.

critical item A purchased good that can have a big effect on profitability but only has a few qualified suppliers.

critical path The path in a PERT diagram with no slack.

critical path method (CPM) A method for planning projects that uses shortest paths.

critical tasks Tasks on the critical path with no slack.

Crosby's 14 steps The steps Crosby suggests for guiding quality improvement.

cross docking A warehousing approach whereby large shipments come in and are broken into smaller shipments to several locations.

customer experience The result of a service process in terms of customer emotions.

customer interaction The degree of customer involvement in the delivery of a service.

customer relationship management (CRM) A methodology for creating mutually beneficial relations between consumers and service providers.

customer relationship management systems (CRMSs) Information systems used to manage customer-related data.

customer-driven excellence A quality management approach based on understanding customers and striving to satisfy their needs.

customer The beneficiary of a specific supply chain or operation.

cycle counting A repetitive procedure for counting inventory on a regular basis—often quarterly or annually. Often coupled with ABC analysis.

cyclical effects Long-term, repetitive patterns in a time series that are often macroeconomic in nature, such as the business cycle or the boom-bust cycle of the world economy. These effects sometimes last 20 years or longer and are difficult to identify in data.

debriefing session A meeting that the negotiation team holds soon after the negotiation that provides accurate and timely feedback.

defect An irregularity or problem with a larger unit.

defective unit A unit that, as a whole, is not acceptable or does not meet performance requirements.

Delphi method An iterative forecasting method using professional judgment.

demand management A proactive balancing of scarce business resources with demand.

Deming's 14 points for management The underpinnings for modern quality thinking.

dependent demand Demand that is calculated from the requirements for some parent item.

dependent variable (y) The predicted variable in a regression model.

derived demand Demand created as managers conceptualize forecasts and guess at future demand; it exists only on paper.

deseasonalizing a forecast or decomposing a time series The act of removing seasonal variation from a time series to estimate trend more closely.

deservitization Reduction of face-to-face interaction in a service setting.

design A process of applying imagination to invent new products and services.

design for disassembly Designing products so that they can be taken apart easily.

design for manufacturing (DFM) A system of design that facilitates the making of products.

detailed capacity plan A plan performed on a computer to ensure that daily production plans are reasonable.

deterministic reorder points Reorder points computed when there is no variation in demand.

differentiation strategy A generic strategy that emphasizes providing special value to customers in a way that is difficult for competitors to replicate.

direct interaction A description of the interaction of two entities in a PCN diagram.

direct spend category Includes any material or service that is part of the final product.

disaggregation Breaking product families into individual products and components of products.

discontinuous design The process of designing products that are complete changes from existing products.

diseconomies of scale When the production of more units results in higher average cost per item.

dispersion The width of a distribution.

DMAIC An acronym used in Six Sigma that stands for define, measure, analyze, improve, and control.

do-it-yourself Self-serve.

double exponential smoothing (DES) A naive model that gets closer to a trend by smoothing out the irregular component in a time series with stable demand.

economic order quantity (EOQ) The order quantity (Q) at which total annualized inventory-related costs are minimized.

economy of scale Producing more so that the average cost of production for the item decreases.

efficiency The proportion of time that work is being performed.

efficiency percentage A metric that accounts for some of the problems with the design capacity measure; because less than full capacity utilization is often preferable, the adjusted number gives us a better measure of capacity usage.

electronic data interchange (EDI) The computer-to-computer interchange of formatted messages such as documents, planning information, and monetary instruments.

end consumer The ultimate beneficiary or the individual or individuals whose needs are satisfied by an operation.

enhancement The improvement of the experience of current customers.

enterprise resource planning (ERP) system A powerful database system used to manage the whole enterprise, including finances, material requirements planning, human resources, production, customer relationship management, accounting, and most everything else.

entity A service provider, a customer, or a supplier in a PCN diagram.

execution Performing the work necessary to complete the project.

expectation-perception gap The difference between what customers expect and what they receive from a service provider.

expediting or crashing Applying more resources to a project task to reduce its expected completion time.

extended process The chain of activities from raw materials to final customer.

external customers The outside-of-company end beneficiaries of work.

failure modes and effects analysis (FMEA) A process used to consider each component of a system, identifying, analyzing, and documenting the possible failure modes within a system and the effects of each failure on the system and the user.

finished goods inventory Products that are waiting to be sold to the customer.

finite replenishment rate inventory model An inventory model used when product cannot be received at the full order quantity.

fishbone diagram A tool of quality used to identify the causes of problems.

Fisher strategy model A model developed by Marshall Fisher that matches capabilities with customer needs.

five S's A lean approach to simplifying the working environment.

fixed time period models Inventory models for ordering in regular time intervals, such as weekly or monthly, to stabilize purchasing and shipping schedules.

fixed-position layouts Layouts in which the product stays in one place while machines are rolled in and out to perform needed processing steps.

flexibility A supply chain's ability to respond to changes in customer needs or requirements.

flexible manufacturing system (FMS) A process that represents a trade-off between mass assembly operations and job shops by providing moderate levels of flexibility with moderate production volumes.

focus strategy A generic strategy that emphasizes select customers or markets.

forecast An assertion about the future whose outcome has not yet been seen.

forecasting The process of creating an assertion about the future.

forward integration When a firm moves forward in the supply chain not only to provide products but also to help customers with the use of the products.

Four I's of SC&O management Impacting, improving, innovating, and integrating.

freight forwarder An individual or company that facilitates moving product from producer to final destination.

front office Service steps involving the customer with the service provider.

functional project organization An organizational form in which employees stay in a functional area and certain project tasks are assigned to them through their functional manager.

functional strategies or operational subplans One- to two-year goals that help the firm "win a battle but not necessarily the war." These subplans include events like improving product quality through continuous improvement, reducing costs through improving warehouse flows, or improving supplier relationships through giving awards to key suppliers.

Gantt chart A bar chart project management tool.

gap A difference between current quality and desired quality.

gap analysis Quality management using Parasuraman, Zeithamel, and Berry's SERVQUAL tool.

Garvin's eight dimensions of quality Performance, features, reliability, conformance, durability, serviceability, aesthetics, and perceived quality.

geographical dispersion The extent to which a firm is spread out around the globe.

global trade agreements The legal terms necessary to import goods.

globalization Increasing global presence by establishing operations in other parts of the world.

gold plating Adding unnecessary deliverables to a project.

grassroots forecasting Going to the market to get information for new product launches.

green belt A person trained in basic quality tools.

greenfield forecasting methods Forecasting approaches used in new product launches.

hedging Building up inventory in anticipation of unforeseen global supply chain interruptions.

heijunka The practice of "producing a little bit of everything, every day," which is attained by making setup times short.

heuristics Rules used to achieve an objective, such as efficiently using machines and labor.

histogram A bar graph.

horizontal deployment The extent that all departments are *involved* in improvement.

Hoshin Kanri planning Policy deployment through a strategic planning process that utilizes project-based improvement.

hub and spoke system A method used to reduce the number of trucks or other carriers needed for shipping when networks of cities are involved in the delivery.

hybrid SOP A planning strategy that involves any combination of the *pure strategies* (level and chase).

impacting Effectively managing core processes that affect customers.

improving The act of making processes, products, and people better.

in-process inspection Quality inspection performed during the production process.

independent demand Forecasted demand.

independent processing The steps an entity performs in a PCN diagram where it does not interact with other entities.

independent variable (x) The explanatory variable in a regression model.

indirect spend category Includes all the spending that supports the operations of a firm, encompassing everything from cafeteria services to spare parts for factory equipment.

information flows Data that moves throughout the supply chain.

initiation Beginning project steps, including scoping and chartering projects.

innovating Large-scale, sudden improvement.

inspection ratio The ratio between the cost of inspection and the cost of failure resulting from a particular step in the process.

integrating Collaboration and cooperation between stakeholders in a supply chain.

internal customers Customers within a firm such as the users of a company print shop.

inventory A store of goods and stocks for some future (either near-term or long-term) use.

inventory management Using tools and strategies to achieve a balance between inventory costs and customer service.

inventory status file A database that knows when items will be in stock as well as the current inventory levels.

inventory velocity The rate at which firms use up their inventory.

irregular component or noise component Random variation that occurs in any time series.

ISO 9000 A global standard for quality.

jidoka A lean method that gives employees the authority to stop the production line when a problem has occurred, which triggers a machine stop.

job shop A processing facility that can produce a variety of products in fairly low quantities.

Juran's trilogy Juran's interrelated points of planning, control, and improvement.

kaizen Continual improvement.

kanban A card system for controlling the flow of materials through a process.

ladder FMS An FMS that allows for parts and assemblies to move in a variety of different directions to receive the needed processing.

lagging capacity Capacity is increased only when increasing demand justifies the increase in capacity.

landed cost The total cost to get the product to the consumer.

lead time The period between placing and receiving an order.

leading capacity Capacity is added incrementally in anticipation of increasing demand.

lean Managing and improving processes to reduce waste.

lean management Reducing waste in a methodical manner to optimize processes.

lean/Six Sigma Combining waste reduction with quality management to guide improvement and change in organizations.

level SOP A planning strategy that is accomplished by varying inventory levels.

leverage item A purchased item that has the potential to affect profit, typically because it is associated with a high level of expenditures while also having many qualified sources of supply.

licensing The sale of a product under another trademark in another region of the world.

life-cycle costing Using value analysis to identify total costs from a supply chain–environmental perspective.

line balancing A process of allocating tasks to process workstations in an efficient manner.

little q quality Tactical quality issues.

load-distance model A model used in designing functional layouts where movement is minimized.

logisticians Business professionals dedicated to analyzing and coordinating the transportation, storage, and distribution of supplies, materials, commodities, and finished goods.

logistics The transportation and storage of goods and materials.

logistics management From the Council of Supply Chain Management Professionals: "That part of supply chain management that plans, implements, and controls the efficient and effective forward and reverse flow and storage of goods, services, and related information between the point of origin and the point of consumption to meet customers' requirements."

loyalty The feeling of affiliation a customer has with a firm.

make-to-order inventory Products sent directly to the customer and not placed in finished goods inventory.

make-to-stock inventory Inventory that is completed and placed into inventory for sale at a later date.

Malcolm Baldrige National Quality Award Criteria for Performance Excellence The guiding document of the Baldrige Award Program.

managing flow Using logistics to regulate the speed of movement of goods through a supply chain.

manufacturing system design The selection of the process technologies that will result in a low-cost, high-quality product.

market pull Continuous development that takes existing products and enhances them to reinvigorate the product life cycle or to create new complementary products.

mass capacity expansion Large-scale capacity expansion with the expectation of high customer demand.

mass customization The process in which standardized components and modules are produced and then assembled or configured only when customers need them.

master black belt Mentors who are experienced black belts who train in Six Sigma projects.

master production schedule (MPS) Portion of the ERP that disaggregates the sales and operations plan from product families to individual products to determine when they will be produced.

matching capacity Capacity is increased at relatively the same rate that demand increases.

material requirements planning (MRP) system The production engine of an ERP system.

matrix team structure A setup in which an employee works part-time on a project team and continues to perform fundamental job assignments.

mean Arithmetic average.

mean absolute deviation (MAD) A measure of forecasting error that tells the average error in a forecast.

mean average percentage error (MAPE) A measure of forecasting error that tracks the average percentage of error.

mean squared error (MSE) A measure of forecasting error used in computing variance.

mean time to repair (MTTR) The mean number of hours it takes to repair the product.

milestones Phases in a project.

monetary flows The movement of money from downstream to upstream.

monitoring and controlling The process of reporting to see that the project plan is being followed.

most likely completion time The best estimate of task completion time.

MRP explosion The process of calculating requirements for components and subassemblies from the demand for finished products.

MRP logic The process of time phasing and calculating requirements for lower-level items from parent items.

multimodal shipping A shipping method contracted with a single carrier or a non-asset-based integrator who works with subcarriers who do various types of shipping. Also known as intermodal shipping.

multiphase queue system A service system involving multiple queues and/or servers.

multiple linear regression A regression model with more than one independent variable.

multiple project assignment matrix A tool for monitoring who is assigned to multiple projects.

Muther's grid A model used in designing functional layouts where behavioral criteria are considered.

N=2 technique Lean acceptance sampling in which the first and last pieces in a shipment are inspected. If supplier documentation shows that the process is stable and capable, the shipment will conform to requirements.

naive forecasting methods Forecasting methods that make no attempt at explaining why demand is increasing or decreasing.

nearshoring Moving production closer to the same country as consumption.

nearsourcing Moving production to a supplier who is geographically closer to where products are sold.

negotiation plan A preparation tool in which the supply manager outlines all the contract terms that need to be negotiated with the supplier.

net promoter score (NPS) A service feedback rating system.

newsvendor analysis A method for making capacity decisions in services that measures the trade-offs between the cost of understocking and the cost of overstocking.

nominal group techniques (NGTs) Brainstorming and team techniques that remove the influence of power and position.

nonrandom variation or special cause variation Variation that results from a specific event, which may be a shift in a process mean or an unexpected occurrence.

North American Free Trade Agreement (NAFTA) An agreement that created a trade bloc consisting of the United States, Canada, and Mexico as an effort to remove trade barriers among these three countries.

offshoring Moving production to another country.

on-time delivery An important performance metric for suppliers.

operating doctrine of inventory management A doctrine that asks two questions of SC&O managers: How much do we order (Q), and when do we place the order (R)?

operational subplans Portions of the strategic plan pertaining to the differing functional areas of the firm that help ensure attainment of strategic objectives.

operations management Managing transformation processes to convert inputs into products and services.

operations strategy Allocating resources within the firm to provide value to customers.

optimistic completion time The shortest time for completing a task.

order qualifiers Necessary attributes that allow a firm to enter into and compete in a market; a firm's strategy must account for these necessities.

order winners Attributes that differentiate a company's products.

out-of-control process A process that exhibits nonrandom variation.

output gap measure A metric that provides a variance measure against design capacity.

outsource To procure from a supplier something that a company has been producing internally.

outsourcing The process of moving production to another firm.

over-the-wall-syndrome A traditional method for design with poor integration and communication.

ownership costs Costs relating to the maintenance and operation of products.

p chart A process chart used to graph the proportion of items in a sample that are defective (nonconforming to specification).

parent items Items that occur at higher levels in a bill of materials.

Pareto's law The 80/20 rule.

periodic inventory systems Inventory models used to calculate order quantities (Q) when orders are placed at fixed intervals such as weekly or monthly, which allows purchasers to combine several orders into one, save time, and sometimes save shipping expense.

pessimistic completion time The longest foreseeable task completion time.

plan, do, check, act (PDCA) cycle Deming's improvement cycle based on the scientific method.

planning Developing a road map for the project.

poka yoke The Japanese term for failsafing.

portfolio model A framework for making purchasing-related strategic management decisions.

postownership costs All costs related to the customer's use and disposition of a purchased item.

predictive analytics The science of using customer data to forecast future behavior.

price analysis The process of comparing supplier prices against one another or against external benchmarks.

pricing A method for increasing demand during slow periods.

probabilistic PERT A method for computing the probability of completing a project in a given period of time.

process The means of making something that is of value to a customer.

process capability The ability of a process to produce a product that meets specification.

process chain network (PCN) diagram A tool that categorizes flowchart steps according to whether or not they involve interaction between entities such as providers and customers.

process charts Graphs designed to signal process workers when nonrandom variation occurs in a process.

process control The act of monitoring a process for its efficacy.

process design Configuring inputs and resources in a way that provides value, enhances quality, and is productive.

process domain The process steps that are the responsibility of a given entity.

process drift Seven points in succession, all increasing or decreasing in a process chart.

process improvement A proactive effort to enhance process performance.

process layout A physical arrangement of equipment and workstations in which like functions are gathered into work centers.

process management The act of executing and controlling the productive functions of a firm.

process maps Flowcharts used to improve a process.

process run Five points in sequence, either above or below the mean.

process tampering Adjusting a process when it exhibits only random variation.

procurement, purchasing, materials, sourcing, and supply management Synonyms for the process of buying and working with suppliers.

product data management (PDM) A method that helps manage both product data and the product development process by tracking the masses of data needed to design, manufacture, support, and maintain products.

product design specification (PDS) A document that demonstrates the design to be implemented and includes major features, uses, and conditions for use of the product.

product design The act of creating new products.

product flows Unidirectional flows of products from upstream to downstream.

product life cycle A graphical representation of the life phases that a product experiences.

product phasing Introducing new products in a sequence that allows for an effective use of capacity.

product traceability A process of tracking products from final use to point of origin.

product/process matrix A visual model that positions process choice as a trade-off between production volume and product variety.

production activity control A method used to coordinate the way that jobs are done on a daily basis, such as loading work centers, sequencing and prioritizing jobs, identifying job start times, job assignments to workstations, and other detailed scheduling.

production kanban A card that orders the production of a part or component.

production smoothing Producing extra inventory during periods of low demand, which is then consumed during periods of high demand.

profit impact The result of either the sheer volume of spend for a particular item or the unique added value from an item.

program evaluation and review technique (PERT) A method for planning and controlling projects using networks.

project A one-time, temporary endeavor with a defined beginning and end.

project charter A document that outlines the primary deliverables, the objective, and the parameters of a project.

project chartering The act of creating a document outlining the deliverables of a project.

project management The act of leading and directing the people and other resources in a project.

pull production The process of not releasing materials until the next stage in production or consumption is ready.

purchasing agent, purchasing manager, buyer, and supply manager Synonyms for people who work in purchasing.

pure project A project to which an employee is assigned full-time.

Q/R systems Inventory models that provide answers to the quantity (Q) and timing (R) operating doctrine questions.

qualifying projects The act of justifying a project financially and strategically.

quality (1) The characteristics of a product or service that bear on its ability to satisfy stated or implied needs. (2) A product or service free of deficiencies.

quality circles Natural work teams made up of workers who are empowered to improve work processes.

quality function deployment (QFD) A method for translating customer requirements into functional design (also called house of quality).

quantity discounts Lowered prices given when higher amounts of an item are purchased.

queue A waiting line.

queue configuration How a waiting line is organized for a given phase of a system.

queue discipline A method for determining who goes next in a waiting line.

queuing psychology The side of queuing theory that emphasizes human behavior.

queuing theory A method for determining customer service system performance and wait times for customers who must wait in lines.

R chart A process control chart used to monitor the dispersion of the process.

random samples To gather samples so that every piece of product has an equal chance of being selected for inspection.

random variation or common cause variation Variation that centers on a mean and occurs with a somewhat consistent amount of dispersion.

randomize To make random.

rapid kaizen Fast improvement focusing on a finite problem.

ratio-to-moving-average method A method for computing seasonal indexes.

raw materials Inputs to production that take the form of either fundamental supplies, such as iron or wood, or subassemblies and components received from suppliers.

relevant costs Inventory-related costs that adjust if you change the amount ordered.

reorder point A signal to replenish an item in inventory.

request for quote (RFQ) or request for proposal (RFP) Contains the specification of what is needed and details the information that must be submitted by a supplier that wishes to be considered for the purchase.

research and development (R&D) The process that firms follow to develop new products or improve existing products.

retention Promoting ongoing and increased business with current customers.

reverse logistics Logistics used to move products up the supply chain. Often used in managing recycling.

risk/return matrix A tool for prioritizing potential projects.

rough-cut capacity planning (RCCP) A planning system that focuses on bottlenecks to ensure that the MPS does not overload production processes or facilities and can be produced given current capacity limitations.

routine item A basic item or supply.

run chart Chart used to plot time series data.

S curve A graph that shows conceptually how cumulative costs are incurred during a project over time.

safety stock Extra stock held in anticipation of variable demand.

sales and operations planning (SOP) System helping managers make decisions related to the creation of schedules that balance demand and supply.

sample A part representing a whole.

satisfaction The extent to which customer needs are met.

SC&O strategy A strategy that encompasses both supply chain management and operations management.

scatter plot A tool of quality used to study the relationship between variables.

scope creep Allowing the deliverables of a project to expand over time.

scope management The act of defining what the team needs to do to complete a project.

scope of work A specification for services.

scorecard A strategic tool to communicate strategic metrics. Often used with suppliers.

seasonal patterns or seasonality Variation that is repetitive and occurs during some fixed time period, such as a day, week, month, or year.

self-service Steps in a service process where the customer performs steps independently of the service provider.

servers or service stations The person providing service in a queuing system.

service capacity planning The process of determining the productive capability needed in a service firm.

service contracts Contracts that guarantee products if they fail during a given time period.

service failures Systemic occurrences that result in dissatisfied customers.

service level The probability that an item will be available in stock for order fulfillment when it is needed during lead time.

service offering A process in which providers ask customers to participate.

service recovery A process to rectify service failures.

service scripts Detailed service encounter guides for use by service providers.

service supply chain management Supply chain management in a service setting.

service supply chains Collaboration between service providers and customers to create value.

service system A service process with waiting line(s) and queue(s).

services The result of services operations.

services operations Production processes wherein each customer is a supplier of process inputs.

servitization The process of integrating service offerings with manufactured products.

SERVQUAL A set of companion surveys used to perform gap analysis in service firms and based on the notion that customers are more satisfied when their perceptions of a service are closely aligned with the service design of the service provider.

SERVQUAL expectations survey An instrument to measure customer expectations of a service.

SERVQUAL perceptions survey An instrument to measure customer perceptions of a service.

seven basic tools The basic tools of quality improvement.

seven managerial quality tools (1) **Affinity diagrams, (2) interrelationship digraphs, (3) tree diagrams, (4) prioritization matrices, (5) matrix diagrams, (6) process decision program charts, and (7) activity network diagrams.**

Shigeo Shingo **Creator of an approach to quality management that includes identifying a group of seven wastes.**

should cost modeling **The process of determining what a product should cost based on its component raw material costs, manufacturing costs, production overheads, and reasonable profit margins.**

simple linear regression **A regression model with only one independent variable.**

simple moving average (SMA) **A naive forecasting technique where prior demand is averaged.**

simple specification **A description given to meet a particular function that does not detail the exact quantities of each ingredient or the precise manner in which a purchased item should be made.**

simultaneity **When the production of services occurs at roughly the same time as customer demand.**

single exponential smoothing (SES) **A naive forecasting model that averages prior demand with a prior forecast.**

single minute exchange of die (SMED) system **Shingo's single minute exchange of die.**

single sourcing **The process of reducing the number of suppliers for a single part to a single supplier.**

SIPOC diagram **A type of process map that includes suppliers, inputs, processing, outputs, and customers.**

situational leadership model **A graph by Hersey and Blanchard that illustrates the correlation between task behavior, relationship behavior, and leadership behavior.**

Six Sigma **An approach to improving product and process through an emphasis on system and product design.**

slack **The difference between the latest possible completion time and the shortest possible completion time.**

smoothing constant **A constant (represented by α) that ranges between 0 and 1 in an exponential smoothing model.**

smoothing effect **The result of reducing random variation in a time series.**

specification **Documentation that tells buyers (and the assigned supply manager) what to buy and the suppliers what is required of them.**

spend analysis **A review of a firm's entire set of purchases. It answers the question, What is the firm spending its money on?**

square root rule **A calculation for calculating safety stock inventory in warehouses, given the number of warehouses.**

stability **Only random variation is present in the process.**

stall built **Another name for a fixed-position layout.**

statistical process control **The application of statistical concepts to the production process to determine if a process displays *stability*.**

statistical thinking **Deming's concept of looking at problems through the lens of data.**

stochastic reorder points **Reorder points used in the more realistic case where demand, while awaiting an order, is variable.**

stockout **The situation that occurs when a customer places an order and there is no stock available to fulfill the order.**

strategic alliances **Strategic ventures with partners and suppliers.**

strategic cost management **Top management focus on price and total ownership costs.**

strategic sourcing **The process of planning, evaluating, implementing, and controlling both highly important and routine sourcing decisions.**

strategy **A long-term plan that defines how the company will win customers, create game-winning capabilities, fit into the competitive environment, and develop relationships.**

strategy content **That which construes a strategy.**

strategy process **The method pursued for creating strategy.**

string method **A simple approach to forecasting using a string to identify trends.**

structured brainstorming **Brainstorming methods following a strict script or format.**

student problem **Procrastination in beginning project tasks.**

supplier award programs **Methods for identifying and rewarding outstanding suppliers.**

supplier development **The process of helping a supplier improve performance in areas such as cost, delivery, and quality.**

supplier management **The processes of forging strong links by identifying what is needed by the firm and then selecting, developing, and actively managing the supply base.**

supplier scorecard **A communication device that serves two key roles for the supply manager: (1) it identifies the supplier performance metrics that are most critical to the supply manager's organization, and (2) it enables the evaluation of suppliers against these key metrics.**

supplier self-assessment **A survey administered to suppliers to determine fit with purchaser needs.**

supplies **Materials stored to support the functioning of the business.**

supply chain and operations (SC&O) **Combining supply chain and operations to serve customers.**

supply chain management **Firms cooperating to create value for customers.**

supply chain quality management (SCQM) **A systems-based approach to performance improvement that leverages opportunities created by upstream and downstream linkages with suppliers and customers.**

supply chain strategy **The supply chain portion of the strategic plan.**

supply risk **The extent to which an item is difficult to source due to a lack of qualified sources, raw material scarcity, lack of substitutes, logistics cost or complexity, and monopoly or oligopoly conditions.**

support processes Processes, such as legal, that support core processes.

surrogate interaction The intersection of two entities in a PCN diagram where there is no direct interaction.

sustainability Proactively managing to save resources and to incorporate "green" production.

sustainability management Improvement-based environmental management systems.

synergistic relationship A relationship between two companies who are committed to working together in a way that the result is greater than the sum of the individual parts.

system availability (SA) The "uptime" or proportion of time that a product or system functions properly.

system for quality improvement A system in which all the variables (e.g., processes, tools, equipment, and people) interact to create a quality result.

system reliability The probability that a system of components will perform the intended function over a specified period of time.

systematic samples Samples ordered by time or sequence.

tactics Short-term steps used to achieve strategic goals.

takt time The required cycle time necessary to meet forecasted needs for a product.

tangibles Products, technology, and other outputs and inputs associated with services.

task precedence Determining which tasks precede and follow other tasks.

technological push Discontinuous development that occurs when a new product is sent to market without a clear idea of how it will be used by the customer.

technology feasibility statement A document used by designers in the design process to assess a variety of issues, such as necessary parameters for performance, manufacturing imperatives, limitations in the physical properties of materials, special considerations, changes in manufacturing technologies, and conditions for quality testing the product. The productive capability of a firm.

theory of constraints A method for managing capacity.

third-party logistics providers Companies that provide all or part of the logistics function for another company.

three cornerstones of sustainable logistics (1) Society, (2) economy, and (3) environment.

three fundamental logistics trade-offs (1) Cost-to-cost trade-off, (2) modal trade-off, and (3) cost-to-service trade-off.

three primary flows of a supply chain Product flows, monetary flows, and information flows.

time phasing Moving backward through time from the delivery date for the completed product to enable releasing orders only when they are needed.

time-perishable capacity Unused capacity (at times of low demand) that is lost forever and cannot be used to meet later demand.

total cost of ownership (TCO) The sum of acquisition, ownership, and postownership costs.

total cost of ownership (TCO) analysis Includes all costs in your analysis of a purchase, not just the purchase price, including acquisition costs, ownership costs, and post-ownership costs.

transactional relationship A relationship in which the buyer has many supplier choices, does not need to share internal company information during the exchange, is purchasing a routine item, does not require technology innovation from the supplier, and does not expect to experience shortages in supply.

transportation method An optimization technique for allocating shipments from sources to destinations.

trend The average rate of change in a time series. In linear regression, it is often referred to as the slope.

two-phase system A configuration of a queuing system with a single waiting line and a different service line.

uncertainty period Used with periodic inventory models, the time between orders (TBO) + order lead time. Using mechanisms such as pricing to level demand.

value The extent to which a firm meets customer needs.

value analysis and value engineering Mapping processes to identify non-value-adding steps.

value chain Inbound logistics, transformation processes, and outbound logistics: the core of what a firm does.

value-added activities Process steps that enhance products and services in a way that makes them more valuable for customers.

value-added logistics services Services that perform functions that are not traditional logistics functions, such as purchasing and production.

variable A continuous measurement such as weight, height, or volume.

vendor-managed inventory (VMI) An arrangement by which the supplier manages the inventory items and the buyer houses the inventory.

vertical deployment The extent that all *levels* of management and workers are actively involved in achieving lean practices.

vertical integration The extent to which the supply chain is outsourced versus being owned by the target firm.

visibility The philosophy that problems and defects should be easy to see and identify.

warehouse A facility for storing inventory.

weighted center of gravity method A method to identify a good (but not necessarily an optimal) location for the placement of a new facility.

weighted moving average (WMA) A naive forecasting model in which previous period data have different weights. Usually, the heavier weight is on the most recent data.

weighted-factor analysis (WFA) A multicriteria decision-making method using weights.

win-win A healthy buyer-supplier relationship.

withdrawal kanban A card that orders the transportation of a part or component.

work breakdown structure (WBS) A brainstorming tool used to plan projects.

work-in-process (WIP) inventory Inventory that has been received and is in the production phase.

x-bar chart A process control chart used to monitor the average of the characteristic being measured.

Name Index

Subject Index

Photo Credits

Cover
AnnaElizabethPhotography/Shutterstock; Alterfalter/Shutterstock; Sirtravelalot/Shutterstock; Olesia Bilkei/123RF; Wavebreakmedia/Shutterstock; Foodcollection/Getty images; Ted S. Warren/AP Images

Chapter 1
p. 1: Ixefra/Getty images; p. 1: Daryl Benson/Photodisc/Getty Images; p. 3: Michael Sparrow/Alamy Stock Photo; p. 7: Lonely Planet Images/Getty Images; p. 8: Grzegorz knec/Alamy Stock Photo; p. 9: Artpixelgraphy Studio/Shutterstock; p. 14: Patrick Seeger/EPA/Alamy Stock Photo; p. 18: Peter Probst/Alamy Stock Photo

Chapter 2
p. 22: Chris Ryan/Caiaimage/Getty Images; p. 24: Grzegorz knec/Alamy Stock Photo; p. 24: Asif Islam/Shutterstock; p. 24: PSL Images/Alamy Stock Photo; p. 26: Rob Wilson/Shutterstock; p. 29: Grzegorz knec/Alamy Stock Photo; p. 29: Cornfield/Shutterstock; p. 29: PSL Images/Alamy Stock Photo; p. 30: Ian Dagnall/Alamy Stock Photo; p. 35: Hans Gutknecht/Los Angeles Daily News/ZUMA Press Inc/Alamy Stock Photo; p. 39: Michael Sparrow/Alamy Stock Photo; p. 42: Peter Probst/Alamy Stock Photo; p. 43: Sheila Fitzgerald/Shutterstock

Chapter 3
p. 47: Wavebreakmedia/Shutterstock; p. 47: PixieMe/Shutterstock; p. 49: Rob245/Fotolia; p. 51: Asif Islam/Shutterstock; p. 61: Tina Manley/Alamy Stock Photo; p. 70: B Christopher/Alamy Stock Photo; p. 70: Jordan Tan/Shutterstock; p. 72: Tina Manley/Alamy Stock Photo; p. 73: Asharkyu/Shutterstock; p. 77: Aleksandr Popov/Fotolia; p. 82: Sirtravelalot/Shutterstock

Chapter 4
p. 93: Lightpoet/Shutterstock; p. 93: Thampapon/Shutterstock; p. 97: Photomans/Shutterstock; p. 98: Jordan Tan/Shutterstock; p. 104: Jfanchin/Shutterstock; p. 105: Zero Creatives/Cultura Creative/Alamy Stock Photo; p. 105: JJM Stock Photography/Alamy Stock Photo; p. 108: Sorbis/Shutterstock; p. 113: James R. Martin/Shutterstock

Chapter 5
p. 122: Ken Wolter/Shutterstock; p. 122: Alex Segre/Alamy Stock Photo; p. 125: Tooykrub/Shutterstock; p. 128: Jfanchin/Shutterstock; p. 129: David Paul Morris/Bloomberg/Getty Images; p. 132: JackF/Fotolia; p. 133: Chrisdorney/Shutterstock; p. 134: TP/Alamy Stock Photo; p. 135: Ed Simons/Alamy Stock Photo; p. 135: PSL Images/Alamy Stock Photo; p. 135: Michael H/The Image Bank/Getty Images; p. 136: Frank Sorge/Agencja Fotograficzna Caro/Alamy Stock Photo; p. 136: Mirko/Fotolia; p. 136: Bst2012/Fotolia; p. 136: Bst2012/Fotolia; p. 136: Carlosseller/Fotolia; p. 136: Monkey Business/Fotolia

Chapter 6
p. 141: Steve Vidler/Alamy Stock Photo; p. 141: Lonely Planet Images/Getty Images; p. 143: Syda Productions/Fotolia; p. 145: Ljupco Smokovski/Fotolia; p. 149: Dmitry Vereshchagin/Fotolia; p. 153: Zoomyimages/Fotolia; p. 157: 360b/Shutterstock; p. 159: Kurhan/Fotolia

Chapter 7
p. 167: Juan Camilo Bernal/Shutterstock; p. 170: PhotoEdit/Alamy Stock Photo; p. 172: Makoto Watanabe/SOURCENEXT/Alamy Stock Photo; p. 173: 360b/Shutterstock; p. 181: 360b/Shutterstock; p. 186: 360b/Shutterstock; p. 187: xPACIFICA/Alamy Stock Photo; p. 187: Ted S. Warren/AP Images; p. 188: Vincenzo_Mancuso/Shutterstock

Chapter 8
p. 196: Al Behrman/AP Images; p. 196: Stars and Stripes/Alamy Stock Photo; p. 198: Staff/MCT/Newscom; p. 199: 360b/Shutterstock; p. 204: ESB Professional/Shutterstock; p. 217: Johnny Hawkins/Cartoon Stock; p. 222: Jeffrey Blackler/Alamy Stock Photo; p. 225: Kevin Brine/Shutterstock

Chapter 9
p. 243: ArtmannWitte/Shutterstock; p. 245: Melinda Sue Gordon/Columbia Pictures/Courtesy Everett Collection; p. 251: Javier Larrea/Age Fotostock/Alamy Stock Photo; p. 255: ESB Professional/Shutterstock; p. 255: George Sheldon/Shuttestock; p. 258: Sheila Fitzgerald/Shutterstock; p. 263: Robert Llewellyn/Imagestate Media Partners Limited/Impact Photos/Alamy Stock Photo

Chapter 10
p. 274: Kadmy/Fotolia; p. 281: Anna Hoychuk/Shutterstock; p. 283: NetPhotos/Alamy Stock Photo; p. 285: George Sheldon/Shuttestock; p. 287: Andrew Holt/Alamy Stock Photo; p. 294: Ditty_about summer/Shutterstock

Chapter 11
p. 306: Richyrichimages/E+/Getty Images; p. 307: Michael Dwyer/Alamy Stock Photo; p. 309: Nirot Sriprasit/123RF; p. 311: Andrew Holt/Alamy Stock Photo; p. 318: 360b/Shutterstock; p. 319: Torsakarin/Fotolia; p. 320: Testing/Shutterstock; p. 321: EPA/Jens Wolf/Dpa picture alliance/Alamy Stock Photo; p. 326: Tony Waltham/Robertharding/Alamy Stock Photo; p. 326: Kenna Love/Alamy Stock Photo; p. 326: Peter Probst/Alamy Stock Photo; p. 327: James Hardy/PhotoAlto/Alamy Stock Photo; p. 327: Photographee.eu/Fotolia; p. 327: Federico Rostagno/Fotolia; p. 327: Leeyiutung/Fotolia; p. 328: Federico Rostagno/Fotolia; p. 328: Leeyiutung/Fotolia; p. 328: Photographee.eu/Fotolia; p. 328: Art Allianz/Fotolia; p. 328: Charles Amundson/Fotolia; p. 328: Karen Gentry/Fotolia; p. 329: Rabbit75_fot/Fotolia

Chapter 12
p. 339: Lonely Planet Images/Getty Images; p. 339: Stephen Barnes/Alamy Stock Photo; p. 341: Dell/Fotolia; p. 341: Bev/Fotolia; p. 352: Gino Santa Maria/Fotolia; p. 362: 360b/Shutterstock; p. 370: Steve Dunwell/Age Fotostock/Alamy Stock Photo

Chapter 13
p. 382: Leekris/Fotolia; p. 384: Peek Creative Collective/Shutterstock; p. 388: Chris Ryan/OJO Images Ltd/Alamy Stock Photo; p. 389: Steve Dunwell/Age Fotostock/Alamy Stock Photo; p. 390: Jonathan Weiss/Shutterstock; p. 392: Richard Drew/AP Images; p. 396: SDBBusiness/Alamy Stock Photo; p. 402: Fabian von Poser/imageBROKER/Alamy Stock Photo; p. 403: Dutourdumonde/Fotolia

Chapter 14

p. 410: Acfotodesign/F1online digitale Bildagentur GmbH/Alamy Stock Photo; p. 414: Kiim Kulish/Corbis Historical/Getty Images; p. 428: Evan El-Amin/Shutterstock; p. 429: Jonathan Weiss/Shutterstock; p. 430: Prachaya Roekdeethaweesab/Shutterstock; p. 436: B Brown/Shutterstock

Chapter 15

p. 453: Africa Studio/Fotolia; p. 457: Stephen Barnes/Alamy Stock Photo; p. 458: Science photo/Fotolia; p. 463: Prachaya Roekdeethaweesab/Shutterstock; p. 463: Olesia Bilkei/123RF; p. 463: Petinov Sergey Mihilovich/Shutterstock; p. 465: Andrew Blue/Fotolia; p. 465: Frenta/Fotolia; p. 466: Rostislav Sedlacek/Fotolia; p. 467: Leszekglasner/Fotolia; p. 469: CoolKengzz/Shutterstock

Multi

Fenton one/Shutterstock; Rtguest/Shutterstock